Jacobean and Caroline Dramatists

Dictionary of Literary Biography

Documentary Series

Yearbooks

Concise Series

Dictionary of Literary Biography • Volume Fifty-eight

Jacobean and Caroline Dramatists

Edited by
Fredson Bowers
University of Virginia

A Bruccoli Clark Layman Book
Gale Research Company • Book Tower • Detroit, Michigan 48226

Manufactured by Edwards Brothers, Inc.
Ann Arbor, Michigan
Printed in the United States of America

Library of Congress Cataloging-in-Publication Data

Jacobean and Caroline dramatists.

   (Dictionary of literary biography; v. 58)
   "A Bruccoli Clark Layman book."
   Includes index.
   1.English drama—17th century—History and criticism.
2. English drama—17th century—Bio-bibliography. 3. Dramatists, English—17th century—Biography—Dictionaries.
I. Bowers, Fredson Thayer. II. Series.
PR671.J33 1987 822'.3'09 [B] 87-8645
ISBN 0-8103-1736-2

Contents

Plan of the Series

. . . Almost the most prodigious asset of a country, and perhaps its most precious possession, is its native literary product—when that product is fine and noble and enduring.

Mark Twain*

The advisory board, the editors, and the publisher of the *Dictionary of Literary Biography* are joined in endorsing Mark Twain's declaration. The literature of a nation provides an inexhaustible resource of permanent worth. It is our expectation that this endeavor will make literature and its creators better understood and more accessible to students and the literate public, while satisfying the standards of teachers and scholars.

To meet these requirements, *literary biography* has been construed in terms of the author's achievement. The most important thing about a writer is his writing. Accordingly, the entries in *DLB* are career biographies, tracing the development of the author's canon and the evolution of his reputation.

The publication plan for *DLB* resulted from two years of preparation. The project was proposed to Bruccoli Clark by Frederick G. Ruffner, president of the Gale Research Company, in November 1975. After specimen entries were prepared and typeset, an advisory board was formed to refine the entry format and develop the series rationale. In meetings held during 1976, the publisher, series editors, and advisory board approved the scheme for a comprehensive biographical dictionary of persons who contributed to North American literature. Editorial work on the first volume began in January 1977, and it was published in 1978.

In order to make *DLB* more than a reference tool and to compile volumes that individually have claim to status as literary history, it was decided to organize volumes by topic or period or genre. Each of these freestanding volumes provides a biographical-bibliographical guide and overview for a particular area of literature. We are convinced that this organization—as opposed to a single alphabet method—constitutes a valuable innovation in the presentation of reference material. The volume

plan necessarily requires many decisions for the placement and treatment of authors who might properly be included in two or three volumes. In some instances a major figure will be included in separate volumes, but with different entries emphasizing the aspect of his career appropriate to each volume. Ernest Hemingway, for example, is represented in *American Writers in Paris, 1920-1939* by an entry focusing on his expatriate apprenticeship; he is also in *American Novelists, 1910-1945* with an entry surveying his entire career. Each volume includes a cumulative index of subject authors and articles. The final *DLB* volume will be a comprehensive index to the entire series.

With volume ten in 1982 it was decided to enlarge the scope of *DLB*. By the end of 1986 twenty-one volumes treating British literature had been published, and volumes for Commonwealth and Modern European literature were in progress. The series has been further augmented by the *DLB Yearbooks* (since 1981) which update published entries and add new entries to keep the *DLB* current with contemporary activity. There have also been occasional *DLB Documentary Series* volumes which provide biographical and critical background source materials for figures whose work is judged to have particular interest for students. One of these companion volumes is entirely devoted to Tennessee Williams.

The purpose of *DLB* is not only to provide reliable information in a convenient format but also to place the figures in the larger perspective of literary history and to offer appraisals of their accomplishments by qualified scholars.

We define literature as the *intellectual commerce of a nation:* not merely as belles lettres but as that ample and complex process by which ideas are generated, shaped, and transmitted. *DLB* entries are not limited to "creative writers" but extend to other figures who in this time and in this way influenced the mind of a people. Thus the series encompasses historians, journalists, publishers, and screenwriters. By this means readers of *DLB* may be aided to perceive literature not as cult scripture in the keeping of cultural high priests but as at the center of a nation's life.

DLB includes the major writers appropriate to each volume and those standing in the ranks immediately behind them. Scholarly and critical coun-

---

*From an unpublished section of Mark Twain's autobiography, copyright © by the Mark Twain Company.

sel has been sought in deciding which minor figures to include and how full their entries should be. Wherever possible, useful references are made to figures who do not warrant separate entries.

Each *DLB* volume has a volume editor responsible for planning the volume, selecting the figures for inclusion, and assigning the entries. Volume editors are also responsible for preparing, where appropriate, appendices surveying the major periodicals and literary and intellectual movements for their volumes, as well as lists of further readings. Work on the series as a whole is coordinated at the Bruccoli Clark Layman editorial center in Columbia, South Carolina, where the editorial staff is responsible for the accuracy of the published volumes.

One feature that distinguishes *DLB* is the illustration policy—its concern with the iconography of literature. Just as an author is influenced by his surroundings, so is the reader's understanding of the author enhanced by a knowledge of his environment. Therefore *DLB* volumes include not only drawings, paintings, and photographs of authors, often depicting them at various stages in their careers, but also illustrations of their families and places where they lived. Title pages are regularly reproduced in facsimile along with dust jackets for modern authors. The dust jackets are a special fea-

ture of *DLB* because they often document better than anything else the way in which an author's work was launched in its own time. Specimens of the writers' manuscripts are included when feasible.

A supplement to *DLB*—tentatively titled *A Guide, Chronology, and Glossary for American Literature*—will outline the history of literature in North America and trace the influences that shaped it. This volume will provide a framework for the study of American literature by means of chronological tables, literary affiliation charts, glossarial entries, and concise surveys of the major movements. It has been planned to stand on its own as a vade mecum, providing a ready-reference guide to the study of American literature as well as a companion to the *DLB* volumes for American literature.

Samuel Johnson rightly decreed that "The chief glory of every people arises from its authors." The purpose of the *Dictionary of Literary Biography* is to compile literary history in the surest way available to us—by accurate and comprehensive treatment of the lives and work of those who contributed to it.

The *DLB* Advisory Board

Foreword

The Renaissance in England reached its full flowering in the reign of Queen Elizabeth I (1558-1603). By common consent the drama of the Elizabethan period (in which we loosely include the reigns of James I and Charles I) up to the Closing of the Theaters by the Commonwealth in 1642 produced the period's greatest literature, which has not been surpassed since its day. Yet a paradox intrudes itself here, for at the time plays were not thought of as "literature," which was taken to be of higher seriousness and value. Indeed, when in 1616 Ben Jonson collected his plays under the title of *Works,* a name reserved for proper literature, there was a certain amount of sniggering at his presumption. Under few circumstances were plays even thought of as an art form. Instead they were generally taken as providing a simple and unintellectual form of amusement, something on the order of a commercial moving picture of today, except that in Elizabethan days plays were not considered to be entirely suitable for a respectable moral person to view or to read. More sermons were printed than any other type of book. It was a commonplace of the drama's opponents that tragedies encouraged great crimes and comedy gave countenance to and even taught various forms of knavery and immorality.

One factor in this view was the general dislike of the puritanical city fathers of the City of London, who succeeded in banishing the outdoor playhouses to the suburbs where they flourished among the taverns and houses of ill-repute, what would now be called the "red-light district." Moreover, the city authorities gave to the actors the general status of rogues and vagabonds and thus forced them to seek the protection of some great lord, or even of the King or Queen, who accepted them as servants and thus gave them a legal being. In addition to their moral disapprobation the aldermen of London had a practical reason for disliking the crowds that thronged the playhouses. Not only did the throngs occasionally provoke riots, especially when apprentices went on a rampage in celebration of some event, but more particularly the congregation of large crowds increased the danger of the plague, which was always present during these years. Indeed, the theaters were automatically banned whenever the weekly deaths from the plague rose

above a certain number, often being closed in the summer but occasionally for many other months. In such times the out-of-work actors were likely to tour the provinces, where they traveled from town to town, acting in whatever places could be used as makeshift stages, for otherwise they would starve.

The typical Elizabethan theater was an outdoor building, open to the sky, holding several thousand people. The groundlings—the poorer sort—stood in the pit before the stage through the whole performance. The more prosperous bourgeoisie and the gentry sat in higher-priced galleries that surrounded the thrust-out stage on three sides, whereas a few select noblemen, or aspirants to public attention, could rent the Lords' Rooms, set above and to the side of the stage. Sometimes spectators were permitted to sit on stools on the very stage itself. From at least 1576, however, the choristers of the Chapel and of Paul's were permitted to act plays in Blackfriars, a building turned into an indoor theater in a district removed from the City's jurisdiction. Boy actors always took the female parts on the Elizabethan stage, but these all-boy companies became so popular after their regular establishment at Blackfriars after Michaelmas 1600 as to give rise to the well-known discussion between Hamlet and Rosencrantz about the "little eyases" who have displaced the adult companies in public esteem. About 1607-1608 the adult companies invaded these so-called private theaters and took them over for their own use, acting both here and in their larger public open-air theaters, in part according to the season.

Plays in the public theaters were acted in daylight without intermission. Much to their advantage, such plays were designed to appeal to the whole spectrum of the London populace from the highest to the lowest. The private indoor theater, on the other hand, exacted a stiff entrance fee and was attended almost exclusively by the gentry and nobility. Two or three brief intermissions were provided with music for entertainment.

Some plays were acted both outdoors and indoors, just as Shakespeare's company used both the public Globe and the private Blackfriars theaters. But a more or less separate repertoire began to develop according to the tastes of the different audiences for which each theater was designed, a split not always with happy effects for the drama. Plays for the public theaters might sometimes be written down to the lowest level of the populace, yet ordinarily they chose a middle course and thus their appeal was universal from apprentice to lord and has remained so to the present day. The indoor theaters, on the other hand, fostered a clique audience, which enjoyed in-plays aimed at their special group, plays that at one time were especially satirical of individuals and at all times were likely to be highly artificial in plotting and characterization, as we find in Beaumont and Fletcher's popular plays aimed at the upper classes. The seeds of the decadence that was to overtake the theater in Caroline times were being sown.

The Court, always in need of amusement, had patronized and protected the theater from the beginning, and if plays like Thomas Edwards's or John Lyly's were written especially for it, the result at the time was an increase in sophistication for which the popular drama was badly in need. During Shakepeare's day both Elizabeth and James ordered the theater's best plays to be presented at Court, but under Charles increasingly a court coterie of dramatists sprang up who aimed their plays at the relatively idle fashionable court audience and lost touch with the popular theater and its lifeblood in their effort to please the King and his courtiers. Such plays were determinedly artificial and mannered and, unfortunately, began to influence the public stage. The elaborate and costly masques, given exclusively at court for royal entertainment on feast days and state occasions, represent a special genre. For the delectation of the vulgar some of the dramatists began to insert masquelike scenes in their plays purely for entertainment value and with little dramatic motivation.

One reason for the preeminence of the Elizabethan drama at its height was its native tradition that was able to overcome attempts to imitate the frigid classicism of the continental European drama, especially the French. This popular tradition was established early. English drama began as little dialogues, or tropes, inserted in the Latin Mass on such church festivals as Easter and Christmas. It rapidly outgrew the church and came under the civic protection of the trade guilds so that in the fifteenth and early-sixteenth centuries citizens acted cycles or series of little plays each of which dramatized some one event in the whole biblical history of mankind from Creation to the Day of Judgment. These so-called miracle or mystery plays

Part of Mathias Merian's View of London *in about 1600 showing the playhouses of Bankside, outside the jurisdiction of the London city fathers: the Swan (number 39), the Beargarden (number 38), and the first Globe (number 37) with the Rose between it and the river. The Globe and the Swan are shown too close to the river and the Rose is located incorrectly (from J. L. Gottfried's* Neuwe Archontologia Cosmica, 1638)*.

A performance of a miracle play on a pageant wagon

were acted on scaffolds but also on top of pageant wagons that were drawn from station to station in the streets to repeat the performance before a fresh group of townspeople, followed by the next wagon, and so on. Devout as these plays were in their subject matter, some of them made sturdy attempts at realistic characterization. Moreover, in certain plays the course of realistic true-to-life narrative began to edge out the pious sentiments and formal religious presentation. The Cain and Abel story, as elaborated, rang true to real life in its portrait of surly anger and jealousy. Abraham and Isaac acquired true pathos verging on tragedy. Secular events intruded. For instance, in *The Second Shep-*

herds' Play most of the action is taken up with the sheep-stealing activities and ultimate detection of a rascal named Mak until such time as the angelic voices announce the birth of Jesus to the shepherds. Noah was given a shrewish wife who refused to leave her gossips to enter the ark and had to be carried in by force after belaboring her husband unmercifully.

Occasional allegorical characters made their appearance in these miracle plays, but it was only when the popular drama fell into the hands of groups of itinerant actors that it became secularized, even in allegorical terms, in what came to be known as the morality play. Here the allegorical

Virtues and Vices took over the dramatized conflict for the soul of Mankind, a conflict that increasingly was developed in terms of real-life incidents and problems as in the best of this type, the well-known *Everyman*. In another development that attracted the popular audience, emphasis began to be placed on crude comedy, focused in the person of a character known as the Vice. Starting as an evil tempter of man, the Vice bit by bit grew into a trickster, with more merriment than evil in his makeup, and the basic plot of man's temptation, fall, and forgiveness began to treat more subjects, like methods of education, or satire on manners, with the moral emphasis considerably subdued.

The turn in the drama's development came when in the universities, in the schools for training the professions like the Inns of Court, in the households of noblemen, and especially in the royal court the demand for entertainment called in a new kind of professional dramatist, like John Heywood for instance, playwrights who first writing for amateur performances soon turned to providing plays for touring bands of actors playing in inn yards, a structure that had a profound effect on the later Elizabethan theater. The rising tide of demand for entertainment brought in as actors for the court under Henry VIII, and then for the public under Elizabeth, the chorister Children of the Chapel Royal for whom Lyly wrote. The training ground was prepared for dramatists who would mix the popular with the courtly tradition for a wider audience in London and the provinces, and the true form of the drama was born as both writing for the stage and acting became profitable occupations that attracted university graduates like Greene, Peele, and Marlowe, whose plays were acted not only in inn yards but in newly built theaters for professional acting companies.

The most convenient division for the forms of drama in its final development is that of History, Comedy, and Tragedy, the categories adopted in Shakespeare's First Folio of 1623.

History plays were early popular, in some small part because their events provided ready-made plots that carried the aura of truth but chiefly because dramatized English history appealed to the patriotic fervor before and after the Armada years and the skirmishes on the Continent in which England took part against its traditional enemies France and Spain. As an art, history had been slow to develop in Elizabethan times and confined itself mainly to chronicles, that is, to recording with little comment or interpretation the main public events of each year, in chronological order, intermixing political and military actions of importance with trivial accounts of natural wonders, storms, monstrous births, and particularly sensational murders. The usual early history play, known as a chronicle-history, narrated its active subjects with little more order than the chronicles and with very small recognition of the cause and effect of the tides of history, the interaction of royal supremacy with the commons, the constant conflict of king and nobles for power. Such plays, as most commonly read now in Shakespeare's *Henry VI* trilogy, made little effort to shape action into an artistic plot with a beginning, a middle, and an end. In something of a dead-end situation, romantic comedy was tried in order to piece out an historical background, as in Greene's *Scottish History of James IV*. To Marlowe in his two-part *Tamburlaine* goes the credit of first forcing scattered historical events into some sort of meaningful pattern. In the later *Edward II* he was the first to attempt to analyze history in terms of personalities, of characterization, and the opposing political forces of King, barons, and commons. In his *Richard III* Shakespeare learned from Marlowe's *Tamburlaine* the unifying force that could be given to history by concentrating on a powerful dominant character who controlled the action. In his *Richard II* he learned from Marlowe the anatomy of weakness and the disease that overtook a kingdom governed by a willful king more concerned with his own private emotions and pleasures than with the national welfare. The apotheosis, the high point of the chronicle-history, came with Shakespeare's *Henry V*, but before that he had unified history as dramatic action and as dramatic fiction into a play in which the characters as individuals and as historical figures merged into one, and the dramatic story line becomes more important than the historical events. This was the celebrated first part of *Henry IV* in which history and comedy form a single strand. In such plays as *Julius Caesar* and *Antony and Cleopatra*, or *Macbeth*, the union is so perfect that the history can no longer be felt as an independent action. Character and historical events are swept up into the purest form of tragedy.

Elizabethan comedy separated itself, at least for a time, into three recognizable groups. There is romantic comedy as in Greene's *Friar Bacon and Friar Bungay*, Dekker's *Old Fortunatus*, Shakespeare's *As You Like It* and *Twelfth Night*. Ben Jonson formulated the comedy of humours in *Every Man in His Humour*, and in his masterpieces *Volpone* and *The Alchemist* he combined these humours with an intrigue plot to create the ultimate in this form of comedy. In some part stemming from Jonson's an-

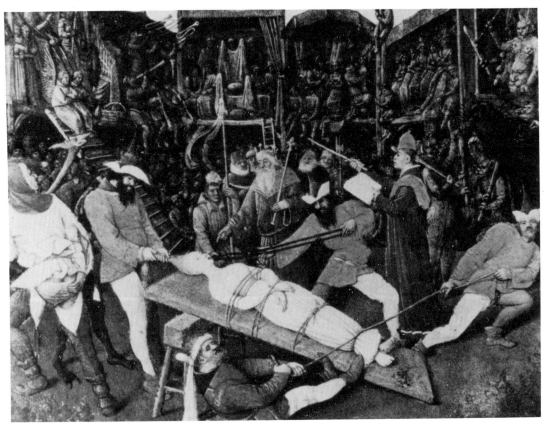

The torture of St. Apollonia in a miracle play. This miniature by Jean Fouquet is the only known medieval illustration of the action in such a play (from Les Heures d'Etienne Chevalier, *circa 1460; by permission of the Musée Condé, Chantilly)*.

tiromantic comic theories, comedies of bourgeois London life were popular, like Dekker and Webster's *Westward Ho!*, Middleton's *Michaelmas Term*, or Jonson, Chapman, and Marston's *Eastward Ho!* Indeed, these became the prevailing form of comedy for some years when dramatists found it difficult to emulate Shakespeare's romantic comedy and could only merge it into a new form of tragicomedy as in Beaumont and Fletcher's *Philaster*. Comedies of manners, in the later sense of the reaction between personality and social codes, were always present in Shakespeare but did not usurp the main plot line. Some few comedies of manners like Fletcher's *Wild-Goose Chase* anticipate what was to develop fully in the Restoration, although Shirley's *Lady of Pleasure* can also be considered as a forerunner.

The clever slave of the Roman comedy of Plautus and Terence gave rise to Brainworm in Jonson's *Every Man in His Humour* and to countless other Elizabethan servants who were more quick-witted than their masters and who amused the audience and kept the plot rolling by manipulating their superiors. But a more far-reaching influence helped to shape the form and attitude of Elizabethan comedy. In a broad sense this was the doctrine of decorum. If we dig beneath the surface manifestation of decorum as form, such as whether in tragedy violent action must be narrated, not performed—a matter of far more moment to the French than to the English, who ignored it—we may see that decorum is associated with character first, and only then with plot, which is the summation of actions appropriate for given characters and not a force independent of character. Decorum was the moving principle of Roman comedy and (though in a less obvious manner) was strongly operative in Senecan Roman tragedy. According to the principle of decorum established in Roman comedy, an old man is supposed to be appreciative of his own wisdom derived from experience but often hardened into formulas of conduct, and thus he will not value the instincts and opinions of youth. He is suspicious but easily deceived, inclined to be loquacious, overly careful of family position and wealth, conservative, and is opposed to all change.

A young man is supposed to be ardent, generous, brave, ruled in his actions more by his emotions than by his reason, and so on. This decorum was not only personal but was also applied to the various conditions of mankind. A merchant was supposed to be prudent, cautious, peaceable; a soldier, valiant, quarrelsome, honorable. The characters of all trades and professions thus became codified. It was as indecorous for a merchant to swagger like a bravo as for a swineherd to possess a refined sensibility. When an opposite to the system was exhibited for satirical purposes, as in the person of the braggart soldier, it was usually made clear that the person was, in fact, no soldier but a pretender to military life.

When in *The Defense of Poesy* Sir Philip Sidney remarked that "comedy is an imitation of the common errors of our life," he was enunciating perhaps the strongest theme of the doctrine of decorum, which reserved comedy for low or middle actions in private bourgeois life beneath the level of greatness; and tragedy for the important affairs of great men, whose private actions must always have public repercussions. (It is clear how romantic comedy broke with this tradition and created a decorum of its own which had no relation to the classical formulas.) Especially under the influence of Ben Jonson, it was held in comedy that actions of private men were to concern the common errors of ordinary life, for Jonson the moralist was fixed in his purpose that comedy was the agent of reform and by exposing abuses should warn the audience against being deceived by similar deceptions or falling into similar irrational ways of thought and action (humours). This moral purpose never left the comedy of ordinary life during the Elizabethan period, for indeed it constituted one of the arguments that the stage did not teach vice by its exhibition of faulty actions but instead exposed these by showing their invariable lack of success as a warning to the audience. That this stance became more lip service than conviction among the dramatists does not affect the general attitude.

Although decorum was a fixed principle in the portrayal of Virtues and Vices in the early morality play, as the popular drama became more secularized and the moral intent more ostensible than real, the degeneration of the morality play's initial high seriousness was accompanied inevitably by degeneration in the consistency of word and action in the characters if the entertainment of the audience was thereby served. That ambiguous figure of the Vice may be something of an example, for a dramatist grappling with new material did not always draw a clear line between mischievousness and deadly corruption aimed at the damnation of the soul, or even between firmly held virtue and formal priggishness.

When the morality play finally surrendered to pure comedy, the principle of decorum imposed a much-needed discipline on the new dramatists, especially the more learned. Ready to hand from Roman comedy was a whole parade of stock figures with characteristics already formulated and tested for dramatic effect. When the Roman comedy was consciously imitated, the transition was a natural one of clever slave to Merygreke in *Ralph Roister Doister* or Diccon in *Gammer Gurton's Needle,* classicized Vices with their fangs drawn in an English setting. A more extreme application and extension of decorum may be observed even in such a potpourri as Greene's *Friar Bacon and Friar Bungay* where social classes are carefully distinguished, as in the calculated wooing of Margaret by Lacy, Earl of Lincoln, and the court paid her by Lambert and Serlsby, mere country gentlemen of her own class. We also see decorum relied on as a substitute for dramatic explanation of action. Lacy's cruel (and, to modern sensibility, meaningless) testing of Margaret's constancy is never motivated. Obviously, Greene did not feel it necessary to explain the reasons for the trick to an audience accustomed to the whims of the great ones. It would seem obvious, according to Greene, that Lacy's action must be suitable for a nobleman in his position. Dekker's *Patient Grissill* has a similar but more highly developed theme.

Whenever plot is predominant, characters are likely to sink into types, of course. Type characters abounded on the English stage, even encouraged in part by the automatic application of a watered-down Jonsonian theory of humours, or overriding passions and tendencies of thought governing action; but it is one of the glories of the Elizabethan drama that there was a constant pressure to break through these standardized molds of form. Decorum and type formulas are usually associated with an emphasis on manners, or a picture of ways of life as represented in the adjustment of character to social position and customs, and the problems that arise when individuality acts to change the rules of the game. The comedy of manners is usually associated with high life, but it need not be; as in Jonson, occupation can take the place of social position in the seesaw of conflict, for the bourgeoisie and even low-life characters have their manners as well as their betters. Yet it was a distinctive manifestation of the Elizabethan delight in individuality

The inn yard at the White Hart, Southwark, where plays were performed on a temporary platform

instead of formulas that led Ben Jonson to give at least as much attention to the eccentricities of human nature in their humours as he did to the characteristics of social types. The distinction is already drawn in *Every Man in His Humour*. The elder Knowell is the ever-careful father of classical comedy, a figure of complete decorum for his age and station. Brainworm is a slightly modified clever slave. But Cob can scarcely be called a characteristic water drawer; Bobadill breaks the bounds of the formal braggart soldier by the inclusion of many other characteristics; and Justice Clements's private amusement in the power of his office is not typical of Justices of the Peace, as Thomas Cash's inbuilt faithfulness is, in contrast, typical of the careful journeyman. Kitely is interesting because in type he is a merchant but in humour he is an irrationally jealous man. The shell of decorum of occupation is broken, and manners are considerably broadened, by packing into him personal attributes that have little or nothing to do with the attributes of his profession. His comic actions may be judged according to ideas of decorum, of what was suitable

for a jealous man to do or say; but these have little connection with the more formal concept of decorous action and words suitable for a merchant. Jonson interchanges one concept for the other, back and forth; but only in a single occasion in this play does he make dramatic use of a conflict between them, as when Kitely cannot bear to leave his merchandise unattended while he pursues what he regards as his faithless wife.

In sum, although in various of their manifestations the humours that dominated Elizabethan comedy reinforced the theory of decorum in manners, as in the model comedy *Eastward Ho!*, nevertheless the seeds of character interest that drove humours away from types and toward unique portraits of individualized fixations substituted another rationale to displace classical decorum with Elizabethan variety: the rationale of inner faithfulness to a coherent individual in his own terms. The terrible picture of Harry Dampit in Middleton's *A Trick to Catch the Old One* goes far beyond any contribution that the theory of decorum ever made to the type of a usurer. Correspondingly, the

The first Globe theater, which burned to the ground on 29 June 1613 (from J. C. Visscher's View of London, *1616)*

great dramatic character of Sir Giles Overreach in Massinger's *A New Way to Pay Old Debts* is faithful to an internal rationale that transcends the usurer of stage tradition. The tendency of Elizabethan comedy, thus, was to free itself from the limitation of formal type decorum as a dramatic principle, and to substitute inner coherence in its own terms of observation, a rationale that placed decorum on a raised level of truth to nature unknown in its classical antecedents except in the most general terms.

On the other hand, some argument may be made for the reverse operation in tragedy. Few Elizabethan dramatists except Shakespeare were affected by the Aristotelian concept of the protag-

onist of moderate virtue who yet has some unsuspected flaw through which tragedy strikes and so enforces the justice of the fatal ending. Instead, the red glare of Seneca's villains enraptured most playwrights. Shakespeare could create a unique villain in Macbeth, who was as little Senecan as he was Aristotelian. Working more within the standard Elizabethan tradition, Webster could yet transcend convention not only by the imaginative power of his realistic portraits of vice but also by his ability to intermingle humanity in such persons as Bosola, Brachiano, and Vittoria.

In 1615 one of the puritanical opponents of the stage, J. Greene, in his *Refutation of the Apology for Actors,* tried to instill repugnance in his readers by a description of the vices of tragedy: "The *Tragedies* discourseth of lamentable fortunes, extreme affects, horrible villainies, rapines, murthers, spoils, tyrannies, and the like." And a little later he is more specific: "The matter of *Tragedies* is haughtiness, arrogancy, ambition, pride, injury, anger, wrath, envy, hatred, contention, warre, murther, cruelty, rapine, incest, . . . rebellions, treasons, killing, . . . treachery, villany, &c., and all kinds of heroyck evils whatsoever." To such diatribes the actors could only respond that though their tragedies did portray the evil deeds of evil men; yet these criminals always came to a bad end and thus the cause of virtue was served by showing the inevitable defeat of vice. Yet it could not be concealed that "all kinds of heroyck evils whatsoever" performed by appropriate villains was what the Elizabethans took over as the action and character that fulfilled tragic decorum. The popular Elizabethan villain play stemmed directly from this narrowing of the matter of tragedy from Shakespeare's huge canvas of tragically flawed good men to the appropriate deeds of great villains. This limited tragic concept led to a limited number of plot formulas and to a stiffening of the formulas of characterization that contrasts with the freedom with which character and plot were exploited in Shakespearean tragedy.

The explanation for this paradox is not far to seek. The common association of tragedy with the exhibition of vicious character in action could thrill the audience with horror, but despite the actors' protestations it could scarcely purge in the manner that comedy proposed for its end. Members of the audience could perhaps see something of themselves and their own experiences on the comic stage and thereby be led to a self-consciousness that was the prerequisite for reform; but the ability to identify with blackest villainy was strictly limited, as Aristotle had long before observed. The Elizabethan comic dramatists had found in Plautus and Terence a strict formula for comedy which they proceeded to broaden and make meaningful by a strong infusion of variety, and its peculiar order of truth, that followed on sympathetic, or at least intimate, observation of real life. The Elizabethan tragic dramatists found in Seneca a formula that was as rigid in its springs of action as the Roman comedy, though less formal in the organization of the plot line and its details. However, the Senecan desertion of the Aristotelian balanced principle in protagonist and plot forced the Elizabethan tragic dramatists away from the realities of observation and into a world of imagination

where their fantasies could not match in artistic validity the lively curiosity about the differences in human nature which alone could break the writers loose from the limitations of formal tragic decorum in character and plot, if we define classical not as Greek (the Greek drama being largely unknown to the Elizabethans) but as Senecan.

Indeed, the Elizabethan tragedians tended to impose a formula on themselves, with the result that the usual Elizabethan villain is likely to be more rigidly typed than his Senecan prototypes. In this process the extraordinary Elizabethan preoccupation with Machiavellism stifled much individuality in character portrayal and channeled villainous motivation into a relatively few standard patterns. (Not all dramatists were capable of the larger view held by Marston in *The Malcontent* of Italian villainy.) It follows that interest in individual character gives place to an emphasis on conventionally motivated startling action. For instance, we know little of the original Marlovian concept of the latter half of *The Jew of Malta*, but the noteworthy degeneration of character when the attention is diverted to intrigue in the plot is either a symptom of an inherent flaw caused by a catering to Machiavel or—perhaps as likely—the effect of the imposition of degenerate Caroline dramatic values on the revision of an old play.

The pernicious influence of Machiavellism was far-reaching. It led to the association of tragic passion exclusively with ambition, lust, envy, hatred, vice, and thus with the establishment of the villain as the protagonist of the usual Elizabethan tragedy, Shakespeare apart. It also led to an action based mainly on intrigue. The Elizabethans were thoroughly horrified with what they had heard of Machiavelli's *The Prince*. They did not understand its cool analysis of the facts of life among the Italian petty tyrants but took its objectivity for approval of every kind of breaking of faith, conscienceless action, and the free use of murder as a political weapon. The lurid stories told in histories of Italy, and the sometimes equally lurid tales in the Italian *novelle* only confirmed an initial anti-Catholic distrust of Italy as the land of poisoners, lust, hypocrisy, and bloodshed. In all this mixture of truth and fantasy the Elizabethans could bring little of their own observation or experience in common humanity to bear. The thrill of an alien villainy rampant in an alien civilization took the place of identification with tragic action and protagonist.

As the period wore on, the absoluteness of formulary Machiavellian villainy blotted out the subtler earlier attempts at portraying the essentially

The interior of the first Globe theater. The groundlings stood in the pit and more-prosperous theatergoers sat in the gallery, in the lords' rooms, and on the stage itself.

good protagonist like Hamlet or Othello and the balance of pity and fear that accompanied his expiatory downfall. When tragic catharsis, at the heart of the Aristotelian principle of decorum, was pushed aside by the coarser shock effects of horror and amazement, the reign of terror that passed for tragic decorum of character and action on the imagined Senecan stage completed its conquest of the minor Elizabethan tragic dramatist.

As the drama passed the first quarter of the seventeenth century, comedy remained lively though growing farther away from the Shakespearean romantic ideal and tending either toward tragicomedy or the continued studies of middle life, with emphasis on intrigue beginning to take the place of humours. Following Fletcher, some tendency may be observed, as in Shirley's *Lady of Pleasure,* for comedy to study the manners of the upper classes instead of the bourgeoisie or the lower orders. When Shakespeare grew somewhat out of fashion, Beaumont and Fletcher usurped the greater popularity. Not only in his unaided works but also in his frequent association with Massinger, Field, Rowley, and Shirley either as collaborators or revisers, Fletcher was a major force in the deterioration of the ethical seriousness of the

earlier drama and its attempts to hold the mirror up to nature whether in realistic or idealistic contexts. Although to the Jacobean and Caroline audiences Beaumont and Fletcher's characters reflected accurately the manners and sentiments that they fancied were—or should have been—their ideals, the present day thinks differently. We now recognize the coarseness of moral fiber characteristic of their plays; the complete artificiality and extravagance of sentiment held by the heroes of their tragicomedies and tragedies like *Philaster, The Maid's Tragedy, A Wife for a Month, A King and No King,* or *The Loyal Subject;* the fawning adulation lavished on the monarchical principle stemming from the divine right of kings; the sudden and unmotivated changes in character according to the arbitrary demands of the plot, including the abrupt repentance of evil characters; the constant sexuality of theme and outlook, the titillations of incestuous passion that turns out to be legitimate after all—this essentially cheap sensationalism helped lead to the decline of the drama. On the other hand, some of Fletcher's comedies can hold their own today, and without question he had a true comic gift for plotting and characterization. It is the essential falseness of his tragicomedies of court life and their basic sentimentality and extravagance that led his imitators astray and without question fostered, ultimately, the peculiar genre of Restoration heroic tragedy.

A few dramatists were fascinated by plots based on abnormal psychology, even though the theme had always been latent in the earlier portraits of Italian ducal villains out of Machiavelli and the histories. John Ford's *'Tis Pity She's a Whore* offers a powerful picture of incestuous love until the play collapses in the Grand Guignol extravagances of the catastrophe. Ford's *The Broken Heart* attempts a study of thwarted love in a complex web of platonic conventions. The most extraordinary psychological probing of situation and character appears in Middleton and Rowley's *The Changeling*,

which paints unsparingly the degeneration of a woman fatally caught up in an abnormal, even diseased, sexual passion that had started in disgust and in physical as well as psychic repugnance.

The latter days of the drama could not equal the energy, the variety, and the delight found in the Renaissance spirit of the earlier plays, reaching its height, of course, in the unique poetic drama of Shakespeare. The need to stimulate an increasingly jaded audience by sensationalism in tragedy, regardless of consistency of theme and characterization, and by increasing the sexual charge in comedy, led to a marked decline in the ethical seriousness of the dramatic form in the hands of minor playwrights. Major dramatists like Middleton, Massinger, and Shirley, on the other hand, did

The second Globe theater (incorrectly labeled "Beere bayting h"), built on the site of the first, was opened in late spring 1614 (from Wenceslaus Hollar's "Long View" of London, engraved in 1644 and published in 1647)

succeed in maintaining some semblance of a higher aim in tragedy and tragicomedy and of social criticism in comedy by their very professionalism operating through authentic literary talent. The drama brought to a close by the Commonwealth inhibition had grown tired and had declined from its earlier height, but it was cut off while it still shone, even though palely, with the reflected glow from its great period of most astonishing Renaissance vigor and magnificence.

—Fredson Bowers

DLB 58: Jacobean and Caroline Dramatists, is a companion to the forthcoming *DLB* volume *Elizabethan Dramatists.* Because many dramatists whose careers began during the reign of Elizabeth I (1558-1603) continued writing during the reign of James I (1603-1625) and in some cases into the reign of Charles I (1625-1649) as well, there are playwrights in each volume who might justifiably have been included in the other.

At the beginning of each entry in these volumes there are lists of an author's play productions and books. Because records for the period are incomplete, the productions listed under the first rubric are the first known performances of plays, and the dates and locations of these productions are sometimes matters of conjecture based on the best available evidence. Many of the texts for plays written in the period are no longer in existence, though some of these plays are mentioned in contemporary documents. If the author of the entry has evidence that a lost play was produced, it is listed under play productions. The reader should be aware that many of these playwrights may have written or helped to write other plays that are unknown to modern scholars or that remain unattributed or misattributed.

Many plays were published anonymously or were erroneously attributed by their first publish-

ers, and the authorship of some is still unresolved. Attributions of the plays listed under both play productions and books are based on the contributors' assessments of most recent scholarship and are not necessarily the same as authors' names listed on title pages of plays' first editions.

Under the play productions rubrics and in the body of the text these entries refer to plays by the titles by which they are now most commonly known, employing modern spellings. Under the books rubrics, while titles are frequently shortened, the spellings of the first printings of surviving books are transcribed as they appear on the original title pages, with the following exceptions: long *s* is transcribed *s,* and for books printed after 1601 *u* and *v* and *i* and *j* are sometimes transcribed according to modern usage ("have" and "use" for "haue" and "vse," "joy" and "filii" for "ioy" and "filij," for example). Imprints are listed as they appear on title pages, but, in cases where a printer, publisher, or bookseller is known but not printed on the title page, the name is added. The authorities for the publication information in this volume are *A Short-Title Catalogue of Books Printed in England, Scotland, & Ireland and of English Books Printed Abroad 1475-1640,* compiled by A. W. Pollard and G. R. Redgrave, second edition, revised and enlarged, begun by W. A. Jackson and F. S. Ferguson, completed by Katharine F. Pantzer (2 volumes, 1976, 1986); and A *Short-Title Catalogue of Books Printed in England, Scotland, Ireland, Wales and British America and of English Books Printed In Other Countries, 1641-1700,* compiled by Donald Wing, revised and enlarged edition (3 volumes, 1972-   ).

At the end of listings of first editions, under the subheading "Editions," authors of entries have listed the most authoritative later texts of the subjects' works. Quotations in this volume are drawn from these editions.

A general bibliography of works relating to the playwrights in both these *DLB* volumes will be published in the *Elizabethan Dramatists* volume.

Acknowledgments

This book was produced by Bruccoli Clark Layman, Inc. Karen L. Rood, senior editor for the *Dictionary of Literary Biography* series, was the in-house editor.

Copyediting supervisor is Patricia Coate. Production coordinator is Kimberly Casey. Typesetting supervisor is Laura Ingram. Lucia Tarbox is editorial assistant. The production staff includes Rowena Betts, David R. Bowdler, Mary S. Dye, Charles Egleston, Gabrielle Elliott, Kathleen M. Flanagan, Joyce Fowler, Karen Fritz, Judith K. Ingle, Judith E. McCray, Janet Phelps, Joan Price, and Joycelyn R. Smith. Jean W. Ross is permissions editor. Joseph Caldwell, photography editor, and Joseph Matthew Bruccoli did photographic copy work for the volume.

Walter W. Ross and Rhonda Marshall did the library research with the assistance of the staff at the Thomas Cooper Library of the University of South Carolina: Lynn Barron, Daniel Boice, Connie Crider, Kathy Eckman, Michael Freeman, Gary Geer, David L. Haggard, Jens Holley, Marcia Martin, Dana Rabon, Jean Rhyne, Jan Squire, Ellen Tillett, and Virginia Weathers.

Special thanks are due to Tom Lange of the Henry E. Huntington Library and Art Gallery, Charles Mann of the Pennsylvania State University Library, and William Cagle of the Lilly Library, Indiana University, for their help in providing illustrations.

Jacobean and Caroline Dramatists

Dictionary of Literary Biography

Francis Beaumont and John Fletcher

Cyrus Hoy
University of Rochester

Francis Beaumont
BIRTH: Grace-Dieu, Leicester, circa 1584, to Francis and Anne Pierrepoint Beaumont.
EDUCATION: Broadgates Hall (now Pembroke College), Oxford, 1597.
MARRIAGE: 1613 or 1614 to Ursula Isley; children: Elizabeth, Frances.
DEATH: Sundridge Hall, Kent, 6 March 1616.

John Fletcher
BIRTH: Rye, Sussex, December 1579, to Richard and Elizabeth Holland Fletcher.
EDUCATION: Fletcher may have attended Bene't College (now Corpus Christi), Cambridge, and been awarded the degrees of B.A. (1595) and M.A. (1598).
DEATH: London, August 1625.

PLAY PRODUCTIONS: *The Woman Hater*, by Beaumont and Fletcher, London, Paul's theater, circa 1606;
The Knight of the Burning Pestle, by Beaumont, London, Blackfriars theater, circa 1607;
The Noble Gentleman, probably by Beaumont, later revised by Fletcher (and perhaps others), London, Paul's theater (?), circa 1607;
Love's Cure, or The Martial Maid, by Beaumont and Fletcher, later revised by Philip Massinger, London, Paul's theater (?), circa 1607;
The Faithful Shepherdess, by Fletcher, London, Blackfriars theater, circa 1608;
Philaster, or Love Lies a-Bleeding, by Beaumont and Fletcher, London, Blackfriars theater, circa 1609;
The Coxcomb, by Beaumont and Fletcher, London, Whitefriars theater, circa 1609;

Cupid's Revenge, by Beaumont and Fletcher, London, Whitefriars theater, circa 1611;
The Woman's Prize or The Tamer Tamed, by Fletcher, London, Whitefriars theater, circa 1611;
The Night Walker or The Little Thief, by Fletcher, London, Whitefriars theater, circa 1611;
The Maid's Tragedy, by Beaumont and Fletcher, London, Blackfriars theater, circa 1611;
A King and No King, by Beaumont and Fletcher, London, Blackfriars theater, circa 1611;
The Captain, by Beaumont and Fletcher, London, Blackfriars theater, circa 1611;
Bonduca, by Fletcher, London, Blackfriars theater, circa 1611;
Valentinian, by Fletcher, London, Blackfriars theater, circa 1612;
Monsieur Thomas, or Father's Own Son, by Fletcher, London, Whitefriars theater, circa 1612;
Four Plays, or Moral Representations in One, by Fletcher and Nathan Field, unknown theater, circa 1612;
Cardenio, by Fletcher and William Shakespeare, London, at Court, winter 1612-1613;
The Masque of the Inner Temple and Gray's Inn, by Beaumont, London, Whitehall Palace, Banqueting House, 20 February 1613;
The Two Noble Kinsmen, by Fletcher and Shakespeare, London, Blackfriars theater, circa 1613;
Henry VIII, by Fletcher and Shakespeare, London, Globe theater, 1613;
The Honest Man's Fortune, by Fletcher, Field, and Massinger, London, Whitefriars theater, circa 1613;
Wit Without Money, by Fletcher, London, Whitefriars theater, circa 1614;

The Scornful Lady, by Beaumont and Fletcher, London, Porter's Hall theater, circa 1615;

Thierry and Theodoret, by Beaumont, Fletcher, and Massinger, London, Blackfriars theater, circa 1615;

Beggars' Bush, by Beaumont, Fletcher, and Massinger, London, Blackfriars theater, circa 1615;

Love's Pilgrimage, by Beaumont and Fletcher, London, Blackfriars theater, circa 1616;

The Nice Valour, or the Passionate Madman, possibly by Fletcher, but mainly the work of Thomas Middleton, unknown theater, circa 1616;

Wit at Several Weapons, possibly by Fletcher, later revised by Middleton and William Rowley, unknown theater, circa 1616;

The Mad Lover, by Fletcher, London, Blackfriars theater, circa 1616;

The Queen of Corinth, by Fletcher, Massinger, and Field, London, Blackfriars theater, circa 1617;

The Chances, by Fletcher, London, Blackfriars theater, circa 1617;

The Jeweller of Amsterdam, by Fletcher, Massinger, and Field, London, Blackfriars theater, circa 1617-1619(?);

The Knight of Malta, by Fletcher, Massinger, and Field, London, Blackfriars theater, circa 1618;

The Loyal Subject, by Fletcher, London, Blackfriars theater, 1618;

The Humourous Lieutenant, or Demetrius and Enanthe, by Fletcher, London, Blackfriars theater, circa 1619;

The Bloody Brother, or Rollo Duke of Normandy, by Fletcher, Massinger, and others (perhaps Ben Jonson and George Chapman), London, Blackfriars theater, circa 1619;

Sir John van Olden Barnavelt, by Fletcher and Massinger, London, Blackfriars theater, August 1619;

The Custom of the Country, by Fletcher and Massinger, London, Blackfriars theater, circa 1619;

The False One, by Fletcher and Massinger, London, Blackfriars theater, circa 1620;

The Laws of Candy (perhaps the work of John Ford), London, Blackfriars theater, circa 1620;

Women Pleased, by Fletcher, London, Blackfriars theater, circa 1620;

The Island Princess, by Fletcher, London, Blackfriars theater, circa 1621;

John Fletcher (by permission of the National Portrait Gallery, London) and Francis Beaumont (by permission of Hugh Sackville West, agent for Knowle Estates)

The Double Marriage, by Fletcher and Massinger, London, Blackfriars theater, circa 1621;

The Pilgrim, by Fletcher, London, Blackfriars theater, circa 1621;

The Wild Goose Chase, by Fletcher, London, Blackfriars theater, circa 1621;

The Prophetess, by Fletcher and Massinger, London, Blackfriars theater, licensed 14 May 1622;

The Sea Voyage, by Fletcher and Massinger, London, Blackfriars theater, licensed 22 June 1622;

The Spanish Curate, by Fletcher and Massinger, London, Blackfriars theater, licensed 24 October 1622;

The Little French Lawyer, by Fletcher and Massinger, London, Blackfriars theater, circa 1623;

The Maid in the Mill, by Fletcher and Rowley, London, Blackfriars theater, licensed 29 August 1623;

The Lovers' Progress, by Fletcher (apparently licensed 6 December 1623 as *The Wandering Lovers;* revised by Massinger as *Cleander,* licensed 7 May 1634), London, Blackfriars theater;

The Devil of Dowgate, or Usury Put to Use, by Fletcher, London, Blackfriars theater, licensed 17 October 1623;

A Wife for a Month, by Fletcher, London, Blackfriars theater, licensed 27 May 1624;

Rule a Wife and Have a Wife, by Fletcher, London, Blackfriars theater, licensed 19 October 1624;

The Elder Brother, by Fletcher and Massinger, London, Blackfriars theater, circa 1625;

The Fair Maid of the Inn, by Fletcher, Massinger (and perhaps John Webster and John Ford), London, Blackfriars theater, licensed 22 January 1626;

A Very Woman (Massinger's revision of an unidentified play by Fletcher and Massinger of circa 1619-1622), London, Blackfriars theater, licensed 6 June 1634.

BOOKS: *Salmacis and Hermaphroditus,* by Beaumont (London: Printed by S. Stafford for J. Hodgets, 1602);

The Woman Hater, by Beaumont and Fletcher (London: Printed by R. Raworth & sold by J. Hodgets, 1607);

The Faithfull Shepheardesse, by Fletcher (London: Printed by E. Allde for R. Bonian & H. Walley, 1609?);

The Knight of the Burning Pestle, by Beaumont (London: Printed by N. Okes for W. Burre, 1613);

The Masque of the Inner Temple and Grayes Inne, by Beaumont (London: Printed by F. Kingston for G. Norton, 1613);

Cupid's Revenge, by Beaumont and Fletcher (London: Printed by T. Creede for Josias Harison, 1615);

The Scornful Ladie, by Beaumont and Fletcher (London: Printed by J. Beale for M. Partrich, 1616);

A King and No King, by Beaumont and Fletcher (London: Printed by J. Beale for T. Walkley, 1619);

The Maides Tragedy, by Beaumont and Fletcher (London: Printed by N. Okes for F. Constable, 1619);

Phylaster, or Love Lyes a Bleeding, by Beaumont and Fletcher (London: Printed by N. Okes for T. Walkley, 1621);

The Tragedy of Thierry King of France and His Brother Theodoret, by Beaumont, Fletcher, and Philip Massinger (London: Printed by N. Okes for T. Walkley, 1621);

Henry VIII, by Fletcher and William Shakespeare, in *Mr. William Shakespeares Comedies, Histories, & Tragedies* (London: Printed by Isaac Jaggard & Ed. Blount, 1623);

The Two Noble Kinsman, by Fletcher and Shakespeare (London: Printed by T. Cotes for J. Waterson, 1634);

The Elder Brother, by Fletcher and Massinger (London: Printed by F. Kingston for J. Waterson & J. Benson, 1637);

The Bloody Brother, by Fletcher, Massinger, and others (perhaps Ben Jonson and George Chapman) (London: Printed by R. Bishop for T. Allott & J. Crook, 1639); republished as *The Tragœdy of Rollo Duke of Normandy* (Oxford: Printed by L. Lichfield, 1640);

Monsieur Thomas, by Fletcher (London: Printed by T. Harper for J. Waterson, 1639);

Wit Without Money, by Fletcher (London: Printed by T. Cotes for A. Crooke & W. Cooke, 1639);

Poems, by Beaumont (London: Printed by R. Hodgkinson for W. Wethered & L. Blaikelocke, 1640; enlarged edition, London: Printed for Laurence Blaikelocke, 1653); republished as *Poems: The Golden Remains of Francis Beaumont and John Fletcher* (London: Printed for W. Hope, 1660);

The Night-Walker, or The Little Theife, by Fletcher, revised by James Shirley (London: Printed by T. Cotes for A. Crooke & W. Cooke, 1640);

Rule a Wife and Have a Wife, by Fletcher (Oxford: Printed by L. Lichfield, 1640);

Comedies and Tragedies Written by Francis Beaumont and John Fletcher, Gentlemen. Never printed before, and now published by the Authours Originall Copies (London: Printed for Humphrey Robinson & Humphrey Moseley, 1647)—comprises *The Mad Lover, The Spanish Curate, The Little French Lawyer, The Custom of the Country, The Noble Gentleman, The Captain, Beggars' Bush, The Coxcomb, The False One, The Chances, The Loyal Subject, The Laws of Candy, The Lovers' Progress, The Island Princess, The Humourous Lieutenant, The Nice Valour or the Passionate Madman, The Maid in the Mill, The Prophetess, The Tragedy of Bonduca, The Sea Voyage, The Double Marriage, The Pilgrim, The Knight of Malta, The Woman's Prize or The Tamer Tamed, Love's Cure or The Martial Maid, The Honest Man's Fortune, The Queen of Corinth, Women Pleased, A Wife for a Month, Wit at Several Weapons, The Tragedy of Valentinian, The Fair Maid of the Inn, Love's Pilgrimage, The Masque of the Inner Temple and Gray's Inn, Four Plays or Moral Representations in One;*

The Wild Goose Chase, by Fletcher (London, 1652);

A Very Woman, Massinger's revision of an unidentified play by Fletcher and Massinger of circa 1619-1622, in *Three New Playes . . . Written By Philip Massenger* (London: Printed for Humphrey Moseley, 1655);

Fifty Comedies and Tragedies. Written by Francis Beaumont and John Fletcher, Gent. All in one Volume. Published by the Authours Originall Copies, the Songs to each Play being added (London: Printed by J. Macock for John Martyn, Henry Herringman & Richard Marriot, 1679)—comprises the contents of the 1647 folio and *The Maid's Tragedy, Philaster, A King and No King, The Scornful Lady, The Elder Brother, Wit Without Money, The Faithful Shepherdess, Rule a Wife and Have a Wife, Monsieur Thomas, The Bloody Brother or Rollo Duke of Normandy, The Wild Goose Chase, The Knight of the Burning Pestle, The Night Walker, Cupid's Revenge, The Two Noble Kinsmen, Thierry and Theodoret, The Woman Hater* (the volume contains fifty-two plays, including erroneously James Shirley's *The Coronation*).

Editions: *The Works of Beaumont and Fletcher,* edited by Alexander Dyce, 11 volumes (London: Moxon, 1843-1846);

The Dramatic Works in the Beaumont and Fletcher Canon, Fredson Bowers, general editor, 6 volumes to date (Cambridge: Cambridge University Press, 1966-   ).

OTHER: *Certain Elegies Done by Sundrie Excellent Wits,* includes nondramatic poems by Beaumont (London: Printed by B. Alsop for M. Patriche, 1618).

Francis Beaumont and John Fletcher began to work together as dramatists around 1606-1607, and in the course of the next half-dozen years wrote some of the most successful plays of the Jacobean theater, plays that continued to hold the stage a century later. They wrote both comedies and tragedies, but they seem to have had their first success in the newly fashionable genre of tragicomedy, a form that provided a potentially tragic plot with a happy ending. Their emergence as playwrights coincided with the closing years of Shakespeare's career in the theater, and critics have long noted the tragicomic shape of Shakespeare's last plays. Shakespeare's *Cymbeline* and Beaumont and Fletcher's *Philaster* display some notable similarities of plot and tone, but the date of each play is so uncertain (both seem to have been written circa 1609) that it is impossible to say which influenced the other. The vogue of tragicomedy was in the air. Shakespeare himself had experimented with it several years before, in *Measure for Measure* (circa 1603-1604), but the success of the younger dramatists with the form may have encouraged him to explore its possibilities even further in plays such as *Cymbeline, The Winter's Tale,* and *The Tempest.* Tragicomedy dominated the London stage throughout the rest of the period, until the closing of the theaters in 1642, and the model for later Jacobean and Caroline tragicomedy was provided by plays such as Beaumont and Fletcher's *Philaster* and *A King and No King,* and the many plays Fletcher wrote either alone or in collaboration with other dramatists after his association with Beaumont ended.

The period of their collaboration did not, in fact, last long. Beaumont married an heiress sometime around 1613 or 1614, and his career as a playwright seems to have ended then. He died in 1616. By that time, Fletcher had succeeded Shakespeare as principal dramatist for London's leading acting company, the King's Men, and he wrote steadily for the stage until his death in August 1625. However, the initial impression of Beaumont and Fletcher as a team persisted. Beaumont, at most, could have had a share in no more than twelve of the fifty-four plays in the Beaumont and Fletcher canon, but when a collection of these plays was published in 1647, it bore the title *Comedies and Tragedies, Written by Francis Beaumont and John*

Fletcher, Gentlemen. There were those at the time who protested that many of the plays in this 1647 folio collection were the unaided work of Fletcher, or of Fletcher in collaboration with dramatists (especially Philip Massinger) other than Beaumont. The protests went unheeded, however, and when in 1679 the plays in the 1647 folio were republished together with the plays that had previously been printed in individual quarto editions (which the 1647 folio had excluded), this second, 1679 folio was titled *Fifty Comedies and Tragedies. Written by Francis Beaumont and John Fletcher, Gent.* The 1679 folio defined the corpus of plays adopted (with occasional additions and subtractions) in all later editions, and the canon continues to be designated as Beaumont and Fletcher's. The two playwrights seem fated to be irrevocably linked in English literary history, and the linkage is one that their contemporary audiences fostered. Thomas Fuller, writing in 1662 (in *The Histories of the Worthies of England*), compared them to "Castor and Pollux (most happy when in conjunction)."

Both dramatists were members of distinguished families, that of Beaumont being especially venerable: it was connected with some of the oldest and noblest families in England (Nevil, Hastings, Talbot, Cavendish), including a royal one (Plantagenet). The Beaumonts were landed gentry, some of the land in their country seat in Leicestershire having been recently acquired from the dissolution of the Nunnery of Grace-Dieu in Charnwood Forest. Beaumont's father (also named Francis) was a lawyer and judge; he was a member of Parliament in 1572, made sergeant-at-law in 1589, and in 1593 appointed one of the Queen's Justices of the Court of Common Pleas. Beaumont the dramatist was born about 1584. On 4 February 1597 he (along with his two older brothers, Henry and John) entered Broadgates Hall (now Pembroke College), Oxford; the matriculation entry describes him as twelve years of age at the time of his admission. When his father died a year later (22 April 1598) the funeral certificate gives the approximate ages of the dead man's four children: Henry, John, and Elizabeth are said to be, respectively, seventeen, fourteen, and nine years of age, "or thereabouts," and Francis is said to be "of thirteen years or more." On 3 November 1600 he entered the Inner Temple, where his two older brothers had preceded him and where their father and grandfather had prepared for legal careers. Though it is impossible to say how seriously Beaumont ever intended to study law, and while it is apparent that after about 1605 his interests had turned decisively

to the theater, he maintained his identification with the Inner Temple throughout his career as a playwright. In 1613, not long before his marriage and retirement from the London theatrical scene, when the Inner Temple joined forces with Gray's Inn to present a masque in honor of the Princess Elizabeth's marriage, it was Beaumont who wrote it. London's inns of court provided an atmosphere that he would have found congenial. His fellow students were aristocrats like himself; there was much interest in poetry and the drama (students at the inns of court were notorious playgoers), and annually there was presented a series of high-spirited revels to celebrate the Christmas season. On one such occasion (sometime between around 1601 and 1605) Beaumont presented a burlesque, "Grammar Lecture," cast in the form of a mock-pedantic explication of the parts of speech amusingly wrenched to convey cynical admonitions to

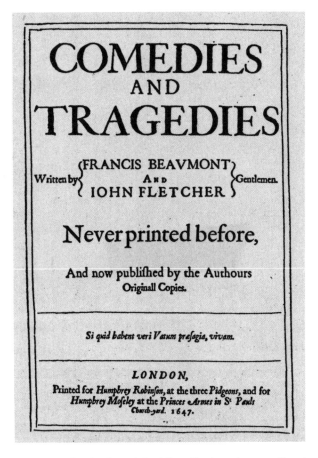

Title page for the first of the folio collections that contributed to the impression that Beaumont and Fletcher always wrote as a team. In fact, Beaumont had a hand in only six of the thirty-five plays in this volume (American Art Association Anderson Galleries, sale no. 4240, 11-12 March 1936).

his audience of sophisticated fellow students. Its flashes of witty satire and its vein of extravagant mockery anticipate the ironic inventions that he would soon be putting on the stage.

This was not Beaumont's only literary performance in these early years. In 1602 his Ovidian narrative poem, *Salmacis and Hermaphroditus,* was published anonymously, the same year in which his brother John's mock-heroic poem, *The Metamorphosis of Tobacco,* was published, also anonymously, with some commendatory verses signed "F. B." *Salmacis and Hermaphroditus* contains an introductory sonnet signed "I. B." (that is, "J. B."). The brothers were evidently exchanging poetical compliments, and both were soon moving in literary circles. In the eighth eclogue of his *Poems Lyric and Pastoral* (entered in the Stationers' Register on 19 April 1606), Michael Drayton pays tribute to Mirtilla who is "in the Muses joyes" and who dwells in Charnwood by the river Soar, sister "to those hopefull Boyes," Thirsis and Palmeo: a tribute that is generally assumed to have reference to Elizabeth Beaumont and her two brothers, Francis and John. This suggests that Drayton's lines were written sometime after 10 July 1605, when Henry Beaumont, the eldest brother and head of the family, died. By his will, witnessed by Francis Beaumont and probated February 1606, Sir Henry left half of his private estate to his sister, Elizabeth, and the other half to be divided equally between John and Francis. John succeeded him as head of the family.

The Beaumont family had strong Roman Catholic loyalties. Francis Beaumont's grandmother, mother, uncle, and even his father before he became a judge had been active recusants. Before the end of the year 1605, the dramatist's cousin, Anne Vaux, would be implicated in the Gunpowder Plot. Soon after he succeeded to the family estate at Grace-Dieu in the summer of 1605, John Beaumont was penalized for his own recusancy. As a result, sometime before October 1605 the profits of his recusancy had been allotted to Sir James Sempill, a boyhood companion of King James. Two-thirds of John Beaumont's lands and all his goods were forfeited to the king, and in 1607 they were formally granted to Sempill, who was still profiting from them as late as 1615. John Beaumont, as a recusant, was now required to live at Grace-Dieu and confined to his house there. With the income from the family estate thus severely curtailed, Francis Beaumont's decision to write for the theater may have been prompted in part, at least, by financial need.

In the case of John Fletcher financial necessity seems almost certainly to have dictated the choice of his profession as a writer for the stage. For the decade or so preceding the beginning of his career as a dramatist, Fletcher had been an orphan. His father had died in 1596, leaving a large burden of debts and nine children, of whom the future playwright, then aged seventeen, was one (his mother had died about 1594). The family fortunes had changed drastically since his birth in December 1579 at Rye, in Sussex, where his father, Richard Fletcher, was minister of the local church. In the following years, the father had had a career of some prominence in the Anglican church: he had been appointed successively Chaplain to the Queen, Dean of Peterborough, Bishop of Bristol, Bishop of Worcester, and in 1594, Bishop of London. Richard Fletcher enjoyed the favor of the Queen, who entrusted him with important missions (as Dean of Peterborough he was chaplain to Mary, Queen of Scots, and had witnessed her execution); he had a house in Chelsea and counted among his friends such counsellors to the Queen as Lord Burghley, Anthony Bacon, Sir Francis Drake, and the Earl of Essex. But in 1595 Richard Fletcher made a most improper second marriage with one Lady Baker, a widow with a notorious past. The Queen suspended him from his office for a year, before the end of which he had died. Whether his son the future dramatist was the John Fletcher who entered Bene't College (now Corpus Christi), Cambridge, in 1591 is uncertain (the name was common), but plausible; Richard Fletcher had once been associated with that college. If the identification is allowed, then John Fletcher the dramatist became B.A. in 1595 and M.A. in 1598. He may have spent some of the years until he was able to fend for himself with his Uncle Giles, the diplomat and author of a notable book on Russia (published in 1591), and with his young cousins, Giles, Jr., and Phineas, who would earn minor places in English literary history as imitators of the poetical manner of Edmund Spenser.

The earliest extant play to exhibit Beaumont and Fletcher working together is a comedy titled *The Woman Hater,* entered in the Stationers' Register on 20 May 1607 and published that year in a quarto edition, the title page of which names no author (the 1648 edition attributed the play to Fletcher while the 1649 edition listed Beaumont and Fletcher as authors; uncertainty of this sort is characteristic of seventeenth-century title-page attributions). Though the play is substantially the work of Beaumont, Fletcher's hand can be traced in at least five scenes, chiefly through his use of certain linguistic forms (notably his preference for the pronoun *ye* for *you*) that Beaumont rarely if ever employed. The play's Italian setting provides the usual veil (familiar in so much of Renaissance English comedy) for satirizing the affectations and the humors of contemporary London life. Its models are the recent satiric comedies of John Marston (such as *The Fawn, The Dutch Courtesan*), and the series of comedies of humors and "comical satires" that Ben Jonson had been presenting on the London stage over the past half-dozen years (*Every Man in his Humour, Every Man Out of his Humour, Cynthia's Revel's, Poetaster*, and most recently, *Volpone*).

The Woman Hater seems to have made no particular impression on its initial audiences. John Dryden, writing many years later (in *An Essay of Dramatick Poesy*, 1668) reported that *Philaster* was the first play that brought Beaumont and Fletcher "in esteem . . . : for before that, they had written two or three very unsuccessfully." *The Woman Hater* was probably one of these. The two others were plays that each dramatist had written independently early in his career: Beaumont's *The Knight of the Burning Pestle*, and Fletcher's *The Faithful Shepherdess*. The composition date of each is uncertain. Nothing is known of either until it appeared in print, and neither play was published until some indeterminate time after it was first performed. *The Knight of the Burning Pestle* was probably written and unsuccessfully acted in 1607 (it was first printed in 1613). *The Faithful Shepherdess* seems to have been presented only to be rejected by audiences in 1608 (it was published in an undated quarto that was probably printed in 1609). Each play is highly characteristic of its author.

The Knight of the Burning Pestle is the only play of Beaumont's sole authorship that we have, and it provides us with a rare opportunity to witness the full ensemble of his comic artistry operating without interference from another quarter: his talents for satire, parody, and burlesque provide the play with a remarkably rich palette of comic shadings that complement and set each other off as effortlessly as the play's three principals (Grocer, Wife, and Apprentice) move back and forth between audience and stage, incorporating their own play into the one that the designated actors are trying to present. *The Knight* mocks the plot materials and the rhetoric of some of the most popular plays of the period: chauvinistic tales of young Englishmen engaged in chivalric exploits in exotic landscapes, such as Thomas Heywood's *Four Pren-*

tices of London, or John Day, William Rowley, and George Wilkins's *Travels of Three English Brothers*; celebrations of the charitable and philanthropic acts of London citizens, such as Heywood's *If You Know Not Me, You Know Nobody*, or Thomas Dekker's *The Shoemakers' Holiday*; bourgeois comedies of love involving London citizens, their daughters, and their apprentices, and recounting the triumph of true affection over the objections of mercantile-minded parents (as again, in *The Shoemakers' Holiday*); plays of romantic adventure such as the anonymous *Mucedorus*. In a prefatory note the printer of the 1613 edition of *The Knight* suggests that a reason why the play was "utterly rejected" when it was first acted was the failure of audiences to understand "the privy marke of *Ironie* about it." Irony in *The Knight* is not a matter of separate speeches or scenes directed to familiar satiric targets; rather, it is inherent in the very phenomenon Beaumont is out to represent, namely, the distance that sep-

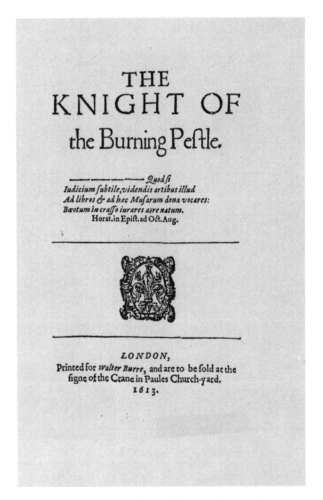

Title page for the 1613 edition of the only known play written by Beaumont alone (Bodleian Library, Oxford)

arates the lives of ordinary London citizens from the various romantic fantasies—of knight-errantry, of love and marriage, of the means to fame and fortune—that dazzle their imaginations. However, plays of the sort that Beaumont is parodying in *The Knight* recognized no ironic distance between the facts of middle-class London life and the glamorous dreams that fed the imaginative life of its citizenry, and it is quite likely that the play's first audiences mistook it for another instance of the sort of play it satirizes. Its chief structural novelty—whereby its action has the appearance of being periodically derailed as the Grocer and his wife invade the stage from the audience—may have contributed to the incomprehension with which it was first greeted. Eventually, audiences came to terms with the play, and it appears in theatrical repertoires throughout the rest of the period, until the closing of the theaters. It is Beaumont's finest achievement, and one of the most brilliant examples of the mock heroic

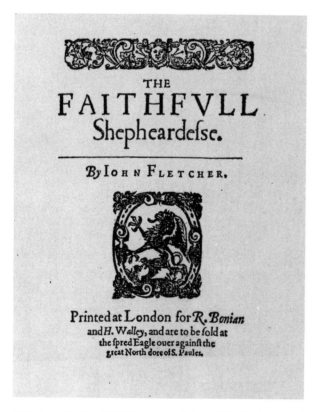

Title page for the 1609(?) quarto edition of Fletcher's pastoral tragicomedy, prefixed by commendatory verses by Beaumont, Ben Jonson, George Chapman, and Nathan Field, all of whom assured potential readers that the play had failed in the theater because it made too great a demand on the intelligence of the average playgoer (Anderson Galleries, sale no. 2077, 20-21 May 1926)

and of literary burlesque in English comic literature.

Fletcher's *The Faithful Shepherdess* is a very different kind of play: a pastoral tragicomedy inspired by Giovanni Battista Guarini's *Il Pastor Fido* (1590), though Fletcher's play has very little direct connection with that celebrated work. Where Beaumont's *Knight* is the product of the dramatist's amused observation of the humorous absurdities flourishing around him in contemporary London, *The Faithful Shepherdess* is very much a product of Fletcher's literary imagination. The play's setting is the conventional landscape of pastoral poetry—forests, arbors, bosky dells, with caves and charmed fountains and altars to the god Pan—populated with a typically pastoral dramatis personae: shepherds, shepherdesses, satyrs, river gods, and priests of Pan. The play celebrates the power of chastity (which accounts for its appeal to the young Milton, a few years later, when he came to write *Comus*). The power is personified in the figure of Clorin, the faithful shepherdess of the title, who, her beloved having died, has vowed to lead a retired life of virginal purity; this preserves her knowledge, possessed since her youth, of "the dark hidden vertuous use of hearbs"; as a result, she is greatly gifted in the arts of healing. The other principal characters are arranged in a spectrum of passional self-control that extends from Clorin's awesome continence through various degrees of sexual indiscretion to uninhibited lust. Each prowls the forest darkness from dusk to dawn during the single night of the play's action, seeking a partner and encountering various forms of frustration and mayhem in the process (twice in the play a young man stabs the young woman whom he loves but believes to be unfaithful, thereby anticipating what would become a notorious scene in *Philaster*). The elaborate, often shrill, testimonials to the power of chastity contained in the play's poetry exist in strained opposition to the sexual frenzy that informs its action. When the play was published, no attempt was made to conceal its failure in the theater. Fletcher's fellow playwrights (Beaumont, Ben Jonson, George Chapman, Nathan Field) rallied to the occasion by assuring him, in commendatory verses prefixed to the undated quarto edition, that what he had written had been too good for the stage; that its poetical excellencies had been, in effect, its undoing, since they made demands on the intelligence of the average audience that most members thereof were incapable of meeting. *The Faithful Shepherdess* never established itself on the seventeenth-century English stage, but if audiences found it unsatisfactory as a play, readers long admired it as a poem. It has a certain importance in the history of seventeenth-century English drama because it provided the occasion for Fletcher's famous definition of tragicomedy. In his address "To the Reader" printed in the undated quarto text of the play, he describes it as "a pastoral tragicomedy" and suggests that it failed in the theater because audiences came to it with false expectations concerning each term. As for "pastoral," audiences assumed "a play of country hired shepherds in gray cloaks, with curtailed dogs in strings, sometimes laughing together, and sometimes killing one another; and, missing Whitsun-ales, cream, wassail, and morris-dances, began to be angry." As for "tragi-comedy," such a play "is not so called in respect of mirth and killing, but in respect it wants deaths, which is enough to make it no tragedy, yet brings some near it, which is enough to make it no comedy, which must be a representation of familiar people, with such kind of trouble as no life be questioned; so that a god is as lawful in this as in a tragedy, and mean [that is, common] people as in a comedy."

Fletcher's comments are based on Guarini's *Il Compendio della poesia tragicomica*, published in 1601 in defense of his own pastoral tragicomedy, *Il Pastor Fido*. Tragicomedy had been attacked by Italian critics as illegitimate because Aristotle had made no provision for such a genre in the *Poetics*, where he had acknowledged only tragedy and comedy, and because tragicomedy has no distinct properties of its own but consists merely of a combination of tragic and comic elements. In defending the integrity of the genre Guarini explains how the author of a tragicomedy, far from mechanically combining the elements of tragedy and comedy, judiciously selects what is requisite from each: he takes from tragedy its great persons but not its great action, a plot which is verisimilar but not true, passions that have been moved but are tempered, tragedy's pleasure but not its sadness, "its danger but not its death; from comedy it takes laughter that is not excessive, modest amusement, feigned difficulty, happy reversal, and above all the comic order."

This selective combination of the requisite elements of tragedy and comedy, Guarini is prepared to claim, can result in a new dramatic genre that is superior to the two conventional ones: "It is much more noble than simple tragedy or simple comedy, as that which does not inflict on us atrocious events and horrible and inhumane sights, such as blood and deaths, and which, on the other hand, does not cause us to be so relaxed in laughter that we

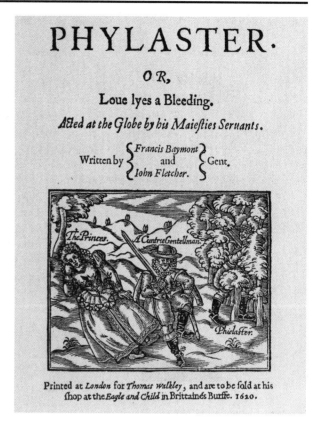

Title page for the 1620 quarto edition of one of Beaumont and Fletcher's most successful tragicomedies (Bodleian Library, Oxford)

sin against the modesty and decorum of a well-bred man. And truly if today men understood well how to compose tragicomedy (for it is not an easy thing to do), no other drama should be put on the stage, for tragicomedy is able to include all the good qualities of dramatic poetry and to reject all the bad ones; it can delight all dispositions, all ages, and all tastes—something that is not true of the other two, tragedy and comedy, which are at fault because they go to excess." Tragicomedy was to be the genre in which Beaumont and Fletcher would have two of their most notable stage successes (*Philaster* and *A King and No King*), and it would be the genre which—after Beaumont's retirement—Fletcher, writing alone and in collaboration with other dramatists, would popularize to an extent that would profoundly influence the nature of English drama throughout the rest of the seventeenth century.

The composition date of *Philaster* is uncertain. It was not published until 1620, but a decade earlier John Davies of Hereford had referred to it under its subtitle, *Love lies a-Bleeding* (along with *The Faithful Shepherdess*), in epigram 206 of his *Scourge of*

Folly, entered in the Stationers' Register on 8 October 1610. Resemblances have often been noted between the titular figure and two of Shakespeare's most famous tragic heroes, Hamlet and Othello. Philaster, like Hamlet, is the son of a king whose kingdom has been usurped by a tyrant; the tyrant tolerates his continued residence at what had been his father's court because the kingdom's subjects love him, but he plans to divert the line of succession from Philaster to his daughter, the Princess Arathusa, whom he intends to marry to a Spanish prince. But Philaster also loves Arathusa and believes that she returns his love. When courtly slander causes him to doubt her faith, an Othello-like fury descends upon him, and he tries to kill the princess. The Shakespearean resemblances are certainly superficial, but ought not to be dismissed. Regularly in the Beaumont and Fletcher plays, there are signs that the authors are reworking sit-

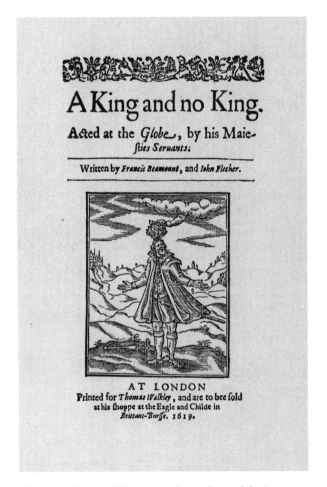

Title page for the 1619 quarto edition of one of the Beaumont and Fletcher tragicomedies that served as models for later Jacobean and Caroline plays written in that popular genre (Bodleian Library, Oxford)

uations from Shakespeare's recent plays, or placing one or another of his characters in altered dramatic circumstances. Philaster has a young page, Bellario, who unknown to him is in fact a young girl in disguise; she loves him, and finds herself—in the manner of Viola in Shakespeare's *Twelfth Night*—pleading the cause of the man she loves to the woman (Arathusa) whom he loves. Bellario is the person with whom, as courtly gossip would have it, Arathusa has been unfaithful to Philaster. There is a moment in the final act of *Twelfth Night* when the Duke, believing his page (the still-disguised Viola) to be his rival for the love of Olivia, threatens to kill the supposed boy. This is the sort of Shakespearean hint Beaumont and Fletcher are fond of developing. Philaster, having wounded Arathusa, wounds Bellario as well. The character of Philaster seems designed to represent a normally gentle prince driven to the brink of madness by melancholy occasioned by his displacement as heir to his father's kingdom and by sexual jealousy occasioned by his supposed displacement in the affections of Arathusa. His behavior is certainly erratic (as Hamlet's is, when the antic disposition is upon him), and his wild swings of mood—from trust to doubt, from proud confidence to pathetic helplessness—give to his movement through the play a quality of comic iteration. On this score, it is worth remembering that Guarini (in a passage already quoted) had stressed that, among the elements of comedy that the tragicomic dramatist will select for his work, he will include "above all the comic order." He will also include, according to Guarini, "feigned difficulty" and "happy reversal." In *Philaster* the feigned difficulty concerns the disguised Bellario and the accusations made against this character and Arathusa. When, at the end of the play, Bellario at last reveals her true identity, the charges against Arathusa fall to the ground, and Philaster's dark fortunes reverse themselves as happily as thought could wish. Arathusa is his, her father accepts him as son-in-law (the Spanish prince is dismissed) and restores to him his rightful place in the kingdom.

A King and No King, which was acted at Court on 26 December 1611 and had been licensed for performance earlier in the same year, centers on another unstable protagonist, King Arbaces, whose pride in his self-sufficiency is severely shaken when he returns from his wars to find that his sister, Panthaea, has grown into a beautiful woman in his absence, and that he is falling in love with her, and she with him. Arbaces's desperate impulse to surrender to his incestuous desires at the same time that he is appalled by them is conveyed in some of

Beaumont and Fletcher's most bravura scenes (they seem mainly to be the work of Beaumont). Arbaces is the sort of dramatic figure who—like a Medea or a Macbeth—knows what is the right way but yet is willfully prepared to pursue the wrong one; his self-awareness on this score seals his march toward disaster with what would seem to be an inexorable finality, but in the manner of Guarinian tragicomedy, we discover as *A King and No King* nears its end that we have been in the presence of a feigned difficulty, and that a happy reversal is in prospect. Arbaces and Panthaea are not brother and sister after all. She is, in fact, the queen of what he has thought of as his realm, and by being unkinged, he is free to marry her. For all the tense agonizing that has occurred at the center of the play, *A King and No King* preserves the comic order, as Guarini has said that a tragicomedy should, by surrounding Arbaces with a shrewdly observed group of friends, counsellors, and court hangers-on whose response to his plight provides a critique by turns sympathetic and ironical of his extravagant behavior.

The Maid's Tragedy seems to have been written and acted in the period between Beaumont and Fletcher's most famous tragicomedies (it is assumed to have been in existence by 31 October 1611 when the Master of the Revels, licensing an anonymous play without a title, named it a "Second Maiden's Tragedy"). At the center of the play is another overwrought male protagonist, Amintor, who, though he has been betrothed to marry Aspatia, has at the King's command married instead Evadne, sister to his friend, the great general Melantius. What he does not know is that Evadne is the King's mistress, and that the marriage has been arranged to protect her reputation. She announces this fact to Amintor on their wedding night and goes on to declare her intention never to consummate their marriage. The play explores the consequences for all the parties to this sensational situation: Amintor's humiliation and rage, the grief of the abandoned Aspatia, the violent confrontation of brother and sister when Melantius learns why Evadne has married his friend. Amintor's impulse to revenge his honor by assaulting the man who has, in effect, made him a cuckold, is paralyzed by his reverence for the divinity that surrounds the person of a king. Melantius is not so awed; he works his sister to a proper sense of her shame with the result that she murders the king in his bed. Aspatia brings about her own death at the hands of Amintor, who thereupon commits suicide.

These three plays made Beaumont and Fletcher famous. That all three were produced by

the King's Men (London's most prestigious acting company, of which Shakespeare was a principal shareholder and principal dramatist) is a measure of the success the two playwrights had achieved within a period of rather less than four years. Their first plays had been produced by companies of boy actors: *The Woman Hater* by Paul's boys, at their theater in the precincts of St. Paul's Cathedral; *The Knight of the Burning Pestle* and *The Faithful Shepherdess* by the Children of the Queen's Revels at their theater in Blackfriars. When, in the summer of 1608, the King's Men took over the lease of the enclosed Blackfriars theater for use as a winter headquarters and proceeded henceforth to produce plays in it as well as in their open-air Globe theater, it may have seemed to them wise to employ the services of a pair of dramatists whose skill at entertaining Blackfriars audiences was beginning to be noticed. Prior to *Philaster*, they had written

Title page for the 1619 quarto edition of the play that, with Philaster *and* A King and No King, *made Beaumont and Fletcher famous with London theatergoers (Bodleian Library, Oxford)*

other plays besides *The Woman Hater, The Knight of the Burning Pestle,* and *The Faithful Shepherdess,* though a good deal of uncertainty surrounds the composition of some of them. There are a number of plays in the Beaumont and Fletcher canon that seem to date from this early period, but there is no external evidence that might help to establish just when they were written; many of these did not appear in print until the folio collection of 1647, and some appear there in versions that have been revised by other hands (a prologue or epilogue frequently announces the fact of revision). A comedy such as *Love's Cure, or The Martial Maid,* for example, is very probably one of Beaumont and Fletcher's earliest collaborations (it has close ties of characterization and language to *The Woman Hater* and may have been written for the company at Paul's), but the 1647 folio text of the play has been extensively revised by Philip Massinger. *The Noble Gentleman* seems originally to have been a play of Beaumont's sole authorship, but in its extant text

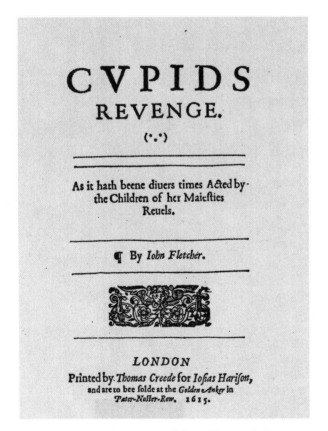

Title page for the 1615 quarto edition of the tragedy Beaumont and Fletcher based on material from Sir Philip Sydney's Arcadia. Despite the title-page attribution to Fletcher alone, the play is the work of both playwrights (Anderson Galleries, sale no. 2077, 20-21 May 1926)

it has been revised by Fletcher and perhaps by others. Even after they had been taken up by the King's Men, Beaumont and Fletcher continued to write for the Queen's Revels, now performing at a new theater in Whitefriars. It was for this children's company that they wrote (circa 1609) their very witty comedy of *The Coxcomb* (its plot suggested by the story of "The Curious Impertinent" in part one of Cervantes's *Don Quixote;* it was performed at Court on 2 or 3 November 1612). It was also for this boys' company that they wrote (circa 1611) their lurid tragedy, *Cupid's Revenge* (based on material from Sir Philip Sydney's *Arcadia;* performances at Court recorded on 5 January 1612, 1 January 1613, and either 9 January or 27 February 1613). For the King's Men they wrote (circa 1611) another play about a woman hater, this one titled *The Captain* (it was performed at Court during the season 1612-1613).

The Court season of 1612-1613 was particularly rich in productions of plays, due to the festivities surrounding the marriage of the Princess Elizabeth to Frederick V, the Elector Palatine, and the head of the league of Protestant princes in Germany. Shortly after his arrival in England in October 1612, the festivities had been interrupted by the death of Prince Henry on 7 November 1612. After a suitable period of mourning, the wedding took place on 14 February 1613. *The Masque of the Inner Temple and Gray's Inn* (with verses by Beaumont), prepared by the members of those inns of court in honor of the occasion, was scheduled for performance on 16 February. Since the "device" or theme of the masque was the marriage of the Thames to the Rhine, the masquers deemed it appropriate to go from their rendezvous at Winchester Place in Southwark to Whitehall Palace by water and did so in an elaborate (and very costly) procession of barges and galleys. Upon their arrival, however, they found the palace so crowded with people that it was impossible for them to make their way to the hall where they were to perform. Thus the explanation in the printed text of the masque, which may be true so far as it goes. But it was also rumored that King James, exhausted from having watched masques on the two previous nights (Thomas Campion's *The Lords' Masque* on the 14th, and George Chapman's *Masque of the Middle Temple and Lincoln's Inn* on the 15th), pronounced himself incapable of watching another on this occasion. The masquers were invited back four nights later, and Beaumont's creation was staged in the Banqueting House at Whitehall on 20 February.

Beaumont's career as a dramatist was drawing to an end, and with it his life in London, including his life with Fletcher, which years later John Aubrey described (perhaps a bit fancifully) in a much-quoted passage: "They lived together on the Bankside, not far from the Play-house, both batchelors; lay together; had one Wench in the house between them, which they did so admire; the same cloathes and cloake, etc.; between them." But Beaumont—sometime during 1613 or 1614—put his bachelor life behind him and married an heiress, Ursula Isley, of Sundridge Hall, Kent. A daughter, Elizabeth, was born in either 1614 or 1615, and another daughter, named Frances, was born a few months after his death on 6 March 1616. He was buried in the Poets' Corner of Westminster Abbey, only the third English writer (after Chaucer and Spenser) to be so honored.

But either before retiring to his wife's country estate, or in the intervals of his life as a country gentleman during his last months, he contributed to four more plays. Beaumont and Fletcher's *The Scornful Lady* is a brilliant comedy of manners; according to the title page of the play's 1616 quarto edition, it was acted by the Children of the Queen's Revels in the Blackfriars, a statement which, if true, means that it was staged in 1615 during the brief period when the Queen's Revels company, having left Whitefriars, performed in a new theater in the precinct of Blackfriars known as Porter's Hall. Beaumont also has a share with Fletcher in three plays for the King's company that seem to have been staged after his death: *Love's Pilgrimage*, a romantic comedy; *Thierry and Theodoret*, a tragedy; and another comedy, *Beggar's Bush*. *Love's Pilgrimage* must have been one of the last plays on which the two dramatists collaborated. The source of the play, Cervantes's story, *Las dos doncellas*, in his *Novelas Exemplares*, was not allowed for publication in Spain until August 1613. A French translation was published in 1615. There is some evidence that the play was acted in 1616. It was not printed until the publication of the 1647 folio, where the text of the play's opening scene unaccountably contains two sizable passages (of 21 and 111 lines respectively) that duplicate passages in II.ii and III.i of Jonson's *The New Inn*, acted by the King's Men in January 1629 and printed in 1631, after the deaths of both Beaumont and Fletcher. Though Beaumont contributed, with Fletcher, to *Thierry and Theodoret*, and to *Beggar's Bush*, a third dramatist, Philip Massinger, has a share in each of these as well. In the years immediately following, Massinger would be Fletcher's principal collaborator, and it would appear that

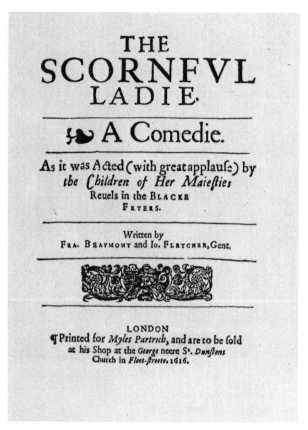

Title page for the 1616 quarto edition of one of the last plays that Beaumont wrote with Fletcher (Bodleian Library, Oxford)

Fletcher joined forces with him now, either in anticipation of Beaumont's retirement, or to take over Beaumont's unfinished shares in these two plays.

In the last years of Beaumont and Fletcher's collaboration, from about 1611 on, Fletcher's career seems to have been moving in its own independent direction. Two signs are notable: Fletcher began to do what Beaumont never did in those years, wrote plays alone; Fletcher collaborated with Shakespeare on three plays, a suggestive sign that he was being groomed to succeed Shakespeare (who was about to retire) as principal dramatist for the King's Men. Shakespeare's *The Tempest* (produced in 1611) is often taken to be his valediction to the theater, but in fact he wrote three more plays, and Fletcher aided him in each of them. The first seems to have been *Cardenio*, acted at Court during the busy Christmas-revels season of 1612-1613, and again before the Savoyard ambassador on 8 June 1613. The play is lost. From its title, one assumes it to have been based on the story of Cardenio in chapters 23-37 of part one of Cervantes's *Don Quixote*. The next Shakespeare-Fletcher collaboration was probably *The Two Noble Kinsmen,* a dramatization of Chaucer's *Knight's Tale.* Since the play uses material from Beaumont's *The Masque of the Inner Temple and Gray's Inn,* it is usually assumed to have been written not long after the performance of that masque on 20 February 1613. The play was printed in 1634 with a title-page attribution to Shakespeare and Fletcher. The third Shakespeare-Fletcher collaboration was *Henry VIII.* Its date is well established since it is described as a new play in accounts of the performance of it that took place at the Globe on 29 June 1613, in the course of which fire broke out and destroyed the theater. The play was first printed (without reference to Fletcher) in the 1623 folio collection of Shakespeare's plays.

After the failure on stage of his *The Faithful Shepherdess,* Fletcher seems to have resumed his career as an independent dramatist with a series of comedies written for companies other than the King's. The first of these seems to be *The Woman's Prize, or the Tamer Tamed,* a farcical exploitation of Shakespeare's *The Taming of the Shrew,* written sometime near the end of 1610 or early in 1611 for an unknown company (by 1633 it had passed into the possession of the King's). There follows a trio of lively comedies set in London and environs and centering on the amorous and/or monetary intrigues of feckless young gentlemen: *The Night Walker, or The Little Thief* (1611, for either the Queen's Revels or the newly formed company patronized by Lady Elizabeth; the text of the only extant substantive edition of the play, that of the 1640 quarto, had been revised by James Shirley in 1633); *Monsieur Thomas, or Father's Own Son* (circa 1612, for either the Queen's Revels or Lady Elizabeth's; one of the play's sources is the "Histoire de Cellidee, Thamyre et Calidon" in *L'Astrée de Messire Honoré d'Urfé,* part two, published in Paris in February 1610); and *Wit Without Money* (circa 1614; probably for Lady Elizabeth's; the play seems to have been revised in 1620). Other work that Fletcher undertook with companies other than the King's during this period involved his collaboration with the actor turned dramatist Nathan Field, which seems to have begun in a series of one-act plays, framed with an induction and an epilogue, titled *Four Plays, or Moral Representations, in One* (circa 1612; the auspices under which this was produced are unknown; the piece may have been designed for a private entertainment). The year 1613 found both Fletcher and Massinger aiding Field in a tragicomedy titled *The Honest Man's Fortune* for Lady Elizabeth's (the shares of Fletcher and Massinger are comparatively small).

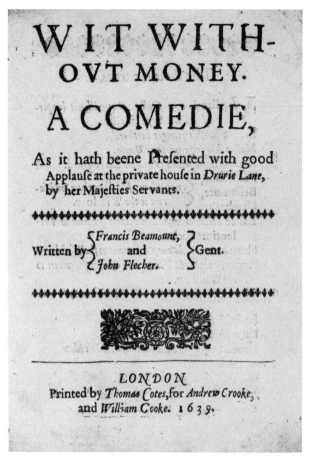

Title page for the 1639 quarto edition of a play Fletcher wrote circa 1614 and probably revised in 1620 (Henry E. Huntington Library and Art Gallery)

Fletcher seems to have launched his work as an independent dramatist for the King's Men with *Bonduca* (circa 1611), a historical tragedy of Roman Britain. Another tragedy, *Valentinian,* shortly followed (circa 1612), for which he again turned for a source to part two of *L'Astrée de Messire Honoré d'Urfé* (the "Histoire d'Eudoxe, Valentinian, et Ursace"). With this play, Fletcher's work in tragedy virtually ended. It had never loomed large in his output. He had helped Beaumont with *Cupid's Revenge* and *The Maid's Tragedy;* he would shortly be contributing (with Beaumont and Massinger) to *Thierry and Theodoret;* three of his future collaborations (*The Bloody Brother, Barnavelt, The Double Marriage*) would be tragedies; but the remaining plays that he would write without a collaborator would be either comedies or tragicomedies.

One of his most successful tragicomedies, *The Mad Lover,* appeared in 1616 (it was acted at Court on 5 January 1617). The play's bizarre plot is typical of the tendency in Fletcherian tragicomedy to deal in dramatic improbabilities with unabashed rhetorical assurance and to concoct histrionic effects that are a heady compound of sentiment and wit. The heroic and idealistic and more than a little naive protagonist of *The Mad Lover*, smitten with the beauty of a sophisticated court lady, offers her his heart, and she, in ironic mood, takes him at his word, whereupon, undaunted, he sets about making plans for having that organ removed from his body and sent to her. The play dramatizes—in terms at once tender and mocking—the means by which he is persuaded that he can go on living honorably without giving the lady what she had consented to receive.

The *Novelas Exemplares* of Cervantes had provided the plot for *Love's Pilgrimage*, and around this time (probably in 1617), Fletcher used another of these, *La Señora Cornelia*, for the plot of one of his best comedies, *The Chances* (the text of the play that appears in the 1647 folio was revised circa 1627, shortly after Fletcher's death).

The collaboration of Fletcher, Massinger, and Field that had produced *The Honest Man's Fortune* in 1613 continued in these years, now for the King's Men. In the period circa 1617-1619, the three dramatists wrote three plays together, though one (*The Jeweller of Amsterdam*) is lost. Of the two extant tragicomedies, *The Queen of Corinth* is notable for the use in its plot of one of the *controversiae* of Seneca the Elder. *Controversiae* were declamations of a judicial kind, used in the oratorical schools of ancient Rome as rhetorical exercises in the training of young orators. The declamations consisted of arguments in support of or in opposition to hypothetical cases that posed legal or ethical dilemmas. The cases were contrived to be as intricate and as paradoxical as possible, the better to test the

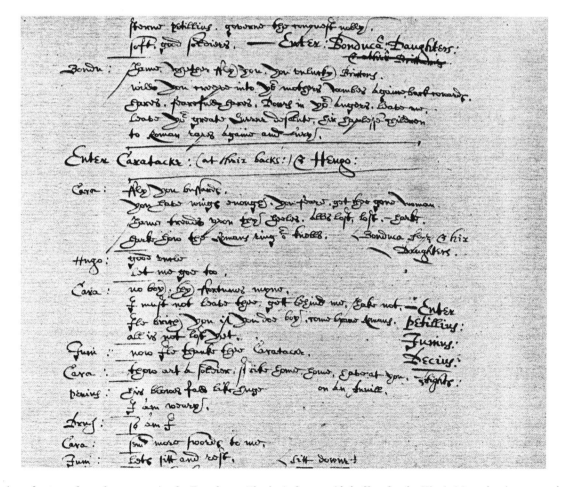

A portion of a page from the manuscript for Bonduca, *Fletcher's first unaided effort for the King's Men, that is preserved in the British Library. This manuscript is thought to be a fair copy made for a private collector by a Mr. Knight, a bookholder for the King's Men, some ten to twenty years before the play was published in the 1647 collection of Beaumont and Fletcher's plays (Add. MS 36758; by permission of the British Library)*

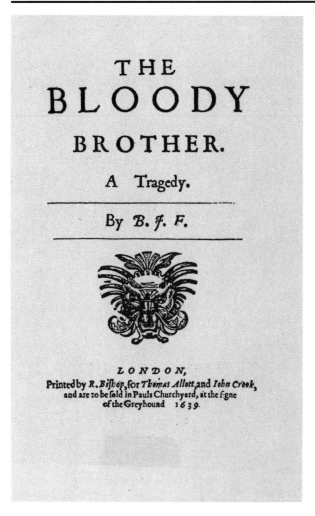

THE
BLOODY
BROTHER.

A Tragedy.

By *B. J. F.*

LONDON,
Printed by *R. Bishop,* for *Thomas Allott,* and *Iohn Crook,*
and are to be sold in Pauls Churchyard, at the signe
of the Greyhound 1639.

After Beaumont's retirement to the life of a country gentleman, Fletcher collaborated with Philip Massinger (and perhaps Ben Jonson and George Chapman) on this tragedy (E. H. C. Oliphant, The Plays of Beaumont and Fletcher, *1927)*

argumentative and rhetorical skills of the student. The *controversia* that provides the climax of *The Queen of Corinth* concerns the sentence that is to be meted out to a man who has raped two women, when one woman demands his death and the other demands that he marry her without a dowry, the law of the land permitting either penalty. This is the sort of difficulty that tragicomedy, as Guarini defined it, was created to solve. In the play, the man (contrary to his belief) has not raped two women, but has raped one woman twice, she being in disguise on the second occasion. The problem concerning the conflicting penalties vanishes when this is revealed. The difficulty has been feigned, just as Guarini said it should be, and by the end of the play, matters have turned to "unexpected com-

edy," as one character puts it. In addition to *The Queen of Corinth*, at least two other plays in the Beaumont and Fletcher canon (*The Laws of Candy* and *The Double Marriage*) are based on one or more of the *controversiae* of Seneca, and the example of these Latin oratorical exercises has had an effect on the design of Fletcherian tragicomedy, specifically with regard to the extravagantly contrived dramatic situations that often comprise its plots, and the elaborate rhetoric that ornaments its speeches in moments of dramatic crisis. Not long after *The Queen of Corinth*, Fletcher, Massinger, and Field wrote another tragicomedy, *The Knight of Malta*.

Field died in 1619 or 1620, and it may have been in an effort to replace him that about this time Fletcher and Massinger teamed up with two other dramatists (who have been conjectured to have been Ben Jonson and George Chapman) to produce a violent tragedy that is variantly titled *The Bloody Brother* (in a quarto edition published in 1639), and *Rollo Duke of Normandy* (in another quarto edition with a somewhat different text published in 1640). The play poses some of the most complicated problems, textual and authorial, in the Beaumont and Fletcher canon. In addition to having been one of its original authors, Massinger seems to have revised at least parts of it at some later date. And somebody has transported into the play (in a somewhat variant version) the song beginning "Take ô take those lips away" from Shakespeare's *Measure for Measure*.

After this experiment in a four-way collaboration, Fletcher seems to have preferred working with a single partner when he was not working alone. From around 1619 until his death six years later, his dramatic output alternates between plays of his own unaided authorship, and collaborations with Massinger. After *The Mad Lover*, his next unaided play seems to have been *The Loyal Subject*, known to have been licensed for performance on 16 November 1618. For details concerning its Moscow setting, Fletcher drew on his uncle Giles's book (published in 1591) on the Russian "commonwealth." During the summer of 1619 Fletcher and Massinger quickly wrote another tragedy, this one dealing with recent political events in Holland: the downfall and execution of the Dutch patriot, Sir John van Olden Barnavelt, whose name gives to the play its title. The play was of great contemporary interest, for religious as well as for political reasons: the conflict of Calvinism and Arminianism is an aspect of political intrigue that leads to Barnavelt's downfall. Not surprisingly, the play ran into censorship problems when the King's Men were ready to put it on the stage; its scheduled opening on 14 August 1619 was suppressed by the order of the bishop of London. What is surprising is that by 27 August, the players had found means to perform the play, and it is said to have had many spectators and to have received applause. However, it was never printed in the seventeenth century and so appears in neither of the Beaumont and Fletcher folios. It is preserved in a manuscript in the British Library and was not published until 1883.

The last half dozen years of Fletcher's career, until his death in the summer of 1625, were immensely productive. His name is associated with some twenty plays, of which seven are works of his unaided authorship. During the first half of this period (from circa 1619 until early 1622), evidence for determining the dates of these plays continues to be scant, as it is for many of the plays that conjecturally belong to the half dozen years prior to 1619. After May 1622 evidence survives from the records of the Master of the Revels, Sir Henry Herbert, concerning the dates when plays were licensed for production, and this provides at least a basic chronology for the last two decades of the Jacobean and Caroline stage, before the closing of the theaters in September 1642. Thus the dates for Fletcher's plays in the last three years of his life can be established with far greater certainty than at any other period of his career.

The plays of Fletcher's unaided authorship that seem to belong to the period 1619-1622 are: *The Humourous Lieutenant* (the play's title in the 1647 folio; a somewhat longer manuscript text of the play exists with the title *Demetrius and Enanthe*), one of Fletcher's most enduringly popular tragicomedies; *Women Pleased* (Fletcher's dramatization of Chaucer's *Wife of Bath's Tale;* it has been suggested that the play is a revision of an earlier one, but the evidence is inconclusive); *The Island Princess* (performed at Court on 26 December 1621); *The Pilgrim,* one of Fletcher's best comedies (written between 18 September 1621—when the English version of the play's principal source, Lope de Vega's *El Peregrino en su Patria,* was entered in the Stationers' Register—and New Year's Day, 1622, when the play was performed at Court); *The Wild Goose Chase* (acted at Court during the same 1621-1622 Christmas season as *The Island Princess* and *The Pilgrim*), Fletcher's most brilliant comedy, and one that seems to have been a particular favorite with contemporary audiences.

Interspersed with Fletcher's five unaided plays during the period 1619-1622 are four collab-

orations with Massinger (including *Barnavelt,* already mentioned). *The Custom of the Country* was probably written in either 1619 or 1620. The source of the play's main plot, Cervantes's *Persiles y Sigismunda,* was printed in Spanish in 1617, in French in 1618, and in English in 1619; the English translation was entered in the Stationers' Register on 22 February 1619, and the authors of the play made use of it. The play was popular and profitable, facts not inconsistent with the notorious reputation it gained for its scenes set in a male brothel. Dryden, at the end of the century, when the Restoration stage was under attack for immorality, replied indignantly (in *Preface to the Fables*) that "There is more bawdry in one play of Fletcher's called *The Custom of the Country,* than in all ours together." *The False One,* Fletcher and Massinger's dramatization of the affairs of Caesar and Cleopatra, appears to date from the same period (circa 1620). *The Double Marriage* is probably a product of 1621. One of the most interesting tragedies in the Beaumont and Fletcher canon, it draws its plot material from a number of sources: Thomas Danett's translation of *The Historie of Philip de Commines* (1596); Cervantes's *Don Quixote,* part two, first published in English in 1620; and no less than two *controversiae* of Seneca ("The Daughter of the Pirate Chief" and "The Woman Tortured by the Tyrant because of Her Husband").

About this time another play printed in the 1647 Beaumont and Fletcher folio, *The Laws of Candy,* drew on a Senecan *controversia* for its source. Its authorship is a matter of considerable uncertainty. Massinger certainly had nothing to do with it, and Fletcher seems to have had very little. The play has been attributed to John Ford, whose career as a dramatist was getting under way in these years, and there is some internal (but no external) evidence for the attribution. It may be noted here that the status of two other plays printed in the 1647 folio is equally anomalous: *The Nice Valour, or The Passionate Madman* (for which dates ranging from circa 1615 to 1625 have been posited) seems to be mainly the work of Thomas Middleton; Fletcher's share in it, if any, is minimal. The play may originally have been a Fletcherian original that Middleton has revised. *Wit at Several Weapons* (for which dates ranging from circa 1609 to 1620 have been suggested) seems—at least in the text that has come down to us—to be the work of Middleton and his frequent collaborator, William Rowley.

The grounds for assigning dates to plays become very much more secure with the commencement in May 1622 of the surviving records of Sir

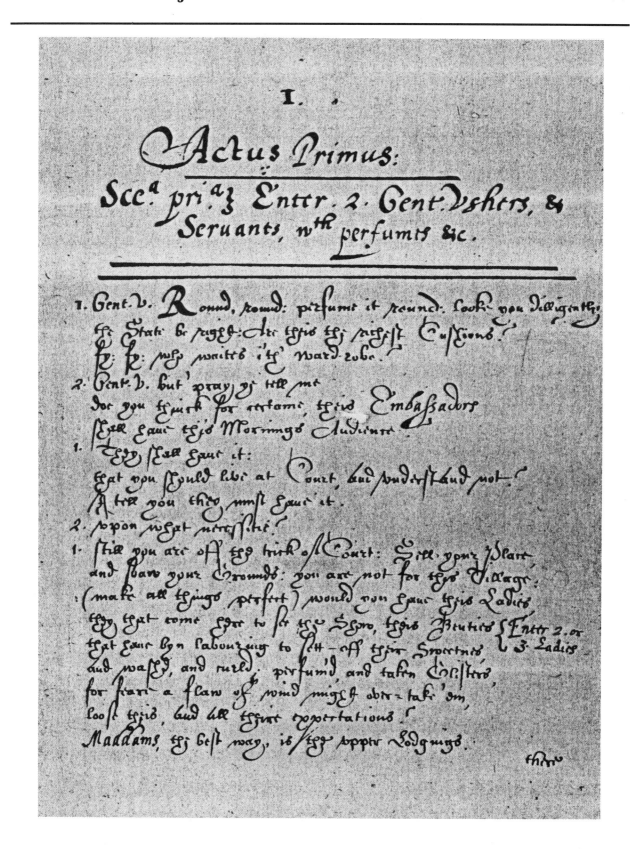

Page from Demetrius and Enanthe, *the longer manuscript version of the play by Fletcher published in the 1647 folio collection of Beaumont and Fletcher's plays as* The Humourous Lieutenant. *This manuscript is a fair copy made by the scribe Ralph Crane in 1625 and is now in the library of Lord Harlech (Brogyntyn MS 42; by permission of Lord Harlech).*

Henry Herbert's licenses for the performance of new (or newly revised) plays. From now until the end of his career, Fletcher's unaided work and his collaboration with Massinger and others can be seen in a remarkably secure chronological sequence. Fletcher and Massinger's work together in the summer of 1622 is clear from Herbert's records. Their tragicomedy, *The Prophetess,* was licensed on 14 May; their romantic comedy, *The Sea Voyage,* on 22 June; and another romantic comedy, *The Spanish Curate,* on 24 October. In the months that followed, Fletcher and Massinger seem to have recast the dramatic design of *The Spanish Curate* in a new piece titled *The Little French Lawyer,* but the result is an uneasy and often incoherent blend of romantic comedy and farce (*The Little French Lawyer* is not mentioned by Herbert, but the surviving transcript of his records is not complete).

On 29 August 1623 Herbert licensed "a new Comedy," *The Maid in the Mill,* and reports it to have been "written by Fletcher, and Rowley," thereby announcing that Fletcher had taken on a new collaborator. William Rowley was a popular actor who, in the course of the previous two decades, had written some unmemorable plays of his own, and—more memorably—had collaborated with Thomas Middleton on quite a good play, *A Fair Quarrel,* and on a great one, *The Changeling.* In 1621, two years before joining forces with Fletcher in *The Maid in the Mill,* Rowley had made a notable contribution (both as actor and part-author) to one of the finest plays of the 1620s, *The Witch of Edmonton,* in which he collaborated with Thomas Dekker and John Ford. Rowley specialized in playing fat, clownish young men, and he is presumed to have written for himself, and acted, the role of Bustofa, the miller's son, in the play that he and Fletcher wrote together.

That Fletcher should have turned to a new collaborator may suggest a change in his association with Massinger, who had virtually grown up professionally under Fletcher's wing. Since working with Fletcher and Field on *The Honest Man's Fortune* in 1613 (apparently his first assignment as a dramatist; he was thirty years old at that time), Massinger had been almost exclusively employed in assisting Fletcher in his various collaborative teams. Occasionally Massinger made moves in new directions. He and Field wrote a tragedy (*The Fatal Dowry*) together (circa 1619). He wrote another tragedy (*The Virgin Martyr*) with Dekker (1620). These were tentative moves in the direction of a career as an independent dramatist. It is difficult to judge the pace of his movement toward this goal because so many of his plays are lost, but by 1623 when Fletcher turned to Rowley to assist him in writing *The Maid in the Mill,* Massinger seems to have written three unaided plays (*The Maid of Honour, The Duke of Milan,* and *The Bondman*). The remaining plays with which his and Fletcher's names have been associated seem, as often as not, to be old plays Massinger revised after Fletcher's death rather than plays on which the two dramatists actively collaborated in the last years of Fletcher's life. This is certainly the case with the play known in the 1647 folio as *The Lovers' Progress;* it contains a prologue declaring it to be an old play of Fletcher's that has been extensively revised. It has been plausibly identified with the play titled *The Wandering Lovers,* licensed by Herbert and attributed by him to Fletcher on 6 December 1623. It has also been identified with "The tragedy of *Cleander*" which Herbert licensed and attributed to Massinger on 7 May 1634. "The Wandering Lovers" would be an apt title for *The Lovers' Progress;* and though the play is a strange mixture of tragedy and tragicomedy, it is a tragedy for the character named Cleander, who is killed in the course of it. Fletcher's *The Wandering Lovers* seems then to have been transformed by Massinger into *Cleander,* and that eventually came to be called *The Lovers' Progress,* a play that clearly contains the work of both dramatists.

A somewhat similar fate seems to have overtaken the play now known as *A Very Woman.* Herbert licensed a play of this title as the work of Massinger on 6 June 1634. Unlike *The Lovers' Progress,* it was not included in the 1647 Beaumont and Fletcher folio and did not appear in print until 1655 when it was included among Massinger's *Three New Plays,* where it is prefaced with a prologue acknowledging it to be an old play that has been revised. The original play has not been identified, but there is evidence from the 1655 text to support the view that it was a Fletcher-Massinger collaboration, and that Massinger's revision of the play in 1634 (when it was licensed anew) was directed chiefly at his own share, and that he left Fletcher's original portion essentially intact.

The comedy titled *The Elder Brother* is sometimes said to be a play left unfinished at the time of Fletcher's death and completed by Massinger, but it seems more likely to be an actual collaboration between the two, with Massinger furnishing the first and last acts, as he often did in his collaborative work (such as in *The False One, The Queen of Corinth*) and as he would do again in *The Fair Maid of the Inn.* This seems to have been the last play on which Fletcher worked. In licensing it on

22 January 1626, Herbert attributed it to Fletcher alone, but by then the dramatist had been dead for five months, and his share in the play is suspiciously small. Massinger is certainly present in the play, and so, it would seem, are two other dramatists who have been conjecturally identified as Webster and Ford. One or both may have been called in after Fletcher's death to complete his share. Before he died, however, Fletcher had written three more unaided plays. A comedy, *The Devil of Dowgate, or Usury Put to Use*, licensed by Herbert on 17 October 1623, is lost. There remains another tragicomedy, *A Wife for a Month*, licensed by Herbert on 27 May 1624, and one of Fletcher's liveliest comedies, *Rule a Wife and Have a Wife*, licensed on 19 October 1624.

Fletcher died in August 1625 at the height of the plague epidemic that had been gradually worsening in London since March. For the week ending 18 August, the death toll was 4,463. It diminished a bit for the week ending 25 August, but still stood at a devastating 4,218. The theaters had been closed for months. According to Aubrey, "a knight of Norfolk (or Suffolke)" invited Fletcher into the country, but he stayed in London in order to have a suit of clothes made, "and while it was making, fell sick of the plague and died." He was buried in the Church of St. Saviour's, Southwark, on 29 August 1625.

At the time of his death, the Beaumont and Fletcher plays dominated the London stage. Virtually all of them were the property of the King's company, and the King's was the premier acting company in London. Also it was the company that performed most frequently at Court. Between 1615 and 1642, the King's Men performed 114 times at Court. Of these performances, 41 were plays from the Beaumont and Fletcher corpus, 15 were plays by Shakespeare, and 7 were plays by Ben Jonson. The preference for tragicomedy on the part of Jacobean and Caroline audiences has a great deal to do with the popularity of the Beaumont and Fletcher plays over those of Shakespeare and Jonson in these years. Tragicomedy presented audiences with interesting moral and ethical dilemmas that could arouse their fervent attention but spare them any really profound emotional involvement of the sort that tragedy at its most powerful would bring about. Tragedy was not the preferred dramatic form in the later Jacobean and Caroline theater. It did not disappear from the stage, but it cannot be said to have flourished in the final decades of English Renaissance drama (that is, from the death of Shakespeare to the closing of the the-

aters). What flourished in these years was tragicomedy. This is evident not only from the success of the Beaumont and Fletcher plays in themselves but from the extent to which other dramatists of the period imitated them. Once plays such as *Philaster* and *A King and No King, The Mad Lover*, and *The Loyal Subject* had made their impact, every dramatist of the period tried his hand at tragicomedy at one time or another, including Webster (*The Devil's Law Case*); Middleton (*More Dissemblers Besides Women, No Wit, No Helps Like a Woman's, The Witch, A Fair Quarrel*); Dekker (*Match Me in London*); Heywood (*The Captives, A Challenge to Beauty*); Ford (*The Lover's Melancholy*). Tragicomedy is central to the work of the principal dramatists writing for the stage in the late 1620s and the 1630s (Massinger, James Shirley, Richard Brome, Sir William Davenant) and it looms large in the offerings of the period's minor dramatists (Lodowick Carlell, Henry Glapthorne, Thomas Killigrew, William Cartwright).

As for Beaumont and Fletcher's comedy, it is a happy transference of Shakespeare's comedy of romantic love from Illyria and the Forest of Arden to the sort of fashionable urban society that Jonson had brought on the stage in *Epicoene*. Beaumont and Fletcher's admiration for Jonson is a matter of record. Both wrote commendatory verses for the published editions of Jonson's *Volpone* (1607) and *Catiline* (1611), and Beaumont contributed a prefatory poem to the 1609 edition of *Epicoene*. The 1647 folio contains Beaumont's famous verse letter to Jonson, written during a visit to the country where he finds himself thinking longingly of his meeting with Jonson and others at the Mermaid Tavern, and of the brilliant conversation that went forth there. By contrast, he ruefully considers how rusticated his own wit is growing in the absence of such stimulating companions. He is dazzled to remember the wit that blazed at the Mermaid:

> wit that might warrant be
> For the whole City to talke foolishly
> Till that were cancel'd, and when that was gone,
> We left an aire behind us, which alone,
> Was able to make the two next companies
> Right witty; though but downright fools, more wise.

There is much mention of the wit of both Beaumont and Fletcher in the forty-odd folio pages of commendatory verses that preface the 1647 edition of their *Comedies and Tragedies*. Aubrey, on the authority of John Earle, reports that Fletcher had an overabundance of the quality, and that "Beau-

·mont's maine Businesse was to lop the overflowings of Mr. Fletcher's luxuriant Fancy and flowing Witt." Throughout the seventeenth century, wit (in the sense of imaginative ingenuity, and an ability to make connections among incongruous elements) is a convenient means of signifying what is special about the Beaumont and Fletcher plays. One of the speakers in Dryden's *An Essay of Dramatick Poesy* observes that Beaumont and Fletcher "had with the advantage of *Shakespeare*'s wit, which was their precedent, great natural gifts, improv'd by study," and he goes on to praise their special excellencies:

> Their plots were generally more regular than *Shakespeare*'s, especially those which were made before *Beaumont*'s death; and they understood and imitated the conversation of Gentlemen much better; whose wilde debaucheries, and quickness of wit in reparties, no Poet before them could paint as they have done. Humour, which *Ben. Johnson* deriv'd from particular persons, they made it not their business to describe: they represented all the passions very lively, but above all, Love.... Their Playes are now the most pleasant and frequent entertainments of the Stage; two of theirs being acted through the year for one of *Shakespeare*'s or *Johnsons*: the reason is, because there is a certain gayety in their Comedies, and Pathos in their more serious Playes, which suits generally with all mens humours. *Shakespeares* language is likewise a little obsolete, and *Ben. Johnson*'s wit comes short of theirs.

If anything had been needed to make Beaumont and Fletcher jointly one with Shakespeare and Jonson in the triumvirate of great English dramatists, it was the publication of the 1647 folio edition of their plays: an edition that matched the 1616 collection of Jonson's and the 1623 collection of Shakespeare's. It is ironic, therefore, that by the time the second folio volume of their plays was published in 1679, their great reputation had begun to dim. Dryden's own later criticism is far more severe concerning the Beaumont and Fletcher plays than the remarks in *An Essay of Dramatick Poesy* had been. In the preface to *An Evening's Love* (1671), after acknowledging that "no man ever will decry wit, but he who despairs of it himself," he goes on to declare (on the authority of Cowley) that one may have too much of a good thing ("rather than all wit let there be none"), and he deplores "the superfluity and wast of wit" in Fletcher and Shakespeare. Later still, in 1679, in the preface to

John Fletcher (by permission of the Earl of Clarendon)

Troilus and Cressida ("The Grounds of Criticism in Tragedy"), Dryden, commenting on "manners" (that is, the inclinations that move a character to action), finds both Shakespeare and Fletcher inferior to Jonson on this score, but Fletcher is decidedly inferior to Shakespeare:

> 'Tis one of the excellencies of *Shakespear*, that the manners of his persons are generally apparent; and you see their bent and inclinations. *Fletcher* comes far short of him in this, as indeed he does almost in every thing: there are but glimmerings of manners in most of his Comedies, which run upon adventures: and in his Tragedies, *Rollo, Otto* [in *Rollo Duke of Normandy*], the *King and No King, Melantius* [in *The Maid's Tragedy*], and many others of his best, are but Pictures shown you in the twi-light; you know not whether they resemble vice, or virtue, and they are either good, bad, or indifferent, as the present Scene requires it.

In this last point Dryden sounds a note that persists in criticism of the Beaumont and Fletcher plays to the present day: the Protean nature of their characters, with their striking capacity to change from one scene to the next, may make for continually surprising stage situations, but these are often achieved at the expense of a character's dramatic consistency and motivation.

As for Dryden's reference to Fletcher (rather than to Beaumont and Fletcher) in discussing the weaknesses of these plays: he anticipates the tendency of later critics to spare Beaumont and to hold Fletcher accountable for all the defects on exhibit in the plays of the Beaumont and Fletcher corpus, despite the fact that his sense of authorial divisions within the corpus is very uncertain (none of the three plays to which he alludes is the unaided work of Fletcher).

Twentieth-century studies of the problems of authorship which these plays pose have made possible a more just appraisal of the poetic and dramatic talents of the two playwrights. Since Fletcher wrote a large number of unaided plays, the characteristics of his poetic and dramatic style can be studied with considerable thoroughness. The case of Beaumont is more difficult. We have only one play that is solely his (*The Knight of the Burning Pestle*). The language of his masque does not shed much light on the language of the plays to which he contributed; nor do his nondramatic poems (*Salmacis and Hermaphroditus*, "The Remedy of Love," the verse letter to Jonson, his various commendatory poems, his "Elegy on the Lady Markham," his "Epistle to the Countess of Rutland" and his "Elegy" on her death, his "Funeral Elegy on the Death of Lady Penelope Clifton"). Beaumont's nondramatic poems are not themselves without authorial problems. Those poems that have just been named are the ones that seem most likely to be his, but they appear in posthumous collections (1618, 1640, 1653, 1660) amid other poems whose attribution to Beaumont seems very questionable. Massinger's share in the Beaumont and Fletcher plays is now fully recognized, and the extent of it is clearly defined, since Massinger, like Fletcher, has left a large number of unaided plays that provide criteria for identifying his work in plays of divided or uncertain authorship. What now emerges clearly from an examination of the Beaumont and Fletcher corpus is that Fletcher's collaboration with Beaumont was different from his collaboration with Massinger or any other dramatist with whom he worked.

The Beaumont-Fletcher collaboration was obviously very close. Beaumont seems usually to have given the final form to their plays (perhaps in the process of bringing Fletcher's reputedly luxuriant fancy and overflowing wit under control), but the plays themselves seem to have been jointly designed, and the language of the two dramatists has been carefully blended to make for a virtually seamless verbal text. Perhaps if one had a clearer idea of Beaumont's unaided style, his share in the collaborative works could be more readily determined, but this is by no means certain, for Fletcher's own very distinctive style which emerges with great clarity from his unaided work is much less readily apparent in the collaborations with Beaumont. When Fletcher collaborated with Massinger, however, their respective shares of a given play could not be more apparent, not only because of their stylistic differences one from another, but because they divided the various acts and scenes of the play on distinctly authorial lines. Beaumont and Fletcher often seem to have sat together in the same room and worked together on the same scene. Fletcher and Massinger seem to have drawn up a scenario for a play and then, on the basis of it, having decided which dramatist would write which scenes, gone their separate ways. When Massinger's work appears in the same scene with Fletcher's, it is a sign, not that the two are writing the scene together, but that Massinger is revising (probably after Fletcher's death) what Fletcher originally wrote.

Fletcher is the constant in the fifty-odd plays of the Beaumont and Fletcher corpus, but Fletcher writing with Beaumont is one thing, Fletcher writing alone is another, and Fletcher writing with his various post-Beaumont collaborators is something else again. The Beaumont-Fletcher collaborations such as *Philaster, The Maid's Tragedy, A King and No King*, have a rare blend of pathos and irony along with a poetic sublety that vanishes from the corpus when Beaumont withdraws. Fletcher's own plays have a histronic and rhetorical extravagance that makes one understand how indeed Beaumont may have exercised a controlling force on Fletcher's wit. They are products of a very shrewd instinct for theatrical artifice, with their improbable plots, volatile characters, and bravura emotional range that extends from sentimental passion to heroic self-control, and that provides occasion for the display of the most effulgent virtue and sinister vice. The best of them—*Valentinian, The Mad Lover, The Loyal Subject, The Humourous Lieutenant, A Wife for a Month*—prepare the way for the baroque tragedy and tragicomedy of the Restoration theater. Fletcher's collaborations with Massinger are most successful when his comic energies can be played off against Massinger's moral earnestness, as in *The*

Custom of the Country, The Spanish Curate, The Prophetess, The Sea Voyage.

The Beaumont and Fletcher plays have never regained the esteem in which they were held during the half century after Fletcher's death, and it is unlikely that they will ever hold the stage again. They are, nonetheless, theatrical artifacts of considerable aesthetic interest, for they are products of an important cultural moment in the history of the English stage. After Marlowe and Shakespeare's work in tragedy, after Shakespeare and Jonson's work in comedy, what direction was English drama to take? The Beaumont and Fletcher plays are the threefold answer. They seek to refine the heritage of Marlowe and Shakespeare in tragedy (as in *The Maid's Tragedy*); they seek to accommodate the romantic and satiric traditions of Shakespearean and Jonsonian comedy in a new comic blend (as in *The Scornful Lady, Monsieur Thomas, The Wild Goose Chase, The Pilgrim, The Chances, Rule a Wife and Have a Wife*); and they seek to explore and to define the space between the classically sanctioned tragic and comic genres by addressing themselves to the creation of a new, third genre (in the celebrated series of tragicomedies produced over a fifteen-year period, from *Philaster* to *A Wife for a Month*). Whatever audiences of future centuries might think of these plays, there is ample evidence that audiences of the middle decades of the seventeenth century found them highly satisfactory. When, during the Interregnum, it was not possible to see them on the stage, sometime-audiences could find pleasure in reading them in the 1647 folio. When, at the Restoration, the theaters were reopened, it was the Beaumont and Fletcher plays which, for the next twenty years, dominated the repertoire, and the heroic tragedies and the double-plot tragicomedies of Dryden and his contemporaries were created in their image. No one who seeks to understand the course of English dramatic history in the seventeenth century can afford to ignore them.

Bibliographies:
Samuel A. Tannenbaum, *Beaumont and Fletcher: A Concise Bibliography* (New York: Privately printed, 1938); supplement, by Samuel A. and Dorothy R. Tannenbaum (New York: Privately printed, 1946);
C. A. Pennel and William P. Williams, *Elizabethan Bibliographies, Supplement VIII: Francis Beaumont and John Fletcher, 1937-1965* (London: Nether Press, 1968);

Terence P. Logan and Denzell S. Smith, eds., *A Survey and Bibliography of Recent Studies in English Renaissance Drama: The Later Jacobean Dramatists* (Lincoln: Nebraska University Press, 1978).

References:
Joseph Quincy Adams, ed., *The Dramatic Records of Sir Henry Herbert, Master of the Revels, 1623-1673* (New Haven: Yale University Press, 1917);
John Aubrey, *Brief Lives: Edited from the Original Manuscripts and With a Life of John Aubrey by Oliver Lawson Dick* (Ann Arbor: University of Michigan Press, 1957);
Gerald Eades Bentley, *The Jacobean and Caroline Stage*, 7 volumes (Oxford: Oxford University Press, 1941-1968);
E. K. Chambers, *The Elizabethan Stage*, 4 volumes (Oxford: Clarendon Press, 1923);
John Dryden, *An Essay of Dramatick Poesy*, in *The Works of John Dryden*, volume 17: *Prose 1668-1691*, edited by Samuel Holt Monk, A. E. Wallace Maurer, Vinton A. Dearing, R. V. LeClercq, and Maximillian E. Novak (Berkeley, Los Angeles & London: University of California Press, 1971), pp. 3-81;
Dryden, Preface to *An Evening's Love*, in *The Works of John Dryden*, volume 10: *Plays: The Tempest, Tyrannick Love, An Evening's Love*, edited by Novak and George Robert Guffey (Berkeley, Los Angeles & London: University of California Press, 1970), pp. 202-213;
Dryden, Preface to *Troilus and Cressida*, in *The Works of John Dryden*, volume 13: *Plays: All for Love, Oedipus, Troilus and Cressida*, edited by Novak, Guffey, and Alan Roper (Berkeley, Los Angeles & London: University of California Press, 1984), pp. 225-248;
Mark Eccles, "A Biographical Dictionary of Elizabethan Authors," *Huntington Library Quarterly*, 5 (April 1942): 281-302;
Charles Mills Gayley, *Beaumont, the Dramatist* (New York: Century, 1914);
Allan H. Gilbert, ed., *Literary Criticism: Plato to Dryden* (New York: American Book Co., 1940);
Cyrus Hoy, "The Shares of Fletcher and his Collaborators in the Beaumont and Fletcher Canon," 7 parts, *Studies in Bibliography*, 8 (1956): 124-146; 9 (1957): 143-162; 11 (1958): 85-99; 12 (1959): 91-116; 13 (1960): 77-108; 14 (1961): 45-67; 15 (1962): 71-90;

Arthur Colby Sprague, *Beaumont and Fletcher on the Restoration Stage* (Cambridge: Harvard University Press, 1926);

Eugene M. Waith, *The Pattern of Tragicomedy in Beaumont and Fletcher* (New Haven: Yale University Press, 1952).

Papers:

Beaumont's "Grammar Lecture" is preserved in Sloane MS. 1709 in the British Library and has been published by Mark Eccles in *Review of English Studies*, 16 (October 1940): 402-414. The manuscripts for seven of the plays in the Beaumont and Fletcher corpus have been preserved: *Sir John van Olden Barnavelt* (BL MS Add. 18653 in the British Library), *Beggars' Bush* (MS in the Lambarde volume, Folger Shakespeare Library), *Bonduca* (Add. MS 36758 in the British Library), *The Honest Man's Fortune* (MS Dyce 9 in the Victoria and Albert Museum), *The Elder Brother* (MS Egerton 1994 in the British Library), *The Humourous Lieutenant* (titled *Demetrius and Enanthe;* Brogyntyn MS 42 in the library of Lord Harlech at Brogyntyn, Oswestry), *The Woman's Prize* (MS in the Lambarde volume, Folger Shakespeare Library).

Richard Brome
(circa 1590-1652)

John S. Nania

PLAY PRODUCTIONS: *A Fault in Friendship,* by Brome and [?] Johnson, London, Red Bull theater(?), 1623;

The Lovesick Maid, London, Blackfriars theater, licensed February 1629;

The City Wit, London, Salisbury Court theater, 1629;

The Northern Lass, London, Blackfriars theater, 1629;

The Queen's Exchange, London, Blackfriars theater, 1632(?);

The Novella, London, Blackfriars theater, 1632;

The Weeding of the Covent Garden, London, Blackfriars theater, 1632;

The Late Lancashire Witches, by Brome and Thomas Heywood, London, Globe theater, 1634;

The Apprentice's Prize, by Brome and Heywood, London, Blackfriars theater(?), circa 1634(?);

The Life and Death of Sir Martin Skink, by Brome and Heywood, London, Blackfriars theater(?), circa 1634(?);

The Sparagus Garden, London, Salisbury Court theater, 1635;

The Queen and Concubine, London, Salisbury Court theater, 1635;

The New Academy, London, Salisbury Court theater, 1635(?);

The English Moor, London, Salisbury Court theater, 1637;

The Love-sick Court, London, Salisbury Court theater, 1638(?);

The Damoiselle, London, Salisbury Court theater, 1638;

The Antipodes, London, Salisbury Court theater, 1638;

A Mad Couple Well Match'd, London, Cockpit theater, 1639;

The Jewish Gentleman, London, Salisbury Court theater or Cockpit theater(?), before 1640;

The Court Beggar, London, Cockpit theater, 1640;

A Jovial Crew, London, Cockpit theater, 1641.

BOOKS: *The Northern Lasse* (London: Printed by A. Mathewes & sold by N. Vavasour, 1632);

The Late Lancashire Witches, by Brome and Thomas Heywood (London: Printed by T. Harper for B. Fisher, 1634);

The Antipodes: a Comedie (London: Printed by J. Okes for F. Constable, 1640);

The Sparagus Garden: A Comedie (London: Printed by J. Okes for F. Constable, 1640);

A Joviall Crew: or, The Merry Beggars (London: Printed by J. Y. for E. D. & N. E., 1652);

Five New Playes, viz. *The Madd Couple Well Matcht. The Novella. The Court Beggar. City Witt. Damoiselle* (London: Printed for Humphrey Moseley, Richard Marriot & Thomas Dring, 1653);

Portrait of Richard Brome by T. Cross from the 1633 quarto edition of Five New Playes *(Henry E. Huntington Library and Art Gallery)*

The Queenes Exchange, A Comedy (London: Printed for Henry Brome, 1657);

Five New Playes, viz. *The English Moor, or The Mock Marriage. The Love-sick Court, or The Ambitious Politique. Covent Garden Weeded. The New Academy, or The New Exchange. The Queen and Concubine* (London: Printed for A. Crook & H. Brome, 1659).

Edition: *The Dramatic Works of Richard Brome,* 3 volumes (London: John Pearson, 1873).

As is the case with many English Renaissance dramatists, little is known about Richard Brome's personal life. It is generally accepted that he was born around 1590 and probably not in London. By 1614 Brome was living in the city, for the induction to Ben Jonson's *Bartholomew Fair* mentions "his [Jonson's] man, Master Brome, behind the arras." Scholars have suggested Brome came to London after joining an acting company engaged in touring the provinces. What is meant by the phrase "his man" is open to debate. It may be either that Brome was Jonson's servant or that he was an actor in whom Jonson recognized some potential

as a dramatist and decided to assist in achieving that goal. Whatever the exact nature of the relationship, Jonson states in his commendatory poem to Brome's play *The Northern Lass* that he taught his protégé the art of play writing.

From the mid 1620s until the close of the theaters in 1642, Brome wrote as many as nineteen plays (sixteen comedies are extant) for a variety of acting companies including the King's Men, Shakespeare's old acting troupe. From all available accounts, his plays were generally well received. Critics debate over Brome's stature as a dramatist, but there is no arguing the fact that he was a popular playwright. After the close of the theaters, Brome only wrote a small number of poems before dying in poverty.

No one would be so bold as to claim Richard Brome as one of the two or three greatest dramatists of the 1600s; however, all of Brome's plays are skillfully constructed, and the case can be made that some of his later comedies are truly outstanding works of theater that surpass the efforts of contemporaries.

Another reason not to ignore Brome's plays is that in them one finds many of the characters, plots, conventions, and genres employed by William Shakespeare, Ben Jonson, Francis Beaumont and John Fletcher, Thomas Middleton, Thomas Dekker, and others. But Brome is no plagiarist; he borrows from other playwrights and then creates a unique comic vision which attempts to demonstrate that theater is an effective weapon against melancholy, his age's pervasive disease.

Many of Richard Brome's plays may be described as city comedies. This group of realistic, intrigue plays, like the rather hard to define label of city comedy, covers a wide range of dramatic modes. Each of these plays may be regarded as an experiment, a necessary preparation for his final masterpieces.

Brome was influenced by Jonson to the extent that he borrowed subject matter, dramatic situations, and characters from the man who "fathered" the genre of city comedy. What Brome did not borrow from Jonson was his sharp, unrelenting satiric tone. For Brome's use of romantic sentiment, we might look to another dramatist who claimed him as a "son," Thomas Dekker.

The speaker of the prologue to *The Northern Lass* says to the audience that the author "implores your laughter" and "would see you merry." Brome's method for creating mirth is similar to Dekker's—a combination of realism, romance, and sentiment. The comic realism is supplied by a complicated intrigue plot, the romance by the wooing and marriage of lovers, and the sentiment by the naiveté of the fifteen-year-old Constance, the northern lass. The prefatory poem makes it clear that her presence in the play, complete with a north-country accent, made it a success.

Sentimentality never again played such a significant part in Brome's city comedies, although it never completely vanished—and we should not expect it to disappear from comedies dealing with the trials and tribulations of young lovers and lost children. Brome's satire, a few thrusts at purchasers of knighthoods, gentlemen ushers, and social climbers, effectively anchors the play in the 1630s. The intrigue, like that in all of Brome's plays, is complex, and as usual, it centers on a group of well-motivated tricksters. Even in this first exciting play by Brome we see him suggesting that melancholy can be cured by the use of theatrical, self-conscious plotting.

Two of Brome's plays rest squarely in the prodigal-son dramatic tradition. Thomas Middleton and the anonymous author of *The London Prodigal* set the genre's extremes of tone—from ironic detachment to straightforward morality. In *The City Wit*, Brome's earliest extant play, he manipulates the conventions of the prodigal-son story. Crasy, the apparent prodigal, uses theatrical deceptions to prove that his honesty, not his lack of wit, led to his downfall. Because he has chosen to be charitable in a corrupt world, a world in which each character acts solely for himself, he appears to be a fool and a prodigal. In contrast to the typical prodigal, Crasy does not "reform" himself. Instead he disguises himself and reforms the society which cast him out. *The City Wit* combines the self-conscious Middletonian and Jonsonian intrigue with a moral point of view. Brome's contribution to city comedy is the creation of a likable, effective, and moral trickster.

A Mad Couple Well Match'd is in many ways a more conventional prodigal-son play. George Careless, a wild gallant, tries to kick his way into his uncle Sir Oliver Thrivewell's good graces for the umpteenth time while simultaneously attempting to seduce Lady Thrivewell. But his repulsive lust, Oliver Thrivewell's good nature, and Lady Thrivewell's virtue and wit prevent the audience from identifying with him.

The ending of the play is more typical of a romantic comedy than a prodigal-son play. Fitzgerrard is reunited with his sister Amie, who has been missing for two years. Lord Lovely refuses to marry her because she is not his social equal, but he promises to give her £200 a year for life and to

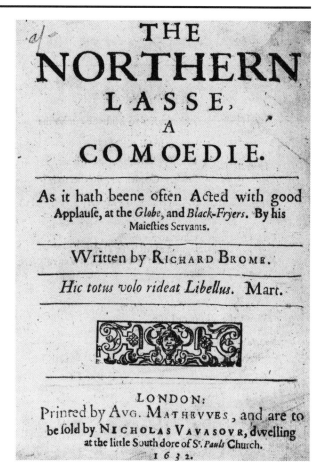

Title page for the 1632 quarto edition of Brome's first published play (Henry E. Huntington Library and Art Gallery)

match her vow of chastity. Likewise, Careless announces he will change his ways, but he also has the good fortune to marry the humorous and wealthy widow Mrs. Crostill and to be accepted by his uncle as his heir, if he behaves. Wat joins Careless in marriage by taking Phoebe, and both Lady Thrivewell and Mrs. Crostill give her money. Finally, Saleware is forced to recognize that his wife has made him a cuckold, but instead of casting her off, he warns her "we will be friends no more, but loving man and wife henceforward."

John Fletcher is an obvious influence on Brome. In Fletcher's comedies Brome found the fully realized, witty, and aggressive heroine; battles between the sexes; and romance conventions galore (disguised lovers, bed tricks, and recognition devices). Witty women are not particular to Fletcher's city comedies; they certainly occupy a prominent place in Shakespeare's romantic comedies. Shakespeare's heroines do not hesitate to disguise themselves in order to achieve their ends, but, with a few exceptions, they do not engage in elaborate theatrical deceptions. These women disguise themselves in order to examine the nature of romantic love. The medium of wit they use to educate the men is language, while Fletcher's women generally defeat their male opponents by elaborate and sustained trickery, and as a result, they are much more aggressive than Shakespeare's heroines. The witty women who appear in Brome's plays fall in the Fletcherian tradition.

The Sparagus Garden's central action is standard New Comedy fare. After parents block the marriage of the young lovers, Samuel and his friends devise a number of tricks which eventually allow the couple to marry and gain their parents' approval. What is particularly Bromian about the schemes of Samuel and his friends is their self-conscious theatricality. The tricksters have visited the theater and seen both romantic comedies (where they have learned love triumphs) and satires. They apply this knowledge of theater to their problems, and, employing a popular plot device (a pillow used to simulate pregnancy), they bring about a comic resolution.

In this play Brome shows the audience that theatrics can cure disordered minds. Samuel's plots cure his and Annabel's lovesickness, and the comic resolution cures Striker and reconciles him with his old adversary Touchwood. Furthermore, Rebecca, a witty woman in the Fletcherian tradition, purposely pretends to be the sinful woman her husband imagines her to be in order to cure him of his jealousy. A further variation of the theme of curing sickness concerns Tim Hoyden's desire to be a gentleman. Moneylacks uses conventional medical techniques—bleeding, dieting, purging—to convince the country fool he is actually a gentleman. However, it is the discovery of his noble parentage (made possible by a recognition device) which actually transforms him.

The New Academy, which is similar to Brome's other city comedies, is a romantic comedy that incorporates the dramatist's usual thematic interests. There are lost sons and daughters, mistaken identities, and marriages. Two subplots draw on the conventions of city comedy, and Hannah, yet another woman in the Fletcherian tradition, devises tricks which simultaneously cure her husband of his indifference and Valentine of his lustfulness.

Ben Jonson made his strong dislike for popular romance known on many occasions. Since Brome could not look to his master for inspiration or guidance while writing tragicomedies, it is appropriate to compare two of them, *The Queen's Ex-*

change and *The Queen and Concubine,* to the romantic comedies and romances of Shakespeare. Critics have described the dramatic structure of Shakespeare's comedies and romances in various ways; yet each agrees that the center of his plays always contains characters who have become confused about their identity and the identity of others. Most often these identity problems are brought about by dreamlike experiences and impenetrable disguises. The loss of identity actually proves to be fortunate because it leads to the finding of a more stable, fuller, and more flexible identity. What makes this losing of an old identity and the finding of a new one possible is that man is guided by a providential plan: he is an actor in a play written by God for the stage of the world.

Although *The Queen's Exchange,* Brome's earliest tragicomedy, has no known source, it is influenced by Shakespeare's tragedies, romantic comedies, and romances. While Brome borrows certain plot devices from *Macbeth* and *King Lear,* other devices, such as the presence of look-alike characters and the theme of love melancholy, recall *The Comedy of Errors* and *Twelfth Night.* Furthermore, the use of dreams, role playing, and the theme of suffering which leads to redemption recalls the romances. Even though this drama may be considered immature and imitative, it plays an important role in Brome's development.

The more mature *The Queen and Concubine* has two main sources, a tale in Robert Greene's *Penelope's Web* and Shakespeare's *The Winter's Tale.* The manner in which Brome expands and alters Greene's slight inset story in *Penelope's Web* strongly suggests that he was influenced by *The Winter's Tale* in particular and the structural pattern of Shakespearean comedy and romance in general. Eulalia and Gonzago bear a great resemblance to their counterparts in Shakespeare's play, Leontes and Hermione. Both Leontes and Gonzago become mad with jealousy, although Brome makes Gonzago's sickness slightly more credible by having Alinda confirm his suspicions with false witnesses. Both Hermione and Eulalia are patient, obedient, and virtuous women who are forced by events to suffer a great injustice, and both women are later reunited with their penitent husbands. Brome's play differs most from *The Winter's Tale* in its lack of a subplot involving young lovers, although Eulalia resembles Perdita in that she spends her exile in a pastoral setting.

Both of Brome's tragicomedies use Shakespearean plot devices and themes: providence intervenes in both plays; the court world is presented as corrupt at the outset of the plays, but it is later purged of its undesirable qualities; court life is generally compared to a transitory dream world, while the conclusion of each play presents a stable world characterized by love, harmony, and order; and finally, the tragicomic pattern of each play depicts man's fall and redemption. Brome, like Shakespeare, believes in man's ability to transform himself into something wonderful and virtuous. In these two tragicomedies dreams play a central role in describing these transformations, while the therapeutic power of role playing is only hinted at.

Shakespeare's comedies and romances were not the only plays to influence Brome's tragicomedies. John Fletcher and his various collaborators produced a large number of tragicomedies, romantic comedies, and comedies of trickery which Brome is sure to have known well. Both Fletcher and Shakespeare used the same conventions, but the manner in which they treat these conventions varies a great deal.

Fletcher's tragicomedies present theatrical, self-conscious worlds. The dramatic language is highly rhetorical and intensely emotional. The characters themselves are protean: they constantly put on disguises, act out roles, and seem to change their very natures from moment to moment. The plots invariably contain surprises which usually take the form of characters revealing or discovering their true identities during the final scenes. His characters lose themselves in dreams of honor, friendship, and love; when their dreams are threatened, they become sick or mad, and the actions of the plays provide cures. These plays reveal worlds that are in a constant state of flux: appearances cannot be separated from reality; ideals are undercut, and fortune, rather than providence, seems to control men's destinies. For Fletcher, life is theatrical because man is constantly searching for a satisfactory role; for Shakespeare, life is theatrical because man is an actor in a play written by a providential author.

The Love-sick Court resembles Fletcher's tragicomedies, but it is also a burlesque of Cavalier drama, a distinct type of drama loosely based on Fletcher's works. Cavalier drama sprang from Queen Henrietta Maria's keen interest in theater and her attempt to establish a court of Platonic love in England. This royal interest in theater convinced several courtiers and even some skillful poets that they could win favor by writing plays which combined the ideals of *preciosité* (refined sentiments, a code of etiquette, and a Platonic theory of love) with romance.

The Cavalier dramatists used the full range of romance conventions, and they especially enjoyed depicting the conflict between love and friendship and employing the recovered-child theme. What distinguishes their plays from Fletcher's tragicomedies is their lack of both theatricality and humor. Whereas Fletcher, who made his living by writing for the public theater, was an extremely skillful dramatist whose plays produced a maximum of theatrical effect, the Cavalier playwrights, who wrote primarily for the specialized tastes of the court, were generally amateurs—they wrote romances in dramatic form rather than dramatic romances.

Although Brome admired Fletcher, he was a leading critic of the Cavalier dramatists, objecting most to their emphasis on spectacle and story at the expense of meaning and mirth and asserting that their inclusion of the ideals of *preciosité* made their plays incomprehensible.

As the title suggests, virtually everyone in *The Love-sick Court* suffers from some sort of sickness. The King of Thessaly is mentally ill because his subjects threaten to revolt unless he names a successor to the throne, preferably the madly ambitious Stratocles. Eudina is sick because she is in love with two brothers, Philocles and Philargus, and cannot choose between them. The brothers are thought to be mad because they would rather glorify their friendship than decide which one of them is to marry the princess and thus save the kingdom from rebellion. Placilla grows sick because she falls hopelessly in love with her brother Philocles, while Themile, the mother of the twins, seems very upset because the midwife Garula threatens to reveal a horrible secret.

The extent to which love sickness and other varieties of madness infect the court is in itself absurd, but there are other clues that suggest the play is a burlesque. Most important, the characters in the comic subplot consciously imitate the actions (including lengthy debates on the conflict between love and friendship) of the main characters, thus mocking the seriousness of the main plot. Brome concludes his attack on Cavalier drama by creating an absurd comic resolution, complete with marriages between characters who do not love one another and who are not even of the same generation.

The Love-sick Court leaves no doubt that it is a burlesque of the absurdities of Cavalier drama and, by extension, Fletcherian comedy at its most outrageous. Both the fantastic plot and the exaggerated language effectively satirize plays containing sprawling, uncontrolled plots and numerous debates which invariably bring the action to a standstill.

Nearly everyone who wrote commendatory poems for Brome's plays referred to Jonson as the younger man's instructor in the art of drama. One reason is that Brome often looked to Jonson's plays for inspiration. He directly recalls his master in the play *The Weeding of the Covent Garden*. Like Jonson's *Bartholomew Fair*, Brome's play contains a multitude of topical allusions and place references which firmly anchor it in seventeenth-century London. It also contains the character Cockbrain, a justice of the peace, who proudly identifies himself with Jonson's seeker of enormities, Adam Overdo. As in *Bartholomew Fair*, the validity of authority is questioned, but Brome focused his attention on the exercise of parental rather than civil authority, undoubtedly because he was more interested in writing festive comedy than a biting satire on society with a qualified "happy" ending.

Brome's play concludes with the formation of a large family through three marriages, two of which are based on love. Cockbrain plays a small and rather farcical part in the play; he punishes no one and merely asks the undesirable characters to leave the precinct. The garden is weeded; it becomes a paradise.

A comparison of Brome's *The Court Beggar* to Jonson's *The Devil Is an Ass,* a play whose satiric tone is harsher than *Bartholomew Fair*'s, also proves instructive. If *The Devil Is an Ass* is stripped of its morality frame the plays become structurally similar; both contain two interrelated plots. One plot in *The Devil Is an Ass* is an intrigue of adultery, while the other is an intrigue of financial trickery. *The Court Beggar* contains a conventional New Comedy intrigue (young lovers overcoming parental opposition) rather than an adultery plot, while the subplot involves financial trickery. Although Brome's satire attacks many of the same abuses as Jonson's, it is never as intense. Furthermore, the transformations of Mendicant, Strangelove, and Ferdinando and the marriage of Frederick and Charissa prevent the satiric tone from becoming a dominant force in the play.

The comparison of these four plays suggests that when Brome echoed one of Jonson's plays he did not do so slavishly; there is a radical shift in tone. Brome included satire in his plays, but stripping men of their masks and exposing their vices and follies was not his main interest. While Jonson saw himself as a modern-day Horace whose job was to comment on and possibly correct the behavior of society, Brome, in conventional New Comedies,

focused his attention on the family. He portrayed the cruelty of parents and guardians who attempt to prevent the marriages of young lovers and the inevitable triumph of romantic love. His plays end with reunions, reconciliations, and marriages, never with the fragmentation of families or society.

In his early and middle comedies, Jonson satirized characters who use shape shifting to gull their fellowman and who wear masks to present a false self to society. Brome, while using Jonsonian situations and humor characters, showed the positive effects of role playing. His characters use theater or theatrical situations to cure others suffering from madness or melancholy. Paradoxically, Jonson believed in the power of the theater to educate the audience, but within his plays he satirized theatricality as a mode of existence. Brome believed that comic mirth could cure the audience's melancholy and humorous behavior and dramatized that process within his plays. Jonson's uneasiness with the theater is one reason for his satiric tone; Brome saw only the positive effects theater could have on an audience and as a result wrote comedies which are more romantic than satiric, more optimistic than pessimistic.

When critics call Brome the son of Jonson, they are almost always referring to the obvious similarities between Brome's plays and Jonson's satires. Brome, however, is much more the son of the Jonson who wrote the court masques and the final plays, especially *The Staple of News* and *The New Inn.*

Between 1616 and 1626 Jonson's primary literary endeavor was writing court masques, incredibly expensive dramatic spectacles designed to pay homage to James I's divine powers of kingship. The fully realized Jonson masque is divided into two parts. The first, the antimasque, contains comic characters whose very natures invert and mock the artistic and moral virtues celebrated in the succeeding main masque. King James, positioned in the very middle of the royal audience, is praised as the source of great and powerful virtue, and it is he who is ultimately responsible for effortlessly banishing the antimasque and inspiring the beautiful poetry, music, and dance of the main masque. These entertainments were part flattery and part demonstration of noble behavior. Members of the audience learned by watching, and then they got to put their newly acquired understanding into action by dancing in the revels that followed. The revels allowed the audience to participate in the spectacle and as such actualized the "all-the-world-is-a-stage" metaphor that is a key part of Jonson's final plays.

Jonson's experimentation in his final plays—often referred to as the "dotages"—manifests itself in a variety of ways. The tone of the last plays is less satiric; their romantic conclusions focus on character reformation, the reunion of lost family members, and marriage; and the poet figures effect dramatic conversions within the play world. Furthermore, these plays suggest appearance and playacting are not always synonymous with deception; they can, on the contrary, assist in the revelation of truths. Finally, these plays are structurally complex because they are self-conscious: not only are there plays within plays, but the audience is constantly reminded that it is watching a play in which people watch other people watching plays. Jonson used the all-the-world-is-a-stage metaphor in order to include the theater audience in his plays and then reform them through a sense of participation.

Brome's final and best plays display the influence of the later Jonson. He uses antimasque images of a world turned upside down and insubstantial dreams to describe the corrupt, mutable world. He strives to make the audience feel as if it is participating in the plays, not by including revels, but by constructing the plays around a central metaphor—all the world is a stage. Finally, he demonstrates an optimistic view of life in general and theater in particular by showing that playacting can cure sick minds.

In *The English Moor*, the children of two old gentlemen and close friends, Meanwell and Rashly, think their fathers quarreled, fought a duel, and died. The duel makes the two families hate each other. Dionisia Meanwell desperately wants her brother Arthur to revenge their father's death, but he refuses to do so because he is secretly in love with Lucy Rashly. Theophilus Rashly does not seek revenge because he has problems of his own: Testy has married his niece Milicent, Theophilus's love, to Quicksands, an old usurer—a situation that causes Theophilus to display his uncontrollable passion and great impatience.

Each of Rashly's and Meanwell's sons and daughters suffers from some sort of psychological distress. While Dionisia displays her grief over the death of her father by passionately desiring revenge, her brother Arthur acts melancholy because he cannot see his love. Dionisia mistakes his sadness for unmanly grief and demands he "cure" himself by taking action against the Rashly family. Lucy, like Arthur, suffers from lovesickness, but because she is so passive, she does nothing to remedy the situation. Lovesickness along with impatience makes Theophilus explosively passionate. Yet his

fear that anything he might do would in some way endanger Milicent makes it impossible for him to attempt to rescue her.

Quicksands thinks himself witty. For thirty days he disguises Milicent as a Moor. She thinks there is something immoral about being disguised as a black woman because the blackness blots out "Heaven's workmanship," but the old usurer assures her there is nothing sinful about the disguise since the queen and her ladies once dressed as Moors in a court masque (a reference to Jonson's first two masques, *The Masque of Blackness* and *The Masque of Beauty*). Quicksands later tells Milicent that to mock his abusers he will hold a feast, during which she will reveal her true identity in a masque. Quicksands casts himself in the role of King James, whose presence turns Moors white in Jonson's *The Masque of Beauty* and *The Gypsies Metamorphosed*. Of course Quicksands has none of the virtues that either masque assigns to James; his masque is in fact a moral inversion. Wealth and false wit, instead of virtue and true art, are supposed to effect the transformation. And his plot ultimately fails.

Act five contains a startling surprise: Rashly and Winlose appear in an inn outside of London, where they explain their disappearance to the host. Rashly acknowledges the theatricality of their scheme by comparing it to "old play-plots" in which fathers test their prodigal sons. With this information, the audience realizes that the first four acts of *The English Moor* are a play within a larger play. Like Pennyboy Canter in Jonson's *The Staple of News*, but without his direct control, Meanwell and Rashly have constructed a prodigal-son play. But the fathers have decided to solve two problems at once. Six years earlier they were involved in a lawsuit against Winlose which destroyed him and his family. They have used their year in France to "redeem" Winlose from prison and thus ease their consciences. The play concludes with conventional romance ending: families reunite, lovers marry, and villains reform. But most important, all these events combine to cure each character of melancholy.

The English Moor and *The Damoiselle* are alike in structure and intent. The central device in *The Damoiselle* is a lottery, which is to take place at the new Ordinary, an inn which attracts customers with free food and drink. The inn recalls Jonson's inn, the Light Heart (in *The New Inn*); in each play the inn's host wears a disguise and directs a plot which involves disguising a man as a woman.

In Brome's play the innkeeper is Dryground, an old decayed knight, who disguises himself as

Page from the manuscript for The English Moor *preserved at Lichfield Cathedral. This manuscript is a fair copy of the play thought to have been made by Brome himself (by permission of the Dean and Chapter of Lichfield Cathedral)*

Humphrey Osbright. Apparently the winner is to get to sleep with Frances (the Damoiselle), Osbright's daughter. The lottery, however, is only a front for Dryground's plans to reform and to make restitution to a number of characters. With the money he has borrowed from Vermine at the start of the play, he bails Wat, Vermine's prodigal son, out of jail, and he rents his tavern, where he harbors Alice, Vermine's runaway daughter, whom he hopes to marry to Brookeall's son. He also attempts to relieve Brookeall financially, in restitution for having seduced and then abandoned Brookeall's sister, Elinor, long ago.

The play's action takes various twists and turns due primarily to the "plays" directed by Dryground. One brings about Wat's reformation and his marriage to Dryground's daughter. Another reforms Wat's father, a vicious usurer. A by-product of Dryground's scheming is his recovery of his abandoned lover. The reunion of Dryground and Elinor is the play's emotional highlight, and this action, as one character notes, was not designed by man: "That Fortune is not blind, that shew'd me way/To Father, Friends, and Husband in one day." In *The Damoiselle* fortune is able to outdo art because the world is a comic theater.

Brome's two most impressive plays, *The Antipodes* and *A Jovial Crew*, are refinements of *The English Moor* and *The Damoiselle*. *The Antipodes* is at once a highly original play and a gathering together of a variety of dramatic and literary sources. The play draws upon Brome's previous plays in its investigation of melancholy, dreams, and the all-the-world-is-a-stage metaphor and in its emphasis on providing mirth. Its self-consciousness, romance conventions, and the use of the masque recall Jonson's *The New Inn*, while its satiric elements recall many of his city comedies. The play's originality lies in the way Brome combines all these elements to create an entertaining and highly complex drama.

Unlike *The Damoiselle*, which resembles *The New Inn* in its use of an inn as a theater in which plots cause hidden identities to be revealed, *The Antipodes* is set not in an inn but almost entirely in Letoy's house in London which "in substance is an amphitheater/Of exercise and pleasure." At first Letoy's love for theater seems extravagant, but we soon learn that he, with the aid of Doctor Hughball, cures people of melancholy with theatrics.

Ostensibly, Letoy's cure of Peregrine is the central action. At the start of the play, Blaze tells the sorrow-stricken Joyless, Peregrine's father, about Doctor Hughball and Letoy and sends his wife for the doctor. Under questioning, Joyless reveals that his son suffers from "a most deep melancholy" caused by his infatuation with the idea of traveling to distant lands. When he was almost twenty he wanted to go on a voyage, but his parents would not allow him to go. Instead they tried to remove his desire to travel by marrying him to Martha. This cure failed. Peregrine remained lost in his fantasies, and Martha became mad because the marriage went unconsummated.

When Doctor Hughball examines Peregrine, he does not try to destroy his illusions; instead he goes along with them and invites him on a trip to the Antipodes. After deciding to journey specifically to anti-London, the doctor has Peregrine drink a toast to the voyage, and Peregrine falls asleep because the drink was drugged. Peregrine awakens twelve hours later to be told the eight-month journey to the Antipodes is over. Although he is convinced he has arrived in the Antipodes,

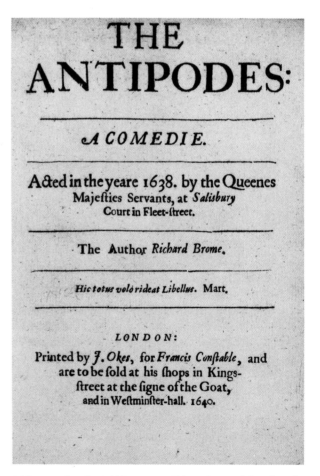

Title page for the 1640 quarto edition of one of the plays for which Brome drew on the lessons of his mentor, Ben Jonson (Henry E. Huntington Library and Art Gallery)

he is actually on the stage of Letoy's theater. Letoy's actors play roles which confirm the doctor's previous description of the upside-down nature of Antipodean behavior. Peregrine shortly proclaims himself King of the Antipodes and finds everything he sees amusing. Eventually he puts on a disguise so that he can mix freely with his countrymen. Now that he can see events more clearly, he is struck by the absurdities and injustices of Antipodean behavior and plans to implement reforms. Once he shows this ability to distinguish right from wrong, he is almost cured. It is time for the final step. The people of the kingdom celebrate their King's presence, and their Queen (who is actually Martha) offers herself in marriage to Peregrine in order to legitimize his kingship. They marry and consummate their love. With his dreams of travel and Letoy's play behind him, Peregrine regains his sanity, and he and his wife begin a normal life together.

Peregrine is not the only member of the Joyless family to suffer from melancholy. Just as Martha and Peregrine's marriage threatens to fall apart because it has not been consummated, Joyless's jealousy and his wife's reaction to it threaten to leave them childless. During his first marriage Joyless did not know what sadness meant, but, because he is now married to the much younger Diana, he suffers from extreme jealousy. He has no knowledge his cure is being undertaken at the same time as that of Peregrine, but it becomes evident to the audience when the doctor tells Letoy he has instructed Diana to spur her husband's jealousy. In act five Joyless's fears appear to have some basis. He watches Letoy attempt to seduce Diana, but promises of wealth and pleasure and threats of force and slander do not move her. She states that she was only putting on a show of disobedience and that she wants no part of a cure which will make her husband what he already fears he is. Letoy ends the seduction with the recognition that Diana is "invincible." This whole scene is a play, and Joyless is the intended audience. When he rejoins his wife, he praises her virtue and announces he is cured of his jealousy.

In another sense the attempted seduction of Diana was not a deceit; it was a serious test of her moral character, and she proved herself virtuous. In response to the test Letoy announces that he, not Master Truelock, is Diana's father, and he explains that he once suffered horribly from groundless jealousy and as a result abandoned Diana's mother. At this point in the play it becomes clear that Peregrine's cure is really a by-play in Letoy's testing and reunion with his daughter.

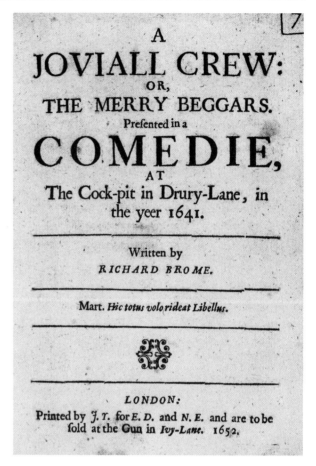

A
JOVIALL CREW:
OR,
THE MERRY BEGGARS.
Presented in a
COMEDIE,
AT
The Cock-pit in Drury-Lane, in
the yeer 1641.

Written by
RICHARD BROME.

Mart. *Hic totus volo rideat Libellus.*

LONDON:
Printed by *J. T.* for *E. D.* and *N. E.* and are to be
sold at the Gun in *Ivy-Lane.* 1652.

*Title page for the 1652 quarto edition of Brome's last play
(Henry E. Huntington Library and Art Gallery)*

Participation in Letoy's plays cures Peregrine of his desire to travel, Martha of her inability to consummate her marriage, Joyless of his jealousy, and Diana of her misguided desire for sexual fulfillment. And because Letoy is an actor as well as a spectator, he takes the final step in curing his own jealousy by acknowledging Diana as his daughter. For each member of the Joyless family the method of therapy is virtually the same: each is involved in an action which brings his fantasy to life, but the fantasy's extreme nature, when observed in the mirror of drama, makes the patient reject it and return to normal.

Brome is not content to cure only the characters in the play; he plans to cure the audience as well with the same theatrical technique. The melancholy of Joyless and his family reflects the melancholy Londoners suffered during the plague. Moreover, the audience, like Joyless's family, will lose its sorrow in the theater. The spectators within the play ultimately become actors and are, as a result, cured. The members of the audience must also become actors on the world's stage in order to be cured.

Although *A Jovial Crew* is more original than *The Antipodes*, it draws upon many of the same sources. But what most distinguishes it from the earlier play is that it is written from Peregrine's point of view, not Letoy's. Patrico, the author, director, actor, remains in the background until the end of the play, and he must rely on providence and nature to bring about the comic resolution. Whereas Letoy's art triumphs over diseased nature in *The Antipodes*, nature, with the aid of the art of theater, triumphs in *A Jovial Crew*.

The play begins with Oldrents telling his friend Hearty that the prophecy of a gypsy fortune-teller named Patrico has "afflicted" him and given him bad dreams. Patrico has told him that both his daughters, the only heirs to his great wealth, will become beggars. His sadness is increased by the desire of his honest steward Springlove to give up his office and spend the summer with the beggars who are visiting the Oldrentses' estate.

Oldrents's melancholy behavior finally prompts his daughters to leave home with their lovers, join the beggars, and thus fulfill Patrico's prophecy. Quickly the young women discover that life with the beggars is nowhere as utopian as it appeared from a distance, and they decide to return home. To celebrate their return to their father and to cheer him up, they offer to perform a play for him with the assistance of Patrico. He is given a list of titles to choose from and rejects *The Two Lost Daughters*, *The Vagrant Steward*, *The Old Squire and the Fortune-teller*, and *The Beggar's Prophecy* because they all recall the reasons for his melancholy. The play he does choose is *The Merry Beggars* (the subtitle of *A Jovial Crew*), no doubt because it appears to answer his desire for mirth. The play, however, proves to be a reenactment of *A Jovial Crew*. It begins with Patrico telling Oldrents's fortune, but for the first time we find out what lies behind it: Oldrents's grandfather cheated a "thriftless" heir of half of his lands and as a result made him and his descendants beggars.

After Oldrents has seen enough of the play, Patrico reveals his true identity: he is the grandson of the man whom Oldrents's grandfather ruined. Patrico then discloses yet another secret: he had a sister, also a beggar, whom Oldrents seduced, and she died a few days after giving birth to his son. The son is none other than Springlove. Oldrents responds to this revelation by acknowledging the justice of his fate and applauding "great providence."

All but the very end of *A Jovial Crew* is equivalent to Peregrine's visit to the Antipodes and Joyless and Diana's unknowing participation in Letoy's play. In both plays melancholy characters live in upside-down worlds. In *A Jovial Crew* characters of high birth transform themselves into beggars in order to avoid melancholy and restraint, and Oldrents vainly tries to become mirthful in order to forget his problems. At the end of the play these characters, unable to block out certain realities, return to the everyday world and become cured of their melancholy. Like the characters in Shakespeare's comedies and romances, they lose themselves to find themselves. *A Jovial Crew* differs from *The Antipodes* in that the audience has no idea these characters are participating in a larger play whose improvising author and director remains hidden until the last moment. And Patrico is not solely responsible for the comic resolution; he is aided by providence.

Brome's two best plays, *The Antipodes* and *A Jovial Crew*, are distinguished from his earlier plays by their structure, which is provided by the all-the-world-is-a-stage metaphor. Brome found himself as a dramatist by boldly exploiting a metaphor he had casually employed previously. What also links Brome's last two plays is their insistence that theater and the mirth it provides are effective cures for the melancholy which threatens to dissolve that tie that binds parents to their children and lovers to one another. Brome suggests that mirth, when combined with a realistic appraisal of the everyday world rather than the desire to escape it completely, can overcome the miseries of an imperfect world.

References:

Jackson Cope, "Richard Brome: The World as Antipodes," in his *The Theater and the Dream: From Metaphor to Form in Renaissance Drama* (Baltimore: Johns Hopkins University Press, 1973);

Joe Lee Davis, *The Sons of Ben* (Detroit: Wayne State University Press, 1967);

R. J. Kaufmann, *Richard Brome: Caroline Dramatist* (New York: Columbia University Press, 1961);

Catherine M. Shaw, *Richard Brome* (Boston: Twayne, 1980).

Papers:

A manuscript copy of *The English Moor*, thought to be in Brome's hand, is preserved at Lichfield Cathedral.

Thomas Campion

(12 February 1567-1 March 1620)

David Lindley
University of Leeds

PLAY PRODUCTIONS: *The Lord Hay's Masque*, London, at Court, 6 January 1607;

The Lords' Masque, London, at Court, 14 February 1613;

The Caversham Entertainment, near Reading, Caversham House, 27-28 April 1613;

The Somerset Masque, London, at Court, 26 December 1613.

BOOKS: *Thomæ Campiani Poemata* (London: Printed by R. Field, 1595);

A Booke of Ayres, by Campion and Philip Rosseter (London: Printed by P. Short, by the assent of T. Morley, 1601);

Observations in the Art of English Poesie (London: Printed by R. Field for A. Wise, 1602);

The Discription of a Maske, Presented before the Kinges Maiestie at White-Hall on Twelfth Night last, in honour of the Lord Hayes, and his Bride, Daughter and Heire to the Honourable the Lord Dennye (London: Printed by J. Windet for J. Brown, 1607);

A Relation Of The Late Royall Entertainment given By The Right Honourable The Lord Knowles, at Cawsome House neere Redding: to our most Gracious Queene, Queene Anne in her Progresse toward the Bathe, upon the seven and eight and twentie dayes of Aprill 1613. Whereunto is annexed the Description, Speeches and Songs of the Lords Maske, presented in the Banqueting House on the Mariage night of the High and Mightie, Count Palatine, and the Royally descended the Ladie Elizabeth (London: Printed by W. Stansby for J. Budge, 1613);

Songs of Mourning (London: Printed by T. Snodham for J. Browne, 1613);

Two Bookes of Ayres (London: Printed by T. Snodham for M. Lownes & J. Browne, 1613?);

The Description of a Maske. Presented in the Banqueting roome at Whitehall on Saint Stephens Night last, at the Mariage of the Right Honourable the Earle of Somerset: And the right noble the Lady Francis Howard (London: Printed by E. Allde & T. Snodham for L. Lisle, 1614);

The Third and Fourth Bookes of Ayres (London: Printed by T. Snodham, 1617?);

A New Way of Making Fowre parts in Counter-point (London, 1617?);

The Ayres that were sung and played, at Brougham Castle in Westmerland in the Kings Entertainment (London: Printed by Thomas Snodham, 1618);

Thomæ Campiani Epigrammatum Libri II (London: Printed by E. Griffin, 1619).

OBSERVATIONS
in the Art of English
Poesie.

By *Thomas Campion.*

Wherein it is demonstratiuely prooued, and by example confirmed, that the English toong will receiue eight seuerall kinds of numbers, proper to it selfe, which are all in this booke set forth, and were neuer before this time by any man attempted.

Printed at London by RICHARD FIELD for *Andrew Wise.* 1602.

Title page for the 1602 octavo edition for Campion's treatise on poetic meter (Bodleian Library, Oxford)

Editions: *Campion's Works,* edited by Percival Vivian (Oxford: Clarendon Press, 1909);

The Lords' Masque, edited by I. A. Shapiro, in *A Book of Masques,* edited by T. J. B. Spencer and Stanley Wells (Cambridge: Cambridge University Press, 1967), pp. 95-124;

The Works of Thomas Campion, edited by Walter R. Davis (Garden City: Doubleday, 1967; London: Faber & Faber, 1969);

Four Hundred Songs and Dances from the Stuart Masque, edited by Andrew J. Sabol (Providence: Brown University Press, 1968);

The Lord Hay's Masque and *The Lords' Masque,* in *Inigo Jones: The Theatre of the Stuart Court,* volume 1, by Stephen Orgel and Roy Strong (London: Sotheby Parke Bernet/Berkeley: University of California Press, 1973), pp. 115-121, 241-252;

De Puluerea Coniuratione (On The Gunpowder Plot), edited by David Lindley, with translations and additional notes by Robin Sowerby, *Leeds Texts and Monographs,* new series 9 (1987).

Thomas Campion made a varied contribution to the arts of his period. Perhaps best known today as the composer of music and lyrics for more than one hundred songs for voice and lute, he was equally celebrated in his own time for his Latin poetry. He wrote a theoretical treatise on versification urging the adoption of classical quantitative meters in English, and a music textbook which was sufficiently forward-looking to be republished throughout the seventeenth century. His contribution to the dramatic literature of the age consists of four masques, works which have been unjustly condemned by most modern critics. While there can be no doubt that Ben Jonson is the dominant figure in the history of the Jacobean masque, Campion's works are fine examples of the genre.

Campion was born on 12 February 1567 in the parish of St. Andrew's Holborn. By 1580 his father, John Campion, a cursitor of the Court of Chancery, and his mother, Lucy, were both dead, leaving him in the care of his mother's third husband, Augustine Steward, and his new wife, Anne Sisley. In 1581 he was sent to Peterhouse, Cambridge, where he remained until 1584, leaving without taking a degree. Two years later he was admitted to Gray's Inn. He acquired no legal qualification, but during the time of his connection with the inn he must have begun his writing career. His connection with drama and the masque also began at this time. In 1588 he acted a part in a comedy presented before Lord Burleigh and other noble-

men, and in 1594 he contributed at least one lyric to *The Masque of Proteus,* a highly significant work in the establishing of the masque form. It is probable that in 1591-1592 Campion joined Robert Devereux, Second Earl of Essex, on his unsuccessful expedition to aid Henry IV of France against the Catholic League in Normandy.

In 1595 Campion's publishing career began with the appearance of *Thomæ Campiani Poemata* (though five songs probably by Campion had been included with other poems appended to Thomas Newman's unauthorized edition of Sir Philip Sidney's *Astrophel and Stella* in 1591). In 1601 Campion and his friend Philip Rosseter jointly published *A Booke of Ayres,* the first half of which was by Campion. Rosseter's dedication of this work to Sir Thomas Monson indicates that Campion had for some time been under the protection of this important musical patron, who was himself a client of the powerful Howard family. This relationship was to be of considerable significance for Campion's future. After the publication in 1602 of his treatise on meter, *Observations in the Art of English Poesie,* it is assumed that Campion traveled on the Continent. In any event he received the degree of M.D. from the University of Caen in February 1605 and practiced medicine for the rest of his life.

Campion's masque-writing career began in 1607, when on 6 January *The Lord Hay's Masque* was performed at court to celebrate the marriage of King James's Scottish favorite James Hay to Honora Denny.

Summarizing a masque text, its meaning and significance, is no easy task. Music and spectacle, which play a vital role in the genre, are not easy to reconstruct in the imagination. Furthermore, the poet's ambition to lay hold on some more-removed mystery (in Jonson's phrase) means that the critic is involved in the explication of myth and symbol. Finally, since a masque grows out of a specific occasion, it is only when the context of an individual work is fully understood that layers of political implication can be uncovered.

The Lord Hay's Masque is notable for the detail with which its musical arrangements are described. Three separate groups of musicians were disposed in different places, their antiphonal sound contributing to the work's dramatic effect, and their climactic conjunction in full chorus to praise James I emphatically underlining the masque's panegyric. The published text also contains an amusing record of a failure in the scene designer's art, when trees that parted to reveal the masquers within failed to disappear "either by the simplicity, negligence, or

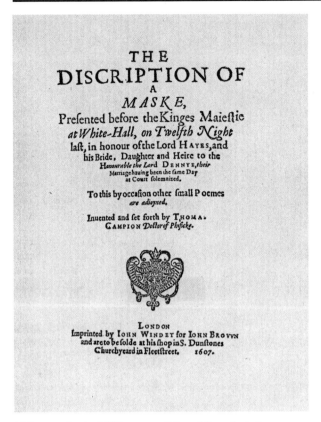

THE
DISCRIPTION OF
A
MASKE,
Prefented before the Kinges Maieftie
at *White-Hall, on Twelfth Night*
laft, in honour of the Lord H AYES, and
his Bride, Daughter and Heire to the
Honourable the Lord D ENNYE,*their*
Marriage hauing been the fame Day
at Court folemnized.

To this by occafion other fmall Poemes
are adioyned,

Inuented and fet forth by T,HOMA,
CAMPION *Doctor of Phyficke.*

LONDON
Imprinted by IOHN WINDET for IOHN BROVVN
and are to be folde at his fhop in S. Dunftones
Churchyeard in Fleetftreet,   1607.

Title page for the 1607 quarto edition of Campion's first masque
(British Library)

conspiracy of the painter," as Campion testily remarked.

The narrative of the masque concerns nine Knights of Apollo who have been imprisoned in trees by Diana, goddess of chastity, for their temerity in seeking to seduce her nymphs. By the mediation of Hesperus, Diana is reconciled, the knights are released and, after paying homage to Diana's tree, are free to join in the revels to celebrate the marriage.

The device is appropriate to its occasion in that the concord of the three deities, Apollo, Venus (Hesperus), and Diana, figures the elemental concord between male heat and female cold that marriage brings about. The masque urges on the couple a temperate and lasting love.

This marriage between a Scotsman and an Englishwoman also served as an emblem of the union between Scotland and England that James had urgently prosecuted since 1603, when, already James VI of Scotland, he had become James I of England. Campion shows himself fully aware of this political dimension. For while the overall direction of the masque serves to commend the

union, much of its detail shows an awareness of the problems that hindered the success of the scheme. Most notably, in choosing Diana as the defender of the female (English) side of the match he alludes to the memory of Queen Elizabeth, and by making the knights' homage to her tree the climax of their restoration he articulates the English concern at the intemperance of James's court and his excessive reward of Scottish followers. At the same time, however, English spectators are reminded that Elizabeth had consented to James's succession and therefore to the union of countries it brought about. The masque as a whole indicates the need for love to replace ancient hostility between the nations. The balanced attitude Campion strikes suited Robert Cecil and Thomas Howard, who probably commissioned and paid for the masque, but it seems typical also of the author's personality as it reveals itself in his poetry and in his later masques.

After this work Campion published virtually nothing for six years, but late in 1612 he was commissioned to provide a masque for the extensive celebrations of the wedding of Princess Elizabeth to Frederick, Elector Palatine. Perhaps it was Jonson's absence from the country that made room for him, and his connection, through Monson, with Thomas Howard, the Lord Chamberlain that secured this prestigious responsibility. The preparations were, however, interrupted by the death of Prince Henry on 6 November 1612. To this sad event Campion responded by publishing his *Songs of Mourning* with music by Giovanni Coprario. In his dedication of this work to Frederick he promised that he would soon be singing "delayed wedding songs," and the promise was fulfilled on 14 February 1613, with the performance of *The Lords' Masque.*

For this work Campion collaborated with Inigo Jones. Where in his previous masque he had cause for complaint against the scene designer, here he was full of praise for Jones's "extraordinarie industrie and skill," especially in his contrivance of a ballet of moving stars. This particularly ingenious device elicited admiring comment from the Venetian ambassador.

It is not only the setting of this masque which marks an advance on earlier work, for the work begins with an antimasque of madmen as foil to the main masque, following the formal innovation introduced by Jonson some four years previously.

The masque itself is complex. Two sets of masquers are involved. The first set, eight lords, represents the dancing stars, and they are brought

Engraving of a Knight of Apollo published in the 1607 quarto edition of The Lord Hay's Masque *(Stephen Orgel and Roy Strong,* Inigo Jones, *1973)*

down by Prometheus, the mythical stealer of fire from heaven. The second set of eight ladies has been turned into statues by Jove in his anger at Prometheus's theft. Jove relents, and four by four the ladies are brought to life, joining in dance with the lords. In a striking variation of the usual masque form the social dances which follow do not bring the masque to a close. Instead the prophetess Sibylla appears, flanked by statues of the bride and groom. She prophesies a happy future for the couple, and then the spectators are invited to contemplate the statues of the couple before turning to honor "the life those figures bear."

The elaborate surface of the masque shadows a serious and ambitious moral design. The program seems based on the Platonic doctrine of the four furies which lead men from earth to celestial contemplation. It begins with the distinction of Poetic Fury from mere madmen in the antimasque and culminates in the presentation of Frederick and Elizabeth as types of Love at the end of the

masque. At the same time Campion is able to explore the problem of how such mysteries may be revealed in art, as Orpheus and Entheus, representing poetry and music, are joined by Prometheus the maker of images. Campion's part in the contriving of the masque is figured in the first two, Inigo Jones's in the third.

Throughout this masque Campion addresses the question of the relationship of masque image to the reality it idealized, and he insists upon the necessity of the masquers' remembering the significance of the roles they play, making clear his didactic purpose.

This marriage was, of course, a highly significant political event. The wedding of Elizabeth to a Protestant was seen as committing James to the anti-Spanish cause in Europe and raised hopes among some fervent souls of a new crusade against Catholicism. Campion presents a much more restrained attitude. The work as a whole seems to support a pacific line that accorded much more closely with James's own inclinations, and perhaps alludes to his policy of balancing this Protestant match with a Catholic marriage for his son. But whether or not that is the case, there can be no doubt that Campion responded to this most demanding commission with an extraordinarily ambitious work, whose meaning is only available after detailed consideration of its iconology and political address.

The political attitude of this masque must have commended itself to the Howard family, since Campion was entrusted by them with two more commissions within the next twelve months. Queen Anne, on her progress to Bath after her daughter's wedding, stayed at Caversham near Reading, the home of Sir William Knollys, who was related to the Howards by marriage.

The Caversham Entertainment is a slighter piece than the other masques. When the Queen approached the house on 27 April she was greeted by a Cynick who attempted to bar the way. A Traveller countered his arguments, and the Queen proceeded toward the house to be greeted at various points by a Keeper and a Gardiner with appropriate verses, songs, and dances. Campion here manipulates fairly standard pastoral figures with grace, for the sequence of meetings is so contrived that the nearer the Queen approached to the house the more sophisticated her welcome became.

The following night the Queen was entertained after supper by a masque indoors. Cynick, Traveller, and Gardiner reappear in a brief, almost Jonsonian antimasque which is interrupted by Sil-

Inigo Jones's costume design for the lords who played dancing stars in Campion's The Lords' Masque *(Stephen Orgel and Roy Strong,* Inigo Jones, *1973)*

vanus. He then introduces the eight masquers in their elegantly pastoral attire.

The lack of any scenic device and the somewhat old-fashioned role of Sylvanus as presenter of the disguising are typical of the necessarily more limited scope of masques away from the court. Within these limits Campion contrived a graceful if not profound work exploiting rather different conventions from those of his larger-scale masques.

It was probably in this same year that Campion brought out his *Two Bookes of Ayres,* dedicated to the Earl of Cumberland and his son. But at the end of the year it was again to a Howard commission that Campion responded, with his masque for the marriage of Suffolk's daughter Frances to Robert Carr, Earl of Somerset.

The Somerset Masque, presented on 26 December 1613, is interesting in a number of ways. Because Inigo Jones was away, Campion had to avail himself of the services of Constantine de' Servi, and

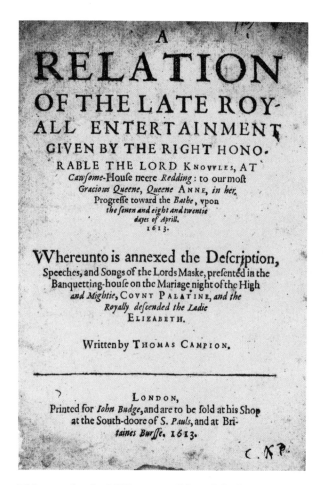

A

RELATION

OF THE LATE ROY-
ALL ENTERTAINMENT
GIVEN BY THE RIGHT HONO-
RABLE THE LORD Knovvles, AT
Cawsome-House neere *Redding*: to ourmost
Gracious Queene, Queene ANNE, *in her*,
Progresse toward the *Bathe*, vpon
*the seuen and eight and twentie
dayes of April*.
1613.

VVhereunto is annexed the Description,
Speeches, and Songs of the Lords Maske, presented in the
Banquetting-house on the Mariage night of the High
and Mightie, COVNT PALATINE, *and the
Royally descended the Ladie*
ELIZABETH.

Written by THOMAS CAMPION.

LONDON,
Printed for *Iohn Budge,* and are to be sold at his Shop
at the South-doore of S. *Pauls,* and at Bri-
taines Burffe. 1613.

C. K P.

Title page for the 1613 quarto edition of the first masque on which Campion collaborated with Inigo Jones (Henry E. Huntington Library and Art Gallery)

once again he had cause for complaint. He wrote: "he, being too much of him selfe, and no way to be drawne to impart his intentions, fayled so farre in the assurance he gave, that the mayne invention, even at the last cast, was of force drawne into a farre narrower compasse then was from the beginning intended." One can only conjecture how seriously this affected the masque, but the comment does serve to underline the extent to which any court masque was a collaborative enterprise, and it alerts a text-orientated critic to the significance of the scene designer's part in the work's devising.

Also noteworthy is the fact that Nicholas Lanier began his career as a composer of masque music with a setting of the lyric "Bring away this Sacred Tree" in a highly declamatory style. The masque is significant in the history of the evolution of musical style, and this song marks a major step in the advance toward a quasi-operatic manner.

Campion himself signaled a departure from his earlier style when in the prologue to the published text he dismissed old-fashioned myth, instead grounding his "whole Invention upon Inchauntments and several transformations." He is here following closely the tendencies of French court entertainment and reflecting his career-long interest in French music and poetry.

Catullus's narrative of the marriage of Peleus and Thetis underlies *The Somerset Masque.* Twelve masquers have been prevented by enchantment from attending the marriage. The consequences of the enchanters' power are demonstrated in a series of discordant dances, but their disharmony is dispelled by the entrance of Eternitie and the Destinies. Queen Anne is invited to pluck a bough from their sacred tree, and the knights are thus freed to dance in honor of the couple. After the revels a brief coda sees skippers emerge from Thames barges and perform a dance before the masque draws to its close.

This masque has an altogether more rhetorical and assertive character than the earlier works, with much less emphasis upon the education of the masquers themselves. The reason is not far to seek, for the circumstances of its composition were peculiarly difficult.

The marriage of Frances Howard to Robert Carr, the King's chief favorite, was a signal triumph in political terms for the Howard clan. It was made possible by Frances's divorce from the Earl of Essex, to whom she had been married as a child in 1606. The divorce hearing, blatantly rigged by the King, granted Frances her freedom on the grounds of Essex's impotence toward her. It occasioned a great deal of salacious gossip and many outbursts of moral indignation.

It was this scandal that *The Somerset Masque* confronted directly. Error, Rumour, Curiosity, and Credulity are the enchanters whose inhibition of the celebrations the masque overcomes. The work is therefore directed out at the audience in a defiant attempt to persuade them of the propriety of the marriage. Queen Anne's blessing on the marriage was more than conventional flattery, since it was the relaxation of her opposition to the match that allowed it to be celebrated in London rather than at the bride's home. Furthermore, the gift of children that the Destinies promised the couple is itself an explicit defense of the divorce, since Essex's impotence would have denied Frances the legitimate possibility of procreation.

It is tempting to see this masque as a glaring example of the obsequious and unthinking flattery proffered to his patron by a court poet. But a case can be made that Campion, like Chapman in his poem *Andromeda Liberata* (which has significant similarities with the masque), saw the marriage as a real attempt to bring court faction together, and as a morally defensible liberation of a woman from the prison of a nonmarriage.

But though such an attitude was possible in 1613, it could scarcely be sustained when, in 1615, it was revealed that Frances Howard, possibly with Carr's collusion, had caused the murder of Sir Thomas Overbury in the Tower of London just before the divorce was granted. These disclosures had important consequences for Campion. His patron Thomas Monson had been instrumental in replacing William Wade as Lieutenant of the Tower with Sir Gervase Elwes, a man more amenable to Frances's designs. Campion himself had collected a large sum of money from Elwes to be given to Monson as payment for procuring the position. He was questioned, but cleared of any guilty knowledge. Monson was not so fortunate. Though never charged, and protesting his innocence, he was imprisoned until 1617. While it is impossible to be absolutely certain, it would seem unlikely that Campion or Monson had any inkling of the dark consequences of their actions.

When Monson was released Campion published his *The Third and Fourth Bookes of Ayres* with a dedication congratulating Monson on his fortitude, which the poet had been able to observe when attending him as his physician. Many of the lyrics in *The Third Booke* speak of disillusionment with the faithlessness of the world, perhaps reflecting something of Campion's own feelings at the betrayal of

the idealized picture of Frances Howard and of court society he had created in *The Somerset Masque*.

It is possible that Campion contributed to the entertainment of King James when he visited the Earl of Cumberland in August 1617 on his return from Scotland. *The Ayres that were sung and played, at Brougham Castle* were published the following year with music by George Mason and John Earsden but no acknowledgment of the writer of the words. Campion had been connected with the Clifford family; a letter cited by Percival Vivian, the editor of the 1909 edition of Campion's works, seems to indicate some degree of involvement with the entertainment of the King, and one or two of the lyrics echo Campion's Latin poems faintly. Unfortunately, whether or not Campion did write these poems, it is impossible to reconstruct from them any real idea of the character of the entertainment in which they figured.

Campion's last work, *Epigrammatum Libri II*, revising and considerably extending his first Latin publication, appeared in 1619. This publication did not, however, include the recently discovered *De Puluerea Coniuratione*, which survives in a single manuscript (Sidney Sussex MS 59). Probably written between 1615 and 1618, it is Campion's most ambitious Latin work. The epical treatment of the Gunpowder Plot is dedicated to the King, and may well represent an effort to regain the favor lost in the aftermath of the Overbury murder. Campion died on 1 March 1620 and was buried at St. Dunstan's in the West, Fleet Street. In his will he left his entire estate, valued at twenty-two pounds, to his old friend Philip Rosseter, wishing that it "had bin farr more."

The smallness of his estate and the fact that he produced no major masques after 1613 may well be connected with the decline of his patrons' fortunes that followed the Overbury trial. Monson suffered financially, and the Howard family's political influence began a decline that culminated in the Earl of Suffolk's removal from office in 1618.

Of Campion's personality it is impossible to write with any certainty. In one of his epigrams he indicates that he was spare of build, and an anonymous poem of circa 1611 implies that he was talkative: "How now Doctor Champion, musicks and poesies stout Champion,/Will you nere leave prating?" The masques suggest that he was balanced in his political attitudes, conservative in temperament, yet able to criticize the excesses of the Jacobean court.

Campion's masques are significant examples of their kind. In them may be traced the evolution of the early Jacobean masque, its music and scene design. Each of them offers an interesting gloss on the significant political events they celebrated. If their symbolism is fully and sympathetically understood then often-repeated criticism of Campion's lack of structural ability is shown to be false, and Stephen Orgel's censure of Campion's political flaccidity revealed as unjust. For though *The Somerset Masque* exposes the strains that any poet must have felt in idealizing the increasingly unideal court of King James, Campion managed in all his works to serve his patrons, satisfy the panegyric necessity of the form, and yet not lose sight of the didactic and moral seriousness that alone could give weight to these transitory shows and preserve his own integrity.

References:

A. Leigh DeNeef, "Structure and Theme in Campion's *The Lords Maske,*" *Studies in English Literature,* 17 (Winter 1977): 95-103;

David Lindley, "Campion's *Lord Hay's Masque* and Anglo-Scottish Union," *Huntington Library Quarterly,* 43 (Winter 1979): 1-11;

Lindley, *Thomas Campion* (Leiden: E. J. Brill, 1986);

Lindley, "Who Paid for Campion's *Lord Hay's Masque?,*" *Notes and Queries,* new series 27 (April 1979): 144;

Edward Lowbury, Timothy Salter, and Alison Young, *Thomas Campion* (London: Chatto & Windus, 1970);

Wilfred Mellers, *Harmonious Meeting* (London: Dobson, 1965);

Stephen Orgel, *The Jonsonian Masque* (Cambridge: Harvard University Press, 1967);

John Orrell, "The agent of Savoy at *The Somerset Masque,*" *Review of English Studies,* 28 (1977): 301-304;

Paul Reyher, *Les Masques Anglais* (Paris & London: Hachette et Cie, 1909);

Ian Spink, "Campion's Entertainment at Brougham Castle, 1617," in *Music in English Renaissance Drama,* edited by John H. Long (Lexington: University of Kentucky Press, 1968), pp. 57-74;

Enid Welsford, *The Court Masque* (Cambridge: Cambridge University Press, 1927).

Lodowick Carlell
(1602-1675)

Karen Wood
University of California, Berkeley

PLAY PRODUCTIONS: *Osmond, the Great Turk, or the Noble Servant,* London, Blackfriars theater(?), 1622;

The Deserving Favorite, London, at Court, circa 1622-1629(?);

The Spartan Ladies, London, Blackfriars theater(?), 1634;

Arviragus and Philicia, parts 1 and 2, London, Blackfriars theater, 1636;

The Fool Would Be a Favorite; Or, The Discreet Lover, London, Salisbury Court theater, circa 1637-1642;

The Passionate Lovers, part 1, London, Somerset House, 10 July 1638; London, Cockpit (Whitehall Palace), 18 December 1638; part 2, London, Cockpit (Whitehall Palace), 20 December 1638.

BOOKS: *The Deserving Favorite* (London: Printed by W. Stansby for M. Rhodes, 1629);

Arviragus and Philicia. As It Was Acted. The First and Second Part (London: Printed by J. Norton for J. Crooke & R. Sergier, 1639);

The Passionate Lovers, A Tragi-Comedy. The First and Second Parts (London: Printed for Humphrey Moseley, 1655);

Two New Playes. Viz. 1. The Fool would be a Favourit: or, The Discreet Lover. 2. Osmond, the Great Turk: or, The Noble Servant (London: Printed for Humphrey Moseley, 1657).

Editions: *The Deserving Favorite,* edited by Charles H. Gray (Chicago: University of Chicago Press, 1905);

Two New Playes. Viz. I. The Fool Would Be a Favorite: or the Discreet Lover, II. Osmond the Great Turk: or the Noble Servant, edited by Allardyce Nicoll (Waltham Saint Lawrence: Golden Cockerel Press, 1926).

OTHER: Pierre Corneille, *Heraclius, Emperor of the East,* translated by Carlell (London: Printed for John Starkey, 1664).

Lodowick Carlell enjoyed considerable success as a dramatist and courtier during the reigns of James I and Charles I. A favorite throughout his life of Queen Henrietta Maria, and probably an accomplished outdoorsman, he held many court posts, most of which were connected with the hunt. His plays, performed by the King's and Queen's Companies, were romances about love and honor, whose heroes were princes and courtiers, idealized figures endowed with superhuman moral capabilities.

Carlell (also spelled Carlisle, Carliell, Carlile) was born in 1602 at Brydekirk in Dumfriesshire, Scotland. His family was impoverished, but old and well connected, tracing its descent from Sir Ade (or Adam) Karleolo, an Annandale landowner of the twelfth century and a vassal of William de Bruce. (The family also claimed as an ancestor King Duncan, who was murdered by Macbeth and others in 1039; a famous modern descendant was Thomas Carlyle.) Carlell's mother was Margaret Cunningham Carlell. His father, Herbert (or Robert) Carlell of Brydekirk (1558-1632), was appointed warden in his district in 1586, bred hounds for James IV of Scotland (later James I of England), and served the King as royal huntsman. He may also have been the author of "Britaine's Glorie," a patriotic allegorical poem written in 1619. The dramatist's uncle, Alexander Carlell, served James as yeoman pricker of the hounds.

Along with this venerable side, the Carlell family had a lawless and disreputable one as well. Contemporary records describe some of the Carlells as "poor burgesses and indwellers of Dumfries, not with £100 each in free gear" and as "brokin men [outlaws], thevis and malefactouris." The family history includes regular involvement in feuds, border skirmishes, thefts of livestock on a large scale, and other acts of violence. One Robert Carlile (not Lodowick's father) was executed for murder.

Dumfriesshire, at the western border between Scotland and England, was in the late-sixteenth and early-seventeenth centuries both lawless and economically depressed. The soil of Annan was of extremely poor quality, and the region had been devastated by the Earl of Essex in 1570. These two factors had combined to produce such poverty that the people of the region could not provide themselves with a church and had to be allowed, under special dispensation from James I in 1609, to worship in Annan Castle itself.

Exactly when or by what means Lodowick Carlell went to court we do not know. He may have been brought to James's attention while the King was at Dumfries in 1617. During this visit, James was entertained by Carlell's maternal relations and may have been solicited on the young man's behalf by them, by Lodowick's father, and even by the powerful figure whom Charles H. Gray proposes was Lodowick's godfather, Lodovic Stuart, Duke of Lennox and Richmond. A young manhood spent at court would be consistent with the absence of Carlell's name from university records and with the reference in the dedication to *The Deserving Favorite*

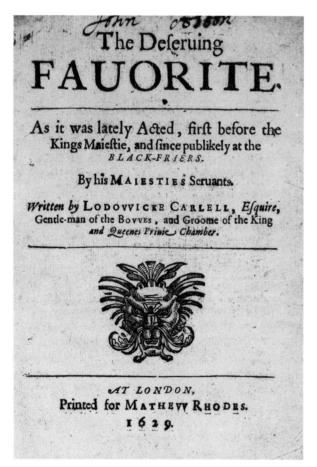

Title page for the 1629 quarto edition of the play Carlell wrote to please the courtly-love coterie surrounding Queen Henrietta Maria (Henry E. Huntington Library and Art Gallery)

to the author's "knowne want of Learning." At any rate, a letter written in 1621 tells us that in that year Carlell applied for the wardship of a young man, Walter Mildmay, and that his application was supported by the King. Carlell was, then, at court by that time and in a position of favor that could allow him to participate in and to profit from the exploitive wardship system under which a courtier could, as Christopher Hill explains, "make what profit he could out of [a ward's] estate during the minority, and . . . marry the heir or heiress to some needy kinsman of his own."

Carlell began writing plays in the 1620s. His first work, *Osmond, the Great Turk,* performed in 1622, is a tragedy that depicts events following the Turkish conquest of Constantinople in 1453. Its hero, Osmond, virtually perfect in duty and fidelity to the Emperor, is the focus of the play's advocacy of monarchic absolutism and the divine right of kings.

In 1626 Carlell married Joan Palmer, daughter of "William Palmer, Gent. of St. James Park . . . at St. Faith's, London," and in 1629 he published the first edition of *The Deserving Favorite* (the date of its first performance is unknown), a tragicomedy built upon the conventions of romance which were to become typical of Carlell's work in general: the separation and reunion of friends, family members, or lovers; false death and resurrection; disguise; and remoteness of setting. This play also began, along with Walter Montague's *The Shepherd's Paradise,* the vogue of writing plays for Queen Henrietta Maria's "new love" coterie. The title page of this edition names Carlell as "Gentleman of the Bowes, and Groome of the King and Queenes Priuie Chamber," and an entry for this year in *The Booke of Establishment,* the Queen's book of household expenses, mentions Carlell as Groom of the Privy Chamber and as huntsman. From this year on came a steady stream of appointments for Carlell. The *Exchequer Accounts* list him as Groom of the Privy Chamber in 1630, as Master of the Bows in 1631, as Keeper of the Hounds in 1631-1633. Thomas Dekker's dedication to the 1631 edition of his play *Match Me in London* reveals something about Carlell's importance at court at this time: by means of an elaborate compliment, rendered in allusive language, Dekker asks Carlell to use his influence to bring about a production of Dekker's play at court. By 1636 Carlell had been made one of two keepers at the royal deer park at Richmond and had been given a lodge there.

During the 1630s Carlell produced four more highly successful plays, two of these in ten acts. *The*

Title page for the 1639 twelvemo edition of Carlell's first ten-act tragicomedy (Henry E. Huntington Library and Art Gallery)

Spartan Ladies, a nonextant comedy, was performed in 1634, according to an entry for that year in Sir Humphrey Mildmay's diary and account book. (This play is also named in Sir Humphrey Moseley's advertisement to Thomas Middleton's *More Dissemblers Besides Women* in 1657 and in a 1669 playlist belonging to the King's Company. It was registered with the Stationers' Company on 4 September 1646.) *Arviragus and Philicia,* a ten-act tragicomedy about the adventures of a deposed Pictish prince, was performed at least three times at court in 1636. The play's fourth performance was given at Blackfriars and was attended by the Queen, whose attendance at the public theater was a high compliment to the dramatist. It was revived in 1672 with a prologue by John Dryden praising the play's native elements. *The Passionate Lovers,* another ten-act tragicomedy, was presented in 1638 with sets by Inigo Jones. Set in fictitious lands, it is about the

amorous exploits of two brother-princes.

The performance dates of *The Fool Would Be a Favorite* are not known. In 1657 the play was published with *Osmond, the Great Turk* in *Two New Playes,* with a title-page announcement that both plays were "often acted by the Queen's Majesty's Servants with great applause"; as the Queen's Company operated between 1637 and 1642, the play was probably performed at some time during those years. Conclusive evidence, however, about the dates or even the auspices of these plays is not available.

This play represents something of a departure from Carlell's other plays. For while the main plot is a heroic romance, the comic subplot is a satire, using the conventions of realism, about an idiotic and rich young man from the country who arrives at court ready to be swindled by two enterprising courtiers offering to "sell" him a favorite's place there, and who composes and appears in a bombastic, and occasionally, obscene parody of a Carlell romance. *The Fool Would Be a Favorite,* like a great many other plays of its period, makes fun of pretenders to courtly attainments, among whom Carlell includes himself: he, like the fool in his play, came to court with his father's help and took up play writing. But the play's deeper satiric purpose is to make us think not only about the ways in which those who are not ostensibly fools may commit acts of folly but also about the belief at the heart of the courtly way of life in the courtier's superior capacity for intellectual, aesthetic, and moral refinement, a consequence of which was the type of play in whose noble, nearly faultless characters, engaged in discussion of serious moral themes, a courtly audience could see itself reflected.

In 1642 the courtier's circumstances were altered. When the civil war began, Carlell, who did not enter combat, contributed £1500 to the Royal Exchequer. (James E. Ruoff believes that this amount was Carlell's entire fortune.) In 1649 Parliament gave Richmond Park to the city of London with the recommendation that the keepers be retained, provided that they were found to be "faithful servants." Carlell, then, may have been permitted to remain at his home there. Moreover, his name appears neither among those of the nobility whose property was confiscated nor among those of royalist emigrés to France.

He may well have escaped the worst effects of this period of unrest, but he did not escape adversity. In 1660 Charles II, probably at the Queen Mother's request, granted Carlell £200 per annum and "the office of keeping the house or Lodge

Inigo Jones's costume design for a druid in Carlell's The Passionate Lovers *(Stephen Orgel and Roy Strong,* Inigo Jones, *1973)*

within the Greate Parke neere Richmond," along with other privileges. Carlell never received the full amount of this pension, and of the £1500 he gave to the royalist cause, only £100 were repaid. That the circumstances of the last years of Carlell's life were not comfortable can be judged from his widow's will, which stated in 1677 that the still unpaid Exchequer debt and the "arrears" of the £200 per annum pension would be used to settle debts. In 1698 Eleanor Carlile, the dramatist's niece, in extreme destitution, petitioned the Crown for the return of the Exchequer contribution. (She was granted £20 by royal warrant and "such ane allowance yearly . . . as upon examination of her circum-

stances it shall be found they deserve. . . .")

In 1664 Carlell published his translation of Corneille's tragedy, *Heraclius, Emperor of the East,* with the intention, according to the play's dedication, of pleasing the Queen Mother, who "loves plays of that kind." The play is also dedicated to Charles, "for the subject of it is the Restoration of a gallant Prince to his just inheritance, many years after the unjust and horrid murder of a Saint-like Father." This translation was never acted. (The anonymous translation which was performed by the Duke's Men is nonextant.)

In 1671, probably for pecuniary reasons, Carlell turned over the ownership of New Park and other property in Scotland to his great-nephew, Adam Carliel. For the remainder of his life, he resided in St. Martin-in-the-Fields. The exact day of his death is unknown, but he was buried at Petersham on 21 August 1675. Buried with him are his son James, who predeceased him by seven years, and his widow Joan, who died in 1678.

Ruoff, though intensely critical of Carlell's plays, calls them "reminiscent of gorgeous Renaissance tapestries richly textured with multitudes of inanimate figures and exotic vestments." The comparison applies in several ways. Like tapestries, these plays inform us about their time, reflecting the preferences and the nature of the court which received them so enthusiastically. The prologue to *The Deserving Favorite* suggests the appeal of Carlell's plays in general to a courtly audience obsessed with romantic love and its refining power:

Great Love, this play is thine,
Worke Miracles, and shew thy selfe Diuine;
Change these rude lines into a sweet smooth Straine,
Which were the weak effects of a dull Braine:
If in this Prologue Contradictions moue,
That best expresses: it was writ by Love.

Henrietta Maria and her coterie subscribed to the Neoplatonic ideals of courtly love which endowed romantic love with immense and transcendent moral significance by making it the means of approaching the divine. The courtly lover's mistress was the full embodiment of earthly virtue, and in serving her, the lover served virtue itself. He could thus undergo, through the love of his mistress, moral refinement and even redemption from vice. "Honor," as Ruoff points out, "within the 'new love' code, was next in importance after love: without it, love was impossible."

Carlell's plays attempt to define the various kinds of love and their relations to one another. Which is most important, they ask, the love between friends, between lovers, between brothers, or between sovereign and subject? How are these kinds of love to be reconciled? The characters—princes and courtiers presented for the most part as sublime examples of constancy, devotion, and self-sacrifice—repeatedly find themselves in situations which develop into tests of moral capability (from which the plays derive considerable dramatic momentum). Such tests are, invariably, survived with dazzling fortitude by those who undergo them. Carlell's characters do not emerge as individuals, and they appear to lack interior motivation; but for Carlell it is the moral example that matters. The audience's task is to admire and to imitate. Carlell's evil characters—Cleon, Iacomo, Adrastus—are also generalized representations, but of vice; they are repugnant examples to be shunned.

Perhaps the most striking feature of Carlell's plays is their escapism. While they do depict evil and suffering, the confirmed virtue of individual characters has the power to avert general catastrophe and to revoke the destructive consequences of error. Entirely excluded, however, is contemporary experience, including any detectable hint of the philosophical developments and epistemological uncertainties of the time. The new science, the deterioration of the Stuart monarchy, the political, economic, and religious turbulence of the 1630s: all have been effectively banished. In their removal from the world of seventeenth-century England, Carlell's plays reflect the isolation of Charles and

THE
PASSIONATE
LOVERS,
A
TRAGI-COMEDY.

The First and Second Parts.

Twice prefented before the K I N G and
Que E N s Majefties at *Somerfet-Houfe,*
and very often at the Private Houfe in
Black-Friars, with great Applaufe,

By his late MAJESTIES Servants.

Written by
LODOWICK CARLELL, Gent.

LONDON,
Printed for *Humphrey Mofeley*, and are to be
fold at his fhop at the fign of the *Prince's Arms*
in St. *Pauls* Church-yard. 1 6 5 5.

Title page for a 1655 octavo edition of Carlell's second ten-act tragicomedy, produced in 1638 with sets by Inigo Jones (Henry E. Huntington Library and Art Gallery)

his court from the nation as a whole. They are symptoms of the illness whose crisis would be the Puritan revolution.

References: ·

Charles H. Gray, *Lodowick Carliell* (Chicago: University of Chicago Press, 1905);

Christopher Hill, *Century of Revolution* (New York: Norton, 1961);

Allardyce Nicoll, Introduction to *The Tragedy of Osmond, the Great Turk, or, the Noble Servant* (Waltham Saint Lawrence: Golden Cockerel Press, 1926);

James E. Ruoff, Introduction to "A Critical Edition of Arviragus and Philicia," Ph.D. dissertation, University of Pennsylvania, 1954.

Papers:

A manuscript for part one of *Arviragus and Philicia* is at the Bodleian Library (MS. Eng. Misc.d), and a manuscript for part two is in Lord Leconfield's library at Petworth.

Robert Daborne
(circa 1580-23 March 1628)

Donald S. Lawless

PLAY PRODUCTIONS: *The Poor Man's Comfort,* London, Whitefriars theater(?), 1611(?);

A Christian Turned Turk, London, Whitefriars theater(?), 1611(?);

Machiavel and the Devil, London, Swan theater(?) or Whitefriars theater(?), 11 August 1613(?);

The Arraignment of London (The Bellman of London?), by Daborne and Cyril Tourneur, London, Whitefriars theater(?) or Swan theater(?), after circa 9 December 1613;

The Owl, London, Whitefriars theater(?), or Swan theater(?), after 28 March 1614;

The She Saint, London, Whitefriars theater(?), or Swan theater(?), or Hope theater(?), after 2 April 1614.

BOOKS: *A Christian Turn'd Turke: or, The Tragicall Lives and Deaths of the Two Famous Pyrates, Ward and Dansiker* (London: Printed by N. Okes for William Barrenger, 1612);

Sermon Preached in the Cathedrall Church of Waterford, in Febr. 1617. Before the Justices of Assize (London: Printed by G. Eld for H. Gosson, 1618);

The Poor-Mans Comfort. A Tragi-Comedy (London: Printed for Robert Pollard & John Sweeting, 1655).

Editions: *A Christian Turned Turk,* edited by A. E. H. Swaen, *Anglia,* 20 (1898): 188-256;

The Poor Man's Comfort, edited by Kenneth Palmer, Malone Society Reprints (Oxford: Oxford University Press, 1955).

OTHER: Christopher Brooke(?), *The Ghost of Richard the Third,* includes commendatory verses by Daborne (London: Printed by G. Eld for L. Lisle, 1614); republished, with an introduction and notes by J. Payne Collier, as Shakespeare Society Publication no. 22 (London: Printed for the Shakespeare Society, 1844);

John Taylor, *The Nipping or Snipping of Abuses,* includes commendatory verses by Daborne (London: Printed by E. Griffin for N. Butler, 1614).

Robert Daborne, a minor Jacobean playwright and clergyman, is of interest today mainly because of his series of letters to theatrical entrepreneur Philip Henslowe, which show Henslowe's relations with the dramatists in his employ and which also shed light upon theatrical and dramatic practices of the Jacobean and, presumably, the Elizabethan periods. Daborne is of interest too because of his associations with a number of other dramatists of his time.

Robert Daborne was the son of Robert Daborne, citizen and haberdasher of London, and of his wife, Susanna (née Traves), who were licensed to wed on 20 November 1578. The exact date of his birth is unknown, but it may be roughly estimated to have been about 1580 since, as Peter Holloway has pointed out, Daborne matriculated sizar from King's College, Cambridge, in 1598, from which university he was presumably granted both B. A. and M. A. degrees (the title page of the quarto edition of *The Poor Man's Comfort* describes him as "Master of Arts"). Robert Daborne the elder belonged to a family that had long resided at Guildford, Surrey. He owned, or at least had an interest in, Guildford Castle, the ancient seat of the family, but he was also a London merchant or craftsman. Whether his son was born at Guildford is not known. In the prologue to *A Christian Turned Turk* Daborne states that his *"owne discent . . . [was] not obscure but generous."*

According to C. L'Estrange Ewen, Daborne went "to London in 1607 upon finding the life of a country gentleman beyond his means." The basis for this date is unknown, but documentary evidence shows that Daborne was certainly there by the middle of 1609 at the latest. He was by that time married to Anne, the daughter of Robert Younger, an attorney of the Common Pleas, and his wife, Elizabeth. Daborne and Anne then had a family.

Some light is thrown on Daborne's activities in the autumn and winter of 1609 by a Chancery suit (1610), which two of his wife's brothers, Thomas and Edward Younger, brought against him and two others—William Taylor of Lincoln's Inn, a kinsman of Daborne's by marriage, and Philip Kingman—over their parents' estate. It appears that on 20 August 1609 Robert Daborne went to his father-in-law and asked to be allowed to go with his wife and children to the Youngers' home in Shoreditch for the remainder of his wife's pregnancy and for a month or six weeks after her delivery. The young couple had, it was said, "noe settled dwelling place" and Daborne was too poor to provide for his family; so Robert Younger welcomed them to Shoreditch. The Dabornes were not, perhaps, wholly dependent on Younger's charity, for Daborne, his supporters had heard, had agreed to contribute to the expenses of the household and also had a legal interest in the house itself. While the Dabornes were there, Elizabeth Younger died (20 October 1609). Daborne and his wife, Kingman had heard, helped to care for her during her final illness, and out of gratitude Mrs. Younger gave Daborne certain things in the Shoreditch house, as well as a lease on property on Fleet Street.

A month later (20 November 1609), Robert Younger also died. After the elder Younger's death, either Thomas or Edward Younger, or perhaps both, in company with others, were alleged to have entered the house at Shoreditch and forced the Dabornes to leave. Daborne, it was said, retorted with a legal action and recovered possession of the house at Shoreditch. Mrs. Daborne and her brother John (who, according to Taylor, also got, along with Daborne, possession of the house and to whom, the same defendant thought, the right of possession belonged) were said to have received authorization to administer their father's estate. Thereafter John Younger and Daborne, it was claimed, sold Robert Younger's goods or part of them.

The plaintiffs, however, said that they had obtained letters of administration and attempted to enter upon their father's estate but were prevented from doing so by Daborne, who refused to surrender Robert Younger's house and goods. Consequently, they began the suit in Chancery. Moreover, they further asserted that on 21 October 1609 Daborne, with the assistance of Kingman and Taylor, broke open Robert Younger's study, cupboard, and chests and secretly took away goods valued at £250; some of these goods were divided among the three, and the rest were sold. Also, additional goods worth £120, they said, were removed, along with a number of obligations and bonds by which Daborne and others were indebted to Robert Younger. Furthermore, they claimed that the same three also removed legal documents, including an obligation by which Daborne stood bound to one Gregory Mylam for £50. The outcome of this case is unknown, as all the papers belonging to it do not appear to be extant.

During these early years Daborne was connected with the theater. On 4 January 1610 he became, along with Philip Rosseter and others, a patentee of the Children of the Queen's Revels. But exactly when he began to write plays is unknown. His first published play, *A Christian Turned Turk*, appeared in 1612, and its date of composition falls between late 1610 and 1 February 1612, when it was entered in the Stationers' Register (Baldwin Maxwell assigns 1611 as a "perhaps more likely" date). In an address "To the Knowing Reader" prefacing this play, Daborne speaks of his *"former labors,"* and Maxwell thinks it seems "not improbable" that *The Poor Man's Comfort* was one of them (the original edition of this play did not appear, however, until 1655). Gerald Eades Bentley dates *The Poor Man's Comfort* as no earlier than 1610 and no later than 1617, while E. K. Chambers suggests that circa 1617 "is as likely a date as another" on the basis of a possible allusion to attempts to save Porters' Hall theater from destruction. Kenneth Palmer, the play's latest editor, accepting Chambers's suggestion, states that the lines concerned "would be topical at any time from the end of September 1615 until at least 27 January 1617." But Maxwell thinks that the allusion under consideration "seems clearly not to the suppression of Rosseter's Blackfriars theatre but to the hall recently organized company of London porters." Maxwell also suggests that Daborne was working on this play and *A Christian Turned Turk* "at about the same time" because of, for one thing, "Several identical or practically identical speeches" in each play.

Moreover, he also notes that, in 1613-1614 at least, Daborne appears to have begun work on a new drama before finishing the one or more he had started already. Maxwell observes, furthermore, that certain plot features in *The Poor Man's Comfort* (derived by Daborne from his source material) also appear in *A Christian Turned Turk*, and these similarities suggest to him "the strong probability" that *The Poor Man's Comfort* is the earlier work.

The Poor Man's Comfort, a tragicomedy with pastoral elements, has as its source William Warner's *Pan His Syrinx* (1584), from which part seven furnished the primary plot (with some additions by the dramatist himself), and part five some of the matter for the subplot. The main plot concerns Lucius, Urania, and Gisbert. Lucius, a nobleman

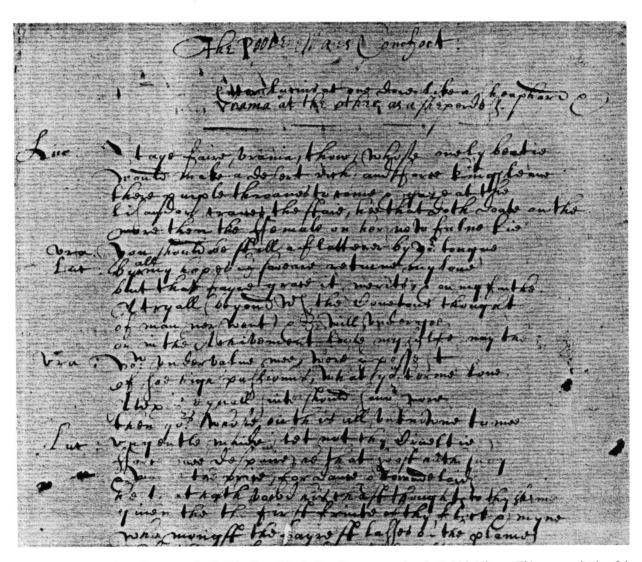

A portion of a page from the manuscript for The Poor Man's Comfort *preserved at the British Library. This manuscript is a fair copy made by an unknown scribe, circa 1600-1650 (MS Egerton 1994, fols 268-292; by permission of the British Library).*

of Thessaly, is exiled and, disguised as Lisander, goes to Arcady, where he serves Gisbert, a shepherd, and falls in love with Gisbert's daughter Urania. Eventually Gisbert gives Lucius his daughter's hand, as well as his lodge and flocks. On his wedding day Lucius learns that he has been restored to his noble rights and property, and he quickly abandons his wife and sells the lodge and flocks. Gisbert goes off in search of justice, eventually securing it from King Ferdinand, who deprives Lucius of his noble rights and lands, ordering him to find Urania (who is searching for him) within four days or suffer death. Earlier Lucius had been involved with a prostitute named Flavia (in whose service Urania was for a time), whom he later kills after she has attacked Urania, with whom he has become reconciled. Gisbert (who has been made a senator) tries Lucius and Urania and sentences them to death, but they are pardoned by King Ferdinand. The subplot deals with Sigismond, King Ferdinand's son, and Adelizia, daughter of Valerio, King of Sicily. Ferdinand, upon the defeat of his usurper nephew Oswell, wants his lords to make Sigismond king but is told that the prince is suffering from "strange distractions." Eventually Sigismond regains his sanity, and, despite shipwreck and a plot against her by the wicked Oswell, Adelizia is to marry Sigismond, as Ferdinand had arranged.

In *The Poor Man's Comfort* an important theme is that base men are swayed by position, wealth, and power, but great men are "Iust & good." Another is that true love, unlike lust, is spiritual and is not marred by "any outward Accident." Daborne handles these themes well through the actions of various characters, but this may well be due largely to the fact that in the main plot, as Wallace A. Bacon points out, he followed his source closely (while making some additions of his own).

The title page of the original edition of *The Poor Man's Comfort* (1655) states that the play "was divers times Acted at the *Cock-pit* in *Drury Lane*," but, as Bentley says, "title-pages generally refer to the latest performances." If the play was written in 1611, it was presumably performed originally by the Children of the Queen's Revels (of which company Daborne is known to have been a patentee) at Whitefriars.

As previously noted, Daborne's *A Christian Turned Turk* may have been written in 1611 and, if so, it was presumably acted by the Children of the Queen's Revels at the Whitefriars. Its main plot is, as the subtitle of the first edition suggests, about

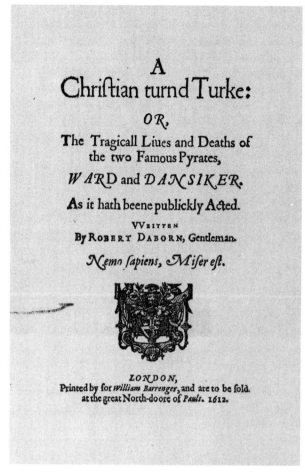

Title page for the 1612 quarto edition of Daborne's first published play (Cambridge University Library)

"Two Famous Pyrates, Ward and Dansiker," but there is more about Ward. The opening scene shows him and his men taking captive some strangers who have been invited aboard his ship. Later he and his associates capture a ship which is carrying Alizia, on her way to join her betrothed, young Raymond. Eventually Ward and his crew reach Tunis, and while there he "turns Turk" (becomes a Moslem) in order to marry a Turkish woman named Voada. His apostasy, rather than his career as a pirate, was Daborne's main concern, as he says in the prologue to the play. Because of his apostasy, Ward is caught up in a series of events that end in his death (before which he repents). Daborne's account of Ward's activities in Tunis is, according to Maxwell, "almost wholly Daborne's creation." Dansiker (having repented of his career as a pirate) is also in Tunis on two occasions in the play, trying to destroy the pirates and their apparatus there. On his first venture he succeeds in destroying some ships in the harbor of Tunis, while capturing others and taking them away under his control. On his second venture, however, he is put to death by order of the governor. Moreover, the play has a subplot which concerns Alizia and her betrothed, who reunite only to meet their deaths.

One of the main themes of the play is that, in the words of the Chorus, "*No course that violent is, secure can last,*" and Daborne shows the truth of this statement in his treatment of Ward, a notorious pirate, and Dansiker, who, though he has renounced piracy, uses violence in his efforts to destroy the pirates in Tunis. Another is that "heauen is iust," as Ward says in his farewell speech. The play is highly illustrative of this point, as the author presents a number of characters who are justly punished because of their evil deeds. Still another theme is that, in the words of the Chorus again, "*Designes are mens, their sway the gods do owe.*" In this work the plans of various characters, including Dansiker, are thwarted.

In 1612, the same year that *A Christian Turned Turk* was published, Daborne's father made his will on 23 August and died shortly thereafter. Significantly, the testator did not mention his son Robert; he left his wife, Susanna, all his estate (after the satisfaction of his debts): Guildford Castle; property in Blackfriars, London; land in Aldenham; and the lease of Lyne farm in Newdigate, Surrey. Not long afterward Mrs. Daborne (her husband's executrix) and several creditors of her late husband began a suit in Chancery (the Bill of Complaint is dated 26 November 1612) against Robert Daborne the younger. The elder Robert Daborne, the plaintiffs said, left a personal estate amounting to little or nothing and was indebted to various persons, including all the plaintiffs save Susanna. Moreover, according to the complainants, the deceased held by lease certain lands and tenements in the Blackfriars, which he had mortgaged at some time to Henry Goodyer, his son-in-law and now a plaintiff in the case. Selling this property was the means by which the elder Daborne's debts could be paid, and the younger Daborne was requested to join in the sale thereof. At first he is said to have seemed willing and to have promised to do so, but he later refused to become a party to their sale. Indeed it was also said that he hindered the sale, pretending to have some interest in, or title to, some or all of the property. It was further alleged that he owed his father £600 or thereabouts and was the chief cause of his father's indebtedness.

The following year Daborne was associated with Philip Henslowe, but exactly when that association began is uncertain. As Chambers writes, after noting that Daborne became one of the patentees of the Queen's Revels in 1610: "Presumably he wrote for this company, and when they amalgamated with the Lady Elizabeth's in 1613 came into relations with Henslowe, who acted as paymaster for the combination." Fortunately the letters from Daborne to Henslowe, as well as a number of related documents, which have been preserved, shed some light on the relations between the two and, what is also of importance, acquaint us with several of the playwright's compositions. A few of the letters are undated, but the rest cover the period from 17 April 1613 to circa 31 July 1614.

Between 17 April 1613 and 2 April 1614 Daborne appears to have been at work on at least four or possibly six plays, all of which are now lost. On 17 April 1613 he signed an agreement with Henslowe to write a play titled *Machiavel and the Devil*, which was to be delivered to him on or before 31 May following (the end of Easter Term). The play, which may possibly have been based upon, as Frederick Gard Fleay and Walter W. Greg suggest, the old *Machiavel* revived by Strange's Men in 1592, appears to have been near completion on 25 June 1613. Greg is probably right in thinking that it was completed about the end of that month, and he conjectures that it "was probably the 'new play' acted 11 Aug."

Even before the completion of *Machiavel and the Devil*, Daborne appears to have been at work on another play, *The Arraignment of London*, for in a letter of 5 June 1613 he told Henslowe that he had given an act from a work of this title to Cyril Tourneur to write. In another letter, dated 23 August 1613, to Henslowe, Daborne says: "J pray s^r goe forward wth that reasonable bargayn for the Bellman we will hav but twelv pownds and the overplus of the second day. . . ." In a note appended to this letter, Henslowe refers to the play as "the bellman of London." And Greg had "little doubt that *The Bellman of London* was the same as the *Arraignment of London*, and was founded on Dekker's tract of the same title, 1608, and its sequel *Lanthorn and Candlelight, or the Bellman's second Night-walk*, 1609." The date of completion of Daborne and Tourneur's play is unrecorded, but Greg thinks that it was the one delivered to Henslowe before 9 December 1613. Chambers, in volume two of *The Elizabethan Stage*, questions Greg's identification, thinking that "*The Arraignment* seems to have been too nearly finished on 5 June for this identification" and that *The Bellman of London* "was probably a sequel" (perhaps with Tourneur again as Daborne's collaborator). Yet in volume three of this same

To the Knowing Reader.

AS no argument more proueth the excellency of Poesy then the contempt is throwne vpon it by silken gulls and ignorant Cittizens, so there is no blemish taketh from the beauty of this onely All-comprehending-art, so much as the same where-with her owne professors brand her, for I may truely vary that of the Tragœdian, Quemcunq; poëtam vides, miserum dicas, I speake it especially in regard of that free title better times allowed this heauenly Science, now made captiue by each vnworthy hand; in recouery whereof I haue, so farre as my weake power extended, procured the publishing this oppressed and much martird Tragedy, not that I promise to my selfe any reputation hereby, or affect to see my name in Print, vsherd with new praises, for feare the Reader should call in question their iudgements that giue applause in the action; for had this wind moued me, I had preuented others shame in subscribing some of my former labors, or let them gone out the in diuels name alone: which since impudence will not suffer, I am content they passe together, it is then to publish my innocence concerning the wrong of worthy personages, together with doing some right to the much-suffering Actors that hath caused my name to cast it selfe in the common rack of censure, accompanied with so weak comforts, as this Triuiall worke can giue it, and that my gratitude may be in the first place, I must in dispight of any iustly neglected

A 3   Cinnicke

To the Reader.

Cynnicke confesse to haue receiued so much worthy respect, & approued so much generous honesty in this, that with any indifferent hazard, I will study to make good their losse, and my gratitude. I write this, led by no Mercinary hopes to share in their Fortunes, which hath so put out somes eyes, that measuring others sight by their owne weakenesse gaue her out for blind; but led by that spirit knoweth no sinne equall to ingratitude: As far the former imputation, granting all obiections, I cleere my selfe by these two positions, No man can faine any ill of a Parricide, the greater alway including the lesse; this being so tollerable, especially in Oratory, which is an vnseparable branch of Poesy, that it subsists not without aggranation; the second is, No man can intitle another to his crimes, for, Alia est cognatio culpæ, alia sanguinis, from which I so farre abhorre, as my owne discent is not obscure but generous, if this will not giue satisfaction, know I liue vnder too safe a law to feare the stab of a Roaring boy, and for any wrong, Equo marte, I forgiue it, daring thus far to boast my knowledge, that I cannot be a coward, I write succinctly, knowing the bounds of an Epistle, she rather because I wish no other perusers, then those to whom I dedicate my selfe; though herein I speak against the Printers profit, if these accept my impolished labours, I promise the next shall be coockt for the stomacks of the Criticall messe it selfe. Sanabimur si separemur a cœtu.

The

The Prologue.

ALL faire content dwell here, & may our straines
Giue you that choice delight which crownes our
Our subiect's low, yet to your eyes presents (paines.
Deeds high in bloud, in bloud of Innocents:
Transcends them low, and your inuention calles
To name the sinne beyond this blacke deed falles.
What heretofore set others pennes aworke,
Was ward turn'd Pyrate, ours is ward turn'd Turke.
Their triuiall Scœnes might best affoord to show
The basenesse of his birth, how from below
Ambition oft takes roote, makes men forsake
The good the'enioy, yet know not. Our Muse doth
A higher pitch, leauing his Pyracy (take
To reach the heart it selfe of villany.
What to that period makes the neerest way,
Our Scœne pursues, you must supose his stay
Hath lately beene vpon the Irish Shore,
Where wanting men he inuites some strangers ore
Into his Barke, in height of wine and game,
He slips his anchor, and reueales his name.
There fate succedes, and to your gentle view
We giue not what we could, but what know true.
Our Ship's aflote, we feare nor rockes nor sands,
Knowing we are inuiron'd with your helping hands.

Drammatis

Drammatis Personæ.

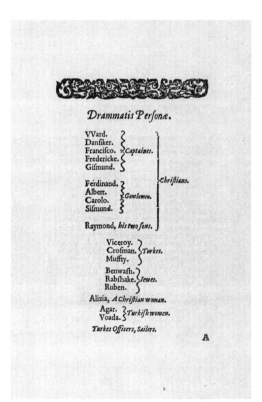

Daborne's address to the reader, the prologue, and the dramatis personae from the 1612 quarto edition of A Christian Turned Turk (Cambridge University Library)

work Chambers lists *The Arraignment of London* as "probably identical with *The Bellman of London*."

To this same year may belong an unnamed play in which Daborne had a part. While he, along with Philip Massinger and Nathan Field, was imprisoned in the Clink, Field wrote Henslowe a letter (to which Daborne and Massinger added postscripts), requesting five pounds so that the three could be bailed out. Part of Field's letter suggested that Henslowe would earn more than that amount from the play they were going to send him. And Daborne's postscript to the letter reads: "The mony shall be abated out of the mony remayns for the play of m^r ffletcher & owrs." From the foregoing

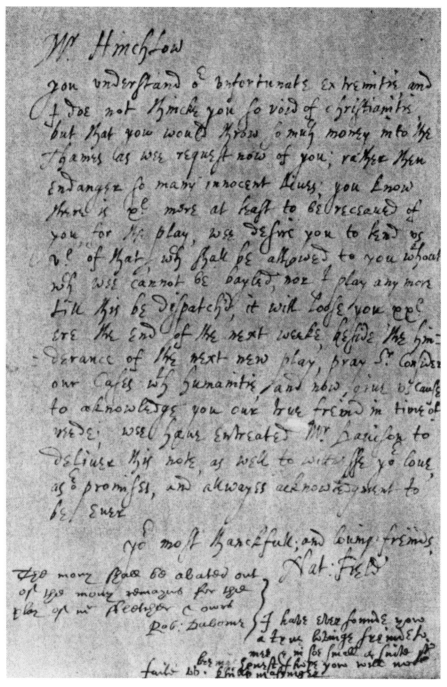

Letter to Philip Henslowe from Nathan Field with postscripts by Daborne and Philip Massinger, probably written in early July 1613 (MS I, art. 68; by permission of Dulwich College, London)

it appears that Daborne had a hand in this play for Henslowe in which Massinger, Field, and John Fletcher also participated. This letter is undated, but Greg suggests that it probably dates from early July 1613, and he thinks that this drama was also the one referred to in another letter to Henslowe, in which Field speaks of conferring with Daborne about the plot for a play which was to be finished upon 1 August. This letter, too, is undated, but Greg tentatively dates it "the end of June 1613." Greg also thinks that Daborne was referring to this play in two other letters. In a 30 July 1613 letter to Henslowe, Daborne spoke of the delivery of "o^r play" to Henslowe on 5 August following, and in an undated letter (which Greg tentatively dates a short time after 5 August 1613) to Henslowe, Daborne said that he thought that he deserved as much money as Massinger and beseeched him to "make vp my mony even wth mr messengers which is to let me have X^s more." Finally, it may be noted that there have been attempts to identify this unnamed play (Fleay, for example, thought that it was *The Honest Man's Fortune*).

In a letter of 9 December 1613 to Henslowe, Daborne spoke of another play suitable to Henslowe's public house, which was undoubtedly, as Greg thinks, *The Owl*, for on the next day Daborne signed a bond with Henslowe to deliver a play of this title to him by 10 February 1614. Later, on 11 March 1614, the playwright sent Henslowe "papers which wants but one short scean of the whole play"; moreover, in the same letter he spoke of "this play" and "the other which shall be finished wth all expedition." Greg suggests that the second play was *The She Saint*. Then in a letter of 28 March of that year, Daborne told Henslowe that he now had "a full play," which Greg identifies as *The Owl*, and he received the final payment for it on the following day. Shortly thereafter, on 2 April 1614, Henslowe advanced eight shillings to Daborne "in earneste of the shee saynte," about which nothing further is heard, but Greg conjectures that it "may have been delivered by the following Aug."

Daborne's plays of 1613-1614 were written, both Chambers and Greg think, for the Lady Elizabeth's company. There would seem to be no reason to dispute this supposition, since, as previously pointed out, this company was amalgamated in 1613 with the Queen's Revels company, of which Daborne was a patentee. According to Samuel Schoenbaum's revised edition of Alfred Harbage's *Annals of English Drama* (1964), during the period in question the Lady Elizabeth's company acted at the Whitefriars theater in 1613-1614, at the Hope theater in 1614-1615, and at the Swan theater from 1611 until about 1615. It would seem therefore that each of the plays Daborne was engaged in writing between 17 April 1613 and 2 April 1614 was, with the possible exception of *The She Saint*, produced originally at the Whitefriars or the Swan. *The She Saint* may have been originally put on at the Hope, which is thought to have opened in autumn 1614, or else at the Whitefriars or the Swan.

Unless Daborne's dramatic activities in the period under consideration were unusual, it seems reasonable to suppose that he wrote other plays that are now lost. As already noted, Fleay thought that *The Honest Man's Fortune* was the play referred to in Field's letter, and a number of others have conjectured that Daborne may have had a hand in some of the other plays of the Beaumont and Fletcher canon; but Cyrus Hoy denies that Daborne collaborated on any play of questionable authorship in that canon.

Daborne's correspondence with Henslowe sheds some light on his private affairs. He appears to have been in need of money as he requested advances from Henslowe. He was also involved in litigation.

In 1614 commendatory verses by Daborne appeared in John Taylor's *The Nipping or Snipping of Abuses* and *The Ghost of Richard the Third*, probably written by Christopher Brooke. The following year Daborne and Massinger were signatories to a bond with Henslowe. By 6 January of the next year he had married a woman whose first name was Frances. On 20 March 1615 he witnessed an agreement between Alleyn and Meade and the actors at the Hope. Daborne and his wife were in London for at least part of each year through 1617. Palmer points out that "Mrs. Daborne at least was in London to depose in the suit *Henslowe v. Henslowe* on 10 September [1616]," and Daborne (or, in certain years, he and his wife) is noted in the "Token Books" of St. Saviour's Church in Southwark from 1612 through 1617.

The next step that Daborne took is indeed surprising: he abandonec the theater, went to Ireland, and, while there, became a clergyman. According to C. L'Estrange Ewen, Daborne went there in 1616, and W. H. Grattan Flood believes that he was ordained in that year. But it does not appear that he had been ordained yet on 28 November 1617 for in a letter under that date to Richard Boyle, Baron of Youghall, one Evan Owens wrote: "Right honorable, I am gyven to vnderstand that Mr Coote hath sould his Archdeaconshipp to M^r dawburne that dwelleth at Tallowe, tenante to

Mr Cornelius. And this morning he ys gon to waterford to my lord Bushopp aboute that business, (and tis supposed to take his orders): yf he shall haue that place I feare your Lordship shall fynd him a very turbulent person." Irish practice was lax, and he may have taken orders only after buying his office. At all events, he had become a clergyman by February 1618, when he preached, in the Cathedral of Waterford, an assize sermon (published that same year).

Daborne became Chancellor of Waterford in 1619, Prebendary of Lismore in 1620, and Dean of Lismore in 1621. (As Henry Cotton noted, "His patent, dated June 14, contained a clause uniting the prebend of Disert and Kilmoleran to the deanery. . . .") He was also, during the course of his career, a Fellow of Youghal College. He died on 23 March 1628.

Today Daborne's correspondence with Henslowe is certainly not forgotten, but his plays are not produced and are generally read only by specialists in English drama. *The Poor Man's Comfort* was revived in 1661, but that seems to have been the last time a play of Daborne's was produced on the professional stage. This play and *A Christian Turned Turk*, his only other extant play, were not reprinted until the close of the nineteenth century (1898-1899), but, more recently, *The Poor Man's Comfort* was edited for the Malone Society (1955). *A Christian Turned Turk* is a poor play, being loosely constructed and confusing in places, and it would receive a low rating from modern critics. *The Poor Man's Comfort*, however, is a better drama in respect to its craftsmanship, and the critics would presumably call it a competent work. While Wallace A. Bacon writes that its main plot "owed its success largely" to its source, he also points out that in both the main plot and the subplot Daborne made additions of his own. What Daborne's lost plays were like we have, of course, no way of knowing; therefore, we cannot treat the matter of his development.

References:

Wallace A. Bacon, "The Source of Robert Daborne's *The Poor Man's Comfort*," *Modern Language Notes*, 57 (May 1942): 345-348;

Gerald Eades Bentley, *The Jacobean and Caroline Stage*, 7 volumes (Oxford: Clarendon Press, 1941-1968);

E. K. Chambers, *The Elizabethan Stage*, 4 volumes (Oxford: Clarendon Press, 1951);

Chambers and W. W. Greg, eds., License for the Children of the Queen's Revels, 4 January 1610, in Malone Society *Collections*, volume 1, part 3 (London: Printed for the Malone Society at the Oxford University Press, 1909), pp. 271-272;

Henry Cotton, *Fasti Ecclesiæ Hibernicæ: The Succession of the Prelates and Members of the Cathedral Bodies in Ireland*, volume 1, revised and enlarged (Dublin: Hodges & Smith, 1851), pp. 146, 167, 190;

C. L'Estrange Ewen, *Lording Barry, Poet and Pirate* (London: Printed for the Author, 1938);

Frederick Gard Fleay, *A Biographical Chronicle of the English Drama 1559-1642*, 2 volumes (London: Reeves & Turner, 1891), I: 195-196;

W. H. Grattan Flood, "Fennor and Daborne at Youghal in 1618," *Modern Language Review*, 20 (July 1925): 321-322;

Walter W. Greg, ed., *Henslowe Papers, Being Documents Supplementary to Henslowe's Diary* (London: A. H. Bullen, 1907);

Greg, ed., *Henslowe's Diary*, 2 volumes (London: A. H. Bullen, 1904-1908), I: 13-14; II: 20, 141-143, 152;

Alexander B. Grosart, ed., *The Lismore Papers*, first series, *Autobiographical Notes, Remembrances and Diaries of Sir Richard Boyle, First and "Great" Earl of Cork* (London: Chiswick Press, 1886), II: 41;

Grosart, ed., *The Lismore Papers*, second series, *Selections from the Private and Public (or State) Correspondence of Sir Richard Boyle, First and "Great" Earl of Cork* (London: Chiswick Press, 1887-1888), II: 112-113; IV: 185;

Alfred Harbage, *Annals of English Drama 975-1700*, second edition, revised by Samuel Schoenbaum (Philadelphia: University of Pennsylvania Press, 1964; London: Methuen, 1964), pp. 96-107, 299;

Peter Holloway, "Robert Daborne: Some New Information," *Notes and Queries*, 221 (May-June 1976): 222;

Cyrus Hoy, "The Shares of Fletcher and His Collaborators in the Beaumont and Fletcher Canon," part 7, *Studies in Bibliography*, 15 (1962): 71-90;

Donald S. Lawless, "*The Ghost of Richard the Third* Revisited," *Notes and Queries*, 227 (December 1982): 491-492;

Lawless, "Massinger and His Associates," Ph.D. dissertation, University of Birmingham, 1965, pp. 204-220;

Lawless, "Philip Kingman: Some New Information," *Notes and Queries*, 224 (April 1979): 141-142;

Lawless, "Robert Daborne, Senior," *Notes and Queries*, 222 (December 1977): 514-516;

Lawless, "Some New Light on Robert Daborne," *Notes and Queries*, 224 (April 1979): 142-143;

Baldwin Maxwell, "Notes on Robert Daborne's Extant Plays," *Philological Quarterly*, 50 (January 1971): 85-98;

E. H. C. Oliphant, *The Plays of Beaumont and Fletcher: An Attempt to Determine Their Respective Shares and the Shares of Others* (New Haven: Yale University Press/London: Oxford University Press, 1927).

Papers:

Daborne's correspondence with Henslowe, various bonds of his, and other documents are preserved at Dulwich College (the College of God's Gift), London. A manuscript for *The Poor Man's Comfort* is at the British Library (MS. Egerton 1994, fols. 268-292).

Sir William Davenant
(February 1606-7 April 1668)

Irby B. Cauthen, Jr.
University of Virginia

PLAY PRODUCTIONS: *The Cruel Brother: A Tragedy*, London, Blackfriars theater, 1627;

The Colonel (later retitled *The Siege*), London, unknown theater, licensed 22 July 1629;

The Just Italian, London, Blackfriars theater, licensed 2 October 1629;

The Wits: A Comedy, London, Blackfriars theater, mid January 1634;

Love and Honor, London, Blackfriars theater, 12 December 1634;

The Temple of Love: A Masque, London, Whitehall, 10 February 1635;

News from Plymouth, London, Globe theater, licensed 1 August 1635;

The Platonic Lovers: A Tragicomedy, London, Blackfriars theater, 1636;

The Triumphs of the Prince D'Amour: A Masque, London, Middle Temple, 23 February 1636;

Britannia Triumphans: A Masque, London, Whitehall, 8 January 1638;

Luminalia, or The Festival of Light, Personated in a Masque, London, Whitehall, 6 February 1638;

The Unfortunate Lovers: A Tragedy, London, Blackfriars theater, 23 April 1638;

The Fair Favorite, London, Cockpit theater, 20 November 1638;

Salmacida Spolia: A Masque, London, Whitehall, 21 January 1640;

The First Day's Entertainment at Rutland House, by Declamations and Music: After the Manner of the Ancients, London, Rutland House, May 1656;

The Siege of Rhodes (Part 1), London, Rutland House, September 1656; (Parts 1 and 2), London, Duke's Playhouse, 1661;

The Cruelty of the Spaniards in Peru, London, Cockpit theater, July 1658;

The History of Sir Francis Drake, London, Cockpit theater, Winter 1658-1659;

The Law Against Lovers, adapted from William Shakespeare's *Measure for Measure* and *Much Ado About Nothing*, London, Duke's Playhouse, 1662;

Playhouse to be Let, London, Duke's Playhouse, 1663;

Macbeth: A Tragedy, adapted from Shakespeare's *Macbeth*, London, Duke's Playhouse, 1663;

The Rivals: A Comedy, adapted in part from Shakespeare and John Fletcher's *The Two Noble Kinsmen*, London, Duke's Playhouse, 1664;

The Tempest, or the Enchanted Island, adapted by Davenant and John Dryden from Shakespeare's *The Tempest*, London, Duke's Playhouse, 7 November 1667;

The Man's the Master: A Comedy, adapted from Paul Scarron's *Le Maître Valet*, London, Duke's Playhouse, 1668.

BOOKS: *The Tragedy of Albovine, King of the Lombards* (London: Printed by F. Kingston for R. Moore, 1629);

The Cruell Brother. A Tragedy (London: Printed by A. Mathewes for J. Waterson, 1630);

The Just Italian (London: Printed by T. Harper for J. Waterson, 1630);

The Temple of Love: A Masque (London: Printed for T. Walkley, 1635);

The Witts. A Comedie (London: Printed by A. Mathewes for R. Meighen, 1636);

The Platonick Lovers. A Tragæcomedy (London: Printed by A. Mathewes for R. Meighen, 1636);

The Triumphs of the Prince D'Amour. A Masque (London: Printed by A. Mathewes for R. Meighen, 1636);

Britannia Triumphans: A Masque (London: Printed by J. Haviland for T. Walkley, 1637);

Luminalia, Or The Festivall of Light (London: Printed by J. Haviland for T. Walkley, 1637);

Madagascar; With Other Poems (London: Printed by J. Haviland for T. Walkley, 1638);

Salmacida Spolia. A Masque (London: Printed by T. Harper for T. Walkley, 1640);

The Unfortunate Lovers: A Tragedie (London: Printed by R. H. & sold by Francis Coles, 1643);

Love and Honor (London: Printed for Humphrey Robinson & Humphrey Moseley, 1649);

A Discourse Upon Gondibert. An Heroick Poem (Paris: Chez Matthieu Guillemot, 1650);

Gondibert: An Heroic Poem (London: Printed by Tho. Newcomb for John Holden, 1651);

The Siege of Rhodes, part 1 (London: Printed by J. M. for H. Herringman, 1656); part 1 (revised) and part 2 (London: Printed for Henry Herringman, 1663);

The First Days Entertainment at Rutland House, By Declamations and Musick: After the Manner of the Ancients (London: Printed by J. M. for H. Herringman, 1657);

The Cruelty of the Spaniards in Peru (London: Printed for Henry Herringman, 1658);

The History of Sr Francis Drake . . . The First Part (London: Printed for Henry Herringman, 1659);

Poem Upon His Sacred Majestics Most Happy Return to His Dominions (London: Printed for H. Herringman, 1660);

Poem to the King's Most Sacred Majesty (London: Printed for Henry Herringman, 1663);

The Rivals: A Comedy, adapted from William Shakespeare and John Fletcher's *The Two Noble Kinsmen* (London: Printed for William Cademan, 1668);

The Man's the Master: A Comedy, adapted from Paul Scarron's *Le Maître Valet* (London: Printed for Henry Herringman, 1669);

The Works of Sr William D'avenant K^t Consisting of Those Which Were Formerly Printed, and Those Which He Design'd for the Press (London: Printed by T. N. for Henry Herringman, 1673)—comprises *Gondibert; Madagascar, with Other Poems; Poems on Several Occasions, Never Before Printed; Declamations at Rutland-House; Three Masques at Whitehall: Cœlum Britannicum* (by Thomas Carew, possibly with the assistance of Davenant); *The Temple of Love*, and *The Triumphs of the Prince D'Amour; The Siege of Rhodes*, parts 1 and 2; *Playhouse to Be Let, Containing The History of Sir Francis Drake, and The Cruelty of the Spaniards in Peru; The Unfortunate Lovers; The Wits; Love and Honor; The Law Against Lovers; The Man's the Master; The Platonic Lovers; The Tragedy of Albovine; The Just Italian; The Cruel Brother; News from Plymouth; The Distresses; The Siege; The Fair Favorite;*

Macbeth, A Tragedy, adapted from Shakespeare's *Macbeth* (London: Printed for P. Chetwin, 1674);

The Seventh and Last Canto of the Third Book of Gondibert, Never Yet Printed (London: Printed for W. Miller & J. Watts, 1685);

The Tempest, or The Enchanted Island. A Comedy, adapted by Davenant and John Dryden from Shakespeare's *The Tempest* (London: Printed by J. M. for Herringman & sold by R. Bentley, 1690).

Editions: *The Dramatic Works of Sir William D'Avenant, with Prefatory Memoir and Notes*, 5 volumes, edited by J. Maidment and W. H. Logan (Edinburgh: W. Paterson, 1872-1874)—comprises *Albovine, The Cruel Brother, The Just Italian, The Temple of Love, The Prince D'Amour, The Platonic Lovers, The Wits, Britannia Triumphans, Salmacida Spolia, The Unfortunate Lovers, Love and Honor, Entertainment at Rutland House, The Siege of Rhodes, Playhouse to be Let, News from Plymouth, The Fair Favorite, The Distresses, The Siege, The Man's the Master, The Law Against Lovers, The Rivals, Macbeth, The Tempest;*

The Tempest, in *Shakespearean Adaptations*, edited by Montague Summers (London: Cape, 1922);

Selected Poems of Sir William Davenant, edited by Douglas Bush (Cambridge, Mass.: Willow Press, 1943);

The portrait of Davenant by William Faithorne that was published in the 1673 folio collection of his works, prepared for the printer by Davenant's wife after his death (from an undated Pickering & Chatto catalogue)

The Wits, in *Six Caroline Plays,* edited by A. S. Knowland (London: Oxford University Press, 1962);

Macbeth, in *Five Restoration Adaptations of Shakespeare,* edited by Christopher Spencer (Urbana: University of Illinois Press, 1965);

Salmacida Spolia, in *A Book of Masques,* edited by T. J. B. Spencer and Stanley Wells (Cambridge: Cambridge University Press, 1967);

The Law Against Lovers, introduction by A. M. Gibbs (London: Cornmarket, 1970);

The Rivals, introduction by Kenneth Muir (London: Cornmarket, 1970);

The Triumphs of the Prince D'Amour and *Britannia Triumphans,* in *Trois Masques à la Cour de Charles Ier d'Angleterre,* edited by Murray Lefkowitz (Paris: Editions Centre National, 1970);

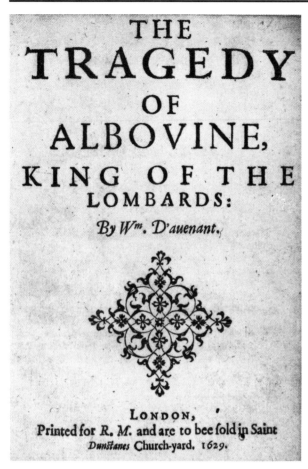

THE
TRAGEDY
OF
ALBOVINE,
KING OF THE
LOMBARDS:

By Wm. D'auenant.

LONDON,
Printed for *R. M.* and are to bee fold in Saint
Dunstanes Church-yard. 1629.

Title page for the 1629 quarto edition of Davenant's first play, which no acting company would accept for production (Henry E. Huntington Library and Art Gallery)

Gondibert, edited by David F. Gladish (Oxford: Clarendon Press, 1971);

News from Plymouth [parallel English and Italian texts], edited by Maria Crino (Verona: Fiorini, 1972);

The Shorter Poems and Songs from the Plays and Masques, edited by A. M. Gibbs (Oxford: Clarendon Press, 1972);

The Siege of Rhodes, parts 1 and 2, edited by Ann-Mari Hedback (Uppsala: Acta Universitatis Upsaliensia, 1973);

The Temple of Love, Britannia Triumphans, Luminalia, and *Salmacida Spolia,* in *Inigo Jones: The Theatre of the Stuart Court,* edited by Stephen Orgel and Roy Strong (London: Sotheby Parke Bernet, 1973).

Sir William Davenant (or D'Avenant), dramatist and theater manager, poet and courtier, is a link between the older Elizabethan and Jacobean drama and the new Restoration drama. From his innovations improving the platform stage our modern playhouse is derived; he refined the genre of the heroic drama with the accompanying themes of love and honor; by tradition he first brought women onto the English stage; and his dramas influenced those of the next several generations, particularly John Dryden's. If he is remembered only for his "adaptations" of Shakespeare we do him disservice.

Davenant was born in Oxford in late February 1606, the son of John Davenant, vinter and proprietor of the Crown Tavern, who at his death was mayor of Oxford, and Jane Shepherd Davenant. William Shakespeare, who lodged at the Crown "once a year," according to John Aubrey, may have been his godfather and, according to subsequent gossip, his natural father as well. The source of this rumor seems to have been Samuel Butler, whose report of a comment by Davenant was recorded by Aubrey: "it seemed to him [Davenant] that he writ with the very same spirit that Shakespeare [did], and seemed content enough to be called his son." Davenant never claimed he was Shakespeare's son, and his reference to the kinship is probably an acknowledgment of literary debtedness.

Davenant was educated in Oxford at St. Paul's Parish under Edward Sylvester, "a noted Latinist and Grecian," according to Anthony à Wood; Aubrey adds that Davenant "was drawn from school before he was ripe enough," but at twelve he had written an "Ode in Rememberance of Shakespeare." In 1620-1621 he went to Lincoln College at Oxford, leaving, because of his father's death, to become page to the Duchess of Richmond. Wood says Davenant "wanted much of university learning"; but he also remarks on the playwright's "high and noble flights in the poetical faculty" and styles him the "Sweet swan of Isis."

After several years of service to the Duchess, Davenant entered the household of Fulke Greville, Lord Brooke, friend of Philip Sidney and Edmund Spenser, where he served most likely as a clerk until Greville's murder in 1628. During his intermittent stay at Brooke House, broken by his residence in the Middle Temple, Davenant's dramatic career began. Here he wrote four plays: *The Tragedy of Albovine, King of the Lombards,* a revenge tragedy completed in 1627, which the actors declined to produce (it was published in 1629), and *The Cruel Brother,* another tragedy of the same year which was acted in Blackfriars; also *The Colonel,* a tragicomedy that was retitled *The Siege* when it was published in 1673, and *The Just Italian,* both acted in 1629.

His career as courtier, begun with service in the houses of Richmond and Brooke, led to his joining the blundering first expedition of the Duke of Buckingham in the 1627 siege of the Isle of Rhé; he may have been in the second, 1628 expedition as well. For the rest of his life, save during a three-year illness, he served the court in various ways—in literature and in military and diplomatic service.

After he was cashiered out of Buckingham's forces, riddled as they were by incompetence and contagion, he contracted syphilis, or, as it was called then, the Grand Pox. For three years, probably in poverty, he endured a treatment of mercury that saved his life but marked him for the rest of it. His disfigured nose, a consequence of the disease and its treatment, was an object of ridicule by his enemies and of tolerant acceptance by his friends. They recognized that "His art was high, though his nose was low." At least one person who commented on his nose suffered for it. During his recuperation, probably incensed by a low jest, Davenant attacked a tapster, Thomas Warren of Braintree, with his rapier and wounded him several times. Warren died a few days later. Davenant, who fled to Holland, was convicted of murder and his property sequestrated. But because the King was petitioned for his pardon, he was able to return to England in 1633. A full pardon was not granted until five years later. Despite his nose, Queen Henrietta Maria received him into her service through the intercession of his friend Endymion Porter.

His first play presented before the court on 28 January 1634, *The Wits,* was "well liked." One of his most successful plays, it reflects Jonsonian humors and satire and anticipates the Restoration wits and witwouds. Another Jonsonian realistic comedy, *News from Plymouth,* was written in 1635 for a vacation audience at the Globe and for the replenishment of a lean purse; as he wrote in a burlesque poem,

> Forth he steals, to Globe does run,
> And smiles and vows four acts are done;
> ....
> And all to get (as Poets use)
> Some coin in pouch to solace muse.

Love and Honor, acted at Blackfriars theater on 12 December 1634, is based on Fletcherian Neoplatonism and anticipates the later heroic drama where characters represent abstract ideals, especially virtue and honor. Samuel Pepys was so de-

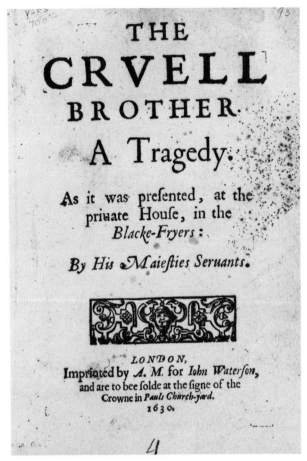

Title page for the 1630 quarto edition of one of the plays Davenant wrote while in the service of Fulke Greville, Lord Brooke (Henry E. Huntington Library and Art Gallery)

lighted with the tragicomedy that he saw it three times during its revival after the Restoration. The play, which reflects the Queen's interest in French romances and seems to have pleased the "courtly love" coterie surrounding her, secured him his first commission from her, a masque celebrating Platonic love. *The Temple of Love,* presented at Whitehall on 10 February 1635, praises love and comments with careful wit on Platonic nonsense. It secured the Queen's servant his livery. Based on the same idea, *The Platonic Lovers* (produced in 1636) did not succeed, most likely because it played too lightly with Platonic idealism to be well received by those, like the Queen, who cherished it.

His second masque, the *Triumphs of the Prince D'Amour,* was written in three days to celebrate the visit of the King's young nephews and produced before them at Court on 23 February 1636. It is a series of semicomic spectacles ending with a table of refreshments for all. The Queen, who had put

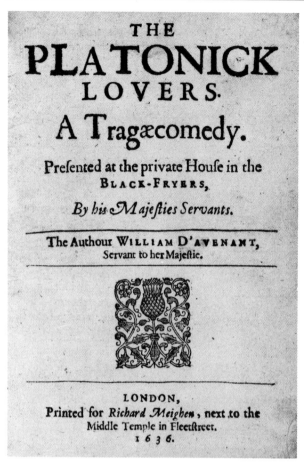

THE
PLATONICK
LOVERS.
A Tragæcomedy.

Prefented at the private Houfe in the
BLACK-FRYERS,

By his Majefties Servants.

The Authour WILLIAM D'AVENANT,
Servant to her Majeftie.

LONDON,
Printed for Richard Meighen, next to the
Middle Temple in Fleetftreet.
1 6 3 6.

Title page for the 1636 quarto edition of the play in which Davenant satirized the Platonic idealism espoused by Queen Henrietta Maria and her courtly-love coterie (Henry E. Huntington Library and Art Gallery)

on "a citizen's habit" for the occasion, "liked it very well," Sir Henry Herbert tells us.

In these halcyon days, Davenant was gaining favor with the court and his fellow poets; he was friend to the Queen and had a wide acquaintance among poets such as Sir John Suckling, Thomas Carew, Henry Vaughan, and George Sandys. On 13 December 1638 King Charles granted him an annuity of £100; there is no mention in the grant of the office of poet laureate, a term not used officially until Dryden's appointment. But Davenant was so accepted, even without the title, by his contemporaries, as Jonson had been by his.

After his annuity was granted, Davenant worked with the well-known architect and set designer Inigo Jones, now estranged from Jonson, in the production of three masques, by now a dying form in the impoverished court: *Britannia Triumphans; Luminalia, or The Festival of Light* (both acted

in 1638); and *Salmacida Spolia* (performed in 1640). In *Salmacida Spolia,* the last of the Caroline masques, the Queen, then pregnant, made her entrance descending by a theatrical device from a cloud.

Besides his court productions, he briefly managed the Cockpit theater in Drury Lane, where he had already seen his plays produced, replacing William Beeston, from June 1640 to his arrest for complicity in a plot against Parliament in May 1641. The popular *The Unfortunate Lovers* (1638), a revenge play, had three command performances, was later given by his rival Thomas Killigrew, and was acted as a tribute to the writer on the day after his death. *The Fair Favorite* (1638), a tragicomedy, may reflect again his respect for the court and his idealized portraits of royalty. His last play before the civil war, *The Distresses, or the Spanish Lovers* (written in 1639, but probably not produced), has been noted for its anticipation of Restoration drama in its witty repartee and in its portraits of the rake and the independent woman. It appeared in the folio edition of his works (1673).

Before his career was interrupted by the war, he had established himself not only as a playwright and manager, but as a poet by the publication of *Madagascar; With Other Poems* in 1638. Hoping for a laureateship, he wrote to royalty and courtiers, even honoring with an "Epick Ode" the Queen's dwarf; the book includes elegies, epithalamia, and other occasional poems. He pays respectful tributes to, among others, Shakespeare and Jonson, whose influence, along with other Renaissance poets, he acknowledges. But his dramatic career came to an end, not only with the closing of the theaters in 1642, but with his arrest for treason the previous year and his flight to France.

His service during the civil war was that of an ardent and faithful royalist. A messenger of the Crown, a supply officer, a privateer, he generously—perhaps too generously—spent his own funds for arms and ammunition. For his service he was knighted at the siege of Gloucester in September 1643. After the execution of Charles I, Davenant served his son, who named him treasurer of the colony of Virginia and, to replace Lord Baltimore, lieutenant-governor of Maryland. Davenant, his ship, and his crew were captured by Parliamentarians on 4 May 1650, the day after they sailed from Jersey. In prison, first at Cowes Castle and then in the Tower, he continued work on his epic poem *Gondibert,* which was placed on sale by mid December 1650 though it was dated 1651. Apparently John Milton and others secured his release

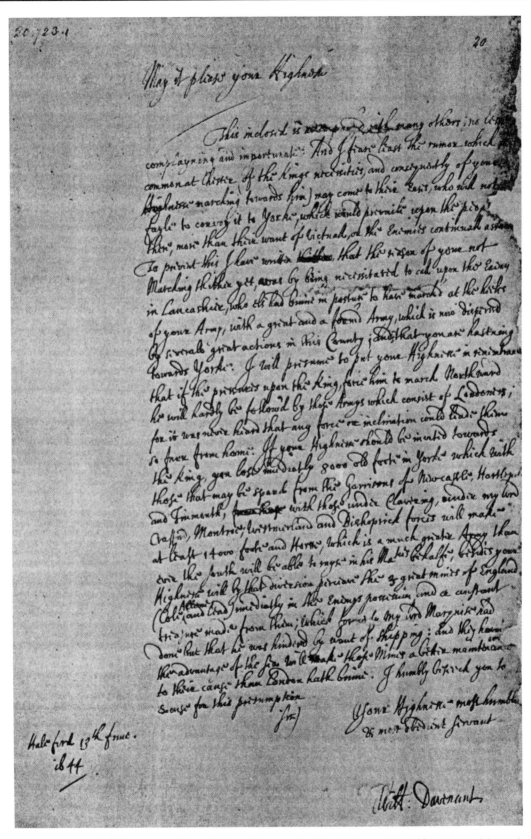

Letter to Prince Rupert in which Davenant offers advice on the conduct of the civil war (MS Addit. 20723, fol. 20; by permission of the British Library)

Inigo Jones's costume designs for four of Davenant's masques: left (top) Indamora, Queen of Narsinga, in The Temple of Love,
(bottom) Britanocles in Britannia Triumphans; *right (top) a masquer in* Luminalia, *(bottom) the Furies in* Salmacida Spolia
(Stephen Orgel and Roy Strong, Inigo Jones, *1973)*

from the Tower in 1652, but he was still under arrest until 1654. Before then he had resumed writing some poetry and drama, especially dramatic and literary "entertainments."

To avoid the restrictions still attached to the words *theater* and *play*, Davenant and others presented *The First Day's Entertainment at Rutland House, by Declamations and Music* in May 1656, a beginning for better things to come. It used music as an auxiliary to the words, as had been done by the ancients. Urged by its success, within three months of 1656 he had composed *The Siege of Rhodes,* part one, "a heroic story in *stillo recitativo*," a play more than an opera. Produced at Rutland House in September 1656, it has been called with more than small justification "the most epoch-making play in the English language."

For this "first heroic drama," there was a platform stage and for the first time a proscenium arch—improving the designs of Inigo Jones for royal masques—a curtain, and five moveable scenes on flats or "shutters." Also notable was the presence in the play of the first Englishwoman, Mrs. Coleman, to act on an English public stage. Henry Lawes, Milton's friend and composer for *Comus,* furnished the music—as he had for *The First Day's Entertainment*—and a protégé of Inigo Jones, John Webb, designed the scenes. Crowds and armies were represented, for the first time on the English stage, on painted canvas. Rutland House could not long hold such entertainments, and by July 1658 the Cockpit was showing *The Cruelty of the Spaniards in Peru,* a succession of songs, declamations, dances, and acrobatics mounted against simple backdrops painted in perspective. Despite its theatricality, the play was written to support Cromwell's war with Spain. *The History of Sir Francis Drake* followed in winter 1658-1659, and a second part of *The Siege of Rhodes,* a full-length, fully equipped play.

The first part of *The Siege of Rhodes* is the story of the siege of 1522, an incident well known to Davenant's contemporaries, when Solyman the Magnificent subdued the city through blockade and assault with 200,000 men. Among the outnum-·bered Rhodians is Alphonso, a visitor to the fortress, who chooses to stay rather than to escape to Sicily and to his new bride, Ianthe, a character invented by Davenant. When *The Siege of Rhodes* was revised for the opening of the more spacious Duke's Playhouse in 1661 Davenant, because he now had more than one actress, added the character Roxalana, who is jealous of the virtuous Ianthe. Roxalana was played by Hester Davenport,

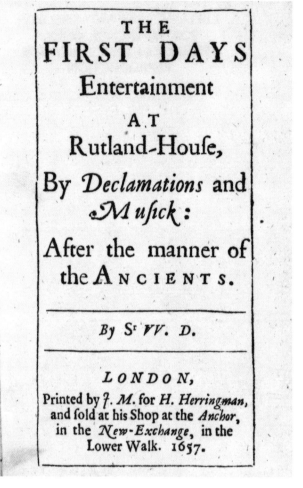

Title page for the 1657 octavo edition of the stage production Davenant mounted in May 1656, his first play since the closing of the theaters in 1642 (Henry E. Huntington Library and Art Gallery)

the first well-known English actress. Part two of *The Siege of Rhodes,* given in alternate performance with part one, is more from Davenant's imagination than from history; it establishes firmly, through Roxalana's conversion by Ianthe's purity, the convention of expressing the conflict of love and honor in heroic couplets.

The first part of the play had been produced under the protectorate without objections, the second after the Restoration of the monarchy. Although Davenant had supported the return of Charles II, he seems to have had little political influence, save in behalf of John Milton who was allowed to come out of hiding but placed under house arrest. However, he continued to serve as poet laureate without pension. But the Restoration

One of John Webb's set designs for the 1656 Rutland House performance of The Siege of Rhodes, *part 1 (from the April-September 1914 issue of the* Burlington Magazine)

allowed him an opportunity to become manager and innovator in the blossoming theater of the time.

He and his great rival, Thomas Killigrew, a favorite of the court, were given a patent to establish a theater and a virtual monopoly on London playhouses. They were first at the Cockpit in Drury Lane until Killigrew took the older and more experienced actors to the Red Bull. Davenant, in turn, after directing his company briefly at Salisbury Court, moved to Lisle's Tennis Court in Lincoln's Inn Fields; the theater there, which became known as the Duke's Playhouse, opened in late June 1661. His company became known by a patent of 1663 as the Duke of York's Players, Killigrew's more elegantly as His Majesty's Players.

At his theater Davenant trained, among others, Thomas Betterton and Henry Harris, admired by some over Betterton; Pepys said that he "was a more airy man." The company also included eight women, four of whom lived with the Davenant family. One of them, Ann Gibbs, became the wife of Thomas Shadwell, the dramatist and poet; another, "Moll" Davis, became a mistress of Charles II.

Old plays formed the basis of the repertoire at the theater; Davenant had exclusive rights to his own work and nine old plays from the King's Company—seven of Shakespeare's, Webster's *The Duchess of Malfi*, and Sir John Denham's *The Sophy*. He rescued others from his old days at the Cockpit and received a few new ones from Sir George Etherege, Dryden, and Shadwell. Samuel Tuke's *Adventures of Five Hours* was given here; its plot had been suggested by the King, and Pepys admired it over Shakespeare.

But Davenant also wrote or altered plays for his theater. The first, *The Law Against Lovers* (produced in 1662), is an altered version of *Measure for Measure* with the importation of the Beatrice-Benedick plot from *Much Ado About Nothing*. His second—and more original—is *Playhouse to be Let* (produced in 1663), "several pieces of different

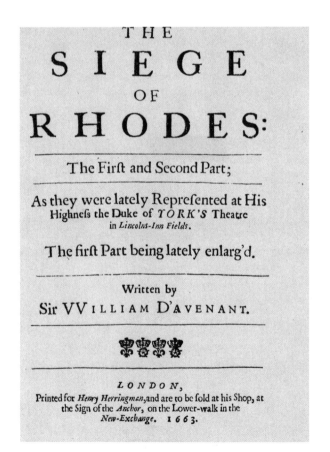

Title page for the 1663 quarto edition of both parts of the play that made theater history with its elaborate staging (Henry E. Huntington Library and Art Gallery)

kinds handsomely tacked together," according to the dramatic historian Langbaine. It is a play about a playhouse where a varied group of performers exhibit their talents and provide the fare for the remainder of the entertainment. One act is Davenant's translation of Molière's *Sganorelle*, the first of his plays to reach the English audience; two other acts revive two of Davenant's own plays, *The History of Sir Francis Drake* and *The Cruelty of the Spaniards in Peru;* and the last act is a burlesque of a popular and now forgotten tragedy. *The Rivals* (produced in 1664) is a free adaptation of *The Two Noble Kinsmen* with two acts, the first and the last, completely new. Considered an improvement upon Shakespeare and Fletcher's original, it was revived for the court as late as 1667. The last of Davenant's dramas is *The Man's the Master* (produced in 1668), a redaction, as Alfred Harbage has pointed out, of Paul Scarron's *Le Maître Valet*, which was found entertaining enough to be given as late as 1775.

But it was in Davenant's handling of Shakespeare's plays at his theater in Lincoln's Inn Fields that he is probably most often remembered. He loved Shakespeare next to idolatry and wanted his audience to share that love. To convince them of that greatness, he recast Shakespeare's plays in the image and taste of his own times. Before one joins unthinkingly the chorus of denigrators, he should cast a critical eye on some Shakespeare productions of our time where a director insists on emerging egotistically from a submerged text; without approving Davenant's meddling, one can at least understand his motivation.

Hamlet, cut and with its diction mutilated, was the first Shakespearean play to be given on Davenant's new picture stage. No succeeding tragedy, it was said, got more reputation and money for the company, partly because Betterton "did the Prince's part beyond imagination"—according to Pepys, who had declared that "the old plays begin to disgust this refined age, since his Majesty's being so long abroad." *Macbeth* was elaborately staged, oddly omitting the apparitions in the last scene with the witches, but enlarging the part of Lady Macduff and suppressing the porter, whose speech seemed too indecorous for such a "refined age." Before the "restored" *Macbeth* was produced in 1774, Londoners saw more than two hundred performances of Davenant's version, which was first acted in 1663.

The Tempest, or the Enchanted Island (produced in 1667), which Davenant adapted from Shakespeare's play with the assistance of John Dryden, was given in this version for nearly two centuries, surely an indication of its theatrical effectiveness.

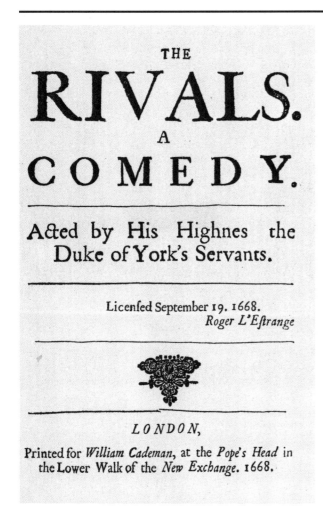

THE

RIVALS.

A

COMEDY.

A&ed by His Highnes the
Duke of York's Servants.

Licenfed September 19. 1668.
Roger L'Eftrange

LONDON,

Printed for *William Cademan,* at the *Pope's Head* in
the Lower Walk of the *New Exchange.* 1668.

Title page for the 1668 quarto edition of the play Davenant partly adapted from William Shakespeare and John Fletcher's The Two Noble Kinsmen *(Bodleian Library, Oxford)*

so popular that the King paid for five performances in the next six months.

In his adaptation, Davenant, knowing his audience, emended for clarity, elegance, and theatricality. Alfred Harbage has written that "as a result, abstract and lyrical passages, those most figurative and imaginative, in a word, most Shakespearean, were recast, abbreviated, or completely excised." Arthur Nethercot deplores Davenant's "violating hand [that] rove murderously among the greatest lines in English literature." That hand resisted no temptation to rewrite and there was no restraining it; what was right, it often wronged.

Although his literary career was chiefly in drama and entertainments, Davenant was a nondramatic poet as well. His early *Madagascar* (1638) was a gallimaufry of adulatory poems worthy of an aspirant to the laureateship. His *Gondibert,* a "Heroick Poem" as he called it, was some years in the making and was published in 1651. Based on admirable intentions—judged and encouraged by Thomas Hobbes—it was his chief occupation during his exile and subsequent imprisonment. Joseph Knight, writing on Davenant in the *Dictionary of National Biography,* pronounced it "a book to be praised rather than read . . . , insufferably dull." For Davenant the poem is of "old, unhappy, far-off things/And battles long ago." It is peopled with an exemplary hero and heroine and, of course, a melodramatic villain, all eighth-century Lombards. The poem's plot is unfinished, and no modern reader—if there are any—could wish for its being a line longer.

His collected *Poems on Several Occasions* was published posthumously in the 1673 folio volume of Davenant's works under the watchful eye of Lady Mary Davenant who, taught well by her husband, saw that the handsome and weighty collection of all his writings was dedicated to Prince Charles. These poems reflect the attitudes of the Cavalier poets and the received tradition of earlier poets, particularly Shakespeare, Jonson, and Donne. This volume contains his best-known lyric, "The lark now leaves his wat'ry nest," a poem whose sensitivity shocks the reader who knows what Davenant could do in meddling with Shakespeare's lines.

Altogether his poems are those of an aspirant to greatness who too largely desired approbation and fame. Without his contributions to the theater, Davenant scarce would be remembered. He died a famous playwright on 7 April 1668. His wife took up his work, and for twenty-two years she occupied herself by finishing the Dorset Garden Theater and

This recasting by an experienced dramatist and his apprentice shows clearly—if in the extreme—the results of adaptation. Miranda, who has never seen a man except her father, is balanced by Hippolito (actually an actress in breeches as the prologue points out), a man who had never seen a woman. By this addition, Miranda must be given a sister, Dorinda. Once such balancing begins, restraint ends, it appears: Caliban gets a sister named for their mother, Sycorax, and Ariel is given a sweetheart, Milcha. The ship's motley crew are joined by Mustacho and Ventoso, adept tricksters who carry the farcical subplot. Much of Shakespeare's lyricism is cut, but there are additional songs, duets, choruses, dances, a drunken hornpipe, and a masque that replaces the original one to Ceres. Perhaps the most effective features of the play were the wind machines. This version of *The Tempest* was managing its business, the first Englishwoman to manage a theater. She was his third wife; his first, whom he married at eighteen, bore him two children but died before they were fully reared. We know little else about her. His second wife, Dame Anne Cademan, whom he married in 1652, was a widow with four sons; she died in 1655 and was buried at St. Andrew's Holborn on 5 March 1655. He married his third wife, Henrietta-Maria du Tremblay, in the same year. He and "Lady Mary," as she was known, had seven sons.

Davenant was buried in Westminster Abbey two days after his death. On a marble stone above his grave is inscribed "O rare Sir Will. Davenant," in imitation of Ben Jonson's epitaph. He was denied a laurel wreath set on his coffin, the finest that Sir John Denham ever saw; Aubrey thought it should have been done.

Although his poems are almost completely forgotten and his plays rarely performed, Davenant has an assured place in English dramatic history. He stands between Shakespeare, whom he acknowledged master, and Dryden, his apprentice. He schooled actors, preserving the Elizabethan traditions and continuing the work of Richard Burbage; the greatest of the Restoration actors, Thomas Betterton, was Davenant's pupil. He gave us a picture stage with its proscenium arch and curtain; his productions—with their greater reliance upon moveable scenery and their elevation of music, song, dance, and elaborate machinery—were significant advances on the Elizabethan private theater. From his innovations is derived our modern theater auditorium. Inspired by the French theater, he was the first to bring women to the English stage. He established the genre of the heroic play and thus influenced two generations of playwrights, Dryden among them. He was an innovator and preserver who marked the beginning of the modern theater by building on the old.

This "inoffensive, good-natured man," as Theophilus Cibber called him, might be remembered also for a story that can be traced to him. He assured his listeners that in his early penniless days Shakespeare held horses outside the Globe theater for the patrons within. In this happier and more human way, Davenant, "the sweet swan of Isis," is linked again with the other of Avon.

Biographies:

Alfred Harbage, *Sir William Davenant, Poet Venturer, 1606-1668* (Philadelphia: University of Pennsylvania Press/London: Oxford University Press, 1935);

Arthur H. Nethercot, *Sir William D'Avenant: Poet Laureate and Playwright-Manager* (Chicago: University of Chicago Press, 1938).

References:

Philip Bordinat and Sophia B. Blaydes, *Sir William Davenant* (Boston: Twayne, 1981);

Peter Dyson, "Changes in Dramatic Perspective: From Shakespeare's *Macbeth* to Davenant's," *Shakespeare Quarterly,* 30 (Summer 1979): 402-407;

James Gellert, "Sir William Davenant's *The Law Against Lovers:* Shakespeare's Problem Comedy and the Restoration Heroic Tradition," *Cahiers Elizabéthains,* no. 16 (October 1979): 27-43;

Wayne H. Phelps, "The Second Night of Davenant's *Salmacida Spolia," Notes and Queries,* 26 (December 1979): 512-513;

Mongi Raddadi, *Davenant's Adaptations of Shakespeare* (Stockholm: Almquist & Wiksell, 1979);

Rudolf Stamm, "Sir William Davenant and Shakespeare's Imagery," *English Studies,* 24 (1942): 65-79, 97-116.

Robert Davenport

(birth date and death date unknown)

Virginia J. Haas
University of Wisconsin-Milwaukee

PLAY PRODUCTIONS: *The City-Night-Cap,* London, Cockpit theater, licensed 14 October 1624;

King John and Matilda, London, Cockpit theater, circa 1628-1634;

A New Trick to Cheat the Devil, London, Cockpit theter, no later than 1639.

BOOKS: *A Pleasant and Witty Comedy: Called, A New Tricke to Cheat the Divell* (London: Printed by J. Okes for H. Blunden, 1639);

A Crowne for a Conquerour; and Too Late to Call Backe Yesterday (London: Printed by E. Purslowe for F. Constable, 1639);

King John and Matilda, A Tragedy (London: Printed for Andrew Pennycuicke, 1655);

The City-Night-Cap: or, Crede Quod Habes, & Habes. A Tragicomedy (London: Printed by Ja: Cottrel for Samuel Speed, 1661).

Editions: *The Works of Robert Davenport,* edited by A. H. Bullen, new series volume 3 of *Old English Plays* (London & Redhill: Privately printed by the Hansard Publishing Union, 1890)—comprises *King John and Matilda, The City-Night-Cap, A New Tricke to Cheat the Divell,* "A Crowne for a Conqueror," "Too Late to Call Backe Yesterday," "A Survey of the Sciences," and commendatory verses;

Robert Davenport's The City-Night-Cap: *A Critical Edition,* edited by Willis J. Monie (New York & London: Garland, 1979);

Robert Davenport's King John and Matilda: *A Critical Edition,* edited by Joyce O. Davis (New York & London: Garland, 1980).

OTHER: Nathanael Richards, *The Tragedy of Messallina, The Roman Empresse,* includes a commendatory poem by Davenport (London: Printed by Tho. Cotes for Daniel Frere, 1640);

Thomas Rawlins, *The Rebellion: A Tragedy,* includes a commendatory poem by Davenport (London: Printed by J. Okes for Daniel Frere, 1640);

"A Spirituall Coward," "A Weeping Convert," "An Acceptable Sacrifice," and "A Valiant Martyr," in *A Little Ark Containing Sundry Pieces of Seventeenth-Century Verse,* edited by G. Thorn-Drury (London: Dobell, 1921).

Almost nothing is known of Robert Davenport's life except that he is the author of three extant plays, a prose character, several poems, and commendatory verses in Nathanael Richards's *The Tragedy of Messallina* and Thomas Rawlins's *The Rebellion,* both published in 1640. Seven other plays are doubtfully associated with Davenport: *Henry the First* (lost), licensed by the Master of the Revels in 1624; *The Pedlar* (probably an erroneous attribution), entered in the Stationers' Register, 1630; *The Pirate* (lost), mentioned in Samuel Sheppard's *Epigraphs, Theological, Philosophical and Romantic* (1651); *Henry the Second* (lost), entered in the Stationers' Register, 1653; *The Woman's Mistaken,* attributed to Thomas Drew and Davenport (lost), entered in the Stationers' Register, 1653; *The Fatal Brothers* (lost), entered in the Stationers' Register, 1660; and *The Politick Queen* (lost), entered in the Stationers' Register, 1660.

No other information about Davenport exists, but from his work and a few records connected with it, some conjectures can be made.

Davenport was first mentioned by Sir Henry Herbert, Master of the Revels, in 1624, when he licensed *Henry the First* and *The City-Night-Cap.* In the dedication to his unpublished poem, "A Dialogue Between Policy and Piety," Davenport beseeches John Bramhall, who became Bishop of Londonderry in 1634, to accept the dialogue as one among "many welcomes"; Davenport writes that his work was "purposely composed for this desired opportunity," and the manuscript is signed "At your Lordships's comandement a servant and poore neighboure Rob Davenport," suggesting that Davenport was then living in Ireland. Thus James McManaway was led to date the work 1635.

The preface in the 1639 quarto edition of *A New Trick to Cheat the Devil* says the work is an or-

phan, "wanting the Father which first begot it."
These words do not necessarily mean that Davenport was dead; they might only indicate that he was elsewhere (perhaps in Ireland) at the time of publication, an idea borne out by the dedication of the separately published poems "Too Late to Call Backe Yesterday" and "To-morrow Comes Not Yet" to Davenport's "noble friends," the actors Richard Robinson and Michael Bowyer (who played King John in Davenport's play): the dedication says the poems "are some expence of [Davenport's] time at sea . . . Virgins that never before kist the Presse"; he was thus still alive in 1639 and had traveled. Though Davenport's commendatory verses were published in the 1640 editions of *The Tragedy of Messallina* and *The Rebellion,* these verses could have been written as early as 1635, when *Messallina* was probably first performed.

The last date associated with Davenport's name is 1655: the epistle to the reader in the first edition of *King John and Matilda,* published in that year, is signed R. D., but there is debate about whether 1655 is the last date for his writing. In *A Little Ark* (1921), G. Thorn-Drury dates the Davenport manuscript containing the prose character "A Valiant Martyr" and the poems "A Spiritual Coward," "A Weeping Convert," and "An Acceptable Sacrifice" as between 1629 and 1643. Thorn-Drury writes that the manuscript's dedication is "very like" that of the undated "A Survey of the Sciences" (first published in *The Works of Robert Davenport,* 1890), but he is wrong. It is actually the 1639 dedication addressed to Robinson and Bowyer that has verbal parallels in "A Survey of the Sciences" (we find "fruites of those faire respects" in one and "fruites of those faire and due respects" in the other, for instance). The dedication in Thorn-Drury's manuscript is more like those for "A Dialogue Between Policy and Piety" and *King John and Matilda* in that all three use the same metaphor for Davenport's work—it is described as an infant in the cradle which can be killed by disapprobation or crowned by approval. Though it has been suggested that the epistle in *King John and Matilda* is a conventional one such as anyone could write, the central metaphor is one Davenport used twice before. Thus he probably wrote this dedication too, though we cannot be certain he wrote it in 1655. In it references to the author are in the second person whereas the first person is used in the other signed dedications; it may be that Davenport died before the play was published, and the personal references in the dedication were changed to accord with this fact.

While much concerning Davenport is uncertain, it is known that his contemporaries linked his name with Shakespeare's, both in the attribution of the lost *Henry the First*—licensed for the King's Men in 1624 but entered in the Stationers' Register by Humphrey Moseley in 1653 as "Henry the first, & Henry the 2d, by Shakespeare, & Davenport"— and in reference to *The Pirate.* Sheppard, in his Epigram 19, is highly laudatory of (and the only source to mention) this lost play; he says that Davenport rivals Shakespeare "though [his] glory's lesse." Hard as it is to decide whether Sheppard is guilty of hyperbole or litotes, we should at least note that he is the forerunner of significant nineteenth-century critics, who found Davenport's plays worthy of favorable notice.

Algernon Swinburne, Victorian poet and critic, devotes a chapter of his *Contemporaries of Shakespeare* (1919) to Davenport, whom he admires: "[he] could write when it pleased him with such masculine purity and simplicity"; of Davenport's three surviving plays, Swinburne found *A New Trick to Cheat the Devil* a masterpiece of sorts, ingeniously and deftly plotted and stylistically "far better and purer than Davenport's other two plays."

We can easily see what Swinburne admired in the plot. Davenport's focus is on middle-class characters; his themes are prodigality and usury. But he underplays traditional comedic elements of courtship and romance to stress a moral message, in this case the dangers implicit in a wife's usurpation of her husband's authority to make a suitable marriage for their daughter. Mistress Anne Changeable, with her father's approval, is to marry a perfectly respectable young man, Slightall. Her mother, however, wanting a title for Anne, promotes the courtship of Lord Skales so glowingly that Anne is ready to accept him and his title, rejecting her betrothed. One meeting with the young nobleman, who is neither handsome nor stately, convinces Anne that Slightall is a better choice. But, because she has rejected him, Slightall has set out to ruin himself through drinking and gambling, and principally through whoring. Before Anne can reclaim him, he has mortgaged his considerable property to a usurer to finance his debauches. Then, miserable and slightly mad, he decides to seek relief from the devil. Anne, aware of this decision, informs her father, who concocts a fantastic scheme in which he convinces Slightall, who really wants nothing to do with Anne, to marry her because she is a she-devil. The demonic plot is meant to fool Anne's mother and Lord Skales as well. It does, and the play ends with the lovers united and

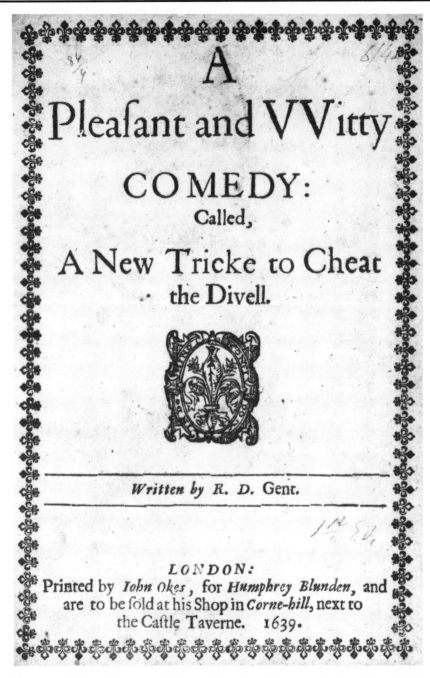

Title page for the 1639 quarto edition of Algernon Swinburne's favorite of Davenport's plays (Henry E. Huntington Library and Art Gallery)

everyone else admirably accepting Anne's rather fickle behavior.

There is a slapstick subplot, probably borrowed from Robert Greene's *Friar Bacon and Friar Bungay* or from an older fable. (W. P. Ker's suggestion of *The Friars of Berwick* as the source is appended to Bullen's edition.) Davenport's subplot is handled "deftly and ingeniously," with true good

humor. Two extraordinarily innocent friars, John and Bernard, who are locked out of their cloister, ask a citizen's wife to give them a night's lodging. The wife, who proves to be unfaithful as well as uncharitable, nearly refuses the two entry because, as she says bitingly, men of their "rank and place,/ Whose lusts have all bin question'd . . . have drawne/Good women of best rumour and report/

Into foul scandall." They find her concern for her virtue so admirable that they make no objection when, after telling them there is no food, she locks them in a cold attic. At first the cold alone keeps Friar John awake, but soon he smells roast chicken. Spying on this "modest dame," he sees her welcome the local constable, who lets the audience know this is not his first visit. The two plan to share the pullet, white bread, strong wine, and then her bed. When her husband comes home unexpectedly, she has to stow wine, bread, chicken, and lover in a handy spot. Friar John watches her subterfuge and hears her shrewish treatment of her husband: she has a cold; the fire is out; and she is *not* cooking supper. On discovering the friars in his attic, the husband insists on sharing a cup with them. But Friar John is not so easily satisfied. He assures the group that he can provide bread, claret, and roast chicken through some innocent conjuring; and he proceeds to do just that—while the wife mutters under her breath that she would like to poison him. Puckish Friar John says his last trick will be to call up the spirit who provided the feast. Of course the demon's own shape is too terrible to look at, so John will require that it appear in the recognizable form of—the local constable. By the time the husband has followed John's instructions to beat and kick the demon out of his house, it is daylight: as the friars take their leave, John charitably admonishes the husband to "make much of your good Dame,/ And thinke no worse of your good officer . . . in whose forme/[The demon] so late appear'd." While the two plots do not really mesh, each provides pleasure.

Set as poetry, the text is irregular, but the language is, as Swinburne suggests, a "natural and fitting raiment for the fresh and virile humour of dialogue and situation." Act 1, scene 1, in which Anne's mother dazzles her with the perquisites of being Lady Skales, is a satire of the middle-class tendency to be awed by titles and the deference they command. As her mother and Skales's representative dangle gems of preferment before her, Anne seems totally brainless, echoing with questions her mother's most banal observations. "Think what it is to be my Lady *Anne*," her mother says, and she responds, "My Lady *Anne*?" Her mother continues: her servants will have to bow when she so much as nods, bending so low their farthingales will "kisse their heels," and she will have "Footmen, Pages, and your gentlemen Ushers,/Walke bare before you." Anne responds, "Bare before me? Well." Dim-witted and shallow as she is made to seem here, she appears far more clever in act 2, scene 1,

when she comes to realize that titles are not very important after all. Lord Skales has just kissed her, to her disappointment, for Slightall kisses better. As for her mother's notion that Lord Skales is honorable simply because he was born an aristocrat, Anne disagrees. She asks her mother, "in what place of his body lyes [honor]; In the face or foot, the Crowne or toe,/The Body, arme, or legge, the back, or bosome,/Without him, or within? I see no more/In him than in another Gentleman." Davenport redeems the audience's estimate of Anne's intelligence by having her utter the Falstaffian parody and returning her to middle-class good sense quickly.

Davenport creates a solid and admirable citizen-character in Master Changeable and the usurer is suitably smarmy; he balances a true servant against a crafty and disloyal one without sentimentality. The dialogue is sprightly and vigorous. The play is a competent example of its type though most critics do not rank it as Davenport's best.

That ranking is usually reserved for *King John and Matilda*. In his *Extracts from the Garrick Plays* (1827), Charles Lamb writes of the "passion and poetry" of the play, noting that even though the repentance of King John is "out of nature . . . supposing the possibility, nothing is truer than the way in which it is handled." A. H. Bullen finds "more spirit and energy" in this play than in most old historical plays. In *The English History Play in the Age of Shakespeare* (1957), Irving Ribner says that out of an early Chettle and Munday play (*The Death of Robin, Earl of Huntington*) and "unhistorical folk legendry . . . Davenport constructed a tragedy of considerable power, developing the plot and characters of his source far beyond anything of which Chettle and Munday were capable." In her critical edition (1980) Joyce O. Davis demonstrates that the changes Davenport made in emphasis, dramatic structure, development of action, and character motivation reflect a dramatist skilled in stagecraft.

Davenport deals with the enmity which develops between King John and his barons, led by the patriotic Fitzwater, when he breaks the conditions enunciated in the Magna Carta and, in addition, lustfully and illicitly pursues Fitzwater's chaste daughter, Matilda. Refusing to give in to the King's passion, she takes refuge at Dunmow Abbey. When John realizes he will never have her, he directs two sycophantic followers, his confessor and Lord Brand, to poison Matilda. In a parallel subplot, Brand, at King John's instigation, imprisons Lady Bruce, wife of a rebellious baron, and her

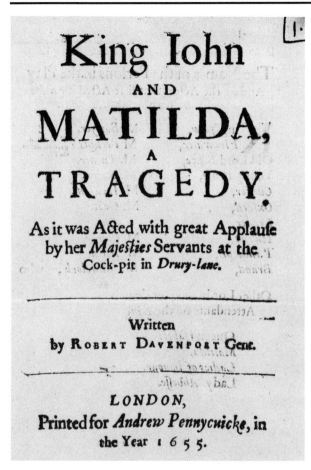

King Iohn
AND
MATILDA,
A
TRAGEDY.

As it was Acted with great Applause
by her *Majesties* Servants at the
Cock-pit in *Drury-lane*.

Written
by R O B E R T D A V E N P O R T Gent.

LONDON,
Printed for *Andrew Pennycuicke*, in
the Year 1 6 5 5.

*Title page for the 1655 quarto edition of the Davenport play
that Charles Lamb praised for its "passion and poetry" (Henry
E. Huntington Library and Art Gallery)*

young son. Lady Bruce and her son are being starved to death, but given the choice of submitting to Brand's sexual advances or continuing to starve, she and her son agree it is better to die. John's private sins—his wrongful pursuit of Matilda plus the deaths of the three innocents—are grievous.

His public aberrations might seem every bit as horrible to a seventeenth-century audience: King John submits his power and part of his wealth to the Pope (a foreign power in the minds of both John's barons and Davenport's audience) in order to be free of interdiction; he listens to "state mice" who seek their own advancement; he ignores the sound advice and complaints of those nobles whose devotion is only to England. In King John, Davenport creates a political portrait of a king whose behavior reminds the audience that the intolerable monarch relies on—and in this case strains to the limit—the Tudor doctrine of passive obedience. Against John, Davenport balances characters who

espouse the rightful order and governance of England; typical is Fitzwater, who reminds the nobles that they must bear a little of John's tyranny for "faith he is the King," who tries to do the right thing "till the fit comes on him." Fitzwater also halts a proposal to offer the English crown to the French king, since he knows that England would undergo a "heavier stroke" from a foreign power than John could ever inflict.

Davenport's poetry, as Davis points out, does not soar; his language might echo that of Shakespeare's histories, but it does not come near Shakespeare in rhetorical or dramatic inventiveness. His melding of personal and political transgressions "exalts the honor and the power of true virtue and [shows] the . . . chaos which inevitably ensues when a king becomes a lustful tyrant," says Davis.

Davenport's virtue is that he does not pretend to metaphysical depth: he keeps the plot moving swiftly, introduces some striking twists (John's unexpected repentance and conversion is one of the more startling ones), and gives some deft touches to his characterizations (Brand is so much John's man that his bluntly lecherous proposals to the starving Lady Bruce take on a tragicomic overtone as they parallel John's more sophisticated attempts to seduce Matilda). Davenport the dramatist gives the audience a good show.

The City-Night-Cap, the last of his plays to be published, has closely linked parallel plots, the Lorenzo/Abstemia one based primarily on Robert Greene's *Philomela*. This part of the play attracted the favorable attention of Washington Irving, whose mention of Davenport's play in his *Bracebridge Hall* (1822) informed or reminded a large number of readers of its existence. Praising Davenport for "bravely attempting to awaken dramatic interest in favor of a woman, even after she was married," when the great defect of the plays and novels read by young women was that they "teach [women] how to be heroines, but leave them totally at a loss when they come to be wives," Irving delighted in the story of how Abstemia, unjustly suspected and accused of infidelity by her jealous husband, Lorenzo, never fails in her love for him and demonstrates "gentle, uncomplaining, womanly fortitude under wrongs and sorrows."

A modern audience would also wonder at her charity and tolerance: like Shakespeare's Leontes, Lorenzo becomes unreasonably jealous of a woman universally regarded as chaste, charming, and honest. The play begins with Lorenzo insisting that his best friend, Philippo, attempt to seduce Abstemia, though Philippo points out the fact that she has

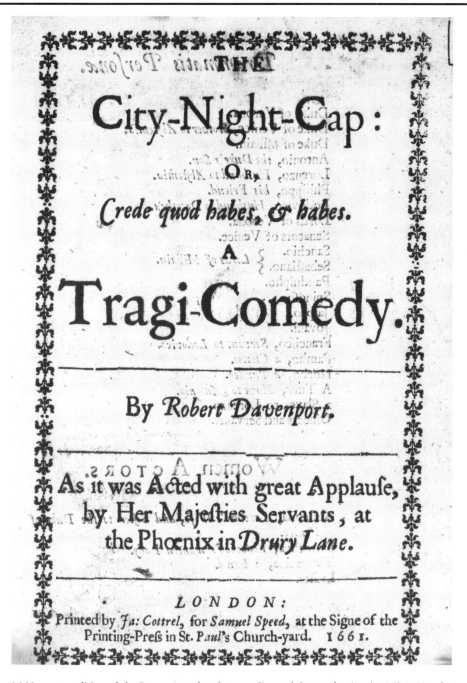

THE

City-Night-Cap:

OR

Crede quod habes, & habes.

A

Tragi-Comedy.

By *Robert Davenport.*

As it was Acted with great Applause,
by Her Majesties Servants, at
the Phœnix in *Drury Lane.*

LONDON:
Printed by *Ja: Cottrel,* for *Samuel Speed,* at the Signe of the
Printing-Press in St. *Paul's* Church-yard. 1661.

Title page for the 1661 quarto edition of the Davenport play that was licensed for production in 1624. Nearly two centuries later Washington Irving praised it for "bravely attempting to awaken dramatic interest in favor of a woman, even after she was married" (Henry E. Huntington Library and Art Gallery).

rejected him twice. He agrees to try once more, hoping that a third failure will assure Lorenzo of his wife's virtue. It does not: like Othello, Lorenzo will read into the meeting between Philippo and Abstemia what he wishes before publicly accusing them of betraying him. On the perjured testimony of two of his slaves, Lorenzo is granted a divorce.

Philippo, banished from Verona, turns to Abstemia's brother, the Duke of Venice, for help in proving her innocence. Abstemia somehow finds her way to a brothel in Milan, misdirected to this "house where gentlewomen lodge" by an unknown Samaritan. There she is forced to fight off the advances of the son of the Duke of Milan—young

Antonio (who assures her at one point that her virtue has reformed him). Philippo and her brother clear Abstemia's name and arrange to have Lorenzo sent to find her. In Milan, through a series of plot convolutions, he is accused of Antonio's murder. (A slave dressed in Antonio's clothes has actually been killed.) To save her husband Abstemia confesses to the murder, only to be imprisoned with Lorenzo as his accomplice. Antonio, obviously not reformed, offers to free both if Abstemia will sleep with him. She refuses, but Lorenzo accepts the offer for her. Crushed, she insists she will die for him or with him, but she will not dishonor him and risk her own soul. They are, of course, freed by Antonio, but only after Lorenzo, still thinking they both might die, finally admits she is the pure and devoted wife she has always seemed.

This part of the plot, with echoes of *Othello*, *The Winter's Tale*, and *Measure for Measure*, has enough intriguing twists to hold the reader's attention, but some adept character development adds dimension to the working out of events. Abstemia never becomes the stock "patient Griselda" or a type of Shakespeare's Isabella because Davenport shows her as a woman realistic enough to establish her own moral criteria and tough enough to adhere to them. In addition he uses a funny, bawdy secondary plot (which Irving completely ignores) to insure that his audience will not only admire Abstemia but also develop some tolerance for Lorenzo.

In the Dorothea/Lodovico plot, the husband constantly brags about his wife's modesty and fidelity. Lodovico is not exceptionally bright, but like Lorenzo, he works hard to convince himself that what he says he believes is actually the truth: not surprisingly, his favorite maxim (used as a subtitle for the play) is *crede quod habes, & habes*—believe you have it, and you have it. He insists to himself and all his friends that, having a chaste wife, he cannot have cuckold's horns. He is as insistently foolish about his wife as Lorenzo is about Abstemia.

In public, he notes, his wife will not "kiss nor drink nor [allow lewd] talk"—she even makes her husband's favorite servant, Francisco, change the lyrics of a song from "prick her finger" to "hurt her finger." But when Francisco reveals that he is a gentleman of Milan, who, having heard of her unshakeable chastity, resolved to seduce her, she is not upset. His favorite maxim—"Extreams .in vertue, are but clouds to vice:/She'll do in the dark, who is i'th'day too nice"—prompts him to ask if she will sleep with him, and she arranges to do it that very night. She concocts an elaborate scheme to convince Lodovico that she and Francisco are testing each other's fidelity to their lord, since the scheme leaves the two free to bed each other. Three months later, masquerading as her father-confessor to assure himself she has only venial sins to admit, Lodovico is startled when she confesses her infidelity and admits that her pregnancy is a result of it. The "friar" imposes a horrifying penance on her: at a masque her husband is giving that night, she must publicly tell him that the child she carries is not his and then name the real father. Dorothea obeys the letter of the penance, if not the spirit of it: she tells of having a dream in which "Frank" is the lawful father of her child. Lodovico also appears in her dream. He makes the child cry and Dorothea asks him to leave, reminding him that he has no right to say anything since he is not the child's father. While this ploy momentarily surprises Lodovico, he does find a way to reveal the truth about his wife.

Bawdily funny as it is, the subplot is Davenport's clever stratagem for strengthening our regard for the characters of the main plot: Dorothea's casual disregard for honor and husband, those things Abstemia will defend with her life, makes Abstemia's integrity all the more appealing. Lodovico's self-delusion is not of the same sort as Lorenzo's, but as we can sympathize with Lodovico's stupidity, so we can find a little tolerance for Lorenzo's terrible behavior (if Abstemia's forgiveness were not enough to make us react more kindly to him). Davenport manages all these elements in a highly entertaining way.

Though *King John and Matilda* was published after the Restoration (a second edition being printed in 1662), no records indicate any performances in that period, and his work does not seem to have played on any modern stage. Furthermore there is no definitive study of his surviving plays and poems; yet a mild revival of interest might have been sparked by the publication of the Renaissance Drama Series' critical editions of *King John and Matilda* (1980) and *The City-Night-Cap* (1979). That his plays do entertain is reason enough for preventing Robert Davenport from becoming a forgotten playwright.

Bibliography:

Terence P. Logan and Denzell S. Smith, eds., *The Later Jacobean and Caroline Dramatists* (Lincoln & London: University of Nebraska Press, 1978), pp. 232-234.

References:

William A. Armstrong, ed., *Elizabethan History Plays* (London: Oxford University Press, 1965);

Joyce O. Davis, Introduction to *Robert Davenport's* King John and Matilda: *A Critical Edition*, edited by Davis (New York & London: Garland, 1980);

James S. Dean, "Borrowings from Robert Greene's *Philomela* in Robert Davenport's *The City-Night-Cap*," *Notes and Queries*, 13 (August 1966): 302-303;

Paul Dean, "Davenport's *King John and Matilda:* Some Borrowings," *Notes and Queries*, 28 (April 1981): 174;

Alexander Leggatt, *Citizen Comedy in the Age of Shakespeare* (Toronto: University of Toronto Press, 1973);

James G. McManaway, "A Manuscript of Davenport's 'Policy without Piety,' " *Notes and Queries*, 170 (March 1936): 295;

W. J. Olive, "Davenant and Davenport," *Notes and Queries*, 194 (July 1949): 320;

Olive, "Davenport's Debt to Shakespeare in *The City-Night-Cap*," *Journal of English and Germanic Philology*, 49 (July 1950): 333-344;

Olive, "Shakespeare Parody in Davenport's *A New Tricke to Cheat the Divell*," *Modern Language Notes*, 66 (June 1951): 478-480.

Papers:
The Folger Library has an untitled manuscript for *The-City-Night-Cap* (MS. 1478.2) and the manuscript for "A Dialogue Between Policy and Piety" (MS. 1919.3).

Sir John Denham

(1615-10 March 1669)

Larry S. Champion
North Carolina State University

BOOKS: *The Sophy* (London: Printed by Richard Hearne for Thomas Walkley, 1642);

Coopers Hill. A Poeme (London: Printed for Tho. Walkley, 1642);

The Anatomy of Play (London: Printed by G. P. for Nicholas Bourne, 1651);

Poems and Translations, With The Sophy (London: Printed for H. Herringman, 1668).

Editions: *The Poetical Works of Sir John Denham*, edited by Theodore Howard Banks, Jr. (New Haven: Yale University Press/London: Oxford University Press, 1928);

Expans'd Heiroglyphicks: A Critical Edition of Sir John Denham's Coopers Hill, edited by Brendan O. Hehir (Berkeley: University of California Press, 1969).

John Denham's reputation as a playwright rests solely upon "*A Tragedy*, called *The Sophy*," entered in the *Stationers' Register* on 6 August 1642 by Thomas Walkley and published in the same year in folio form. Reprinted three times in *Poems and Translations, With* The Sophy (1668, reprinted 1671

and 1684), the play perhaps was never acted either prior to the closing of the theaters in 1642 or during the Restoration. There is no firm evidence to support the statement on the title page of the 1642 edition that it "was acted at the Private House in Black Friars by his Majesties Servants." The possibility of a court performance—inferred from the existence of "The Prologue at Court" included by Theodore H. Banks in *The Poetical Works of Sir John Denham* (1928)—has totally vanished since the prologue is now known to belong to William Habington's *The Queen of Aragon*. Nor did William Davenant ever exercise his option to produce *The Sophy*, listed in 1660 as one of the "ancient Playes" he was granted the privilege "of reformeing . . . and making fitt for the Company of Actors appointed vnder his direction."

The political realities of Denham's world, which literally prevented further development of whatever dramatic talents he possessed, prompted Alfred Harbage's observation that he "might have made a first-rate dramatist." Born in 1615 in Dublin to Sir John Denham, who was one of the Barons of the Exchequer, and his second wife, Eleanor Moore, he was taken to England within two years. The location of his early schooling is uncertain, but he was enrolled at Trinity College, Oxford, by November 1631, and in his *Athenae Oxonienses* (1691-1692) Anthony à Wood reported that in 1634 he was "examined . . . for the degree of Bach. of Arts." From Oxford he proceeded to the study of law at Lincoln's Inn in London, and he was admitted to the bar in 1639. Meantime he had married Anne Cotton on 25 June 1634, and his father had died on 6 January 1639, leaving him a considerable estate. Three years later *The Sophy*, Denham's first publication, prompted Edmund Waller's euphoric observation that the author of this tragedy, "admired by all ingenious men, . . . broke out like the Irish Rebellion, threescore thousand strong, when no body was aware, or in the least suspected it."

The outbreak of open war between Charles I and the Parliament prevented Denham's pursuit of either legal or literary ambitions. In 1642 he published *Cooper's Hill*, destined to be his best-known poem, but by October of that year, as High Sheriff for Surrey and Governor of Farnham Castle, he had taken up arms for the Royalists, and by December he became a prisoner of war in London for a brief period. He was imprisoned again on 23 January 1646; but, on orders issued directly by the House of Commons, he was exchanged for a certain Major Harris who was held prisoner by the Royalists. Apparently he was never a major figure in the King's cause, but he was a devoted and faithful one, whether engaged in the siege of Dartmouth (January 1646) or the battle for Exeter (April 1646), in France in the company of Queen Henrietta Maria for nearly a year (from May 1646 to March 1647), in London as informant (1647-1648), or in Poland from 1649 to 1651 by Charles's appointment to raise money (ultimately more than £10,000) from the King's Scottish subjects in that country. Even though his estates were confiscated, his friendship with the Earl of Pembroke helped him avoid total devastation in those darkest days. With the Restoration of the monarchy in 1660 his fortunes improved. He succeeded Inigo Jones (and preceded Christopher Wren) as Surveyor of the Works; and, although not a few complained that he lacked the necessary architectural skills, he was responsible for overseeing the construction of Burlington House and Greenwich Palace and for considerable improvements in the paving of the London streets. Other and even more significant honors followed. At the coronation of Charles II Denham was made Knight of the Bath, and he was

named "Clerk of the Works in the Tower of London and in all his majesty's honors, castles, etc. reserved for his abode." In April 1661 he was returned to Parliament from Old Sarum, County Wilts, and in May 1663 he was elected a member of the Royal Society. The prosperity of his final years was marred, however, by domestic and physical difficulties. His first wife had died sometime between 1643 and 1647; his second wife, Margaret Brooke, whom he married on 25 May 1665, was almost thirty years his junior and became notorious in 1665 as the Duke of York's mistress. Rumor blamed his brief period of madness in the following year, probably occasioned by paresis, on the embarrassment and indignation occasioned by his cuckoldry. His wife's mysterious death in 1668 prompted additional rumors, but an autopsy revealed no trace of poison. His sanity restored, Denham returned to Parliament and to his duties as Surveyor of the Works during his final years, dying in his office, probably of apoplexy, on 10 March 1669, with burial following in the Poets' Corner of Westminster Abbey.

The Sophy, written at a time when the struggle between the Royalists and the Puritans was taking definitive shape, is a tragedy of political intrigue. King Abbas of Persia, having gained the throne through the murders of a brother and his father, is persuaded by his corrupt adviser Haly, who is ambitious to establish a dynasty he can dominate, that his son Mirza is plotting for the throne. Acting upon the direct order of the misled ruler, Haly and his attendants attack Mirza, blind him, and cast him into prison. Guiltless of anything more than the desire for martial glory, the mutilated prince decides that he can best achieve vengeance by killing his daughter Fatyma, on whom the grandfather dotes. Only a last-minute change of heart, even as he holds the knife at the young girl's throat, prevents this grisly deed, as he determines to be ruled by reason and to leave revenge to the gods. Meanwhile, Turkish soldiers befriended earlier by Mirza return in disguise to Persia to avenge their friend, but Haly manages to have them arrested. Pursuing his plan to eliminate both Abbas and Mirza and to establish a figurehead on the throne, the Machiavel has poison administered to both, then reunites them even as he informs the father of his son's innocence. Following a poignant scene of anguish and reconciliation and at the moment of the King's death, Prince Mirza's army arrives led by two honest courtiers. Haly is betrayed by his confidant, and Sophy, Mirza's son, ascends the throne. The new ruler, though regretful that his reign must begin

The only known likeness of Denham, depicting him at about age four, is the small figure at left on the monument in Egham Parish Church to Lady Cicely Denham (his father's first wife, right), Lady Eleanor Denham (the playwright's mother, left), and the daughter with whom Lady Eleanor died in childbirth

"in blood," nonetheless pronounces that the sentence of execution against the conspirators is a "cruel piety" by which to bring "justice to [his] fathers soul." Defiant to the end, Haly refuses to beg for mercy or to "condescend to parley/With foolish hope."

It is understandably tempting to consider the dramatic action as an allegory of the political events in England. Banks sees King Abbas, for example, as a reflection of "Charles cut off from his people and surrounded by his 'evil counsellors' " and the Caliph, who readily plots with the King against his son, as a depiction of "those clergy against whom the 'root and branch' bill was aimed, specifically, perhaps, Archbishop Laud." Such attempts, though, are ultimately myopic since even a brief consideration of Denham's departure from his source clearly indicates that the tragedy can be used to support neither faction in the political strife.

Othello, perhaps, in a very broad sense suggested salient elements of characterization, the King like Shakespeare's Moor succumbing to jealousy framed in most circumstantial terms, "Honest Haly" like Iago spinning his evil web and then smil-

THE
SOPHY.

As it was acted at the Private Houfe in Black Friars
by his Majefties Servants.

LONDON,
Printed by *Richard Hearne* for *Thomas Walkley,* and
are to be fold at his fhop at the Signe of the
Flying Horfe betweene York-houfe
and BritainesBurfe· 1642.

Title page for the 1642 folio edition of Denham's only play
(Henry E. Huntington Library and Art Gallery)

ing in the face of torture and death, Mirza like Desdemona unsuspecting and guileless in the opening scenes. The principal source, however, is Thomas Herbert's *A Relation of Some Years Travel Begun Anno 1626, into Afrique and The Greater Asia,* in which Mirza does indeed kill Fatyma, then poisons himself, after which Abbas dies, leaving Sophy as his successor. Denham introduces the villainous Haly as the instigator of the father's jealousy and as the murderer by poison of both father and son; and in his version Mirza contemplates but does not enact the murder of his daughter. These alterations obviously enhance the dramatic quality by creating strong character interactions—the conniving manipulator whose ambition is to seize and consolidate his power behind the throne; the aging and gullible old ruler who, like Lear, allows insinuation and innuendo to assume monstrous proportions and to lead him into a destructive rage for which his later remorse is no less pitiable; and the virtuous son, to whom malicious thoughts are as alien as political

ambitions, but who is so free of evil himself that he fails to observe and protect himself from it in those around him. No less firmly drawn are lesser characters such as the faithful wife, whose love extends beyond physical fortune and finds greatest expression in times of physical adversity. In lines reminiscent of Donne's "Valediction" she assures the blinded Mirza that

These outward beauties are but the props and scaffolds
On which we built our love, which now made perfect,
Stands without these supports: nor is my flame
So earthy as to need the dull material fuel
Of eyes, or lips, or cheeks, still to be kindled,
And blown by appetite, or else t'expire.

Fatyma too is devoted to her father, readily offering to give him one of her eyes, even as he vengefully considers taking her life.

The two dynamic characters are Abbas and Mirza, the father only at the point of death discovering Haly's villainy and repenting of his disastrous misdeeds and the son in prison caught between the hot-blooded desire to repay misery in kind and the moral outrage prompted by such considerations. Mirza, in fact, by act three emerges clearly as the protagonist of a drama that represents a striking variation upon the revenge play popular on the stage from Thomas Kyd's *The Spanish Tragedy* in the late 1580s to John Shirley's *The Cardinal* in 1641. Denham's stage world is completely without metaphysical dimensions by which the central figure is directed to his revenge by some ghostly mandate. Here the victim is his own potential revenger; the focal point of the action is the internalized struggle in act four through which Mirza, like Charlemont in Cyril Tourneur's *The Atheist's Tragedy,* ultimately determines that vengeance is not man's prerogative. In a soliloquy early in act four he vows to "live/Only to die revenged" and invokes "Revenge [to] ascend, and bear the Scepter/O're all my passions." But his wife's words of love and consolation shake his resolve, and he describes himself as "Tost like a ship 'twixt two encountring tides!"; though love would "fain return," revenge, "now the Porter of my soul," refuses entrance. Resolving at the critical second that love is the "nobler passion," he proclaims that he will "carry" his "innocence to th' other world" and that his "brave revenge" will be to raise his mind to such a high constancy that his patience will mock his father's fury, a principle reiterated in a soliloquy in the opening lines of act five. Vengeance is left to the heavens, and the fortuitous arrival of the Prince's army effects justice upon Haly moments after the intriguer has provoked in Abbas a greater agony and remorse than Mirza could ever have achieved. While the Prince dies totally unaware of Haly's role in his tragedy, his perseverance in the face of temptation—and by extension damnation—is without question the action that is intended to provoke the most meaningful response from the reader/spectator.

Equally important in attempting to understand the tragedy in terms of England's political context, Denham's modifications of his source result in a play that projects the danger of extremes, both political and moral. The life wholly dedicated to Machiavellian ambition is no greater threat to society and government than the individual who can be victimized either through gullibility or through naïveté, through a willingness on the one hand to act hastily upon broad assumptions of ulterior motives in others or a highmindedness on the other that prevents until too late the realization that Machiavellian individuals do exist. Aside from the actions of the major characters, the Caliph's willingness to use religion as a cloak for enforcing King Abbas's despotic will provides a particularly apposite example. One courtier bemoans the fact that religion, which should curb tyranny, instead becomes its spur; he says in act four that kings who "seem/To rise to heaven [instead] make heaven stoop to them." A second courtier, however, quickly counters that no less vicious is the "many-headed beast" who conspires with religion to shake "from his neck the royal yoke," who treads on authority and sacred laws "all for God, and his pretended cause." Obviously such a passage provides vindication neither for Monarchists nor Puritan zealots. As Brendan O Hehir observed in his 1968 biography, "Undoubtedly current events were on Denham's mind as he wrote his tragedy, but, insofar as his political opinions are reflected in the text of the play, they are those not of an Anti-Royalist, but of an advocate of moderation and the middle path between political extremes."

The Sophy deserves neither the lavish attention of the seventeenth century nor the general disregard of the twentieth. Echoing Waller's panegyric are commendatory verses by Thomas Prestell (in his *Theophila,* 1652) and allusions to the play such as Jo. Leigh's (in his preface to William Cartwright's *Comedies, Tragicomedies, With Other Poems,* 1651), Samuel Butler's "A Panegyric Upon Sir John Denham's Recovery From His Madness," or those in *Scarron's Comical Romance* (1676), or in the anony-

mous "Session of the Poets" (1697) and *Andromana, or the Merchant's Wife* (1642-1660). By contrast, except for Harbage, critics of the nineteenth and twentieth centuries have given scant notice to Denham. In his *A History of English Dramatic Literature to the Death of Queen Anne* (1875) A. W. Ward points the way with his description of the play as "overrated by Denham's contemporaries." C. F. Tucker Brooke affords it only a single line in *A Literary History of England* (1948), commenting on its "indifferent blank verse"; Denham merits no mention at all in Irving Ribner's *Tudor and Stuart Drama* (1966), and even the twentieth-century editor of Denham's works (1928) dismisses *The Sophy* as a play "of no great importance" that "need not detain us long." Nevertheless, if the play lacks sufficient complication of design and depth of characterization, its plotting is firm and straightforward. The resolution is admittedly contrived, but the situation faced by Prince Mirza is a dilemma that fascinated

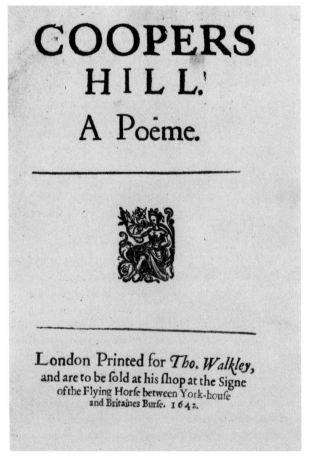

Title page for the 1642 quarto edition of Denham's best-known poem, reprinted at least twenty-four times between 1642 and 1826 (Henry E. Huntington Library and Art Gallery)

Elizabethan and Jacobean dramatists for more than half a century, and the play depicts it with reasonable, if stilted, philosophical and dramaturgic credibility.

Denham's poetic work, especially *Cooper's Hill* (also first printed in 1642), contributed directly to his contemporary popularity; certainly it was the major reason that his literary reputation remained relatively high throughout the eighteenth century. His light verse includes personal, religious, political, and poetical satire; and he translated a considerable body of material from the French, Greek, and Latin—including act five of Corneille's *Horace*. But it was the "local poem," *Cooper's Hill*, printed at least twenty-four times between 1642 and 1826, in addition to nineteen collected editions of his poetry by 1857, that secured his fame for fully a century and a half. He directly influenced such work as Waller's *Poem on St. James's Park,* Dyer's *Grongar Hill,* and Pope's *Windsor Forest;* and Dryden considered him a significant poetic voice that was instrumental in popularizing the closed couplet. Sir John Denham, in a word, was a poet, playwright, courtier, and wit renowned in his own and succeeding generations. Among the last plays written before the closing of the theaters, *The Sophy,* even if it never realized the production claimed on its title page, brought a measure of contemporary fame to its author that ironically for our age has faded to virtual indistinction.

References:

Theodore Howard Banks, Jr., Introduction to *The Poetical Works of Sir John Denham,* edited by Banks (New Haven: Yale University Press/ London: Oxford University Press, 1928), pp. 1-57;

Gerald Eades Bentley, *The Jacobean and Caroline Stage* (Oxford: Clarendon Press, 1956), III: 275-279; V: 1034-1035, 1149-1150;

Herbert Berry, "Sir John Denham at Law," *Modern Philology,* 71 (February 1974): 266-276;

C. F. Tucker Brooke, "The Renaissance," in *A Literary History of England,* edited by A. C. Baugh (New York: Appleton-Century-Crofts, 1948), p. 671;

Anat Feinberg, "The Perspective of Fear in Sir John Denham's *The Sophy,*" *Studia Neophilologica,* 52, no. 2 (1980): 311-322;

Alfred Harbage, *Cavalier Drama* (New York: Modern Language Association of America, 1936), pp. 131-132;

Pierre Legouis, "Un biographie de Sir John Denham (Avec un supplément)," *Etudes Anglaises,* 24 (July-September 1971): 292-297;

Allardyce Nicoll, *A History of English Drama* (Cambridge: Cambridge University Press, 1952), I: 314-315;

Brendan O Hehir, *Harmony From Discords: A Life of Sir John Denham* (Berkeley: University of California Press, 1968);

O Hehir, Introduction to *Expans'd Heiroglyphicks: A Critical Edition of Sir John Denham's* Coopers Hill, edited by O Hehir (Berkeley: University of California Press, 1969), pp. xvii-xxix;

J. H. Walter, "Revenge for Honor: Date, Authorship and Sources," *Review of English Studies,* 13 (October 1937): 425-437;

Adolphus William Ward, *A History of English Dramatic Literature to the Death of Queen Anne* (London: Macmillan, 1875), pp. 148-149.

Nathan Field
(1587-1619 or 1620)

Irby B. Cauthen, Jr.
University of Virginia

PLAY PRODUCTIONS: *A Woman is a Weather-cock,*
London, Whitefriars theater, 1609;
Amends for Ladies, London, Whitefriars theater,
1611;
Four Plays, or Moral Representations, in One, by Field
and John Fletcher, unknown theater, circa
1612;
The Honest Man's Fortune, by Field, Fletcher, and
Philip Massinger, London, Whitefriars the-
ater, circa 1613);
The Queen of Corinth, by Field, Fletcher, and Mas-
singer, London, Blackfriars theater, circa
1617;
The Jeweller of Amsterdam, by Field, Fletcher, and
Massinger, London, Blackfriars theater, circa
1617-1619?;
The Fatal Dowry, by Field and Massinger, London,
Blackfriars theater, circa 1617-1619;
The Knight of Malta, by Field, Fletcher, and Massin-
ger, London, Blackfriars theater, circa 1618.

BOOKS: *A Woman is a Weather-cocke* (London:
Printed by W. Jaggard for J. Budge, 1612);
Amends for Ladies (London: Printed by G. Eld for
M. Walbancke, 1618);
The Fatall Dowry, by Field and Philip Massinger
(London: Printed by J. Norton for F. Con-
stable, 1632);
Four Plays, or Moral Representations, in One, by Field
and John Fletcher; *The Honest Man's Fortune,*
by Field, Fletcher, and Massinger; *The Queen
of Corinth,* by Field, Fletcher, and Massinger;
The Knight of Malta, by Field, Fletcher, and
Massinger, in *Comedies and Tragedies Written by
Francis Beaumont and John Fletcher, Gentlemen*
(London: Printed for Humphrey Robinson &
Humphrey Moseley, 1647).
Editions: *The Plays of Nathan Field,* edited by Wil-
liam Peery (Austin: University of Texas Press,
1950)—comprises *A Woman is a Weather-cock*
and *Amends for Ladies;*
The Fatal Dowry, edited by T. A. Dunn (Berkeley:
University of California Press, 1969);

*Nathan Field (by permission of the Governors, Dulwich College
Picture Gallery, London)*

*A Critical Edition of Massinger and Field's The Fatal
Dowry,* edited by Carol Bishop (Salzburg: Institut für Englische Sprache und Literatur,
1976).

OTHER: "To the worthiest Maister Jonson," in
Ben: Jonson his Volpone or the Fox (London:
Printed by George Eld for Thomas Thorpe,
1607);
"To my lov'd friend M. John Fletcher on his Pas-
toral," in *The Faithfull Shephardesse,* by Fletcher
(London: Printed by E. Ailde for R. Bonian
& H. Walley, 1609?);
"To his worthy beloved friend Mr. Ben Jonson,"
in *Catiline his conspiracy,* by Jonson (London:
Printed for Walter Burre, 1611).

Nathan Field, actor, writer of two plays un-
assisted, and collaborator in at least six others, was
chiefly known and highly praised by his contem-

poraries for his acting. He most likely played John Littlewit in Ben Jonson's *Bartholomew Fair,* a play in which Jonson compares him with Burbadge: just before the puppet show Cokes asks, "Which is your Burbadge now? . . . Your best actor, your Field?" Field's name, along with Burbadge's, appears among the "Principall Actors" in the 1623 Shakespeare folio; we do not know what roles he played, but Edmund Malone, the eighteenth-century editor of Shakespeare, believes he "performed female parts." He is ranked next to Burbadge in the cast lists that were published in editions of *The Queen of Corinth,* which he wrote with John Fletcher and Philip Massinger, and Fletcher's *The Loyal Subject.* He is also known to have played in Jonson's *Poetaster* and his *Epicoene,* and his name comes first in the cast lists for Beaumont and Fletcher's *The Coxcomb,* and *The Honest Man's Fortune,* on which he collaborated with Fletcher and Massinger. Even after his death he was remembered; in the 1641 prologue to George Chapman's *Bussy d'Ambois,* he is given this tribute: "Field is gone whose action first did give it name." Only a few years later Henry Vaughan, the poet, in writing "Upon Mr. Fletcher's Plays" (1647), coupled Field with Eliard Swanston, a prominent and admired actor. As late as 1664 Richard Flecknoe in his *Short Discourse* recalled the actor's fame: "In this time were poets and actors in great flourish: Jonson and Shakespeare, with Beaumont and Fletcher, their poets, and Field and Burbadge, their actors."

Nathan Field was born in London and baptized in St. Giles, Cripplegate, on 17 October 1587. His father was the Puritan divine John Field, who, because of his ardent advocacy of reformation within the Church, foreshadowed in his writings the Marprelate controversy, and because of his anti-episcopacy was imprisoned. After his release he, with others, founded the first Presbyterian church in England, some four miles from London. He is connected with Elizabethan dramatic history by his tract on the collapse of the galleries at the Paris Garden on 13 January 1583, *A Godly Exortation, by Occasion of the Late Judgement of God, at Parris-Garden. [As an] Instruction, Concerning the Keeping of the Sabbath Day* (1583), an accident in which many members of the audience at a bearbaiting were injured and some were killed. The Puritan opposed to episcopacy and to dramatic entertainment died in March 1588, spared the knowledge that one of his sons would eventually rise to be Bishop of Hereford and another to become one of the time's most admired actors.

Nathan Field, often confused with his brother Nathaniel, attended St. Paul's School and may have begun his schoolboy's training in drama under Richard Mulcaster, that remarkable headmaster who envisaged education, not in Latin, but in and through English and who declared himself in favor of the schooling of women. St. Paul's was famous for the plays performed there by his schoolboys. They also played every year either at Court or in Middle Temple Hall; the young Field's talents in these plays must have been obvious to others than his elite audiences.

According to F. G. Fleay, in his *A Chronicle History of the London Stage, 1559-1642* (1890), some time before January 1601 Field was "unduly and unjustly taken" by agents acting under the authority of a royal commission for impressing boys for singing in the Chapel Royal; from those so impressed—or kidnapped—emerged not only a choir but a company of boy-actors established at Blackfriars. Though some said they were kept against their wills and suffered from threatened or real punishment for not learning their lines, there may have been as well some compensation. They played on occasion before the Queen—Field may have had a role in *Cynthia's Revels* at Court in 1601. And perhaps as boys they were congenial; it has been conjectured that Jonson read Latin at Blackfriars with Field. At least it must have been more exciting than life at St. Paul's.

Field for some years shared the fame of the Children of the Chapel Royal, renamed successively Children of the Queen's Revels, Children of the Revels, and the Children of the Blackfriars. They became rivals of the great adult companies; described in *Hamlet* as "the eyrie of children, little eyases," the boys carried it away. While Field shared their fame, he must have shared their indiscretions, which included "bitterness, liberal invectives against all estates . . . supposing their juniority to be a privilege for any railing, be it never so violent," according to Thomas Heywood's *An Apology for Actors* (1612). A series of incidents in the plays they performed (some clearly the creation of their directors)—jokes about the Scots (in *Eastward Ho!*, by Jonson, Chapman, and John Marston), veiled references to the Court (in John Day's *Isle of Gulls*), a slighting portrait of the queen of France (Chapman's *The Conspiracy and Tragedy of Charles Duke of Byron*, perhaps), and in the same week a portrait of King James as a violent, blaspheming drunkard—could not be excused, even in the mouths of children. Field may have been imprisoned for his part in some of these plays and most likely joined

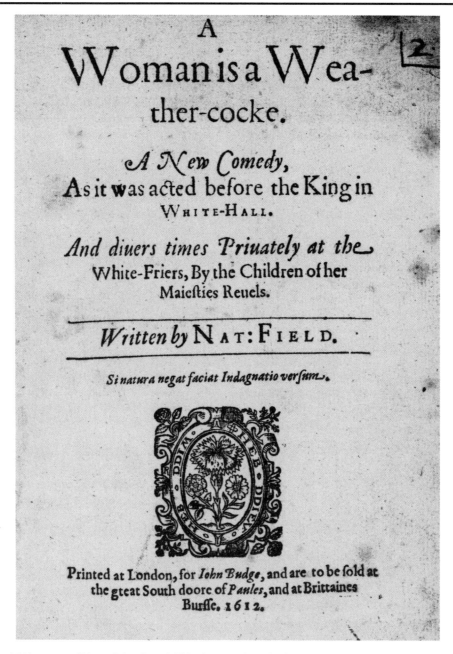

*Title page for the 1612 quarto edition of the play Field built upon the old adage "Know'st not how slight a thing woman is? . . .
[It] is impossible to find a good one" (Henry E. Huntington Library and Art Gallery)*

others there (if he had not been there before) after the royal indignation over Day's *Isle of Gulls*, which they performed in February 1606.

The record of their indiscretions is overshadowed by their artistic achievements: they pioneered a new vein of satiric comedies with two of Jonson's experimental "comical satires" and his *Epicoene* in which Field appeared when he was twenty-two. They performed Marston's major plays after he became manager in 1604. And the company had two of the most notable child actors. One was Salomon Pavy, who "did act . . . Old men so duly/As sooth, the Parcae thought him one,/He play'd so truly," according to Jonson's famous epitaph, written after Pavy died at thirteen. And, of course, the other was Field. The careers of Pavy and Field may suggest that the boy actors followed no slavish and childish imitation of adult behavior. Indeed, as R. A. Foakes conjectures, the company may have looked more and more like a normal adult troupe.

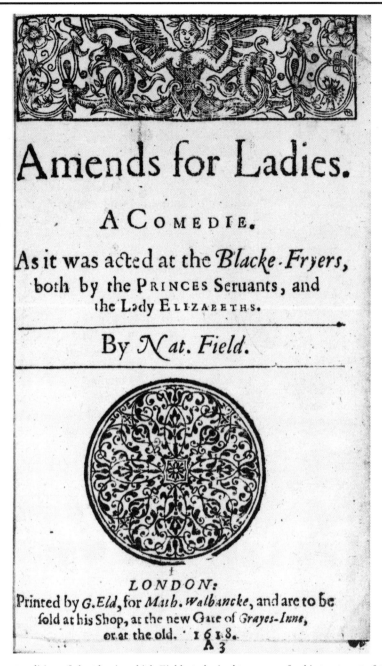

Title page for the 1618 quarto edition of the play in which Field apologized to women for his treatment of them in A Woman is a Weather-cock *(Henry E. Huntington Library and Art Gallery)*

Eventually the boys and their best plays were absorbed into the regular public theater.

In the fall of 1609 the Revels Company was established at the Whitefriars theater, and Field is said to have become manager of the new company. Here his first play, *A Woman is a Weather-cock*, was produced that year. The company was again reorganized as the Second Queen's Revels; only Field of those boys who had entered Blackfriars in about 1600 now remained. For this company he wrote his second play, *Amends for Ladies*, acted by 11 October 1611. After this he wrote for the stage only with collaborators.

A Woman is a Weather-cock is built upon a commonly held cliché: "Know'st not how slight a thing woman is? . . . [It] is impossible to find a good one among them." Mischief and disease mark these "deep dissemblers"; "an eel by the tail's held surer than a woman"—a queer species, it appears, suited principally for comic treatment. In *Amends for Ladies* he withdraws such vitriol and apologizes "to . . . all the sex."

They are slight plays, deriving from the comedies of humors and of manners. Even those who find good writing elsewhere in Field comment on them with not much more than perfunctory praise—his skill in plotting, the mirroring of the contemporary London scene, his "buoyancy of spirit" shown in quick repartee, and his use of classical allusion and apt satire. These rather conventional virtues are balanced by his sacrifice of sincerity for theatrical and farcical effect, his violation of consistency in character, and his taking advantage of his fame as an actor and capitalizing upon it in an attempt to become a dramatist like those he admired and whose works he acted.

Field's company underwent several more reorganizations—first, in 1613 there was a complex financial relationship with Henslowe's group that did not last long; then the next year Field became the leader of the Lady Elizabeth's Men. On 31 October 1614 they played Jonson's *Bartholomew Fair,* where, as John Littlewit, he heard his praises sung by Cokes, who ranked him with Burbadge.

One of his nondramatic writings of about this time deserves notice, for it gives us a rare personal view of the actor. The new minister at St. Mary's Overies, Thomas Sutton, denounced from the pulpit all actors and adjudged them—Field in particular who was in the congregation—damned. Field replied to this invective calmly in "Feild the Players Letter to Mr. Sutton" (1616). He cited Christ who pronounced no "uncharitable and unlimited condemnations"; instead, Field wrote, he "suffered for all men's sins not excepting the player, though in his time there were some." Interestingly, he refers to his reading of the Bible: "God's whole volume—which I have studied as my best part." At the time of his death, Field was not a member of Sutton's parish but of St. Giles-in-the-Fields.

His acting career was not foreshortened by Sutton's insults; he seems to have traveled in the provinces, and in 1617 he removed to the King's Men, where his name appears in the Beaumont and Fletcher plays given there. He joined with Heminge, Condell, and Burbadge in the Signet Bill

which was to secure their right to act at Blackfriars. Finally, on 19 May 1619, he was given new livery.

That is the last reference to his career; he died between June 1619 and August 1620. He had been an actor for nineteen years—since he was thirteen—and was associated with the leading dramatic companies of his time. He had acted, in addition to the plays named here, in others both not known or forgotten. His portrait at Dulwich College, in which he is wearing an embroidered shirt, shows a darkly handsome young man with piercing eyes, his hand placed a bit melodramatically over his heart. One viewer thought that "the unease in his face reflects the precarious existence of a Jacobean actor." But the expression may as well be that of an actor still conscious of his audience and awaiting their applause.

Biographies:

Roberta Florence Brinkley, *Nathan Field, The Actor-Playwright* (New Haven: Yale University Press/London: Oxford University Press, 1928);

Eliane Verhasselt, "A Biography of Nathan Field: Dramatist and Actor," in *Revue belge de philologie et d'histoire,* 25, no. 3-4 (1946-1947): 485-508.

References:

Bertha Hensman, *The Shares of Fletcher, Field and Massinger in Twelve Plays of the Beaumont and Fletcher Canon* (Salzburg: Institut für Englische Sprache und Literatur, 1974);

Cyrus Hoy, "The Shares of Fletcher and His Collaborators in the Beaumont and Fletcher Canon," part 4, *Studies in Bibliography,* 12 (1959): 91-108;

Sheila Huftel, "The Portrait of Nathan Field," *Contemporary Review,* 238 (June 1981): 320-325;

William Peery, Introduction to *The Plays of Nathan Field,* edited by Peery (Austin: University of Texas Press, 1950).

Papers:

There are three letters from Field to Philip Henslowe at Dulwich College (MSI, articles 68, 69, and 100).

John Ford

Paul A. Cantor
University of Virginia

BIRTH: Ilsington, England, baptized 17 April 1586, to Thomas and Elizabeth Ford.

EDUCATION: Exeter College, Oxford, 1601(?).

DEATH: Place and date unknown.

PLAY PRODUCTIONS: *An Ill Beginning Has a Good End,* attributed to Ford, London, at Court, winter 1612-1613;

The Witch of Edmonton, by Ford, Thomas Dekker, and William Rowley, London, Cockpit theater(?), 1621;

The Welsh Ambassador (perhaps a revision of *The Noble Spanish Soldier* by Dekker and John Day), by Dekker and perhaps Ford, unknown theater, circa 1623;

The Sun's Darling, by Ford and Dekker, London, Cockpit theater, March 1624;

The Fairy Knight, by Ford and Dekker, London, Red Bull theater, licensed 11 June 1624;

The Late Murder of the Son upon the Mother, by Ford, Dekker, Rowley, and John Webster, London, Red Bull theater, September 1624;

The Bristow Merchant, by Ford and Dekker, London, Fortune theater, licensed 22 October 1624;

The Lover's Melancholy, London, Blackfriars theater, licensed 24 November 1628;

Beauty in a Trance, London, Cockpit (Whitehall Palace), 28 November 1630;

The Broken Heart, London, Blackfriars theater, circa 1630-1633;

'Tis Pity She's a Whore, London, Phoenix theater, circa 1630-1633;

Love's Sacrifice, London, Phoenix theater, circa 1632-1633;

Perkin Warbeck, London, Phoenix theater, circa 1633-1634;

The Fancies Chaste and Noble, London, Phoenix theater, circa 1635-1636;

The Lady's Trial, London, Phoenix theater, licensed 3 May 1638.

BOOKS: *Fames Memoriall, or The Earle of Devonshire Deceased* (London: Printed by R. Bradock for C. Purset, 1606);

Honor Triumphant. Or the Peeres Challenge, By Armes Defensible, At Tilt. Also the Monarches Meeting (London: Printed by G. Eld for F. Burton, 1606);

Christes Bloodie Sweat. Or the Sonne of God in His Agonie, attributed to Ford (London: Printed by R. Blower, 1613);

The Golden Meane, attributed to Ford (London: Printed by H. Lownes for J. Chorlton, 1613);

A Line of Life. Pointing at the Immortalitie of a Vertuous Name (London: Printed by W. Stansby for N. Butter, 1620);

The Lovers Melancholy (London: Printed by F. Kingston for H. Seile, 1629);

The Broken Heart. A Tragedie (London: Printed by J. Beale for H. Beeston, 1633);

'Tis Pitty Shee's a Whore (London: Printed by N. Okes for R. Collins, 1633);

Loves Sacrifice. A Tragedie (London: Printed by J. Beale for H. Beeston, 1633);

The Chronicle Historie of Perkin Warbeck (London: Printed by T. Purfoot for H. Beeston, 1634);

The Fancies, Chast and Noble (London: Printed by E. Purslowe for H. Seile, 1638);

The Ladies Triall (London: Printed by E. Griffin for H. Shephard, 1639);

The Queen, or The Excellency of Her Sex, attributed to Ford (London: Printed by T. N. for Thomas Heath, 1653);

The Sun's-Darling: A Moral Masque, by Ford and Thomas Dekker (London: Printed by J. Bell for Andrew Penneycuicke, 1656);

The Witch of Edmonton, by Ford, Dekker, and William Rowley (London: Printed by J. Cottrel for Edward Blackmore, 1658).

Editions: *The Works of John Ford,* 3 volumes, edited by Alexander Dyce and William Gifford (London: J. Toovey, 1869)—comprises *The Lover's Melancholy, 'Tis Pity She's a Whore, The Broken Heart, Love's Sacrifice, Perkin Warbeck, The Fancies Chaste and Noble, The Lady's Trial, The Sun's Darling, The Witch of Edmonton, Fame's Memo-*

rial, Poems, Honor Triumphant, A Line of Life; John Ford, edited by Havelock Ellis (London: T. Fisher Unwin, 1888)—comprises *The Lover's Melancholy, 'Tis Pity She's a Whore, The Broken Heart, Love's Sacrifice, Perkin Warbeck;*

John Ford: Three Plays, edited by Keith Sturgess (Harmondsworth, U.K.: Penguin, 1970)—comprises *'Tis Pity She's a Whore, The Broken Heart, Perkin Warbeck.*

John Ford is arguably the last major dramatist of the English Renaissance. Though he is usually discussed along with the Jacobean playwrights, most of his dramatic work falls into the Caroline period. Judging by his plays, Ford himself seems to have had a sense of being a latecomer to the Renaissance dramatic scene. Coming as he did at the end of one of the most productive eras in the history of drama, Ford had a rich heritage to draw upon in shaping his own art. He clearly derived inspiration from his great predecessors, above all, Shakespeare, and his plays often have a reflective character, as if he were consciously harking back to earlier achievements in the genres in which he was working.

And yet the artistic heritage which sustained Ford also presented a challenge to him, the challenge of finding novel themes and stage effects long after writers from Christopher Marlowe to Thomas Middleton seemed to have exhausted the possibilities of Renaissance theater. Ford's attraction to normally taboo themes, such as incest, may be accounted for by his need to get the attention of audiences who thought they had already seen everything there was to see on the stage. It was once common to attribute Ford's choice of subject matter to a kind of moral decadence, as if in portraying incest on the stage he were advocating it in real life. But Ford's exploration of exotic subjects is best explained in aesthetic rather than in moral terms. He had to find a way of revitalizing themes and motifs that had grown stale through repetition in the hands of his predecessors. In his most famous and most shocking play, *'Tis Pity She's a Whore,* Ford takes the potentially hackneyed theme of star-crossed young lovers and gives it a new twist by making the Romeo and Juliet of his play brother and sister. In many respects, Ford pushed Renaissance drama to its limits, and the course his work took suggests that, even if the Puritans had not closed the London theaters in 1642, the Elizabethan dramatic impulse had finally played itself out in the Caroline era.

As is the case with many Renaissance dramatists, little is known about Ford's life. He was born in Ilsington, Devonshire, and baptized on 17 April 1586, the second son of Thomas and Elizabeth Ford. The Fords were evidently a family of country gentlemen; one of Ford's ancestors was granted a coat of arms and his father was a landowner. Ford seems to have been relatively well educated. A John Ford from Devon is listed on the rolls of Exeter College, Oxford, in 1601. In 1602 Ford enrolled at one of the Inns of Court, the Middle Temple, with which he was associated for many years. The Inns of Court provided a general education and specific legal training. We have no way of knowing whether Ford ever actually practiced law, but at the time it was one of the few professions open to young gentlemen who hoped to rise in the world. What evidence we have suggests that Ford ran into a few difficulties. He was expelled from the Middle Temple in the 1605-1606 term for not paying his buttery bill and was not reinstated until 10 June 1608. In 1617 he was suspended along with forty other members of the Middle Temple for wearing mere hats in place of the traditional lawyer's caps. One hesitates to read too much into such a minor incident, but it does suggest that Ford had trouble fitting himself into the conventional role of a lawyer.

The one other piece of evidence perhaps suggesting a rebellious nature in the young John Ford is his father's will. When Thomas Ford died in 1610, he left ten pounds to John but larger sums to John's two younger brothers, an action which hints at some form of parental displeasure with the future dramatist. Ford's older brother, Henry, died in 1616 and left John a legacy amounting to twenty pounds a year for the rest of his life. As sketchy as the details of Ford's life are, the profile he presents is a familiar one: a young man setting out for London to make his fortune but not succeeding in conventional paths, gradually drifting into literary endeavors, and finally hitting upon the theater as his means of livelihood. Ford's career as a dramatist is fairly well documented. At the height of his dramatic powers, he worked for the King's Majesties Servants (Shakespeare's old company) and then joined Beeston's companies at the Phoenix theater in Drury Lane. Among the few contemporary references to Ford, the closest we come to a glimpse into his personality is in an epigram in William Heminges's *Elegy on Randolph's Finger:* "Deep in a dumpe Jack Ford alone was got/With folded arms and melancholy hat." The last work of Ford's to be published under his name appeared in 1639. After that date no records of Ford can be found; we do not even know when or where he died.

Before turning to drama, Ford tried his hand at a few other literary forms. He is generally credited with five nondramatic works, two poems, *Fame's Memorial* (1606) and *Christ's Bloody Sweat* (1613), and three pamphlets, *Honor Triumphant* (1606), *The Golden Mean* (1613), and *A Line of Life* (1620). *Christ's Bloody Sweat* and *The Golden Mean* are only conjecturally attributed to Ford, and he may also have been the author of a prose work called *Sir Thomas Overbury's Ghost* (entered in the Stationers' Register on 25 November 1615), now lost. None of these works has any particular literary merit, and they would probably not be remembered if they were not associated with an author who went on to become an important dramatist. *Fame's Memorial*, an elegy on the death of Charles Blount, Earl of Devonshire and Lord Mountjoy, is of some interest because the poem is dedicated to Blount's widow, Lady Penelope Rich, the Stella of Sir Philip Sidney's sonnet sequence, *Astrophel and Stella*. Some scholars believe that Lady Rich, who was married against her will and who seems to have become involved in a romantic triangle, may have provided a model for a number of Ford's heroines, particularly Penthea in *The Broken Heart*. The prose pamphlets are of interest because they show Ford already concerned with models of virtuous conduct and questions of nobility. The kind of rhetorical and dialectical skill Ford displays in arguing such typical Renaissance topics as "Fair lady was never false" was later to be at the disposal of his characters, such as Giovanni in *'Tis Pity She's a Whore*.

In his nondramatic works, Ford was writing as a literary amateur. Unfortunately the beginnings of his career as a professional dramatist are obscure. In the first of his surviving works he was collaborating with older and more established playwrights. But he may have written a number of plays on his own earlier. For many of Ford's "works" all that survive are the titles and in some cases records of their having been staged; in most cases the attribution to Ford is speculative, and even if he did have a hand in these works, he may not have been the sole author. All one can do is to record the titles of lost works which have been associated with Ford's name: *An Ill Beginning Has a Good End*, *Beauty in a Trance*, *The London Merchant*, *The Royal Combat*, *The Fairy Knight* (written with Thomas Dekker), *The Late Murder of the Son upon the Mother* (with Dekker, William Rowley, and John Webster), and *The Bristow Merchant* (with Dekker). To complicate the picture further, some scholars have tried to

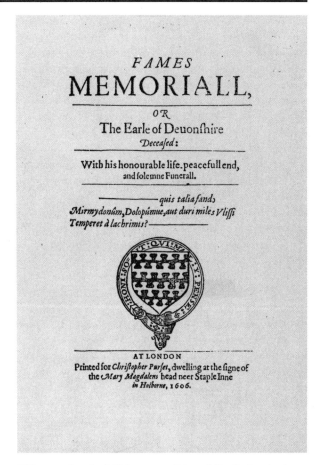

Title page for the 1606 quarto edition of Ford's first book, an elegy for Charles Blount, Earl of Devonshire and Lord Mountjoy (Bodleian Library, Oxford)

ascribe to Ford works credited to other playwrights, such as *The Spanish Gypsy*, published originally as a work by Middleton and Rowley. Even in the case of the established Ford canon, it has proven impossible to determine conclusively the dates of composition for the plays, or even the precise order in which they were written. Thus any attempt to analyze Ford's dramatic career must rest on shaky foundations. It is very difficult to substantiate any hypothesis about his development as a playwright since most of his early works have been lost and we cannot be sure which are his final compositions. The titles of his lost works suggest that the range of his subject matter was greater than appears in his surviving work. In particular, he seems to have devoted more attention to middle-class subjects than one would conclude from the works we have by him. Given the significant gaps in our knowledge about Ford's output as a playwright, the only safe course is to take up his surviving works in their order of publication, which is firmly established.

Though his output is uneven in quality, Ford was in general a consummate man of the theater. The governing principle of his dramas seems to be theatrical effect. For the sake of a striking scene or turn of events, he will sacrifice dramatic probability or consistency of character. Rather than exploring a single plot in depth, he tends to load his plays with multiple plots, so that he can always keep one story line or another moving. In a quintessentially Fordian moment in *Love's Sacrifice*, a "wanton Courtier" named Ferentes is confronted by not just one but three women he has seduced with promises of marriage and abandoned with child. In *The Broken Heart*, the heroine Calantha learns in the space of less than ten lines of the deaths of her father, her best friend, and her betrothed lover.

In terms of subject matter, Ford staked out for himself the theme of thwarted love. He frequently portrays the conflict between romantic passion and other obligations, usually of a social nature. His plays often deal with romantic triangles, and he seems particularly drawn to the theme of sexual jealousy, especially when a man's close friend is the one to arouse his suspicions. Of all the earlier plays which seem to hover in the background of Ford's works, *Othello* casts the broadest shadow.

What is perhaps most distinctive about Ford as a playwright is the clarity, directness, fluidity, and (at its best) the limpid beauty of his dramatic verse, together with his talent for mood painting, especially moods of exquisite sorrow and suffering. His characters are perpetually frustrated in their desires either because they are simply confused about what they want or because their passions pull them in two directions at once. He loves to create characters with an almost self-conscious aristocratic bearing, who pride themselves on maintaining their self-possession in the face of the most calamitous turns of fortune. Noble death scenes, filled with stoic rhetoric, are one of Ford's specialties. At times his characters can become theatrical in their nobility, as if they somehow knew they were on stage playing a part and had decided to play it to the hilt, observing all the proper forms and gestures. In a way Ford's characters seem to share their creator's sense of being a latecomer. They appear to have learned how to behave from watching plays; they are governed in their lives by theatrical models of what it is to be a tragic lover, a noble prince, a jealous husband, or a loyal friend. It is no accident that *Perkin Warbeck* is the most nearly perfect of Ford's creations, for in choosing the theme of a pretender to the throne for this play he finally hit upon the ideal dramatic vehicle for his distinctive vision. Striving to act out the noble role of a storybook king in a world of *Realpolitik*, Perkin becomes an emblem for all of Ford's characters, whose often overheated poetic imaginations are constantly running afoul of the coolly prosaic reality in which they find themselves.

The first play of Ford's which survives is *The Witch of Edmonton*, written in 1621 with the seasoned Elizabethan playwright Thomas Dekker and the perennial collaborator William Rowley. It may have been first performed by the Prince's Servants at the Cockpit theater before the court production at Whitehall Palace on 29 December 1621. The play is in part based on an actual contemporary incident, recounted in Henry Goodcole's *The Wonderfull Discoverie of Elizabeth Sawyer A Witch Late of Edmonton* (1621). The play weaves together two plots. One is the story of Mother Sawyer, an old woman who is accused by the local townspeople of witchcraft so often that she turns to the devil to gain revenge and actually becomes a witch, a crime for which she is eventually sentenced to death. The other plot is the story of a young man named Frank Thorney, who has secretly married a serving maid named Winnifride. When Frank's father insists for financial reasons that he marry a rich yeoman's daughter, Susan Carter, he knowingly commits bigamy and, sinking further into crime, eventually kills Susan in order to be able to escape with Winnifride and his newly acquired wealth. Though Frank temporarily manages to place the blame for the murder on two innocent men, his guilt is discovered in the end, and he too is led off to be executed.

In trying to parcel out the different sections of *The Witch of Edmonton* among its three authors, scholars have quarreled, but the consensus is that Dekker basically handled the Mother Sawyer plot and Ford the Frank Thorney plot (though Dekker may have been largely responsible for creating the character of Susan Carter). As was often the case in his collaborations, Rowley probably did not contribute much to the play: he seems to have written the few comic scenes between a rustic clown named Cuddy Banks and the devil in the form of Mother Sawyer's dog. Though at times crude and simplistic, *The Witch of Edmonton* is in many respects one of the most successful of the few Renaissance attempts at domestic tragedy. With its rural setting and the inevitability with which its protagonists are drawn to their destruction, the play has something of the feel of a Thomas Hardy novel. In its sympathy for the outcast and the financially troubled,

The Witch of Edmonton comes as close as any English Renaissance drama to social protest. Frank is basically a decent young man who is led into bigamy and other crimes in order to save his father's land (and hence his own inheritance). Initially, Mother Sawyer's only crime is being old, and, when she is accused of being a witch, she pointedly turns the tables on her accusers by claiming that the real witches are the beautiful women at court, who bewitch men with their sensual arts, and the wives of London merchants, who magically transform hard-earned wealth into worthless luxuries.

But The Witch of Edmonton stops short of being a modern problem play or sociological drama. Though at times it strongly suggests that the upper classes get away with precisely the crimes for which the middle and lower classes are punished, in the end the play reimposes conventional moral categories on its action. The authors were not quite ready for a purely sociological explanation of events. They have to account for the tragedy they are telling by the only explanatory system they have available: evil spirits, not socioeconomic conditions, are ultimately responsible for what Mother Sawyer and Frank Thorney do. For example, Frank kills Susan as a result of the promptings of the witch's familiar. Despite the effort to associate Frank with evil spirits, he is allowed a sincere repentance at the end and receives forgiveness from all the characters he has injured. Though Ford did not write the whole of The Witch of Edmonton, many critics believe that he was responsible for the play's overall construction. In any case the play is unique in the Ford canon as we have it and adds to our sense of his range as a dramatist. Set in the country rather than in the court, with a cast of common people rather than of aristocrats, and dealing with simple and basic human problems and emotions rather than the convoluted psyches and hyper-sophisticated sentiments of Ford's usual characters, The Witch of Edmonton is proof that when he wanted to, Ford could work within the ordinary range of human experience.

Ford continued his collaboration with Dekker in a masque called The Sun's Darling, licensed on 3 March 1624 and presumably performed at the Cockpit theater and at court. The work was not printed until 1656, and we do not know if what we have is the original version. There are signs that the masque was revised in 1638 or 1639, perhaps for a new court performance. The Sun's Darling is a typical court masque, with elements of a morality play mixed in. It tells the story of the Sun's favorite, Raybright, who tries to cure his melancholy by

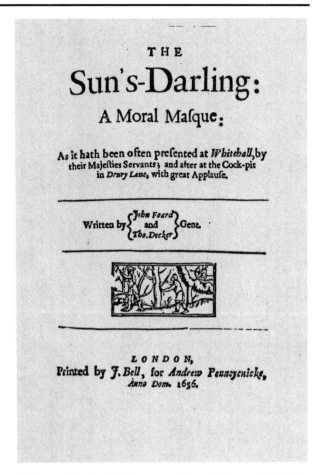

THE
Sun's-Darling:
A Moral Masque:

As it hath been often presented at *Whitehall*, by their Majesties Servants; and after at the Cock-pit in *Drury Lane*, with great Applause.

Written by { John Foard and Tho. Decker } Gent.

LONDON,
Printed by *J. Bell*, for *Andrew Penneycuicke,*
Anno Dom. 1656.

Title page for the 1656 quarto edition of Ford and Dekker's masque (Fredson Bowers, ed., The Dramatic Works of Thomas Dekker, *volume 4, 1961)*

turning to the world of nature. Moving through the four seasons from spring to winter, Raybright foolishly abandons the natural gifts symbolized by his companions Youth, Health, and Delight for the sake of a variety of false pleasures to which he is led by his squire Folly and which are chiefly represented by a figure named Humour. When read, the work comes across as an obvious and on the whole rather tedious allegory; when performed, it was no doubt enlivened by the use of stage spectacle, music, singing, and dancing.

The first of Ford's solo efforts as a dramatist which has come down to us is The Lover's Melancholy, a tragicomedy licensed in 1628, performed according to the title page by the King's Majesties Servants privately at the Blackfriars and publicly at the Globe, and published in 1629. The play tells the story of two mental illnesses which must be cured, in true comic fashion, by means of a series of disguises and mistaken identities. Prince Palador of

Cyprus is suffering from the lover's melancholy of the title as a result of losing his betrothed Eroclea in a series of intrigues involving his now dead father, King Agenor. Eroclea's father, Lord Meleander, has lost his reason as a result of her disappearance. Into this sorrowful and nearly paralyzed world Ford introduces a young lord named Menaphon, who has returned from Greece to see the woman he loves, Thamasta, cousin to Palador. Menaphon is accompanied by a youth from Greece named Parthenophil, whose good looks enchant Thamasta. Though Parthenophil rejects Thamasta's advances, Menaphon grows increasingly jealous of his young friend. When events threaten to take a tragic turn, Parthenophil is revealed to be Eroclea in disguise, thus resolving all difficulties. Eroclea is reunited with Palador, helps to restore her father's mental balance, and permits Menaphon to be reconciled with Thamasta.

Much of the criticism of *The Lover's Melancholy* has focused on Ford's debt to Robert Burton's *The Anatomy of Melancholy* (1621), the great Renaissance compendium of medical, scientific, and psychological knowledge, which Ford does draw upon in portraying the symptoms and cure of his melancholy characters. But Ford's greatest debt is to Shakespeare. *The Lover's Melancholy* is basically a reworking of *Twelfth Night*, with Palador corresponding to Orsino and Eroclea to Viola. Though Ford does not fully grasp Shakespeare's profound understanding of the pitfalls of romantic love, he does follow his master in portraying the way people get locked into sterile poses as a result of living by artificial ideals of conduct generated by literature, especially Petrarchan love poetry. The Prince's physician, Corax, complains that he is failing to follow the regimen of physical exercise his doctor prescribed and is instead wrapped up in books, with the result that his princely activities are "all changed into a sonnet." His courtiers even accuse the Prince of narcissism, claiming that his melancholy, like Orsino's in *Twelfth Night*, is a form of self-indulgence (you are "wrapt up in self-love" he is told in II.i). By using the comic device of mistaken identity to jumble up his characters, Ford is able to break them out of the ruts into which they have fallen and thus to restore psychic health to their community. As in Shakespeare's romantic comedies, the multiple marriages at the end of Ford's play signify the triumph of a realistic and fruitful conception of male-female relationships over the self-imposed melancholy and abstract idealism of the Petrarchan love tradition: "Sorrows are changed to bride-songs."

Ford's other principal debt is to *King Lear*. The mad old Meleander is clearly modeled on Lear, as is evident from a number of striking verbal parallels, such as Meleander's reaction in II.ii when a number of characters come to see him: "I am a weak old man. All these are come/To jeer my ripe calamities/. . . . But I'll outstare ye all." Meleander's contempt in his madness for the luxuries of the court, the way he is finally cured of his madness, and, above all, his reunion scene with his daughter all hark back to *King Lear*. Naturally the comparison cannot work to Ford's advantage. He misses all the tragic complexity and grandeur of Lear and exploits the situation of a mad old man largely for its potential for sentiment. *The Lover's Melancholy* shows how readily Ford was able to adapt Shakespearean material to his own purposes. But the fact that he chose to mix material from one of Shakespeare's greatest tragedies indiscriminately with material from the romantic comedies suggests that Ford's appropriation of Shakespeare resulted not from any deep aesthetic affinity or sympathetic understanding, but from a practical playwright's sense of what in the work of his predecessor had been effective with audiences.

The play Ford probably wrote after *The Lover's Melancholy* is *The Broken Heart,* published in 1633 and evidently the last of his works to be performed by the King's Majesties Servants. *The Broken Heart* is set supposedly in ancient Sparta, but one would search in vain in Thucydides for any Spartans acting as do Ford's. Like so many of Ford's plays, *The Broken Heart* tells a story of love thwarted and vengeance delayed but eventually executed. In a peculiar twist, seemingly more appropriate to comedy than tragedy, the characters have "names fitted to their Qualities." Perhaps Ford was experimenting with the idea of a tragedy of humors. The proud young hero Ithocles ("Honour of loveliness") has incurred the hatred of Orgilus ("Angry") by forcing his sister Penthea ("Complaint") to break her betrothal to Orgilus and marry instead an older and thoroughly distasteful man named Bassanes ("Vexation"). Insanely jealous, Bassanes has made Penthea's life miserable with his suspicions, and in order to ease her burden Orgilus pretends to leave for Athens. In reality he remains in Sparta disguised as a philosophy student, but Penthea rejects his secret advances, even though she still loves him. Meanwhile, Ithocles has grown to regret what he did to his sister and has himself fallen hopelessly in love with Princess Calantha ("Flower of beauty"). When Bassanes discovers Penthea and Ithocles in private conference he accuses Ithocles of having committed incest with his sister. Though grotesquely unjust this charge drives Penthea to despair and destroys her will to live. Before she starves herself to death, however, she manages to win Calantha's love for her brother. But before Ithocles can be wed to Calantha, Penthea's death provokes Orgilus to murder him. Having just become Queen of Sparta, Calantha sentences Orgilus to die, and he chooses to do so by bleeding himself to death on stage. Calantha then expires by the side of her dead lover Ithocles. The deaths of Orgilus and Calantha fulfill two mysterious oracles uttered earlier in the play: "Revenge proves its own executioner" and "The lifeless trunk shall wed the broken heart."

The Broken Heart has proven to be one of the most enduring of Ford's works and has attracted more critical attention than any of his plays, with the exception of *'Tis Pity She's a Whore* and *Perkin Warbeck*. No source has ever been identified for *The*

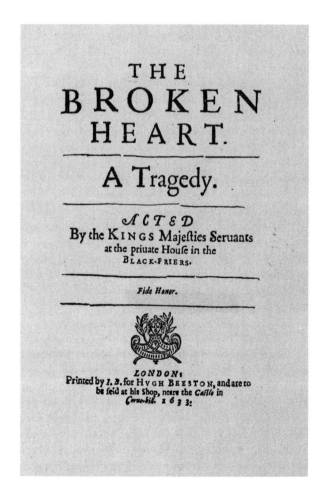

Title page for the 1633 quarto edition of what is probably the last play Ford wrote for the King's Majesties Servants (Bodleian Library, Oxford)

Broken Heart, and it seems to be the most original and perhaps the most personal of all Ford's plays. For once, he steps out of the shadow of Shakespeare and finds his own voice, and a distinctive voice it turns out to be. No Renaissance play focuses so unrelievedly on moments of psychological suffering or sustains so plaintively the accents of grief. With an inexorable dramatic logic Ford pursues his favorite theme: the tragic consequences of any attempt to divert human passions from their chosen paths and channel them instead into lawful but unwanted directions. As one of the characters says: "affections injur'd/By tyranny, or rigor of compulsion,/Like tempest-threaten'd trees unfirmly rooted,/Ne'er spring to timely growth." The frustration and twisting of romantic passion in *The Broken Heart* is so pervasive that the play verges at times on sentimentality. And the fact that the characters' suffering can find no vent in action but is merely something to be endured threatens to give the play a static, almost monotonous quality.

Nevertheless, Ford manages to give a kind of stateliness to the sorrow he portrays. Though a mood of grief suffuses the whole play, the grief is restrained, especially in the way it is expressed. In general the characters tend to understate their sorrows; Calantha sums up the mode of the play when she speaks of "the silent griefs which cut the heartstrings." The laments of Ford's characters, and above all their death scenes, have a ritual air about them, in part because he creates self-conscious characters, who seem to sense that they are on display. Penthea says at one point: "On the stage/Of my mortality, my youth hath acted/Some scenes of vanity," and as Bassanes graciously opens one of Orgilus' veins, he comments on the impression the scene is making: "This pastime/Appears majestical; some high-tun'd poem/Hereafter shall deliver to posterity/The writer's glory and his subject's triumph." For what may be the first time in Ford theatricality becomes both means and end. Wanting to achieve a certain kind of stage effect, Ford creates characters whose theatrical attitude toward their own emotions and circumstances ensures that he will get just the ritualized pattern of grief he wants.

The Broken Heart may have provided the germinal idea for Ford's best-known play, *'Tis Pity She's a Whore*. In the earlier work Ford merely toys with the idea of brother-sister incest; audience reaction may have suggested to him the shock value of building a whole play around the theme. *'Tis Pity She's a Whore* was first published in 1633; because Ford refers to it as "these first fruits of my leisure" in

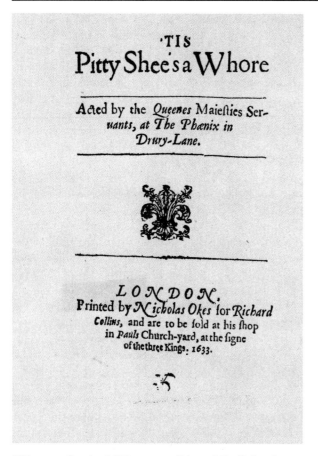

'TIS
Pitty Shee's a Whore

Acted by the *Queenes* Maiesties Seruants, at *The Phœnix in
Drury-Lane.*

L O N D O N.
Printed by *Nicholas Okes* for *Richard
Collins,* and are to be fold at his fhop
in *Pauls* Church-yard, at the figne
of the three Kings. *1633.*

*Title page for the 1633 quarto edition of Ford's best-known
play (Folger Shakespeare Library)*

the dedication, some scholars have argued that it was the first of his major plays and have claimed that it must have been written and performed well before its publication date. But the fact that the title page asserts that the play was performed by the Queen's Majesties Servants suggests that it came later than *The Broken Heart* and may in fact have been the first result of Ford's switch to a new theater company.

The hero of *'Tis Pity She's a Whore* is an impetuous young man named Giovanni, who develops an incestuous longing for his beautiful sister, Annabella. Despite the warnings of a friar named Bonaventura, Giovanni pursues his love for his sister and quickly wins her assent to a passionate affair. In order to conceal the unlawful romance Annabella eventually consents to marry a nobleman named Soranzo. Soranzo has a guilty secret himself, having seduced and abandoned a married woman named Hippolita. Much of the play is devoted to unsuccessful attempts by Hippolita and her husband, Richardetto, to gain revenge on Sor-

anzo. Ford also includes a comic subplot involving a fool named Bergetto who vainly woos Annabella. The secret love of Giovanni and Annabella is finally revealed when Soranzo discovers that he has married a pregnant woman. By the end of the play almost all the characters have been killed off in a sequence of revenges and counterrevenges. Giovanni has the most spectacular death of all. After killing Annabella to preserve the purity of their love, he enters the last scene with her heart on his dagger, murders Soranzo, and is finally killed himself by a gang of banditti specifically hired by Soranzo for the purpose.

Most of the critical debate concerning *'Tis Pity She's a Whore* has understandably centered on Ford's treatment of incest. The play contains many explicit attacks on such an unconventional love, and of course the catastrophic outcome of the romance of Giovanni and Annabella suggests that Ford was warning against the breaking of so basic a social taboo. And yet Ford allows Giovanni to make an unusually spirited and eloquent defense of forbidden love. Moreover, Giovanni and Annabella are by far the most vibrant characters in the play, and, even though their love destroys them, there are strong suggestions that they have in the process attained an intensity of experience from which the crassly conventional characters in the play are barred. *'Tis Pity She's a Whore* has a Marlovian quality: the protagonists are overreachers and perish in their attempt to go beyond the limits of normal humanity, but the forces which oppose them in the scheme of the play hardly have a solid moral basis for their opposition, being involved as they are in a shabby web of sexual intrigue and assassination plots. In the end, *'Tis Pity She's a Whore* seems to turn on the opposition between one grand crime of romantic passion and a series of petty crimes fueled by lust and vengefulness.

Perhaps Ford simply was not interested in analyzing and resolving the moral problem of incest. Had he wished to explore the topic in depth, he would have shown Giovanni's incestuous passion gradually developing and concentrated on Annabella's moral dilemma of whether or not to yield to her brother's advances. But in fact by the second scene Ford already has Giovanni and Annabella pledging their love to each other, and he chooses to fill up the rest of the play with revenge plots instead of giving us further insights into the characters of the young lovers. In short, brother-sister incest is the dramatic premise of *'Tis Pity She's a Whore,* not its sole focus. One might then argue that Ford was driven to the theme by the logic of his historical position as a latecomer in Renaissance drama. Romantic passion thrives on opposition: lovers derive the strength of their emotion from the strength of the obstacles they have to overcome in order to be united. When Shakespeare wrote *Romeo and Juliet,* it was enough that the lovers' parents opposed the match. But Ford was writing in and for a world that had already, as it were, digested the message of *Romeo and Juliet:* that romantic love must be allowed some legitimacy. In *The Broken Heart,* for example, when the young prince Nearchus learns that Calantha is in love with Ithocles, he abandons his suit to her and is willing to let a social inferior take precedence over him because Ithocles has passion on his side. In *'Tis Pity She's a Whore* itself, Annabella's father, unlike Juliet's, makes it clear that he will not force her into a marriage against her wishes: "I would not have her marry wealth but love." In this newly permissive and parentally indulgent environment Ford must search for a form of love that will *not* have the endorsement of society.

Love between brother and sister is the answer to Ford's need for a passion that can still totally isolate his protagonists and drive them to a tragic death. With this one change Ford is able to rewrite *Romeo and Juliet* even to the point of companioning his young hero with a meddling friar and his heroine with a coarse nurse. Supplied with the fresh context of an incestuous situation, all the old clichés of Petrarchan love poetry suddenly regain their vitality, as the lovers really must keep their relationship a secret and face danger and the prospect of death wherever they turn. The situation thus permits Ford's characters the kind of theatricality he savors. Giovanni, for example, seems obsessed with playing the role of a Romeo. As he marches off to the final scene, he prompts himself: "Shrink not, courageous hand, stand up, my heart,/And boldy act my last and greater part." An incestuous love proves to be the only way Giovanni can act the part of a tragic lover in a world that has come to grant more conventional forms of romantic passion their legitimate place in society.

The last of Ford's plays to be published in 1633 is *Love's Sacrifice.* If *'Tis Pity She's a Whore* rewrites *Romeo and Juliet, Love's Sacrifice* is Ford's most sustained effort at rewriting the play that seems to have obsessed him more than any other: *Othello. Love's Sacrifice* tells the story of a peculiar love triangle involving Philippo Caraffa (Duke of Pavia), his beautiful wife, Bianca, and his best friend, Fernando. An Iago-like character named D'Avolos convinces Philippo that Fernando is having an af-

fair with Bianca behind his back. To arouse the Duke's suspicions D'Avolos uses many of Iago's strategies, such as taunting Philippo with the prospect of actually seeing himself cuckolded: "Would you desire, my lord, to see them exchange kisses, sucking one another's lips, nay, begetting an heir to the dukedom?" The difference from *Othello* is that in Ford's play there is a genuine basis for the husband's suspicions. Fernando and Bianca have fallen in love but have taken a vow to keep their relationship Platonic. But when Philippo discovers them in each other's arms, he accuses his wife of adultery and kills her. Protesting their innocence of literal adultery, Fernando poisons himself at Bianca's funeral. Realizing that he has unjustly destroyed his wife and his friend, Philippo also commits suicide, leaving D'Avolos to be punished for his role in precipitating the tragedy.

On the face of it *Love's Sacrifice* ought to be a more plausible drama than *Othello.* After all, D'A-

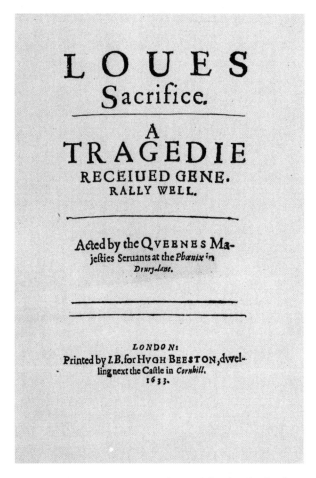

LOUES
Sacrifice.

A
TRAGEDIE
RECEIUED GENE.
RALLY WELL.

Acted by the QVEENES Majesties Seruants at the *Phœnix* in *Drury-lane.*

LONDON:
Printed by I. B. for HVGH BEESTON, dwelling next the Castle in *Cornhill.*
1633.

Title page for the 1633 quarto edition of the play that has been called Ford's attempt to rewrite William Shakespeare's Othello *(Bodleian Library, Oxford)*

To my trueſt friend, my worthieſt
Kinſman, I O H N F O R D of *Grayes-
Inne, Eſquire.*

 HE Title of *this little worke*
(may goodCozen)isin ſence
but the argument of a Dedication ; which being in moſt
writers a *Cuſtome,* in many a
complement, I queſtion not but
your cleere knowledg of my
intents,will in me read as the
earneſt of affection. My am-
bition herein aimes at a faire flight, borne vp on the
double wings of gratitude, for a receiued, and acknow-
ledgement for a continued loue. It is not ſo frequent to
number many kinſmen, & amongſt them ſome friends;
as to preſume on ſome friends, and amongſt them little
friendſhip. But in euery fulneſſe of theſe particulars, I
doe not more partake *through you* (my Cozen) the delight, then enioy the benefit of them. This *Inſcription
to your name,* is onely a faithfull deliuerance to *Memory*
of the truth of my reſpects to *vertue,* and to the equall
A   in

The Epiſtle Dedicatory:

in honour with vertue, *Deſert.* The contempt throwne
on *ſtudies of this kinde,* by ſuch as dote on their owne ſin-
gularity, hath almoſt ſo out-fac'd *Inuention,* and pre-
ſcrib'd *Iudgement* ; that it is more ſafe, more wiſe, to be
ſuſpectedly ſilent, then *modeſtly confident* of opinion, herein. Let me be bold to tell the ſeuerity of *cenſurers,* how
willingly I neglect their practiſe, ſo long as I digreſſe
from no becomming thankfulneſſe. Accept then (my
Cozen) this *witneſſe to Poſteritie* of my conſtancy to
your Merits ; for no *Ties* of blood, no ingagements of
Friendſhip ſhall more juſtly liue a *Preſident,* then the ſin-
cerity of *Both* in the Heart of

I O H N F O R D.

To my friend Mr. I O H N F O R D.

V *Nto this Altar, rich with thy owne ſpice,
I bring one graine, to thy Loues Sacrifice :
And boaſt to ſee thy flames aſcending, while
Perfumes enrich our Ayre from thy ſweet Pile.*

Looke here T H O V *that haſt malice to the Stage,
And Impudence enough for the whole Age ;
Voluminouſly-Ignorant ! be vext
To read this Tragedy, and thy owne be next.*

James Shirley.

The Sceane *P A V Y E.*

The Speakers in this T R A G E D Y.

P *Hillippo Caraſſa,*	Duke of Pavy.
Paulo Baglione,	Vnckle to the Dutcheſſe.
Fernando	Favorite to the Duke.
Ferentes	A wanton Courtier.
Roſeilli	A young Nobleman.
Petruchio	⎱ Two Counſel-
Nibraſſa	⎰ lors of State.
D'auolos	Secretary to the Duke.
Mauruccio	An old Antike.
Giacopo	Servant to *Mauruccio.*
Attendants.	

Women.

B *Iancha*	The Dutcheſſe.
Fiormonda	The Dukes Siſter.
Colona	Daughter to *Petruchio.*
Iulia	Daughter to *Nibraſſa.*
Morona	an old Lady.

Dedicatory letter, commendatory verse by James Shirley, and dramatis personae from the 1633 quarto edition of Love's Sacrifice
(Bodleian Library, Oxford)

volos can point to real evidence in substantiating his accusations, whereas Iago must manufacture his proofs out of thin air and Othello's jealous imagination. Perhaps Ford was trying to correct Shakespeare and show how a true tragedy of jealousy should be written. And yet of the two, it is *Othello* which makes by far the more convincing impression as a drama. Shakespeare makes his tragedy grow out of the natures of his characters so that the story unfolds with a sense of dramatic inevitability. Ford, by contrast, attempts to generate interest, not by following a single intense plot line, but by continually playing with his audience: misleading them, arousing false expectations, springing shocking reversals on them, and in general working to keep them off-balance at all times. In the process, he bends his characters to fit a contrived dramatic pattern to the point where they begin to dissolve as people with firm characters and

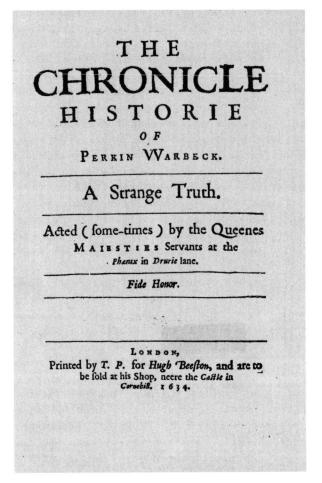

Title page for the 1634 quarto edition of Ford's history play about the last major challenger to the legitimacy of the Tudor line of the British monarchy (King's College, Cambridge)

turn into a series of flexible stage reactions. For example, one comes away from the play with no consistent impression of Bianca. At first she seems to resist Fernando's advances completely, then she seems to want to yield to him completely, and finally she seems determined to resist him completely again. One gets the impression that Ford was thinking in terms of individual brilliant scenes without considering how they might add up to a coherent dramatic whole. Critics have argued that *Love's Sacrifice* achieves a certain consistency through an underlying philosophy of Platonic love derived from a cult which flourished in the court of Charles I under the patronage of his French Queen, Henrietta Maria. But once again this seems to be a case of critics looking for a moral message in Ford, when he was largely concerned with keeping his audience on the edges of their seats.

The one play Ford wrote with any genuine depth is *Perkin Warbeck*, published in 1634. *The Broken Heart* may be the most distinctively "Fordian" of his works and *'Tis Pity She's a Whore* the most theatrically exciting, but *Perkin Warbeck* is his most satisfying work of art, coherent in conception, consistent in execution, and thought-provoking in its implications. It tells the story of the last of the major challenges to the legitimacy of the Tudor line, the appearance of the Yorkist pretender Perkin Warbeck, who claimed to be the younger of Edward IV's two sons (the princes Richard III was supposed to have murdered in the Tower of London). Striving for historical accuracy, Ford based his account on two sources, Thomas Gainsford's *True and Wonderful History of Perkin Warbeck* (1618) and Francis Bacon's *History of the Reign of King Henry VII* (1622). Following Bacon's lead, Ford portrays Henry VII as the model of a modern king, efficient in his administration, concerned about the financial basis of his rule, and never letting any idealistic principles or romantic illusions stand in the way of the realistic securing and exercising of his power. What is lacking in Henry VII is the poetry of kingship, and that is just what the pretender Perkin is able to supply in abundance. Perkin has all the trappings of a king without the substance: he knows how to speak nobly, always has the right gesture at his command, and maintains a regal bearing even in defeat. Though Ford leaves little doubt that Perkin is in fact an impostor, he departs from his sources and never shows the pretender admitting that he is not what he claims to be. We are never sure whether Perkin is consciously trying to deceive the world or is somehow himself deluded by the role he had adopted.

As a result, *Perkin Warbeck* takes on a very modern quality, as if it were a play by Luigi Pirandello or perhaps the William Butler Yeats who wrote *The Player Queen* (1922). Ford's theme seems to be that the player king is in some respects more kinglike than the real king. It is Perkin who inspires the kind of personal loyalty in his followers that one associates with feudal monarchy in all its glory. To add to the romantic aura that surrounds Perkin, Ford gives him the one love interest in the play. He is married to a kinswoman of the Scottish King, Lady Katherine Gordon, who remains faithful to him even when he is captured and sentenced to death by Henry. But Perkin's nobility has a fairy-tale quality to it. He can sound regal in his speeches, but he cannot perform the deeds needed to back up those speeches. In the end he seems to have stepped out of the pages of some book of Arthurian romance and unfortunately to have wandered into a very real world of Machiavellian statecraft and diplomacy, which swiftly destroys him. His chivalry and courtliness, however admirable as personal qualities, are no match for the hardheaded, down-to-earth politics of Henry VII. As a measure of Perkin's failure in worldly terms, Ford shows King James of Scotland, who initially supports the pretender's claim to the throne, gradually coming over to the Tudor party and abandoning the would-be Yorkists. But even in defeat—one might say above all in defeat—Perkin wins our sympathy. His is the pathos of a perpetually lost cause, and one inevitably thinks of *Waverley* when reading Ford's play and of the parallels in Walter Scott's romantic treatment of the doomed supporters of the Stuart pretender. (Both the Ford play and the Scott novel contrast a modern, bourgeois England with a Scotland more in touch with a heroic, aristocratic past.) Living in a world of dreams and poetic aspirations, Perkin has the luxury of never having to dirty his hands with the kind of difficult deeds real kings are called upon to perform. It is easy to be perfectly noble if one never has to get down to the business of actually ruling.

In writing a history play in the 1630s Ford realized that he was attempting to revive a genre that had long been "out of fashion" (to quote his prologue). He clearly had Shakespeare's history plays in mind; one might in fact argue that Ford's choice of subject matter was an attempt to fill in the one gap Shakespeare had left in his sequence, the period between *Richard III* and *Henry VIII*. The history play which seems to have influenced *Perkin Warbeck* most is *Richard II*. Many critics have seen the contrast between Perkin and Henry VII as a re-creation of the contrast between Richard II and and Henry Bolingbroke. Though coming late in the development of the genre, indeed at the very end, *Perkin Warbeck* can justifiably lay claim to being the finest history play in English after Shakespeare. If Ford does not equal Shakespeare's achievement it is because, unlike Shakespeare's protagonists, his main character is not as actively engaged in the process of history. Though Perkin is a historical figure, in a sense history has passed him by; he is a walking anachronism trying to live by a code of kingship now outmoded by the English civil wars. Thus Perkin imperceptibly passes out of the realm of historical action into the realm of pure poetry. His antagonist, Henry, finally expresses his contempt for the pretender in theatrical terms: "The player's on the stage still, 'tis his part;/'A does but act. . . . The lesson, prompted and well conn'd, was moulded/Into familiar dialogue, oft rehearsed/Till, learnt by heart, 'tis now receiv'd for truth." As a man for whom life has become an act, Perkin Warbeck is arguably the quintessential Fordian dramatic figure.

If one had to select a single play that brings the great era of Renaissance drama to a close, *Perkin Warbeck* would be an excellent choice. The era in effect began with the titanic figure of Marlowe's Tamburlaine, who is able to conquer cities merely with the power of his words. Perkin speaks the language of a king, but when he and his party try to talk one of Henry's strongholds into yielding, its defenders stand firm. In Ford's play reality no longer yields to the power of poetry: in fact, reality and poetry seem to be separating out into two distinct realms, with Henry ruling one and Perkin the other. Thus in *Perkin Warbeck* the interaction of poetry and reality, which had given life to so many Renaissance dramas, ceases to be a viable possibility. With reality becoming prosaic and poetry losing touch with reality, it becomes difficult to write the kind of poetic drama that had made Renaissance theater so powerful. Ford himself never seems to have been able to equal his level of achievement in *Perkin Warbeck*. His two plays published after *Perkin Warbeck* show a sad decline in quality, but whether this is to be attributed to the exhaustion of his creative powers we cannot be sure, especially since they may have been written earlier and merely published later.

The Fancies Chaste and Noble, a tragicomedy published in 1638, is Ford's one genuinely repellant work. He titillates his audience with all sorts of sexual innuendo and then in the end tries to show that everything in the play was actually innocent.

The Scene,
The Continent of Great Britayne.

The Persons presented.

Henry the seaventh.
Dawbney.
Sir *William Stanly.*
Oxford.
Surrey.
Bishop of *Durham.*
Vrswicke Chaplaine to
King *Henry.*
Sir *Robert Clifford.*
Lambert Simnell.
Hialas a Spanish Agent.
Constable, Officers, Ser-
vingmen, and Souldiers.

Iames the 4th King of *Scotl.*
Earle of *Huntley.*
Earle of *Crawford.*
Lord *Dalieil.*
Marchmount a He-
rauld.

Perkin Warbeck.
Frion his Secretarie.
Mayor of Cork.
Heron a Mercer.
Sketon a Taylor.
Astly a Scrivener.

Women.

Ladie *Katherine Gourdon,* ——wife to *Perkin,*
Countesse of *Crawford.*
Iane Douglas —— Lady *Kathi.* mayd.

TO

PROLOGVE.

STudyes haue, of this Nature, been of late
So out of fashion, so vnfollow'd; that
It is become more Iustice, to revine
The antick follyes of the Times, then strine
To countenance wise Industrie : no want
Of Art, doth render witt, or lame, or scant,
Or slothfull, in the purchase of fresh bayes;
But want of Truth in Them, who giue the prayse
To their selfe-loue, presuming to out-doe
The Writer, or (for need) the Actor's too.
But such THIS AVTHOVR'S silence best besits's,
Who bidd's Them, be in loue, with their owne witt's:
From Him, to cleerer Iudgement's, wee can say,
Hee shew's a Historie, couch't in a Play:
A Historie of noble mention, knowne,
Famous, and true : most noble, 'cause our owne :
Not forg'd from Italie, from Fraunce, from Spaine,
But Chronicled at Home; as rich in strayne
Of braue Attempts, as ever, fertile Rage
In Action, could beget to grace the Stage,
Wee cannot limitt Scenes, for the whole Land
It selfe, appeard too narrow to with-stand
Competitors for Kingdomes: nor is heere
Vnnecessary mirth forc't, to indeere
A multitude; on these two, rest's the Fate
Of worthy expectation; TRVTH and STATE.

THE

THE
CHRONICLE
HISTORIE OF
PERKIN WARBECK.

Actus primus, Scæna prima.

Enter *King* Henry, Durham, Oxford, Surrey, *Sir* Wil-
liam Stanly, *Lord Chamberlaine, Lord* Dawbny.
The King supported to his Throne by Stanly *and*
Durham.   *A Guard.*

King. STill to be haunted; still to be pursued,
Still to be frighted with false apparitions
Of pageant Majestie, and new-coynd greatnesse,
As if wee were a mockery King in state;
Onely ordaind to lauish sweat and blond
In scorne and laughter to the ghosts of *Yorke,*
Is all below our merits; yet (my Lords,
My friends and Counsailers) yet we sit fast
In our owne royall birth-right; the rent face
And bleeding wounds of *England's* slaughterd people,
Haue beene by vs (as by the best Physitian)
At last both throughly Cur'd, and set in safetie;
And yet for all this glorious worke of peace
Our selfe is scarce secure.

B   *Duri* The

Epilogue.

HEre ha's appear'd, though in a severall fashion,
The Threats of Majestie; the strength of passion;
Hopes of an Empire; change of fortunes; All
What can to Theater's of Greatnesse fall;
Proving their weake foundations : who will please
Amongst such severall Sight's, to censure These
No birth's abortive, nor a bastard-brood
(Shame to a parentage, or fosterhood)
May warrant by their loues, all just excuses,
And often finde a welcome to the Muses.

FINIS.

Dramatis personae, prologue, first page of act one, and epilogue from the 1634 quarto edition of Perkin Warbeck
(King's College, Cambridge)

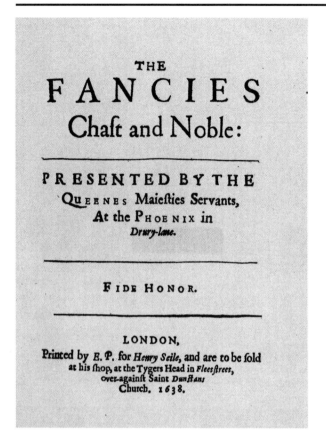

THE
FANCIES
Chaſt and Noble:

PRESENTED BY THE
Queenes Maieſties Servants,
At the Phoenix in
Drury-lane.

FIDE HONOR.

LONDON,
Printed by E. P. for *Henry Seile*, and are to be ſold
at his ſhop, at the Tygers Head in *Fleetſtreet,*
over-againſt Saint *Dunſtans*
Church. 1638.

Title page for the 1638 quarto edition of the Ford play that most closely follows the model of Francis Beaumont and John Fletcher's popular tragicomedies (Bodleian Library, Oxford)

Set in Sienna, the play seems to portray a thoroughly corrupt world in which a young man named Livio is willing to advance his own career by making a whore out of his sister Castamela. He sends her off to the court of the Marquis Octavio, where she joins three young ladies collectively known as "the Fancies." All sorts of rumors circulate concerning the Marquis's collection of females, from the suggestion that he is running a harem to supply his lust to the equally damning assertion that he is impotent and merely keeps the women around for show. Ford fills the play with characters with equally sordid reputations. In the end we learn that the "Fancies" are actually Octavio's nieces, three orphans he has brought up carefully and chastely. All the other characters with reputations for lewdness turn out to be equally misrepresented in Sienna.

Based on the epilogue, one could try to read a moral lesson out of *The Fancies Chaste and Noble* about not trusting first impressions or common opinion. But judging by the way Ford handles the material, he seems to have been interested solely in exploiting it for its prurient interest. The audience cannot help feeling cheated by the end of the play. What drama Ford generates depends wholly on his withholding of information from his characters and the audience. In its dramaturgy, *The Fancies Chaste and Noble* resembles the work of Francis Beaumont and John Fletcher rather than that of Shakespeare. Ford is skillful in the way he manipulates and misleads his viewers or readers, but the skill serves no real artistic purpose. Despite its title, *The Fancies Chaste and Noble* comes as close to pornography as any English Renaissance drama. That all turns out to have been chaste does not make the play noble; indeed it only underlines its hollowness.

The Lady's Trial, published in 1639, is probably Ford's last attempt to come to terms with *Othello*. He tells the story of a Genoese nobleman and soldier named Auria, who has to leave behind his beautiful wife, Spinella, while, like Othello, he goes off to war against the Turks (as a reward for his services Auria becomes governor of Corsica, rather than Cyprus). Auria's best friend, Aurelio, warns him against leaving Spinella alone and unprotected, and in Auria's absence Aurelio becomes convinced that she is having an affair with a young lord named Adurni, especially when he breaks in upon them having supper together. As usual Ford fills the play with subplots which add to the atmosphere of sordidness and sexual infidelity. But Spinella is innocent and was in fact rejecting Adurni's advances when Aurelio discovered them together. Nevertheless, goaded into suspicion by Aurelio, Auria, once he returns to Genoa, feels that he has to subject Spinella to a mock trial. She acquits herself well and in the end is reconciled with her husband.

Ford seems to be going out of his way to write a play in which sexual jealousy does *not* lead to violence and tragedy. Once again, one might read *The Lady's Trial* as an attempt to "correct" *Othello*. As in *Love's Sacrifice*, Ford provides a more substantial basis for his hero's jealousy, and this time the lady's accuser is no villain but a friend genuinely interested in Auria's welfare. Ford might be trying to show a couple coping rationally with a situation that destroyed Othello and Desdemona. Auria has cause to distrust Spinella: he, like Othello, has married a woman much younger than he and, as he says: "disproportion/In years, amongst the married, is a reason/For change of pleasures." Nevertheless, Auria struggles hard to maintain his faith in Spinella and argues to Aurelio: "he deserves no wife/Of worthy quality who does not trust/Her virtue in the proofs of any danger," which might serve as Ford's comment on Othello. In contrast to Desdemona, Spinella will not let anyone get away with falsely accusing her and gives a spirited defense of herself at her "trial." In a way, *The Lady's Trial* is *Othello* with a happy ending presented as the more likely outcome of such a domestic broil. All that is missing from the play is, of course, Othello and Desdemona, he with the profound anguish of his great soul and she with her unquestioning faith in her chosen lord. But perhaps Ford is not consciously commenting on *Othello* in *The Lady's Trial,* but simply searching, as in *The Fancies Chaste and Noble,* for any new dramatic formula to keep his audiences interested. When the theatrical convention was that the slightest hint of sexual infidelity might lead to marital tragedy, to show a couple working out their problems with a degree of candor and emotional restraint became a real novelty on the stage.

One remaining play has come to be included in the Ford canon, a tragicomedy called *The Queen,* published anonymously in 1653. There is no external evidence for attributing the play to Ford, but on the basis of a few verbal parallels and a general resemblance to the situation in a number of Ford's plays, several twentieth-century scholars have claimed that Ford is the author of *The Queen.* The play weaves together two basic plots. One is the story of the Queen of Arragon, who saves a rebel named Alphonso from a sentence of death and marries him, only to have him banish her from his presence, until his adviser Muretto awakens his love for her by first awakening his jealousy, falsely accusing the Queen of having an affair with a young lord at court. The other is the story of the Queen's great general, Velasco, who, out of devotion to his beloved Salassa, consents to refuse all fighting and act like a coward, much to his public disgrace. The two plots come together when Velasco is called upon to serve as the Queen's champion once Alphonso formally accuses her of infidelity. The queen's name is cleared, and all problems are resolved as Velasco weds Salassa and the Queen and Alphonso are reunited. The fact that *The Queen* has certain elements of *Othello* in it, in particular Muretto's Iago-like role in arousing Alphonso's suspicions, suggests that Ford may have had a hand in the play, but it is hardly conclusive. The way the play deals with the perversities of romantic love, and especially Muretto's scheme for curing Alphonso of his misogyny, suggests that *The Queen* may be a companion piece to *The Lover's Melancholy.*

But the aesthetic quality of the play is so low that it could just as easily be the work of an imitator of Ford. One wonders why anyone would go out of his way to include the play in the Ford canon: it adds nothing to our understanding of his art or to our appreciation of his skill or range as a playwright.

The large number of titles associated with Ford's name, as well as the substantial number of plays which have actually come down to us, suggests that he was one of the most successful dramatists of his era. Though his plays have not become standard theatrical repertory, neither have they suffered the total eclipse many Renaissance dramas have undergone. Ford was occasionally revived in the Restoration era: Samuel Pepys attended both *'Tis Pity She's a Whore* and *The Lady's Trial,* neither of which he liked. There are records of performances of *The Lover's Melancholy* and *Perkin Warbeck* in the eighteenth century. The Jacobite threat

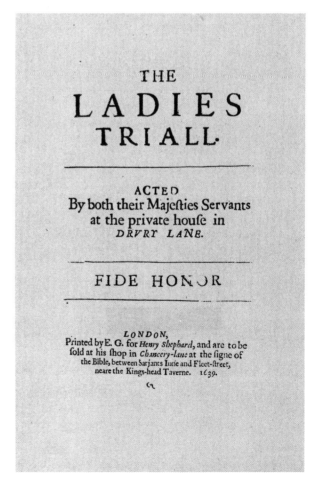

Title page for the 1639 quarto edition of the last play by Ford that is believed to have been staged during his lifetime (Cambridge University Library)

seems to have kept interest in *Perkin Warbeck* alive. It was reprinted in 1714 and was performed at the Goodman's Fields theater on 19 December 1745, presumably as a warning against the latest Stuart uprising. Given its purpose, the play was revised to make Perkin a less attractive character in this production.

In the nineteenth century, Charles Lamb rediscovered Ford and championed him in his *Specimens of English Dramatic Poets* (1808), calling him "of the first order of poets." Ford was soon attacked by some powerful critics, including Francis Jeffrey and William Hazlitt, who said that Ford's plays "seem painted on gauze, or spun out of cobwebs." Critical opinion has swung back and forth between these two extremes ever since, with some critics hailing Ford as a major dramatic and poetic talent and others assailing his works as superficial and empty. The truth lies somewhere in between these two positions. At his worst, Ford could be very bad indeed, but at his best, he was a master dramatic craftsman, and even in the face of the massive accumulated achievement of English Renaissance drama, he managed to carve out a distinctive place for himself. He clearly deserves his current ranking as the best of the Caroline dramatists and one of the most important in the whole Renaissance era. He continues to attract a great deal of attention from critics, and interpretations of his work as a whole and of individual plays have been proliferating. Measured by the demanding standard which in a way he himself invites—the plays of Shakespeare—Ford inevitably appears inferior and lacking in depth. But to be forced to create in the wake of Shakespeare was no easy task, and Ford did not shun the challenge. In two of his best plays, *'Tis Pity She's a Whore* and *Perkin Warbeck*, he showed that something could still be done in genres Shakespeare seemed to have staked out for himself, and

in *The Broken Heart* Ford created a work uniquely his own in style and subject matter. Though not uniform in quality, Ford's plays are at least varied in theme and tone and together constitute one of the most impressive bodies of achievement in Renaissance drama.

References:

Donald K. Anderson, Jr., "John Ford," in *The Later Jacobean and Caroline Dramatists,* edited by Terence P. Logan and Denzell S. Smith (Lincoln: University of Nebraska Press, 1978), pp. 120-151;

Anderson, *John Ford* (New York: Twayne, 1972);

Anne Barton, "He That Plays the King: Ford's *Perkin Warbeck* and the Stuart History Play," in *English Drama: Forms and Development,* edited by Marie Axton and Raymond Williams (Cambridge: Cambridge University Press, 1977), pp. 69-93;

T. S. Eliot, "John Ford," in his *Selected Essays* (New York: Harcourt, Brace, 1950), pp. 170-180;

Una Ellis-Fermor, *The Jacobean Drama* (London: Methuen, 1936);

Arthur Kirsch, *Jacobean Dramatic Perspectives* (Charlottesville: University Press of Virginia, 1972);

Clifford Leech, *John Ford and the Drama of His Time* (London: Chatto & Windus, 1957);

Robert Ornstein, *The Moral Vision of Jacobean Tragedy* (Madison: University of Wisconsin Press, 1960);

Irving Ribner, *Jacobean Tragedy* (London: Methuen, 1962);

L. G. Salingar, "The Decline of Tragedy," in *The Age of Shakespeare,* edited by Boris Ford (Harmondsworth, U.K.: Penguin, 1955);

George F. Sensabaugh, *The Tragic Muse of John Ford* (Stanford: Stanford University Press, 1944).

Henry Glapthorne
(July 1610-1643?)

Charles L. Squier
University of Colorado-Boulder

PLAY PRODUCTIONS: *Argalus and Parthenia,* London, Cockpit theater, between 1632 and 1639;

The Lady's Privilege, London, Cockpit theater, between 1632 and 1640;

Albertus Wallenstein, London, Globe theater, between 1634 and 1639;

The Lady Mother, London, probably Salisbury Court theater, probably 1635;

The Hollander, London, Cockpit theater, licensed 12 March 1636;

Wit in a Constable (perhaps a revision of an earlier play), London, Cockpit theater, 1639.

BOOKS: *The Tragedy of Albertus Wallenstein* (London: Printed by T. Paine for George Hutton, 1639);

Argalus and Parthenia (London: Printed by R. Bishop for Daniel Pakeman, 1639);

Poëms (London: Printed by R. Bishop for Daniel Pakeman, 1639);

The Ladies Priviledge (London: Printed by J. Okes for Francis Constable, 1640);

The Hollander (London: Printed by J. Okes for A. Wilson, 1640);

Wit in a Constable (London: Printed by J. Okes for Francis Constable, 1640);

White-Hall: A Poem (London: Printed for Francis Constable, 1643);

His Majesties Gracious Answer to the Message Sent from the Honourable City of London (London: Printed for Thomas Massam, 1643);

Revenge for Honour, by Glapthorne, wrongly attributed to George Chapman (London: Printed for Richard Marriott, 1654).

Editions: *The Plays and Poems of Henry Glapthorne,* 2 volumes, edited by R. H. Shepherd (London: John Pearson, 1874)—comprises *Argalus and Parthenia, The Hollander, Wit in a Constable, The Tragedy of Albertus Wallenstein, The Lady's Privilege,* and *Poems;*

Revenge for Honour, in *The Tragedies of George Chapman,* edited by Thomas Marc Parrott (London: Rutledge/New York: Dutton, 1910);

The Lady Mother (Oxford: Printed for the Malone Society at the University Press, 1958).

OTHER: Thomas Beedome, *Poems, Divine and Humane,* edited by Glapthorne (London: Printed by E. P. for John Sweeting, 1641).

In less than ten years Henry Glapthorne wrote seven surviving plays, and another four lost plays (*The Duchess of Fernandia, The Noble Husbands, The Noble Trial, The Vestal*) are attributed to him. This production record, as well as a number of his poems ("Prologue to a reviv'd Vacation Play" and "Prologue for *Ezekiel Fen* at his first Acting a Mans Part," for example), probably mark him as a professional playwright attached to a theater and writing speculatively or under contract. A. H. Bullen, who included Glapthorne's *The Lady Mother* in *A Collection of Old English Plays* (1882-1887), observed correctly that "Any one who has had the patience to read the Plays of Henry Glapthorne cannot fail to be amused by the bland persistence with which certain passages are reproduced in one play after another. Glapthorne's stock of fancies was not very extensive, but he puts himself to considerable pains to make the most of them." Glapthorne borrowed from other writers with nearly equal assiduity. He was not an original or especially skilled playwright, but his plays are at least representative of the stock fare of the Caroline stage and illustrate the dramatic practice of a competent, if undistinguished, professional playwright.

Little is known of Glapthorne's life, and contemporary references to him are few. His dedication of his poem *White-Hall* to Richard Lovelace— as well as other dedications and poems—points to his royalist sympathies, but no commendatory verses are directed to Glapthorne, and his social and intellectual contacts can be reconstructed only in a limited way. Theatrically he can be linked to the Cavalier court dramatists and to playwrights in the traditions of both Ben Jonson and John Fletcher.

ARGALUS
AND
PARTHENIA.

As it hath been Acted at the Court before their MAIESTIES:

AND

At the Private-House in DRURY LANE,

By their MAIESTIES Servants.

By HEN. GLAPTHORNE.

LONDON,
Printed by R. BISHOP for DANIEL PAKEMAN,
at the Raine-bow neere the Inner Temple Gate.
1639.

Title page for the 1639 quarto edition of the play that Glapthorne based on four chapters in book one of Sir Philip Sidney's Arcadia
(Henry E. Huntington Library and Art Gallery)

He was baptized on 28 July 1610 in Cambridgeshire at St. Andrew's Church in Whittlesey, the fourth son of a gentleman, Thomas Glapthorne, and the first surviving son of Thomas's third wife, Faith Hatcliffe. The Glapthornes appear to have been a prosperous family. His father became bailiff to Lady Hatton, Sir Edward Coke's wife. His half-brother, George, was a justice of the peace who seems to have raised the ire of his puritanical neighbors and in 1654 was accused of being "a common Swearer, a common Curser, a frequenter of Ale-houses, and an upholder of those of evill fame, . . . a companion of lewd women . . . not fit to be a Law-maker or Parliament man. . . ."

Henry Glapthorne's early education is conjectural, J. H. Walter in a 1936 letter to the *Times*

Literary Supplement opting for Peterborough and R. H. Shepherd, editor of *The Plays and Poems of Henry Glapthorne* (1874), suggesting St. Paul's. His matriculation as a pensioner at Corpus Christi College, Cambridge, at Easter 1624 is the only surviving academic record. Other records are equally sparse.

His mother died in September 1625, and his sister-in-law Priscilla Glapthorne, elegized in his *Poems,* died in August 1629. He may have arrived in London by 1631, and *Argalus and Parthenia,* probably his first play, is likely to have been composed around 1633; but the first certain date is that of the licensing for the stage by Sir Henry Herbert of *Love's Trial, or The Hollander* in March 1636. His *Poëms,* which appeared in 1639, includes one titled "To Lucinda. He being in Prison," but this poem is in a group of conventional verses to one of those insubstantial ladies of seventeenth-century amorous poetry and is doubtful autobiography. Glapthorne edited Thomas Beedome's poems in 1641 and wrote two commendatory poems and the address to the reader. The volume included commendatory verses by the playwright Thomas Nabbes and by Edward May, an actor with King Charles's Men and later with the King's Revels; both were likely to have been Glapthorne's friends.

Five of Glapthorne's own plays were published in 1639 and 1640. This rather odd circumstance suggests a break with the theater and a need for quick cash, perhaps to tide him over until he possibly obtained a post as groom-porter in a nobleman's household. *White-Hall,* dedicated to "my noble Friend and Gossip, Captain *Richard Lovelace,*" which—according to the title page—was written in 1642, was published in 1643. The speaker of the title poem, the palace itself, laments, from a royalist point of view, the current state of Britain. The other poems are elegies to court luminaries, and Glapthorne's attachment to the royalist cause is clear. The baptism of his daughter Lovelace was recorded on 1 July 1642 and the death of his wife, Susan, on 22 March 1643. On 12 January 1643 Richard Herne testified before the House of Lords that "he printed a book, intituled, His Majesty's gracious Answer to the Message sent from the Honourable City of London, concerning Peace: and he said he had it of one Glapthorne, who lived in Fetter Lane." In February 1643 "Glapthorne the Porter," along with Herne and others, was summoned to the House of Lords. Herne was committed to Fleet Prison, but Glapthorne's fate is unknown. He was clearly engaged in royalist political work, and it is quite likely he died in its cause. King Charles

wrote to "Clapthorne Esq." in 1663 and there is a reference to Mr. Clapthorne, a "Poore Knight of Windsor," but it is unlikely that either of these references is to Henry Glapthorne, and he probably died in the 1640s.

Argalus and Parthenia, presumably his first play, is a pastoral tragedy with an overlay of Court Platonism and *préciosité.* It is based on Sir Philip Sidney's *Arcadia,* book one, chapters five through eight. The mutual love of Argalus and Parthenia is thwarted by the marital ambitions of the rough and boastful soldier Demagorgas. When Parthenia rejects him, Demagorgas destroys her beauty by sprinkling a poisonous juice on her face. Argalus, a true Neoplatonic, is still ready to marry her for her "excellent mind," but Parthenia refuses and disappears. When she surfaces again, her beauty is restored, but she denies that she is really Parthenia. After a bout of romantic riddling all is sorted out, and the lovers are united with epithalamic song and dance. Two acts remain, however, in which the conflicts of love, honor, and friendship result in the deaths of both Argalus and Parthenia, through chivalric conflict with Amphialus. A comic subplot involves the clownish shepherd Strephon, whose boast, "My body is the garden, though it walk;/And ther's no woman but may well, To th' worst part about it smell," is representative of much of the humor of the play.

Argalus and Parthenia is a court entertainment in style and action. Apart from the crudities of the comic subplot, the language of the play mixes heroic, pastoral, and courtly romantic dictions. The exaggerated romantic stances and bursts of Neoplatonism were clearly aimed to meet the fashionable tastes of Queen Henrietta Maria and her courtiers. The verse, however, is irregular and inept; *Argalus and Parthenia* is a weak play, but Glapthorne's command of the courtly idiom was clearly competent enough to fill an idle evening at court.

It was acted by Beeston's Boys, but, as G. E. Bentley points out, Beeston did not include it in his repertory list for protection by the Lord Chamberlain. Nonetheless, it was revived in the Restoration, and Samuel Pepys saw it three times, concluding, "though pleasant for the dancing and singing, I do not find it good for any wit or design therein." At one of the productions, however, he revised his opinion because the actress playing Parthenia "had the best legs that ever I saw, and I was very pleased with it." Pepys is often a questionable critic, but in the case of *Argalus and Parthenia* he is sound enough. It is the sort of play in which an actress's legs and the details of production will make a major difference.

The Lady's Privilege is a considerable improvement over *Argalus and Parthenia*. It is a well-constructed and rather skilled tragicomedy which uses virtually all the commonplaces of Caroline drama—love and honor, love versus friendship, honor versus the law, love questions, disguise, and a mixture of heroic and precious language. The title page of the quarto boasts that it was played twice at Whitehall, and it is a typical court play.

The setting is Genoa, to which Admiral Doria has returned from victory over the Turks and is caught up in the romantic complexities of the Ducal court. His beloved, Chrisea, undertakes to test his love and brings him to the brink of death. He is saved by one of those peculiar laws popular with Renaissance dramatists—in this case one that allows a condemned man to be saved by a maiden who agrees to marry him. The requisite maiden is produced, the nuptials celebrated; Chrisea then declares that she has loved Doria all along. Doria's romantic agony is increased with the revelation that the man he is supposed to have killed is alive, and it is resolved with the final revelation that his "bride" is really his loyal pageboy in female disguise. He and Chrisea are free to marry after all. The discoveries of the last act would hardly surprise any moderately alert Caroline theatergoer, but they are efficiently handled. *The Lady's Privilege* has no pretenses, but it shows Glapthorne in control of the language and themes of court *préciosité* as well as the tragicomic tradition of John Fletcher.

Albertus Wallenstein might have been a serious historical tragedy on the fall of General Wallenstein, Duke of Friedland, whose assassination was a major event in what would come to be called the Thirty Years War. Glapthorne, however, essentially depoliticizes and trivializes the historical event by turning Wallenstein into a conventional stage tyrant responsible for the death of his son and of his son's beloved.

The great General Wallenstein, forced into retirement by the emperor, responds by raising a rebellion. His English officers, opportunists ultimately loyal to the emperor, conspire against Wallenstein. The clear potential for a debate over loyalties and issues is not developed. Instead Glapthorne gives his audience a mix of rhetoric—heroic and romantic, comic, and bloody melodramatic.

Although the quarto edition of the play is dedicated to the courtier William Murray, one of the gentlemen of the bedchamber, there is no indication of a court performance. It was played at the Globe in the summer of one of the years 1634, 1635, 1638, or 1639. In 1637 Shakespeare's *Julius Caesar* was revived at the Globe, and echoes of it in *Albertus Wallenstein* suggest composition around that time. Glapthorne seizes every opportunity for a purple passage and never hesitates to slow the action for a burst of similitudes; but songs, bawdry, and murders by sword and rope are supplied in sufficient quantities for a summer audience at the Globe. At best *Albertus Wallenstein* is an interesting repository of Caroline dramatic conventions.

Like *The Lady's Privilege*, which borrows from it—or from which *The Lady Mother* borrows, depending on the resolution of the dates of composition—*The Lady Mother* is a tragicomedy filled with surprising twists and turns and tests of love. The play constantly flirts with perverse tragedy and is turned to tragicomedy by labored improbabilities. A substantial interlarding of knockabout farce underlines the play's basic lack of serious intent; it is finally a rather slipshod entertainment.

The Lady Mother was not published until A. H. Bullen edited the manuscript prompt copy in the British Library. The manuscript contains the license for the play signed by William Blagrave, Deputy to the Master of Revels, dated 15 October 1635. *The Lady Mother* was most probably acted by the King's Revels at Salisbury Court. It is difficult to believe that the players valued the play enough to keep Glapthorne from publishing it in 1640 with his other plays; perhaps even he thought it too careless and imitative a work for publication.

The Lady Mother of the title (Lady Marlove) is a widow apparently gone wrong, almost to the point of becoming a sexual monster. She nearly drives one daughter to suicide by defaming her to her suitor in a love test, and in yet another test she gets her other daughter to woo her own lover for her. The perverse potential of the love-crazed widow is pushed as far as possible with a series of revelations about the Lady Mother's increasing degeneracy.

Lady Marlove's daughters are in turn witty comic combatants in the game of love and tragicomic heroines. The play's country-house setting and drunken steward momentarily recall *Twelfth Night*, but in an instant a jealous lover appears and *Othello* is evoked. The comic turns variously involve country-versus-city jokes, fools wooing witty maidens, and the basic comic standby of drunken farce. Tragicomic heights (of a sort) are reached when Lady Marlove and her son are about to be sent off to prison, trial, and sure hanging for the murder of Thurston, suitor of Clariana. The stage direc-

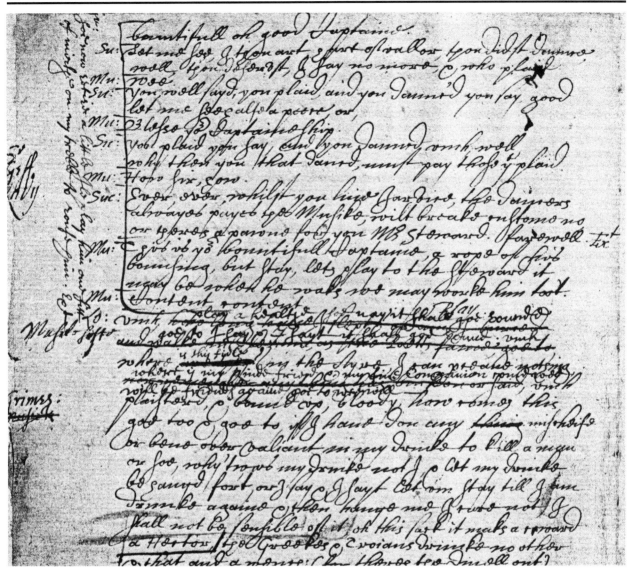

A portion of a page from the manuscript for The Lady Mother *preserved at the British Library. This manuscript is a copy made by an unknown scribe, probably from Glapthorne's foul papers at the time of the play's first production, circa 1635. The revisions on this page and throughout the manuscript are thought to be in Glapthorne's hand (MS Egerton 1994, fols 186-211, by permission of the British Library).*

tions read: "Flourishe Horrid Musicke Enter Death: Gri[mes] and furies," and a masque reveals that Thurston is alive and well, as are the presumed drowned pair of lovers, Bonville and Clarissa. *The Lady Mother* is marked by Glapthorne's notorious autoplagiarism and borrowings from others, his penchant for high-flown language, and his disinterest in motivation and character development of any sort.

The Hollander, or Love's Trial, written for Queen Henrietta's Men and inherited in the stock of plays of Their Majesties Servants, a stronger play than *The Lady Mother,* is an eclectic mix of realistic and romantic, precious comedy. The realistic portion recalls Ben Jonson's *The Alchemist*; a false Doctor of Physicke maintains a bawdy house disguised as a female hospital or, as his wife puts it, "a schoole/ For Female vaulters, and within pretence/Of giving Phy'sicke, give them an over-plus/To their disease." Other parallels are found to Jonson's *The Devil is an Ass,* and *Epicoene,* to James Shirley's *A Fine Companion,* and to Shackerley Marmion's *A Fine Companion* and *Holland's Leaguer.* The play's Jonsonian realism, however, is diffused by an equal amount of Court Platonism. The language and the matter of the play bounce back and forth with surprising

THE
HOLLANDER.

A Comedy written 1635.

The Author
HENRY GLAPTHORNE.

And now Printed as it was then Acted
at the Cock-pit in *Drury lane*, by
their Majesties Servants,
with good allowance.

And at the Court before both their
Majesties.

LONDON:
Printed by *I. Okes*, for *A. Wilson*, and
are to be sold at her shop at Grayes-
Inne Gate in Holborne. 1640.

Title page for the 1640 quarto edition of the Glapthorne play that was produced by Queen Henrietta's Men in 1636 and later by Their Majesties Servants (Henry E. Huntington Library and Art Gallery)

rapidity between realistic gulling comedy and ornate, highly rhetorical, romantic preciosity.

Realistic comedy is developed around the affectation of the naturalized Dutchman, Sconce, who is inducted into the "Knights of the Twibill" by a set of cheating rogues and the humors of the excessively jealous Sir Martin Yellow. The major romantic plot brings together the reformed rake Freewit and the precious Mistress Knowworth, whose exalted standards of sexual conduct generate the complexities of the upper plot.

The Hollander is a potpourri of themes and styles. Glapthorne seems happiest when developing displays of elaborate simile-laden rhetoric. The play is most interesting for the mixture of styles it presents, a rather uneasy alliance of city realism and Court Platonism.

Glapthorne's next comedy, *Wit in a Constable*, is a more consistently Jonsonian comedy of wit. It is a lively, if unoriginal play and makes effective use of a variety of dramatic comic conventions. The witty daughter and niece of Alderman Covet are to be married to a brace of rich fools. True Wits intervene; and, after a number of contretemps, tricks, and disguises, they win the witty girls while the fools are matched to the Constable's daughters. The verbal combat of the male and female wits looks forward to William Congreve, but Glapthorne's language is coarser, and the sexual equality posited in the comedy of manners is essentially absent or at most weakly implied in Glapthorne. Constable Busie and his watch look back to Dogberry in *Measure for Measure*, and Busie dominates

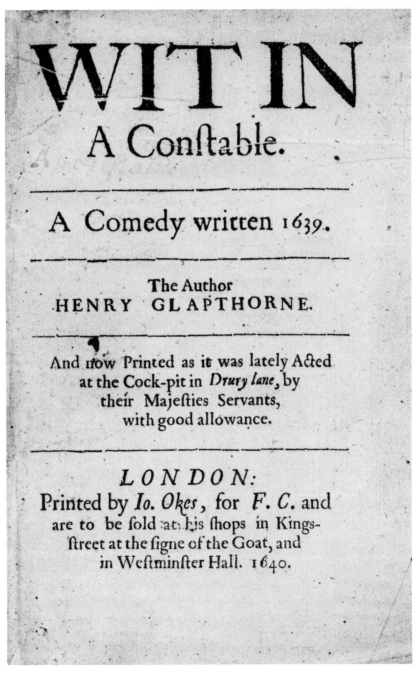

Title page for the 1640 quarto edition of the Glapthorne play that was first produced in 1639 and revived three times during the Restoration (Henry E. Huntington Library and Art Gallery)

the last act, which contains lively tavern comedy and boisterous song as well as the obligatory unwinding of the marriage plots. In *Wit in a Constable* Glapthorne shows himself in command of the comic idiom of his day, producing a lively and competent, if uninspired and unoriginal, work. Records of three Restoration productions attest to a degree of popularity.

Glapthorne's last extant play, *Revenge for Honour,* was included in a list of plays entered in the Stationers' Register by Richard Marriott in 1653 as "The Paraside or Revenge for Honor by Henry Glapthorne"; but when Marriott published the play in 1654, the quarto was attributed to George Chapman. The attribution to Chapman was probably a sales device on Marriott's part. Everything about the play, especially the extensive borrowing of Glapthorne's own lines from his other plays, points to Glapthorne as the author of *Revenge for Honour.*

It is one of Glapthorne's better entertainments, written in the dramatic style of John Fletcher and no doubt improved by revision. The action is set in the exotic court of Almanzor, the Caliph of Arabia, where two half-brothers, reminiscent of Edmund and Edgar in *King Lear,* struggle for power and the love of the immoral Caropia, wife of a "rough lord, a soldier" named Mura.

The Caliph's elder son, Abilqualit, has been having an affair with Caropia, who earlier had rejected the advances of the villainous younger son, Abrahen; the issue of honor arises when Abilqualit confesses to an accusation of rape in order to protect Caropia's reputation. This honorable confession, however, sentences him to the Arabian punishment for rape, blinding.

The action of the play rises to a series of horrific events and surprising turns. After the sentence of blinding has apparently been executed on Abilqualit and seems to have resulted in his death, the Caliph is grief stricken. He wipes his tears with a poisoned handkerchief—conveniently left on Abilqualit's body by his wicked brother—and dies. Abrahen, assuming his brother dead, seizes the throne and wins the treacherous Caropia's hand, but Abilqualit is not dead and stages a counterrevolution. Abrahen then stabs Caropia and kills himself by kissing the poisoned handkerchief. Before she dies, Caropia, a thorough villainess, gratuitously adds to the carnage by fatally stabbing Abilqualit, who has breath enough to moralize before he dies, warning his successor to "shun the temptings" of "lascivious glances," prompting his friend Selinthus to conclude " 'Las, good prince/ He'll die indeed, I fear, he is so full/Of serious thoughts and counsels." The deliberate play for a laugh at the end of the tragedy effectively undermines any tragic pretensions. *Revenge for Honour* boils the pot with a full range of conventional scenes and language; turn follows turn; rhetorical displays, surprise, and dramatic variety are the limits of Glapthorne's ambitions.

If one adds the lost plays to Glapthorne's dramatic output, his production is quantitatively quite respectable for a professional playwright. His inclination to borrow from himself and the frequent looseness of structure in his plays seem to indicate haste and a certain haphazardness. He is not a polished playwright nor original in any way. To call him a dramatic hack may be harsh but accurate. He was one of those playwrights who kept the stage alive with a steady flow of material. He worked easily within the dramatic conventions of the day, and Jonsonian comic realism, Fletcherian tragicomedy, and the *préciosité* of Court Platonism were all in his versifying repertoire. His plays are the work of a theatrical journeyman and of interest as exemplars of common theatrical fare produced by such playwrights.

References:

Gerald Eades Bentley, *The Jacobean and Caroline Stage* (Oxford: Clarendon Press, 1956), IV: 473-497;

Joe Lee Davis, *The Sons of Ben: Jonsonian Comedy in Caroline England* (Detroit: Wayne State University Press, 1967);

B. S. Fields, Jr., "Sidney's Influence: the Evidence of the Publication of the History of *Argalus and Parthenia," English Language Notes,* 17 (December 1979): 98-102;

Clifford Leech, *Shakespeare's Tragedies and Other Studies in Seventeenth Century Drama* (London: Chatto & Windus, 1965);

Chester Linn Shaver, "The Life and Works of Henry Glapthorne," Ph.D. dissertation, Harvard University, 1937;

J. H. Walter, "Henry Glapthorne," *Times Literary Supplement,* 19 September 1936, p. 748;

Walter, "The Plays and Poems of Henry Glapthorne," Ph.D. dissertation, University of London, circa 1935.

Papers:

A manuscript copy of *The Lady Mother* in a scribal hand with additions and corrections possibly in the hand of the author is in the British Library (MS Egerton 1994, folios 186-211).

Thomas Goffe
(circa 1592-July 1629)

Susan Gushee O'Malley
Kingsborough Community College
City University of New York

PLAY PRODUCTIONS: *The Raging Turk, or Bajazet II,* Christ Church, Oxford, circa 1613-1618;

The Tragedy of Orestes, Christ Church, Oxford, circa 1613-1618;

The Courageous Turk, or Amurath the First, Christ Church, Oxford, 21 September 1618;

The Careless Shepherdess, attributed with reservations to Goffe, Christ Church, Oxford, circa 1618-1629(?); revised version, London, Salisbury Court theater, circa 1638;

Phoenissae, Christ Church, Oxford, 1619(?).

BOOKS: *Oratio Funebris habita in ecclesia cathedrali Christi Oxon in obitum viri omni aevo dignissimi Gulielmi Goodwin istius Ecclesiae Decami, etc.* (Oxford: Printed by J. Lichfield & J. Short, 1620);

Deliverance from the Grave. A Sermon Preached at Saint Maries Spittle in London, on Wednesday in Easter weeke last, March 28, 1627 (London: Printed by G. Purslowe for R. Mab, 1627);

The Raging Turke, or, Bajazet the Second. A Tragedie (London: Printed by A. Mathewes for R. Meighen, 1631);

The Couragious Turke, or, Amurath the First. A Tragedie (London: Printed by B. Alsop & T. Fawcett for R. Meighen, 1632);

The Tragedy of Orestes (London: Printed by J. Beale for Richard Meighen, 1633);

The Careles Shepherdess. A Tragi-Comedy Acted Before the King & Queen, attributed, with reservations, to Goffe (London: Printed for Richard Rogers & William Ley, 1656).

Edition: *A Critical Old-Spelling Edition of Thomas Goffe's "The Courageous Turk,"* edited by Susan Gushee O'Malley (New York: Garland, 1979).

OTHER: "Oratio funebris . . . in obitum H. Savilii," in *Ultima linea Savilii* (Oxford: Printed by J. Litchfield & J. Short, 1622).

Thomas Goffe had a distinguished reputation as a playwright during the seventeenth century. In the manuscript for *The Fairy King* (Bodleian MS. Rawlinson 28) Samuel Sheppard praises Goffe's tragedies and compares them to the tragedies of Euripides and Sophocles; the author of *II Crafty Cromwell,* 1648, groups Goffe with Seneca, Sophocles, Shakespeare, Ben Jonson, Euripides, John Webster, and Sir John Suckling; and Samuel Holland in *Don Zara del Fogo* (1656) makes Goffe—with Philip Massinger, Thomas Dekker, Webster, Suckling, William Cartwright, and Thomas Carew—a lifeguard for Shakespeare and John Fletcher. Only three plays are definitely the work of Goffe although many more have been attributed to him.

Thomas Goffe, the son of a clergyman, was born in Essex, England, circa 1592. He attended Westminster School as a Queen's Scholar, and he probably participated in the annual Westminster play. Goffe's fellow students at Westminster included George Herbert; Charles Chauncey, the second president of Harvard University; and the future bishops John Hacket and Henry King, the second of whom was to become Goffe's close friend. From Westminster Goffe was elected on 3 November 1609 to a scholarship for Christ Church, Oxford. After receiving his bachelor of arts from Christ Church on 17 June 1613, Goffe proceeded to take his master of arts on 20 June 1616 and his bachelor of divinity on 3 July 1623, both at Christ Church. In 11 July 1623 Goffe was licensed to preach; he was also incorporated M.A. at Cambridge in 1617.

While Goffe was at Oxford, he gained the reputation of being an able scholar, an excellent preacher, and a good playwright and poet. In 1612 Goffe composed a poem for the miscellany in tribute to Sir Thomas Bodley, and in 1619 some verses on the death of Queen Anne of Denmark, all of which are no longer extant. He also delivered two Latin orations, one at the funeral of William Godwin, the dean of Christ Church who died in 1620, and one in 1622 on the death of Sir Henry Savile, a benefactor and scholar. That Goffe was asked to deliver Savile's funeral oration was a great honor, for Savile, reputed to be the most learned scholar of his day, was warden of Merton College, Oxford, and provost of Eton; he had also helped to prepare the King James version of the Bible, had translated works by Tacitus, had edited works of Xenophon and St. Chrysostom, and had helped Bodley found his library. The funeral oration for Savile was ordered by the vice-chancellor and doctors of Oxford and was delivered publicly to the academicians at the theological school. The oration for Godwin, published at Oxford in 1620, required a second edition within the year and was published in London in 1627; the oration for Savile was published at Oxford in 1622 with verses by the poets of Oxford added to it under the title *Ultima linea Savilii.* There is speculation that Goffe wrote some of the poems in this volume as well.

Goffe was also an active playwright and actor during his stay at Christ Church. His first play was probably *The Raging Turk, or Bajazet II,* a tragedy produced at Christ Church circa 1613-1618 and published posthumously in 1631. Goffe's second play was probably *Orestes,* a tragedy produced at Christ Church circa 1613-1618 and published in 1633. It was followed by his *The Courageous Turk, or Amurath the First,* produced on 21 September 1618 at Christ Church and published in 1632. There is no internal evidence for dating these three plays. The unworkable structure, the crude dialogue, and the heavy-handed use of its source, Richard Knolles's *The Generall Historie of the Turkes,* suggests that *The Raging Turk* is Goffe's first attempt at play writing. The prologue of *The Courageous Turk* speaks of

> our hope which intends
> The sacred Muses Progeny to greet,
> Which under roofe, now the third
> time meet . . .

These lines may mean that this play was Goffe's third to be acted before the audience at Christ Church. In 1656 all three plays were published in one volume as *Three Excellent Tragedies.*

The Raging Turk is the tragedy of Emperor Bajazet II, who desperately tries to hold onto his power amid plotting sons, an usurping brother, and power-hungry bassas. When he tries to pick his successor, confusion reigns, and at least sixteen deaths occur. Bajazet is poisoned, and his grandson Solyman is crowned emperor. Goffe appears to be fascinated with the reputed evil of the Turks and their insatiable greed. Indeed, the subject of Turkish history was popular with Jacobean playwrights.

Goffe's *The Tragedy of Orestes* is the story of Aegisthus's murder of Agamemnon with Clytemnestra's help and Orestes's revenge. Unsure who murdered his father, Orestes and his friend Pylades disguise themselves and let it be rumored that they have killed themselves by jumping off a cliff. Orestes is told that if he brings the bones of his father to Canida, a wise woman who lives in a cave, she will reveal the murderer. When she reveals the truth, Orestes kills the baby born of his mother and Aegisthus and forces them to drink the child's blood. After Aegisthus and Clytemnestra are killed on stage, Orestes is denied the crown and is banished by Tyndarus, Clytemnestra's father. Electra kills herself; Strophius, Pylades's father, dies; and Orestes and Pylades die by running on each other's sword. Thus a Greek myth becomes the subject of a bloody Jacobean revenge tragedy. Although Orestes is initially treated sympathetically, he is

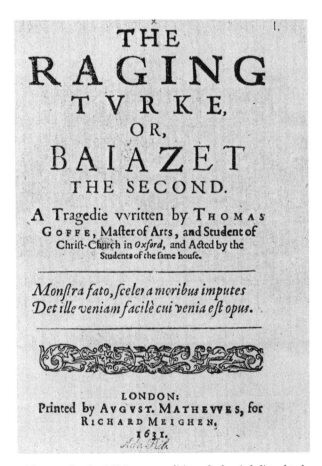

Title page for the 1631 quarto edition of what is believed to be Goffe's first play (National Library of Scotland)

punished by madness and death after he kills his mother.

Goffe's third play, *The Courageous Turk,* structurally breaks into two parts. The first, acts one and two, is concerned with Amurath's passion for his concubine Eumorphe, his officers' discontent with Amurath's affair, and Amurath's beheading of Eumorphe. The second part, acts three through five, is a series of events consisting of Amurath's various war exploits in Servia, the Christians' martial confusion, the marriage of Amurath's son Bajazet to Hatam, Amurath's conflict with his son-in-law Aladin, the mutual stabbing deaths of Amurath and the Christian Captain Cobelitz, and the raising of Bajazet to Emperor with the subsequent death of his brother Jacup. In the first part Goffe shapes his source, Knolles's "The Life of Mahomet," into a dramatic action that moves successfully to the

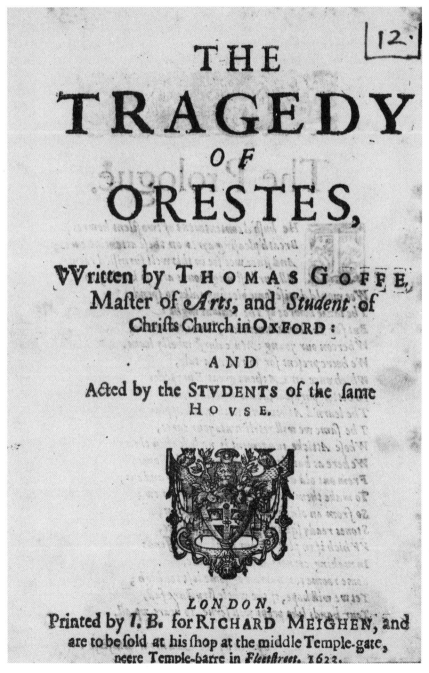

Title page for the 1633 quarto edition of one of the plays Goffe wrote while he was a student at Christ Church, Oxford (Henry E. Huntington Library and Art Gallery)

dramatic climax of the beheading of Eumorphe. In the second part Goffe borrows from his source, Knolles's "The Life of Amurath," without shaping or connecting the events into a plot. Only the dramatic confrontation of Amurath with his daughter, his grandchildren, and his son-in-law—all of whom beg Amurath to spare their lives—is as effective dramatically as the first two acts.

Criticism of *The Courageous Turk* has been unfavorable. In *Elizabethan Drama* (1908) Felix Schelling calls it "all but unendurable" because of its "outrageous rant and bombast." Adolphus Ward in *A History of English Dramatic Literature to the Death of Queen Anne* (1875) calls the play "repulsive bombast." Undoubtedly *The Courageous Turk* contains bombastic lines. The seventeenth-century audience, however, admired it because of the outrageous character of Amurath, the elaborate staging that called for flying devices and blazing heavens with comets and stars, the subject of Turkish history which fascinated the Jacobean audience with its violence and bloodiness, and Goffe's world vision of the frailty of kings and the ultimate reward given to Christians who struggle against heathens on earth. Although influenced by the tradition of revenge tragedy, in comparison with *Orestes* or *The Raging Turk*, *The Courageous Turk* is not a revenge tragedy. Hatred of the Christians and personal aggrandizement, not revenge, are what motivate Amurath.

In *Annals of English Drama 975-1700* (1964) Samuel Schoenbaum assigns to Goffe with reservations *The Careless Shepherdess*, a pastoral probably produced at Christ Church between 1618 and 1629 and later revised and produced by Queen Henrietta's Men in about 1638. W. J. Lawrence in "The Authorship of 'The Careless Shepherdess'" argues against Goffe's authorship because of the statement on the title page that *The Careless Shepherdess* was acted at Salisbury Court, a theater that opened after Goffe's death, and because of the prologue's reference to the author as alive. The catalogue of all printed plays appended to the quarto edition of *The Careless Shepherdess* also adds to the confusion over the authorship of the play. *The Raging Turk* and *The Careless Shepherdess* are omitted, and *The Courageous Turk* and *Orestes* are listed without author.

Gerald Bentley in *The Jacobean and Caroline Stage* (IV, 1956) agrees with Lawrence that the play was not written for Salisbury Court because the lease for the theater was not signed until three weeks before Goffe's burial and because Goffe's academic and clerical career made it unlikely that

he would write for a commercial theater. The play, according to Bentley, was written by Goffe and produced for an Oxford audience between September 1618, the date of the production of *The Courageous Turk*, and July 1629, the month of Goffe's death. Bentley believes, however, that the praeludium and prologue were written for a Salisbury Court production after Goffe's death.

The Careless Shepherdess is different from the three plays definitely attributed to Goffe in structure, language, and theme. It is a pastoral about two young men in love. Philaritus, a son of a wealthy man, loves a shepherdess, Arismena, against his father's wishes, while Lariscus is in love with Casterina, who will not return his affection until her banished father is restored. They are all captured by satyrs but are saved by Casterina's father, who is disguised as a satyr.

Another play attributed to Goffe is the tragedy *Phoenissae*, probably performed at Christ Church in 1619, but now lost. Plays erroneously attributed to Goffe are *I Selimus* (probably by Robert Greene), *The Second Maiden's Tragedy* (perhaps by Middleton or Massinger), and *The Bastard*.

In addition to writing plays at Oxford Goffe acted on several occasions. The prologue to *Orestes* is prefaced by lines "Spoken by the Author himselfe," and there is evidence that Goffe took the part of Polypragmaticus in Burton's Latin play *Philosophaster* on 16 February 1617. There is a surviving manuscript of actor's sides that includes the part of Polypragmaticus, the part of Amurath in *The Courageous Turk*, and the parts of Antonius and Poore in unidentified Latin and English plays respectively. These are known to have been intended for performances at Christ Church. Also appended to the actors' sides is a poem, "A Songe upon ye loss of an Actors voyce, beeinge to play a cheife part in ye Vniversitie." There is speculation that some of the parts in the actor's sides and the poem were written out by Goffe and that he took the parts of Amurath, Antonius, and Poore, in addition to that of Polypragmaticus.

After receiving a bachelor of divinity degree from Christ Church and his license to preach in July 1623, Goffe was asked to be rector of the church in East Clandon, Surrey, in the deanery of Stoke, and promised a salary of about eighty pounds a year. Although Goffe had always claimed to be an enemy of women and was described by some of his acquaintances as another Joseph Swetnam, the author of the popular pamphlet *The Arraignment of Lewd, Idle, Froward, and unconstant Women* (1615), he married the widow of his prede-

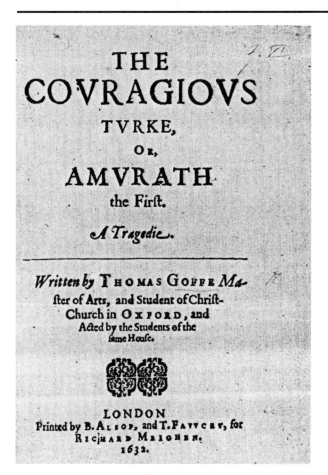

THE COVRAGIOVS

TVRKE,

OR,

AMVRATH

the Firſt.

A Tragedie.

Written by THOMAS GOFFE *Maſter of Arts, and Student of Chriſt-Church in* OXFORD, *and Acted by the Students of the ſame Houſe.*

LONDON

Printed by B. ALſop, and T. Fawcer, for
RICHARD MEIGHEN.
1632.

Title page for the 1632 quarto edition of the play performed at Christ Church, Oxford, on 21 September 1618 (British Library)

cessor, Alexander Adams. According to biographers, she and her children drove Goffe to his grave. John Aubrey in his *Brief Lives* speaks of Goffe's unfortunate marriage as follows:

> His Wife pretended to fall in love with him, by hearing him preach: Upon which, said one Thomas Thimble (one of the Squire Bedell's in Oxford, and his Confident) to him; Do not marry her: if thou dost, she will break thy Heart. He was not obsequious to his Friend's sober Advice, but for her Sake altered his Condition, and cast Anchor here.
>
> One time some of his Oxford Friends made a Visit to him. She look'd upon them with an ill Eye, as if they had come to eat her out of her House and Home (as they say). She provided a Dish of Milk, and some Eggs for Supper, and no more: They perceived her Niggardliness, and that her Husband was inwardly troubled at it (she was wearing the Breeches) so they resolv'd to be merry at Supper, and talk all in Latin, and laugh'd ex-

ceedingly. She was so vex'd at their speaking Latin, that she could not hold, but fell out a Weeping, and rose from the Table. The next day, Mr. Goffe order'd a better Dinner for them, and sent for some Wine: They were merry, and his Friends took their final Leave of Him.

> 'Twas no long Time before this Xantippe made Mr. Thimble's Prediction good; and when he died the last Words he spake were: *Oracle, Oracle, Tom Thimble,* and so he gave up the Ghost.

Another indication that Goffe remained in contact with his Oxford friends during his later years exists in the elegy written late in 1624 for Anne Berkley, the wife of his friend Henry King. In line 118 Goffe calls Anne "my dearest friend." The first ten lines illustrate the quality of this elegy:

> Hir Genial bed enrich't wth chastitie,
> Was crown'd wth triumphes of fertilitie.
> Children were sure, & frequent: eury year
> By a new darling was seal'd currant here.
> Hir Births were Almanakes; & shee ye Root,
> Prognosticated seasons by hir Fruit.
> Thrice happy mother! who, wth out ye sunn,
> Numbring hir blessings, knew ye year was done.
> But now, these Mathematikes being lost,
> Our seasons fall, our reckonings still are crost[.]

While he was rector at East Clandon, Goffe gained a reputation as a sermon writer. Edward Brayley in *A Topographical History of Surrey* claims "his sermons display, together with the quaintness common to the discourses of his time, a fancy and vivacity peculiar to the writer." Only one sermon entitled *Deliverance from the Grave,* which was preached at St. Mary Spittle in London on 28 March 1627, seems to have been published. A sermon for Easter week, it is based on Ezek. 37:13: "And ye shall know that I am the Lord, when I opened your graves, O my people, and brought you out of your graves." The sermon displays Goffe's "fancy and vivacity," as well as his antifeminism when he speaks of the female refugees of the plague:

> Then were your delicate and tender Dames (whom the Sunne in his pride must not looke vpon; and he in all that pride, not so proud as one of them) scorning at another time to grace a Countery Village with their presence; but then glad to shelter themselves vnder an humble Thatch. Come now you pampred Truncks, and see these Bodies a Feast to their

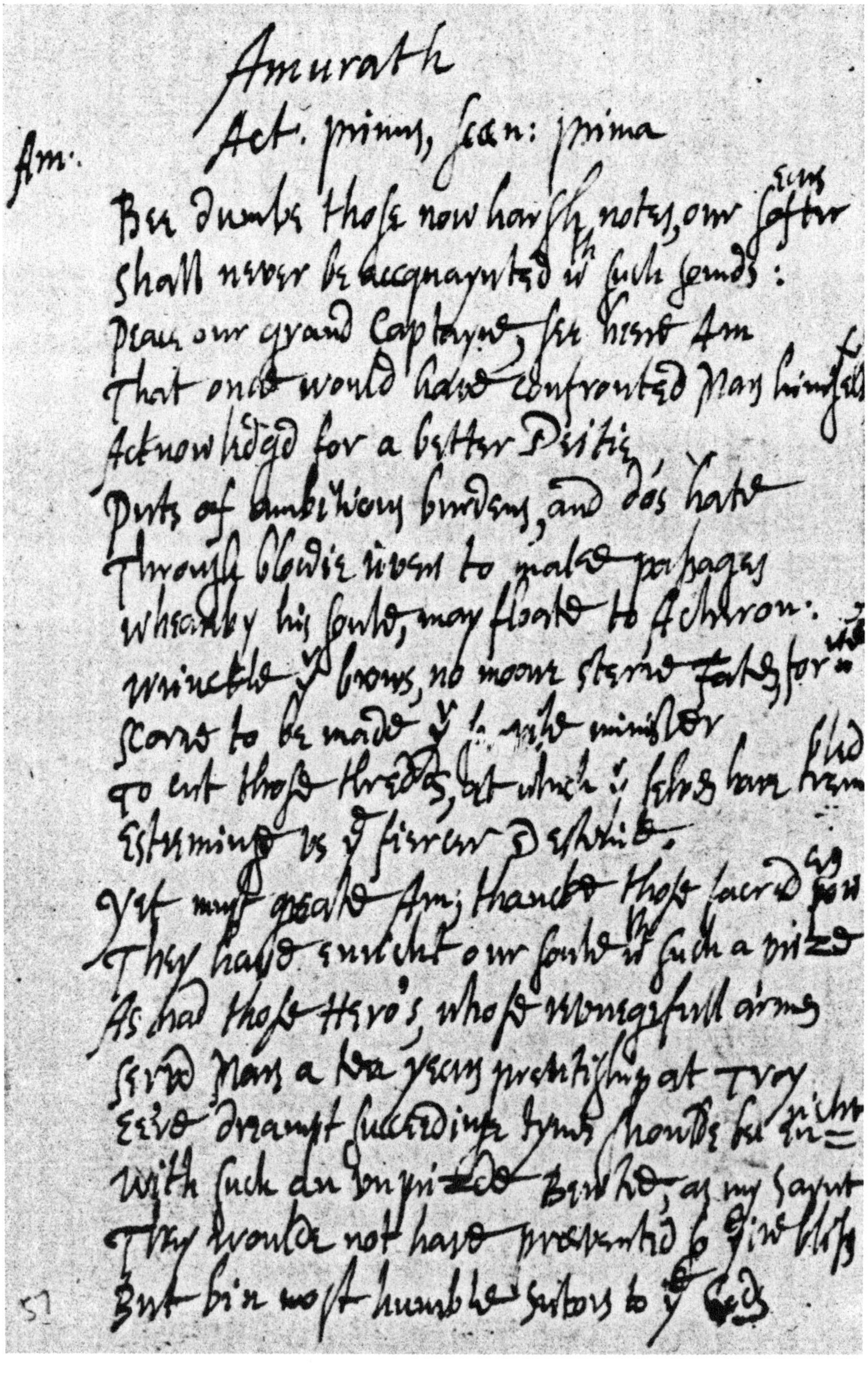

Amurath

Act: primus, Scæn: prima

Am.

Bee dumbe those now harsh notes, our softer
shall never be acquaynted wth such sounds:
Peace our grand Captayne, see here Am
That once would have confronted Mars himselfe
Acknowledgd for a better Deitie,
Puts of ambitious burdens, and dos hate
Through blowdie rivers to make passages
Whearby his soule, may floate to Acheron:
wrinckle ye brows, no more sterne lookes for
scorne to be made ye vyle minister
To cut those threeds, at which ye selues have bin
Esteeming us of fiercer Deitie,
yet must greate Am; thanck those sacred po
They have enricht our soule wth such a prize
As had those Hero's, whose revengefull armes
serve Mars a tea yeares prentishing at Troy
Ever dreampt succeeding tymes should see em
with such an empired brother, as my father
They would not have prevented to give blis
But bin most humble suitors to ye Gods

57

First page from the manuscript for the part of Amurath in The Courageous Turk, *preserved at the Houghton Library, Harvard University. Because this actor's side is thought to be written in Goffe's hand, some scholars have suggested that he played this part in the Christ Church, Oxford, production of his play (MS Thr. 10.1; by permission of the Houghton Library, Harvard University).*

Polypragmaticus:

    Actus primus, Scena prima:

Polyp: Componite, componite, componite inquam ocyus

    Tunicas, togas, barbas, vestes, habitus:

Pant: —— admissionis dies?

Polyp: Certo certius, hodie ad horam decimam

    Dux adsunt, quaque admittendi Academici

    Tu libros nos, quaque instrumenta hæc cape

    Tu pro te feros Mathesin, tu Philosophiam

    Tu medicinam, Ego quamcumque scientiam

Pant: Sed unde scientiam?

Polyp: Unde? Stupes, librum hunc cape

    Et edisce hinc verba quædam

Pant: —— Hæc ubi posito:

Polyp: —Imo? si furnis ad mensam, vel ad collegium

    Cape quadram, erit librum, si sit altera

    Dic esse parallelogrammum rectangulum,

    Secus Rhombum, vel Romboidem, si multilaterum

    Et regulare, Polygonon, secus Trapezium

Pant: —— Egone hæc?

Polyp: Dam scinde in forma tetraedron

    Dic conum, cylindrum, prisma, parallelepipedum

    Habensque semper in promptu hunc circinum

    Describes figuras quasdam Geometricas

An actor's side, believed to be in Goffe's hand, for the role of Polypragmaticus in Robert Burton's Philosophaster *(MS Thr. 10.1, by permission of the Houghton Library, Harvard University)* owne corruption, for whom here no fowle was deare enough, no fish rare enough, to content their wittily-luxurious palats. . . .

Apparently four sermons were preached during that Easter week, whereupon a "rehearser" either praised or criticized them and made his own sermon using the previous four. Goffe's rehearser was very critical of *Deliverance from the Grave,* and Goffe, in indignation, wrote two epistles "To the Reader" attacking the rehearser because he said that he could not understand Goffe's meaning and that Goffe's style was too high. Goffe died in July 1629 and was buried in the middle of the chancel of the church at East Clandon on 27 July 1629.

Thomas Goffe's reputation in the seventeenth century was much greater than it is today. It is curious, however, that a man preparing for the clergy at Oxford and later well known for his Latin orations should write plays so full of bombast, cruelty, and passion. Apparently Goffe the undergraduate was well aware of his audience's fascination with violence and bombast. The use of popular subject matter, the experimentation with stage technique (which indicates a knowledge of the contemporary London stage), and the cruel, bombastic tone used by an Oxford undergraduate who was to become a respected author of Anglican sermons makes a study of the plays important to the understanding of university drama.

References:

W. J. Lawrence, "The Authorship of 'The Careless Shepherdess,' " *Times Literary Supplement,* 24 July 1924, p. 463;

Lawrence, "Goffe's 'The Careless Shepherdess,' " *Modern Language Review,* 14 (1919): 419-421;

Norbert Frank O'Donnell, " 'The Tragedy of Orestes' by Thomas Goffe: A Critical Edition," Ph.D dissertation, Ohio State University, 1950;

Susan Gushee O'Malley, Introduction to *A Critical Old-Spelling Edition of Thomas Goffe's "The Courageous Turk"* (New York: Garland, 1979);

Warner Grenelle Rice, "Turk, Moor, and Persian in English Literature From 1550-1660, with Particular Reference to the Drama," Ph.D dissertation, Harvard University, 1926;

Alvin Thaler, "Thomas Goffe's Praeludium," *Modern Language Notes,* 36 (1921): 337-341.

Papers:

A manuscript for *The Courageous Turk* is at Tabley House, Knutsford, Cheshire, England, in the library of John Leicester-Warren, Esq., under the title *The Tragedy of Amurath, third Tyrant of the Turkes.* The actor's sides for the parts of Polypragmaticus, Amurath, Antonius, and Poore and the poem "A Songe upon ye loss of an Actors voyce, beeing to play a cheife part in ye Vniversitie" (MS Thr. 10. 1), are at the Houghton Library, Harvard University.

Thomas Killigrew

(7 February 1612-19 March 1683)

James C. Bulman
Allegheny College

PLAY PRODUCTIONS: *The Prisoners*, London, Phoenix theater, probably 1635 but no later than 12 May 1636;

Claracilla, London, Phoenix theater, before 12 May 1636;

The Princess, London, Blackfriars theater, before 12 May 1636 or (more likely) after 2 October 1637;

The Parson's Wedding, possibly London, Blackfriars theater, circa 1640; London, Theatre Royal, 1664.

BOOKS: *The Prisoners and Claracilla. Two Tragae-Comedies* (London: Printed by T. Cotes for Andrew Crooke, 1641);

Comedies, and Tragedies (London: Printed for Henry Herringman, 1664)—comprises *The Prisoners; Claricilla; The Princesse, or Love at First Sight; The Parson's Wedding; The Pilgrim; Cicilia & Clorinda, or Love in Arms; Thomaso, or the Wanderer;* and *Bellamira her Dream, or the Love of Shadows.*

Editions: *The Parson's Wedding,* in *Six Caroline Comedies,* edited by A. S. Knowland (New York & London: Oxford University Press, 1962);

Claricilla [1664 text], edited by William T. Reich (New York: Garland, 1980).

Though his career as a playwright began during the Caroline period, Thomas Killigrew is best remembered for his role in Restoration theater. A favorite of Charles II, he and Sir William Davenant secured royal patents to establish rival theater companies—in essence, to monopolize London theater—in 1660. Killigrew, as manager of the King's Company, staged many of the most memorable productions of the period, and he served as Master of the Revels from 1673 to 1677. These achievements have tended to overshadow his aspirations as a dramatist. A member of the literary court that surrounded Henrietta Maria, Queen to Charles I, and later of the court in exile, Killigrew wrote eleven plays, many of them inspired by French heroic romances and intended for a coterie audience.

Only one, *The Parson's Wedding,* achieved popularity. The most ribald of his efforts, this play for a long time contributed to Killigrew's unwarranted reputation as a coarse and unprincipled libertine.

Killigrew was born in 1612 in London, one of twelve children born to Sir Robert Killigrew, who, as a courtier from an ancient Cornish family, achieved prominence for his wit, loyalty, and entrepreneurial spirit. All of Thomas's siblings were involved in life at court. Most notable among them were William, who was knighted by James I, served as captain of a troop of horse guarding Charles I during the civil wars, and later became a playwright; Henry, who was created a Doctor of Divinity by Charles I, later preached to Charles II, and also tried his hand at play writing; and Elizabeth, who served as maid of honor to Henrietta Maria, married Francis Boyle, and became the mistress of Charles II. As fourth son, Thomas apparently had little formal education: he himself jested that he was an "illiterate Courtier." But his love for the theater developed early. Samuel Pepys, dining with Sir John Minnes on Lord Mayor's Day in 1662, was told the way in which Thomas got to see plays when he was a boy: "He would go to the Red Bull, and when the man cried to the boys, 'Who will go and be a devil, and he shall see the play for nothing?' then would he go in and be a devil upon the stage, and so get to see plays." When Killigrew was still young, most likely in 1625 or 1626, he was appointed Page of Honour to Charles I. The court, then, became his university; and he was to attach himself to a circle of courtiers surrounding Henrietta Maria.

Like other Cavaliers in that circle, Killigrew attempted to please the Queen—and to supplement his modest income of £100—with displays of literary talent. His first three plays, amateur attempts at tragicomedy, no doubt appealed to her taste for courtly romance and its exotic contests of love and honor. The first of them, *The Prisoners,* Killigrew wrote in London, circa 1634-1635. The second and third, *The Princess* and *Claracilla* (the spelling was changed to *Claricilla* in the edition of

1664), were written in 1636 in Italy, while he was accompanying the brilliant courtier Walter Montague on his Continental travels. *The Prisoners* and *Claracilla* were acted by the Queen's company at the Phoenix theater in Drury Lane, probably in 1635 and 1636 respectively, and certainly no later than 12 May 1636, when the plague closed the theaters for seventeen months. *The Princess* was most likely performed after the theaters reopened on 2 October 1637, possibly by the King's Men. None of the three was a commercial success.

On 29 June 1636, shortly after returning from the Continent, Killigrew married Cecilia Crofts, maid of honor to the Queen. She bore him a son, Henry, who grew up to be an unscrupulous rake whose reputation has sometimes been confused with that of his father. Cecilia died in January of 1638; and after that, Killigrew began a personal decline. His lavish tastes left him chronically in debt; and to augment his income, he became (like so many courtiers at this time) a "court vulture" who indulged in begging estates—that is, petitioning the King for fines in cash or in confiscated property accrued to the Crown from convicted malefactors. Killigrew wrote *The Parson's Wedding* in 1640 or perhaps 1641, when his fortunes were at a low ebb, probably in part because he thought a bawdy comedy would prove popular with audiences and thus help him to pay off his debts. As the theaters closed shortly thereafter, however, the play probably was not performed until the Restoration.

When civil war broke out, Killigrew remained loyal to the King and served actively as a royal courier or liaison officer. To reward him for his loyalty, Parliament in September 1642 committed him to the custody of the marshall, Sir John Lenthall, "on suspicion for raising arms against Parliament"—a charge not proven. In all likelihood Killigrew was not incarcerated, since he retained his fashionable lodgings at the Piazza in Covent Garden; but his creditors did not forget him, and in May 1643 he petitioned Parliament for protection against actions of debt prosecuted against him. The House of Lords obliged by voiding all suits so long as he was under house arrest; and in July of that year, the Lords ordered that he be exchanged for another prisoner at Oxford and "that he be given a pass to proceed to the Royalist army." When Henrietta Maria sailed for France a year later, in July 1644, Killigrew almost certainly sailed with her.

Killigrew's career in exile is fascinating to trace. At first he seems to have spent time in Paris

Thomas Killigrew at age twenty-six, a copy of a painting by Sir Anthony Van Dyck (by permission of the National Portrait Gallery)

in service to the Queen. By 1647 he was referred to as *Dilectus & fidelis serviens noster* by the Prince of Wales, who sent him on an important mission to Italy, most likely to beg money for the Prince. In 1648 Killigrew was temporarily employed as Groom of the Bedchamber for the Duke of York, who resided in The Hague; but when, on the beheading of Charles I in 1649, the Prince of Wales became king, Killigrew was recalled to the court at Paris and was sent as envoy to Savoy, Florence, and Venice to assert Charles II's royal claim. The assignment at Venice proved to be controversial. After a lukewarm reception by the Venetian Senate and many delays, Killigrew was dismissed in disgrace owing to accusations of debauchery. It was later discovered that the Senate trumped up the charge so as not to antagonize Cromwell, with whose agents the Republic of Venice was negotiating. The presence of an envoy from Charles II had become an embarrassment.

During these years of exile Killigrew wrote seven plays, only one of which, *The Pilgrim*—a tragedy in the style of James Shirley, written in Paris

Page from a letter to an unknown recipient that Killigrew wrote during his tenure as King Charles II's envoy to Venice (American Art Association Anderson Galleries, sale no. 4240, 11-12 March 1936) circa 1645-1646—seems to have been intended for the stage. The other six plays (actually three two-part plays) were closet dramas, composed by Killigrew for his own pleasure and with little concern for the exigencies of theatrical production. Two of the three—*Cicilia & Clorinda* (composed circa 1649-1650) and *Bellamira her Dream* (composed circa 1650-1652)—were written during his residency in Italy and inspired, like his earlier plays, by French heroic romance. The third, *Thomaso, or the Wanderer,* written in Paris circa 1654, is a more comic and autobiographical play about the adventures and amours of exiled courtiers in Madrid. None of these plays was ever performed.

After his dismissal from Venice, Killigrew was quickly restored to royal favor, and on 28 January 1655 he married Charlotte de Hesse, a Dutch heiress with a ten-thousand-pound fortune, by whom he had three sons. He spent the remainder of the exile in Maestricht, where he continued to serve the King and on occasion was employed in the service of the States General. On 23 May 1660 he sailed on board the *Royal Charles* when it carried the King back to England; on the following day Pepys reported that while walking upon the decks, he met a number of distinguished figures, "amongst others, Thomas Killigrew (a merry droll, but a gentleman of great esteem with the King) who told us many merry stories."

Killigrew's wit and drollery must have ingratiated him with Charles. Once back in England he moved swiftly, with Davenant, to secure a monopoly on the theaters. Charles granted Killigrew a patent to form the royal company—the King's Company—and granted Davenant a patent to form the Duke's Company. These patents ordered the two managers to reform the theater in various ways: to introduce actresses on the stage in order to avoid the scandals attendant upon boy actors; to introduce to the public stage the kinds of scenery and music theretofore associated with masques, operas, and pastorals; and not least to revise and clean up the plays in the old repertory. As the favored company, Killigrew's got the choice of older actors such as Charles Hart and Michael Mohun; and as a descendant of the "old" Caroline King's Company, it also had a right to many of Shakespeare's plays and to the cream of the plays of Ben Jonson, Francis Beaumont and John Fletcher, and Shirley. Killigrew was fortunate enough to secure the services of two modern writers as well, John Dryden and William Wycherley, whose work enriched the repertory of the Theatre Royal.

Of the two managers, however, Davenant ultimately proved the more successful. Careful and provident, he took full authority over his fledgling actors. While exercising fiscal restraint, he nonetheless experimented with new forms of theater, such as opera, and built a magnificent new theater at Dorset Garden to house the scenery, music, and dancing required by those forms. Killigrew, on the other hand, exerted less control, both financial and artistic, over his company. In part because he was still plagued with debt, he made veteran actors Mohun, Hart, and John Lacy shareholders with him; and the resulting disagreements among them were damaging to the company. When the newly refurbished Theatre Royal burned in January 1672, the company was paralyzed and began a rapid decline. The second Theatre Royal opened in 1674, but debt forced Killigrew to make over his shares to others. In 1676 he quarreled with his son Charles, who claimed both his father's promise of the managership of the theater and also the office of Master of the Revels, which Killigrew had held since the death of Sir Henry Herbert in 1673. In 1677 Killigrew relinquished both to his son. Charles, however, proved an even poorer manager than his father: his mismanagement continued until the Union of the Theatres in 1682, when Killigrew's company was essentially taken over by the more successful Duke's Company. Killigrew died in March 1683 and was buried in Westminster Abbey.

Although Killigrew's first three plays are usually passed over as amateur attempts to curry royal favor, they in fact are of literary interest as a bridge between Caroline drama and the heroic plays popular during the Restoration. They demonstrate many of the motifs that were hallmarks of later plays. All three had a common source in *Ariane*, a heroic romance by Jean Desmaretz de Saint-Sorlin, published at Paris in 1632 and very much in vogue with the Platonic précieux at both the French and the English courts. Like those longer romances by La Calprenède and de Scudéry, *Ariane* is crowded with pseudo-historical events that take place in fantastic dream countries. The plots of Killigrew's three plays, then—*The Prisoners, The Princess,* and *Claracilla*—though superficially different, are in truth very much alike. They all involve the intrigues of royal lovers in and about Sicily, Sardinia, and Rome: the heroes are gallant; heroines, peerless; villains, blackguardly. Parents obstruct the course of true love; heroines are torn between love for the heroes and the honor of their countries; heroes, between love for the heroines and chivalric

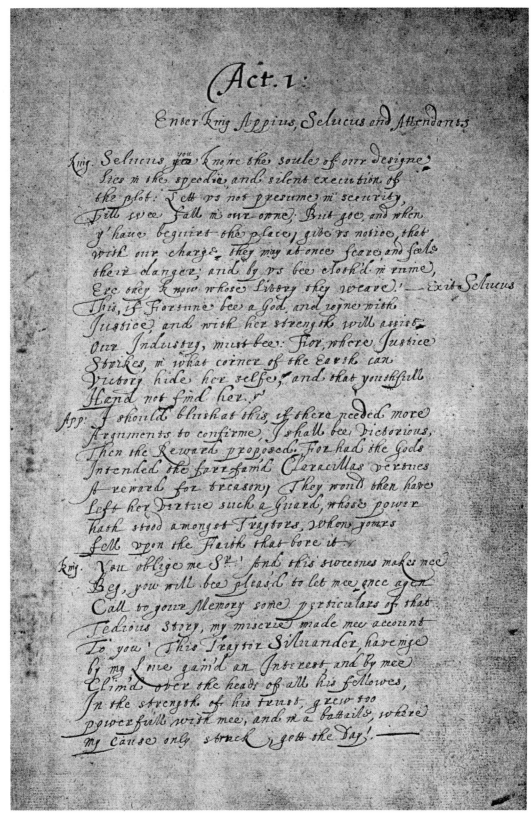

Page from the manuscript for Claracilla *preserved at the Houghton Library, Harvard University. This manuscript, dated 1639, is presumed to be in the hand of a scribe (gift of Friends of the Library; by permission of the Houghton Library, Harvard University).*

friendship with one another. The course of love is obstructed further by storms at sea, by pirate bands (led, of course, by men of quality), by masquerades and disguises; and the plays, like their source, are peppered with the most exalted of sentiments and artificial of emotions. Of the three, the best plotted and theatrically most effective was *Claracilla*. Although Pepys was not much impressed by it, it appears to have had its admirers—witness the facts that it was performed during the Interregnum in 1653, was still in Mohun's repertory at the time of the Restoration, and continued in Killigrew's repertory at the Theatre Royal for another decade.

The Parson's Wedding is altogether different from these early plays; and in many ways, this vulgar comedy of manners obliquely comments on their artificial idealism. Pepys called it an "obscene loose play"; and indeed, it is full of stock scenes from farce. But they are seldom so well executed as in this play. The parson of the title is in fact a secondary character. Victim of a trick played on him by a "Captain" and his raffish friends, he marries the Captain's mistress, a woman named Wanton, on whom he dotes; but she abuses him, robs him, and helps to disgrace him by bringing an aged bawd to his bed, then accusing him of adultery. This action is merely subsidiary to the main plot, however, which focuses on a battle of wits that anticipates many such battles in Restoration comedy. In it, two witty and fortune-hunting gallants plot to win an attractive young widow and her friend from two dull, Platonic lovers who assiduously woo them. The battle lines are drawn on the field of Platonic love: the ladies defend the précieux ideals of Platonic love, even though they are bored with their hypocritical wooers' pledges of constant service; and the gallants attack "the spiritual Nonsence the age calls Platonick Love," even though, at the end, they submit to the conventions of marriage. The gallants' open revolt against submission to the lady is of course an affront to the female sex and cannot be condoned lest the lady lose sovereignty. Yet sovereignty is compromised in a final trick whereby the gallants invade the ladies' bedroom one night and appear at the open window for all to see, thus forcing the ladies into marriage to save their reputations.

Though the play relies heavily on such old devices, its attitudes are Cavalier and its sentiments royalist. It includes satire directed against Parliament and political reform, against dissenting clergy and religious agitators, against the military, and against creditors—all of which fixes the play firmly in the period before the civil wars. The gallants

The portrait of Killigrew by William Faithorne that was published in the 1664 folio edition of his Comedies, and Tragedies *(Maggs Bros., catalogue no. 569, 1932)*

themselves, like Cavaliers of that period, are prototypes for the rakes of Restoration comedy; and the heroines differ from Restoration heroines only insofar as they are not yet fully emancipated from the assumptions of Platonic love. Revealingly, *The Parson's Wedding* is usually anthologized—and it is the *only* play by Killigrew to be anthologized—as a Restoration comedy; and indeed, since it may have been performed for the first time in 1664, that classification may be appropriate. Killigrew cut the text considerably for production and added to the play's titillation by having women play all the roles. Apparently the play was popular: it was revived in 1672, again with all parts played by actresses, and no doubt there were other performances as well.

The Pilgrim is, in certain respects, a better and more polished play. In *Some Account of the English Stage, 1660-1830* (1832) John Genest asserts that it "is a good Tragedy—with judicious alterations it might have been made fit for representation." Indeed, although there is no record of performance, Killigrew might have written *The Pilgrim* for a company of English actors in Paris supported, and finally dissolved, by the Prince of Wales in 1646. Some of the play's motifs hark back to Killigrew's earlier tragicomedies—for instance, the conflict between romantic love and chivalric friendship, the heroes' nice concern with points of honor, the overuse of disguises, tokens, letters. More directly, Killigrew borrowed his plot from a tragicomedy by Shirley called *The Politician*, performed circa 1639-1640. The plot involves intrigue in the household of the Duke of Milan, who has just conquered Pavia and married its Duchess Julia. The Duke has shown favor, too, to the Duchess's son and daughter; but a true Machiavel, Julia schemes against the Duke's son to put her own son (who is the offspring of an adulterous union between Julia and the Count Martino) on the throne. Complications arise because the two princes are best of friends and each

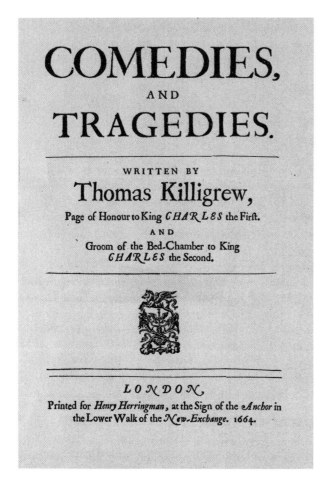

COMEDIES,

AND

TRAGEDIES.

WRITTEN BY

Thomas Killigrew,

Page of Honour to King *CHARLES* the Firſt.

AND

Groom of the Bed-Chamber to King
CHARLES the Second.

LONDON,

Printed for *Henry Herringman*, at the Sign of the *Anchor* in
the Lower Walk of the *New-Exchange*. 1664.

Title page for the folio collection of eight plays by Killigrew

in love with the other's sister. The resultant accidental judgments, casual slaughters, and purposes mistook are as reminiscent of *Hamlet* as they are of *The Politician*; and in fact the whole play, especially in its verbal echoes and in its denouement, owes a great deal to Shakespeare. *The Pilgrim* has flaws: an excessively long trial scene needs to be pruned, and a comic subplot—not at all amusing—is unrelated to the main action. But on the whole, critics agree that this is Killigrew's most promising play.

All of the remaining six plays written in exile are closet drama, not intended for the stage. The six are actually halves of three longer plays: as none of the first parts has a denouement in the fifth act, we may regard the plays justifiably as unwieldy ten-act giants. The first of them, *Cicilia & Clorinda*, is a dramatization of part one, book three of Mademoiselle de Scudéry's *Artamène ou Le Grand Cyrus*, a heroic romance published at Paris in 1649 and enormously popular with readers. The second, *Bellamira her Dream*, is a more fantastical and less coherent play fashioned of material drawn from Arcadian romances, heroic romances, and snatches of old plays. Both of these plays return to Killigrew's favorite locales in Italy (where they were written) and involve absurd plots of families separated, captive princesses, cruel villains, mistaken identities, and fierce duels. Perhaps the most distinguishing feature of *Cicilia & Clorinda* is its remarkable triple duel. Even more than the earlier tragicomedies, however, these plays suffer from a highly artificial rhetoric, extreme verbosity, and inflated emotionalism; and they are best left where Killigrew chose to keep them—in the closet.

The last of his plays, *Thomaso, or the Wanderer*, is entirely different from these heroic plays. Though it has no particular source, it borrows liberally from Fletcher's *The Captain*, Jonson's *Volpone*, Middleton's *Blurt Master Constable*, and Brome's *The Novella*. *Thomaso*, however, is unlike any of these plays. A huge, rollicking comedy of Cavaliers in exile, it is obviously autobiographical, depicting in a broad way encounters that Killigrew (the name Thomaso is a key) may have had on his travels in Spain. Thomaso has come to Madrid in the company of other Cavaliers to woo Serulina, sister of the wealthy Grandee Don Pedro. These Cavaliers are portrayed ambivalently: they are prone to violence, and their attitudes toward sex are liberal. They regard themselves as "Royal and Loyal Fugitives" (part I, I.ii) but are seen by others as "a race of men who have left praying, or hoping for daily bread; and only relye upon nightly drink" (part I, II.iv). Thomaso shows his stripes when he becomes smitten with a Venetian courtesan, Angelica Bianca, whom Don Pedro also desires. Thomaso cannot rival Don Pedro's lavish attentions; but when the English beat the Spaniards on the field, Angelica falls passionately for Thomaso, and much humorous intrigue follows, including a plot by Thomaso's jilted whores to assassinate him. The whores attack the wrong man, and Thomaso escapes to marry Serulina and to secure his fortune—a fate Killigrew would secure for himself the year after he wrote this play.

Thomaso mixes fantasy with realism. In a grotesque subplot, two of Thomaso's companions marry a pair of wealthy Jewish monsters: blinded by greed, they expect a Jonsonian mountebank to restore these freaks to normal form. Informed by a revived interest in magic and astrology, this subplot makes its point, however absurdly; and indeed, had Killigrew revised the play for the stage, it might have proved popular with Restoration audiences. As it turned out, though, *Thomaso* found a place in theater history only because it inspired others. As a record of the experiences of exiled Cavaliers, it informed the tone and attitudes of the "Spanish" plays of the Restoration far more than letters or legal documents did. It inspired Richard Flecknoe to lampoon Killigrew in *The Life of Thomaso the Wanderer* (1667). Most important, it provided the source for the best and most popular of Aphra Behn's comedies, *The Rover; or, The Banish't Cavaliers*, produced at Dorset Garden in 1677. The second part of *The Rover*, which included two comic monsters based on those in *Thomaso*, followed in 1680.

Behn's postscript to the first edition of *The Rover* implies that she had been accused of plagiarism and, furthermore, hints that she had not asked Killigrew's permission. Her denial of these charges is worth noting:

> This Play had been sooner in Print, but for a Report about the town (made by some either very Malitious or very Ignorant) that 'twas Thomaso alter'd; . . . That I have stoln some hints from it may be a proof, that I valu'd it more than to pretend to alter it, had I had the Dexterity of some Poets, who are not more Expert in stealing than in the Art of Concealing. . . . I will only say the Plot and Bus'ness (not to boast on't) is my own: as for the Words and Characters, I leave the Reader to judge and compare 'em with Thomaso, to whom I recommend the great Entertainment of reading it.

It is both ironic and somehow fitting that for a playwright of no great talent, Killigrew's most lasting legacy should be a play we know only indirectly, through adaptation by another, and finer, playwright.

Biographies:

Alfred Harbage, *Thomas Killigrew: Cavalier Dramatist, 1612-83* (Philadelphia: University of Pennsylvania Press, 1930; reprinted, New York: Benjamin Blom, 1967);

Montague Summers, "Thomas Killigrew, and the History of the Theatres until the Union, 1682," in his *The Playhouse of Pepys* (New York: Macmillan, 1935), pp. 65-145.

References:

Gerald Eades Bentley, *The Jacobean and Caroline Stage*, volume 4 (Oxford: Clarendon Press, 1956), pp. 694-710;

Alfred Harbage, *Cavalier Drama: An Historical and Critical Supplement to the Study of the Elizabethan and Restoration Stage* (New York: Modern Language Association of America, 1936);

Leslie Hotson, *The Commonwealth and Restoration Stage* (Cambridge: Harvard University Press, 1928), pp. 176-280;

Robert D. Hume, *The Development of English Drama in the Late Seventeenth Century* (Oxford: Clarendon Press, 1976);

W. R. Keast, "Killigrew's Use of Donne in 'The Parson's Wedding,'" *Modern Language Review*, 45 (October 1950): 512-515;

John Loftis, *The Spanish Plays of Neoclassical England* (New Haven: Yale University Press, 1973);

Allardyce Nicoll, *A History of Restoration Drama, 1660-1700* (Cambridge: Cambridge University Press, 1923);

Lois Potter, "The Plays and the Playwrights, 1642-60," in *The Revels History of Drama in English*, edited by Philip Edwards and others (London: Methuen, 1981), IV: 263-279;

John Harrington Smith, *The Gay Couple in Restoration Comedy* (Cambridge: Harvard University Press, 1948);

J. W. Stoye, "The Whereabouts of Thomas Killigrew 1639-41," *Review of English Studies*, 25 (July 1949): 245-248;

William Van Lennep, "Thomas Killigrew Prepares His Plays for Production," in *Joseph Quincy Adams Memorial Studies*, edited by James G. McManaway, Giles E. Dawson, and Edwin E. Willoughby (Washington, D.C.: Folger Shakespeare Library, 1948).

Papers:
Killigrew's copy of *Comedies, and Tragedies* (1664)—in which he heavily cut the text of *The Parson's Wedding* (apparently for the performance of the play for an all-female cast—is preserved in the library of Worcester College, Oxford. A manuscript of *Cicilia & Clorinda* is located in the Folger Shakespeare Library (MS 4458), bound in two separate folios, and the Castle Howard Library houses a manuscript of *Claracilla* dated 1639. Copies of a newsletter concerning the possessed Ursuline nuns of Tours, dated Orleans, 7 December 1635 and originally addressed to Lord Goring, may be found in the British Library (MSS 27402, f.70), in the Ashmolean (MSS 800, 3, ff.21-27), and at Trinity College, Dublin (MSS 1665). The letter was printed in the *European Magazine* (1803): 102-106.

Shakerley Marmion
(January 1603-1639)

Allan P. Green

PLAY PRODUCTIONS: *Holland's Leaguer,* London, Salisbury Court theater, December 1631;

A Fine Companion, London, Salisbury Court theater, circa 1632-1633;

The Antiquary, London, Cockpit theater, winter 1634-1635(?).

BOOKS: *Hollands Leaguer. An Excellent Comedy* (London: Printed by J. Beale for J. Grove, 1632);

A Fine Companion (London: Printed by A. Mathewes for R. Meighen, 1633);

A Morall Poem, Intituled The Legend of Cupid and Psyche (London: Printed by N. & J. Oakes & sold by H. Sheppard, 1637);

The Antiquary. A Comedy (London: Printed by F. K. for I. W. & F. E., 1641).

Editions: *The Dramatic Works of Shakerley Marmion,* edited by James Maidment and W. H. Logan (Edinburgh: W. Paterson, 1875)—comprises *Holland's Leaguer, A Fine Companion, The Antiquary;*

The Legend of Cupid and Psyche, in volume 2 of *Minor Poets of the Caroline Period,* 3 volumes, edited by George Saintsbury (Oxford: Clarendon Press, 1905-1921).

Dramatist, poet, and soldier, Shakerley Marmion in his brief career as a playwright employed Ben Jonson's classical "rules" chiefly to promote the Platonic love cult that arose at the court of Queen Henrietta Maria in the early 1630s. In his elegy to Jonson, which appeared in *Ionsonus Virbius* (1638), Marmion freely acknowledged that his muse was Jonson's ("Made by adoption *free* and *genuine*") and offered this cogent self-criticism:

> Nature has afforded me a slight
> And easie *Muse,* yet one that takes her flight
> Above the *vulgar* pitch.

In a revealing passage of this elegy, Marmion offered an insight into what Jonson's "rules" meant to an aspiring playwright of the time:

> For whether He [Jonson], like a fine thread does *file*
> His terser Poems in a *Comick stile,*
> Or treates of *tragick furies,* and him list,
> To draw his *lines* out with a stronger *twist:*
> *Minervas,* nor *Arachnes* loome can show
> Such curious tracts; nor does the Spring bestow
> Such glories on the Field, or *Flora's* Bowers,
> As His *works* smile with *Figures,* or with Flowrs.
> Never did so much strength, or such a spell
> Of *art,* and eloquence of papers dwell.
> For whil'st that he in colours, *full* and *true,*
> Mens *natures, fancies,* and their *humours* drew
> In *method, order, matter, sence* and *grace,*
> Fitting each person to his *time* and *place;*
> Knowing to *move,* to *slacke,* or to make *haste,*
> Binding the *middle* with the *first* and *last:*
> He fram'd all *minds,* and did all *passions* stirre,
> And with a *bridle* guide the Theater.

Born in January 1603, Shakerley Marmion was baptized in the parish church at Aynho, Northamptonshire, on the twenty-first of the month. His father, Shakerley Marmion, Sr., was a country gentleman who had held minor commissions in the county. The dramatist was one of four children: his sisters, Mary and Francisca, were baptized at Aynho in 1601 and 1604, respectively, while his brother, Richard, was baptized there in 1607. During the dramatist's childhood, his father's fortunes were declining. Neither of his sisters seems to have married, and his brother, Richard, unlike the dramatist, did not attend either university; he married and became a London goldsmith, which may explain Marmion's fondness for metaphors drawn from metalworking.

The dramatist's mother, Mary, was the only daughter of Bartrobe Lukin of London, a self-made man who had risen from yeoman stock to become a clerk of the Court of Wards and Liveries and who owned a house in London's Fleet Street and property in Barking, Essex. He provided his daughter with the substantial dowry of £800 upon her marriage to Shakerley Marmion, Sr., which took place on 16 June 1600 at St. Dunstan's-in-the-West, Fleet Street.

The Marmions of Aynho, Northamptonshire, can trace their descent from the Baron Robert Marmion I, who entered England with William the Conqueror, fought at Hastings, and was rewarded for his service with vast English estates. The dramatist's descent from the baronial family of Marmion is through branches of the family at Adwell and Checkendon, in Oxfordshire. His more immediate progenitor was Henry Marmion, a younger son of William Marmion of Adwell (died 1530), who, as a young man, established himself at Gloucester, where he was twice chosen mayor. Henry Marmion's son, Thomas, was the dramatist's grandfather, and it was he who founded the Marmion line at Aynho when, about 1568, he married Anne Shakerley, the youngest of five daughters of Rowland Shakerley, a mercer of London and Aynho. Thomas Marmion, a lawyer of Lincoln's Inn, bought the shares in the manor held by his wife's sisters and died in 1583. Two years later, his widow married Anthony Morgan, a local landowner, and by the terms of her marriage settlement she made her eldest son, Shakerley, the dramatist's father, responsible for the debts and legacies of her first husband's will.

At the time of his mother's second marriage, Shakerley Marmion, Sr., was a boy of eight. According to the terms of his mother's marriage settlement, he was held liable not only for the support of three brothers and a sister, all young and living at Aynho, but also for the accommodation in the manor house of his mother and stepfather and for the stabling for their horses. Anne Morgan died at Aynho in 1605, four years after the marriage of her eldest son. After her death Bartrobe Lukin persuaded his son-in-law to sign a statute staple, which he evidently hoped would ensure that the manor would pass to the eldest son and heir, Shakerley Marmion, Jr., the future dramatist.

After the death of his father-in-law, Shakerley Marmion, Sr., tried to sell the manor in order to pay the debts and legacies of his father's will and his own debts, which he said in court were largely in consequence of having to borrow money at high rates of interest. The proposed sale was challenged in court by Bartrobe Lukin's widow and her only son, Thomas, on the grounds that the statute staple made the sale illegal, but in 1616 Shakerley Marmion, Sr., successfully sued his in-laws in the Chancery Court for the right to sell the property. The sympathy for the disinherited heir apparent in the plays of Shakerley Marmion, Jr., seems, then, to have an autobiographical basis. Though, as the court stipulated, £3,000 of the £5,200 profit from the sale was used to buy a lease of the Rectory Manor at Adderbury, in Oxfordshire, which it was believed would provide an income sufficient to maintain Shakerley Marmion, Sr., and his family, the father's later years seem also to have been darkened by debt. He is almost certainly the Shakerley Marmion who was buried at St. Margaret's, Westminster, in 1642, surviving his son by three years. The fact that the father was not buried beside "Mary the wife of Shakerley Marmion," who was buried in the church of St. Bartholomew-the-Great, Smithfield, London, in 1632, suggests that the dramatist's parents had been estranged during the later years of their marriage. Though the dramatist's burial place is uncertain, it has been conjectured that he seems to have chosen to be buried in the same place as his mother.

Anthony à Wood is the source of most of the facts—and errors—that we have about Marmion. Wood's charges that the dramatist and his father had dissipated the family's fortune have now been refuted by the Aynho Estate Documents, which have been available only since 1960.

The future dramatist attended the Free School at Thame, in Oxfordshire, where he doubtless acquired that love of the Latin classics to which his plays attest. In 1617 he became a gentleman commoner of Wadham College, Oxford, receiving a B.A. degree in 1622 and an M.A. in 1624. A commission rebel was issued for Marmion's apprehension by the Chancery Court of London in June of 1624, or about the time he left Oxford, but the case records for "Spencer Potts vs. Shakerley Marmion" give no indication of the nature of the charge, though it is likely to have been a criminal one.

The years 1624 to 1629 are blank in Marmion's biography, but it is likely that he spent much of this period living outside the law in the London suburbs and in foreign military service. His plays give ample evidence that he knew the life of the suburbs well. Wood says that he served in the Low Countries under Sir Sigismund Ziszan. Though there is no record of a license to pass beyond the seas for Marmion, the records of the period are incomplete. Moreover, if he were a fugitive from justice, he could not have gotten one. If Marmion did serve under Ziszan, he would have been out of England for most of 1626. The establishment of his friendship with Jonson also belongs to this period, but whether this friendship began before or after Marmion's military service is not known. Certainly, the "boon Delphic god" presiding over the wits at the Devil Tavern in Marmion's *A Fine Companion* (II.iv) is Jonson, and the characterization is clearly based on personal experience.

In an indictment dated 1629 the Middlesex Grand Jury charged Marmion with having assaulted one Edward Moore with a sword in the highway of St. Giles' parish and having wounded him in the head the previous July. Shakerley Marmion, Sr., posted twenty pounds of the bail money and one Richard Browne a like sum. The case is marked "extra" in the margin, which W. W. Greg interpreted as meaning that Marmion was still at large in September of 1629, thereby forfeiting his bail money.

In the new decade Marmion turned from soldiering and dissipation to play writing. His few occasional verses reveal little about his literary friendships. His elegy to Jonson is deeply felt and sincere, and one can only draw from it the fact that he had learned the dramatic art from Jonson. He wrote three poems for books by Thomas Heywood and called Heywood a friend. Perhaps he admired Heywood more than later generations because he regarded Heywood, like Jonson, as a master of the intrigue comedy. He wrote his last play, *The Antiquary*, for the same company—the Queen's Company—for which Heywood and another master of intrigue comedy, Philip Massinger, were writing in the 1630s. In *The Antiquary* Marmion's title character puns on the title of Massinger's *A New Way to Pay Old Debts*. Marmion seems to be indebted to James Shirley, who was also writing for the company during that period, for the spirit in which he portrays Aurelio and Lucretia in *The Antiquary*.

After writing only three plays, Marmion's dramatic career was brought to a sudden end in the middle of the decade. Why he wrote no more plays is not clear, though the extended closing of the theaters by plague for much of 1636 and 1637 may have been the cause. In 1637 appeared his long mythological poem, *The Legend of Cupid and Psyche*, and the following year his elegy to Jonson marked his final appearance in print.

Toward the close of his life, Marmion turned again to soldiering. Wood says that he was a valued friend of Sir John Suckling and that Suckling persuaded him to join the cavalry troop which he had raised at his own expense in 1639, after Parliament had refused the money, to ride north against the Scottish convenanters. Marmion got no farther than York, where, according to Wood, he fell ill and was conveyed back to London at Suckling's expense. He died there not long after and was "obscurely buried"—to use Wood's phrase—in the church of St. Bartholomew, in Smithfield, London. Wood did not specify which church of St. Bartholomew in Smithfield the dramatist was buried in, and the records of neither St. Bartholomew-the-Great nor St. Bartholomew-the-Less mentions the burial of the dramatist; but it is probable that he was buried near his mother in the church of St. Bartholomew-the-Great.

Marmion's first play, *Holland's Leaguer*, licensed in December of 1631, was performed by the Prince Charles' Men at the Salisbury Court theater on six successive days in that month, said to have been one of the longest runs of the period. Prince Charles' Men, a newly organized company, had moved into the Salisbury Court theater in December of 1631, and Marmion's play was their opening production. The comedy contrasts three gallants, who repair to a realistically depicted brothel—there actually was a brothel called Holland's Leaguer on the Bankside—to be gulled by a pair of Platonic lovers. The play reads like a first effort written according to Jonson's "rules." Like Jonson, Marmion is fond of quoting the Latin satirists, particularly Juvenal.

According to Marmion's letter, prefacing the 1632 quarto edition of the play, *Holland's Leaguer* was well received at Salisbury Court, and he repeated this statement in the prologue to his second

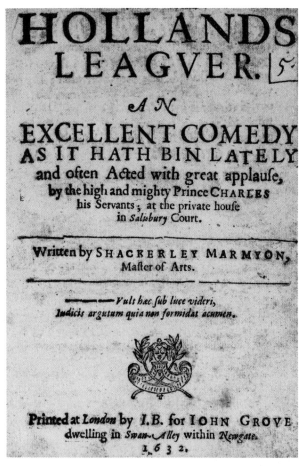

Title page for the 1632 quarto edition of Marmion's first play (Henry E. Huntington Library and Art Gallery)

comedy, which was written for the same company. In the published version of *Holland's Leaguer,* it was also noted that the "reformations" of Sir Henry Herbert, the Master of the Revels, were to be "strictly observed." In his letter prefacing the play Marmion defended himself against the charge of indecency, calling himself "a reprover, not an interpreter of wickedness." Though he was required to remove some offensive passages before publication, some obscene dialogue remains in the play as we have it. Yet if Marmion's self-defense would not have satisfied a Puritan, it would have satisfied a wit.

In *Holland's Leaguer* the Platonic lovers, who spurn sensual pleasure in favor of idealized sentiment, are Philautus, a conceited young man, and Faustina, a paragon of good counsel who, unlike Philautus, is aware of the improbable fact that they are brother and sister. In a long scene in act three, Faustina, promoting the new love doctrine, instructs her brother that true manly honor is to be

won on the field of battle. Since no development of a love intrigue between a brother and sister is possible—barring criminal conduct—the situation is undramatic, promoting only poetic exordiums such as:

> I would have you proceed and seek for fame
> In brave exploits, like those that snatch their honour
> Out of the talons of the Roman Eagle,
> And pull her golden feathers in the field.
> Those are brave men, not you that stay at home,
> And dress yourself up, like a pageant,
> With thousand antic and exotic shapes;
> That make an idol of a looking glass,
> Sprucing yourself two hours by it, with such
> Gestures and postures, that a waiting wench
> Would be ashamed of you, and then come forth
> T' adore your mistress' fan or tell your dream,
> Ravish a kiss from her white glove, and then
> Compare it with her hand, to praise her gown,
> Her Tire, and discourse of the fashion:
> Make discovery, which lady paints, which not,
> Which lord plays best at gleek, which best at racket.
> These are fine elements!

The speech demonstrates Marmion's strength as a keen observer of his society, but unfortunately, the social satirist is unable to make sufficiently dramatic use of his insights. The harangue is merely meant to inspire Philautus to give up vanity and to learn true manly honor in the school of war in Holland. In *A Fine Companion* Marmion makes more effective drama of his insights into society, and in a sense he goes beyond Jonson in his portraits of fops and witty young women, for, unlike Jonson, Marmion does not deviate from mere folly into what a later age would call neurosis. It can also be said that he did not have the genius to do so, but his portraits are more realistic than Jonson's and, therefore, closer to the character types found on the Restoration stage.

The play's underplot concerning the gulling of three gallants provides some compensation for the dramatic deficiency of the main plot. Invited to the war in Holland, the three gallants, under the direction of the "projector" Agurtes, set off to assault the fortified Holland's Leaguer. Agurtes, with his disciple, Autolicus, is reminiscent of many similar figures in Jonson's plays, and his function of plot manipulator is the same. He provides Marmion with a mouthpiece for what must have been his own observations of London low life. Agurtes' fear of what will become of him once he is old and no longer able to cheat for a living is a real one, and in II.iii he envisions such a time that:

I am grown so poor, that all my goods
Are shipt away i'th bottom of a sculler.
And then be driven t'inhabit some blind nook
I' th' suburbs, and my utmost refuge be
To keep a bawdy house, and be carted.

Agurtes need fear no such fate while there
are boobies like Capritio, the younger brother of
Philautus's wife, Triphoena. Capritio has come up
to London with his tutor, Miscellanio, intent on
becoming a gallant. The pupil and his tutor are
joined by Trimalchio, the beloved of Triphoena,
in the assault upon the brothel. Trimalchio is another who has come up to London to dissipate,
having inherited the manor upon the death of his
father. Agurtes trips up each of the gallants by
impersonating first a constable and then a justice
of the peace, managing to marry each to a woman
of humble station by convincing the gallants that
the women are ladies. Thus, Trimalchio is con-

vinced to marry Agurtes' daughter, Milliscent; Capritio is duped into marrying Milliscent's maid,
Margery; and Miscellanio is fobbed off on Triphoena's maid, Quartilla. These antics are handled
briskly, with no sympathy wasted.

Marmion's second comedy, *A Fine Companion*,
was also performed by Prince Charles' Men at the
Salisbury Court theater. Because the license to perform the play is not extant, the exact date of production is unknown, but in the play's prologue,
spoken by a Critic and the Author, we learn from
the Author that the same audience "crown[ed] our
infant muse, whose celestial/Applause she heard at
her first entrance"—a reference to the reception
of *Holland's Leaguer*. There is further evidence in
the prologue that no more than one season could
have separated these plays. The Critic appears to
be referring to Jonson's *The Magnetic Lady* (licensed
in October 1632) when he bids the Author to

Remember, if you please, what entertainment
Some of your tribe have had that have took pains
To be contemn'd, and laught at by the vulgar,
And then ascrib'd it to their ignorance.

Of equal interest is the Critic's comment about
those "poetasters," who, "without art or learning
. . . usurp the stage, and touch with impure hands/
The lofty buskin, and the comic style." The sentiments are clearly Marmion's.

In a letter dedicating the play to his kinsman
Sir Ralph Dutton which prefaces the 1633 quarto
edition of *A Fine Companion*, Marmion stated that
his play "hath often pleas'd, and without intermission." Moreover, we learn from the quarto title
page that the play was "acted before the king and
queen at Whitehall." The date of the royal performance is unknown, but it was probably in the
winter season 1632-1633, or about the same period
as the public performance.

Unlike his first essay at the dramatic form,
which is written entirely in verse, Marmion's second
comedy alternates prose and verse scenes. The handling of the plot is much more adept, and Marmion
integrates his Platonic lovers into the action so that
the undramatic attitudinizing of his first effort is
largely avoided. The basic intrigue formula remains the same, however.

The play contrasts two brothers. Before the
play's action begins, Aurelio, the elder, has been
disinherited because he and his father were in love
with the same woman, Valeria, the elder daughter
of the usurer Littlegood. The younger brother,
Careless (the "fine companion" of the title), has

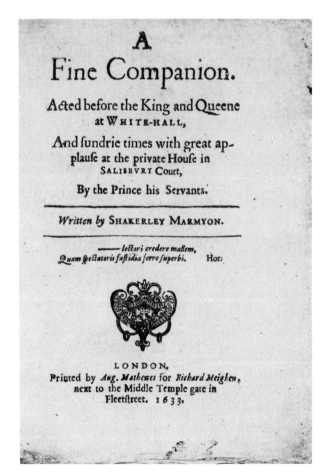

*Title page for the 1633 quarto edition of the play that, according
to Marmion's preface, "hath often pleas'd, and without intermission" (Henry E. Huntington Library and Art Gallery)*

inherited the family's lands and mortgaged them to the hilt to support a life of dissipation in London. Aurelio and Valeria express their love for each other in the rhetorical set speeches of Platonic lovers and agree to part, at Aurelio's insistence, because his fortune is unworthy of her.

While Valeria is all sensibility, her younger sister, Aemilia, being all sense, provides an apt contrast. A precursor of the typical heroine of the Restoration stage, she is witty and resourceful and feels the equal of any man. Her portrait posits a society in which men and women meet as equals. A conventional situation of comedy transpires when Aemilia's father thrusts old Dotario upon her as his candidate for her hand. The young woman heaps insults upon Dotario for his presumption and has no difficulty whatever in eloping with her beloved Careless, who has disguised himself as Dotario.

Valeria's father intends her for the fop Spruse, whose consultation with his tailor in I.iii must be one of the earliest instances of a scene that was to become a stock-in-trade of the Restoration dramatists. Although it might be argued that Spruse is patterned on Jonson's Fastidious Brisk of *Every Man out of His Humour*, the real source of the characterization is Marmion's observation. When Spruse is rejected by Valeria, his love quickly turns to hate, and, seeking revenge, he slanders the young woman's good name to Aurelio, who too readily accepts Spruse's falsehoods as the truth. After some difficulty, Aurelio's devoted friend Fido manages to persuade the deluded lover of Valeria's honesty. Fido, like Agurtes in Marmion's first play, also functions as a plot manipulator, suggesting that Valeria feign madness. This ruse causes Spruse to repent and to aid the lovers by suggesting to Littlegood that he call in a doctor for his daughter. The doctor proves to be Aurelio in disguise, and he takes Valeria off to church. Thus Littlegood, upon whom no tears are wasted, is duped out of both of his daughters.

The subplot of *A Fine Companion* chiefly promotes the antics of the braggart Captain Whibble, whose characterization probably owes more to Jonson's Bobadil in *Every Man in His Humour* than to Shakespeare's Falstaff. Whibble speaks a language reminiscent of his greater progenitors: "There's a wench has her suburb tricks about her, I warrant you. Hold there Bellerophon! take thy Ocyrois, and mount her like Phlegon." The action of the subplot concerns the gulling of Littlegood's booby son, Lackwit, who is initiated into the brotherhood of the Red Lattice tavern in Southwark by being made to pay for their drinking and whoring. But Captain Whibble receives his comeuppance when Careless, who has supported him in his madcap life, is made to see that the captain will slander him as readily as another—a realization which completes Careless's reformation. The captain ends up marrying the hostess of the Red Lattice and turning tapster. The machinations of the subplot seem insufficiently realized, and certainly Captain Whibble's sidekick, Lieutenant Sterne, is but the shadow of a character.

Marmion's final comedy, *The Antiquary*, is the only one of his plays to have been republished in the eighteenth- and nineteenth-century collections of old English plays. It was included by Robert Dodsley in *A Select Collection of Old Plays* (1744, new editions 1780 and 1826); Sir Walter Scott, who is said to have admired the play, published it in his *The Ancient British Drama* (1810); and W. Carew Hazlitt included it in his *A Select Collection of Old English Plays* (1875).

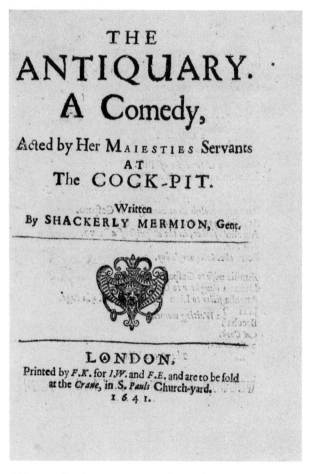

Title page for the 1641 quarto edition of Marmion's last play (Henry E. Huntington Library and Art Gallery)

The license for the play, which was performed by the Queen's Company at the Cockpit (or Phoenix) theater, is not extant, but internal evidence, which stops short of being conclusive, suggests the winter season of 1634-1635. The play was not published until 1641, about two years after Marmion's death. That he had nothing to do with the publication is apparent from an examination of the text. Evidence of authorial supervision is totally absent. There is no dedicatory letter prefacing the play, as was the case with Marmion's two earlier comedies, and there are inconsistencies in the names of the characters and in the setting.

Nor does this volume contain any evidence regarding the play's reception. Why Marmion should have changed companies is also a mystery. It might be noted, however, that his tendency toward realistic social comedy may have led him to the Queen's Company, one of whose best-known dramatists, James Shirley, wrote this type of comedy.

In *The Antiquary*, Marmion repeats familiar situations and characters, even to the point of using the same names. This play also has its Aurelio, who is in love with Lucretia, the daughter of Lorenzo, a gentleman of Venice. But in depicting these two lovers, Marmion holds up to ridicule the Platonic love that he had treated so sympathetically in his first two comedies. When Aurelio utters his high-flown sentiments beneath Lucretia's window to the accompaniment of music, the young lady rejects them as "a language you are studied in." Repeating the situation he had already used in *A Fine Companion*, Marmion has Lucretia's father foist old Moccinigo upon her as a suitor. Angered when he is spurned by the girl, Moccinigo hires a bravo, who is Aurelio's father in disguise, to murder Aurelio. When Lucretia discovers that she loves Aurelio after all, she saves him from the plot against his life by persuading the bravo that murder is a heinous crime. If Lucretia's changed attitude toward Aurelio seems unmotivated, it should be remembered that such sudden shifts are common in intrigue comedy.

Lucretia swallows her pride and goes as a penitent to Aurelio, but instead of forgiving her, Aurelio heaps scorn and abuse upon her. Fido disabuses Aurelio of his mistaken view of Lucretia, and Aurelio wins the young woman by appearing on her balcony in the morning and greeting his friends in the street below with the news that he and Lucretia are man and wife. The trick is like a tale from an Elizabethan jest book, and, if it seems to conventional morality to be blackmail, in the in-

trigue comedy it is meant to be merely amusing.

The Antiquary, like Marmion's two earlier plays, also has its fop. He is Petrutio, an Italianate Englishman—despite the fact that the play is set in Venice—who derives ultimately from John Lyly's popular prose romance, *Euphues* (1579), and the figure has many dramatic incarnations in the plays of the period. Petrutio attributes it to "vallainous destiny" that he is not instantly recognized by the Duke as a great man and employed on affairs of state. Petrutio's father, Gasparo, who dotes upon his son, is, by Jonson's definition, a humorous character because he is blinded by conceit. While in the company of Lorenzo, Gasparo encounters his son, freshly returned from his travels. Immediately and quite improbably, Lorenzo offers the conceited young man his daughter Lucretia's hand in marriage, which the young man, with unseemly arrogance, as quickly rejects. Lorenzo seeks revenge, but Lionell, who is the nephew of Veterano (the Antiquary of the play's title) and, with the Duke, chief plot manipulator, prevents any dire consequences by persuading Lorenzo to take his sister, Angelia—disguised as a boy—into his house as a page. Amusing consequences issue from this far-fetched scheme: not only does Aemilia, Lorenzo's wife, attempt the virtue of the "page," but, when her husband charges her with infidelity, she is able to turn the tables on him—with Lionell's help—by charging him with introducing his mistress into their home disguised as a youth. After similar manipulations, Lionell, with the aid of the Duke, succeeds in marrying Angelia, disguised now as the Duke's "sister," to Petrutio, whose fate as a "gull" is arguably too good for him; still his reformation augurs a better character in the future.

Another aspect of the subplot involves the gulling of Veterano, the Antiquary. An indiscriminate lover of old things—hints for his characterization were drawn from John Earle's character of "An Antiquary" in *Micro-Cosmographia* (1628)—Veterano is an innocuous old fool, and his gulling by his nephew, Lionell, abetted by the Duke, is not without a certain cruelty that most readers of the play probably find difficult to accept. Because his uncle has refused to support him in the life of gallantry and folly to which he aspires, Lionell—with the help of the Duke—gets money from the old man by selling him bogus manuscripts for exorbitant sums. Deprived of his "treasures" by the "Duke" (Lionell in disguise) on the grounds that they are too valuable to be in the hands of a private citizen, Veterano is brought before the "Duke" in a drunken state and wearing fool's motley and made to beg for his collections. But, when Lionell reveals his true identity, the old man generously grants him enough money to live on. Only once is Veterano allowed to express a positive view of his mania, and then, in II.v, he merely notes that the cause of the fashions and diseases brought daily from overseas is to be found in "the neglect of these useful instructions which antiquity has set down." Veterano is a feeble social critic, but the play offers interesting insights into a society that Marmion clearly regarded as crassly material and morally corrupt.

The plot of *The Antiquary* is more complicated than those of Marmion's two earlier comedies. Moreover, the Platonic love interest portrayed in the relationship of Aurelio and Lucretia is largely subordinated to the demands of a comedy of intrigue. Unlike Marmion's earlier portrayals of Platonic lovers, Aurelio and Lucretia are both active and resourceful individuals. Here Marmion is treating Platonic love not with deference, but with satire.

In 1637 Marmion concluded his literary career—save for his elegy to Jonson—with a more than 2,000 line mythological poem entitled *The Legend of Cupid and Psyche*. That the poem was dedicated to Frederick, Prince Elector of the Palatine, confirms Marmion's Royalist sympathies. The poem, which largely lacks the vividness and immediacy of Marmion's plays, is at least three-quarters translation from the Latin of Apuleius's *The Golden Ass*. The remaining lines are mainly Marmion's, though some few are from other classical authors.

Marmion is an adequate translator of his source, but it is significant that his additions are better than the parts he translates. If the poem reads rather unevenly, it is because the additions, which are in the mock-heroic vein and have the effect of humanizing the characters, stand head and shoulders above the translated portions. What is more, they are at times at variance with the intent of the original. Apuleius intends an allegory of the Soul (Psyche), who, through her love of Desire (Cupid), is purified of all sensual longings and brought, finally, to the true marriage of souls.

Marmion makes his originals into something like characters in his plays. Thus Cupid, although he begins as the mischievous boy of legend, is then described and shown to behave like a young man. Moreover, his mother, Venus, shown at her toilet attended by the Graces, is really a petulant lady of Caroline society and resembles Belinda attended by her sylphs in Alexander Pope's *The Rape of the*

Lock (1712-1714). Marmion's interest in humanizing the legend is made clear from the fact that he drew several lines from act four of his then-unpublished play, *The Antiquary*, for his description of Cupid and Psyche's first love encounter. In the poem we read:

> My armes shall be they Spheare to wander in,
> Circles about with spells, to charme they feares,
> Instead of *Morpheus* to provoke they teares,
> With horrid dreames, *Venus* shall thee entrance
> With thousand shapes of wanton dalliance.

And in the play:

> My armes shall be thy spaer to wander in,
> Circled about with spels to charm those fears;
> And, when thou sleep'st, *Cupid* shall crown thy
>   slumbers
> With thousand shapes of lustfull dalliance.

Significantly in his poem Marmion does not dwell upon sensual details. Indeed, his conclusion of this invitation to dalliance, which is entirely his own addition to his source, has a comic abruptness:

> And having said so, he made haste to bed.
> Enjoy'd his spouse, and got her Maydenhead.

This quarrying of his own work—the only instance of its kind in Marmion—suggests that in 1637 he had given up the idea of writing for the stage and probably did not intend to publish his last play. He was not, however, to find a career as a poet, although his long poem, if little read, is still readable.

Marmion remains a minor figure in the history of English dramatic literature; yet he richly deserves the praise of Swinburne, who wrote in his "Sonnets of English Dramatic Poets" of "Marmion, whose verse keeps always keen and fine/The perfume of their Apollonian wine." A sweet and graceful writer, if not profound (as Swinburne's praise implies), he was yet able to adapt Jonson's classical rules of comedy to his own interests, which lay largely in the Platonic-love theme and the conventions of the intrigue comedy. Moreover, like Shirley and others, Marmion, in his portraits of high-spirited young men and women, showed himself to be a keen observer of contemporary society. He foreshadowed Restoration drama, where the relations between the sexes are founded upon an absolute social equality.

References:

Allan P. Green, "Shakerley Marmion, Caroline Dramatist and Poet, 1603-1639," Ph.D dissertation, Rutgers University, 1974;

Green, "Shakerley Marmion, Dramatist: Declared an Outlaw in 1624?," in *The Yearbook of English Studies*, edited by G. K. Hunter and C. J. Rawson (Leeds: Modern Humanities Research Association, 1977), pp. 81-85;

Green, "Shakerley Marmion, Dramatist (1603-1639): His Descent from the Marmions of Adwell, Oxon.," *Notes and Queries*, new series 24 (April 1977): 124;

Green, "Shakerley Marmion, Dramatist: The Dates of His Military Service in the Low Countries," *Notes and Queries*, new series 23 (May-June 1976): 222.

John Marston

George L. Geckle
University of South Carolina

BIRTH: Wardington, Oxfordshire, baptized 7 October 1576, to John and Mary Guarsi Marston.

EDUCATION: B.A., Brasenose College, Oxford, February 1594.

MARRIAGE: 1605 to Mary Wilkes; son: John.

DEATH: Aldermanbury, London, 25 June 1634.

PLAY PRODUCTIONS: *Histriomastix*, London, Middle Temple, 1598-1599;

Lust's Dominion (presumably the same play as *The Spanish Moor's Tragedy*), by Marston, Thomas Dekker, John Day, and William Haughton, London, Rose theater, Spring 1600;

Jack Drum's Entertainment, London, Paul's theater, 1600;

Antonio and Mellida, London, Paul's theater, 1600;

Antonio's Revenge, London, Paul's theater, 1600;

What You Will, London, Paul's theater, 1601;

The Malcontent, London, Blackfriars theater, 1602-1603;

Parasitaster, or The Fawn, London, Blackfriars theater, 1604;

Eastward Ho, by Marston, George Chapman, and Ben Jonson, London, Blackfriars theater, 1604-1605;

The Dutch Courtesan, London, Blackfriars theater, 1605;

The Wonder of Women, or The Tragedy of Sophonisba, London, Blackfriars theater, 1606;

The Spectacle presented to the Sacred Majesties Of Great Britain, and Denmark as they Passed through London, London, 31 July 1606;

The Entertainment of the Dowager-Countess of Darby, Ashby-de-la Zouch in Leicester, 1607;

The Insatiate Countess, by Marston and William Barksted, London, Whitefriars theater, 1608(?).

BOOKS: *The Metamorphosis of Pigmalions Image. And Certaine Satyres* (London: Printed by J. Roberts for E. Matts, 1598);

The Scourge of Villanie. Three Bookes of Satyres (London: Printed by J. Roberts & sold by J. Buzbie, 1598);

Jacke Drums Entertainment: Or, The Comedie of Pasquill and Katherine (London: Printed by T. Creede for R. Olive, 1601);

The History of Antonio and Mellida (London: Printed by R. Bradock for M. Lownes & T. Fisher, 1602);

Antonios Revenge (London: Printed by R. Bradock for T. Fisher, 1602);

The Malcontent (London: Printed by V. Simmes for W. Aspley, 1604);

Eastward Hoe, by Marston, George Chapman, and Ben Jonson (London: Printed by G. Eld for W. Aspley, 1605);

The Dutch Courtezan (London: Printed by T. Purfoote for J. Hodgets, 1605);

Parasitaster, or The Fawne (London: Printed by T. Purfoote for W. Cotton, 1606);

The Wonder of Women, or The Tragedie of Sophonisba (London: Printed by J. Windet, 1606);

What You Will (London: Printed by G. Eld for T. Thorppe, 1607);

Histrio-mastix: Or, The Player whipt (London: Printed by G. Eld for T. Thorp, 1610);

The Insatiate Countesse, by Marston and William Barksted (London: Printed by T. Snodham for T. Archer, 1613);

The Workes of M^r. J. Marston (London: Printed by A. Mathewes for W. Sheares, 1633); republished as *Tragedies and Comedies* (London: Printed by A. Mathewes for W. Sheares, 1633)—comprises *Antonio and Mellida, Antonio's Revenge, The Wonder of Women* (or *Sopho-*

nisba), *What You Will, Parasitaster* (or *The Fawn*), and *The Dutch Courtesan;*

Comedies, Tragi-comedies; & Tragedies, Nonce Collection (London, 1652)—comprises *The Malcontent, What You Will, The Dutch Courtesan, The Wonder of Women* (or *Sophonisba*), *Parasitaster* (or *The Fawn*), *Antonio and Mellida, Antonio's Revenge,* and *The Insatiate Countess;*

Lust's Dominion, or The Lascivious Queen (presumably the same play as *The Spanish Moor's Tragedy*), by Marston, Thomas Dekker, John Day, and William Haughton (London: Printed for F. K. & sold by Robert Pollard, 1657).

Editions: *The Plays of John Marston,* 3 volumes, edited by H. Harvey Wood (Edinburgh: Oliver & Boyd, 1934-1939)—comprises *Antonio and Mellida, Antonio's Revenge, The Malcontent, Sophonisba, The Dutch Courtesan, The Fawn, What You Will, The Insatiate Countess, Eastward Ho, Jack Drum's Entertainment,* and *Histriomastix;*

The Poems of John Marston, edited by Arnold Davenport (Liverpool: Liverpool University Press, 1961);

The Malcontent, edited by M. L. Wine, Regents Renaissance Drama Series (Lincoln: University of Nebraska Press, 1964);

Antonio and Mellida: The First Part, edited by G. K. Hunter, Regents Renaissance Drama Series (Lincoln: University of Nebraska Press, 1965);

Antonio's Revenge: The Second Part of Antonio and Mellida, edited by G. K. Hunter, Regents Renaissance Drama Series (Lincoln: University of Nebraska Press, 1965);

The Dutch Courtesan, edited by M. L. Wine, Regents Renaissance Drama Series (Lincoln: University of Nebraska Press, 1965);

The Fawn, edited by Gerald A. Smith, Regents Renaissance Drama Series (Lincoln: University of Nebraska Press, 1965);

The Malcontent, edited by Bernard Harris, The New Mermaids Series (London: Benn, 1967);

The Malcontent, edited by George K. Hunter, The Revels Plays (London: Methuen, 1975);

Antonio's Revenge, edited by W. Reavley Gair, The Revels Plays (Manchester: Manchester University Press/Baltimore: Johns Hopkins University Press, 1978);

The Fawn, edited by Davis A. Blostein, The Revels Plays (Manchester: Manchester University Press/Baltimore: The Johns Hopkins University Press, 1978);

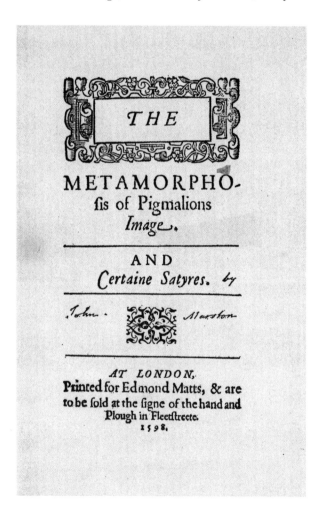

Title page for the 1598 octavo edition of Marston's first book (British Library)

The Wonder of Women or The Tragedy of Sophonisba,
  edited by William Kemp (New York: Garland,
  1979);
The Insatiate Countess, edited by Giorgio Melchiori,
  The Revels Plays (Manchester: Manchester
  University Press, 1984).

Aside from his reputation as a playwright,
John Marston has for the most part been recognized from his own time to the present as a satirist,
a malcontent, and a generally cantankerous individual. His contemporaries thought of him as a
good verse satirist, but coarse and indecent, and
one extended portrait of him in the anonymous
play *The Return from Parnassus* (written circa 1600)
is particularly unflattering and at the same time
revealing:

> What *Monsier Kinsayder,* lifting vp your legge and
>   pissing against the world, put vp man, put vp for
>   shame.
> Methinks he is a Ruffin in his stile,
> Withouten bands or garters ornament,
> He quaffes a cup of Frenchmans Helicon.
> Then royster doyster in his oylie tearmes,
> Cuts, thrusts, and foynes at whomesoeuer he meets.
> And strowes about Ram ally meditations.
> Tut what cares he for modest close coucht termes,
> Cleanly to gird our looser libertines.
> Giue him plaine naked words stript from their shirts
> That might beseeme plaine dealing *Aretine:*
> I there is one that backes a paper steed
> And manageth a penknife gallantly.
> Strikes his poinado at a buttons breadth,
> Brings the great battering ram of tearmes to townes
> And at first volly of his Caunon shot,
> Batters the walles of the old fusty world.

W. Kinsayder was Marston's pseudonym in *The
Scourge of Villainy,* a collection of verse satires that,
along with *The Metamorphosis of Pygmalion's Image
and Certain Satires,* launched his literary career in
1598. *The Metamorphosis* is an erotic poem, deemed
pornographic by some critics, but defended as satiric by Marston himself. The satires *are* crude and
harsh, but deliberately so, it seems, because Marston draws attention to himself in *The Scourge of
Villainy* twice as "a sharpe fangd Satyrist." His peculiar style indeed ranges from the "Ruffin" (that
is, Ruffian) to "the great battering ram of tearmes,"
and his great contemporary Ben Jonson managed
a marvelous burlesque of Marston in *Poetaster, or
His Arraignment* (produced in 1601), which concluded with the administering of an emetic to the
hapless Rufus Laberious Crispinus (alias John Mar-

ston, who was, it seems a red head, hence "rufus"),
causing him to disgorge such vocabulary as *"retrograde—reciprocall—incubus," "glibbery—lubricall—
defunct," "spurious—snotteries," "barmy froth,"
"Puffy—inflate—turgidous—ventositous," "oblatrant—
furibund—fatuate—strenuous,"* and *"Snarling gusts—
quaking custard,"* several of which terms can actually
be found in Marston's poems and early plays.

John Marston was born in Wardington, Oxfordshire, and baptized on 7 October 1576 in the
church of St. Mary Magdalene. His father, John
Marston, was a gentleman and member of the Middle Temple and had property in Wardington and
Cropredy, Oxfordshire, and Coventry. The playwright's mother, Mary Guarsi of Wardington, was
the daughter of Andrew Guarsi, an Italian surgeon.
Marston's parents married on 19 September 1575,
and he was their only child. Nothing is known of
the young Marston's early education, but he ma-

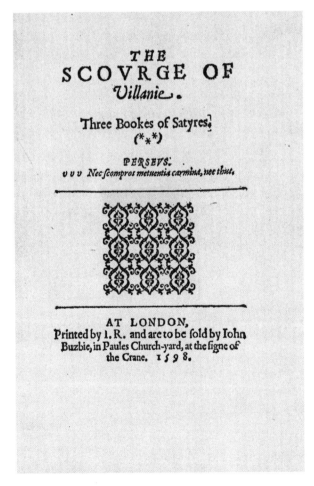

*Title page for the 1598 octavo edition of the collection of verse
satires in which Marston, writing under the pseudonym W.
Kinsayder, twice calls himself "a sharpe fangd Satyrist" (Anderson Galleries, sale no. 2077, 20-21 May 1926)*

triculated at Brasenose College, Oxford, on 4 February 1592. He was admitted to the B.A. degree at Oxford on 6 February 1594 and formally concluded "determination" (disputations) on 23 March 1594.

Although he was admitted to the Society of the Middle Temple on 2 August 1592 (while the elder Marston was holding office as a reader), he seems not to have established residency there until November 1595. Thereafter, there are records that he was at the Middle Temple at least intermittently through 21 November 1606. He was not always in good graces; for on 14 October 1601 he was expelled for "nonpayment of commons and other causes." He was "restored to the Fellowship" a few weeks later. It is during this period also that John Manningham of the Middle Temple recorded in his famous diary the following anecdote about Marston (dated 21 November 1602):

> Jo. Marstone the last Christmas when he daunct with Alderman Mores wives daughter, a Spaniard borne, fell into a strang commendacion of her witt and beauty. When he had done, shee thought to pay him home, and told him she though[t] he was a poet. "'Tis true," said he, "for poetes fayne, and lye, and so dyd I when I commended your beauty, for you are exceeding foule."

We can see that Marston was early on building the reputation that later earned him mention with George Chapman, Jonson, and Shakespeare as one of the "pregnant witts of these our times" in William Camden's *Remaines* (1605) and as someone "in great renown for his wit and ingenuity in sixteen hundred and six," according to Anthony à Wood in his *Athenae Oxoniensis* (published in 1692-1692).

Marston's intellectual and social milieu, then, was that of the highly educated, first at Oxford and then at the Middle Temple, where he shared chambers first with his father and later, upon his father's death in November 1599, with another lawyer. The normal expectation would have been that Marston would eventually become a lawyer, but in his father's will there is a bequest of the furniture in his Middle Temple chambers and also his law books to his son John, "wherein I have taken greate paynes with delighte and hoped that my sonne would have proffetted in the studdye of the lawe wherein I bestowed my uttermost indevor but man proposeth and god disposeth." There is no record that Marston was ever called to the bar, and, in fact, the publication of his two volumes of poetry in 1598 would certainly indicate where his real interests resided. However, although *The Scourge of Villainy* was reprinted twice in 1599, Marston did not continue as a verse satirist, perhaps because of the bishops' ban on satire in June 1599. The "Order of Conflagration" of John Whitgift, Archbishop of Canterbury, and Richard Bancroft, Bishop of London, consigned several books, including Marston's, to the fire. Some critics conjecture that Marston turned to dramatic satire as another outlet for his literary talents. More recently, however, it has been argued that he was writing plays before the "Order of Conflagration" because in his father's will there is a canceled passage that refers to "my willful disobedyent sonne," for whom the elder Marston prays, "therein god blesse hym and giue hym trewe knowledge of hymself and to foregoe his delighte in playes vayne studdyes and fooleryes."

If Marston was writing plays well before 1599, instead of just going to the theater or reading other people's plays (which may be the only implication of the canceled passage in his father's will), then such early work seems to have been lost (although Marston's share in *The Insatiate Countess* may well have been written in the early part of his career). E. K. Chambers has noted in *The Elizabethan Stage* (1923) that "On 28 Sept. 1599 Henslowe paid £2, on behalf of the Admiral's, for 'Mr Maxton the new poete.' . . . The title of the play was left blank, and there was no further payment." He goes on to argue "that the £2 was meant to make up a complete sum of £6 10S. for *The King of Scots*, and that Marston was the 'other Jentellman' who collaborated with Chettle, Dekker, and Jonson on that lost play. The setting up of the Paul's boys in 1599 saved Marston from Henslowe." Another theory is that the Henslowe payment was for Marston's part in *Lust's Dominion*, first printed in 1657 and attributed to Christopher Marlowe, but now identified with *The Spanish Moor's Tragedy* and attributed to Marston, Thomas Dekker, John Day, and William Haughton. The only extant play currently and generally attributed to Marston that seems to fit into the time scheme is *Histriomastix: Or, The Player whipt*, which seems likely to have been written for the Middle Temple's Christmas revels of 1598-1599. (It was not entered into the Stationers' Register, where all plays were supposed to be registered before they were printed, until 31 October 1610, and then without attribution.) According to Philip J. Finkelpearl in a persuasive article entitled "John Marston's *Histriomastix* as an Inns of Court Play: A Hypothesis" (1966), there are several pieces of evidence that point to Marston's first play having been written for a special audience, including academic jargon and philosophical arguments in the text, many references to lawyers and law terms (three characters—Voucher, Fourcher, and Champerty—have names derived from technical law terms), and an irascible satirist named Chrisoganus, who seems to have been modeled in part on Ben Jonson, who in the late 1590s was quite close to several members of the Middle Temple.

The audience to which the twenty-two-year-old fledgling playwright was trying to appeal was described by John Stow in *A Survey of London* (1603) as "a whole Uniuersitie, as it were, of students, practisers or pleaders and Iudges of the lawes of this realme, not liuing of common stipends, as in other Uniuersities it is for ye most part done, but of their owne priuate maintenance, as being altogither fed either by their places, or practise, or otherwise by their proper reuenue, or exhibition of parents & friends: for that the yonger sort are either gentlemen, or the sons of gentlemen, or of other most welthie persons." The nature of the *very* learned and privileged audience for Marston's first dramatic production may explain why the play is so highly intellectual in substance.

Histriomastix is a six-act allegorical play that dramatizes the stages through which a commonwealth (England, of course) degenerates from a Golden Age to an Age of Iron and is then renewed through the return of the goddess Astraea, alias Queen Elizabeth. The crucial character in the play is the scholar-poet Chrisoganus, whose name, symbolic of his role, means "begotten of gold" or "golden-born." When the play opens, the allegorical character Peace enters with her handmaidens, Grammer, Logick, Rhetorick, Arithmatick, Geometrie, Musick, and Astronomie—that is, the traditional lower and higher divisions of the liberal arts, or the trivium and quadrivium. The opening speech of Peace indicates the ideal state of affairs:

> Now sit wee high (tryumphant in our sway,)
> Encircled with the seauen-fold flower of Art,
> To tread on Barbarisme with silver feete;
> These, these are adjuncts fit to waite on *Peace*,
> Who beeing courted by most searching spirits,
> Have always borne themselves in God-like state,
> With lofty foreheads, higher then the starres.

The problems involved in maintaining such a state become immediately apparent when some nobles arrive and fail to recognize these "adjuncts fit to waite on *Peace*." Being duly informed, each noble chooses "a spowsall mate," but Chrisoganus, who

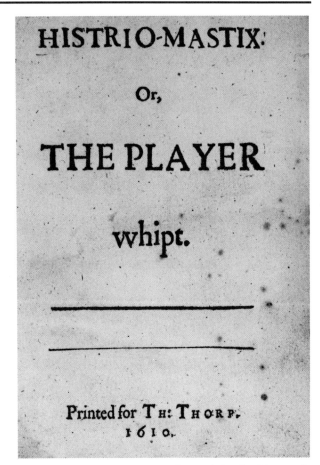

HISTRIO-MASTIX:

Or,

THE PLAYER

whipt.

Printed for Th: Thorp.
1610.

Title page for the 1610 quarto edition of the play Marston is believed to have written for the Middle Temple's Christmas revels of 1598-1599 (Henry E. Huntington Library and Art Gallery)

has recognized the liberal arts, chooses to be the servant of all. He launches into a discourse on epistemology that concludes that arithmetic is the most exact art of the quadrivium, being most "Abjunct from sencive matter." (The passage echoes one in Satyre VIII of *The Scourge of Villainy* and leaves the nobles, if not a modern reader, impressed.)

The remainder of act one involves the formation of Sir Oliver Owlet's players (Marston's send-up of the public companies), an interchange between some merchants and lawyers, who choose to spend their afternoon "hearinge the Mathematickes read" by Chrisoganus instead of going to a play, and a concluding masque. At the conclusion of act one, Peace resigns her crown to her daughter Plenty, who enters in act two with her attendants, Plutus and Bacchus. The movement is toward a materialistic age, and the nobles, merchants, and lawyers now reject the golden lore of Chrisoganus for the pastime of hunting and hawking, while the newly formed players, whose playwright is named Posthast, decide to rehearse "the new plot of the prodigall childe," appropriate for a new age of profligacy.

Further degeneration occurs in act three as Pride, attended by Vaine-glory, Hypocrisie, and Contempt, "turnes her houre." The merchants and lawyers and their wives all display an outrageous capacity for materialism and vanity. The nobles foolishly dismiss their servants in order to support instead "rich lac'd sutes/And straight lac'd mutton" (that is, unchaste women). Even the players show arrogance as they reject the services of Chrisoganus for the "rotten stuffs" of "goosequillian *Posthast.*" The act ends as each "estate" grows envious of the others, and Envy then ascends to power.

Acts four and five rapidly bring further changes for the worse. In act four the four groups of people grow so envious of one another that all vestiges of civilized behavior are discarded. The inevitable happens, and, as act five begins, Warre, attended by Ambition, Fury, Horror, and Ruine, ascends Envy's throne. Finally, in act six we learn, as Chrisoganus says, that "Justice hath whips to scourge impiety" (an allusive pun on the play's title), as Poverty enters with her attendants, Famine, Sicknesse, Bondage, and Sluttishnesse. The ruined nobles now turn back to Chrisoganus for counsel and are advised, "First entertaine submission in your soules/To frame true concord in one unity." Chrisoganus concludes: "For law is that which Love and Peace maintaine." The lawyers and merchants also now ask for Peace again, the unrepentant players are shipped out of the country, and Peace returns with Plenty.

The implied pattern that has become explicit is one of the endless turning of the Wheel of Fortune, and, in fact, in Ludovic Lalanne's *Le Livre de Fortune: Recueil de Deux Cents Dessins Inedits de Jean Cousin* (manuscript dated 1568), there is a plate that shows six figures on a wheel that clearly reflects the underlying structure of Marston's play. The inscription reads: "Ex: Divitiis Svperbia, Ex: Spera Bellvm, Ex: Bello Pavpertas, Ex: Pavper Hvmilita, Ex: Hvmilitate: Pax, Ex: Paca Divitiae." In Marston's play, however, the endless revolution is stopped by the appearance of "*Astraea* ushered by *Fame,* supported by *Fortitude* and *Religion,* followed by *Virginity* and *Artes.*" In a long speech Peace resigns her throne to Astraea—"*Peaces* patronesse, *Heavens* miracle,/*Vertues* honour, *Earths* admiration,/*Chastities* Crowne, Justice perfection"—who ascends in the guise of Queen Elizabeth:

Still breath[e] our glory, the worlds *Empresse*
Religions Gardian, *Peaces* patronesse;
Now flourish Arts, the Queene of *Peace* doth raigne,
Vertue triumph, now shee doth sway the stemme,
Who gives to *Vertue,* honours Diadem.

The conclusion of *Histriomastix* reflects an allegorical tradition in which Queen Elizabeth was associated with the goddess of Justice, who at the end of the Golden Age of Saturn left earth (with her comrade Chastity, as Juvenal tells us in his Satire VI) to reign in heaven as Virgo. Because of Queen Elizabeth, it is implied, England is not subject to the vagaries of Dame Fortuna.

Although it is not in many respects a particularly accomplished play, *Histriomastix* does reflect the concerns Marston was to return to many times throughout his dramatic career. As one might expect from an educated Elizabethan, the themes of social and political order and the values of spiritual and intellectual attainment are crucial to Marston's first play. Likewise, the use of a social critic or satirist who is both part of the action and yet stands detached from it is a recurring figure in the succeeding plays. Finally, the structural devices of multiple plot strands and the Wheel of Fortune appear in many of the later dramatic works. *Histriomastix* is in both its virtues and defects indicative of Marston's future career as a playwright.

Marston's next play was *Jack Drum's Entertainment: Or The Comedy of Pasquill and Katherine.* According to the records of the Stationers' Company, *Jack Drum's Entertainment* was first entered on 8 September 1600 and was described as "*a commedy . . . diuerse tymes acted by the Children of Paules.*" The play was probably written in 1600 and marks Marston's first professional connection with the Children of Paul's, a newly revived company of boy actors with whom such playwrights as George Chapman, Thomas Dekker, Thomas Middleton, and John Webster were also associated, Although it has many of the morality-play characteristics of *Histriomastix,* *Jack Drum's Entertainment* also reveals Marston's developing interest in romantic tragicomedy, which soon came to fruition in his next play, *Antonio and Mellida.*

The main plot of *Jack Drum's Entertainment,* the story of Pasquill and Katherine, derives from an anonymous play titled *The Trial of Chivalry* (itself derived from two episodes in Sir Philip Sidney's *Arcadia*). Each play includes a situation in which a villainous rejected suitor disfigures the heroine, whose face is cured and who eventually marries the hero. Each play also contains a situation in which

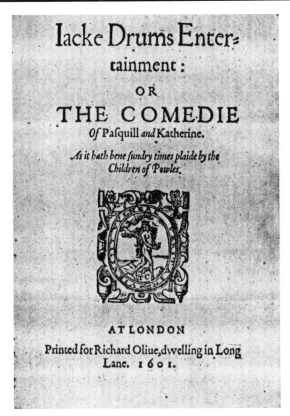

Title page for the 1601 quarto edition of what is probably the first play Marston wrote for the Children of Paul's (Anderson Galleries, sale no. 2077, 20-21 May 1926)

a woman is reunited with her lover, who was believed to be dead. It has been argued that Marston's play is a burlesque of the obviously romantic *The Trial of Chivalry*, which was probably performed circa 1600 by the Earl of Derby's Men, a rival public company. A passage in the introduction to *Jack Drum's Entertainment* in which the audience is informed that the author ". . . vowes not to torment your listning eares/With mouldy fopperies of stale Poetry,/Unpossible drie mustie Fictions," may well be a clue to the intention of Marston's play.

Perhaps also the nature of the rejected suitor in *Jack Drum's Entertainment* is an indication of Marston's attitude. In *The Trial of Chivalry* the suitor is a powerful noble, but in *Jack Drum's Entertainment* he is an aged usurer named Mamon. Marston seems to have derived his character from a late morality play called *The Three Ladies of London* (printed in 1584) and attributed to Robert Wilson. *The Three Ladies of London*, like *Histriomastix*, is concerned with the "estates," and Wilson's allegory concerns the destruction of Love and Conscience on account of Lucre. Mamon in *Jack Drum's Enter-*

tainment serves a function similar to that of Usury, Lady Lucre's secretary, in *The Three Ladies of London*, in that Mamon's antagonistic attitude toward the hospitality of Sir Edward Fortune, father of Katherine and Camelia (the marriageable young women in *Jack Drum's Entertainment*), is similar to Usury's toward Hospitality in the morality play. There are other similarities between Marston's play and *The Three Ladies of London*, and it may be that Wilson's play even suggested to Marston his title, because at one point in the morality play a character named Dissimulation threatens one named Simplicity with "Jack Drum's entertainment."

The full title of Marston's play indicates the major themes. "Jack Drum's entertainment" was a proverbial Elizabethan expression for "a rough reception." The phrase is used in Shakespeare's *All's Well That Ends Well* (produced circa 1602-1603) when the cowardly Parolles is exposed. In Marston's play, the usurer Mamon rejects the opening Whitsuntide festivities and tells Sir Edward Fortune (owner of an estate in the London suburb of Highgate), that he "keep[s] too great a house." Jack Drum, leader of the festivities and servant of Sir Edward, tells his master that he should "give him [Mamon] *Jacke Drums* entertainment." Those who obstruct what C. L. Barber in his *Shakespeare's Festive Comedy* (1959) has called the "saturnalian pattern" of "festive comedies" usually receive rough treatment, and Mamon is no exception. When he later hires the Frenchman John fo de King to murder (unsuccessfully, of course) Pasquill, his rival for Katherine's love, Pasquill beats him. When he then disfigures Katherine, we can expect him to suffer even more, and he does, for his material possessions are destroyed, and he goes mad.

The play contains a subplot in which "Jack Drum's entertainment" is also meted out. John Ellis is beaten by Brabant Jr. for wooing Sir Edward's other daughter, Camelia, but is himself given a rough reception by her because of his poor prospects. Planet, the play's major satirist, revenges Brabant Jr. by rejecting the fickle Camelia when she responds favorably to his seemingly serious pursuit of her. In yet another subplot, Brabant Sr. (the elder brother of Brabant Jr.), as a practical joke, introduces his wife as a courtesan to the lustful John fo de King, but the joke backfires when the Frenchman actually seduces her instead of receiving "Jack Drum's entertainment." In another practical joke, the maid Winifride, who has promised to sleep with both John fo de King and Jack Drum, manages to get Jack Drum (who has arrived early for his assignation) carried off in a sack by the

Introduction and beginning of act one from the 1601 quarto edition of Jack Drum's Entertainment *(British Library)*

unsuspecting Frenchman, who thinks he has Winifride instead.

Jack Drum's Entertainment has, to be sure, many of the elements of farce. It also contains various kinds of satire, some of it poking fun at the absurd rhetorical mannerisms of the young gallants and some of it actually drawing attention to the boy actors themselves. At one point Planet makes fun of Camelia by saying: "fore this Audience,/Put off your cloathes, and you are like a *Banbery* cheese,/ Nothing but paring." Later, Sir Edward Fortune says: "I sawe the Children of *Powles* last night,/And troth they pleasde mee prettie, prettie well,/The Apes in time will do it hansomely." One could emphasize the first part of the play's title, stress such incidents, and call the entire play a burlesque. However, the subtitle directs us to *The Comedy of Pasquill and Katherine.* Although this main plot is certainly not as convincing as some of Shakespeare's romantic relationships, it does not contain overt satire and

is not necessarily a burlesque of romantic heroes and heroines. The behavior and dialogue of Pasquill and Katherine can be viewed as unrealistic, even absurd, but they are not much more so than what we find later with Antonio and Mellida or even Freevill and Beatrice (in *The Dutch Courtesan*). Marston, simply, was never able to write particularly convincing romantic scenes. There is no compelling reason, therefore, to read all of *Jack Drum's Entertainment* as burlesque. The overall mood of the play is festive, like that of some of Shakespeare's comedies, for instance, and the mood is reinforced by many songs and dances. The Pasquill/Katherine plot is primarily romantic, not satiric, in tone. If the play is not particularly satisfying as an artistic whole, it is because Marston attempted more than he could handle at this early stage of his dramatic career.

The same may be said of his next play, *Antonio and Mellida,* probably written late in 1600. It was entered in the records of the Stationers' Company on 24 October 1601 and printed in quarto format in 1602 with the title "THE HISTORY OF Antonio and Mellida. *The first part. As It hath beene sundry times acted, by the children of* Paules. *Written by I. M.*" *Antonio and Mellida* has been variously described by critics as a comedy (with Senecan elements), a burlesque, and a tragicomedy. The comic elements are obvious and consist primarily of the exposure of foolish subplot characters with Italian names (most found in John Florio's 1598 Italian/English dictionary *A Worlde of Wordes*) that indicate their types, such as Balurdo (*balordo:* "a foole"), Castilio Balthazar (probably a reference to Baldassare Castiglione, author of *Il Cortegiano*), Forobosco (*forabosco:* "a sneaking prying busie fellowe"), Catzo (*cazzo:* "a mans priuie member"), Dildo ("a word of obscure origin," according to the *Oxford English Dictionary;* actually, an artificial cazzo), and Matzagente (*mazzagente:* "a killer or queller of people"). The comic tone is set in the dedication to "the most honorably renowned Nobody" in which Marston speaks of his "humorous blood," which has led him "to affect (a little too much) to be seriously fantastical." The induction likewise contributes to the comic, even burlesque, tone as various actors appear "*with parts in their hands, having cloaks cast over their apparel*" and comment on their roles:

Are ye ready, are ye perfect?
....
... But whom act you?
The necessity of the play forceth me to play two
    parts. . . .

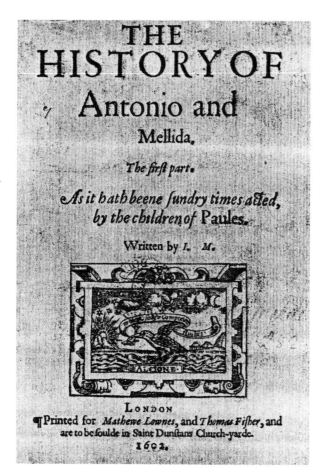

Title page for the 1602 quarto edition of the play that Marston dedicated to "the most honorably renowned Nobody" (Bodleian Library)

....

O, doth he play Forobosco the parasite?

....

Rampum scrampum, mount tufty Tamburlaine!
  What
rattling thunderclap breaks from his lips?

O' 'tis native to his part. For acting a modern
  Bragadoch
under the person of Matzagente. . . .

When the play proper begins, however, the intent of the burlesque element is less certain, even though Antonio appears *"disguised like an Amazon."* (Marston's source here is probably Sidney's *Arcadia.*) His opening lines could be viewed as a burlesque of the sort of hyperbolic rhetoric found in Christopher Marlowe's *Tamburlaine,* already alluded to in the induction:

Heart, wilt not break? And thou, abhorred life,
Wilt thou still breathe in my enraged blood?
Veins, sinews, arteries, why crack ye not,
Burst and divuls'd with anguish of my grief ?

Likewise, Piero (the chief villain) could be seen as a similar sort of burlesque figure in his opening speech:

Victorious Fortune, with triumphant hand,
Hurleth my glory 'bout this ball of earth,
Whilst the Venetian Duke [Piero] is heaved up
On wings of fair success to overlook
The low-cast ruins of his enemies;
To see myself ador'd and Genoa quake,
My fate is firmer than mischance can shake.

Similarly, the various hyperbolically romantic speeches of Antonio (for example, these lines in I.i: "She comes. Creation's purity, admir'd,/Ador'd, amazing rarity, she comes") and the several moments in the play when the characters draw attention to themselves as actors could also indicate that the play is a burlesque of more serious early Elizabethan drama such as *Tamburlaine* or Thomas Kyd's *The Spanish Tragedy.* In fact, Anthony Caputi in his *John Marston, Satirist* (1961) and R. A. Foakes in his "John Marston's Fantastical Plays: *Antonio and Mellida* and *Antonio's Revenge*" (1962) have so argued, both stressing the inherently comic effect of boy actors uttering pretentious speeches.

The problem with taking *Antonio and Mellida* as a parody is that one is then left with the philosophical, serious passages, as well as the characters who utter the neo-Stoic sentiments. One can argue, as Caputi does, that these elements are the only serious part of the play, but then Marston seems to be quite incompetent as a playwright. Or one can ignore these elements, as Foakes does, but then one ignores much of the play. Perhaps a better approach is to view *Antonio and Mellida* as an experiment in the genre of tragicomedy.

Although comedy and tragedy were frequently defined and discussed in the sixteenth and seventeenth centuries, the only satisfactory critical essay on tragicomedy is by Giambattista Guarini in *Il Compendio della poesia tragicomica,* but it was not published until 1601, and it is doubtful that Marston read it before he wrote his more mature and accomplished tragicomedy, *The Malcontent* (produced 1602-1603). Nonetheless, the structure of *Antonio and Mellida* shows that Marston had some concept of the tragicomic genre, probably derived from the practical experience of playwriting and from the knowledge of such peculiar composites of tragedy and comedy (and even history) as Thomas Preston's *Cambises* (published 1569) or Marlowe's *Doctor Faustus* (produced 1594-1597) or even Shakespeare's *1 Henry IV* (produced circa 1596-1597). Marston's *Antonio and Mellida* displays a not uncommon Elizabethan technique of alternating serious and comic scenes and also of admixing tragic characters and Senecan rhetorical passages with satiric types and humorous incidents. What unity the play has derives from its thematic underpinnings, which focus on such themes as fortune, pride, and envy (seen earlier in *Histriomastix* and *Jack Drum's Entertainment*).

Therefore, although Piero's opening speech could be taken as parodic, it can also be taken as a serious utterance in which the character is revealed as a proud ruler who believes, wrongly and foolishly, that he can control the goddess Fortuna. The fact that a boy actor originally played Piero's part is not indicative of a burlesque intention either because there is evidence (as Ejner J. Jensen in "The Style of the Boy Actors," [1968] proves) that the boys were very skillful, convincing actors. Piero, in fact, can be put easily within the context of a Senecan-Machiavellian villain who utters quotations from Senecan tragedy (mostly from the villain Atreus in *Thyestes*) and treats his enemies, Andrugio and his son Antonio, with murderous intent. Andrugio and Antonio, who also quote much Seneca and utter Stoic commonplaces, are likewise to be seen within the context of the conventions of Senecan and revenge tragedy, hence their frequent references to the vagaries of Fortune and the revolutions of her wheel, as in IV.i:

Antonio ....
.... O, what black sin
Hath been committed by our ancient house,
Whose scalding vengeance lights upon our heads,
That thus the world and fortune casts us out
As loathed objects, Ruin's branded slaves.
Andrugio ....
Do not expostulate the heavens' will.
But, O, remember to forget thyself;
Forget remembrance what thou once hast been.
....
I am a-raising of our house, my boy,
Which Fortune will not envy, 'tis so mean
And like the world, all dirt. . . .

In the above passage, Andrugio's Stoicism is obvious, and so also is the collocation of the themes of fortune and envy, themes which are also united with the satiric themes of the play through the comments of Feliche, the play's acerbic critic, who inhabits both worlds with equal uneasiness.

Uneasiness, or indeed awkwardness, is what the reader ultimately comes away feeling after a session with *Antonio and Mellida*. It is a play in which the hero, disguised as an Amazon (of all things) throughout much of the play, twice throws himself upon the ground, has a long love duet with the heroine *in Italian,* and after having escaped from the clutches of his enemy by putting on the disguise of a sailor, reappears at the end by leaping out of a coffin. It is a play in which the court critics, Feliche and his counterpart Rossaline (Mellida's cousin), satirize the court fops and fools for such vices as envy and pride and then reveal themselves to be just as guilty of the same faults. It is, finally, a play in which serious philosophical issues are ultimately discarded, not resolved, so that the playwright could have his hero conclude: "Here ends the comic crosses of true love;/O may the passage most successful prove." These lines take us right back to the end of the induction, where the actor playing Antonio earlier said: "I have heard that those persons, . . . that are but slightly drawn in this comedy, should receive more exact accomplishment in a second part; which, if this obtain gracious acceptance, means to try his fortune." The fact is that a lack of decorum (in the Renaissance sense of fitness of language and action to character type) ruins Marston's *Antonio and Mellida*. Although he may well have intended to write a comedy, he allowed the serious Antonio-Andrugio-Piero plot to throw his play out of balance, to cause it to lack verisimilitude by the standards of either comedy or tragedy. It was not until he composed *The Malcontent* that Marston was

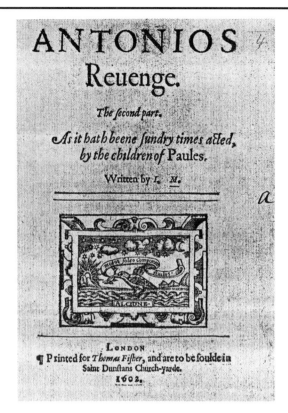

Title page for the 1602 quarto edition of Marston's sequel to Antonio and Mellida *(British Library)*

able to write a successful tragicomedy.

But Marston did write a successful tragedy in his sequel to *Antonio and Mellida*. Entered in the records of the Stationers' Company at the same time (24 October 1601) as *Antonio and Mellida, Antonio's Revenge* was likewise printed in quarto format in 1602—with the title "ANTONIOS Reuenge. *The second part. As it hath beene sundry times acted, by the children of* Paules. Written by *I. M.*" The head title notes that it is "The second part of the Historie of *Antonio and Mellida.*" Whereas *Antonio and Mellida* is primarily comic in tone, *Antonio's Revenge* is probably most fruitfully discussed within the context of the conventions of revenge tragedy. Although some critics, including R. A. Foakes, have tried to argue that *Antonio's Revenge* is a parody of the Kydian revenge play, there seems to be little evidence within the text itself to support such a view.

What most bothers most critics, and leads them to various fanciful conjectures and/or exasperated utterances, is the conclusion of *Antonio's Revenge*. Antonio undergoes extreme hardship and emotional pain, including the murder of his father Andrugio by the villainous Piero, the death of his beloved Mellida (who has been slandered for unchastity by her own father and who expires thinking Antonio himself is dead), and the courtship of his mother Maria by Piero, and is enjoined by Andrugio's ghost to take revenge. Antonio does so in what is one of the most unusual and horrific revenges in all of Elizabethan-Jacobean drama—and then goes off to a monastery with his corevengers, Pandulpho, father of the murdered Feliche, and Alberto, a courtier.

Most critics and scholars believe that Marston's conclusion to *Antonio's Revenge* is an ethical disaster because the chief revengers, Antonio and Pandulpho, are not, say, killed off at the end, as are Hieronimo (in *The Spanish Tragedy*) and Hamlet, or arrested for murder, as are Vindice and Hippolito in *The Revenger's Tragedy* (published 1607). I would argue, however, that Marston was quite aware of what he was doing in *Antonio's Revenge*, both in terms of the play's morality and its place within the tradition and conventions of Senecan revenge tragedy.

Much has been written about the relationship of *Antonio's Revenge* to Shakespeare's *Hamlet*, the first performance of which is usually dated 1600-1601. There are many plot similarities: the hero's father (Hamlet I/Andrugio) is poisoned by the villain (Claudius/Piero) before the play opens; the ghost of the murdered father reveals the crime and enjoins revenge on his son; the villain attempts to remove the son from the scene; the villain courts the widow (Gertrude/Maria); the hero delays and also acts mad to avoid suspicion; the hero eventually effects revenge on the murderer of his father. On the other hand, as G. K. Hunter has cogently argued in the introduction to his Regents Renaissance Drama Series edition of *Antonio's Revenge* (1965), we find an "astonishing lack of verbal correspondence between the plays, astonishing, that is, given the structural similarities." Hunter further points out, as have others, that if Marston did not imitate Shakespeare, then Shakespeare may have imitated Marston. Since the production date of Marston's play is probably 1600, that is a possibility. However, most recently Harold Jenkins in the introduction to his Arden edition of *Hamlet* (1982), has made a strong case for Marston's indebtedness to Shakespeare's play, which he believes was therefore on stage in 1599-1600.

Another possible line of indebtedness can be found in Thomas Kyd's *The Spanish Tragedy* (produced circa 1592), a revenge play that can be viewed as the prototype of all subsequent extant works in the genre. It is in Kyd's play that we first find the use of a ghost who wants revenge, a grief-stricken revenger, delay due to grief and madness (actual in this case), a Machiavellian villain and his accomplice, an Italianate (Spanish was considered to be of the same ilk) setting, long rhetorical speeches, and much discussion by the victims of the miseries of earthly existence. More specifically, as G. K. Hunter notes, "Pandulpho, the just man at court mourning the murder of his virtuous son, is obviously cast in the mold of Hieronimo. . . ."

And, finally, there is another line of influence that seems to inform *Antonio's Revenge:* the Senecan element, previously found in *Antonio and Mellida.* As Fredson Bowers has pointed out in his *Elizabethan Revenge Tragedy 1587-1642* (1940), "Marston who with Webster and Tourneur was one of the most Italianate of Elizabethan dramatists . . . was at the same time one of the most Senecan." The Senecan elements in *Antonio's Revenge* can be found in several passages imitated or quoted from both the nondramatic (*De Remediis Fortuitorum* and *De Providentia*) and dramatic (*Agamemnon, Medea, Octavia, Thyestes*) works attributed to the Roman author. The Stoic philosophy of Pandulpho is replete with Senecan allusions, but the main Senecan thematic and structural influence derives from *Thyestes*, which also served as a source for Shakespeare's *Titus Andronicus* (first produced in 1594).

Both *Thyestes* and *Titus* are crucial to an understanding of Marston's tragedy, especially the morality of the revenge action. It is the so-called "Thyestean banquet" (at which the cuckolded Atreus took revenge upon his brother Thyestes for seducing his wife by serving the sons of Thyestes to him for a meal), found also in Shakespeare's *Titus Andronicus* (where Titus serves up Tamora's sons to her), that is the source for Antonio's grisly murder of Piero's son, Julio, and the subsequent covered-dish presentation to the father. It is probably also *Thyestes* that gave Marston the idea of writing a variation on the Kydian ending (in which the revenger himself suffers death). In *Thyestes* the Ghost of Tantalus is driven from Hades by a Fury, which forces the Ghost to incite Atreus to revenge. In *Antonio's Revenge* the Ghost of Andrugio invokes the same *lex talionis* morality at the play's climax as he approaches the grieving Antonio in III.i:

> Thy pangs of anguish rip my cerecloth up;
> And lo, the ghost of old Andrugio
> Forsakes his coffin. Antonio, revenge!
> I was empoison'd by Piero's hand;
> Revenge my blood! Take spirit, gentle boy.
> Revenge my blood! . . .
>
> . . . .

Alarum Nemesis, rouse up thy blood,
Invent some stratagem of vengeance
Which, but to think on, may like lightning glide
With horror through thy breast. Remember this:
Scelera non ulcisceris, nisi vincis.

The "revenge" motif is both reminiscent of the Senecan dramatic situation—the Latin, which translates, "you do not avenge evil deeds unless you exceed them," is spoken by Atreus in *Thyestes*—and Old Testament measure-for-measure morality. The Ghost's influence is evident because Antonio's very next speech is a quotation from some of the lines of the opening speeches of the Ghost of Tantalus in *Thyestes* as it is being urged on by the Fury. Antonio, then, is being incited to commit atrocities by a supernatural force. He, of course, responds with a "stratagem of vengeance" that includes such horrors as the slaughter of the innocent Julio (dramatically equivalent to the three sons of Thyestes) and the sprinkling of his blood on Andrugio's tomb ("Blood cries for blood; and murder murder craves"), the plucking out of Piero's tongue, and in V.iii the presentation of Julio to Piero as "a dish to feast thy father's gorge." He is not punished for these deeds, but then neither is Atreus punished at the conclusion of *Thyestes*.

The added horror of the mutilated tongue is not derived from *Thyestes* but from the incident in *Titus Andronicus* where Titus's daughter, Lavinia, is ravished and mutilated. Just as *Thyestes* provided Marston with a gruesome pattern of retributive acts, so also did *Titus Andronicus* give him both structural and thematic ideas for his play, such as in the relatively clear-cut contrast between good and evil and in the emphasis on the pathos of the victims. At the end Titus is excused for his version of the Thyestean banquet and other atrocities: "Now judge what cause had Titus to revenge/These wrongs unspeakable, past patience,/Or more than living man could bear." But critics have been hard on Marston and have accused him, unlike Shakespeare, of moral obtuseness, because his revengers are not killed or appropriately punished.

However, if we view *Antonio's Revenge* as being an experiment in the genre of revenge tragedy, or what has sometimes more narrowly been called the "tragedy of blood," we can see that Marston has consciously written with the same sort of intentions that Shakespeare seems to have had. If it all seems more excessive in *Antonio's Revenge*, perhaps that is because Marston's theatricality (which ranges from Piero's walking about with arms smeared with blood, to the hanging and bleeding body of Feliche,

to Julio's death scene, to the strangling on the stage of Strotzo, to the dumping of Feliche's corpse on the reclining Antonio, to the final banquet scene) is more in the Grand Guignol tradition than that of Shakespeare. On the other hand, the emphasis on murderous excess—*Scelera non ulcisceris, nisi vincis*—is found in the action of *Titus Andronicus*, as well as in *Thyestes*.

As for rhetorical excess, the language in Marston's play is no more self-consciously inflated than that in many Elizabethan or Jacobean revenge tragedies. In fact, Marston may have rightly been proud of the "high style" of his play, as he seems to draw attention to it in Antonio's last speech, in which the hero tells us:

Never more woe in lesser plot was found.
And, O, if ever time create a muse
That to th' immortal fame of virgin faith
Dares once engage his pen to write her death,
Presenting it in some black tragedy,
May it prove gracious, may his style be deck'd
With freshest blooms of purest elegance;
May it have gentle presence, and the scenes suck'd up
By calm attention of choice audience;
And when the closing Epilogue appears,
Instead of claps may it obtain but tears.

This concluding speech, a formal lament, is Marston's attempt to place his play within the emotional context found in good Renaissance tragedy, a context reflected in such Shakespearean lines as "For never was a story of more woe/Than this of Juliet and her Romeo" (V.ii) or "You sad Andronici, have done with woes" (V.iii). The First Senator in *Antonio's Revenge* asks as he views the murdered Piero, "Whose hand presents this gory spectacle?" So Fortinbras asks Horatio, "Where is this sight?" To which Horatrio replies, "What is it you would see?/ If aught of woe or wonder, cease your search" (V.ii. 361-63). As J. V. Cunningham has pointed out in *Woe or Wonder: The Emotional Effect of Shakespearean Tragedy* (1951): "Fear, sorrow, and wonder are the emotions explicitly associated with tragedy, not only in *Hamlet,* but generally in the tradition of literary criticism of Shakespeare's day." Marston, we can conclude, had perfectly clear ideas about what he was doing in *Antonio's Revenge.* The play is by no means a failure, and his "choice audience" at the Children of Paul's probably accorded him "calm attention" and then "claps" as well as "tears."

Much has been conjectured about the audiences of the private theaters vis-à-vis the public theaters, and, although both were probably heterogeneous, they probably were different in makeup also. As Philip Finkelpearl has argued in his *John Marston of the Middle Temple: An Elizabethan Dramatist in His Social Setting* (1969): "The audience at these performances was undoubtedly wealthier and, on the average, better educated than that at the large 'public' theaters. The private 'houses' were located very near the Inns of Court; by all accounts the percentage of Inns' members in the audience was high, and the audience was very similar, probably even in age, to the spectrum at the Inns. . . . It is impossible to assess precisely the nature of this audience, but one general term will cover the majority of its members: 'gallants.' . . . Possibly because the price of admission limited the social range, Marston chose to find in such an audience a 'choise selected influence' [see Marston's introduction to *Jack Drum's Entertainment*]. The audience apparently reciprocated his admiration. Almost instantly he seems to have become a successful playwright, and the Children of Paul's was for a time a thriving financial enterprise."

Marston's next and last play for the Children of Paul's, *What You Will*, was not entered in the Stationers' Register until 6 August 1607, the year it was printed in quarto form, but most scholars agree that it was written and performed in 1601. Any discussion of this play has to include at least some reference to the so-called War of the Theaters, or Poetomachia. In his *Poetaster* (1601), Ben Jonson (who was working for a rival company, The Children of the Chapel) wrote in an appendix "To the Reader" that "three yeeres,/They did prouoke me with their petulant stiles/On euery stage," and it is generally agreed upon by scholars that the reference is to Marston and Thomas Dekker, whom Marston supposedly helped (with advice) in *Satiromastix* (first produced in 1601), a play in which Jonson is satirized in the figure of Horace. The quarrel seems to have been quite serious, for Jonson told Drummond of Hawthornden in 1619 that "he had many quarrells with Marston beat him & took his Pistol from him, wrote his Poetaster on him the beginning of y^m were that Marston represented him jn the stage." In *The Elizabethan Stage* (1923) E. K. Chambers succinctly summed up Marston's role in the stage quarrel: "Marston's representation of Jonson as Chrysoganus in *Histriomastix* was complimentary, that as Brabant senior in *Jack Drum's Entertainment* offensive [it has been denied by Finkelpearl that there is any connection with Jonson here]; and it was doubtless the latter that stirred Jonson to retaliate on Marston, perhaps as Hedon in *Cynthia's Revels*, certainly as Crispinus in

The Poetaster. Marston's final blow was with Lampatho Doria in *What You Will*."

It is, in fact, arguable whether the melancholy satirist Lampatho Doria (Italian *lampazo:* "bur," according to Florio's *A Worlde of Wordes*) represents Ben Jonson. Lampatho does have some of the characteristics of the scholar-poet Chrisoganus in *Histriomastix* and is described rather accurately by the critic Quadratus (*quadrato: "fowre-square"*) as "a fustie caske,/Devote to moldy customes of hoary eld"). Lampatho's speeches might remind one of Chrisoganus at times, as, for example, in the following disquisition on the nature of the soul:

> How twas created, how the soule exsistes
> One talkes of motes, the soule was made of motes,
> An other fire, tother light, a third a spark of Star-like nature,
> *Hippo* water, *Anaximenes* ayre,
> *Aristoxenus* Musicke; *Critias* I know not what.
> A company of odde phreneteci

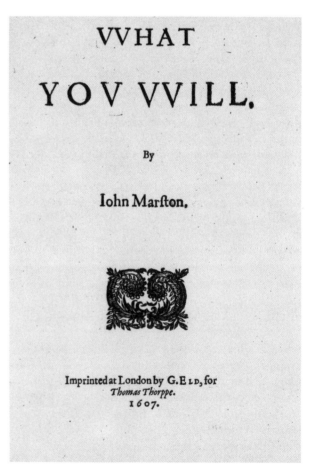

Title page for the 1607 quarto edition of the last play Marston wrote for the Children of Paul's (Henry E. Huntington Library and Art Gallery)

Did eate my youth, and when I crept abroad,
Finding my numnesse in this nimble age,
I fell a railing, but now soft and slow,
I know, I know naught, but I naught do know.
What shall I doe, what plot, what course persew?

(This passage, interestingly, has appealed to two modern American poets, Conrad Aiken and James Dickey.) However, although Lampatho has a philosophical as well as satirical bent and tends to show off his learning, there are no specific defining characteristics that identify him with Jonson. There is at least something that might point to Marston himself, for at one point Quadratus irritably says to Lampatho: "why you *Don Kynsayder*/Thou Canker eaten rusty curre, thou snaffle/To freer spirits." W. Kinsayder was, of course, Marston's own pseudonym in *The Scourge of Villainy*.

However, *What You Will* is not entirely a vehicle for satire, although there is much of that in the play, just as there is in *Jack Drum's Entertainment*, the Marston comedy it most resembles in structure and tone. As in *Jack Drum's Entertainment*, we find self-conscious theatricalism, as at the ends of act two ("So ends our chat, sound Musick for the Act") and act three ("our sceane is donne yet fore we cease wee sing"). We also find the boy actors drawing attention to themselves in the induction (as in the induction in *Antonio and Mellida*) as they mock the fashionable gallants who attended plays and sat on or near the stage ("I so, so, pree thee Tyer-man set *Sineor Snuffe* a fier, he's a chollerick Gentleman, he will take Pepper in the nose instantly, feare not, fore Heaven I wonder they tollerate him so nere the Stage"), and they even refer to the size of the Paul's stage itself ("Let's place our selves within the Curtaines, for good faith the Stage is so very little we shall wrong the generall eye els very much").

It is in the induction that we learn that the play's title is *What You Will*, which, of course, was the subtitle to Shakespeare's *Twelfth Night* (first performed circa 1601-1602), a play involving disguises and mistaken identity that, like Marston's *Jack Drum's Entertainment* and *What You Will*, can be categorized as "festive comedy." Like Shakespeare's comedy, *What You Will* is based upon an Italian play. Marston's main plot derives from Sforza d'Oddi's *I Morti Vivi* (published 1576), a tragicomedy, from which Marston extracted the subplot as the source for his main plot. Marston's basic story, set in Venice, involves the love rivalry of Iacomo ("starke mad, alasse for love") and the foppish Frenchman Laverdure for the supposedly widowed Celia, wife of the merchant Albano ("Tis

skarce three monthes since fortune gave him dead"). Although Celia has rejected the respectable Venetian Iacomo, her uncles, Randolfo and Andrea, want to prevent her match to Laverdure and so disguise a perfumer named Franciscio Soranza as the supposedly deceased Albano. When Albano himself arrives in act three and meets Soranza, who has even been coached to stutter like the merchant, we get the kind of fun associated with Shakespearean disguise-plot mixups. However, Marston's satire against lascivious widows is more in tune with George Chapman's in a play such as *The Widows Tears* (first performed circa 1604-1605), which even has a bizarre Governor akin to the Duke in *What You Will*.

Again as in *Jack Drum's Entertainment*, the title of *What You Will* indicates the play's major themes. In the Renaissance the verb *will* could mean to "desire" or "wish for" something, or as a noun it could mean "carnal desire or appetite," which senses certainly inform the main plot. There was also a proverbial expression "Will and wit strive with you (for the victory)" that can be applied to the entire play, for *wit* in the sense of the rational faculty or reason can be applied to the behavior of those who oppose Celia's ill-considered marriage to Laverdure. And *wit* in the sense of verbal cleverness can be seen as a major consideration in the play's many confrontations between dupes such as Simplicius Faber (Italian *semplice*: "simple-witted") and Laverdure and "wits" such as Quadratus (an Epicure who believes in "exterior sense," or "the five wits"), Lampatho Doria, and Meletza (Celia's sister), as well as such clever pages as Slip, Bydet, and Holifernes (who seem to owe debts to characters and scenes in Shakespeare's *Love's Labour's Lost* and *The Merry Wives of Windsor*).

Although much of *What You Will* is clever and probably would play well in performance, the final judgment on the play has to be agreement with a character in the induction who calls it "a slight toye, lightly composed, to swiftly finisht, ill plotted." Although the denouement contains a series of comic reversals and exposures, there is no resolution of the budding love affair between Lampatho and Meletza, no sense that Lampatho or Quadratus have come to terms with either society or themselves, or any seeming final point to the character and behavior of the mad Duke of Venice, or even to the set satiric schoolroom (act two), and Court of Pages (act three) scenes with the young wits.

To sum up Marston's career with the Children of Paul's, we have to conclude that it was a time of self-conscious experimentation in dramatic form, but a period that produced no completely satisfactory work of dramatic art. Although Marston's last work for Paul's was in 1601, the company continued to perform plays until 1606 (except for a period of some months from March 1603 to probably April 1604 when the theaters were closed because of Queen Elizabeth's illness and then the plague). However, Marston for some unknown reason or reasons seems to have shifted his allegiance to the Blackfriars (and the Children of the Chapel Royal, after 4 February 1604 called the Children of the Queen's [Majesty's] Revels) where he wrote his four best plays, *The Malcontent, The Fawn, The Dutch Courtesan,* and *Sophonisba.* Ultimately, these are the plays on which his reputation as a dramatist must stand or fall.

The most authoritative recent discussion of the text and dating of *The Malcontent* is that of George K. Hunter in his Revels Plays edition (1975). Hunter points out that there were three editions of the play in quarto by the same printer in 1604 and that "all show signs of definitive authorial revision or correction from MS." He further points out that "the Induction added to the third issue (QC) of *The Malcontent* makes it clear that the play was originally performed by a company of boys, the *decimo-sexto* actors from whom the *folio* adult company of Shakespeare and Burbage, the Chamberlain's or King's Men, have stolen it." He also concludes that the original boys' company that performed *The Malcontent,* probably in 1603, was the Children of the Chapel Royal at Blackfriars. Hunter concludes, as have other scholars, that the induction was written by John Webster, who also may have written some of the argumentations (such as those involving the clown Passarello, probably a role added for Robert Armin of the King's Men), although Marston probably wrote most of the additions to the third edition.

The Malcontent itself is considered by most critics to be Marston's finest play (its only rival being *The Dutch Courtesan*). Dedicated to Ben Jonson, who had written *Cynthia's Revels* (produced in late 1600) and *Poetaster* (produced in early 1601) for the Children of the Chapel Royal at Blackfriars, the play shows that Marston had patched up his relationship with the man he here calls "POETAE ELEGANTISSIMO, GRAVISSIMO." Although Marston terms the play a comedy in both the dedication and in his preface "To the Reader," it was registered in the Stationers' Register as a "*tragiecomedia,*" and that generic classification seems to be most fitting. Bernard Harris has argued in his New Mermaids edition of *The Malcontent* (1967) that Marston bor-

rowed from an English translation of Giambattista Guarini's tragicomedy, *Il Pastor Fido* (published in Italy, 1590; English translation, 1602), but it is most likely that Marston derived the structure and tone of his play from reading Guarini's *Il compendio della poesia tragicomedia* (published 1601; appended to an Italian edition of *Il Pastor Fido* in 1602), rather than Guarini's tragicomedy. Allan H. Gilbert translates Guarini's definition of the genre as follows (in his *Literary Criticism: Plato to Dryden,* 1940):

> He who composes tragicomedy takes from tragedy its great persons but not its great action, its verisimilar plot but not its true one, its movement of the feelings but not its disturbance of them, its pleasure but not its sadness, its danger but not its death; from comedy it takes laughter that is not excessive, modest amusement, feigned difficulty, happy reversal, and above all the comic order, of which we shall speak in its place. These components, thus managed, can stand together in a single story, especially when they are handled in a way in accord with their nature and the kind of manners that pertains to them.

The Malcontent fulfills Guarini's requirements nicely, for the "great persons" Duke Altofronto (deposed Duke of Genoa, alias Malevole the malcontent), Maria (imprisoned wife of Altofronto), Pietro (current Duke of Genoa), Aurelia (wife of Pietro and current Duchess of Genoa), Mendoza (aspirant to the throne and lover of Aurelia), and Ferneze (a courtier and aspiring lover of Aurelia) are all part of a "verisimilar plot" of Italianate political intrigue.

This main plot is structured around the basic Wheel of Fortune pattern Marston first used in *Histriomastix,* although in *The Malcontent* we find four rather than six phases, or what Howard R. Patch has termed in *The Goddess Fortuna in Mediaeval Literature* (1927) the "formula of four," a "picture . . . exceedingly familiar in mediaeval art" where the phases are "inscribed respectively, Regno, Regnavi, Sum sine Regno, and Regnabo." Hence, as the play opens we find Duke Altofronto ("*high*" "*forhead,*" according to Florio's *A Worlde of Wordes*) *Sum sine Regno* because he has been thrust out of power by Pietro and Mendoza ("*corrupted*"). As the disguised Malevole ("*malitious, maleuolent*"), however, Altofronto is in the *Regnabo* phase, as he tells Mendoza in I.v: "I once shall rise!" And he then puts the pattern into perspective in a sententious couplet: "No vulgar seed but once may rise

Title page for the third 1604 quarto edition of Marston's first play for the Children of the Chapel Royal, with most of the additions and revisions by Marston and a new induction by John Webster (Maggs Bros., catalogue no. 569, 1932)

and shall;/No king so huge but 'fore he die may fall." Pietro, now *Regno* because he has usurped the throne, is too weak to retain power (or his wife) and becomes *Regnavi* because of the Machiavel Mendoza, who becomes *Regnabo* by plotting to get his rival Ferneze caught in Aurelia's chamber and by laying the blame for her dishonor on Pietro. Although he gains Aurelia's support, Mendoza is soon in trouble because the populace and Aurelia's father, Duke of Florence, turn against them at the same time that Mendoza foolishly employs Malevole in his plots. Mendoza attains the throne, but his moment of triumph—*Regno*—is brief because Malevole, the honest Celso ("*high, noble*"), the badly wounded but recovered Ferneze, and the chastened Pietro combine to bring him down, *sine Regno.*

As we can see, the "formula of four" rise-and-fall structural pattern is peculiarly appropriate for a tragicomedy in which we find "danger but not . . . death," according to Guarini. It is also appropriate for a disguise-plot play in which a railing malcontent can satirize court folly and vice and at the same time control the outcome of the action, hence the "feigned difficulty" and also the "happy reversal" in which rewards and punishments are meted out to friends and foes. It is, finally, "the comic order" that dictates not only the structure but also the tone of *The Malcontent.* As Guarini says (in Gilbert's translation), "the end of tragicomedy" is the "purging with pleasure the sadness of the hearers. This is done in such a way that the imitation, which is the instrumental end, is that which is mixed, and represents a mingling of both tragic and comic events. But the purging, which is the architectonic end, exists only as a single principle, which unites two qualities in one purpose, that of freeing the hearers from melancholy." At the end of the play, then, we are delighted that Malevole (as well as the audience) has been purged of his melancholy, that Altofronto is back on his throne with his faithful wife, Maria, that the repentant Pietro and Aurelia are reconciled, and that Mendoza and Maquerelle are cast out of the comic society.

It can be safely argued, then, that *The Malcontent* is the "*tragiecomedia*" that it was termed in the Stationers' Register. It was a form particularly suited to Marston's dramatic proclivities, for it gave him a structure within which he could be both morally serious and dramatically interesting and effective. It allowed him to achieve for the first time in his career a successful combination of satire and philosophy and to present a diverse range of character types within a well-plotted story frame. For example, whereas in *Histriomastix* or *Antonio's Revenge* Marston dealt with the themes of Fortune and the relationship of men and society to a higher power or set of values, he solved the issues with rather arbitrary devices. In *The Malcontent,* however, the attitudes of the characters toward Fortune and her Wheel are attuned to the structural design of rise and fall. Pietro and Mendoza, for example, choose to trust in Fortune and thereby rise and fall quickly. Mendoza, moreover, as a Machiavellian politician ("politician" and "policy" are common terms in the play) believes that "fortune dotes on impudence" and that "The train of Fortune is borne up by wit," whereas Altofronto/Malevole believes in "heaven's impos'd conditions," or the Christian concept of Providence: "Who doubts of Providence,/That sees this change? A hearty faith to all!/He needs must rise who can no lower fall." Similarly, Mendoza's subplot counterpart, Maquerelle the panderess, who refers to herself as "like Lady Fortune," is willing to do anything, including the destruction of the honor of Aurelia and other wives in the play, in order to improve her fortunes. For Maquerelle, of course, the rising/falling has primarily sexual rather than political implications (". . . we women always note the falling of the one is the rising of the other").

The Malcontent sums up Marston's early literary interests in a mature work of art. It brings together the themes of female chastity, political and social change versus ordered stability, Fortune and Providence. For the select audience at Blackfriars, the original production home of the play, *The Malcontent* with its court setting also provided ample portions of topical satire and was able to cash in on the turn-of-the-century interest in melancholy and malcontentedness. As for the disguise plot, it was to prove to be one of Marston's most effective dramatic structures and found its place again in his next endeavor.

Marston's next play was *Parasitaster, or The Fawn.* Although it was not entered in the Stationers' Register until 12 March 1606, it was probably written around 1604 (and performed after the theaters reopened on 9 April 1604). It is another duke-in-disguise-plot play, like *The Malcontent,* and shows Marston's first interest in John Florio's 1603 English translation of Montaigne's *The Essayes* (from which we can find several borrowings). Like *The Malcontent* it was first performed at Blackfriars, but, as the title pages of the two 1606 quartos tell us, *"by the Children of the Queenes Maiesties Reuels,"* a company that succeeded the Chapel Children and one in which Marston at some point became a shareholder.

As scholars have pointed out, among *The Fawn's* dramatic sources are George Chapman's satiric comedy *All Fools* (produced 1601), itself indebted to Terence's *Adelphi,* and Thomas Middleton's duke-in-disguise-plot play *The Phoenix* (produced 1604).

The Fawn, like *Jack Drum's Entertainment* and *What You Will,* is a comedy that contains both romantic plot elements and topical satire. As with those plays, the title is an indication of Marston's main concerns. In Marston's time, "fawn" could have both noun and verb meanings. In Jonson's *Poetaster,* for instance, we find an instance of the substantive meaning of "fawn" as an "act of fawning; a servile cringe, a wheedling courtesy" when Caesar praises Horace (alias Jonson himself): "Thankes, HORACE for thy free, and holsome sharpnesse:/which pleaseth CAESAR more, then seruile fawnes./'A flatterd prince soone turnes the prince of fooles.' " It is doubtful that *The Fawn* is a response to Jonson's portrayal of Marston as Cris-

pinus in *Poetaster,* but several critics over the years have argued that Marston *is* satirizing King James I in his portrayal of Duke Gonzago, ruler of Urbin, a foolish man given to refer frequently to his own clever wit, profound wisdom, and powers of intuition. As scholars who have worked on Shakespeare's *Measure for Measure* (produced in 1604; another play with a duke in disguise) in recent years have demonstrated, James considered himself to be a statesman and an intellectual. However, there is no contemporary evidence connecting King James with *The Fawn,* and if the satire is there Marston and Queen Anne's company of boys seem to have gone unscathed, as Marston did not when he, Chapman, and Jonson later insulted the King in *Eastward Ho* (produced in 1604-1605).

Fawning or flattery in a courtly setting, at any rate, is the main theme of *The Fawn,* and the basic plot line centers on Hercules, Duke of Ferrara, who sends his son, Tiberio, to Urbin to court Gonzago's daughter, Dulcimel, for Hercules. Deciding to check up on his son, Hercules disguises himself as Faunus, but after meeting several of Urbin's courtiers he changes his mind (and acknowledges his age) and decides to let Tiberio court Dulcimel for himself. Hercules will concentrate on the flatterers, he says in I.ii:

> . . . I now repent
> Severe indictions to some sharp styles;
> Freeness, so't grow not to licentiousness,
> Is grateful to just states. Most spotless kingdom,
> And men, O happy born under good stars,
> Where what is honest you may freely think,
> Speak what you think and write what you do speak,
> Not bound to servile soothings. . . .
> . . . .
> . . . . Since vice is now term'd fashion,
> And most are grown to ill even with defense,
> I vow to waste this most prodigious heat,
> That falls into my age like scorching flames
> In depth of numb'd December, in flattering all
> In all of their extremest viciousness,
> Till in their own lov'd race they fall most lame,
> And meet full butt the close of vice's shame.

Hercules (alias John Marston the satirist?) here shows his own rhetorical powers in his tropes and figures of speech. (One of the attributes of the mythological Hercules in the Renaissance was eloquence.)

The court of Gonzago, however, is filled not with those who speak in freeness, but those given to "servile soothings" and other abuses of language and social relationships. These include Herod

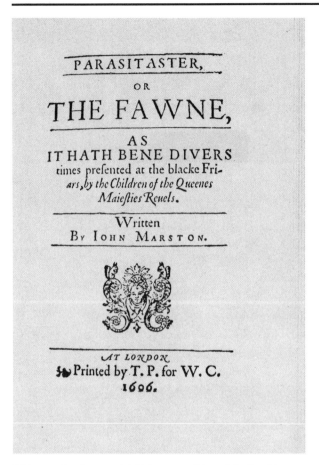

PARASITASTER,

OR

THE FAWNE,

AS
IT HATH BENE DIVERS
times prefented at the blacke Friars, by the Children of the Queenes
Maiefties Reuels.

Written
By IOHN MARSTON.

AT LONDON,
Printed by T. P. for W. C.
1606.

Title page for the second 1606 quarto edition of the first Marston play produced after the reopening of the theaters in 1604 (Victoria and Albert Museum)

Frappatore (the Christian name is probably derived from the medieval drama's braggart tyrant; the surname means "*a bragger, a boaster,*" according to Florio's *A Worlde of Wordes*), who is having an adulterous affair with Donna Garbetza ("*sowrenes, tartnes, sharpenes*"), wife of the sickly Sir Amoroso Debile-Dosso ("*weake*" "*backe*"), brother of Herod. Herod, however, is untrue to Donna Garbetza, and when his affair with the court laundress, Puttota ("*a prettie trull*"), is revealed, Donna Garbetza says that she's pregnant with Herod's child and that he's ruined his chances for the inheritance. In another perverse relationship Don Zuccone ("*a gull, a ninnie*") has neglected his wife sexually for four years, and Donna Zoya ("*a gemme, a iewell*") announces that she's pregnant in order to get him to reject her so that she can then be rid of him. Hercules wanders around the court flattering and then mocking these and other fops and fools while at the same time dazzling the courtiers (and audience) with his own verbal pyrotechnics in the form of

witty paradoxes, false syllogisms, and mock encomiums—all set off with a veritable index of tropes and figures of speech.

The entire play is concerned more with the uses and abuses of language than it is with varieties of love. For though we have abnormal sexual relationships in the two groups described above (adultery versus abstinence), and though we have a character named Nymphadoro (described in the dramatis personae as "*a young courtier and a common lover*") who says in III.i that he's "in love with all women," and though we even have a romantic subplot that dramatizes an ideal love affair in the case of Tiberio and Dulcimel (a witty woman in the mold of *Antonio and Mellida's* Rossaline), the main plot and themes of *The Fawn* revolve around rhetoric. This is made clear not only in the speeches of Hercules but also in those of Gonzago, who takes pride in his own rhetorical abilities—"My Lord Granuffo, pray ye note my phrase" (III.ii); "Did we not shake the prince with energy?" (III.i); "as we are princes, scholars, and have read *Cicero de Oratore*" (IV.i)—although he turns out to be as foolish as any of his courtiers and is arraigned at the conclusion of the play in Cupid's Parliament. It is in this "Parliament" that Cupid metes out comic punishments to the deserving with Hercules acting as "reader" of statutes and witness. Thus Nymphadoro in V.i is arraigned for his "plurality of mistresses" and is "committed to the ship of fools, without either bail or mainprize"; Sir Amoroso is called to account for impotence, or "counterfeiting of Cupid's royal coin," and also "pressed to sail in the ship of fools"; likewise, Herod is sent to the ship of fools for violating "An act against forgers of love letters, false braggarts of ladies' favors, and vain boasters of counterfeit tokens"; Don Zuccone is charged with violating "An act against slanderers of Cupid's liege, ladies' names, and lewd defamers of their honors," but repents and is reconciled with Donna Zoya; Granuffo (described in the dramatis personae as "*a silent lord*") is arraigned for "seeming wise only by silence"; and the final exposure is of Gonzago, who by trying to prevent the union of Tiberio and Dulcimel has violated "An act against privy conspiracies" through "presumptuous wisdom," and as he himself concludes: "There is no folly to protested wit."

The basic premise in *The Fawn* is that rhetoric is a powerful tool that must be used properly. As Philip J. Finkelpearl has shown in "The Use of the Middle Temple's Christmas Revels in Marston's *The Fawne*" (1967), the Parliament of Cupid was most likely derived from a Middle Temple Christmas festivity in which a Lord of Misrule called the "Prince d'Amour" arraigned various types of lovers before a jury. Even though there is no evidence that *The Fawn* was performed at the Middle Temple, the private theater audience at Blackfriars would certainly have contained lawyers and other educated people who made their livings by the use (or abuse) of rhetoric and would have appreciated Marston's "in(n)" jokes. However, although the play is basically satiric and comic in tone, the major underlying issues—the social and political consequences of misuse of language coupled with self-deceit—are serious. Marston, in this respect, would undoubtedly have agreed with a passage in Ben Jonson's *Timber: or, Discoveries:* "Wheresoever, manners, and fashions are corrupted, Language is. It imitates the publicke riot. The excess of Feasts, and apparell, are the notes of a sick state; and the wantonnesse of language, of a sick mind."

Marston's work on *Eastward Ho,* a collaborative effort with Jonson and George Chapman, is generally believed to be his next dramatic effort. The play was probably written in 1604-1605 and was first published in quarto in 1605. It was performed at the Blackfriars by the Children of the Queen's Revels. Most of the convincing work on the attribution of shares has been by Chapman's and Jonson's editors, and few Marston scholars, with the exception of Morse S. Allen in *The Satire of John Marston* (1920) and Anthony Caputi in *John Marston, Satirist* (1961), have had much to say about Marston's contribution to the comedy. However, a recent detailed study of the authorship problem, D. J. Lake's "*Eastward Ho:* Linguistic Evidence for Authorship" (1981), has corroborated most earlier informed opinion that generally Marston is responsible for act one (and perhaps part of II.i), Chapman for acts two-four, and Jonson for act five. In other words, Marston began *Eastward Ho,* a so-called London or city comedy, and thus provided the framework for the main plot, which involves Master Touchstone, a goldsmith, and the fortunes of his daughters, one proud and the other humble, and his apprentices, the prodigal Quicksilver and the industrious Golding. The "touchstone" of the play's value system is bourgeois morality. As Caputi has argued, it seems likely that Marston's work on *Eastward Ho* influenced his other city play, *The Dutch Courtesan* (produced in 1605). Nonetheless, in *The Dutch Courtesan* Marston's interests lie not in a good-natured exposure of prodigal sons, fops, vain women, and usurers, which is the basic subject matter of *Eastward Ho,* but in the probing of the sexual and moral nature of men and women.

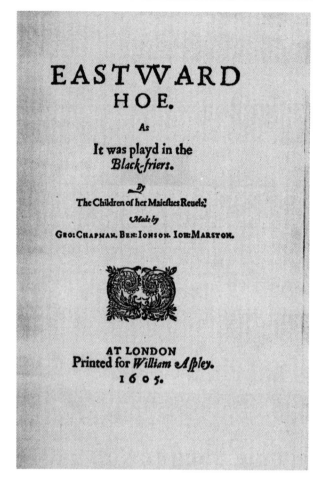

Title page for the 1605 quarto edition of the play that angered King James I because of its slighting references to the Scots (Victoria and Albert Museum)

Aside from the attribution of shares, which is by no means definitively settled, one of the most interesting issues involving *Eastward Ho* is the fact that it got the three playwrights into serious trouble with King James (either in performance or in printed form) because of a couple of slighting references (in III.iii and IV.i) to the Scots. Jonson refers to the incident in his *Conversations with Drummond of Hawthornden* in a passage just before the one about his "many quarrells with Marston": "he was delated [informed against] by Sr James Murray [a fairly recently knighted Scot] to the King for writing something against the Scots jn a play Eastward hoe & voluntarily Imprissonned himself w^t Chapman and Marston, who had written it amongst y^m. the report was that they should then had their ears cutt & noses. after y^r delivery he banqueted all his friends. . . ." All escaped imprisonment without mutilation, and it is uncertain that Marston ever

THE
Dutch Courtezan.

AS

IT WAS PLAYD IN THE
Blacke-Friars, by the Children
of her Maiesties Reuels.

VVritten
By IOHN MARSTON.

AT LONDON,
¶ Printed by T. P. for Iohn Hodgets,
and are to be sould at his shop in
Paules Church-yard. 1605.

Title page for the 1605 quarto edition of the play in which Marston reverses Ben Jonson's dictum that playwrights should provide moral lessons to their audiences, stating in his prologue: "We strive not to instruct, but to delight" (Henry E. Huntington Library and Art Gallery)

was in prison, for in letters to various supporters Chapman and Jonson mention only themselves as being so confined, and Chapman even disclaims his or Jonson's responsibility at all for the offensive passages.

Although it is not unlikely that Marston was responsible for the offensive passages in *Eastward Ho* (though III.iii and IV.i are usually assigned to Chapman), there is no factual evidence to convict him. The reason he is often indicted is because some scholars (the most convincing is Philip J. Finkelpearl in his *John Marston of the Middle Temple*) have seen anti-James I references in other plays by Marston, such as a slighting remark about "Signior S. *Andrew Iaques*" (V.v) in the first quarto of *The Malcontent* in which the "*Iaques*" was removed from the second and third quartos, the supposition that Gonzago in *The Fawn* was modeled on the King,

and a subplot trick in act two of *The Dutch Courtesan* in which a jokester named Cocledemoy dresses up like a barber, calls himself Andrew [the patron saint of Scotland] Shark, and hoodwinks (or "shaves") a London vintner named Mulligrub out of some money.

The Dutch Courtesan was probably written in 1605, soon after Marston's collaborative work on *Eastward Ho*. It was entered in the Stationers' Register on 26 June 1605, and the title page of the 1605 quarto indicates that like *The Fawn* and *Eastward Ho* it was played at Blackfriars "by the Children *of her Maiesties Reuels.*" Like *Eastward Ho* it is a city comedy, actually, it may be argued, a tragicomedy because it includes the distinct possibility of hanging ("danger but not . . . death," in Guarini's terms) for two characters, Malheureux and Mulligrub. Like *The Fawn* it makes use of John Florio's 1603 translation of Montaigne's *Essayes*, such large use, in fact, that the thought of *The Dutch Courtesan* is permeated with Montaigne's views on sexuality, marriage, friendship, and morality. Perhaps these themes were of especial interest to Marston at this time because he got married in 1605 to Mary Wilkes, only daughter of Dr. William Wilkes, the rector of Barford St. Martin in Wiltshire. (Their only child, John, died an infant in 1624.) Perhaps too, the pervasive moral discussions in *The Dutch Courtesan* can be traced to the influence of Marston's new (or soon-to-be) father-in-law, for Ben Jonson years later in his *Conversations with Drummond* sarcastically said: "Marston wrott his Father jn Lawes preachings & his Father jn Law his Commedies."

Marston and Jonson may have been having one of their "many quarrells" in 1605 because the prologue to *The Dutch Courtesan* seems in the line "We strive not to instruct, but to delight" to allude to the common reverse Jonsonian dictum in his critical pronouncements (such as in the prologue to *Volpone*, produced in 1606), where the emphasis is on instruction. Whatever the personal conflicts or theoretical critical positions of Jonson and Marston, *The Dutch Courtesan* certainly does emphasize serious issues, as is made clear in the *Fabulae Argumentum*, which asserts: "*The difference betwixt the love of a courtesan and a wife is the full scope of the play, which, intermixed with the deceits of a witty city jester, fills up the comedy.*" Although the play contains only one married woman, the subplot character Mistress Mulligrub, wife to the vintner Master Mulligrub (the victim of Cocledemoy, the "witty city jester"), the main plot is indeed concerned with both the love *of* or *pertaining to* a courtesan and to a wife and the common courtesan's type of love versus the faithful wife's type of love. Thus, we have the cavalier attitude of Freevill, described aptly by Gustav Cross in his excellent "Marston, Montaigne, and Morality: *The Dutch Courtezan* Reconsidered" (1960), as "Montaigne's 'natural man,' forerunner of the libertine or *honnête homme* who features so largely in later seventeenth-century literature." When the play opens, Freevill has already discarded the courtesan Franceschina because he is now courting the chaste (and marriageable) Beatrice. His puritanical friend Malheureux (unhappy, unfortunate), however, lectures him about sins of the flesh and goes with Freevill to see Franceschina: "Well, I'll go to make her loathe the shame she's in./The sight of vice augments the hate of sin." Freevill replies: "The sight of vice augments the hate of sin/Very fine, perdy!" The predictable occurs, and in scene two Malheureux falls in love with the beautiful courtesan: "Now cold blood defend me!/What a proportion afflicts me!" The references to "cold blood" and "proportion" allude to the Renaissance concepts of physiology and psychology that inform the theory of the four humors. Malheureux's "cold blood" indicates that he, like Angelo in Shakespeare's *Measure for Measure,* is probably of a melancholic complexion (or "proportion"). Such a temperament was supposedly prone to violent afflictions of love. The more sanguine Freevill—who has a "well-humor'd cheek"—is better able to control his affections.

Malheureux's lack of control becomes evident when in I.ii he immediately begins to question societal and Christian values—"Are strumpets, then, such things so delicate?/Can custom spoil what nature made so good?"—but even agrees momentarily to kill Freevill at the behest of the vengeful Franceschina. What he shows is a lack of the cardinal (or natural) virtue of temperance, which was the foundation stone of both classical and Christian ethical attitudes related to right reason, the mean, natural law, and the control of sexual passion and anger (the concupiscible and irascible appetites). Marston's sources for knowledge of temperance (and the other cardinal virtues—fortitude, prudence, and justice) could have been Cicero's *De Officiis* (alluded to in I.ii and II.i) or any of several Renaissance treatises such as Thomas Elyot's *The Book Named the Governor* (1531) or Pierre de la Primauday's *The French Academie* (English translation, 1586). Most likely with his educational background, Marston knew several books on the subject. However, it is certain that he read John Florio's 1603 translation of Michel de Montaigne's *The Essayes*

because there are over forty borrowings from it in *The Dutch Courtesan* and about half are from the essay "*Upon some verses of* Virgill." The main thesis of the essay is the need for moderation in all things, especially in sexual matters, and an emphasis upon moderation or the mean is evident in Marston's play.

Not only are both Malheureux (concupiscent) and Franceschina (concupiscent and irascible) guilty of immoderation or intemperance, but so is Freevill when he subjects Beatrice to great anguish by pretending to have been murdered by Malheureux so that he can teach him a lesson *and* test her love (or patience). Crispinella, Beatrice's cousin and another of Marston's witty female critics in the mode of Rossaline in *Antonio and Mellida*, takes him to task in V.ii for what he calls "my immeasurably loving," and Beatrice herself makes the telling point in the same scene: "there's nothing sweet to man but mean." Franceschina, of course, is the main source of the trouble in the main plot, and although as a beautiful courtesan she might retain some audience sympathy among the gallants in the audience, her vicious plot to destroy Beatrice, Freevill, and Malheureux ultimately costs her all support, as it did the courtesan in Marston's narrative source, *Le Premier Livre Des Bergeries De Juliette* (1587) by Nicolas de Montreux.

There is a similar emphasis upon temperance (or the lack of it) in the subplot of *The Dutch Courtesan*. Mistress Mulligrub indicates that she is not a particularly chaste woman, and at one point we learn that she and her husband belong to the Family of Love (an Anabaptist sect that was often accused of immorality and that seems to have especially perturbed James I), among whose members is Mary Faugh, Franceschina's bawd. Master Mulligrub himself is prone to outbursts of temper and is sorely tried by Cocledemoy, who continually dupes him and steals his goods, once in each act, in fact. After the final practical joke in V.ii (involving a stolen cloak), Mulligrub the vintner is the victim, ironically, of the "choler of a justice wrong'd in wine" and sentenced to be hanged. However, he, like Malheureux, is saved at the foot of the gallows because he acknowledges his own faults (which include running a dishonest tavern) and asks forgiveness. Mulligrub, in short, can now temper his anger, just as Malheureux has tempered his sexual passion.

Although the main unifying element in *The Dutch Courtesan* is the concept of temperance, there is also evidence that Marston was concerned with the other cardinal virtues, that is, fortitude (Mal-

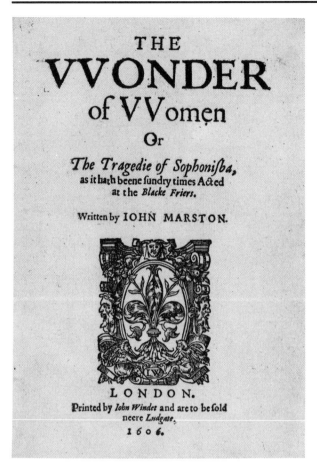

THE
VVONDER
of VVomen
Or
The Tragedie of Sophonifba,
as it hath beene fundry times Acted
at the *Blacke Friers.*

Written by IOHN MARSTON.

LONDON.
Printed by *Iohn Windet* and are to be fold
neere *Ludgate.*
1 6 o 6.

Title page for the 1606 quarto edition of the play for which Marston drew on works by the Latin historians Appian and Livy (Henry E. Huntington Library and Art Gallery)

heureux is deficient here), prudence (Mulligrub shows none), and justice (the denouement involves trials and gallows, and Franceschina is sent to prison). The thematic framework fits nicely within the dramatic structure of tragicomedy, so that Marston was able to combine such disparate elements as topical satire of contemporary types (such as Tysefew, "*a blunt gallant,*" and Caqueteur, "*a prattling gull,*" wooers of Crispinella) with a serious exploration of the sexual and moral nature of mankind in civilized society.

It has been argued, most recently and convincingly by Harry Keyishian in "Dekker's *Whore* and Marston's *Courtesan*" (1967), that *The Dutch Courtesan* is "a satiric protest against Dekker's sentimental treatment of the reformed prostitute Bellafront" in *1 The Honest Whore* (produced in 1604). Nonetheless, there is contemporary evidence that not everybody understood Marston's intentions, for one Anthony Nixon in a book entitled *The*

Blacke yeare (1606), seems to be referring to Marston's play in the following passage: "others haue good wittes, but so criticall, that they arraigne other mens works at the Tribunall seate of euery censurious *Aristarchs* [grammarian and critic, circa 150 B.C.] vnderstanding, when their owne are sacrificed in Paules Churchyard for bringing in the *Dutch Curtezan* to corrupt English conditions, and sent away *Westward* for carping both at Court, Cittie and countrie." It is difficult to say what "sent away *Westward*" means. E. K. Chambers thinks it refers to the troubles (with Chapman and Jonson) over *Eastward Ho* and indicates that Marston did escape imprisonment. Whatever the reference, Marston's next play, perhaps his last, shows him dramatizing a much safer subject.

The last play attributed wholly to Marston is *Sophonisba*. It was entered in the records of the Stationers' Company on 17 March 1606 and printed in quarto form in the same year with the title "THE WONDER of Women Or *The Tragedie of Sophonisba,* as it hath beene sundry times Acted at the *Blacke Friers, Written by* IOHN MARSTON." According to E. K. Chambers in *The Elizabethan Stage:* "The mention of Blackfriars without the name of a company points to a performance after [Queen] Anne's patronage had been withdrawn from the Revels boys, late in 1605 or early in 1606. . . ." Because Marston (presumably) mentioned on the title page of a second edition of *The Fawn* in 1606 that the play was "now corrected of many faults, which by reason of the Authors absence, were let slip in the first edition," Anthony Caputi has asserted that "it is reasonable to assume that he wrote this second tragedy in the second half of 1605 and early in 1606, perhaps during his enforced exile after the *Eastward Ho* scandal. . . . [Marston] was out of London when the first edition of *The Fawn* appeared, sometime after March 12, 1606, the date of the Stationers' entry, and for all we know he may have been in continuous exile until he returned sometime before July 31, 1606, for the *City Pageant* [presented (in Latin) to James I and the visiting King of Denmark], an event that indicates that King James had forgiven him."

In the second edition of *The Fawn* Marston appended several lines to the preface ("To My Equal Reader") that obviously allude to the printing of the first edition and also to the forthcoming *Sophonisba:* "Reader, know that I have perused this copy to make some satisfaction for the first faulty impression; yet so urgent hath been my business, that some errors have still passed, which thy discretion may amend. Comedies are writ to be spoken, not read. Remember the life of these things consists in action, and for your such courteous survey of my pen, I will present a tragedy to you which shall boldly abide the most curious perusal." Marston's pride in *Sophonisba* is evident both in his preface ("To the Generall Reader"), where he says, *"Know that I have not labored in this poeme, to tie my selfe to relate any thing as an historian but to inlarge every thing as a Poet, To transcribe Authors, quote authorities, & translate Latin prose orations into English black* [blank]*-verse, hath in this subject beene the least aime of my studies,"* and in his epilogue, where he speaks of *"words well senc'd* [full of meaning, sententious], *best suting subject grave,/Noble true story."* Scholars have argued that the preface may contain a slap at Ben Jonson, a distinct possibility, because in the preface ("To the Readers") to *Sejanus* (published 1605), Jonson argued: "if in truth of Argument, dignity of Persons, grauity and height of Elocution, fulnesse and frequencie of Sentence, I haue discharg'd the other offices of a *Tragick* writer, let not the absence of these *Formes* ["the strict Lawes of *Time*" and "a proper *Chorus*"] be imputed to me," and further asserted, "least in some nice nostrill, the *Quotations* might sauour affected, I doe let you know, that I abhor nothing more; and haue only done it to shew my integrity in the *Story.* . . ." Even though Marston wrote a dedicatory poem for the 1605 quarto of *Sejanus,* he may well have taken issue later with what he considered to be Jonson's pedantic approach to his sources.

Marston's attitude toward his sources in *Sophonisba* is indeed that of a poet and not a historian. His main sources were *The second part of Appian of Alexandria,* translated by W. B. (1578), and *The Romane Historie Written by T. Livius of Padva,* translated by Philemon Holland (1600). Most of Marston's basic story—which involves the rivalry of the Libyan Kings Massinissa and Syphax for the love of Sophonisba, daughter of Asdruball of Carthage—is derived from Appian's version of the Punic Wars of 205-203 B.C. In this story the noble Asdruball engages Sophonisba to the Numidian Massinissa, son of a king, but when Syphax, also in love with Sophonisba, invades Carthage and joins forces with the Roman Scipio, the Carthaginians turn Sophonisba over to Syphax in order to get his support. When the aggrieved Massinissa decides to go over to Scipio's side, Asdruball and other Carthaginians decide to dispatch him, but he escapes the attempt. Whereas in Appian Sophonisba is engaged to Massinissa and is a virgin, in Livy she is married to Syphax and is presented as a sexually alluring woman who, after Syphax's defeat in battle, appeals for protection to Massinissa, who is an ally of Scipio, but who succumbs to her wiles. In both Appian's and Livy's versions Syphax blames Sophonisba for his break with Rome, and in both versions the apprehensive Scipio demands that Massinissa turn the temptress over to him. Massinissa solves his problem—fidelity either to Sophonisba or to Rome—in both versions by bringing poison to Sophonisba, who commits suicide.

From Appian Marston derived most of his plot and basic characterization, but from Livy he derived hints for the psychological characterization of such people as Syphax and Massinissa. In Marston's play, however, Sophonisba is a truly noble virgin martyr and patriot, and Massinissa is also considerably more noble than in the sources. Syphax, on the other hand, is totally depraved in the play, and, as if to show his contempt for Jonson's "truth of Argument" and "integrity in the *Story,*" Marston went to Lucan's *Pharsalia* and found a Thessalian witch named Erichtho (specialty: necrophagia), who is invoked by Syphax to aid him in seducing Sophonisba but instead ends up in bed with the horrified Syphax. The theatrical effect must have been stunning.

Marston seems to have read widely for *Sophonisba,* and there are indications that he borrowed some material for the Syphax/Erichtho incident from the Cupid and Psyche legend in Lucius Apuleius's *Golden Ass,* translated by William Adlington (1566), and may even have derived hints for the characterization of Sophonisba—"a female glory/ (The wonder of a constancie so fixt/That fate it selfe might grow envious)," says Marston's prologue—from the faithful Psyche. Other sources include hints for the characterization of a Carthaginian Senator named Gelosso from Nicholas de Montreux's *Sophonisbe* (1601) and intellectual substance, again, from John Florio's 1603 translation of Montaigne's *Essayes,* especially the essay *"Of profit and honestie,"* which deals with the difference between expediency and true morality.

The seriousness with which Marston treated *Sophonisba* is evident throughout. The play, like Marston's other tragedy, *Antonio's Revenge,* has Senecan elements in it, both in the Stoicism exhibited by Sophonisba and in the rhetoric and plot devices, but it is at the same time not a closet drama. The major theme of the play is concerned with integrity and fidelity, more particularly with swearing and forswearing or the keeping or breaking of vows. Sophonisba is the Wonder of Women because she chooses suicide rather than "vowes base breach," which is the fault (or crime) of most of the other

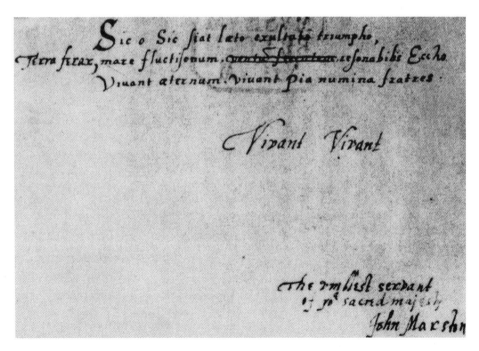

After that the Recorder in the
name of the Cittye had Saluted
the Maiesties of great Brittaine
and Denmarck with this short
Oration. ── ─

Serenissime, Augustissime Rex: quid enim
Reges dicam, quos non tam conjunctio sanguinis
quam communio pietatis vnum fecit?

Anni sunt quinquaginta plus minus, à quo
Regem Iel vnum aspeximus, nunc duos
simul contemplamur adoramur :·
Quapropter antiqua civitas LONDON
nova ista condecorata gloria.
Triumphat gaudio, salutat precibus,
Majestatis. binam hanc majestatem.·

Sic o Sic fiat laeto exultato triumpho,
Terra ferax, mare fluctisonum. ~~verbo fecerunt~~ resonabilis Echo
Viuant aeternum. Viuant pia numina fratres·

Vivant Vivant

The rmliest servant
of yo' sacred majesty
John Marshn

Portions of pages from the manuscript describing the city pageant Marston wrote to celebrate the London visit of King Christian IV of Denmark. Now preserved at the British Library, this manuscript is for the most part a scribe's copy, but the last four lines (on the second sheet above) are believed to be in Marston's own hand (MS Royal 18 A. XXXI; by permission of the British Library).

major characters in the play both in their private and public lives.

After *Sophonisba* Marston's own life seems to have undergone radical changes. He wrote a masque called *The Entertainment of the Dowager-Countess of Darby* in 1607, and until fairly recently it has been understood that he worked on at least one more play, *The Insatiate Countess,* but left it unfinished and left the theater in 1608. *The Insatiate Countess* was first published in quarto in 1613, and the title page describes it as "A TRAGEDIE: Acted at White-Fryers. Written by IOHN MARSTON." In three of what were once (until the 1940s) the six known copies, the name of the author has been cut out of the title. Another quarto was printed in 1616, but no mention is made on the title page of the type of play it was, where it was acted, or who wrote it. In 1631 another quarto was published, and the title page (containing Marston's name) and bibliographical collation both indicate that the edition was printed from the 1613 quarto. However, in another 1631 issue of *The Insatiate Countess* the original title page has been replaced with one that lists it as a tragedy performed at Whitefriars and written by "William Barksteed," or Barksted (as his name is more commonly spelled).

The fact that Barksted's name is on one of the 1631 title pages of *The Insatiate Countess* would probably not have caused such controversy if there were not other external evidence to associate him with the authorship of the play. However, in 1887 A. H. Bullen, editor of *The Works of John Marston,* pointed out that two lines in the concluding speech of the play—"Night, like a Masque, is entred heavens great hall,/With thousand Torches ushering the way:"—are taken verbatim from Barksted's long narrative poem *Mirrha The Mother of Adonis: Or, Lustes Prodegies* (1607). In 1896 a scholar named Roscoe Addison Small noted that there are fourteen passages (two of them verbatim parallels) derived from *Mirrha* and another long narrative poem by Barksted entitled *Hiren: Or, The faire Greeke* (1611). He concluded that Barksted probably wrote most of the play. Later, E. K. Chambers agreed and added: "It may be conjectured that Marston left the fragment when he got into trouble for the second time in 1608 [Marston was committed to Newgate for an unspecified offence on 8 June 1608], and that the revision was more probably for the Queen's Revels at Whitefriars in 1609-11 than for the conjoint Queen's Revels and Lady Elizabeth's in 1613." H. Harvey Wood, editor of *The Plays of John Marston,* disagreed with Small (and, by implication, with Chambers) and concluded: "Echoes of Marston are more frequent and more obvious in the play than the traces of Barksteed, undeniable as these may be: indeed, the play as a whole could, in my opinion, be attributed to no other hand, on stylistic evidence, than Marston's."

The attribution controversy has raged ever since, and recently it has been pointed out there are two more copies of the 1613 quarto. It seems that one Lewis Machin's name appears with that of one William Bacster (undoubtedly Barksted) on a cancel that replaces the original title page in the copy of the 1613 quarto at the Folger Shakespeare Library. E. K. Chambers tells us that Machin "is probably the L.M. who contributed 'eglogs' to the *Mirrha* (1607) of the King's Revels actor William Barksted." Indeed, Machin did append three short Ovidian narrative poems to *Mirrha.* He also wrote a short dedicatory poem to Barksted's work. In "*The Insatiate Countess:* Linguistic Evidence for Authorship" (1981), D. J. Lake has concluded that neither Barksted nor Machin (of whose work there are no clearly direct parallels in *The Insatiate Countess*) wrote enough for us to "identify the non-Marstonian hand or hands." Most recently, though, Giorgio Melchiori in his Revels Plays edition (1984) of *The Insatiate Countess* has argued that "Marston devised the plot and underplot of the play, wrote a first draft of Act I, part of II.i, some speeches and outlines of the rest, particularly II.ii, II.iv and, to a lesser extent, III.iv, IV.ii and V.i." He further asserts that Barksted and Machin, both of whom are known to have worked for the Children of the King's Revels (which performed at Whitefriars 1607-1609), and perhaps someone else, "revised and added to the parts written by Marston and completed the rest of the play." Finally, a "third layer" of work, including the addition of V.ii, was performed by "a new hack writer or one who had already worked on the play." Melchiori concludes: "Marston's part cannot be later than 1607 or early 1608." However, in "Marston's Early Contribution to 'The Insatiate Countess' " (1977), Michael Scott has argued that Marston may well have written his share of the tragedy early in his literary career. Scott's most telling point is that *The Insatiate Countess* shows no evidence of the influence of Montaigne's *Essayes.* There is also stylistic evidence that would indicate an early date, and we might recall the canceled passage in Marston's father's will about "my willful disobedyent sonne" and "his delighte in playes."

If we look again, briefly, at Marston's early plays, we find some interesting things. For exam-

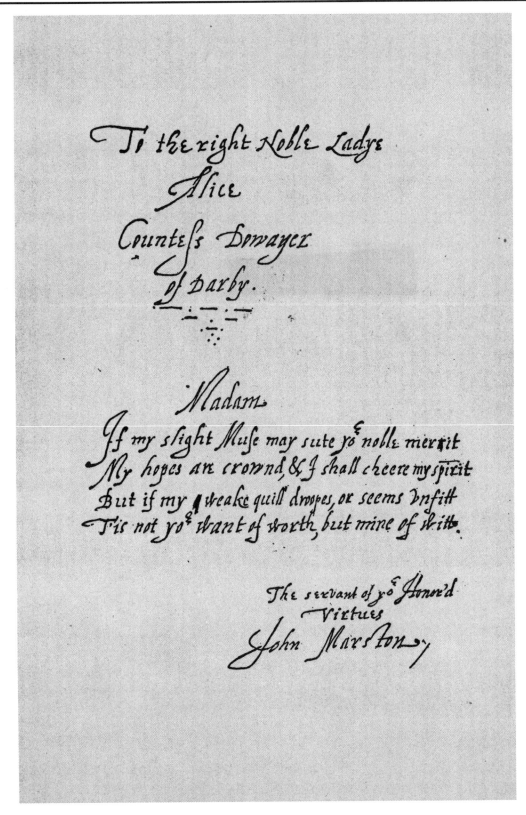

Address to Countess Alice of Darby, in a scribal hand and signed by Marston, from the manuscript for The Entertainment of the Dowager-Countess of Darby *that is preserved at the Henry E. Huntington Library and Art Gallery. This manuscript is believed to be the scribal copy Marston had made for presentation to the countess (E. L. 34. B9; by permission of the Henry E. Huntington Library).*

ple, in *Histriomastix* the thematic emphasis is upon social order. In *Jack Drum's Entertainment* there is much ado about courtship. In the *Antonio* plays, the assault upon female chastity is a major indication of the degeneracy of Piero's Italianate court. In *The Insatiate Countess,* which also has an Italianate setting, we have three stories, all involving sexual relationships: 1) the story of the widowed Countess Isabella, who is a nymphomaniac, derived from the tale of "The Countesse of Celant" in William Painter's *The second Tome of the Palace of Pleasure* (1567); 2) the story of Mendosa and the widowed Lady Lentulus, which deals with a sexual relationship within the context of honor and the Lady's vows, derived from Painter's "Two Gentlewomen of Venice"; and 3) the Rogero-Thais, Claridiana-Abigail comic plot, which revolves around revenge by means of attempted cuckoldry, found also in "Two Gentlewomen of Venice." Furthermore, in terms of structure, Marston's early plays, with the exception of *Antonio's Revenge,* are not well plotted. In *Histriomastix, Jack Drum's Entertainment,* and *Antonio and Mellida,* Marston tried, rather unsuccessfully, to handle several plot strands and alternate serious and comic scenes, which is the case again in *The Insatiate Countess.* But *The Insatiate Countess,* a tragedy (there are two deaths, Count Massino's in act four and Isabella's in act five), is more like *Antonio's Revenge* than Marston's other and later tragedy, *Sophonisba,* in terms of its imagery.

It is conceivable, then, that Marston drafted at least the serious plots of *The Insatiate Countess*—those of Isabella and Mendosa/Lady Lentulus—both of which contain the usual Marstonian moral earnestness, sometime around 1599-1600, but for unknown reasons left them unfinished as he went on to write all of his other plays, first for the Children of Paul's and later for the Queen's Revels at Blackfriars and the Children of the Blackfriars. Why he left the stage is another mystery, but E. K. Chambers has conjectured that he was sent to Newgate on 8 June 1608 because "he was the author of the [non-extant] Blackfriars play . . . which hit at James's explorations after Scottish silver. He [then] disappeared, selling his interest in the Blackfriars company, then or in 1605, to Robert Keysar. . . ." Philip Finkelpearl agrees with Chambers and adds that an epigram by John Davies of Hereford in *The Scourge of Folly* (1610) contains lines which confirm Marston's decision to enter the Church: "Thy *Male-content,* or, *Malecontentednesse/* Hath made thee change thy *Muse* as some do gesse./ . . . ./*Thou shalt be prais'd; and kept from want and wo;/So, blest are* Crosses, *that* do *blesse us so.*"

Marston was ordained deacon on 24 September 1609 and ordained priest on 24 December of the same year (both in the parish church at Stanton Harcourt, Oxfordshire). It is known that he worked as a clergyman with his father-in-law at Barford St. Martin, Wiltshire, in 1610 at least, and he received the living of Christchurch, Hampshire, in 1616 (the same year he seems to have been robbed on the highway). His new position as a clergyman would explain why his name was removed from the title pages of several quartos of *The Insatiate Countess* and also from the entire second edition of his collected works, printed for William Sheares in 1633. He seems to have spent the rest of his life as a clergyman, but he ended it where he began his literary career, for his funeral certificate tells us that he "died in Aldermanbury at his house there on the 25th daye of June 1634 & was conveyed from thence to the Middle Temple where in the Quier of the Temple Church he lyeth interred by his father."

Bibliographies:

Cecil M. McCulley, "John Marston," in *The New Intellectuals,* edited by Terence P. Logan and Denzell S. Smith (Lincoln: Univeristy of Nebraska Press, 1977), pp. 171-247;

Kenneth Tucker, *John Marston: A Reference Guide* (Boston: G. K. Hall, 1985).

References:

Morse S. Allen, *The Satire of John Marston* (Columbus, Ohio: Privately printed, 1920);

Michael C. Andrews, "*Jack Drum's Entertainment* as Burlesque," *Renaissance Quarterly,* 24 (Summer 1971): 226-231;

A. José Axelrad, *Un Malcontent Élizabéthain: John Marston (1576-1634)* (Paris: Didier, 1955);

Philip J. Ayres, "Marston's *Antonio's Revenge:* The Morality of the Revenging Hero," *Studies in English Literature,* 12 (Spring 1972): 359-374;

Allen Bergson, "The Ironic Tragedies of Marston and Chapman: Notes on Jacobean Tragic Form," *Journal of English and Germanic Philology,* 69 (October 1970): 613-630;

Ellen Berland, "The Function of Irony in Marston's *Antonio and Mellida,*" *Studies in Philology,* 66 (October 1969): 739-755;

Fredson Bowers, *Elizabethan Revenge Tragedy 1587-1642* (Princeton: Princeton University Press, 1940);

Robert E. Brettle, "Bibliographical Notes on Some Marston Quartos and Early Collected Editions," *Library*, new series 8 (December 1927): 336-348;

Brettle, "*Eastward Ho*, 1605. By Chapman, Jonson, and Marston. Bibliography, and Circumstances of Production," *Library*, new series 9 (December 1928): 287-302;

Brettle, "John Marston, Dramatist at Oxford, 1591(?)-1594, 1609," *Review of English Studies*, 3 (October 1927): 398-405;

Brettle, "John Marston, Dramatist: Some New Facts about His Life," *Modern Language Review*, 22 (January 1927): 7-14;

Brettle, "Marston Born in Oxfordshire," *Modern Language Review*, 22 (July 1927): 317-319;

Brettle, "Notes on John Marston," *Review of English Studies*, new series 13 (1962): 390-393;

Brettle, "The 'Poet Marston' Letter to Sir Gervase Clifton, 1607," *Review of English Studies*, 4 (April 1928): 212-214;

Oscar James Campbell, *Comicall Satyre and Shakespeare's "Troilus and Cressida"* (San Marino, Cal.: Huntington Library, 1938);

Anthony Caputi, *John Marston, Satirist* (Ithaca: Cornell University Press, 1961);

E. K. Chambers, *The Elizabethan Stage*, 4 volumes (Oxford: Clarendon Press, 1923);

John Scott Colley, *John Marston's Theatrical Drama*, Salzburg Studies in English Literature: Jacobean Drama Studies (Salzburg: Universität Salzburg, 1974);

Gustav Cross, "Marston, Montaigne, and Morality: *The Dutch Courtezan* Reconsidered," *ELH*, 27 (March 1960): 30-43;

Cross, "The Retrograde Genius of John Marston," *Review of English Literature*, 2 (October 1961): 19-27;

Gilbert R. Davis, "The Characterization of Mamon in *Jack Drum's Entertainment*," *English Language Notes*, 3 (September 1965): 22-24;

Madeleine Doran, *Endeavors of Art: A Study of Form in Elizabethan Drama* (Madison: University of Wisconsin Press, 1954);

T. S. Eliot, "John Marston," in his *Elizabethan Essays* (London: Faber & Faber, 1934);

Una Ellis-Fermor, "John Marston," in her *The Jacobean Drama: An Interpretation*, third edition, revised (London: Methuen, 1953), pp. 77-97;

Philip J. Finkelpearl, *John Marston of the Middle Temple: An Elizabethan Dramatist in His Social Setting* (Cambridge: Harvard University Press, 1969);

Finkelpearl, "John Marston's *Histriomastix* as an Inns of Court Play: A Hypothesis," *Huntington Library Quarterly*, 29 (May 1966): 223-234;

Finkelpearl, "The Use of the Middle Temple's Christmas Revels in Marston's *The Fawne*," *Studies in Philology*, 64 (April 1967): 199-209;

R. A. Foakes, "John Marston's Fantastical Plays: *Antonio and Mellida* and *Antonio's Revenge*," *Philological Quarterly*, 41 (January 1962): 229-239;

Foakes, "Mr. Levin and 'Good Bad Drama,'" *Essays in Criticism*, 22 (July 1972): 327-329;

Foakes, *Shakespeare: The Dark Comedies to the Last Plays: From Satire to Celebration* (Charlottesville: University Press of Virginia, 1971);

George L. Geckle, *John Marston's Drama: Themes, Images, Sources* (Rutherford, N.J.: Fairleigh Dickinson University Press, 1980);

Brian Gibbons, "The Giddy Sea of Humour: Marston's First Contribution," in his *Jacobean City Comedy: A Study of Satiric Plays by Jonson, Marston and Middleton* (Cambridge: Harvard University Press, 1968), pp. 83-104;

Donna B. Hamilton, "Language as Theme in *The Dutch Courtesan*," *Renaissance Drama*, new series 5 (1972): 75-87;

Michael Higgins, "The Convention of the Stoic Hero as Handled by Marston," *Modern Language Review*, 39 (October 1944): 338-346;

G. K. Hunter, "English Folly and Italian Vice: *The Moral Landscape of John Marston*," in *Jacobean Theater*, edited by John Russell Brown and Bernard Harris, Stratford-upon-Avon Studies, no. 1 (London: Arnold, 1960), pp. 85-111;

R. W. Ingram, *John Marston*, Twayne's English Authors Series (Boston: Twayne, 1978);

Ingram, "Marston, Old or New Elizabethan," *Humanities Association of Canada Bulletin*, 17 (1966): 19-26;

Ingram, "The Use of Music in the Plays of Marston," *Music and Letters*, 37 (April 1956): 154-164;

James L. Jackson, "Sources of the Subplot of Marston's *The Dutch Courtezan*," *Philological Quarterly*, 31 (April 1952): 223-224;

Ejner J. Jensen, "The Boy Actors: Plays and Playing," *Research Opportunities in Renaissance Drama*, 18 (1975): 5-11;

Jensen, "The Style of the Boy Actors," *Comparative Drama*, 2 (Summer 1968): 100-114;

Jensen, "Theme and Imagery in *The Malcontent*," *Studies in English Literature*, 10 (Spring 1970): 367-384;

Joel Kaplan, "John Marston's *Fawn*: A Saturnalian Satire," *Studies in English Literature*, 9 (Spring 1969): 335-350;

Alvin Kernan, *The Cankered Muse: Satire of the English Renaissance,* Yale Studies in English, volume 142 (New Haven: Yale University Press, 1959);

Kernan, "John Marston's Play *Histriomastix,*" *Modern Language Quarterly,* 19 (June 1958): 134-140;

Harry Keyishian, "Dekker's *Whore* and Marston's *Courtesan,*" *English Language Notes,* 4 (June 1967): 261-266;

Christian Kiefer, "Music and Marston's *The Malcontent,*" *Studies in Philology,* 51 (January 1954): 163-171;

Arthur Kirsch, "Marston," in his *Jacobean Dramatic Perspectives* (Charlottesville: University Press of Virginia, 1972), pp. 25-37;

D. J. Lake, "*Eastward Ho:* Linguistic Evidence for Authorship," *Notes and Queries,* new series 28 (April 1981): 158-166;

Lake, "*The Insatiate Countess:* Linguistic Evidence for Authorship," *Notes and Queries,* new series 28 (April 1981): 166-170;

Richard Levin, "The New *New Inn* and the Proliferation of Good Bad Drama," *Essays in Criticism,* 22 (January 1972): 41-47;

Levin, "The Proof of the Parody," *Essays in Criticism* (July 1974): 312-317;

John J. O'Connor, "The Chief Source of Marston's *Dutch Courtezan,*" *Studies in Philology,* 54 (October 1957): 509-515;

David G. O'Neill, "The Commencement of Marston's Career as a Dramatist," *Review of English Studies,* new series 22 (November 1971): 442-445;

Robert Ornstein, "John Marston, Beaumont and Fletcher," in his *The Moral Vision of Jacobean Tragedy* (Madison: University of Wisconsin Press, 1960), pp. 151-169;

John Peter, "John Marston's Plays," *Scrutiny,* 17 (Summer 1950): 132-153;

Peter, "Marston's Use of Seneca," *Notes and Queries,* new series 1 (April 1954): 145-149;

Robert K. Presson, "Marston's *Dutch Courtezan:* The Study of an Attitude in Adaptation," *Journal of English and Germanic Philology,* 55 (1956): 406-413;

Samuel Schoenbaum, "The Precarious Balance of John Marston," *PMLA,* 67 (December 1952): 1069-1078;

Michael Scott, *John Marston's Plays: Theme, Structure and Performance* (London: Macmillan, 1968; New York: Barnes & Noble, 1978);

Scott, "Marston's Early Contribution to 'The Insatiate Countess,' " *Notes and Queries,* new series 24 (April 1977): 116-117;

Michael Shapiro, *Children of the Revels: The Boy Companies of Shakespeare's Time and Their Plays* (New York: Columbia University Press, 1977);

William W. E. Slights, " 'Elder in a deform'd church': The Function of Marston's Malcontent," *Studies in English Literature,* 13 (Spring 1973): 360-373;

Slights, "Political Morality and the Ending of *The Malcontent,*" *Modern Philology,* 69 (November 1971): 138-139;

Roscoe Addison Small, "The Authorship and Date of the Insatiate Countess," *Studies and Notes in Philology and Literature* (Harvard University), 5 (1896): 227-282;

Small, *The Stage-Quarrel Between Ben Jonson and the So-Called Poetasters* (Breslau: M. & H. Marcus, 1899);

Theodore Spencer, "John Marston," *Criterion,* 13 (July 1934): 581-599;

Elmer Edgar Stoll, "Shakespeare, Marston, and the Malcontent Type," *Modern Philology,* 3 (January 1906): 281-303;

Albert H. Tricomi, "John Marston's Manuscripts," *Huntington Library Quarterly,* 43 (Spring 1980): 87-102;

Albert W. Upton, "Allusions to James I and His Court in Marston's *Fawn* and Beaumont's *Woman Hater,*" *PMLA,* 44 (December 1929): 1048-1065;

Peter Ure, "John Marston's *Sophonisba:* A Reconsideration," *Durham University Journal,* new series 10 (June 1949): 81-90;

T. F. Wharton, "*The Malcontent* and 'Dreams, Visions, Fantasies,' " *Essays in Criticism,* 24 (July 1974): 261-274;

Wharton, "Old Marston or New Marston: The *Antonio* Plays," *Essays in Criticism,* 25 (July 1975): 357-369;

Paul M. Zall, "John Marston, Moralist," *ELH,* 20 (September 1953): 186-193.

Papers:

A manuscript for *The Spectacle* is in the British Library (Royal Mss. 18A XXXI) and is signed by Marston. A manuscript for *The Entertainment* is in the Henry E. Huntington Library (E.L. 34.B9). There is one authenticated holograph letter: "Poet Marston" to Sir Gervase Clifton, manuscript CLC 567, University of Nottingham.

Philip Massinger
(November 1583-March 1640)

Philip Edwards
University of Liverpool

PLAY PRODUCTIONS: *The Honest Man's Fortune,* by Massinger(?), John Fletcher, and Nathan Field, London, Whitefriars theater, circa 1613;

Thierry and Theodoret, by Massinger, Fletcher, and Francis Beaumont, London, Blackfriars theater, circa 1615;

Beggar's Bush, by Massinger, Beaumont, and Fletcher, London, Blackfriars theater, circa 1615;

The Queen of Corinth, by Massinger, Fletcher, and Nathan Field, London, Blackfriars theater, circa 1617;

The Jeweller of Amsterdam, by Massinger, Fletcher, and Field, Blackfriars theater, circa 1617;

The Fatal Dowry, by Massinger and Field, London, Blackfriars theater, circa 1617-1619;

The Knight of Malta, by Massinger, Fletcher, and Field, London, Blackfriars theater, circa 1618;

The Bloody Brother, or Rollo Duke of Normandy, by Massinger(?), Fletcher, and others (perhaps Ben Jonson and George Chapman), London, Blackfriars theater, circa 1619;

Sir John van Olden Barnavelt, by Massinger and Fletcher, London, Blackfriars theater, August 1619;

The Custom of the Country, by Massinger and Fletcher, London, Blackfriars theater, circa 1619;

The False One, by Massinger and Fletcher, London, Blackfriars theater, circa 1619;

The Virgin Martyr, by Massinger and Thomas Dekker, London, Red Bull theater, October 1620;

The Double Marriage, by Massinger and Fletcher, London, Blackfriars theater, circa 1621;

The Maid of Honour, by Massinger, London, Phoenix theater, circa 1621-1622;

The Duke of Milan, by Massinger, London, Blackfriars theater, circa 1621-1622;

The Prophetess, by Massinger and Fletcher, London, Blackfriars theater, licensed 14 May 1622;

The Sea Voyage, by Massinger and Fletcher, London, Blackfriars theater, licensed 22 June 1622;

The Spanish Curate, by Massinger and Fletcher, London, Blackfriars theater, licensed 24 October 1622;

The Little French Lawyer, by Massinger and Fletcher, London, Blackfriars theater, circa 1623;

The Bondman, by Massinger, London, Phoenix theater, 1623;

The Renegado, by Massinger, London, Phoenix theater, 1624;

The Parliament of Love, by Massinger, London, Phoenix theater, licensed 1624;

The Spanish Viceroy, by Massinger, London, Blackfriars theater, 1624;

The Unnatural Combat, by Massinger, London, Globe theater, circa 1624-1625;

The Elder Brother, by Massinger and Fletcher, London, Blackfriars theater, circa 1625;

Love's Cure, by Beaumont and Fletcher, revised by Massinger, London, Blackfriars theater, circa 1625;

A New Way to Pay Old Debts, by Massinger, London, Phoenix theater, 1625;

The Fair Maid of the Inn, by Massinger(?), Fletcher (and perhaps John Webster and John Ford), London, Blackfriars theater, licensed 22 January 1626;

The Roman Actor, by Massinger, London, Blackfriars theater, 1626;

The Judge, by Massinger, London, Blackfriars theater, 1627;

The Great Duke of Florence, by Massinger, London, Phoenix theater, 1627;

The Picture, by Massinger, London, Globe theater and Blackfriars theater, 1629;

Minerva's Sacrifice, by Massinger, London, Blackfriars theater, 1629;

Believe As You List, by Massinger, London, Globe theater and Blackfriars theater, licensed 6 May 1631;

The Emperor of the East, by Massinger, London, Blackfriars theater, 1631;

The Unfortunate Piety, by Massinger, London, Globe theater and Blackfriars theater, 1631;

The portrait of Massinger by Thomas Cross published in the 1655 quarto edition of Three New Playes (*from* The Plays and Poems of Philip Massinger, *edited by Philip Edwards and Colin Gibson, 1976*)

The City Madam, by Massinger, London, Blackfriars theater, 1632;

The Guardian, by Massinger, London, Blackfriars theater, 1633;

Cleander (The Lovers' Progress), Massinger's revision of a play by Fletcher, London, Blackfriars theater, licensed 7 May 1634;

A Very Woman (Massinger's revision of an unidentified play by Fletcher and Massinger of circa 1619-1622), London, Blackfriars theater, licensed 6 June 1634;

The Orator, by Massinger, London, Blackfriars theater, 1635;

The Bashful Lover, by Massinger, London, Blackfriars theater, 1636;

The King and the Subject (perhaps the same play as *The Tyrant*), by Massinger, London, Blackfriars theater, 1638;

Alexius or the Chaste Gallant / Lover, by Massinger, London, Blackfriars theater, 1639;

The Fair Anchoress of Pausilippo, by Massinger, London, Blackfriars theater, 1640.

BOOKS: *The Tragedy of Thierry King of France and His Brother Theodoret,* by Massinger, Francis Beaumont, and John Fletcher (London: Printed by N. Okes for T. Walkley, 1621);

The Virgin Martir, A Tragedie, by Massinger and Thomas Dekker (London: Printed by B. Alsop for T. Jones, 1622);

The Duke of Millaine. A Tragœdie (London: Printed by B. Alsop for E. Blackmore, 1623);

The Bond-Man: An Antient Storie (London: Printed by E. Allde for J. Harison & E. Blackmore, 1624);

The Roman Actor: A Tragœdie (London: Printed by B. Alsop & T. Fawcett for R. Allot, 1629);

The Renegado, A Tragœcomedie (London: Printed by A. Mathewes for J. Waterson, 1630);

The Picture: A Tragœcomœdie (London: Printed by J. Norton for T. Walkley, 1630);

The Maid of Honour (London: Printed by J. Beale for R. Allot, 1632);

The Fatall Dowry: A Tragedy, by Massinger and Nathan Field (London: Printed by J. Norton for F. Constable, 1632);

The Emperour of the East. A Tragœ-Comœedie (London: Printed by T. Harper for J. Waterson, 1632);

A New Way to Pay Old Debts: A Comoedie (London: Printed by E. Purslowe for H. Seyle, 1633);

The Great Duke of Florence. A Comicall Historie (London: Printed by M. Flesher for J. Marriot, 1636);

The Elder Brother, by Massinger and Fletcher (London: Printed by F. Kingston for J. Waterson & J. Benson, 1637);

The Unnaturall Combat. A Tragedie (London: Printed by E. Griffin for J. Waterson, 1639);

The Bloody Brother, by Massinger(?), Fletcher, and others (perhaps Ben Jonson and George Chapman) (London: Printed by R. Bishop for T. Allott & J. Crook, 1639); republished as *The Tragoedy of Rollo Duke of Normandy* (Oxford: Printed by L. Litchfield, 1640);

The Honest Man's Fortune, by Massinger(?), Fletcher, and Field; *Beggars' Bush,* by Massinger, Beaumont and Fletcher; *The Queen of Corinth,* by Massinger, Fletcher, and Field; *The Knight of Malta,* by Massinger, Fletcher, and Field; *The Custom of the Country,* by Massinger and Fletcher; *The False One,* by Massinger and Fletcher; *The Double Marriage,* by Massinger and Fletcher; *The Prophetess,* by Massinger and Fletcher; *The Sea Voyage,* by Massinger and Fletcher; *The Spanish Curate,* by Massinger and Fletcher; *The Little French Lawyer,* by Massinger and Fletcher; *The Fair Maid of the Inn,* by Massinger(?), Fletcher (and perhaps John Webster and John Ford); *Love's Cure,* by Beaumont and Fletcher, revised by Massinger; *The Lovers' Progress,* by Fletcher, revised by Massinger; in *Comedies and Tragedies Written by Francis Beaumont and John Fletcher, Gentlemen* (London: Printed for Humphrey Robinson & Humphrey Moseley, 1647);

Three New Playes (London: Printed by T. Newcombe for Humphrey Moseley, 1655)—comprises *A Very Woman, The Guardian,* and *The Bashful Lover;*

The City Madam (London: Printed by J. Bell for Andrew Pennycuicke, 1658).

Editions: *Sir John van Olden Barnavelt,* by Massinger and Fletcher, edited by Wilhelmina P. Frijlinck (Amsterdam: Van Dorsen, 1922);

The Dramatic Works of Beaumont and Fletcher, Fredson Bowers, general editor, 6 volumes to date (Cambridge: Cambridge University Press, 1966-);

The Plays and Poems of Philip Massinger, 5 volumes, edited by Philip Edwards and Colin Gibson (Oxford: Clarendon Press, 1976).

As the leading dramatist of London's major theatrical company, the King's Men, during Charles I's reign, Philip Massinger had the distinction of holding a post which had been occupied by William Shakespeare until 1616 and then by John Fletcher until 1625. He was the author or part-author of well over fifty plays. Some of these are lost, known to us only by their titles. A most important part of his output, the twelve or more plays that he wrote in collaboration with John Fletcher, were published, without any acknowledgment of his participation, in the "Beaumont and Fletcher" folio of 1647.

In his own plays Massinger went on to exploit the vein of romantic tragicomedy that John Fletcher had successfully initiated early in the Jacobean period; but he wrote several tragedies, of which *The Roman Actor* was the best known. He also wrote two satirical social comedies, *A New Way to Pay Old Debts* and *The City Madam,* and his posthumous recognition has depended almost entirely on this pair. *A New Way to Pay Old Debts* was probably the most popular play outside Shakespeare on the English and American stages in the late-eighteenth and early-nineteenth centuries, attracting all the major actors to the role of the unscrupulous financier Sir Giles Overreach. Massinger's reputation waned in the late-nineteenth and early-twentieth centuries as critical attention focused more and more on other Jacobean and Caroline dramatists, such as John Webster, Cyril Tourneur, Thomas Middleton, and John Ford. More recently, an increased interest in the social and political matrix of seventeenth-century drama has encouraged a new attention to Massinger's plays, within whose florid plots can be found searching explorations of social change and the operation of political power.

Philip Massinger was born into the gentry, something that he could never forget. His father, Arthur Massinger, had been a fellow of Merton College, Oxford until his marriage to Anne Crompton, daughter of a well-to-do merchant, in 1579, when he entered the service of one of the greatest noblemen in the land, the Earl of Pembroke, as his confidential agent. He was also a member of Parliament. Massinger was brought up in a gentleman's family within the ambience of august aristocracy. That his adult life did not continue in this environment seems to have been a severe disappointment to him, but he heroically supported what he considered to be the values of the nobility in the less-favored circumstances in which he wrote his many plays.

His baptism was recorded in Salisbury in Wiltshire (not far from Wilton, the Pembroke home) on 24 November 1583. He entered St. Alban Hall, Oxford, in 1602 but never graduated. The death of his father in 1603 may well have left him not only impoverished but deprived of the expectations of patronage that his father's association with the exalted Pembrokes offered. We do not hear of Massinger again for ten years, and then we find him in prison for debt, along with two other playwrights, Nathan Field and Robert Daborne, appealing to the theater impresario Philip Henslowe to bail them out. This episode is conjectured to have taken place in 1613. It appears from the letter that the penurious trio were all working on an unidentified play with Fletcher at the time of their arrest. A year or two later, Massinger and Field were again collaborating with Fletcher (as may be inferred from stylistic evidence) on two plays printed in the Beaumont and Fletcher canon, *The Queen of Corinth* and *The Knight of Malta*; Fletcher and Massinger then worked together on a play on contemporary events, *Sir John van Olden Barnavelt*. In about 1617-1619 Massinger and Field collaborated on the play which is usually counted the first in the Massinger canon, *The Fatal Dowry*, which was followed by *The Virgin Martyr*, a collaboration between Massinger and Thomas Dekker. What Massinger had been working on for Henslowe with those other dramatists about the year 1613, or when it was he entered into the play-writing business, is impossible to say. A revealing letter which he wrote to William Herbert, Earl of Pembroke (undated, probably 1615-1620), shows him recognizing his vocation as a poet but lamenting that he is unable to secure the patronage which alone could provide a livelihood for a writer. Hoping to find a "noble favorer" in Pembroke, he referred disparagingly to what penury forced him to write as "those toys I would not father," his authorship being known only to his fellow dramatists and to the actors.

It does not seem that Massinger had much success with William Herbert, though his brother, Philip, who succeeded him in 1630, may have been more generous. Massinger enjoyed a certain amount of patronage but never had the financial security necessary to free him from the subservience and toil of writing for the public theater. After 1625, when it is most likely that as regular dramatist for the King's Men he was under some sort of contract, his circumstances and security must have improved, and though he never ceased to grumble at his poverty and lack of artistic freedom, a recently discovered poem that he wrote about 1630 shows a sturdy pride in being a professional dramatist—as one would expect from the author of *The Roman Actor*. Massinger made a virtue of necessity.

When working with Fletcher Massinger was of course the junior partner, writing to order, but it is evident that he was given a lot of the more serious work to do, big scenes in which moral dilemmas are worked through or defiant victims face their accusers. *Sir John van Olden Barnavelt*, however, might be considered his play as much as Fletcher's. The history in this play was extremely recent. The elderly statesman Barnavelt had been executed—following a travesty of judicial process—by the Prince of Orange, his ally during many years of the struggle for Dutch independence, on 12 May 1619. The play was being performed in London in August. It is not surprising that authority was nervous. The manuscript of the play is extant, showing the alterations demanded by the Master of the Revels, anxious to give no public offense to King James or to Spain. As soon as the play was mounted it was banned by the Bishop of London; but the players found some way around the prohibition, and the play was a popular success. Massinger and Fletcher's treatment of this tragic conflict in the precariously independent Dutch republic is politically favorable to the Dutch Prince Maurice, but they created a strong and masterful presence for the proud irascible patriot, who is prepared to exploit religious differences and armed force to hold back the rise of his younger rival. It is a pity this excellent play is not better known.

There could be no greater contrast with *Barnavelt* than *The Virgin Martyr*, a lurid piece of hagiography whose Counter-Reformation features have been influential in suggesting that Massinger was a Catholic. It is the story of Dorothea, persecuted under Diocletian. Spirits good and evil in human guise walk the stage to prosecute the attack on Dorothea or support her in the sufferings which are lubriciously set before the audience, including finally "Her head struck off."

It is in his collaboration with Nathan Field in *The Fatal Dowry* that we first recognize the characteristic elevation and severity of Massinger's moral stance. A hero with an unrelenting and old-fashioned moral code tries to find his way in a slick and corrupt society whose highest objectives are money and sex. The partnership of the two dramatists is ideal since Massinger can eloquently voice the sternness of the hero Charalois while Field's free-running satirical wit splendidly presents the shallowness and affectation of the people who surround him. Massinger had learned from Fletcher (or had taught Fletcher?) the great usefulness as a source of plots for plays of the collection of imaginary law cases put together by Seneca the Elder in the first century A.D. These *controversiae* always have intriguing dilemmas at their center. The question at the heart of *The Fatal Dowry* is how far personal gratitude should interfere with the claims of justice. Charalois's selfless honor has inspired Rochfort not only to pay his debts for him but also to offer him his daughter in marriage. This is the fatal dowry, because the daughter has no intention of letting marriage interrupt her liaison with another man. Charalois finds his wife and her lover flagrante delicto and kills them both. He refuses to admit that his indebtedness to his father-in-law should have influenced what he regards as the absolute claims of justice, and he dies steadfast in that belief.

In the early 1620s Massinger was busy collaborating with Fletcher in plays for the King's Men to be performed at Blackfriars or at the Globe and in writing the first plays of his sole authorship for the companies working for Christopher Beeston at the recently opened Phoenix theater (otherwise known as the Cockpit) in Drury Lane. One of these early independent plays, however, *The Duke of*

Milan, was accepted by the King's Men. It is a fine study of a duke (Sforza) so infatuated with his wife (Marcelia) that he refuses to contemplate the possibility that she might outlive him and marry again. So he orders his favorite to kill her should he fail to return from an expedition. Sforza has absolute power in his domain; the play is one of several studies by Massinger of the corrupting influence of autocracy on both the ruler and the ruled. The favorite to whom Sforza has given his secret instructions has his own reasons for wanting revenge on his patron, and he simply tells Marcelia what her husband's possessive jealousy has proposed. Her pathetic effort to assert her rights as an independent person eventually provokes the blind fury of Sforza and her death at his hands.

The explosive chemistry of psychological weakness and political strength is developed in *The Duke of Milan* in a plot which, like most of Massinger's, has the intricacy of opera. The final resolution of these elaborate plots nearly always requires the revelation of something that has been kept secret from the audience as well as the characters—generally the question of someone's identity or a previous crime. These sensational plots with the extreme emotions which they generate sometimes seem an incongruous medium for exploring moral, social, and political problems; and it is perhaps not surprising that the existence of these problems has been overlooked. The portrait in this play of the overbearing male voluptuously cowering in sexual submissiveness to a woman he can dominate by the power that society gives to men, even if they are not rulers, was a favorite of Massinger's, and he reworked Sforza's overweening and masochistic jealousy in both *The Bondman* and *The Picture*.

How directly Massinger commented on the political events of his time has been a matter of considerable debate. As early as 1779 Thomas Davies suggested that the uncomplimentary portrayals of autocratic rulers and their time-serving favorites might be glancing at James I, Charles I and Buckingham. He characterized Massinger as an opponent of "arbitrary power" and "despotic principles," and drew particular attention to *The Maid of Honour* as an attack on James for being so slack in offering aid to his son-in-law, the Elector Palatine, in the Thirty Years War. A century later the celebrated historian S. R. Gardiner wrote an article in which he identified Massinger as a supporter of the Earl of Pembroke's opposition to James's policies, singling out many passages and incidents in the plays as direct if veiled topical allusions. A hundred years later still, Gardiner's role

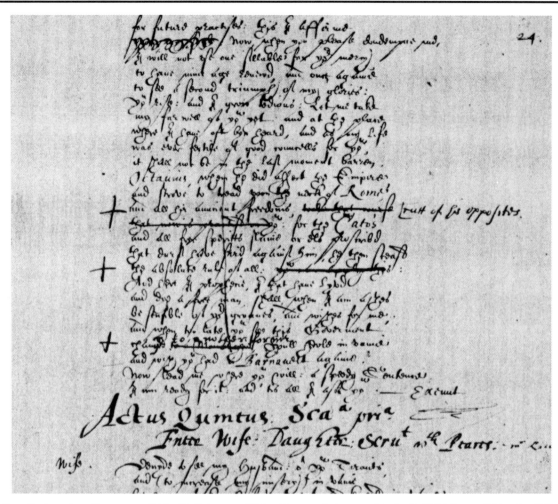

A portion of a page from the manuscript for Sir John van Olden Barnavelt *preserved in the British Library. This copy of Massinger and Fletcher's play is in the hand of the scribe Ralph Crane and was submitted to George Buc, Master of the Revels, who censored the play (see lines marked with crosses above) prior to its first production in 1619 (MS Add. 18653; by permission of the British Library).*

for Massinger as a direct "opposition" commentator has been revived by a number of critics, including Margot Heinemann, Martin Butler, and Annabel Patterson. This new wave of interest in Massinger as a political dramatist sensitive to and concerned about the grave constitutional issues of his time is very welcome, but the attempts to identify the characters and happenings of his plays with actual people and events are rarely convincing. The plays reflect the issues of his time at a deeper level than that of personal allusion or of encouraging support for particular parties at particular junctures. To see *The Maid of Honour* as an attack on James's dilatory and evasive tactics as regards helping the Elector Palatine necessarily entails misreading the play.

King Roberto of Sicily in *The Maid of Honour* is indeed a cautious, self-protective monarch, afraid to commit himself or engage in a forthright foreign policy, and he also runs a most objectionable favorite, Fulgentio. His romantic half-brother Bertoldo pleads the cause of honor in advocating aid for the Duke of Urbin in his hour of need in his war against Siena. He makes specific comparison of the island state of Sicily and that of England, urging that overseas ventures are essential for survival:

> Nature did
> Design us to be warriors, and to break through
> Our ring the sea, by which we are environed;

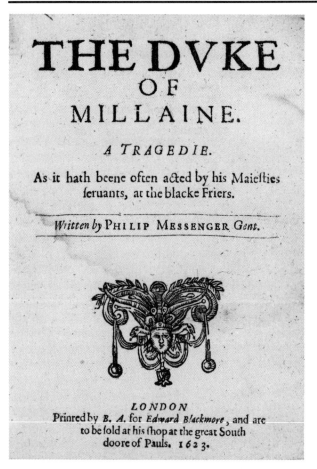

Title page for the 1623 quarto edition of one of the first plays entirely written by Massinger (Henry E. Huntington Library and Art Gallery)

And we by force must fetch in what is wanting
Or precious to us.

The king despises imperialism, however:

            Let other monarchs
Contend to be made glorious by proud war
And with the blood of their poor subjects purchase
Increase of empire.

But, like the king in *All's Well That Ends Well,* he is prepared to allow Sicilian volunteers to go to the aid of Urbin.

    Bertoldo is in love with a rich woman, Camiola. She loves him too, but one reason why she will not accept his proposal of marriage is that she does not approve of his renouncing the vow of celibacy which he has made as a Knight of Malta. She changes her mind, however, when he is taken prisoner in his ill-starred military adventure. This war has turned out to be a shabby and discreditable business, rash and dishonorable from the begin-

ning, and not in any way a theme for honor and renown. Bertoldo finds his ransom paid by Camiola, and a marriage is arranged. But he quickly yields to the superior attractions of a duchess and forswears his vow to Camiola. In the play's surprising ending the duchess learns the truth about Bertoldo and yields him to Camiola; Camiola, instead of accepting her penitent spouse like Helena in *All's Well That Ends Well,* spurns him and takes the veil. This striking rejection by Camiola of a husband is a striking rejection by Massinger of the conventional comic or tragicomic ending. A woman who has learned of the shallowness and perfidy of men has the courage not to deny her knowledge by submitting to their yoke.

    Since Bertoldo, the champion of military intervention, is totally discredited by the end of the play, it is impossible to accept the view that the play advocates a campaign on behalf of the Elector Palatine. Recently Annabel Patterson, accepting that

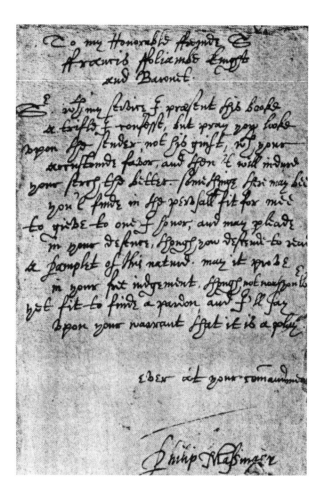

Inscription by Massinger in a copy of the 1623 quarto edition of The Duke of Milan *(Dyce Collection, 6323; by permission of the Victoria and Albert Museum)*

Title page for the 1624 quarto edition of the play Massinger set in Sicily during the classical period (from the 1932 Princeton University Press edition of The Bondman, *edited from the first quarto by Benjamin Townley Spencer)*

general and submit to the ignominy of being rallied into activity by a woman, Cleora. The distinction in these two plays between an oversea adventure and a defense of the homeland is just the sort of thing Massinger loved to insist on. The aristocrats of Sicily are rotten with wealth and idleness. They depend on their slaves, and when they have actually been organized to march away to fight the invader, the slaves make the most of their opportunity and rise in rebellion. Massinger demonstrates the justice of their protest against cruelty, injustice, and oppression without sentimentalizing the slaves or disguising the wildfire anarchy of their rebellion. The leader of the slaves, Marullo, makes a point of protecting Cleora, so that when the army returns and puts down the revolt, she, being deeply impressed by his bearing, protects him, and actually rejects the man she is engaged to marry (her social equal but a domineering snob) in order to accept

the play is "a metaphor for the Palatinate crisis," has argued that Massinger was more concerned to provide "a critique of values" than simple propaganda, and that the play yields "no consistent allegory of international relations" (*Censorship and Interpretation*, 1984). It seems more fruitful to drop the idea of the play as "metaphor." Too close a focus on the Palatinate crisis may well blind us to the way in which, as he unfolds Bertoldo's heedless irresponsibility in war and in love (the main concern of the play), Massinger uses him to question the whole notion of colonialism as well as military adventurism.

Critical confusion about the political direction of *The Maid of Honour* is understandable because in his next play, *The Bondman*, Massinger *must* be backing the appeal to a state to emerge from its slothful inactivity and fight. Sicily (now in the classical period) has fallen into a lethargy so shameful that she is incapable of fighting off an invading army, and the citizens have to import a foreign

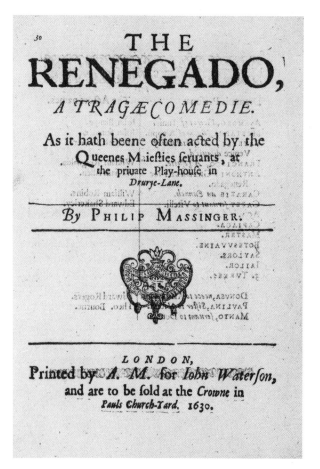

Title page for the 1630 quarto edition of a Massinger play produced in 1624 by Lady Elizabeth's Company and later by their successors at the Phoenix theater, Queen Henrietta's Men (Henry E. Huntington Library and Art Gallery)

the slave's love. But this time Massinger cannot bring himself to follow the logic of his own moral position. Marullo the slave-leader turns out to be Pisander, a gentleman who was a suitor for Cleora's hand but was turned away by her family. He has returned in disguise to try his luck again. So there is a happy ending.

The moral test which Massinger devises of divesting the suitor of the appurtenances of class and presenting him to the woman in unprivileged meanness is one which Cleora passes successfully in this play. The same device appears in another play, *A Very Woman*, originally a collaboration with Fletcher, which Massinger rewrote toward the end of his career (1634). Here it is the woman herself (Almira) who has spurned the suitor, who returns as a slave (Antonio). She finds him much more interesting and attractive as a slave than he was as a gentleman. The attraction is sexual rather than ideological; Almira (chauvinistically the "very woman") is irredeemably shallow. But there is a dismally conventional ending when Antonio (restored to himself) is complaisant enough to accept the woman who liked him only in degradation.

In *The Renegado* Massinger turned from political and social to religious issues with a remarkable story of the clash of Christian and Moslem faiths in Tunis under Ottoman rule. Massinger put his story together from tales of Cervantes bolstered by his own reading in Turkish history. Grimaldi, the renegade, committed a mad act of sacrilege in Venice as the priest celebrated mass, then kidnapped Paulina and sold her to the viceroy of Tunis, with whom he has taken service. As the play opens, we find in Tunis not only Grimaldi and the imprisoned Paulina but also the offended priest

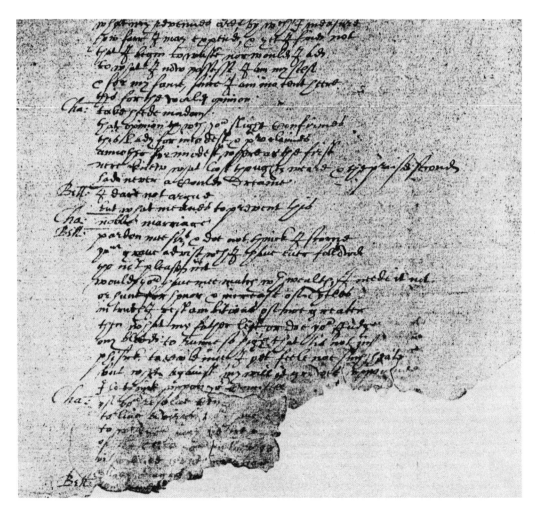

A portion of a page from the manuscript for The Parliament of Love *that is preserved in the Victoria and Albert Museum. This manuscript is in the hand of a scribe and may be the copy of the play submitted to Sir Henry Herbert, Master of the Revels, for licensing in 1624 (Dyce Collection; by permission of the Victoria and Albert Museum).*

(Francisco) and Paulina's brother, Vitelli, searching for her. Vitelli, alas, is seduced by no less a person than the niece of the great emperor Amurath, Donusa. His fall is swiftly followed by total contrition, but his faith is to be tested to its full because, the guilty pair having been found out, they can be allowed to live only if Donusa converts him to Islam. But he manages to convert her to Christianity, and the couple prepares for death. However, in the parallel plot Grimaldi has undergone a dramatic reconversion, sinking into despair of ever receiving pardon for his earlier sacrilege until assured of forgiveness by the Jesuit Francisco. Grimaldi, Francisco, and Paulina ingeniously combine forces to free Donusa and Vitelli from prison, and all escape from Tunis.

Christianity in *The Renegado* is entirely Catholic, as it is in *The Virgin Martyr* and *The Maid of Honour.* So it is not in the least surprising that since early in the nineteenth century the inference has been drawn that Massinger himself was a Catholic. There is no external evidence for this. In spite of the obvious sympathy for Catholicism in the plays, there is a certain vagueness of detail about it and it is more than possible that in drama Massinger was free to indulge an emotional bias that he was disinclined to acknowledge or develop in his personal life. However this may be, Massinger must have felt some confidence that his audience at the Phoenix for both *The Maid of Honour* and *The Renegado* would take pleasure in plays with a strong religious content couched in Catholic terms. The Catholic sympathy in the plays makes it yet harder to accept Massinger as the champion of European Protestantism, espousing the cause of the Elector Palatine.

The Renegado was certainly a success on the stage; when it was published in 1630, six years after its first performance, the title page spoke of its being "often acted" at "the private playhouse in Drury-lane." Massinger's other play licensed in 1624, *The Parliament of Love,* was almost certainly a failure. It may never have reached the stage (though it was licensed for performance), and Massinger never published it. (A manuscript survived in mutilated form, and the play was first printed in 1805.) Its main interest is in its being yet another attack on the predatory male; the play leads up to the multiple discomfiture of self-confident would-be seducers.

The Unnatural Combat, which was written about this time for the King's Men and acted at the Globe, is probably Massinger's least successful tragedy. The hero-villain, Malefort, the admiral of

Marseilles, kills his renegade son in a duel and then conceives an incestuous passion for his own daughter Theocrine. Heavy work is made of his lascivious gloating over her beauty. Though his conscience prevents him from violating her, Theocrine is raped nevertheless as an act of revenge by a disappointed suitor. The last scene brings in the ghosts of Malefort's dead son and Malefort's wife, "her face leperous," whom we learn Malefort had murdered. In spite of Malefort's repentance the stage direction has it that "He's killed with a flash of lightning." The violence of the passions and the incidents are no greater than those of a Webster play, but one is hard put to find the violence a language for anything except sensationalism.

Massinger designated only two of his plays as comedies, *A New Way to Pay Old Debts* (produced in 1625) and *The City Madam* (produced in 1632). These are satirical comedies dealing with contemporary economic and social conditions. Two other

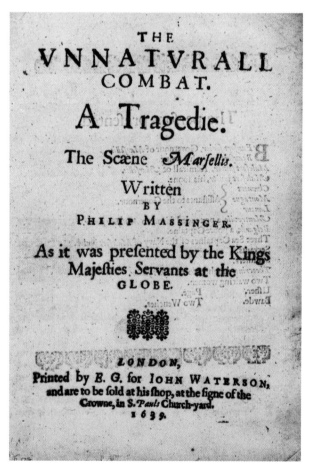

Title page for the 1639 quarto edition of a Massinger tragedy produced by the King's Men in about 1624 or 1625 (Henry E. Huntington Library and Art Gallery)

plays which could well be called comedies, *The Great Duke of Florence* (produced in 1627) and *The Guardian* (produced in 1633), have romantic plots and settings but are designated "comical history" on their title pages. Even so, only four comedies among so many plays is a very small proportion; Massinger was a grave and serious writer, and light-heartedness was not his strong point. Nevertheless, *A New Way to Pay Old Debts* is his best-known play, and two hundred years after its first performance, the great actors of the London stage in the early nineteenth century, J. P. Kemble, Edmund Kean, J. P. Booth, vied with one another in the part of the tyrannical villain, Sir Giles Overreach.

A New Way to Pay Old Debts, set in the Nottinghamshire countryside, deals with the major social crisis of the decline in the power and status of the old landed gentry in face of the encroachment of commercial wealth. Welborne, the hero, a gentleman of honorable descent, has irresponsibly frittered away his patrimony on drink, women, and gambling. The play tells how he regains both his

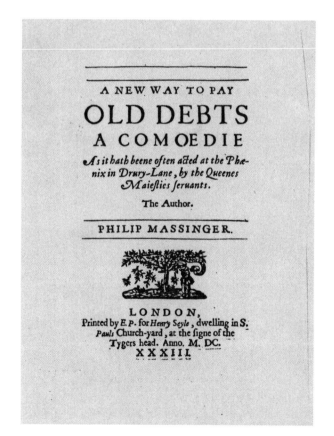

Title page for the 1633 quarto edition of one of Massinger's best-known plays, which continued to be popular with British and American audiences through the early nineteenth century (Sotheby Parke Bernet, 15 December 1982)

honor and his inheritance, the family lands, which his debts forced him to make over to his uncle, Sir Giles Overreach.

Sir Giles is an immensely ambitious and unscrupulous financier who has managed to marry into the gentry and obtain a knighthood (presumably by purchase). His pleasure in enriching himself is equaled only by his delight in ruining the gentry. His Achilles heel is his passion to make his entry into the upper aristocracy—by marrying his daughter Margaret to Lord Lovell. This towering figure is felled by three deceptions: the pretense by Welborne that he is to marry Lady Alworth—which makes Overreach advance him money in the hope of ensnaring her estates too; the pretense that Margaret is going off to marry Lord Lovell when she actually marries her young man, Tom Alworth; and the final revelation that the deeds consigning his nephew's estates to him had been written in invisible ink. Kean's acting of Overreach's insane rage on his discovery that he has been so totally outwitted terrified those on stage as well as in the audience.

A New Way to Pay Old Debts has to be seen as a kind of therapeutic rite, in which a social class finds satisfaction in making a model of what it most fears and destroying it. Lands are restored to those who properly deserve them, tarnished honor is brightened, and the extortioner is annihilated. Massinger's acute observation of the social particularities of his day is not well matched by what seems to be his nostalgic fervor for the feudal rights and obligations of the nobility. As will be seen, his later comedy, *The City Madam*, works strongly toward an accommodation of the aristocratic and the commercial worlds.

Although *A New Way to Pay Old Debts* and *The Great Duke of Florence* were written for the Phoenix theater, the death of John Fletcher in 1625 gave Massinger the position of leading dramatist with the King's Men at the Blackfriars and the Globe. He may have designed *The Roman Actor* (produced in 1626) as a special inaugural play. It stands with *Believe As You List* as his best tragedy. Not only does it have the assurance and control that *The Unnatural Combat* entirely lacks, but it embodies an argument about the social function of drama that declares the confidence Massinger had come to place in the profession which he had perhaps only half-willingly entered. The play deals with the overbearing cruelty of the emperor Domitian (in a manner reminiscent of Jonson's *Sejanus*), ruthlessly doing away with those whom he suspects of opposing him, or those who stand in the way of his desires, like the husband of Domitia. But he has a soft spot for his actors, led by Paris. Yet Paris is brought before the senate by the time-serving Aretinus to answer charges of scandalous comment on the state in his plays:

> You are they
> That search into the secrets of the time,
> And under feigned names on the stage present
> Actions not to be touched at.

Paris eloquently defends drama as a major moral force in society, providing persuasive images of honor and discrediting viciousness. To the charge that its portraits of vice can be interpreted as slanders on great men, Paris shrugs his shoulders; if a great man feels himself traduced when the theater presents the story of a corrupt judge, "we cannot help it." If the cap fits, wear it.

The insistence on drama's right to engage itself with the major moral issues of the day while disclaiming political intrigue and lampooning is one of three separate statements made about drama in the course of the play.

The second comes by way of a prolonged incident in which Paris lends his skill to cure a miser of avarice by means of a play. But instead of being properly shamed by the portrayal of himself, the miser, though absorbed by the story, is unmoved and unchanged. The implication is that the moral force of drama in society does not operate by means of sensational "cures" of individuals.

The third statement, tragic for Paris, shows Domitia conceiving a passion for him as he acts the part of a lover in a play. She tries to seduce him, and they are discovered by the emperor. The emperor insists on acting in a play with Paris and stabs him during the action.

Such is the power of the theater! For all his determination, Paris cannot cure the miser; the emotional impact of the drama is outside his control and is quite incalculable; it twice brings him into conflict with authority—the second time in a fatal conflict with his patron.

The continuing paradox of the English drama since the time of Elizabeth is clearly indicated in *The Roman Actor*. The theater was cherished by a monarchy which protected it against its many enemies and ill-wishers in society and government, and yet was so jealous of its prerogative that it could be merciless to its nursling on the least fancy or suspicion of insult. And the more drama exercised its responsibilities, the more vulnerable it was to attack.

Massinger never suffered imprisonment, as Jonson did for the outspokenness or fancied offense of his plays. But the presence of the hovering censor has already been seen in the difficulties of the early play of *Barnavelt*. A famous incident occurred at the other end of Massinger's career, in 1638, over a play (now lost) called *The King and the Subject*. King Charles read the manuscript of the play and, coming across a passage in which a ruler justified himself for levying illegal taxes, he wrote in the margin: "This is too insolent, and to be changed."

But the major act of government control affecting Massinger concerned his next great tragedy, *Believe As You List*. In 1630 Massinger composed a play about an issue which had created a considerable stir in Europe thirty years earlier. Don Sebastian, the young king of Portugal, was supposed to have been killed in Morocco in 1578

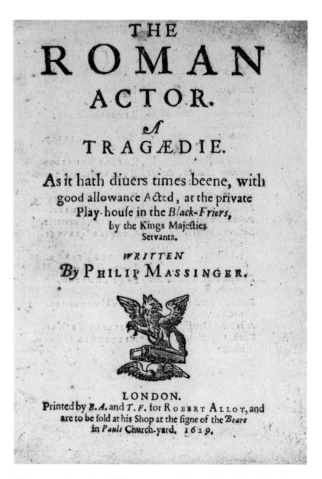

THE
ROMAN
ACTOR.
A
TRAGÆDIE.

As it hath diuers times beene, with good allowance Acted, at the private Play-houfe in the *Black-Friers*, by the Kings Majefties Servants.

WRITTEN
By PHILIP MASSINGER.

LONDON.
Printed by *B. A.* and *T. F.* for ROBERT ALLOT, and are to be fold at his Shop at the figne of the *Beare* in *Pauls* Church-yard. 1629.

Title page for the 1629 quarto edition of the first Massinger play produced by the King's Men after the death of John Fletcher in 1625 had led to Massinger's appointment as the company's chief dramatist (Henry E. Huntington Library and Art Gallery) on his romantic and ill-advised expedition against the infidel. His death led to the annexation of Portugal by Spain. But many believed that Sebastian had not in fact died; one of those who claimed to be the lost king sought support in the courts of Europe at the turn of the century and was finally executed by the Spaniards in 1603. Massinger submitted his play to the Master of the Revels, Sir Henry Herbert, who banned it outright, "because it did contain dangerous matter, as the deposing of Sebastian, king of Portugal, by Philip the Second, and there being a peace sworn 'twixt the kings of England and Spain." This peace between England and Spain was very recent, having been signed the previous November. The treaty involved England's rejection of the claims of Elector Frederick, and Herbert may have felt that the danger of the play lay not only in the unfavorable light in which Spain was shown in its relation with Portugal, but also in the possible identification of Sebastian with the forlorn exiled "winter king" of Bohemia.

Massinger refused to jettison his play. In the next few months he rewrote it, with great ingenuity transferring his story back 1,800 years to relate it to a Syrian, Antiochus the Great, who was defeated by the Romans. Massinger's manuscript of this rewritten play still survives (in the British Library) and at the end of it is Sir Henry Herbert's license for this new version: "This play, called *Believe As You List,* may be acted. This 6 of May, 1631. Henry Herbert."

The earlier version of the play is not extant, but there is every indication that Massinger adhered as closely as he could to the language and the incidents of the original as he put the Portuguese pretender into his new dress as Antiochus, the defeated king of Syria. Massinger gave great dignity to the figure of his hero, who returns from supposed death to rescue his country from vassalage. It is essential for Rome to discredit this potential focus of rebellion, and to intimidate those who are willing to support him. The Roman envoy Flaminius is a brilliant portrayal of the devoted servant of the imperial idea, ready to adopt whatever tactics may be needed to destroy what threatens that idea. He pursues and hounds Antiochus, who is rejected and betrayed by the timidity and fear of those who acknowledge his rights. When finally Flaminius has Antiochus in his power, he first tries to persuade him to confess himself an imposter; he then tries humiliation and degradation before sending him to the galleys. Against all this persecution and brainwashing Antiochus holds out:

> Do what you please.
> I am in your power, but still Antiochus,
> King of the lower Asia, no impostor.

The real political importance of the play lies not in immediate reference to contemporary events but in providing a myth for an England forsaken by its ancient protector and abandoned to a fierce modernity. The title, *Believe As You List,* reveals the secret of the play's message. In this respect the revision of the play may have obscured the force of the original, for there is no doubt about the new hero's genuineness. The point about the man who claimed to be Don Sebastian (like the man who claimed to be Edward IV in Ford's companion play, *Perkin Warbeck*) is that one cannot be certain whether the claimant was counterfeit or genuine. Such men demanded faith, and that faith could be awoken by the nobility of bearing which these mysterious persons evinced. Those who know what monarchy is recognize that it is these men, and not their replacements, who are the true rulers of their lands. Nostalgic like *A New Way to Pay Old Debts,* *Believe As You List* differs in leaving its ending open, with Antiochus neither dead nor triumphant.

Between *The Roman Actor* and *Believe As You List* Massinger wrote (along with some plays that have not survived) two fairly lighthearted romantic plays, *The Great Duke of Florence* (produced in 1627) and *The Picture* (produced in 1629), which again show the sensitivity, unusual for his time, with which he approached the male/female relationship. *The Great Duke of Florence* demonstrates the insidious growth of corruption when the promptings of natural desire try to accommodate themselves within the constraints of an autocratic court. The duke's favorite (Sanazarro) and his heir (Giovanni) are involved in an entanglement of deceit as each tries to obtain the beautiful Lidia and forestall their master's interest in her. The Massingerian sternness emerges (inevitably) in depicting the favorite's inconstancy in deserting his Fiorinda for Lidia. The final forgiveness by the duke and Fiorinda, a rather moving recognition of the frailty of everyone, places the conclusion somewhere between the unexpected severity of *The Maid of Honour* and the tired surrender to the happy ending in *A Very Woman.*

The Picture, too, has a notable ending. The play gives us a splendidly conceived example of masculine complacency and self-approval in Mathias, who goes off to the wars with a magic picture to keep him up-to-date on his wife's fidelity. But

A portion of a page from the manuscript for Believe As You List, *Massinger's revision of an earlier play (now lost) that Sir Henry Herbert had refused to license for production. This manuscript, in the playwright's own hand and now preserved at the British Library, is the copy of the new version that was submitted to Herbert, who licensed it in May 1631 (MS Egerton 2828, fol. 12[b]; by permission of the British Library).*

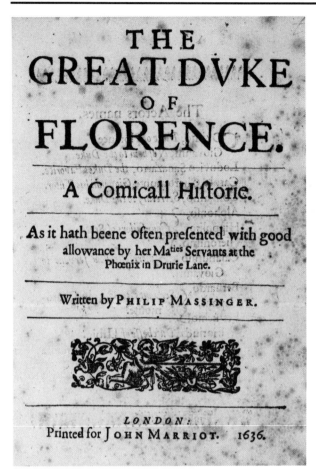

Title page for the 1636 quarto edition of one of the last plays Massinger wrote for Queen Henrietta's Men at the Phoenix theater. It was produced there in 1627, after Massinger had left the company to write for the King's Men (Henry E. Huntington Library and Art Gallery).

his own fidelity proves more fragile. When on his return the play seems to be sliding easily toward forgiveness all round, Massinger moves into almost a Shavian mode as Sophia absolutely refuses to reconcile herself to her husband and sues for a divorce—less because he has been unfaithful than because he so unwarrantably distrusted her. Massinger allows her to relent in the end without compromising the challenge she has made to double standards in sexual morality.

By the year 1630, with Massinger aged forty-seven, it is evident that his career was running into some kind of trouble. He became involved in a quarrel which concerned both the Blackfriars and the Phoenix theaters. On the one side were William Davenant, Thomas Carew, and an influential section of the Blackfriars audience, and on the other the professional playwrights James Shirley and

Massinger. The prologues for *The Emperor of the East* (produced 1631; published 1632) speak of those who "delight to misapply whatever he shall write" and "the envy [that is, malice] of some Catos of the stage." A friend, Henry Parker, actually wrote of "a hissing crowd." Two years later, Massinger's prologue to *The Guardian* suggests that two of his plays had failed, and that Massinger had therefore stopped writing:

> After twice putting forth to sea, his fame
> Shipwrecked in either, and his once known name
> In two year's silence buried . . .
> Our author weighs up anchors, and once more
> Forsaking the security of the shore,
> Resolves to prove his fortune. . . .

Certainly *The Emperor of the East* is not a particularly exciting play. Unusually, Massinger went to Byzantine history of the fifth century for his

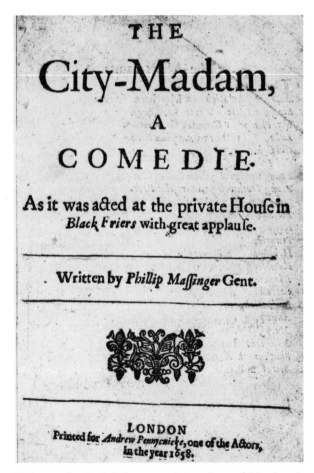

Title page for the 1658 quarto edition of one of Massinger's comedies about the social conflict between the rising merchant class and the aristocracy (Henry E. Huntington Library and Art Gallery)

story. The conflict between the emperor Theodosius and his austere sister Pulcheria is presented in a way that almost suggests a satire on what Massinger's source called "the holy court." The introduction of several scenes of overt satire on malpractices at Charles I's court involving a "projector," an informer, and a "master of the manners" enforce the feeling of subversiveness. But frequent and blatant plagiarism of Shakespearian scenes toward the end of the play point to tired writing, and the uncertain tone of the play may simply be a weakness of control.

Massinger's very positive satirical talents were unambiguously exploited in *The City Madam* (produced in 1632), a fine play which was frequently acted in an adapted version in the late-eighteenth and early-nineteenth centuries. The play centers on the household of a highly successful and wealthy London merchant, Sir John Frugal. He has a foolish wife, who encourages the expensive tastes and social ambitions of their two daughters. There is a rich social mix of city and country, nobility and common people in those who are attracted to the household as suitors for the daughters, apprentices in the countinghouse, or clients of the merchants. One suitor is the son of a peer of the realm, Lord Lacy (also in attendance), whose ancestral lands are mortgaged to Sir John. The most interesting inmate is Luke, Sir John's brother, ruined by his profligacy and now a humble and unctuous pensioner of his successful brother. The main action of the play is a deception by which, to test Luke and chasten the women, Luke is put in charge of the household. He very soon reveals himself for the covetous and corrupt petty tyrant he really is. His eventual downfall is accompanied by a general reconciliation. Commerce and the aristocracy may consort together to their mutual advantage and even intermarry provided that the city people (especially the women) show in their general demeanor a proper respect for "the distance 'twixt the City and the Court." The nobility graciously accept the alliances which their pecuniary needs force on them, so long as the outward signs of their social superiority are maintained.

The City Madam shows Massinger in a much less exposed position than in *A New Way to Pay Old Debts*. Overreach has mellowed into Sir John Frugal and the austere Lord Lovell has mellowed into Lord Lacy. The threat to the gentry is no longer in the financier as such but in the class hatred of Luke, which the play optimistically believes can be contained. Both plays, however, can be said to combine rather simplistic notions of the resolution of social conflict with very shrewd observation of social groupings and class distinction in the England of Charles I.

There is no further indication of Massinger's problems with his audience. It would seem from the mention of several plays now lost that he was reasonably active writing plays until his death, but apart from the revision of *A Very Woman*, only two further plays survive, *The Guardian* (produced in 1633) and *The Bashful Lover* (produced in 1636). The latter is a thin and rather uninteresting play, but *The Guardian*, Massinger's only venture into farce, is a tour de force. Massinger seems to delight in mocking the conventions of the Fletcherian tragicomedy he so long had served. A banished nobleman, Severino, lives a Robin Hood life with a company of bandits. Back in town, his prudish

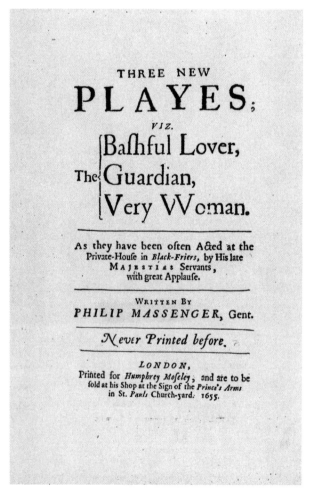

Title page for the 1655 octavo edition of two late Massinger plays and Massinger's late revision of A Very Woman, *an earlier collaboration with John Fletcher (Anderson Galleries, sale no. 1890, 8-9 December 1924)*

wife, Iolante, scolds her daughter for her immodesty but soon falls desperately in love with a stranger. In a brilliant night scene of cross-purposes and mistaken identity, the astonished husband finds himself taking part in an assignation intended for his wife's lover, the daughter absconds with the wrong man, and the "right" man (Adorio) finds he has abducted the maid. The darkness has in fact straightened out perverse intentions, for even Adorio is in the end content when by a ludicrous revelation it is found that the maid is of noble birth. In this lighthearted play Massinger took a holiday from his own moral sternness.

Massinger published eleven of his plays. During his lifetime the play began to enjoy more of an independent life as a literary object, though the traditional jealousy of the theatrical companies over their property still made it unusual for a play to be published within a year or two of its first performance. There is evidence that Massinger was accustomed to visit the printing house to check the printing of his plays, and nearly all his plays appeared with elaborate dedications to actual or prospective patrons, and commendatory verses from friends. The fact that Massinger published no less than five of his plays—some of them quite old—between 1630 and 1632 may well have something to do with the theater quarrel of that time and the apparent decline of his popularity. It also seems that in 1632 Massinger was thinking of bringing out a volume of his collected plays. He bound up all eight of the plays published by that time and made extensive corrections to the texts in ink. This venture never went any further, but the copies

Edmund Kean as Sir Giles Overreach in an early-nineteenth-century production of A New Way to Pay Old Debts; *oil sketch attributed to George Clint, circa 1820 (by permission of the Director of the Victoria and Albert Museum)*

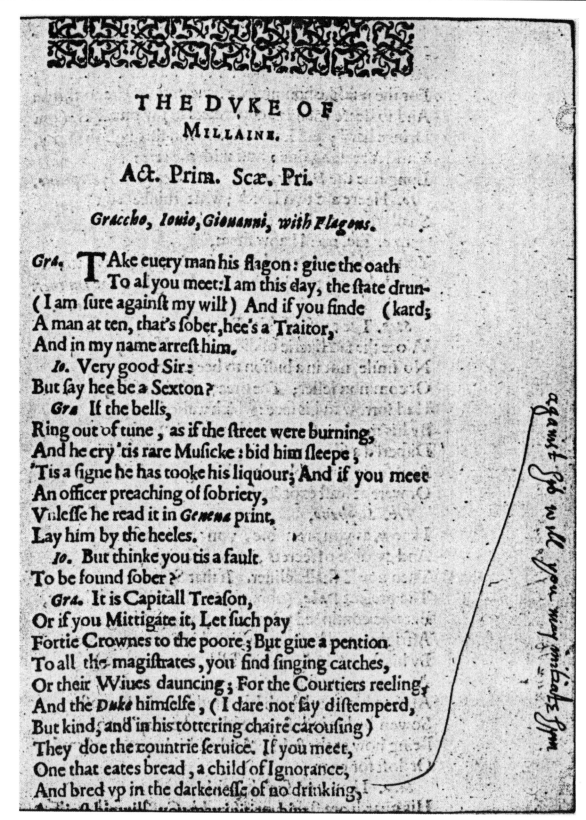

THE DVKE OF
MILLAINE.

Act. Prim. Scæ. Pri.

Graccho, Iouio, Giouanni, with Flagons.

Gra. TAke euery man his flagon: giue the oath
  To al you meet: I am this day, the state drun-
(I am sure against my will) And if you finde (kard;
A man at ten, that's sober, hee's a Traitor,
And in my name arrest him.

 Io. Very good Sir:
But say hee be a Sexton?

 Gra If the bells,
Ring out of tune, as if the street were burning,
And he cry 'tis rare Musicke: bid him sleepe;
'Tis a signe he has tooke his liquour; And if you meet
An officer preaching of sobriety,
Vnlesse he read it in *Genena* print,
Lay him by the heeles.

 Io. But thinke you tis a fault.
To be found sober?

 Gra. It is Capitall Treason,
Or if you Mittigate it, Let such pay
Fortie Crownes to the poore; But giue a pention.
To all the magistrates, you find singing catches,
Or their Wiues dauncing; For the Courtiers reeling,
And the *Duke* himselfe, (I dare not say distemper'd,
But kind, and in his tottering chaire carousing)
They doe the countrie seruice. If you meet,
One that eates bread, a child of Ignorance,
And bred vp in the darkenesse of no drinking,

Pages with Massinger's corrections from the volume of eight of his plays that he had bound together in 1632 (by permission of the Folger Shakespeare Library)

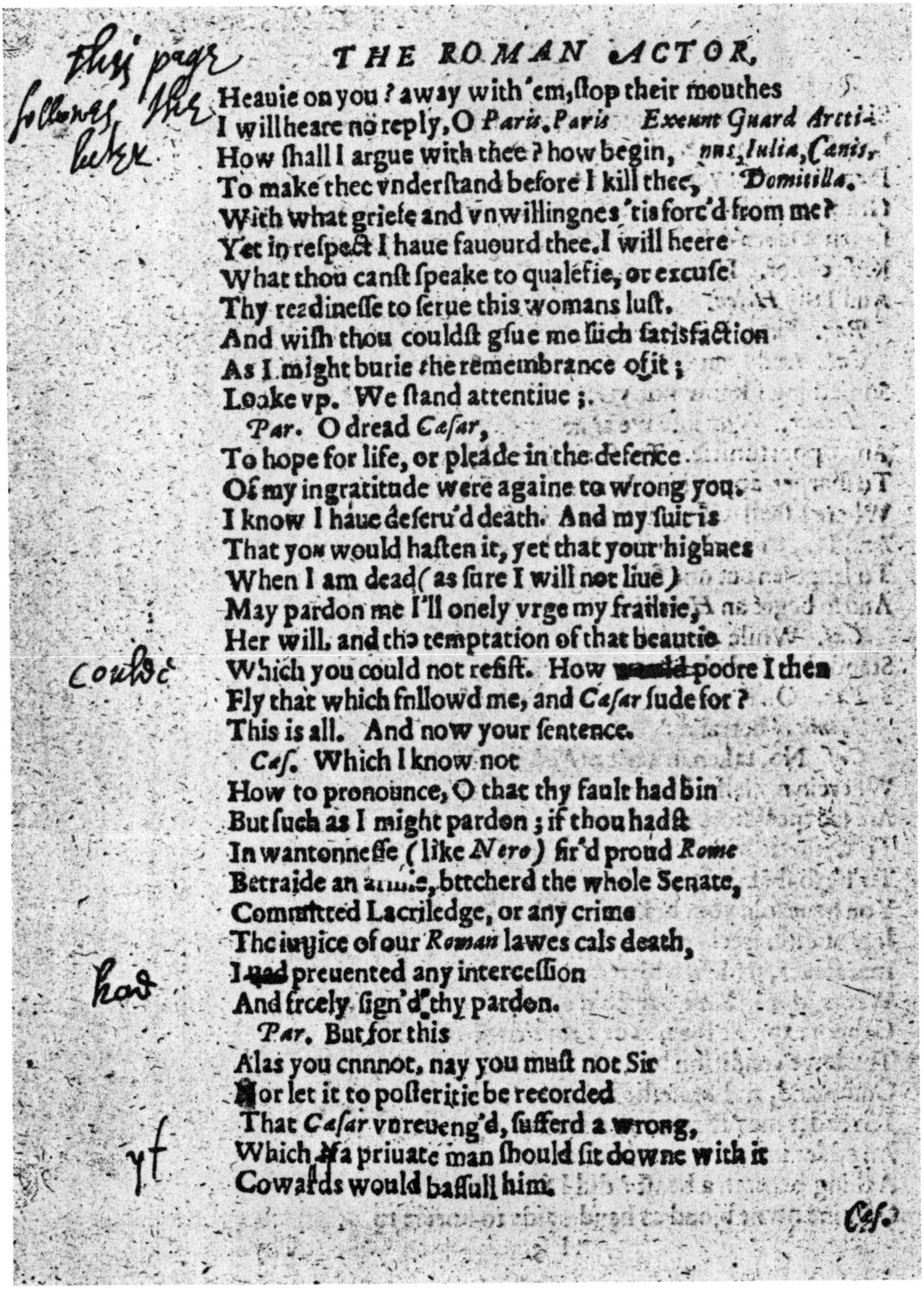

this page
followes the
later

THE ROMAN ACTOR.

Heauie on you? away with 'em, stop their mouthes
I will heare no reply, O *Paris. Paris*   *Exeunt Guard Aretinus, Iulia, Canis,*
How shall I argue with thee? how begin,   *Domitilla.*
To make thee vnderstand before I kill thee,
With what griefe and vnwillingnes 'tis forc'd from me?
Yet in respect I haue fauourd thee. I will heere
What thou canst speake to qualefie, or excuse
Thy readinesse to serue this womans lust.
And wish thou couldst giue me such satisfaction
As I might burie the remembrance of it;
Looke vp. We stand attentiue;.
  Par. O dread *Cæsar,*
To hope for life, or pleade in the defence
Of my ingratitude were againe to wrong you.
I know I haue deseru'd death. And my suit is
That you would hasten it, yet that your highnes
When I am dead (as sure I will not liue)
May pardon me I'll onely vrge my frailtie,
Her will, and the temptation of that beautie

coulde

Which you could not resist. How could poore I then
Fly that which followd me, and *Cæsar* sude for?
This is all. And now your sentence.
  Cæs. Which I know not
How to pronounce, O that thy fault had bin
But such as I might pardon; if thou hadst
In wantonnesse (like *Nero*) fir'd proud *Rome*
Betraide an armie, btrcherd the whole Senate,

had

Committed Lacriledge, or any crime
The iustice of our *Roman* lawes cals death,
I had preuented any intercession
And freely sign'd thy pardon.
  Par. But for this
Alas you cannot, nay you must not Sir

yt

Nor let it to posteritie be recorded
That *Cæsar* vnreueng'd, sufferd a wrong,
Which if a priuate man should sit downe with it
Cowards would baffull him.   *Cæs.*

(now in the Folger Shakespeare Library) have survived, a unique example of a dramatist of this period working over his printed text.

Massinger died in March 1640 and was buried by the side of John Fletcher in St. Saviour's, Southwark (now Southwark Cathedral). We know very little about his personal life, where he lived, whether he was married, whether he had children, whether he was a practicing Catholic. Like most Tudor and Stuart dramatists, he lives almost exclusively in his plays.

Massinger's plays continued to be popular when the theaters opened again at the Restoration, and in the eighteenth century he stood with Shakespeare, Jonson, Beaumont and Fletcher to represent the drama of his time. Garrick brought *A New Way* back to the stage in 1748, and the first of many collected editions appeared in 1759. In the early nineteenth century all the romantic poets read him—Coleridge with especial thoroughness—while on the stage Kean was giving his famous renderings of Sir Giles Overreach. William Gifford brought out a major edition of the plays in 1805, and in 1830 they were published in an edition "adapted for family reading . . . by the omission of objectionable passages."

Later in the nineteenth century Massinger's reputation began to wane as the esteem for Marlowe, Middleton, Webster, and Ford began to increase. The growing opinion that his writing was insufficiently imaginative culminated in a famous essay of 1920 by T. S. Eliot, which more or less extinguished critical and theatrical interest in Massinger for fifty years. The recent revival of interest has been largely due to a renewed perception of the political content of his work.

Massinger's defects are not hard to locate. He is repetitive. The reader becomes very familiar with certain types of situation and certain types of character and the language that goes with these situations and characters. And if his great strength is his moral concern, his weakness is to allow his characters to preach and sermonize rather tediously. The question of Massinger's dramatic language is not so easily settled. The smooth and even tenor of his diction and the expectedness of his imagery make his language much less poetically interesting than that of Middleton, Marston, or Webster. But his dialogue is conceived as debate and belongs in a rhetoric of persuasion as the characters try to convince, rebut, challenge, assert, deny. The audiences at the Phoenix or the Blackfriars were alert to the shaping of arguments, quick to detect the fallacies of self-interested reasoners or admire the defiance of the embattled victim. Massinger's verse has had all too little chance to prove itself in the medium of the theater.

It is Massinger's continuous concern for values that justifies his position as an important writer. The wildest of his plays, for all their extravagance of plot and emotion, are also steady examinations of what constitutes worth in human conduct. If we sometimes find it difficult to endorse his standards, we should reflect that his plays present some remarkable challenges to the standards of his own time, particularly as regards the submissiveness of women and the assumptions of masculine superiority. Massinger is not sentimental about his women characters, and could in fact accept stereotypes of their frailty, but it is notable how many of his plays take up the cudgels on behalf of the rights of women to their independence.

Bibliographies:

Samuel A. and Dorothy R. Tannenbaum, *Philip Massinger (A Concise Bibliography)* (New York: S. A. Tannenbaum, 1938);

C. A. Pennel and William P. Williams, *Elizabethan Bibliographies, Supplement VIII: Beaumont-Fletcher-Massinger* (London: Nether Press, 1968).

Biography:

Donald S. Lawless, *Philip Massinger and his Associates* (Muncie: Ball State University, 1967).

References:

Robert Hamilton Ball, *The Amazing Career of Sir Giles Overreach* (Princeton: Princeton University Press, 1939);

Peter Beal, "Massinger at Bay: Unpublished Verses in a War of the Theatres," *Yearbook of English Studies*, 10 (1980): 190-204;

Martin Butler, "Massinger's *The City Madam* and the Caroline Audience," *Renaissance Drama*, new series 13 (1982): 157-187;

Maurice Chelli, *Le Drame de Massinger* (Lyons: Audin, 1923);

Chelli, *Étude sur la collaboration de Massinger avec Fletcher et son groupe* (Paris, 1926);

A. H. Cruickshank, *Philip Massinger* (Oxford: Blackwell, 1920);

T. A. Dunn, *Philip Massinger: The Man and the Playwright* (Edinburgh: Nelson for the University College of Ghana, 1957);

Philip Edwards, "Massinger the Censor," in *Essays on Shakespeare and Elizabethan Drama in Honor of Hardin Craig*, edited by Richard Hosley (Columbia: University of Missouri Press, 1962), pp. 341-350;

Edwards, "The Royal Pretenders in Massinger and Ford," in *Essays and Studies 1974,* edited by Kenneth Muir (London: Murray for the English Association, 1974), pp. 18-36; republished in Edwards's *Threshold of a Nation: A Study in English and Irish Drama* (Cambridge: Cambridge University Press, 1979);

T. S. Eliot, "Philip Massinger," in his *The Sacred Wood* (London: Methuen, 1920); republished in *Selected Essays* (London: Faber & Faber, 1932);

Robert A. Fothergill, "The Dramatic Experience of Massinger's *The City Madam* and *A New Way to Pay Old Debts,*" *University of Toronto Quarterly,* 43 (Fall 1973): 68-86;

S. R. Gardiner, "The Political Element in Massinger," *Contemporary Review,* 28 (1876): 495-507;

Colin Gibson, "Massinger's Use of his Sources for *The Roman Actor,*" *AUMLA,* 15 (1961): 60-72;

Roma Gill, " 'Necessitie of State': Massinger's *Believe As You List,*" *English Studies,* 46 (1965): 407-416;

Allen Gross, "Contemporary Politics in Massinger," *Studies in English Literature,* 6 (Spring 1966): 279-290;

Margot Heinemann, *Puritanism and Theatre: Thomas Middleton and Opposition Drama under the Early Stuarts* (Cambridge: Cambridge University Press, 1980);

Douglas Howard, ed., *Philip Massinger: A Critical Reassessment* (Cambridge: Cambridge University Press, 1985);

Annabel Patterson, *Censorship and Interpretation: The Conditions of Writing and Reading in Early Modern England* (Madison: University of Wisconsin Press, 1984);

Leslie Stephen, "Massinger," in his *Hours in a Library* (London: Smith, Elder, 1879), pp. 1-49;

Patricia Thomson, "The Old Way and the New Way in Dekker and Massinger," *Modern Language Review,* 51 (April 1956): 168-178.

Papers:

The manuscript for Massinger's play *Believe As You List* is one of the most important theatrical documents of his time. It is his revised version of the play, written after the censor had objected to the original version, and it is in his own hand but with many additions and alterations made by the "bookkeeper" in preparing the play for the stage. The manuscript is in the British Library (Egerton 2828). There is a manuscript for one other play, *The Parliament of Love,* in the Victoria and Albert Museum in London (Dyce collection) but it is not in Massinger's hand.

About 1633 Massinger had eight of his previously published plays bound together in a single volume. Possibly he was thinking of publishing a collection of his works; possibly he wanted the volume as a gift to a patron. He made extensive ink corrections in a number of the plays: *The Bondman, The Renegado, The Emperor of the East, The Roman Actor.* The other plays he did not annotate: *The Picture, The Fatal Dowry, The Maid of Honour, The Duke of Milan.* This unique collection of printed plays with a seventeenth-century dramatist's own corrections is now in the Folger Shakespeare Library, Washington, D.C.

The manuscript for *Sir John van Olden Barnavelt* (by Massinger and Fletcher) in the hand of the scrivener to the King's Men, Ralph Crane, is in the British Library (Additional MS. 18653).

Manuscripts (not autograph) for two of Massinger's poems, "The Copy of a Letter" and "A New Year's Gift," are in the library of Trinity College, Dublin. A copy of *The Duke of Milan,* with a verse inscription in Massinger's own hand to Sir Francis Foljambe, is in the Victoria and Albert Museum (Dyce collection). "London's Lamentable Estate," in the hand of Ralph Crane, is in the Bodleian Library, Oxford (MS. Rawl. poet. 61). Three manuscripts (not autograph) for "The Virgin's Character" are extant, in the Bodleian, the British Library, and Harvard Library. "Sero sed Serio," in the hand of an unknown scribe, is in the British Library (Ms. Royal 18A. xx). The recently discovered poem "A Charm for a Libeller" comes from a manuscript (not in Massinger's hand) in the Berkshire Record Office, Reading, England.

The begging letter written by Massinger, Robert Daborne, and Nathan Field from a debtors' prison to Philip Henslowe is among the Henslowe papers in Dulwich College, London.

Thomas May

(1595 or 1596-13 November 1650)

Irby B. Cauthen, Jr.
University of Virginia

PLAY PRODUCTIONS: *The Heir: An Excellent Comedy*, London, Red Bull theater, 1620;

The Tragedy of Cleopatra, Queen of Egypt, London, unknown theater, 1626;

The Tragedy of Julia Agrippina, Empress of Rome, London, unknown theater, 1628;

The Old Couple: A Comedy, London, unknown theater, 1636.

BOOKS: *The Heire, An Excellent Comedie* (London: Printed by B. Alsop for T. Jones, 1622);

Barclay His Argenis: or, The Loves of Poliarchus and Argenis, verse translations by May and prose translations by Kingesmill Long (London: Printed by G. Purslowe for H. Seile, 1625); May's verse translations republished in *John Barclay His Argenis*, prose translations by Sir Robert Le Grys (London: Printed by Felix Kyngston for Richard Meighen & Henry Seile, 1628);

Lucan's Pharsalia: Or, The Civill Warres of Rome, Betweene Pompey the Great, and Julius Caesar. The Three First Bookes, translated by May (London: Printed by J. Norton & A. Mathewes & sold by M. Law, 1626);

Lucan's Pharsalia. . . . The Whole Ten Bookes, translated by May (London: Printed by A. Mathewes for T. Jones & J. Marriott, 1627);

Virgil's Georgicks, translated by May (London: Printed by H. Lownes for T. Walkley, 1628);

Selected Epigrams of Martial, translated by May (London: Printed by H. Lownes for T. Walkley, 1629);

A Continuation of Lucan's Historicall Poem Till the Death of Julius Caesar (London: Printed by J. Haviland for J. Boler, 1630); republished in May's original Latin as *Supplementum Lucani* (London, 1640);

The Mirrour of Mindes, or, Barclay's Icon Animorum, translated by May (London: Printed by J. Norton for T. Walkley, 1631);

The Tragedy of Antigone (London: Printed by T. Harper for B. Fisher, 1631);

The Reigne of King Henry the Second (London: Printed by A. Mathewes & J. Beale for B. Fisher, 1633);

The Victorious Reigne of King Edward the Third (London: Printed by J. Beale? for T. Walkley & B. Fisher, 1635);

The Tragedie of Cleopatra (London: Printed by T. Harper for T. Walkley, 1639);

The Tragedy of Julia Agrippina (London: Printed by R. Hodgkinsonne for T. Walkley, 1639);

Observations on the Effects of Former Parliaments (London, 1642);

A True Relation from Hull of the Present State and Condition It Is in (London: Printed by G. Dexter for John Bull, 1643);

The History of the Parliament of England, Which Began November the third, M.DC.XL. With a Short and Necessary View of Some Precedent Years (London: Printed by Moses Bell for George Thomason, 1647);

Historiae Parliamenti Angliae Brevarium (London: Printed by Charles Sumpter & sold by Thomas Bruster, 1650); translated into English as *A Breviary of the History of the Parliament of England* (London: Printed by B. White for T. Brewster & O. Moule, 1650);

The Old Couple. A Comedy (London: Printed by J. Cottrel for Samuel Speed, 1658).

Edition: *The Old Couple*, edited by Sister M. Simplicia Fitzgibbons (Washington, D.C.: Catholic University of America Press, 1943).

Thomas May, playwright, poet, translator, and historian, lived a life marred by ephemeral success and lasting disappointments. His expectations of becoming a country squire, even a justice of the peace, fell to nothing at the death of his improvident father. The home that he had anticipated inheriting sold, he spent his life in London, moving in circles distinguished for literary talent and courtly grace; this corpulent man afflicted with a stammer was relegated to the periphery of a group that knew him for his geniality among his "very friends" and for his weak jests. His closest ties with them seem to have been a series of perfunctory commendatory poems for his works. As a Jacobean man of letters, he played the role of a minor character, an attendant lord, a writer dedicated to received traditions without the imagination to remake them for his own. His plays were not popular, unsuited as they were to his audience's taste; in the next century Samuel Johnson praised his Latin poetry, but Thomas Warton denigrated it as more akin to parody. Late in his life—for a short five years—he worked assiduously for the Parliamentarians, turning his back on a king who had scarce befriended him but whose commands he had obeyed. Some of his acquaintances never forgave the treason; they held him in contempt even in death. One of the few ways he is now remembered, if at all, is by Andrew Marvell's poem "Tom May's Death," where he is characterized as a "most servile wit and mercenary pen." Buried in Westminster Abbey, his body was removed by or-

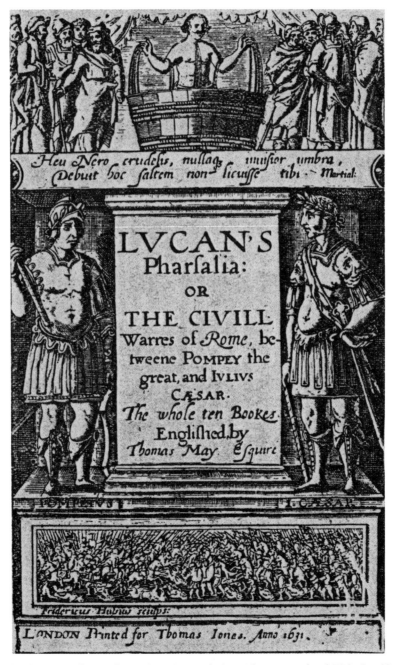

Engraved title page for the 1631 edition of one of May's translations (from an undated Pickering & Chatto catalogue)

der of Charles II and reinterred outside; a rival poet and dramatist, Sir William Davenant, later took May's place. Even his effulgent Latin epitaph by Marchamont Needham was taken away and turned upside down in St. Benedict's Chapel. So passed a life not unproductive but undistinguished.

Thomas May was born in the parish of Burwash, Sussex, in late 1595 or early 1596. A few years afterward, his father bought Mayfield, a manor house sometimes known as "the palace" because of its previous ownership by the Archbishop of Canterbury. The house came with some 9,000 acres of land, pasture, mead, and heath, a mark of his family's rise in the emerging economy of Elizabethan England; this notable acquisition was accompanied by his father's knighthood in 1603.

In 1609, when he was fourteen, the future playwright was admitted fellow-commoner to Sidney Sussex College, Cambridge, a college denounced by William Laud, Archbishop of Canterbury, as a nursery of Puritanism and sedition. That characterization was remembered by Cromwell; for when he seized all the plate of other Cambridge colleges, he spared that of Sidney Sussex, earning himself a place in the list of the college's benefactors. At Cambridge May distinguished himself as a classical scholar, a training that would follow him for the rest of his life and mark his work. He was graduated B.A. in 1613; a little more than a year later he entered Gray's Inn. He had little hope, however, of becoming a barrister because of an "imperfection of speech, which was a great mortification to him, and kept him from entertaining any discourse but in the company of his very friends," according to the Earl of Clarendon. His residence at Gray's Inn must have allowed him, however, to attend the theaters and to enjoy, if even vicariously, the life of the young literati about town.

After his early successes, his father died in 1616, having squandered away his fortune and his land by improvidence. His son's inheritance must have been small. Edward, Earl of Clarendon, declared that this young man whose "parts of art and nature were very good had only an annuity left him, not proportionate to a liberal education." And thus, out of necessity and some daring—not out of talent—May turned to writing to enlarge his annuity.

He turned first—and quickly—to comedies: *The Heir* was performed by the Revels Company in 1620. Another comedy, *The Old Couple,* may have been acted the year before but seems more likely to have been written, as Sister M. Simplicia Fitz-

gibbons conjectures, closer to its performance in 1636. For his Roman tragedies of Cleopatra and of Julia Agrippina, acted in 1626 and 1628, he drew upon his classical training—as he did for his drama on Antigone, an unproduced play that A. G. Chester, May's biographer, believes to have been written circa 1627. May's Latin play *Julius Caesar,* written between 1625 and 1630, perhaps for a performance at the Inns of Court or at Sidney Sussex College, has disappeared.

May's dramas reflect English dramatic traditions and materials without revitalization, save for disparate combinations of elements, for his contemporary audiences. For *The Heir* he appropriated elements from at least four Shakespearean plays, a central situation from Jonson, and even (as Chester points out) details from Barnaby Riche's *Farewell to the Military Profession. The Old Couple,* the most original of his plays, attempts Jonsonian satire and realism coupled with Fletcherian romanticism. *The Lives and Characters of the English Dramatick Poets* (1699), Charles Gildon's continuation of Gerard Langbaine's *An Account of the English Dramatick Poets* (1691), said of *The Old Couple* that "the chief design of it seems to be against covetousness." Its sympathetic twentieth-century editor, Sister M. Simplicia Fitzgibbons, admits that May "is laborious rather than inspired" in this play, which "is neither excellent nor distinguished."

His Roman tragedies appear to follow Jonson's attempts to portray history in a dramatic but accurate form. Chester believes it "pleasant to think" that May "received lessons in making plays from the distinguished veteran of the theatres," and it would seem so. For *Antigone* he drew upon Seneca, Statius, and Lucan—even his own translation of the *Pharsalia.* Chester points out that May's dependence upon Sophocles' *Antigone* is that of an innovator, for which he must be given credit. There is no record, Chester says, of an English version, either translation or adaptation, earlier than May's.

May did not commit himself to writing "good, solid" but undistinguished plays. He began another, more compatible career as a translator: Lucan's *Pharsalia,* praised by Jonson, and his continuation of it, translated from his own Latin, down to the death of Caesar; Virgil's *Georgics;* John Barclay's *Argenis* and *Icon Animorum;* and other works. These translations formed the most solid basis for his reputation; he was remembered for them into the eighteenth century. His dedications to these works surely brought him to the attention of some of the nobility, and his continuation of Lucan, dedicated to James I, before the court. He

Page from the manuscript for The Tragedy of Cleopatra *preserved at the British Library. This manuscript is thought to be a fair copy made by May at some time before the publication of the 1639 twelvemo edition of the play (MS Royal 18 c vii; by permission of the British Library)*

The engraved portrait of Edward III published in the 1635 edition of one of the historical poems May wrote at the command of Charles I (from an undated Pickering & Chatto catalogue)

received "a very considerable donative from the king," Clarendon reported, and Anthony à Wood described him as "graciously countenanced by King Charles I and his royal court." His two historical poems on Henry II and Edward III were written at the command of Charles I and contain effusive dedicatory epistles to that monarch.

Still, he was on the outer fringes of court life; if he had been a favorite or even well known, he would have been recognized by the Lord Chamberlain, Earl of Montgomery, who broke his staff over May's shoulder for his coming "athwart my Lord Chamberlain." But the King did call him "my poet," and Montgomery apologized with a gift of money. The King also recommended him for the post of historian of the city of London, just vacated by Jonson's death, but the aldermen did not appoint anyone to fill the office for two years nor did the King push for his candidate. With Jonson's death, there was an unofficial poet laureateship vacant. May lost that, too, to the more able, more courtly Davenant.

Perhaps embittered by Davenant's success, perhaps remembering his Puritan training at Sidney Sussex, and perhaps even with the hope of steady employment, he chose in 1640 the side of Parliament against the King. Clarendon had the harshest words on May's apostasy: he "prostituted himself to the vile office of celebrating the infamous acts of those who were in rebellion against the king; which he did so meanly, that he seemed to all men to have lost his wits, when he left his honesty; and so shortly after died miserable and neglected, and deserves to be forgotten."

By 1645 he had become, after some years as apologist for the Parliamentarians, the secretary of Parliament; for his work in preparing defenses of Parliament in Latin for continental readers, he received a steady income, other than his annuity, for the first time in his adult life. From this post came his most important prose work, his *History of the Parliament of England* (1647), which John Milton relied upon in writing *Eikonoklastes* (1649), though he seems not to have known May well. A Latin work that followed was subsequently translated as *A Breviary of the History of Parliament*. His last assignment, first given to Milton then to May, was to translate into Latin a declaration of Parliament upon the marching of their army to Scotland. It was never finished, for May died on 13 November 1650.

In his *Brief Lives* John Aubrey included a bizarre account of his death: he "came to his death after drinking [,] with his chin tied with his cap (being fat); suffocated." By the command of the Council of State he was buried in Westminster Abbey next to William Camden, the antiquarian, with an elaborate epitaph above the grave. In 1661, however, Charles II had May's body, along with others, disinterred and reburied in the adjoining churchyard. It was ironic that Sir William Davenant, one of his old rivals, was buried in 1668 where May's corpulent body had once briefly rested.

Biography:

Allan Griffith Chester, *Thomas May: Man of Letters, 1595-1650* (Philadelphia: University of Pennsylvania, 1932).

References:

J. Wilkes Berry, "Thomas May's 'The Tragedie of Cleopatra,'" *Discourse*, 11 (1968): 67-75;

H. Neville Davies, "Dryden's *All For Love* and Thomas May's *The Tragedie of Cleopatra...*," *Notes and Queries*, new series 12 (1965): 139-144;

Wayne H. Phelps, "Two Notes on Thomas May," *Notes and Queries*, new series 26 (1979): 412-415;

Christine Rees, "'Tom May's Death' and Ben Jonson's Ghost: A Study in Marvell's Satiric Method," *Modern Language Review*, 71 (1976): 481-488.

Papers:

The British Library has manuscripts for *The Tragedy of Cleopatra* and *The Reign of King Henry the Second*.

Thomas Middleton

T. H. Howard-Hill
University of South Carolina

BIRTH: London, circa 18 April 1580, to William and Anne Snow Middleton.

EDUCATION: Queen's College, Oxford, 1598-1601.

MARRIAGE: circa 1602 to Magdalen Marbeck; child: Edward.

DEATH: Newington Butts, circa 4 July 1627.

PLAY PRODUCTIONS: *Caesar's Fall or The Two Shapes,* by Middleton, Anthony Munday, John Webster, and Michael Drayton, London, Fortune theater, May 1602;

Randall, Earl of Chester, London, Fortune theater, 1602;

"Speech of Zeal" in *The Magnificent Entertainment Given to King James upon his Passage Through London,* by Thomas Dekker, London, 1604;

The Honest Whore, part 1, by Middleton and Dekker, London, Fortune theater, 1604;

The Phoenix, London, Song school near St. Paul's Cathedral, circa 1604;

A Trick to Catch the Old One, London, Song school near St. Paul's Cathedral, circa 1605;

Your Five Gallants, London, Song school near St. Paul's Cathedral, circa 1605;

Timon of Athens, by Middleton and William Shakespeare, London Globe theater, circa 1605;

A Mad World My Masters, London, Song school near St. Paul's Cathedral, circa 1606;

Michaelmas Term, London, Song school near St. Paul's Cathedral, circa 1606;

The Puritan, or The Widow of Watling Street, London, Song school near St. Paul's Cathedral, circa 1606;

The Viper and her Brood, London, Blackfriars theater, 1606;

The Revenger's Tragedy, London, Globe theater, circa 1606;

A Yorkshire Tragedy, London, Globe theater, circa 1606;

The Second Maiden's Tragedy, London, Blackfriars theater, 1611;

The Roaring Girl or Moll Cutpurse, by Middleton and Dekker, London, Fortune theater, 1611;

No Wit, No Help Like a Woman's, London, Swan theater, circa 1611;

The New River Entertainment, London, 29 September 1613;

A Chaste Maid in Cheapside, London, Swan theater, circa 1613;

The Triumphs of Truth, a Solemnity, London, 29 October 1613;

Wit at Several Weapons, by Middleton and William Rowley, London, circa 1613-1615;

The Mask of Cupid, London, 4 January 1614;

The Witch, London, Blackfriars theater, circa 1614;

The Nice Valour, or the Passionate Madman, by Middleton (possibly with John Fletcher), London, circa 1616;

Civitatis Amor, The City's Love; an Entertainment, London, 4 November 1616;

The Widow, London, Blackfriars theater, circa 1616;

The Triumphs of Honor and Industry, A Solemnity, London, 29 October 1617;

A Fair Quarrel, by Middleton and Rowley, London, Hope(?) theater, circa 1617;

The Mayor of Queenborough, or Hengist King of Kent, London, circa 1618;

The Old Law, or A New Way to Please You, by Middleton and Rowley, London, circa 1618;

The Inner Temple Masque, or Masque of Heroes, London, Inner Temple, 6 January-2 February 1619;

More Dissemblers Besides Women, London, Blackfriars theater, circa 1619;

The Triumphs of Love and Antiquity, A Noble Solemnity, London, 29 October 1619;

A Courtly Masque; the Device Called the World Tossed at Tennis, by Middleton and Rowley, London, Cockpit theater, 1620;

Anything for a Quiet Life, by Middleton and Webster, London, Blackfriars theater, circa 1621;

Women Beware Women, London, Blackfriars theater, circa 1621;

The Sun in Aries, A Noble Solemnity, by Middleton and Munday, London, 29 October 1621;

Woodcut portrait of Middleton from the Bodleian Malone copy of Your Five Gallants *(245[1]; Bodleian Library)*

The Changeling, by Middleton and Rowley, London, Cockpit theater, 1622;

An Invention for the Service of Edward Barkham, London, Guildhall, 1622;

The Triumphs of Honor and Virtue, A Noble Solemnity, London, 29 October 1622;

The Puritan Maid, Modest Wife, and Wanton Widow, London, circa 1623;

The Triumphs of Integrity, A Noble Solemnity, London, 29 October 1623;

A Game at Chess, London, Globe theater, 6-16 August 1624;

The Triumphs of Health and Prosperity, London, 30 October 1626;

The Conqueror's Custom, London, circa 1626.

BOOKS: *The Wisdome of Solomon Paraphrased* (London: Printed by V. Sims, 1597);

Micro-Cynicon: Sixe Snarling Satyres (London: Printed by T. Creede for T. Bushnell, 1599);

The Ghost of Lucrece (London: Printed by V. Simmes, 1600);

The Ant, and the Nightingale: or Father Hubburds Tales (London: Printed by T. Creede for T. Bushnell, sold by J. Chorlton, 1604);

The Blacke Booke (London: Printed by T. Creede for J. Chorlton, 1604);

The Honest Whore, part 1, by Middleton and Thomas Dekker (London: Printed by V. Simmes & others for J. Hodgets, 1604);

Platoes Cap. Cast at This Yeare 1604 Being Leape-Yeere, (London: Printed by T. Purfoot for J. Chorlton, 1604);

The Meeting of Gallants at an Ordinarie; or, The Walkes in Powles, by Middleton and Dekker (London: Printed by T. Creede, sold by M. Lawe, 1604);

Michaelmas Terme (London: Printed by T. Purfoot & E. Allde for A. Johnson, 1607);

The Phoenix (London: Printed by E. Allde for A. Johnson, 1607);

The Puritaine, or The Widdow of Watling-Streete (London: Printed by G. Eld, 1607);

The Revengers Tragœdie (London: Printed by G. Eld, 1607);

A Mad World, My Masters (London: Printed by H. Ballard for W. Burre, 1608);

A Trick to Catch the Old-One (London: Printed by G. Eld, 1608);

A Yorkshire Tragedy (London: Printed by R. B. for T. Pavier, 1608);

Your Five Gallants (London: Printed by G. Eld for R. Bonian, 1608);

Sir Robert Sherley, Sent Ambassadour in the Name of the King of Persia, to Sigismond the Third, King of Poland. His Royal Entertainement in Cracovia (London: Printed by J. Windet for J. Budge, 1609);

The Two Gates of Salvation or The Mariage of the Old and New Testament (London: Printed by N. Okes, 1609); republished as *The Mariage of the Old and New Testament* (London: Printed by N. Okes, 1620); republished again as *Gods Parliament-House: or The Marriage of the Old and New Testament* (London: Printed by J. Okes, 1627);

The Roaring Girle, or Moll Cut-Purse, by Middleton and Dekker (London: Printed by N. Okes for T. Archer, 1611);

The Triumphs of Truth. A Solemnity at the Establishment of Sir. T. Middleton, Lord Maior (London: Printed by N. Okes, 1613); enlarged as *The Triumphs of Truth . . . Shewing also his Lordships Entertainment upon Michaelmas Day Last* (London: Printed by N. Okes, 1613);

Civitatis Amor. The Cities Love. An Entertainment by Water (London: Printed by N. Okes for T. Archer, 1616);

A Faire Quarrell, by Middleton and William Rowley (London: Printed by G. Eld for J. Trundle, sold by E. Wright, 1617);

The Tryumphs of Honor and Industry. A Solemnity at the Establishment of G. Bowles, Lord Maior (London: Printed by N. Okes, 1617);

The Inner-Temple Masque. Or Masque of Heroes (London: Printed by W. Stansby for J. Browne, 1619);

The Triumphs of Love and Antiquity. An Honourable Solemnitie at the Establishment of Sir W. Cockayn, Lord Maior (London: Printed by N. Okes, 1619);

A Courtly Masque: the Device Called the World Tost at Tennis, by Middleton and Rowley (London: Printed by G. Purslowe, sold by E. Wright, 1620);

Honorable Entertainments, Compos'de for the Service of This Noble Cittie (London: Printed by G. Eld, 1621);

The Sunne in Aries. A Noble Solemnity at the Establishment of E. Barkham, Lord Maior, by Middleton and Anthony Munday (London: Printed by E. Allde for H. Gosson, 1621);

The Triumphs of Honor and Vertue. A Noble Solemnitie, at the Establishment of P. Proby, Lord Maior (London: Printed by N. Okes, 1622);

The Life of Tymon of Athens, by Middleton and William Shakespeare, in *Mr. William Shakespeares Comedies, Histories, & Tragedies* (London: Printed by I. Jaggard, and E. Blount, 1623);

The Triumphs of Integrity. A Noble Solemnity at the Establishment of M. Lumley, Lord Maior (London: Printed by N. Okes, 1623);

A Gam^e at Chæss (London, 1625);

The Triumphs of Health and Prosperity. A Noble Solemnity at the Inauguration of C. Hacket, Lord Maior (London: Printed by N. Okes, 1626);

A Chast Mayd in Cheape-Side (London: Printed for F. Constable, 1630);

The Bloodie Banquet, by Middleton and Dekker; revised, probably by Robert Davenport (London: Printed by T. Cotes, 1639);

The Nice Valour, by Middleton (possibly with John Fletcher); *Wit at Several Weapons*, by Middleton and Rowley, in *Comedies and Tragedies Written by Francis Beaumont and John Fletcher, Gentleman* (London: Printed for Humphrey Robinson & Humphrey Moseley, 1647);

The Widdow (London: Printed for Humphrey Moseley, 1652);

The Changeling, by Middleton and Rowley (London: Printed for Humphrey Moseley, 1653);

The Excellent Comedy, Called the Old Law, or A New Way to Please You, by Middleton and Rowley (London: Printed for Edward Archer, 1656);

No Wit, No Help Like a Woman's, by Middleton, possibly revised by James Shirley (London: Printed for Humphrey Moseley, 1657);

Two New Playes, viz. More Dissemblers Besides Women . . . Women Beware Women (London: Printed for Humphrey Moseley, 1657);

The Mayor of Quinborough (London: Printed for Henry Herringman, 1661);

Any Thing for a Quiet Life, by Middleton and John Webster (London: Printed by T. Johnson for F. Kirkman & H. Marsh, 1662);

A Tragi-Coomedie, Called The Witch (London: Printed by J. Nichols, 1778);

The Second Maiden's Tragedy (London: Printed for C. Baldwin, 1824).

Editions: *The Works of Thomas Middleton,* 8 volumes, edited by A. H. Bullen (London: Nimmo, 1885-1886)—comprises *The Phoenix; Michaelmas Term; The Mayor of Queenborough; The Old Law; A Trick to Catch the Old One; Your Five Gallants; A Mad World, My Masters; The Roaring Girl; A Faire Quarrel; No Help, No Wit Like a Woman's; A Chaste Maid in Cheapside; The Window; Anything for a Quiet Life; The Witch; The Changeling; Women Beware Women; More Dissemblers Besides Women; A Game at Chess; The World Tossed at Tennis; The Inner Temple Masque; Part of the Entertainment to King James; The Triumphs of Truth, and The Entertainment at the Opening of the New River; Civitas Amor; The Triumphs of Honour and Industry; The Triumphs of Love and Antiquity; The Sun in Aries; The Triumphs of Honour and Virtue; An Invention; The Triumphs of Integrity; The Triumphs of Health and Prosperity; The Black Book; Father Hubbard's Tales; Micro-Cynicon; The Wisdom of Solomon Paraphrased; Sir Robert Sherley;* and other works, misattributed to Middleton;

The Meeting of Gallants at an Ordinary, in *The Plague Pamphlets of Thomas Dekker,* edited by Frank P. Wilson (Oxford: Clarendon Press, 1925);

A Game at Chesse, by Thomas Middleton, edited by R. Cecil Bald (Cambridge: Cambridge University Press, 1929);

The Ghost of Lucrece, by Thomas Middleton, edited by Joseph Quincy Adams (New York & London: Scribners, 1937);

Hengist, King of Kent; or, The Mayor of Queenborough, by Thomas Middleton, edited by Bald (New York & London: Scribners, 1938);

The Changeling; Thomas Middleton & William Rowley, edited by Nigel W. Bawcutt (London: Methuen, 1958);

A Fair Quarrel, by Middleton and Rowley, edited by R. V. Holdsworth (London: Benn, 1974);

Women Beware Women; Thomas Middleton, edited by J. Ronnie Mulryne (Manchester: Manchester University Press, 1975);

The Second Maid's Tragedy, edited by Anne Lancashire (Manchester: Manchester University Press, 1978);

"The Revenger's Tragedy," Attributed to Thomas Middleton, A Facsimile of the 1607/08 Quarto, edited by MacDonald P. Jackson (Rutherford: Fairleigh Dickinson University Press, 1983).

OTHER: Zeal's Speech, in *The Magnificent Entertainment: Given to King James, upon His Passage through London,* by Thomas Dekker (London: Printed by T. Creede, H. Lownes, E. Allde & others for T. Man the Younger, 1604).

For twenty years at the beginning of the seventeenth century only a handful of men rivaled Thomas Middleton as a writer for the English stage, and now only Shakespeare and Jonson are held his superiors. He shared Jonson's satiric temper but lacked his weight; if he felt Shakespeare's deep interest in common humanity, he gave no expression to it in his plays. As poets Shakespeare and Middleton hardly bear comparison. As skillful a dramatic writer as Shakespeare was, the poet was not long subordinated to demands of the theater; he thought in images. Even when a Shakespearean speech is deeply impressed with the character of the speaker in the play, it may be enjoyed as poetry; it has interest detached from the character and situation. For Middleton in most part it is otherwise. He abandoned the poetic aspirations of his youth once he started to write for the stage. Scarcely an extended passage in his plays could be detached for an anthology; few playwrights lend themselves less well to quotation. The theatrical context is almost everything. His plays in the main are firmly plotted, with intricate parts deftly subordinated to one another, and the action moves briskly to ends which, in the comedies at least, are rarely predictable or commonplace. The deep theatricality of the situations gives his plain colloquial style a peculiar power for which one would search in vain if a speech were anthologized. As an ironist Middleton was second to none of his contemporaries; situational ambivalences and speeches of unwitting double meaning, together with his usually unornamented language, are especially congenial to modern readers and relished by the audiences of those few works which have been played in this century: *The Revenger's Tragedy, Women Beware Women, The Changeling,* and a few of his comedies.

Middleton's present reputation is largely the creation of pioneering nineteenth-century scholars although the last decade has seen a significant increase in the scholarly attention given to his works. His reputation has suffered from the fact that as a craftsman (rather than an artist) of the theater, he was quick to follow the dictates of contemporary taste, thus obliging himself to write in styles (such as Fletcherian tragicomedy) for which apparently he had little sympathy or enthusiasm. Some of his plays were written in collaboration with other authors, and only recently has scholarship soundly established his claim to anonymous or spuriously attributed plays formerly denied his pen. The most prominent titles are *The Puritan, The Revenger's Tragedy, A Yorkshire Tragedy,* and *The Second Maiden's Tragedy.* Other works formerly attributed to him, often with negligible cause, have been identified as the works of different authors. Among these are *Blurt, Master Constable* (by Dekker, written circa 1601-1602), *The Family of Love* (probably written by Dekker, circa 1602-1603), *The True Narration of the Entertainment of His Royal Majesty* (published anonymously in 1603), *The Birth of Merlin* (a collaboration between Rowley and another, circa 1608), *The Peacemaker* (published in 1618 by a Thomas Middleton probably not the dramatist), and *The Spanish Gypsy* (by John Ford and others, produced in 1623). These reattributions make his start upon a theatrical career a little later than it had earlier been believed to be, and they significantly advance and strengthen his connection with the King's Men. Knowledge of his canon is probably as secure now as it can be made from internal investigations within the limitations of present external evidence. He is best remembered for a handful of early comedies and his part in three powerful tragedies (*The Revenger's Tragedy, Women Beware Women,* and *The Changeling*) which rank among the greatest of the age.

Middleton's plays, notably his comedies, draw extensively on his experience of London life from a middle position in society. For the greater part of his working life he was a professional playwright with no apparent aspirations, as Jonson had for instance, to exalt the products of his craft to the status of art. Like Jonson's stepfather, however, Middleton's father was a bricklayer, whose pros-

perity would in modern times elevate his occupational title to that of builder or even building contractor. William Middleton in fact bore arms and a crest; he was therefore in all but occupation a gentleman, and despite his early death his son received an appropriate education. No details survive of Thomas Middleton's education before he matriculated at Queen's College, Oxford in April 1598. He embarked there on studies of rhetoric and logic with some arithmetic and music, which in usual course would have led to the Bachelor of Arts degree. However, as David George discovered, Middleton did not complete his studies and took no degree. Mark Eccles reports that on 8 February 1601 a tenant of one of the family's properties testified in court that the young Middleton was then in London "accompaninge the players."

Middleton's premature departure from Oxford was only partly impelled by the disputes over his father's estate which involved him as beneficiary from his early years. By the time William Middleton died in January 1586, he had acquired interests in two substantial properties, one being four acres of land by the Curtain theater with several tenements which he had improved himself. His estate was valued at something over £335, of which a third was to be divided between Thomas and his younger sister, Avis or Alice (born 1582). Anne Middleton herself added another forty pounds to each child's portion, making each heir of the other. However, her motherly concern for her children's future prosperity was substantially nullified by her early remarriage to Thomas Harvey. He claimed to be a grocer but had lost what fortune he had with Sir Richard Grenville's expedition to Roanoke Island. A property-owning wife must have seemed a good solution for his financial problems but in short time husband and wife were quarreling bitterly over the control of William Middleton's bequests. The intermittent troubles—interminably chronicled in legal dispositions—were further complicated when Avis, having married Allan Waterer, a cloth worker of Shoreditch, and claimed her inheritance (3 August 1598), returned with her husband to her mother's house, to everyone's discomfort. In short time Waterer successively allied himself with Harvey to wrest control of the properties from Middleton's mother and then competed with Harvey for absolute dominion. On 3 December 1599 Middleton sold his brother-in-law his half-interest in the lease of property of Limehouse. On 10 June 1600 when Middleton was still at Oxford, Harvey sued his wife and son-in-law Waterer in the Court of Requests to obtain control of the family property. However, Mildred G. Christian notes that on 28 June 1600 Middleton sold Waterer his half share of the Curtain and Holywell properties for money "paid and disbursed for my advancement and preferment in the University of Oxford where I am now a student and for my maintenance with meat, drink and apparel and other necessaries." Peter G. Phialas believes it possible that he returned to London on 6 December 1600 to testify in court, but Eccles observes that there is no evidence of his actual appearance in court. However, Middleton was evidently in London at the end of 1600, as the deposition of 8 February 1601 maintained, keeping company not only with "the players" but also possibly with their writers. Phialas suggests that Middleton is one of three poets, with Dekker and Marston, ridiculed in *Jack Drum's Entertainment* (produced in 1600) by a character representing Jonson, but the references are brief and the identification doubtful. However, according to Eccles, on 21 April 1601, a few days after attaining his majority, he appeared before the Lord Mayor and aldermen of the city to acknowledge receipt of the last part of his father's bequest. The amount, twenty-five pounds, should have been sufficient to have seen him through the remaining three terms of residence in Oxford. Middleton, however, chose to continue the career in the theater to which, it seems, he was already committed.

Setting aside for the moment the attractions of a literary career for a young man who had already demonstrated his devotion to the muse in three published poems, it is possible that another more pressing consideration urged him to relinquish his studies. Some time before 1603, according to Eccles, Middleton married Magdalen Marbeck, granddaughter of the well-known musician and theologian John Marbecke, organist of St. George's Chapel, Windsor. Her brother Thomas was an actor with the Admiral's company, named in the plot for *1 Tamar Cham*, an old play by an unknown author revived in 1602, when Middleton started to write for the company. Although Eccles suggests that Middleton "met his wife through his association with the Admiral's Men," for whom he started to write plays in the same year, he might well have met her somewhat earlier; the necessity to support a wife and household could then have determined his choice to seek employment as a dramatist.

In any event his early compositions reveal an interest in literature which was not readily accommodated within formal curricula. Published in 1597 when he was only seventeen years old, before his sojourn at Queen's, *The Wisdome of Solomon Par-*

aphrased was a pious exercise in metrics. Stultifying long—nearly five thousand verses—it is undoubtedly one of the period's most deservedly unread poems. Its only modern editor, A. H. Bullen, having "read at various times much indifferent verse and much execrable verse," could "conscientiously state that [it] is the most damnable piece of flatness that has ever fallen in my way." With admirable though misplaced confidence in his achievement the poet dedicated the poem to Robert Devereux, Earl of Essex, at that time the greatest man of the realm. There is no record that the dedication was profitable. Middleton's next poem was dedicated to William, second Baron Compton, of Compton Wynyates in Warwickshire, perhaps, as Joseph Quincy Adams mentions, in anticipation of the patron's generosity on account of his marriage in 1599 to the heiress of the "fabulously rich" Sir John Spencer. A continuation and imitation of the style of Shakespeare's *The Rape of Lucrece* (1594), Middleton's *The Ghost of Lucrece*, published in 1600 but written in 1598-1599 while he was at Oxford, adopts the complaint form popularized in England by *The Mirror for Magistrates*. Again, so far as is known, the young poet's industry went unrewarded. In the same period he experimented with formal satire, probably encouraged by the success of Joseph Hall's *Virgidemiarum* (1597-1598), but his *Micro-Cynicon: Sixe Snarling Satyres* (1599) brought Middleton no greater literary success. With six other satirical works it was burned in Stationers' Hall on 4 June 1599 by order of the Archbishop of Canterbury: consequently copies of it are rare. His satiric barbs were aimed at conventional objects of satire—the usurer, the prodigal, the lady, the sharper, the "ingle" (boy favorite), and the fool—but the subjects and tone which characterize Middleton's London comedies are foreshadowed here for the first time in his youthful work. Nevertheless, the failure of his early ventures in poetry to secure patronage, the financial problems which persistently distracted him from his university studies, and—possibly—the imminence of marriage may well have combined with his existing interest in the theater to turn him finally toward the stage.

Middleton is first documented as a playwright by an entry in Philip Henslowe's *Diary* for 22 May 1602 when he shared five pounds with Anthony Munday, John Webster, and Michael Drayton in earnest of a tragedy called *Caesar's Fall or The Two Shapes;* it has not survived. Those named and Thomas Dekker received a final payment of three pounds on 29 May. Philip Henslowe served as banker for the Lord Admiral's company of actors,

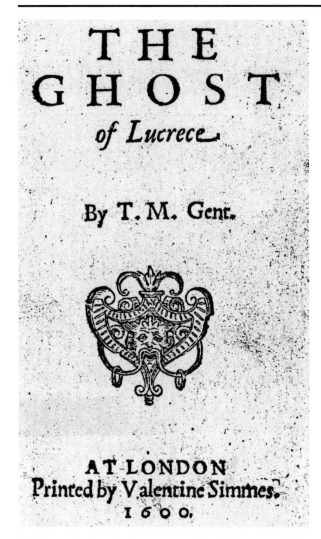

Title page for the only known copy of the 1600 octavo edition of the long poem Middleton wrote in 1598-1599, while he was a student at Oxford (Folger Shakespeare Library)

closed the London theaters from 19 March for more than a year (except for a few short periods) until 9 April 1604. Like many of his fellow dramatists, Middleton turned to pamphleteering for an income. On the basis of an eyewitness account of the execution of a Francis Clarke at Winchester on 29 November 1603, later incorporated in Edmund Howe's 1615 continuation of John Stowe's *Annals of England* and signed T. M., R. Cecil Bald has Middleton there and at nearby Newbury at the end of 1603, having left London to escape the plague. Bald cites as support passages in Middleton's *Michaelmas Term* (II.iii.226-229) and *A Mad World My Masters* (IV.iii.102-107), plays which seem to him to have been written by the middle of 1604. *The Ant and the Nightingale or Father Hubbard's Tales* was licensed for publication on 3 January 1604 with a

who at that time played at the Fortune theater, which Henslowe had built with Edward Alleyn, the company's principal actor, in 1600. Another lost, unnamed, and presumably unfinished play for Worcester's company netted him an earnest of one pound on 3 October 1602. On 21 October, Henslowe paid Middleton four pounds in part payment for a lost history play, *Randall, Earl of Chester,* and a final payment of two pounds on 9 November. Shortly afterward on 14 December he was paid five shillings for a prologue and epilogue for a performance of Robert Greene's *Friar Bacon and Friar Bungay* (written circa 1589) at Court. However, Middleton's relative prosperity did not last. Queen Elizabeth's illness, which led to her death on 24 March 1603, and a virulent outbreak of plague

Title page for the 1604 quarto edition, with annotations by John Philip Kemble, of Dekker and Middleton's popular comedy (Anderson Galleries, sale no. 2077, 20-21 May 1926)

satirical dedication to "Sir Christopher Clutchfist," a "pinching patron and the Muses' bad paymaster" who never gave "the poor Muse-suckers a penny"; Middleton doubtless recalled his early lack of success in securing patronage. On 22 March of the same year *The Black Book* was entered in the Stationers' Register. Continuing the exposure of city villainy and folly of such pamphlets as Thomas Nashe's *Pierce Penniless, His Supplication to the Devil* (1592), Middleton's work is notable for the introductory verse presenting "Lucifer ascending, as prologue to his own play," which looks forward to the induction of his *A Game at Chess* (produced in 1624). It is the most accomplished of his miscellaneous writings thus far.

Quite early in 1604, as plague deaths abated, Middleton was writing plays again. Another pamphlet published anonymously in 1604, *The Meeting of Gallants at an Ordinary*, is often attributed to Dekker, but, according to David J. Lake, linguistic details suggest that Middleton had a substantial part in it as well. He definitely contributed the speech of Zeal to Dekker's *Magnificent Entertainment Given to King James upon His Passage Through London* on 15 March, and Henslowe records a payment also in March of five pounds to Dekker and Middleton in earnest of *The Honest Whore*, part one, a comedy written mainly by Dekker for Prince Henry's Men, a continuation of the Admiral's company. On 9 November 1604 the play was entered for publication in the Stationers' Register. The relationship of Middleton and Dekker during Middleton's apprenticeship in the profession was unusually close so that for many works it is difficult to distinguish the contribution of one from the other's. Collaboration was the rule among the playwrights who looked mainly to Henslowe for commissions, and Middleton and Dekker seemed to have worked together in almost seamless unity of style. *Blurt, Master Constable* and *The Family of Love* were long held to be Middleton's earliest surviving plays but recent investigations by D. J. Lake and M. P. Jackson confirm the suggestions of previous scholars that the first play is certainly and the second probably entirely by Dekker. Middleton's hand in part one of *The Honest Whore* is most apparent in I.v and III.iii, but there are intermittent passages in other scenes which testify to the closeness of their collaboration.

At this point (14 March 1604) Henslowe's *Diary* ceases to note payments for plays; hereafter the dates of many of Middleton's compositions are less precisely determined. (The years given after titles are usually the dates assigned in Samuel Schoenbaum's 1964 revision of Alfred Harbage's *Annals*

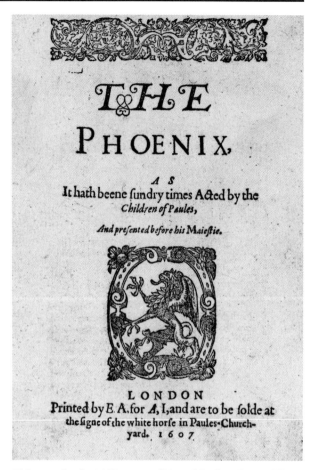

Title page for the 1607 quarto edition of the first play Middleton wrote for Paul's Boys (Henry E. Huntington Library and Art Gallery)

of English Drama.) Around this time (1603-1604) he started to write for the Paul's Boys, children of the song school and, sometimes, of the grammar school of St. Paul's Cathedral who performed near the cathedral. The plays were all comedies: *The Phoenix* (produced circa 1604), *A Trick to Catch the Old One* (produced circa 1605), *Your Five Gallants* (produced circa 1605), *A Mad World My Masters* (produced circa 1606), *Michaelmas Term* (produced circa 1606), and *The Puritan* (produced circa 1606). Short summaries of these comedies show the extent of their common indebtedness to Middleton's close observation of the disreputable side of London life. In *The Phoenix* Middleton uses the plot device of the prince who assays the condition of his country by traveling around it in disguise. Phoenix, son of the Duke of Ferrara, soon encounters a gallery of notable villains, among them Tangle, an "old busy turbulent fellow, a villanous maltworm, that eats holes into poor men's causes," and Falso, a justice of peace and a bribe taker whose rascally servants occupy themselves with highway robberies. Even more odious characters are Proditor, a treacherous lord, and the wastrel sea Captain who in his greed arranges to sell his wife; here Middleton drew on his mother's experience with his stepfather, Thomas Harvey. The play ends in the manner of Shakespeare's *Measure for Measure* with the Prince's exposure of the vicious characters before the Duke; and a temperate speech of Quieto, the one honest man Phoenix encountered, brings the lively intrigues to a satisfying moral conclusion.

Intrigue is equally strong in *A Trick to Catch the Old One,* where a young gallant, Witgood, has improvidently mortgaged his property to his usurious uncle, Lucre. Repenting and desiring to make a new life, Witgood pretends to be about to marry a rich widow who is in fact a courtesan, his accomplice in the plot to ensnare his uncle. Lucre seeks the widow for himself but has a rival in One-

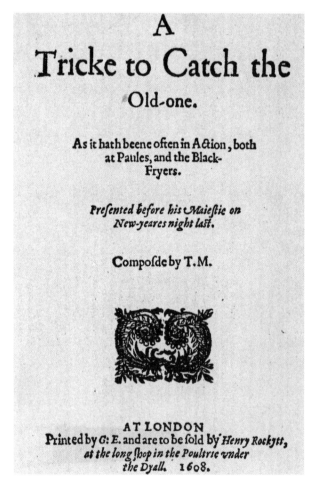

A
Tricke to Catch the
Old-one.

As it hath beene often in Action, both
at Paules, and the Black-
Fryers.

*Prefented before his Maieftie on
New-yeares night laft.*

Compofde by T.M.

AT LONDON
Printed by G: E. and are to be fold by *Henry Rockytt,*
at the long fhop in the Poultrie vnder
the Dyall. 1608.

Title page for the second issue of the 1608 quarto edition (Anderson Galleries, sale no. 2078, 24-25 May 1926)

siphorous Hoard, his inveterate enemy, who carries the complacent widow away to marry her. Lucre allies himself with his nephew, whom he adopts as his heir, and gives up his mortgages, but is too late to prevent the widow's marriage to Hoard. However, Witgood, asserting a precontract of marriage with the widow, alarms Hoard into buying off his other creditors, and they proceed to a wedding feast where finally the whole process is revealed. But all ends well when the courtesan declares herself almost spotless, Hoard accepts his lot, and Witgood affirms his reformation.

Your Five Gallants has been described by Richard H. Barker as "a reworking of the material in *The Black Book*" in that the characters "are not so much human beings as illustrations—illustrations of various underworld tricks and swindles." The five gallants are Frippery, the broker-gallant, Primero, the bawd-gallant, Goldstone, the cheating-gallant, Pursenet, the pocket-gallant, and Tailby, the whore-gallant; in the play they function according to their characterizations, being motivated by cynicism, lust, and greed. The dramatist allows them to expose their natures through a series of episodes in the first four acts observed by Fitsgrave, who provides a moral commentary. In the fifth act Fitsgrave tricks the gallants into revealing their true natures in a masque, whereafter he somewhat peremptorily assigns their punishments. The play is neither as amusing nor satisfying as Middleton's two previous comedies, its interest for a great part being confined to its depiction of the common vices of London life. *A Mad World My Masters,* on the other hand, is a sparkling comedy of intrigue in the manner of *A Trick to Catch the Old One.* Follywit, the protagonist of the main plot, is a variation of Witgood in the other play. Follywit, however, does not seek reformation but intends to live upon his wits. The object of his schemes is his wealthy grandfather, Sir Bounteous Progress, whose hospitality cries to be taken advantage of. Follywit enters his grandfather's luxurious house disguised as Lord Owemuch, is entertained, and during the night robs him. To conceal his crime he ties up himself as well as Sir Bounteous, who in the morning insists on compensating his guest for his presumed loss. Encouraged by that success Follywit robs again, this time disguised as his grandfather's courtesan, with whom later he falls in love, encouraged by her skillfully assumed modesty. Another more elaborate deception follows, but Follywit is discovered at last; he excuses himself, insisting that he has not only reformed but has married a virginal gentlewoman.

Your fiue Gallants.

As it hath beene often in Action at the Black-friers.

Written by T.Middleton.

Imprinted at London for Richard Bonian, dwelling at the figne of the Spred-Eagle, right ouer-againft the great North dore of Saint Paules Church.

Title page for the 1608 quarto edition of the play that has been described as Middleton's "reworking" of the depiction of the vices of London life in his 1604 prose pamphlet The Blacke Booke *(Anderson Galleries, sale no. 2078, 24-25 May 1926)*

In V.ii Sir Bounteous reveals that Follywit has outwitted himself: "When he has gull'd all, then is himself the last"; his wife is a courtesan.

Social pretension and greed rather than folly drive the plot of *Michaelmas Term,* another comedy of intrigue. Ephestian Quomodo, a draper, plots to acquire and enjoy the estate of a young heir, Easy. His financial machinations prove successful but in the last act Quomodo overreaches himself by pretending to be dead in order to test his family's reaction. His confederates cheat him, his son rejoices, his daughter marries the wrong suitor, and his wife quickly remarries—the bankrupted Easy. Quomodo has difficulty in proving that he is still alive and loses Easy's estate in the process.

Although *The Puritan, or The Widow of Watling Street* claimed on the title page of the 1607 quarto edition to have been "written by W. S." and was printed in later collections of Shakespeare's works,

the attribution has been uniformly rejected. Recent studies by Lake and Jackson strongly confirm its position in the Middleton canon earlier suggested by F. G. Fleay, Bullen, and others. George Pie-Board, a scholar and a citizen, and Peter Skirmish, an old soldier, resolve in I.ii to thrive by "shifts, wiles, and forgeries," the first disguised as a fortune-teller, the second as a conjurer. Pie-Board's invention fastens on the situation of the Puritan widow, Lady Plus, whom he had overheard forswearing remarriage to one of her daughters. An associated design, to free Captain Idle, Skirmish's friend, is pursued with the aid of Nicholas Saint-Tantlings, the captain's kinsman and a servant to the widow. Nicholas is persuaded to rob his mistress's brother, Sir Godfrey, of his golden chain; he would not steal it, he says in I.iv: "I must not steal; that's the word, the literal, *thou shalt not steal,*" but robbing is something else. Pie-Board is now able confidently to predict that Sir Godfrey will have a loss and other matters that convince the widow to retract her vow not to remarry, in order to release her husband's soul from purgatory. Nicholas tells Sir Godfrey that a conjurer lying in the Marshalsea prison will restore the chain; Sir Godfrey buys release for Captain Idle disguised as a conjurer, who with Pie-Board conjures up the chain. The conspirators win the hands of the widow and her elder daughter, but the wedding ceremonies are forestalled when a disgruntled Skirmish exposes the impostures; the widow and her daughter readily transfer their affections to more respectable objects, their longtime suitors. Pie-Board and the Captain are attractive, manly characters for whom Middleton dictates no punishment. On the other hand the "virtuous" characters are fools and hypocrites whose just reward is to be paired off at the end of the play.

Apart from *The Phoenix,* which to an extent is more somber than Middleton's other comedies for the Paul's Children, his early comedies may be characterized generally as realistic farces. (The apparent oxymoron may be applied to the whole body of Middleton's work in the comic kind for the public stage.) The realism is found in the detailed depictions of the excesses of middle- and lower-class London manners and attitudes; many of the rogues and fools are rendered in meticulous detail so that they would be easily recognized by audiences with knowledge of the complex city life of which the plays treat. On the other hand, some of the characters are grotesques who in some important respects seem scarcely to inhabit a real world. The extravagance of their language and reactions, the

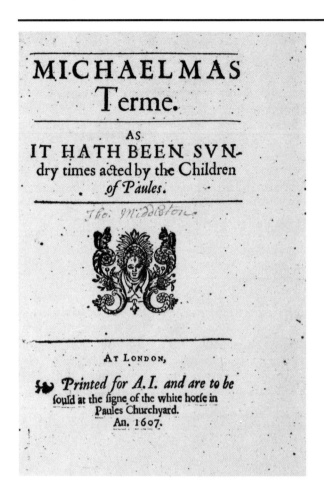

Title pages for the 1607 and 1608 quarto editions of comedies Middleton wrote for Paul's Boys (Henry E. Huntington Library and Art Gallery)

general implausibility of the situations in which they act, and the buffoonery which is oftentimes allowed by the frequent use of disguise are elements of farce. To be sure morality is present, but it only infrequently intrudes on the audiences' attention in long speeches. Audiences indeed are more likely to enjoy the exposure of follies and vices which the playwright does not demand they identify in themselves. As befits comedies in which deception and intrigue supply the essential structure of the plots, ironic contrasts of intention and consequence, as well as the often unwitting commentary of characters on their own and others' conduct, produce usually satisfactory outcomes of plots recoiling on the heads of their progenitors. Such reversals are sometimes the only punishments Middleton metes out to his merely foolish as distinct from vicious characters, and, as has been seen, the pervasive folly of the world they inhabit allows such relatively deserving rascals as Pie-Board and

Follywit to escape serious consequences.

The three years from early 1604 to the end of 1606 were intensely productive for Middleton. However, the Paul's company apparently ceased to play around the middle of 1606; its last documented performance was on 30 July. Shortly afterward, in 1607 and 1608 many of their plays, including those by Middleton mentioned earlier, were sold for publication; Middleton was obliged to find alternative employment for his pen. In May 1606 he handed over to Robert Keysar, Master of the Blackfriars, another children's company, a manuscript of *The Viper and Her Brood* in satisfaction of a bond. The tragedy is known only from the lawsuit which mentions it. Because this is his only known association with that company it is not unlikely that Keysar's dissatisfaction over his dealings with Middleton obliged the playwright to look elsewhere for income. In short time he embarked on a series of tragedies for the King's Men, the preeminent company of players which owned Shakespeare and John Fletcher as their principal playwrights.

The best of these and Middleton's first masterpiece in the genre was *The Revenger's Tragedy* (produced circa 1606), long attributed to Cyril Tourneur but recently proved by Lake and Jackson to be Middleton's without possibility of reasonable doubt. (See also the entry on Cyril Tourneur.) The tautly plotted play is so complex as almost to defy intelligible characterization without summary. For the death of his mistress, Vindice bitterly vows vengeance on the voluptuous old Duke who poisoned her. Disguised as a serviceable malcontent, Piato, he enters the service of Lussurioso, the Duke's heir, who rivals him in lechery. The Duchess, the Duke's second wife, incestuously loves his illegitimate son, Spurio; and the Duchess's youngest son, Junior, has raped the virtuous wife of Antonio, a nobleman; she has poisoned herself. At the end of the first act Lussurioso employs Vindice-Piato to seduce his own sister, Castiza, into the prince's bed. Vindice tempts his mother, Gratiana, to suborn her daughter and is appalled when she undertakes the task. Meanwhile, Spurio decides to disinherit Lussurioso by discovering him in bed with Castiza, which to prevent Vindice-Piato reveals the Duchess's infamy. Intending to surprise Spurio with the Duchess, Lussurioso mistakenly attacks the Duke and is imprisoned; Supervacuo and Ambitioso, his envious brothers, scheme to have him killed, but the plot goes awry, and Junior is executed instead. Soon afterward, Vindice-Piato and his brother Hippolito lead the Duke to an assignation in a secluded place. Vindice dresses the skull of his dead mistress as a puppet and poisons its mouth; the Duke kisses it and dies after having been presented with the view of his wife embracing Spurio. Lussurioso resents Piato's responsibility in the crime he almost committed against his father and seeks Hippolito's aid to be revenged upon him. Hippolito introduces Vindice in his own person, and they vow Piato's death. Vindice and Hippolito dress the Duke's body in Piato's disguise to make it appear that Vindice killed Piato and then fled, and together visit their mother to reform her pandarism. In the final act the Duke's body is discovered; Lussurioso succeeds to the throne, and Vindice and Hippolito plot with other noblemen against him. They decide to kill Lussurioso at a banquet and do so in a "masque of revengers." Another "masque of intended murderers" with Ambitioso, Supervacuo, and Spurio finds its task already accomplished; they quarrel over the

throne, killing one another. Carried away by the success of his designs, Vindice reveals his part and he and Hippolito are condemned to execution by Antonio whose revenge had been obtained without active participation in the numerous murders.

The effect of the play is dazzling. The poetry brilliantly sustains a perfervid atmosphere of corruption from which not even the protagonist can secure himself at the end. As their names reveal, the characters are not conceived realistically (although their crimes are substantial enough); Vindice is indebted to revengers developed through such plays as *Hamlet* (produced circa 1600-1601) and Marston's *Antonio's Revenge* (produced in 1600) and *The Malcontent* (produced in 1602-1603); the grotesques of the Duke's family have a complex literary lineage which includes the satirical villains of Middleton's own earlier plays. Morality elements are strongly marked, particularly in the temptations of Gratiana and Castiza, and notably in the subordination of the fine verses which, according to R. Foakes, render emotion and sensation to "commonplace moral generalizations" often expressed as generalising couplets. This common feature of Middleton's style was peculiarly effective to remind the audience of a world of morality from which the play's feverous vices must often have distracted them.

Middleton's second King's company tragedy of this period was *A Yorkshire Tragedy* (produced circa 1606), which the title page of the 1608 edition attributes, like *The Puritan*, to Shakespeare, but just as surely, as Lake and Jackson have established, the play was not his but Middleton's. (See also the entry on *A Yorkshire Tragedy*.) The powerful study of a man driven by guilt into a state of depression ("fearful melancholy") and acts of ferocious violence has many links to Middleton's comedies which treat of young prodigals obsessed with dissipation. The play was based on a pamphlet, *Two Unnatural Murders* (1605), which described the events that took place on 23 April 1605, when Walter Calverley, head of a well-established Yorkshire family, murdered two of his children, wounded his wife, and was taken while on the way to kill his remaining child, who was in the care of a neighbor. Calverley was convicted and pressed to death in August of that year. The play is short, consisting of little more than 700 lines; it was apparently intended for performance with other short plays as its head title describes it as *One of the Four Plays in One*.

According to Jackson, around 1605 Middleton contributed most of I.ii and III, "besides a few other portions here and there," to Shakespeare's

Timon of Athens. In a detailed study of the authorship question shortly to be published by Oxford University Press, R. V. Holdsworth identifies Middleton's share of *Timon of Athens* as I.ii.1-250, III.i.1-III.vi.120, IV.ii.30-50, IV.iii.458-536 (Riverside edition line numbering), amounting to more than a third of the play. Middleton's next complete tragedy for the King's Men was the anonymous *Second Maiden's Tragedy* (written in 1611). There are two related plots. The first concerns a "new usurping Tyrant" who loves the daughter of one of his noblemen, Helvetius. However, she (simply called Lady in the play) loves Govianus, the deposed rightful king, and willingly accepts confinement with him. Helvetius is dispatched to persuade her to the Tyrant's purposes, but Govianus converts Helvetius to his. The Tyrant sends another, whom Govianus within a short space stabs with his sword. Govianus and the Lady make a suicide pact, but when Govianus is unable to accomplish his part, the Lady kills herself, much to his embarrassment when he recovers from a swoon. Disconsolate because the Lady chose death before him, the Tyrant releases Govianus and visits the Lady's tomb, stealing her body. After Govianus arrives, the apparition of the Lady reveals in IV.iv that the Tyrant "In his own private chamber, There he woos me And plies his suit to me. . . ." Govianus makes his way there in disguise and, at the Tyrant's command, paints the face of the body; the Tyrant kisses it and dies from poison added to the paint by Govianus, who reclaims his throne. The romantic sickliness of all this shows Middleton more influenced by John Fletcher here than Marston, but the second plot is more credible.

Anselmus, Govianus's brother, doubts the virtue of his wife and prevails upon his friend Votarius to test it. The Wife (another unnamed character) is tempted to yield and seeks the protection of her trusty waiting woman Leonella, whose lover Bellarius is Votarius's enemy, but Votarius and the Wife become lovers. Votarius directs Anselmus's suspicions toward Bellarius, but Leonella informs on the lovers, who arrange a charade intended to convince Anselmus of his wife's innocence. However, the Wife betrays Votarius, killing him unprepared with a sword; Anselmus then dispatches the "false" informant Leonella, whose death brings Bellarius into the fray. The Wife runs between their swords and dies; Anselmus and Bellarius wound each other and die after informing Govianus—who had come to his brother for advice—what had occurred. In dealing with jealousy, lust, and betrayal in an intrigue plot crafted to his

usual standard Middleton is more comfortable and convincing. Although their crimes are desperate, Anselmus, Votarius, and the Wife—and to some smaller extent Leonella and Bellarius—are depicted with considerable psychological realism. It is the city house rather than the court which at this stage of his career provides Middleton with his best milieu. Nevertheless, both plots are skillfully integrated with parallelism of structure and by contrast (such as the true Lady, the faithless Wife, spiritual and sensual love) and, according to Anne Lancashire, "thus function as dramatic exempla of the rewards of virtue and the evil consequences of vice."

In turning to tragedy for the King's Men, Middleton had not abandoned comedy although his later comedies—with the notable exception of *A Chaste Maid in Cheapside*—are, according to Barker, "less amusing, less original in their material, and less consistent in their point of view." In the

Title page for the 1611 quarto edition of the play Middleton and Dekker based on the real-life story of Mary Frith, who "had long frequented all or most of the disorderly and licentious places in this city . . . usually in the habit of a man" (British Library)

late spring of 1611, according to Cyrus Hoy in his *Thomas Dekker* (1980), Middleton renewed his collaboration with Dekker in a comedy written, like *The Honest Whore,* for Prince Henry's Men. *The Roaring Girl* presented in the character of Moll Cutpurse a sentimentalized portrait of Mary Frith, who, as proceedings before the Bishop of London's Ecclesiastical Court described her, "had long frequented all or most of the disorderly and licentious places in this city . . . usually in the habit of a man." The scenes can be divided equally between the collaborators. "Middleton's unaided work is most evident in II.i and III.i," according to Hoy; Jackson adds II.ii, IV.i, and V.i.

No Wit, No Help Like a Woman's (produced circa 1611) is Middleton's first venture into the style of romantic comedy made fashionable by Beaumont and Fletcher. Philip Twilight has married secretly abroad but passes his wife off to his father, Sir Oliver, as the daughter of his long-lost wife. However, the return of Lady Twilight exposes Philip's deception; further, to his dismay she claims his wife as her daughter indeed. The difficulty is not resolved before the second story is concluded. The wealthy Lady Goldenfleece has appropriated Mistress Low-Water's fortune, but Mistress Low-Water obtains the restitution of her money when she deceives Lady Goldenfleece into a compromising marriage. Lady Goldenfleece finally recounts a conventional tale of infant daughters exchanged, and all characters are reconciled in happiness. In *Wit at Several Weapons,* a comedy that, according to Jackson, was written around 1613-1615 for an unknown company, Middleton joined with another collaborator, the actor William Rowley, who was a leading member of Prince Charles's Men before joining the King's players around August 1623. Linguisitic details indicate that Middleton wrote somewhat more than half the play, I.i, II.i, III, and IV. However, *A Chaste Maid in Cheapside* (produced circa 1613) for the Lady Elizabeth's company was solely Middleton's. Barker praises it as "a great play and in many respects an epitome of all the comic work that Middleton had so far done." The play presents a complexly interwoven tapestry of London characters and manners extending across a wider range than in his previous comedies. As usual the play centers on battles of wits, between four sets of characters. Young Touchwood seeks to marry Moll, the daughter of goldsmith Yellowhammer, on whom he plays three tricks; he manages finally to marry the chaste maid. Yellowhammer's son Tim, a Cambridge dunce being tutored in logic, is set up against the Welshwoman, mistress to Sir

Walter Whorehound. Tim finds himself married to his adversary shortly after his sister marries Touchwood, but Yellowhammer solaces himself in V.iv:

> So fortune seldom deals two marriages
> With one hand, and both lucky; the best is,
> One feast will serve them both.

Touchwood Senior begets so many children that he cannot remain with his wife; on the other hand Sir Oliver Kix cannot get children at all. Touchwood sells him a cure for barrenness and cuckolds him; Sir Oliver, delighted at his wife's fruitfulness, engages to support the Touchwoods and all their children: "Get children, and I'll keep them." But the most ironic reversal occurs in the relationship of Sir Walter Whorehound with Mistress Allwit, by whom he has children, maintaining them and their mother's household along with Allwit, who, entirely complacent about the arrangement, says in I.ii:

> I see these things, but like a happy man,
> I pay for none at all; yet fools think's mine;
> I have the name, and in his gold I shine.

Eventually, seriously wounded in a duel with Young Touchwood, Sir Walter repents his former way of life and forswears his mistress and his children; Allwit's base condition appears about to be revealed. When Young Touchwood is reported dead and Sir Walter asks Allwit for sanctuary, Allwit has the upper hand. He turns Sir Walter away with hypocritical face-saving speeches, and while he is imprisoned for debt the Allwits, "richly furnish'd . . . with household stuff," plan a comfortable future as landlords. Middleton still amuses himself and audiences with the contrivances of his charlatans, fools, and intriguers. There is small security in his comic world for any of them, and even the best, like Touchwood and Moll, can thrive only by their wits. He observes his characters with ironic detachment rather than moral indignation. The controlling principle of his comedies is not so much satire in which the knaves must be stripped naked to the world, receiving the punishment and moral censure due to their offences, but comedy; the restorative vitality of the genre ensures all but the most vicious a share in the happy resolution of all plots and intrigues. Hereafter Middleton turned to more serious concerns; with small exceptions his later comedies show neither the interest in comic devices of his earlier plays nor yet comparable achievement in the comic vein.

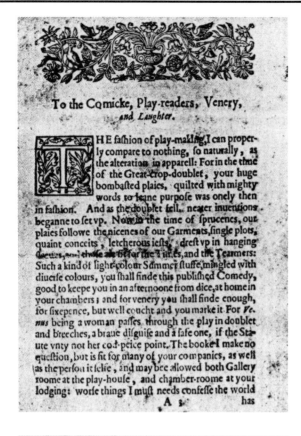

To the Comicke, Play-readers, Venery,
and Laughter.

THE fashion of play-making, I can properly compare to nothing, so naturally, as
the alteration in apparell: For in the time
of the Great-crop-doublet, your huge
bombasted plaies, quilted with mighty
words to leane purpose was onely then
in fashion. And as the doublet fell, neuer inuentions
beganne to set vp. Now in the time of sprucenes, our
plaies followe the nicenes of our Garments, single plots,
quaint conceits, letcherous iests, drest vp in hanging
sleeues, and those are fit for the Times, and the Teamers:
Such a kind of light-colour Sommer stuffe, mingled with
diuerse colours, you shall finde this publisht Comedy,
good to keepe you in an afternoone from dice, at home in
your chambers; and for venery you shall finde enough,
for sixepence, but well couch't and you marke it. For Venus being a woman passes through the play in doublet
and breeches, a braue disguise and a safe one, if the Sta-
ute vnty not her cod-peice point. The booke I make no
question, but is fit for many of your companies, as well
as the person it selfe, and may bee allowed both Gallery
roome at the play-house, and chamber-roome at your
lodging: worse things I must needs confesse the world

A 3   has

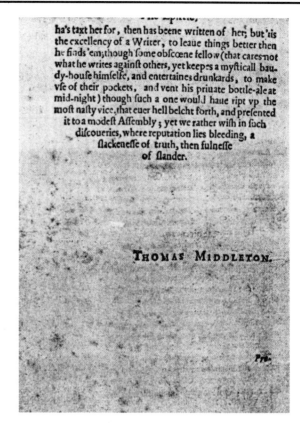

ha's taxt her for, then has beene written of her; but 'tis
the excellency of a Writer, to leaue things better then
he finds 'em; though some obscœne fellow (that cares not
what he writes against others, yet keepes a mysticall bau-
dy-house himselfe, and entertaines drunkards, to make
vse of their pockets, and vent his priuate bottle-ale at
mid-night) though such a one would haue ript vp the
most nasty vice, that euer hell belcht forth, and presented
it to a modest Assembly; yet we rather wish in such
discoueries, where reputation lies bleeding, a
slackenesse of truth, then fulnesse
of slander.

THOMAS MIDDLETON.

Pro.

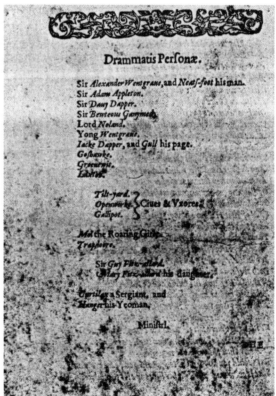

Prologus.

A Play (expected long) makes the Audience looke
For wonders:— that each Scœne should be a booke,
Compos'd to all perfection; each one comes
And brings a play in's head with him: vp he summes,
What he would of a Roaring Girle haue writ;
If that he findes not here, he mewes at it.
Onely we intreate you thinke our Scœne
Cannot speake high (the subiect being but meane)
A Roaring Girle (whose notes till now neuer were)
Shall fill with laughter our vast Theater,
That's all which I dare promise: Tragick passion,
And such graue stuffe, is this day out of fashion.
I see attention sets wide ope her gates
Of hearing, and with couetous listning waites,
To know what Girle, this Roaring Girle should be.
(For of that Tribe are many.) One is shee
That roares at midnight in deepe Tauerne bowles,
That beates the watch, and Constables controuls;
Another roarest th day time, sweares, stabbes, giues braues,
Yet sells her soule to the lust of fooles and slaues.
Both these are Suburbe-roarers. Then there's (besides)
A ciuill Citty-Roaring Girle, whose pride,
Feasting, and riding, shakes her husbands state,
And leaues him Roaring through an yron grate.
None of these Roaring Girles is ours: shee flies
With wings more lofty. Thus her character lyes,
Yet what neede characters? when to giue a gesse,
Is better then the person to expresse;
But would you know who 'tis? would you heare her name?
Shee is cal'd madde Moll; her life, our acts proclaime.

Dramatis

Drammatis Personæ.

Sir Alexander Wentgraue, and Neats-foot his man.
Sir Adam Appleton.
Sir Dauy Dapper.
Sir Beauteous Ganymed,
Lord Noland.
Yong Wentgraue.
Iacke Dapper, and Gull his page.
Goshawke.
Greenewit.
Laxton.

Tilt-yard.
Openworke. Ciues & Vxores
Gallipot.

Mol the Roaring Girle.
Trapdoore.

Sir Guy Fitz-Allard.
Mary Fitz-allard his daughter.

Curtilax a Sergiant, and
Hanger his Yeoman.

Ministrl.

Middleton's epistle to the reader, the prologue, and dramatis personae from the 1611 quarto edition of The Roaring Girl
(British Library)

A

CHAST MAYD

of

CHEAPE-SIDE.

A
Pleafant conceited Comedy
neuer before printed.

As it hath beene often acted at the
Swan on the Banke-fide, by the
Lady ELIZABETH her
Seruants.

By THOMAS MIDELTON Gent.

LONDON,
Printed for *Francis Conftable* dwelling at the
figne of the *Crane* in *Pauls*
Church-yard.
1630.

Title page for the 1630 quarto edition of one of Middleton's later comedies (Anderson Galleries, sale no. 2078, 24-25 May 1926)

In the same year (1613) Middleton embarked on a sequence of civic pageant shows and entertainments, writings which were to prove most lucrative for the rest of his professional life. His first commission for the City of London was to honor Sir Thomas Middleton, who had just been elected the Lord Mayor of London, and his brother, Sir Hugh, a wealthy goldsmith and banker who had constructed at his own cost a public water system between Amwell Head and Arlington. The dramatist's contribution to the inaugural ceremonies on 29 September 1613 was a short speech praising the benefactor and the workers. The *New River Entertainment* appears to have pleased the Lord Mayor for Middleton's next employment was *The Triumphs of Truth*, a pageant for the Lord Mayor's show on 29 October. Each year on the day after he took office the new Lord Mayor went in state from the Guildhall down to the Thames River and from

there by barges to Westminster, to take his oath of office before the Lord Chief Justice. Returning by water, still accompanied by the barges of the great livery companies (grocers', drapers', goldsmiths', for instance), the procession passed the yard of St. Paul's Cathedral, where some of the main shows were mounted, and then returned to Guildhall, stopping occasionally to watch other shows. After dinner at Guildhall the whole procession went to a service at St. Paul's after which the Lord Mayor was escorted home with full ceremony. The organization of the procession—which was paid for by the company to which the new Lord Mayor belonged—was largely the responsibility of the man appointed to design the allegorical shows intended to celebrate the city's prosperity and the civic virtues on which it was founded. The most experienced pageant master of the Jacobean era was Anthony Munday, whose virtual monopoly Middleton interrupted; Munday shared in the production of fifteen Lord Mayors' shows between 1602 and 1623. *The Triumphs of Truth*, which with Middleton's later shows is extensively described by David M. Bergeron, was his finest, the cost of £1,300 borne by the prosperous Grocers' company, making it the most lavish such entertainment of the times. (*The Mask of Cupid*, written by Middleton for a banquet given by the Merchant Taylors' company on 4 January 1614, has not survived.) Munday wrote the shows of the next three years, but in 1616 the rival dramatists were obliged to work together. Munday's Lord Mayor's show in October was followed within a few days by a pageant for the investiture of Charles as Prince of Wales on 4 November, and the thrifty Fishermongers' company used some shows for both events. Middleton was principally responsible for the royal entry, on which the City London spent over £323; his part was titled *Civitatis Amor.*

In 1617, with the election of another Grocer as Lord Mayor, that company turned again to Middleton; his *The Triumphs of Honor and Industry* brought him £282 for his pains in writing the show, finding actors, and paying for the construction and costumes. An eyewitness account by Horatio Busino, chaplain to the Venetian ambassador, relates such spectacular details as how the first "stages" or wagons were "drawn by griffins, lions, camels, or other large animals" and were "laden with bales from which the lads took sundry confections, sugar, nutmegs, dates and ginger, throwing them among the poplace." In 1619 Middleton wrote *The Triumphs of Love and Antiquity* to honor Sir William Cockayne, a Skinner; the pageant is remarkable only in that it is the only show written by Middleton which presents a speech delivered on the river. In the following two years Middleton wrote ten brief entertainments for civic dignitaries, mainly for presentation at dinners. These were published together as *Honourable Entertainments Composed for the Service of this Noble City* in 1621, when he also wrote *The Sun in Aries* with Munday for the show of the Draper, Sir Edward Barkham. (The manuscript of Middleton's *Invention* for a feast at Barkham's house in the Easter holidays, 1622, survives in the Public Record Office.) The Grocers patronized him for the third time in 1622 when he composed *The Triumphs of Honour and Virtue* for the inauguration of Sir Peter Proby, and the next year Middleton and Munday collaborated again on a Lord Mayor's show for the Draper, Sir Martin Lumley, Munday contributing the water part under the title of *The Triumphs of the Golden Fleece* and Middleton the land part, *The Triumphs of Integrity*. There were indications that Middleton's inventiveness in this kind was waning; as it turned out he wrote only one other such show, in 1626, which may be mentioned with the works of his final years.

Around 1614—returning to strict chronology—Middleton began a sequence of plays influenced by the prevailing fashion for romantic tragicomedy. The King's company play, *The Witch*, dated variously between 1609 and 1615 but probably a production of 1614, was the least successful, as much on account of its adoption of the Beaumont and Fletcher formula as despite it. The serious situations are dramatic but incredible, and characters such as the pregnant sixteen-year-old Francisca, who in the early comedies would be engagingly resourceful, are merely depraved and disgusting. An editor of the play, Sir Walter Greg—who read or at least looked through every play printed before 1640—considered it probably the worst play written for the early English stage. Some scholars suggest that it was commissioned mainly to make use of expensive properties made for the single court performance of Ben Jonson's *Masque of Queens* in 1609 but the date is too early for Middleton. Almost its sole interest now is that two of the witches' songs found their way into the 1623 text of Shakespeare's *Macbeth*.

The Nice Valour, or the Passionate Madman (produced circa 1616), first published in the 1647 Beaumont and Fletcher folio, is so Fletcherian in quality that scholars have been reluctant to admit Middleton's share in it. Barker, for instance, writes "The chief character is a hopeless snob with a preposterously refined sense of honor; Middleton could

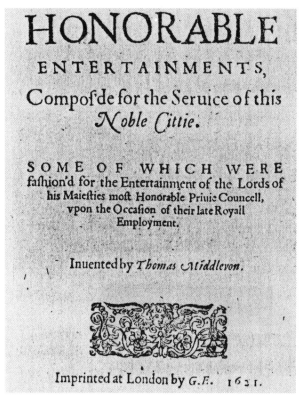

Title page for the only known copy of the 1621 octavo collection of some of Middleton's shorter writings for public occasions (Henry E. Huntington Library and Art Gallery)

by no stretch of the imagination have drawn him"; yet linguistic investigations by Jackson identify Middleton "not merely as reviser but as virtual sole author, at least with respect to the actual writing." In any event Middleton had not hitherto shrunk from the vapid excesses of the romantic style. His next comedy, *The Widow* (written in 1616), for the King's Men, is conventionally romantic in the main and lacks the telling ironies which distinguished his early city comedies.

In 1617 or possibly a little earlier, he returned to collaboration with Rowley in *A Fair Quarrel*, a tragicomedy for Prince Charles's company of which Rowley was a leading member. Middleton's share of the play—"II.i., III.i, III.iii, IV.ii, IV.iii (substantially), and roughly the first hundred lines of I," according to Jackson—comprises the main plot. Captain Ager is resolved to meet his erstwhile friend, the Colonel, in a duel after the Colonel has called him "The son of a whore," an insult that, he says in II.i, "kills At one report two reputations, A mother's and a son's." However, Lady Ager attempts to protect her son from his highly developed sense of honor by pretending that he is a

Page from the manuscript for The Witch *preserved in the Bodleian Library. This manuscript is a fair copy made by the scribe Ralph Crane, probably between 1619 and 1627 (MS Malone 12; by permission of the Bodleian Library)* bastard. Captain Ager meets the Colonel, seeking to resolve their quarrel peaceably, but, called a coward, he fights, leaving the Colonel desperately wounded. Mother and son are reconciled when Lady Ager retracts her lie, but Captain Ager looks forward eagerly to another duel. Lady Ager believes him lost but the serious action dissolves sentimentally in a reconciliation between the Colonel and the Captain, who wins the affection of the Colonel's virtuous sister. Although the play was successfully revived on the stage in recent times, it does not significantly add to Middleton's reputation.

In *The Mayor of Queenborough, or Hengist King of Kent* (written in 1618), a tragedy written for an unknown company (probably the Lady Elizabeth's players) but subsequently the property of the King's Men, the serious concerns are identified by the subtitle. The Saxon Hengist is serviceable to the English king Vortiger, who rewards him with lands in Kent. Having already murdered his predecessor, Constantius, Vortiger becomes infatuated with Roxena, Hengist's daughter, who is, however, the mistress of Horsus, another Saxon. Vortiger employs Horsus to compromise the honor of his wife, Castiza, so that he might marry Roxena. Eventually, Constantius's sons raise arms against Vortiger; he and Horsus quarrel, stab each other, and with Roxena, die. Despite its ultimate origin in Geoffrey of Monmouth's *History, Hengist* is not a history play like Shakespeare's early compositions but rather, in the manner of *Cymbeline,* a melodrama in which the political interest is almost entirely subordinated to a Fletcherian preoccupation with lust, honor, chastity, and betrayal; but even this is muted. Later seventeenth-century audiences delighted in the clownish escapades of the tanner Simon, who became Mayor of Queenborough, and his quarrel with Oliver, a fustian weaver and Puritan, but their scenes, even when amusing, are not conducive to the achievement of the tragic effect. The brilliance of *The Revenger's Tragedy* and *The Changeling* is entirely lacking.

The Old Law (written in 1618), a tragicomedy written in the same period, again for an unknown company, is attributed on the title page of the 1656 edition to Middleton, Rowley, and Philip Massinger but recent linguistic investigations by Lake and Jackson can find no evidence of Massinger's participation in the collaboration. Rowley wrote most of the play, Middleton being "substantially responsible for the writing of II, III.ii, and IV.ii," according to Jackson; these scenes convey most of the tragic matter of the play. The Duke of Epire has decided to put to death all men who have reached the age of eighty. Hippolita, who is regarded as a paragon of wifely virtue, arranges with her husband, Cleanthes, to protect her father-in-law, Leonides, from the edict, but moved by pity at the hypocritical tears of her relative Eugenia, whose old husband has also been condemned, she reveals her secret. Eugenia betrays both the trust and Leonides; he is led away to be executed, leaving Hippolita to reflect in IV.ii that "mine own pity E'en cozen'd me together, and stole from me This secret, which fierce death should not have purchas'd." However, Rowley provides a happy ending in the fifth act.

At the end of the year Middleton wrote *The Inner Temple Masque, or Masque of Heroes,* which was performed between 6 January and 2 February 1619 by professional actors of Prince Charles's company, among them Rowley as Plumporridge. *More Dissemblers Besides Women* appears, according to a 1976 article by Lake, to have been written for the King's Men around the middle of the year. The Cardinal of Milan adores the Duchess because she has pledged herself never to remarry. His nephew Lactantio must dissemble his love for Aurelia in his presence. But it turns out that the Duchess is infatuated with Andrugio, her general, and conceals it by naming Lactantio as her lover; Lactantio has a pregnant mistress disguised as a page and easily transfers his affections from Aurelia to the Duchess; the Cardinal promptly reverses his attitude to widowed chastity in order to favor his family's promotion; and Aurelia deceives Lactantio with Andrugio. Their dissembling turns back on them. With forgiving speeches the Duchess, who has both broken her vow and given up the man she loves, departs the stage for a life of religious seclusion. The comedy lies in the shifts to which the hypocrites are driven for their advantages; the harm their devices bring the noble Duchess comprises the serious outcome of the play. Such warmly human characters cannot survive in a world of that kind.

Later in 1619 Middleton is alleged by J. P. Collier (in his *New Facts Regarding the Life of Shakespeare,* 1835) to have contributed verses "On the Death of Richard Burbage," the great Shakespearian actor, but Joel Kaplan has made a good case for the epitaph as another Collier fabrication. Middleton did collaborate with Rowley on *A Courtly Masque; the Device Called The World Tossed at Tennis* (produced in 1620) for performance by Prince Charles's men before James and the Prince at Denmark House, but the court performance was not given and the play was subsequently altered for public presentation. Later in 1620 Middleton, by now well established as a deviser of Lord Mayor's shows, gained the post of Chronologer to the City of London, an office which, according to Barker, his *Honorable Entertainments* (1621) suggests was "probably intended to include that of Inventor of the City's Honorable Entertainments." Besides the annual salary of six pounds, thirteen shillings, and four pence, raised the next year to ten pounds, Middleton received other substantial amounts from time to time. If he had not been financially secure before, the addition of responsibilities to keep a journal of public events and write speeches of welcome and entertainments for city banquets brought such a handsome addition to his income from play writing that his prosperity was assured for much of the last part of his career. Another comedy for the King's company was written about the same time, with an old collaborator, John Webster. According to Jackson, *Anything for a Quiet Life* (written in 1621) shows Middleton in II.ii, III, IV.ii-iii, and V, with II.iii unassigned. It has been suggested that Webster, whose part covers most of the main plot, may have partially revised Middleton's manuscript. The play is not an important addition to Middleton's canon; Barker dismisses it as "mere farce" while pointing to passages which are "uproariously funny and outrageously indecent."

The King's company tragedy *Women Beware Women* (written in 1621) is another matter, being one of the two works in the genre on which Middleton's reputation rests. Because it was not published until 1653 and the Master of the Revels' license has not survived, dating is especially difficult; it is not possible to be sure that it did not succeed Middleton's other great tragedy *The Changeling* (produced in 1622). Dorothy M. Farr has suggested that in the development of Middleton's art and interest the play would be well placed at the end of 1623 or early 1624. The play is notable for its strong roles for women, befitting the title. The well-born Bianca has fled her city, married to Leantio, a factor or business agent. Welcomed by Leantio's mother, at first she accepts her reduced circumstances and is affectionately reluctant to allow her husband to go about his business; however, when a neighbor, Livia, conspires to provide the Duke of Florence access to her, Bianca cannot withstand his suggestions. Once she is acquainted with sin in II.ii, her husband's house becomes distasteful; she leaves it with the Duke's messenger. Leantio is bought off with the captainship of a fort in III.ii, a scene which unites other plot lines. Livia's brother, Fabritio, seeks to marry his daughter Is-

abella, to the Ward, "a rich young heir" who is also thoroughly foolish; Isabella understandably recoils from the match. Her uncle Hippolito, cherishing an incestuous passion for her, confesses it to his sister Livia, who undertakes to help him. She advises Isabella that she can marry the Ward for her own advantage or not; in any case she is not her father's child, but she must not tell Hippolito that he is not her uncle. Isabella swears, informs Hippolito that she will marry the Ward, and accepts her uncle's love. At the banquet in III.ii all main deceivers are present in ironic juxtaposition: the adulterous Duke, his mistress Bianca, the purchased cuckold Leantio, the falsely betrothed Isabella engaged in an unwittingly incestuous relationship with Hippolito, who must pander his niece to the Ward, and the arch-intriguer Livia. In such company mere fools (Fabritio and the Ward) and knaves (Guardiano, uncle to the Ward) afford welcome contrast. By the end of the scene Livia, who has fallen in love with Leantio, takes him as her lover in III.ii: "Do but love enough, I'll give enough. *Leantio.* Troth then, I'll love enough, and take enough." After Leantio, resplendent in his new finery, confronts Bianca, she complains of his liaison to the Duke, who arranges for Hippolito to challenge Leantio on his sister's behalf. This is no sooner done than the Lord Cardinal, the Duke's brother, severely reprehends his immoral conduct in powerful speeches which convert the Duke, to a point. Satisfied that Leantio will be killed, he determines to marry his widow. Hippolito kills Leantio; the vengeful Livia exposes his incestuous affair with Isabella, and with Guardiano and the Ward they plot in V.i against the Duke's marriage-feast, to which the Cardinal's renewed warnings serve as moral prologue. In due course Livia as Juno kills Isabella, whose presented incense in turn kills her; Guardiano falls through a trapdoor; Hippolito is struck with poisoned arrows shot by cupids, confesses the plot ("Vengeance met Vengeance Like a set match"), and kills himself; the Duke falls after drinking from a poisoned cup which Bianca has prepared for her enemy the Cardinal. Finally in V.ii she drinks from it herself: "Oh the deadly snares that women set for women, without pity Either to soul or honor!"

The masque in V.i—which Middleton employed in similar fashion in *The Revenger's Tragedy*—is sometimes criticized as mere melodrama, providing a conclusion inconsistent with the more naturalistic scenes earlier in the play, but the irony of the revengers turning on each other, often receiving their punishments from the ostensibly benign pastoral figures of the masque, would not have been lost upon the audience. There was in fact nothing left for the characters to do but to die in their damnable perfidy. The prevailing irony so characteristic of Middleton is exquisitely deployed in the tense scene (II.ii) in which Livia occupies the Mother with a game of chess while Bianca escorted by Guardiano confronts the Duke in the gallery above. A parade of double entendres underlines and counterpoints the predicament into which Livia's duplicity has led Bianca. The characters, with the notable exception of the Mother, are for the most part morally worthless, but they are delineated, particularly Livia, Isabella, Bianca, and Leantio, with impressive psychological realism. An audience may be alienated by their moral weakness and the expedients they use to satisfy their desires, but as characters they remain fascinating to the end, not the least because of the dramatist's skill in depicting their helpless awareness of the moral dimensions of their actions: for the worst characters the most condemnatory speeches come from their own mouths. *Women Beware Women* is a masterful theatrical achievement.

Similar qualities characterize *The Changeling* which Middleton wrote with Rowley for the newly organized Lady Elizabeth's company; it was licensed to be acted on 7 May 1622. There is general agreement that Middleton's part in the play consisted of II; III.i-ii, iv; IV.i, ii.17-150; V.i-ii, scenes in which, apart from Rowley's introduction and conclusion, the tragic plot is conducted. Vermandero has betrothed Beatrice to Alonzo de Piracquo, a suitor who becomes an embarrassment when she falls in love with Alsemero. She employs her devoted but detested admirer, De Flores, a malcontent, to murder Alonzo, mistakenly believing that he will accept money as his reward; however, he will be satisfied only by her virginity. For her wedding night Beatrice, no longer a maid, must send her waiting woman Daiphanta in her stead, but she plays her role so zestfully that Beatrice fears that the substitution will be detected to her shame and arranges a diversion. De Flores sets a fire and murders Diaphanta to protect his mistress's honor. However, Alsemero has become suspicious of the new familiarity between Beatrice and De Flores and accuses her of adultery; she defends herself by revealing that she has murdered to marry him. Alsemero is horrified ("Oh, thou art all deform'd!"); De Flores wounds Beatrice, stabs himself, and they die together. Tomazo de Piracquo who has appeared fitfully in the play as a frustrated revenger is satisfied: " . . . my injuries Lie dead before me."

To the perfidious Beatrice the subplot contrasts the faithful Isabella, wife to the jealous Alibius, keeper of a hospital for madmen and fools, which Antonio and Franciscus enter in disguise in order to woo Isabella. The subplot is entirely Rowley's.

The interest of *The Changeling* concentrates almost exclusively on two supreme characters in Jacobean tragedy, Beatrice and De Flores. Their intense relationship inverts the story of Beauty and the Beast because Beatrice has no powers to redeem De Flores but rather leads him to corrupt his willing service into vice, and De Flores remains obdurately a creature of lust. Beatrice, the center of her own world, cannot believe that others' purposes may differ from hers; her horror in III.iv when she realizes that De Flores does not seek money as his reward is almost amusing were it not that it reveals a greater corruption:

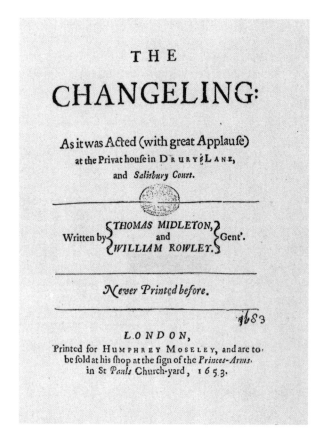

Title page for the 1653 quarto edition of the tragedy Middleton and Rowley wrote for the newly organized Lady Elizabeth's company of actors (British Library)

> *Bea.* Why, 'tis impossible thou canst be so wicked,
>   Or shelter such a cunning cruelty,

To make his death the murderer of my honour!

Morally undeveloped, Beatrice is a willful child who cannot resist the patent attractions of Alsemero, a man who does not scruple to court a woman betrothed in marriage, still less De Flores's obsessive compulsion to enjoy her. She cannot conceive that either her contemptuous treatment of him at the beginning of the play or her employment of him in Alonso's murder could have serious consequences. De Flores does not so much corrupt her as supply the character she lacks from his own depravity. Lacking knowledge of herself and the world of commonplace morality which even De Flores acknowledges in his perversity, her end is inevitable. This is a play of deception and self-deception, of lust masquerading as love, of concern for worldly reputation substituting for moral awareness. Rowley's moral conclusion in V.iii to some may appear a merely conventional balancing of the moral ledger but no one can doubt that Middleton approved and planned it: " . . . justice hath so right The guilty hit, that innocence is quit."

The last five years of Middleton's career were occupied with intermittent civic entertainments and one concluding triumph. His hand has been detected in a comedy for the Red Bull company, *A Match at Midnight* (produced in 1622) but the play is usually included in Rowley's canon. Another comedy, *The Puritan Maid* (produced in 1623), and a tragicomedy, *The Conqueror's Custom* (produced in 1626), which both may have been written at any time after 1601, are lost, and *The Spanish Gypsy*, licensed for performance on 9 July 1623 by the Lady Elizabeth's players, is now assigned by Lake and Jackson to Ford, Dekker, Rowley, and Brome. In the same year Middleton contributed commendatory verses to the first edition of John Webster's tragedy *The Duchess of Malfi*. His most spectacular success was the satirical comedy *A Game at Chess*, licensed for performance on 9 July 1624 and performed by the King's Men at the Globe theater for an unprecedented run of nine performances between 6 and 16 August before it was closed down by order of the Privy Council. Written to benefit from strong anti-Spanish feelings following the breakdown of the arrangements for a marriage between Prince Charles and the Infanta of Spain, the play allegorized the contention between Catholic Spain and Anglican England using the dominant device of chess play, a game at which Spaniards were held to be most skillful. The circumstances of the Spanish marriage itself contributed little directly in the play other than the

conclusion, a "checkmate by discovery" in which the White Knight (Prince Charles) and the White Duke (the Duke of Buckingham) deceive the Black side into revealing their malicious designs for "universal monarchy." The London audiences most relished satirical impersonations of the hated former ambassador in England, Gondomar, who was represented as a scheming Machiavellian, the Black Knight, and the more broadly humorous depiction of the grasping apostate Marco Antonio de Dominis, Archbishop of Spalato, as the Fat Bishop, as well as other touches of contemporary satire. The main action concerns the attempted seduction of the devout but lovesick White Queen's Pawn by the Black Bishop's Pawn, the epitome of what Protestant Englishmen regarded as Jesuit hypocrisy.

The nine consecutive performances of *A Game at Chess* played to packed houses and brought exceptional returns to the players, and numerous references in contemporary letters show that the play created a minor sensation. It was in any event exceptional in the period for the King's Men had gone to unprecedented lengths to impersonate the main satirical characters. For Gondomar, for instance, there are references to the fistula which made him a common laughingstock, and "they counterfeited his person to the life, with all his graces and faces, and had gotten (they say) a cast suit of his apparel for the purpose with his litter" (Chamberlain to Carleton, 21 August 1624; quoted in Bald's edition of the play) for which Middleton provided a spectacular entry at V.i. The success could not be enjoyed for long: the Spanish ambassador complained to King James, who ordered the performances halted, and the Privy Council was commanded to investigate who was responsible for "such insolent and licentious presumption." Although principal actors of the King's Men assured the Privy Council that they had played only what was set down in the play book licensed by the Master of the Revels, the author did not attend with the rest. Apparently Middleton had gone into hiding and was supervising the transcription of the play for sale to private readers and publishers: three editions were published within a year. Middleton's son, Edward, was sent for, doubtless to reveal his father's whereabouts, but surviving documents do not record that the playwright was punished for his share in the most successful play of the period. However, a tradition that Middleton was confined to the Fleet prison for some time, obtaining his release only by a verse petition to the King, although lacking support from official documents, may be true, for the Lord Mayor's show

Title pages for London (1625; British Library) and Leyden (1625?; Bodleian Library) quarto editions of Middleton's highly successful satirical comedy

in October was devised by John Webster, his first experience in civic pageantry.

The extent to which Middleton's last years were clouded by his connection with *A Game at Chess* is unsure. Unless *Women Beware Women* is later than most believe, it seems that he did not write for the King's Men again, or for any other company, and his relations with the civic authorities were shadowed by allegations of "abuses and bad workmanship." A city welcome for Charles I and his newly married queen planned for 1625 was postponed on account of plague and was abandoned on 25 May 1626 by the King's command. Later in the year payments for his *The Triumphs of Health and Prosperity* (produced in 1626), written for the mayoral inauguration for the Draper, Sir Cuthbert Hacket, was delayed on the ground of "ill performance." Within less than a year Middleton died and was buried in the parish church of Newington Butts, in Southwark on the south side of the Thames on 4 July 1627; his wife followed him in the next year on 18 July.

Middleton's death passed unremarked, either by elegiac verses or the publication of a commemorative collection of his works like those of Jonson, Shakespeare, and Beaumont and Fletcher. During his lifetime he had not established a reputation; contemporary references to him are few and perfunctory; only with *A Game at Chess* did he attract much attention. He appears to have received no patronage other than from the City of London and was no more closely attached to any of the acting companies than as an occasional contributor of plays. Yet he left a handful of comedies and tragedies which rank with the best productions of the period. His early satires, such as *The Phoenix* and *Your Five Gallants,* are not attractive, being artificial in form and based on literary sources, with usually conventional low characters who are not well distinguished. In other comedies based on observation of city life, Middleton struck a happier vein; *Michaelmas Term, A Trick to Catch the Old One, A Mad World My Masters,* and *A Chaste Maid in Cheapside* genially fulfill the fundamental conditions of comedy. The young struggle against the old, the dis-

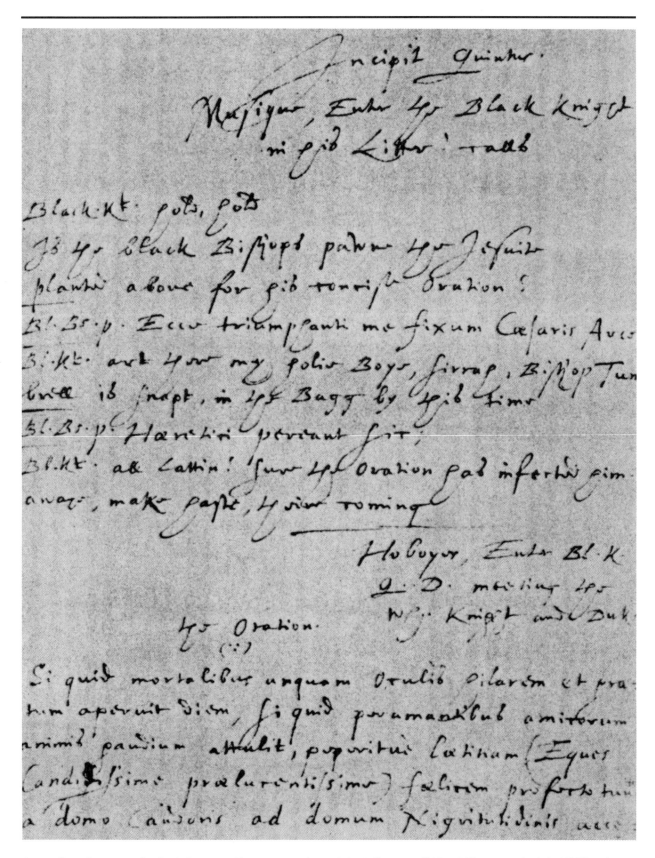

A page from the manuscript for A Game at Chess *preserved at Trinity College, Cambridge. This manuscript is in Middleton's own hand (MS O. 2. 66, fol. 39^b; by permission of Trinity College, Cambridge).*

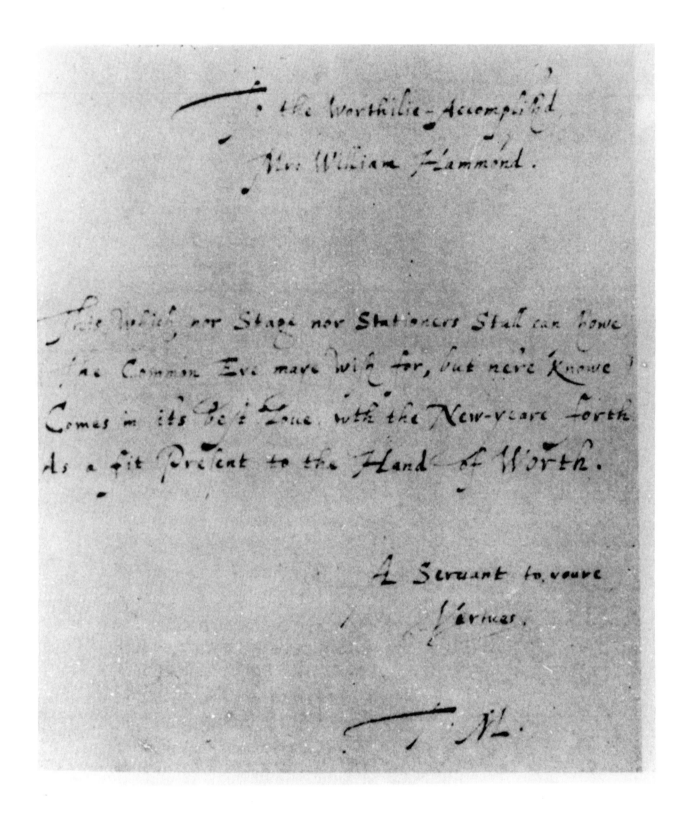

Dedication to William Hammond, in Middleton's hand, in the fair copy of A Game at Chess *made by the scribe Ralph Crane (MS Malone 25, fol. vii[a]; by permission of the Bodleian Library)*

advantaged against the advantaged, the loving against the unloving in brilliantly coordinated interlocking plots of intrigue, pointed with contrastive irony. The merely conventional characters achieve merely conventional rewards; the flawed young men achieve by their wits imperfect satisfactions, all that an imperfect world will allow. The ebullient characters (always vivaciously interesting even when morally blameworthy) together with the brisk pace with which Middleton conducts the action give plays which, in the words of Dorothy Farr, "are still good reading, still very actable and with an audience more witty than squeamish . . . could hardly fail to please."

Without demonstrating the local references and exaggerated mannerisms of the comedies, Middleton's three great tragedies are more to modern taste. Although *The Revenger's Tragedy*, *Women Beware Women*, and *The Changeling* are significantly distinctive achievements in tragedy, they occupy a much narrower range than, say, the Jacobean tragedies of Shakespeare which make more varied claims on the audience's sympathies. In his baroque tragedy of revenge Middleton inaugurated a trenchant examination of corruption as process and product which occupied him in his later plays, *Women Beware Women*, *The Changeling*, and, just as important, in the satirical allegory *A Game at Chess*. These plays do not possess the outward-referring dimension of the tragedies of Shakespeare and, to an extent, Webster; they do not reaffirm an experience of the common strength of human kindness and consequently miss much of the tragic effect. Middleton's plays concern fundamentally ordinary people who to their essential human frailty cannot counterpoise convincing assertions of heroism, justified or not. Life has perplexed them; for the most part they lack the moral knowledge and energy to recognize their fate or to avert it. For a time characters such as Bianca, Beatrice, or De Flores aspire to conditions beyond the natural scope of their characters, but they mistake their way and come at last to awareness of the moral law which they have neglected. The judgments of tragedy are harsher than those of comedy: lack of moral awareness or the strength to act on it dismisses these characters to oblivion. Nevertheless Middleton's tragedies heighten our understanding of a complex world which is as inhospitable to extremes of vices and folly as—Middleton's most attractive female character, the White Queen's Pawn in *A Game at Chess* exemplified—innocent goodness itself.

Bibliographies:

Samuel A. Tannenbaum, *Thomas Middleton, A Concise Bibliography* (New York: Privately printed, 1940);

Dennis G. Donovan, *Thomas Middleton, 1939-1965*, Elizabethan Bibliographies Supplements, no. 1 (London: Nether Press, 1967);

John B. Brooks, "Thomas Middleton," in *The Popular School*, edited by Terence P. Logan and Denzell S. Smith (Lincoln: University of Nebraska Press, 1975), pp. 51-84;

Brooks, "Recent Studies in Middleton, 1971-1981," *English Literary Renaissance*, 14 (Winter 1984): 114-125;

Sara J. Steen, *Thomas Middleton: A Reference Guide* (Boston: G. K. Hall, 1984);

Geraldo V. de Sousa, "Thomas Middleton: Criticism Since T. S. Eliot," *Research Opportunities in Renaissance Drama*, 28 (1985): 73-85;

Dorothy Wolff, *Thomas Middleton: An Annotated Bibliography* (New York: Garland, 1985).

References:

Caroline Asp, *A Study of Thomas Middleton's Tragicomedies* (Salzburg: Institut für Englische Sprache und Literatur, Universität Salzburg, 1974);

Barbara J. Baines, *The Lust Motif in the Plays of Thomas Middleton* (Salzburg: Institut für Englische Sprache und Literatur, Universität Salzburg, 1973);

R. Cecil Bald, "The Chronology of Middleton's Plays," *Modern Language Review*, 32 (January 1937): 33-43;

Bald, "Middleton's Civic Employments," *Modern Philology*, 31 (August 1933): 65-78;

Richard H. Barker, *Thomas Middleton* (New York: Columbia University Press, 1958);

David M. Bergeron, *English Civic Pageantry 1558-1642* (London: Arnold, 1971), pp. 179-200;

Caroline L. Cherry, *The Most Unvaluedst Purchase: Women in the Plays of Thomas Middleton* (Salzburg: Institut für Englische Sprache und Literatur, Universität Salzburg, 1972);

Mildred G. Christian, "Middleton's Residence at Oxford," *Modern Language Notes*, 61 (February 1946): 90-91;

Anthony Covatta, *Thomas Middleton's City Comedies* (Lewisburg: Bucknell University Press, 1973);

Mark Eccles, "Middleton's Birth and Education," *Review of English Studies*, 7 (October 1931): 431-441;

Eccles, " 'Thomas Middleton a Poett,' " *Studies in Philology*, 54 (October 1957): 516-536;

Dorothy M. Farr, *Thomas Middleton and the Drama of Realism; A Study of Some Representative Plays* (Edinburgh: Oliver & Boyd, 1973);

Kenneth Freidenreich, ed., *"Accompaninge the Players": Essays Celebrating Thomas Middleton, 1580-1980* (New York: AMS Press, 1983);

David George, "Thomas Middleton at Oxford," *Modern Language Review,* 65 (October 1970): 734-736;

George, "Thomas Middleton's Sources; a Survey," *Notes and Queries,* 18 (January 1971): 17-24;

Margot Heinemann, *Puritanism and Theatre; Thomas Middleton and Opposition Drama Under the Early Stuarts* (Cambridge: Cambridge University Press, 1980);

David M. Holmes, *The Art of Thomas Middleton* (Oxford: Clarendon Press, 1970);

MacDonald P. Jackson, "An Allusion to Marlowe's *The Jew of Malta* in an Early Seventeenth Century Pamphlet Possibly by Thomas Middleton," *Notes and Queries,* 29 (April 1982): 132-133;

Jackson, *Studies in Attribution; Middleton and Shakespeare* (Salzburg: Institut für Englische Sprache und Literatur, Universität Salzburg, 1979);

Joel H. Kaplan, "Thomas Middleton's Epitaph on the Death of Richard Burbage, and John Payne Collier," *Papers of the Bibliographical Society of America,* 80 (1986): 225-232;

David J. Lake, *The Canon of Thomas Middleton's Plays; Internal Evidence for the Major Problems of Authorship* (Cambridge: Cambridge University Press, 1975);

Lake, "The Date of *More Dissemblers Besides Women,*" *Notes and Queries,* 23 (May-June 1976): 219-221;

John F. McElroy, *Parody and Burlesque in the Tragicomedies of Thomas Middleton* (Salzburg: Institut für Englische Sprache und Literatur, Universität Salzburg, 1972);

Bruno Nauer, *Thomas Middleton; a Study of the Narrative Structures* (Zurich: Juris-Verlag, 1977);

Peter G. Phialas, "Middleton's Early Contact with the Law," *Studies in Philology,* 52 (April 1955): 186-194;

Marilyn Roberts, "A Preliminary Check-List of Productions of Thomas Middleton's Plays," *Research Opportunities in Renaissance Drama,* 28 (1985): 37-61;

George E. Rowe, *Thomas Middleton and the New Comedy Tradition* (Lincoln: University of Nebraska Press, 1979);

Samuel Schoenbaum, *Middleton's Tragedies, A Critical Study* (New York: Columbia University Press, 1955);

Schoenbaum, "Middleton's Tragicomedies," *Modern Philology,* 54 (August 1956): 7-19;

Schoenbaum, "A New Middleton Record," *Modern Language Review,* 55 (January 1960): 82-84;

Louis C. Stagg, *Index to the Figurative Language of the Tragedies of Shakespeare's Chief 17th Century Contemporaries,* revised edition (New York: Garland, 1982);

Sara J. Steen, "The Response to Middleton: His Own Time to Eliot," *Research Opportunities in Renaissance Drama,* 28 (1985): 63-71.

Papers:

Middleton's surviving manuscripts are scattered among various repositories, including the British Library; the Public Record Office; the Bodleian Library; the library at Trinity College, Cambridge; the Folger Shakespeare Library; and the Henry E. Huntington Library and Art Gallery. An annotated checklist is published in *Index to English Literary Manuscripts,* edited by Peter Beal (London: Mansell, 1980), I: 341-346, 632.

Thomas Nabbes
(circa 1605-April 1641)

Norman Sanders
University of Tennessee

PLAY PRODUCTIONS: *Covent Garden,* London, Phoenix (or Cockpit) theater, February(?) 1633;

Tottenham Court, London, Salisbury Court theater, spring(?) 1633;

Hannibal and Scipio, London, Phoenix (or Cockpit) theater, 1635;

The Spring's Glory, possible private production, 1636 or 1637;

Microcosmus, London, Salisbury Court theater, between 24 February and 1 March 1637 or October 1637(?);

A Presentation Intended for the Prince, London, at Court(?), November or December 1637;

The Bride, London, Phoenix (or Cockpit) theater, summer(?) 1638.

BOOKS: *Hannibal and Scipio. An Historicall Tragedy* (London: Printed by Richard Oulton for Charles Greene, 1637);

Microcosmus. A Morall Maske (London: Printed by Richard Oulton for Charles Greene, 1637);

Totenham Court. A Pleasant Comedie (London: Printed by Richard Oulton for Charles Greene, 1638);

Covent Garden: A Pleasant Comedie (London: Printed by Richard Oulton for Charles Greene, sold by N. Fussell, 1638);

The Springs Glorie. Vindicating Love. . . . Moralized in a Maske. With other Poems, Epigrams, Elegies, and Epithalamiums (London: Printed by John Dawson for Charles Greene, sold by N. Fussell, 1638)—includes *A Presentation Intended for the Prince*;

Playes, Maskes, Epigrams, Elegies, and Epithalamiums (London: Printed by John Dawson, sold by N. Fussell, 1639)—comprises *Microcosmus, Hannibal and Scipio, Covent Garden, The Spring's Glory, A Presentation Intended for the Prince, Totenham Court, The Unfortunate Mother,* and *The Bride*;

The Bride, A Comedie (London: Printed by Richard Hodgekinson for Laurence Blaikelocke, 1640);

The Unfortunate Mother: A Tragedie (London: Printed by John Okes for Daniel Frere, 1640).

Editions: *Microcosmus,* in *A Select Collection of Old English Plays,* edited by Robert Dodsley (London, 1744), V: 315-360;

The Works of Thomas Nabbes, 2 volumes, Old English Plays, new series 1-2, edited by A. H. Bullen (London: Privately printed, 1887)—comprises *Covent Garden, Totenham Court, Hannibal and Scipio, The Bride, The Unfortunate Mother, Microcosmus, The Spring's Glory, A Presentation Intended for the Prince,* and *Miscellaneous verses*;

The Spring's Glory, edited by John Russell Brown, in *A Book of Masques in Honour of Allardyce Nicoll* (Cambridge: Cambridge University Press, 1967), pp. 317-336.

OTHER: "A Continuation of the Turkish Historie, From The Yeare Of Our Lord 1628, To The End of the Yeare 1637," an appendix to the fifth edition of Richard Knolles's *The General Historie of the Turkes* (London: Printed by A. Islip, 1638).

Thomas Nabbes's working life as a playwright was spent at the very end of the period which produced the Renaissance English drama—literally in the last decade before the theaters were closed in 1642 for twenty years. Generally considered to be one of that group of writers ("the sons of Ben") who were strongly influenced by the aging Jonson, he actually tried his hand—certainly at city comedy—but also at a variety of other genres including heroic tragedy, the masque, the Italianate intrigue play, tragicomedy, and, most interesting, in *Microcosmus,* the revival of the Tudor morality play.

The year of Nabbes's birth must be deduced from the record of his matriculation at the age of sixteen at Exeter College, Oxford, on 3 May 1621. The same entry indicates that he came from Worcestershire, although at least one county historian claims he was a resident rather than a native, a supposition based on the lack of reference to any indigenous branch of the Nabbes family in the

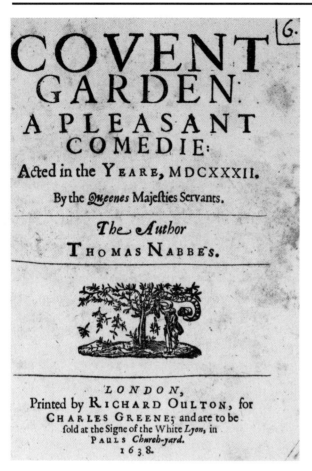

COVENT GARDEN.
A PLEASANT COMEDIE:

Acted in the YEARE, MDCXXXII.

By the Queenes Majefties Servants.

The Author
THOMAS NABBES.

LONDON,
Printed by RICHARD OULTON, for
CHARLES GREENE; and are to be
fold at the Signe of the White Lyon, in
PAULS Church-yard.
1638.

Title page for the 1638 quarto edition of Nabbes's first play, which, according to his dedication to Sir John Suckling, received only "some partiall allowance" from its audience at the Phoenix theater (Henry E. Huntington Library and Art Gallery)

county records. Two of his occasional poems, "An Encomium on the Leaden Steeple at Worcester" and "Upon Excellent Strong Beer Which He drank at the Town of Wich in Worcestershire," have been thought to support his association with the region. There is no record of his having taken a degree at the university, and, again on the evidence of his poetry, he may have spent some of his years before arriving in London in the service of a nobleman or bishop.

Nabbes must have left the provinces for London sometime before 1633, which—from the evidence of the title page of its 1637 quarto edition—is the date his first play, *Covent Garden*, was performed at the Phoenix or Cockpit theater in Drury Lane by Queen Henrietta's Men. From a remark in the quarto's dedication to Sir John Suckling that the audience gave the play only "some partiall allowance," it would appear that his first theatrical

venture was not a blazing success, despite the fact that he clearly planned his subject matter and its treatment with an eye to current popular taste. It is obvious that the play is an attempt to rival, and in some ways to copy, Richard Brome's *The Weeding of Covent Garden*, produced earlier the same year, even though Nabbes protests to the contrary in his prologue. Furthermore, like Brome's comedy, it aimed at catering to the fashion for plays with real-life London settings, which was prevalent in the early 1630s and was also the stimulus for such pieces as Shakerley Marmion's *Holland's Leaguer* (first performed in 1631) and James Shirley's *Hyde Park* (first performed in 1632).

Presumably also with an eye to success, Nabbes works with two kinds of comic materials: two central romantic plots that have as their standards the chic Court Platonism, and the type satire and purging of "humours" derived ultimately from Ben Jonson. However, he is unable to reconcile these two elements and offers a series of scenes alternating between two comic worlds rather than an integrated whole. The standards in the love plots are set by two women: Dorothy Worthy and her youthful stepmother, Lady Worthy. Dorothy is the object of the affections of Artlove, "a compleat gentleman" who is a veritable walking anthology of the ideals of Platonic love: "when a beautious frame/Garnish't with all the lustre of perfection/Invite's the eye, and tells the serching thoughts/It holds a richer minde, with which my soule/Would rather mixe her faculties." Dorothy shows an occasional tendency to mock her lover's high-flown diction by parodying it, but the possibility of such satirical conflict is not developed; and Dorothy herself falls into the same mode when she defends Artlove against her brother's warnings.

Lady Worthy, the young bride of an unsatisfactory, old, and jealous husband, is solicited by her former suitor, Hugh Jerker, a libertine and critic of Artlove's values. She is perhaps the most convincingly drawn character in the play; and, as she pursues the course, so often mapped out in earlier citizen comedies, to deter and reform her suitor and to cure her husband of his jealousy, she displays a noticeable wit and maturity in both the preservation of her virtue and her defense of a single standard of sexual morality.

The satire directed against the minor characters is designed to prick various social and erotic pretensions. In the persons of Jerker's cousin, Jeffrey; Warrant, a law clerk; Spruce, a gentleman usher; and Littleword, a would-be lover and gallant, Nabbes clearly intended a low-life comic counterpoint to the lovers in the main plots. For example, Jeffrey espouses Jerker's "epicurean" credo and indiscriminately makes sexual advances to every woman in the play at a first meeting. Warrant and Spruce, in their pursuit of Lady Worthy's tippling maid, Susan, are tricked into a comic challenge and confrontation which results in an obvious attempt to reprise the *Twelfth Night* duel between Viola and Andrew Aguecheek. Similarly the secondary female characters are fashioned as contrasts to Dorothy and Lady Worthy: Mistress Tongall, the Covent Garden gossip and pander, and Susan, the drunken amorist, live in a mental world of materialism and bawdry far removed from the elevated aspirations of their social superiors.

The two most effective comic characters in the play have little to do with the central action, although both add greatly to the realism. The first of these, Dungworth, is a country gentleman who means to "turn Gallant" by selling "some few dirty Acres" so that he may "buy a knighthood," thus translating his "Farme of *Dirtall* into the Mannor of *No-place*." In various scenes we see him earning the "character" of the country gentleman who aspires unsuccessfully to be a city gallant—a character which his witty servant, Ralph, gives him in the mock trial with which the play ends. The other is Dasher, the host of an ordinary, whose "humour" is to raise the courtly complimenting of his guest to the level of a mania. It is in his tavern that the most theatrically accomplished scenes take place. There and only there does Nabbes shows signs of grasping the comic possibilities of the lively interplay and juxtaposition of characters and dialogue.

Nabbes's second attempt at comedy, *Tottenham Court*, is a better-constructed play. Despite the confusion generated by the conflicting information about the company that performed the play given on the variant issues of the title page for the second quarto edition in 1639, it was probably first staged in 1633 at the Salisbury Court theater, Fleet Street, by either the King's Revels or Prince Charles's Men. As in *Covent Garden*, the action involves the conflict of two standards of morality: that represented by two pairs of romantic lovers and a married couple of the citizen class and that followed by a group of debauched London gallants who make the three women of the first group the objects of their sexual pursuits.

Worthgood, a penniless but "deserving Gentleman," is eloping with his mistress, Bellamie, an heiress, when the play opens. As a result of a vigorous chase by her irate uncle, they lose each other in Marylebone Park and are not reunited until the final scene when the fortuitous death of Worthgood's rich uncle makes him an acceptable husband for Bellamie. The middle scenes concern the adventures of Bellamie and her companion, Cicely, the Marylebone keeper's daughter, who is really Worthgood's natural sister. In a device which looks back to such plays as Jonson's *The New Inn* and *The Case is Altered*, the two girls change identities and find themselves the objects of the attempted seductions by the city lechers: Frank, who is the chief spokesman for the consciousness of class differences that permeates the play and is finally reduced to contemplating marriage as a last resort to win Cicely's favors; George, an obese sensualist who boasts of having taken nineteen maidenheads; and James, a wild Inns of Court man who prefers dancing schools and playhouses to legal cases and documents.

It is clearly Nabbes's aim to present his audience with a lesson in morality. To this end he allows all the female characters to assert at length their idealistic erotic creed. Bellamie, the least colorful of the three, is the most consistent in her belief in the superiority of "the mind's brightness" over "outward beautie"; and Mistress Stitchwell, a Caroline descendant of the merry wives of Shakespeare and Jacobean city comedy, is equally intent on proving that "not every City Wife [is]/Wanton, that onely loves a merry life." It is Cicely, however, who emerges as the chief energetic and imaginative spokeswoman for the faith that "converse which love instructs the soule in" and not "enjoying for your senses pleasure" is the only sound basis for a happy marriage. And it is fitting that she should at the play's end be matched with Sam, Bellamie's brother, who also holds that "Love is a cement/That joynes not earthly parts above, but workes/Upon th' eternall substance, making one/Of two agreeing soules."

Yet while there is no doubting Nabbes's personal endorsement of such Platonic standards, it is striking how vigorously and colorfully all three women pretend to be prostitutes and cuckolding wife in order to gull their would-be seducers and bring them to a final abjurance of their roystering ways. These scenes are the liveliest in the play, and the reader is occasionally struck by the fact that these three models of female virtue do seem to know much about the trade of prostitution and its vocabulary. If Nabbes's plays are indeed the precursors of sentimental comedy as some critics have claimed, then Caroline sentimentality is a far cry from its eighteenth-century counterpart.

In one of the prologues to Nabbes's next play, *Hannibal and Scipio,* there are some lines which suggest that the playwright's financial circumstances had not been improved by his two comedies. He stresses his poverty and takes to task the nobility for not assuming their traditional duties as patrons of the arts. There is every sign too that he had a high opinion of and great hopes for his first tragedy. He draws the audience's attention to its classical features, to its elaborate changing scenery, to the musical interludes between the acts, and he strongly denies the rumors that he has based it on an earlier drama. Indeed, he does seem to have done a good deal of research in order to treat his "rich subject" with the dignity and high style he felt it deserved. There has been much scholarly discussion of possible sources for the play, and many candidates have been brought forward with varying claims to conviction; but Nabbes at least had a detailed knowledge of relevant sections of Plutarch, Livy, Appian, and possibly Polybius.

The paradigms of right conduct and the nature of virtue that subsume Nabbes's city comedies are also at the center of *Hannibal and Scipio,* though here they are treated with a consistently serious tone that strains for the effects of classical drama and the more striking elevations achieved by Shakespeare in his Roman plays. *Hannibal and Scipio* also has epic aspirations. For example, the Nuntius's narration of the Battle of Zama has Homer hovering behind it; Sophonisba's suicide in act three obviously aims at the effects of Cleopatra's final poetic deification; and Hannibal's denunciation of an ungrateful Carthage conveys a whiff of Coriolanus's bitter recriminations. The play is packed with sententious lines on such topics as danger, death, fate, fortune, and ambition which move rather effectively on occasion from their immediate dramatic context to attempt an encapsulation of eternal verities; such as these lines on history's repetitive patterns: "What a strange circulation/Is in time accidents? From victory/Peace is deriv'd; from peace security;/Thence lust, ambition; two maine grounds of jarres:/We fight for peace, and peace again breed's warres."

The episodes from the later careers of the two eponymous heroes that the play dramatizes are in effect illustrations of the belief that "Passion's the noble soules worst enemy." Hannibal's is the first demonstration of continence as in act one he castigates the lasciviousness and effeminacy of his soldiery at Capua. Then, after falling victim to the charms of a Capuan lady himself, he conquers his passion when he perceives that beauty and ease are

HANNIBAL
AND
SCIPIO.
AN HISTORICALL
TRAGEDY.

Acted in the yeare 1635. by the Queenes Majesties Servants, at their Private house in *Drury Lane.*

The Author *Thomas Nabbes.*

Arma virosque cano.

LONDON,
Printed by *Richard Oulton* for *Charles Greene,* and are to be sold at the white Lion in *Pauls* Church-yard. 1637.

Title page for the 1637 quarto edition of Nabbes's first tragedy (Sotheby Parke Bernet, 15 December 1982)

the "onely engines" to ruin military virtue. He foregoes his desire to destroy Rome because political virtue demands a conquest of himself and his personal ambitions. Yet in spite of his spiritual struggles, Hannibal is ultimately a victim of fate and his own pride; he is defeated at Zama, is betrayed into exile by the Carthaginian senate, and kills himself when he feels that his Herculean nature has been violated.

Scipio is clearly designed to contrast to his mighty opposite. He knows that "Fortune's an under power that is her selfe/Commanded by desert"; he recognizes, along with his admiration of the man, that Hannibal's pride is "that disease of vertue"; and at the height of his fame he retires to lead a contemplative life, thus adhering to his tenet that "Man/From outward accidents should not derive/The knowledge of himselfe: for so hee's made/

The creature of beginnings over which/His vertue may command."

On 12 May 1636 a particularly severe epidemic of the plague caused the London theaters to be closed by government restraint, a disastrous cessation of playing that lasted until 2 October 1637, except for one week's intermission in February 1637. The dramatist Richard Brome, a close friend of Nabbes, makes clear in some complimentary verses that the most interesting and original of Nabbes's dramas, *Microcosmus,* was one of the victims of this closure in that its first performance by the Queen's Men at the Salisbury Court theater was delayed. It must have been performed during that single week in February or when the theaters reopened in October.

Nabbes calls this work "A Morall Maske," which accurately describes its curious blend of court-masque and medieval-morality-play elements. At its basis are two commonplaces: the notion of man as microcosm or little world and the metaphor of life as rôles played on the great stage of the world. However, while acts two through five trace the career of an Everyman figure (Physander) acting out the pattern familiar in the psychomachia of the Middle Ages—prosperity-temptation-fall-repentance-salvation—the values demonstrated in the play are closer to those of the secular Tudor interludes than of their medieval stage antecedents. For example, both the vices and the virtues are drawn from the formulations of seventeenth-century natural philosophy rather than twelfth-century Christian doctrine. Thus Physander has to control Choler, Blood, Phlegm, and Melancholy and to cope with Bonus and Malus Genius. He falls prey to the earthy influences of the Five Senses, and tries to withstand the enticements of Sensuality. The characters who finally win him back to moral health have similar philosophical origins: Bellamina, his wife, and her allies, Prudence "the vertue of the mind," Fortitude, and grave Philosophy who "instructs [his] soule in Justice." Even when a familiar medieval dramatic figure, Conscience, makes an appearance, he is defined as "neither power, nor habit, but an act;/To wit an application of that knowledge/That shows the difference."

In the manner of their Tudor predecessors these moral abstractions slip easily and entertainingly into being recognizable human types speaking an idiom appropriate to some dominant "humour." So Seeing is a lubricious Chamberlain, Smelling a scatalogical countryman, Touching an usher-cum-pimp, and Tasting a cook with a relish for describing dishes in a way that induces nausea. And it is to these low-life creations that belongs the verbal vigor which is necessarily lacking in the prosing moral utterances of the virtues. This morality action is prefaced by act one which is virtually a self-contained masque in which Nature and Janus are horrified at the strife among their offspring, the Four Elements, and have to resort to Love, who brings harmony out of these seemingly "contrary matters."

On the evidence of the play's quarto (1637), the production was a very elaborate affair, or at least was intended to be by the author. In the book Nabbes details the striking symbolic costumes worn by each character and supplies the occasions for dramatically functional songs and dances. The staging must also have been spectacular with its fixed setting of "a perspective of ruins" within an arch "adorn'd with brasse figures of Angels and Divels," and the five moveable "scenes" which revealed to the audience by means of screens an appropriate tableau at the main points of psychological change in each act.

The success of *Microcosmus* may well have had a temporary effect for the better on Nabbes's material circumstances, for he married a woman named Bridget sometime in 1637 and was residing in the parish of St. Giles in the Fields, at which church his daughter was christened on 27 May 1638. Clearly he decided to work further the vein he had exploited in his morality play and produced two masques: *The Spring's Glory* and *A Presentation Intended for the Prince His Highness on his Birthday.* By this date the contest between Ben Jonson and Inigo Jones about the relative importance of poetic text and spectacular stage effects in the court masque had long been settled in Jones's favor. Nevertheless, Nabbes as a true "son of Ben" followed his master in emphasizing poetic dialogue at the expense of possible visual delights.

The Spring's Glory reworks the central theme of *Microcosmus.* Ceres and Bacchus represent the standards that are "sensuall onely," Venus and Cupid the love that "moves more in the soule." The claims of these two kinds of affection are submitted to Christmas and Shrovetide, who in a lively debate argue about the superior delights of their respective festivities and give their decision in favor of Bacchus and Ceres. But in an original twist Lent enters to vouch for Venus's supremacy. He introduces an antimasque dance of beggars and heralds Spring, who reconciles the principals and asserts both the traditional pleasures of her season and the virtues of temperance and Platonic love. There is no provision in the masque for the usual entrance of the amateur masquers to perform the final dance; rather Spring leads the others in a "measure" after which they all retire back into the "scene" of Spring herself. There is no evidence that this piece was ever intended for any special occasion. Indeed the absence of great possibilities for spectacle, of attendant masquers, and of any specifically directed compliment in the finale has persuaded at least one scholar that Nabbes may well have designed the text to be a "blank masque" which might be adapted to almost any celebration or even as an unparticularized masquelike entertainment for the public theater.

A Presentation Intended for the Prince, clearly a bid for Court favor in its flattery of the King's eight-year-old son, is made up of three sections. Time berates the almanac makers for not recording those actions "such as may/Challenge deserv'dly a peculiar day/To every owner" and instances the military exploits of the Black Prince. As punishment

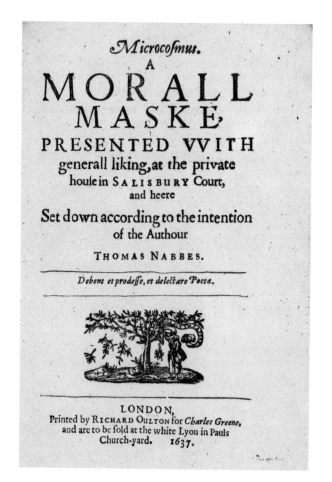

Title page for the 1637 quarto edition of Nabbes's most successful play (Henry E. Huntington Library and Art Gallery)

for their dereliction of duty they are changed into satyrs and perform an antimasque dance at the end of which they are forgiven and retransformed. In the third section Time introduces May, attended by Flora and Vertumnus, who speaks of Charles's royal future, and eight former Princes of Wales perform the final masque song and dance, concluding with the birthday wishes. Again there is no evidence of performance; and while it has been claimed that the Prince's own troupe (for whom Nabbes probably wrote *Tottenham Court*) may have performed it at one of their three Court appearances in November-December 1637, the fact that the Prince's birthday was on 29 May makes this suggestion questionable.

Nabbes's final comedy, *The Bride,* finds him still in pursuit of success, this time by attempting to appeal not to the usual private audience at the Phoenix or Cockpit theater but to the citizen and merchant class whom he hoped apparently to lure away from the delights of Bartholomew or Southwark Fairs during the summer vacation of 1638. So much is clear from his prologue with its aspersions on the "motions in the fayre" and its claim that the author wishes "t'expresse a Citizen a Gentleman."

At the heart of the play are the trials of two lovers, Theophilus and The Bride; but unlike the lovers in the earlier comedies, they derive their frustrations from within themselves as much as from the intrigues of an Iago-like villain, Raven, a cousin of Theophilus. The romantic situation and the direction of the plot are laid out in act one. Goodlove has pretended he wishes to marry The Bride so that he can gain the maximum dowry from her father and then present her to Theophilus, whom he believes to be his adopted son. Theophilus, unaware of his parent's intentions, is in love with The Bride; and, when he finds she reciprocates his affection, encouraged by Raven he elopes with her. The villainous Raven assures the audience that he intends to use this event to supplant his cousin as Goodlove's heir.

The central scenes are devoted to the lovers' struggles with their consciences, as they attempt to reconcile filial piety with their desire for each other and with Raven's schemes to blacken their characters. He manages to separate them by employing his gang of tavern "Blades" at whose hands The Bride narrowly escapes rape. She is subsequently assaulted by the lecherous French cook Kickshaw, and finally Raven tries to murder Theophilus. The last scene effects the reconciliation of the lovers with their parents, Goodlove's discovery that Theophilus is his real son, and the repentance and forgiveness of Raven.

There is no subplot in any real sense, though there is a group of miscellaneous figures only tenuously connected with the lovers' plight: Justice Ferret and his ignorant domineering wife; a pair of foreign merchants; Horton, "an owner of rarities and antiquities"; and "a nimble vintner," Squirrell. Each of these characters takes part in scenes that are palpably the result of the playwright's accurate observation of daily life in Caroline London; but they remain detached set pieces and never generate the liveliness of the low-life doings of *Tottenham Court*. The lovers are just as high-mindedly wedded to their Platonic principles as were their predecessors, though the verse in which they express their beliefs is noticeably more flexible and carries much greater conviction than in the earlier plays. The threat of violence and danger is more real, and the tone is generally darker; yet the reader gets the impression that the elements of evil are never taken to be more than a plot device. Nabbes clearly decided to use the materials of tragicomedy without feeling the responsibility to work out either their dramatic or moral implications.

In his last play, *The Unfortunate Mother*, Nabbes turned again to tragedy; but he greatly reduced his chances of success by placing on himself some rather strange limitations. He ostensibly used the subject matter of the kind of Italianate tragedy popular in the 1630s: lust, intrigue, political ambition, and revenge. But he consciously eschews the "liberty . . . from . . . new establisht custome" and aimed at only "plaine words, and language cleane" rather than "bumbast raptures swelling high." Further, he adheres to the classical ideal of "strict method in't, and every part/Serverely order'd by the rules of Art./A constant Scene: the businesse it intends/The two houres time of action comprehends."

Certainly Nabbes sticks to these principles he enunciates in his "Proeme to the Reader": there are no highly emotional verbal flights and there is very little more flamboyant action than one would find in a play by Racine. But the result is not passionate dignity, rather it is a flat statement of an emotional power and depth which are never successfully realized by either dramatic or verbal means.

The play attempts to link the political and erotic activities at the court of Ferrara. Corvino, a counsellor to the young Duke Macario, strives to get the power of the state into his own hands by a series of unconvincing intrigues: first, by pressing his daughter Melissa to marry the Duke; then by seeking the Dowager Duchess's hand in marriage; and finally by suggesting that one and then the other of his supposed sons—Curio, the court favorite, and Notho, the national military hero—should marry Melissa on the grounds that they are not her brothers but the illegitimate sons of the Duchess. These plans all fail and result in the deaths of his aide, the bawd Cardente, of his two adopted sons, and of the Duchess herself. The romantic elements are connected with the political intrigues only insofar as Corvino's plotting necessitates the breaking up of alliances desired by the young people: Melissa with Fidelio and Spurio with Amanda. A great deal of stage time is also taken up with the results of Amanda's mischievous hinting to Cardente that she is pregnant; but the series of misunderstandings as the bawd attempts to retail this gossip allusively to most of the principal characters seem spun out and stimulate only incredulity in the reader.

If Nabbes intended *The Unfortunate Mother* for production by Beeston's Boys he was disappointed; for the company apparently turned down the play. In 1640 he therefore published the text with a dedication to Richard Braithwaite referring to his resentment against the actors, his "Proeme" stating his dramatic ideals, and a series of commendatory verses (by Edward Benlowes among others) applauding the play's qualities and deploring the actors' decision.

This play was Nabbes's last work for the stage; and the meager official notices of his last days of existence make melancholy reading. The dramatist himself was buried in the parish of St. Giles in the Fields on 6 April 1641. The conditions in which he left his family may be gathered from the records of the burials of his daughter Bridget on 30 June 1642 and his son William on 29 August 1643, and from an entry in the parish's account books for relieving the poor: "1642 to Mrs. Nabbs, a poet's wife, her husband being dead . . . 1 shilling."

Nabbes seems never to have been popular in his own time. Although the writers of the commendatory verses in the quartos of his plays praise his work conventionally enough, there is no special conviction in their claims; and there is no record of any revivals of his works after his death. There was some reference to and quotation from his works in the eighteenth and nineteenth centuries, especially noteworthy being the attentions of Charles Lamb and Algernon Swinburne, and A. H. Bullen's edition of Nabbes's works. During the present century the resistance of his reputation to academic revaluation may perhaps be gauged by the fact that there have only been two book-length studies of him: one by Charlotte Moore in 1918, which is characterized by overpraise and academic dullness; the other R. W. Vince's unpublished dissertation, which stands as the fullest and best study to date but which can find little to admire when Nabbes is seen in the context of the Caroline stage.

References:

Gerald Eades Bentley, *The Jacobean and Caroline Stage* (Oxford: Clarendon Press, 1941-1968), IV: 927-944;

T. W. Craik and C. Leech, gen. eds., *The Revels History of the Drama in English* (London: Methuen, 1981), IV: 233-235;

John P. Cutts, "Thomas Nabbes's *Hannibal and Scipio*," *English Miscellany*, 14 (1963): 73-81;

Joe L. Davis, *The Sons of Ben: Jonsonian Comedy in Caroline England* (Detroit: Wayne State University Press, 1967), pp. 131-135, 137-140, 179-183;

John Freehafer, "Perspective Scenery and the Caroline Playhouses," *Theatre Notebook*, 27 (Spring 1973): 98-113;

Mina Kerr, *The Influence of Ben Jonson on English Comedy 1598-1642* (New York: Appleton, 1912);

T. J. King, "*Hannibal and Scipio* (1637): How 'The Places Sometimes Changed,'" *Theatre Notebook*, 29, no. 1 (1975): 20-22;

J. Koch, "Echte und 'unechte' Masken," *Englische Studien*, 58 (1924): 179-212;

Koch, "Thomas Nabbes, ein zu weinig beachteter Dichter," *Anglia*, 47 (1923): 332-382;

W. J. Lawrence, "The Origin of the Substantive Theatre Masque," *Pre-Restoration Stage Studies* (Cambridge: Harvard University Press, 1927), pp. 325-339;

Theodore Miles, "Place-Realism in a Group of Caroline Plays," *Review of English Studies*, 18 (November 1942): 428-440;

Charlotte Moore, *The Dramatic Works of Thomas Nabbes* (Menasha, Wisc.: George Banta, 1918);

Allardyce Nicoll, *Stuart Masques and the Renaissance Stage* (London: Harrap, 1937);

H. K. Russell, "Tudor and Stuart Dramatizations of the Doctrines of Natural and Moral Philosophy," *Studies in Philology*, 31 (January 1934): 1-27;

A. C. Swinburne, *Contemporaries of Shakespeare* (London: Heinemann, 1919), pp. 253-258;

R. W. Vince, "Morality and Masque: The Context for Thomas Nabbes's *Microcosmus*," *English Studies*, 53 (August 1972): 328-334;

Vince, "Thomas Nabbes's *Hannibal and Scipio*: Sources and Theme," *Studies in English Literature*, 11 (Spring 1971): 327-343;

Enid Welsford, *The Court Masque* (Cambridge: Cambridge University Press, 1927).

Thomas Randolph

(June 1605-March 1635)

Jill L. Levenson
Trinity College, University of Toronto

PLAY PRODUCTIONS: *Aristippus, or The Jovial Philosopher,* Trinity College, Cambridge, 1625 or 1626;

Hey for Honesty, Down with Knavery, Trinity College, Cambridge(?), circa 1626-1628(?);

The Drinking Academy, or The Cheaters' Holiday, London, Westminster(?), between 1626 and 1632(?);

Salting, Trinity College, Cambridge, between late September and mid November 1627;

The Conceited Pedlar, Trinity College, Cambridge, 1627;

The Muses' Looking Glass (The Entertainment), Cambridge, circa 1630(?); London, Salisbury Court theater, late 1630;

Amyntas, or The Impossible Dowry, London, Whitehall Palace, 1631(?);

The Jealous Lovers, Trinity College, Cambridge, March 1632.

BOOKS: *Aristippus, or The Joviall Philosopher. . . . To Which Is Added, The Conceited Pedlar* (London: Printed by T. Harper for J. Marriot, sold by R. Mynne, 1630);

The Jealous Lovers (Cambridge: Printed by T. & J. Buck, printers to the University of Cambridge, 1632);

Cornelianum dolium. Comœdia lepidissima, attributed to Randolph and R. Brathwait (London: Printed by T. Harper for T. Slater & L. Chapman, 1638);

Poems with The Muses Looking-Glasse: and Amyntas (Oxford: Printed by L. Lichfield for F. Bowman, 1638);

A Pleasant Comedie, entituled Hey for Honesty, Down with Knavery (London, 1651);

The Drinking Academy, or The Cheaters' Holiday, edited by Hyder E. Rollins, *PMLA,* 39 (December 1924): 837-871; republished, edited by Rollins and Samuel A. Tannenbaum (Cambridge: Harvard University Press, 1930);

The Fary Knight; or, Oberon the Second, attributed to Randolph, edited by Fredson Thayer Bowers (Chapel Hill: University of North Carolina Press, 1942).

Editions: *Poetical and Dramatic Works of Thomas Randolph,* 2 volumes, edited by W. Carew Hazlitt (London: Reeves & Turner, 1875)—comprises *Aristippus, The Conceited Pedlar, The Jealous Lovers, The Muses' Looking Glass, Amyntas, Hey for Honesty, Poems,* and *Oratio Praevaricatoria;*

The Poems and Amyntas of Thomas Randolph, edited by John Jay Parry (New Haven: Yale University Press, 1917)—includes *Praeludium;*

The Poems of Thomas Randolph, edited by G. Thorn-Drury (London: Etchells & Macdonald, 1929);

Salting, edited by Roslyn Richek, in "Thomas Randolph's *Salting* (1627), Its Text, and John Milton's Sixth Prolusion as Another Salting," *English Literary Renaissance*, 12 (Winter 1982): 113-126.

OTHER: Prologues, Epilogue, and Praeludium, attributed to Randolph, in *The Careless Shepherdess*, attributed to Thomas Goffe (London: Printed for Richard Rogers & William Ley, 1656).

"Of all the minor English poets of his century, Randolph may perhaps be considered as standing at the head." This assessment appears in the first modern edition of Thomas Randolph's works, edited by W. Carew Hazlitt (1875), and it accords with the playwright-poet's reputation during most of the seventeenth century. Until the Restoration, Randolph's literary skills were often compared favorably with those of such luminaries as Shakespeare and Ben Jonson. By the end of the century, however, his reputation went into decline, and it stayed there for the most part until the late-nineteenth and early-twentieth centuries, when a modest number of scholars became interested in his life and writings.

Gerald Eades Bentley has discovered plentiful evidence of Randolph's great popularity during his lifetime and for a generation afterward: numerous poems and anecdotes about Randolph's career occur in seventeenth-century commonplace books; his verses appear in a host of manuscript copies; and during the seventeenth century, almost a hundred allusions to him accumulated, the majority before the Restoration. G. Thorn-Drury, the editor of a 1929 collection of Randolph's poetry, explains that, "While Thomas Randolph was yet alive, and probably before he had completed his four-and-twentieth year, the poetical issue of his brain had been pronounced divine, comparable to Minerva, the issue of the brain of Jove, and before the end of his short life he had come to be regarded if not as the equal of Ben Jonson, at least as one who would be no unworthy successor to him. The tributes published after his death expressed such a sense of the loss to letters which it involved as I think has never attended the death of any other English poet."

According to the generally held seventeenth-century view, therefore, Randolph's early death snuffed out a literary career of extraordinary promise. But once Randolph's aura had faded, it never again regained anything like its original glow; and the few modern scholars who have shown interest in Randolph tend to concentrate rather on matters of fact about his life and works—dates, sources, establishing the canon—than on critical appreciations of his literary output. Their findings demonstrate that although Randolph's drama and verse were judged important by his own era, they have had little influence on English theater or letters since the seventeenth century.

While considerable evidence remains to attest to Randolph's popularity during the seventeenth century, few extant records provide reliable information about his career. As a result his short biography contains more lapses than substance, and its chronology at many points has not been settled. On 15 June 1605 he was either born or baptized as the eldest son of William Randolph (steward to Sir George Goring and to Edward, Lord Zouch) and his wife Elizabeth. At an uncertain date Thomas entered the illustrious Westminster School, which he attended with other potential belletrists such as William Cartwright, William Heminges, and Jasper Mayne. Before he left the school, he may have composed *The Drinking Academy* for performance by Westminster boys.

Anecdotes constitute the major source of data about Randolph's juvenile years, and, if they may be trusted, they indicate that he displayed striking precociousness in the writing of verse. When Randolph was nine years old, according to John Aubrey's report in his *Brief Lives*, "he wrote the history of our Saviour's incarnation in English verse. . . ." By the following year, the gifted child evidently composed English poetry extempore. One admirer pays tribute to the prodigy in lines accompanying the first edition of Randolph's poems (1638): "He lisped wit worthy the press as if that he/Had us'd his cradle for a library."

Randolph's schooling continued at Trinity College, Cambridge, where he was elected to a scholarship in spring 1623, admitted in April 1624, and matriculated in July 1624. His official connections with Cambridge lasted until 1631: he graduated with his B.A. in 1628, was elected a Fellow of Trinity in September 1629, and received his M.A. in July 1631, thus becoming incorporated at Oxford. Most of Randolph's poetry dates from his years at Cambridge, and it begins to appear soon after his arrival. In 1625, for example, he contributed verses to a Cambridge University collection on the marriage of King Charles; in 1626, he produced a long Latin poem for the collection on the death of Francis Bacon (whom he evidently knew).

During his early years at Cambridge, Randolph began to write plays, even though Puritan disapproval of theater had already collapsed the great age of university drama. He definitely composed three dramatic pieces at this time: *Salting, Aristippus,* and *The Conceited Pedlar;* and he may have written early versions of *Hey for Honesty, Amyntas,* and *The Muses' Looking Glass.* Immediately after his undergraduate years, Randolph's dramatic career becomes difficult to follow. Scholars cannot determine precisely how much time he spent in residence at Cambridge and how much in London, where he started to write plays for the professional theater. Sometime around late 1629 and certainly by 1630, he produced comedies for the King's Revels company: *Amyntas* and *The Muses' Looking Glass* were licensed for performance by this troupe during this period. (Bentley, modifying Fleay's conclusions, suggests that Randolph may have been the regular playwright for the King's Revels company at the Salisbury Court theater "perhaps as early as the end of 1629" but more likely 1630.) It appears that for awhile Randolph traveled regularly between London and Cambridge, living the contradictory roles of academic and professional dramatist, and that at one stage he sojourned in London.

While he spent time in London, Randolph had two notable experiences which recur in a number of anecdotes and verses. In the more frivolous episode his little finger was cut off in a tavern fray by an anonymous gentleman. This incident prompted two humorous poems by Randolph—"A finger's loss (I speak it not in sport)/Will make a verse a foot too short. . . ."—and one by his former Westminster schoolfellow Heminges. In the more important encounter Jonson adopted Randolph into the Tribe of Ben. Although this adoption happened in fact, narrative accounts about it are apocryphal. According to one often repeated version of the story by William Winstanley, an impoverished and embarrassed Randolph diffidently sought Jonson out at the Devil Tavern among his eminent poetic friends: "he peep'd in the Room where they were, which being espied by *Ben. Johnson,* and seeing him in a Scholars thredbare habit, *John Bo-peep,* says he, come in, which accordingly he did, when immediately they began to rime upon the meanness of his Clothes, asking him, If he could not make a Verse? and withal to call for his Quart of Sack; there being four of them, he immediately thus replied, 'I *John Bo-peep,* to you four sheep,/ With each one his good fleece,/If that you are willing to give me five shilling,/'Tis fifteen pence a

A nineteenth-century drawing of Randolph's birthplace, Newnham-cum-Badley in Northamptonshire

233

piece.' By *Jesus*, quoth *Ben. Johnson*, (his usual Oath) I believe this is my Son *Randolph*, which being made known to them, he was kindly entertained into their company, and *Ben. Johnson* ever after called him Son."

Randolph seems to have returned to Cambridge before July 1631, when he received his M.A. He wrote *The Jealous Lovers* for performance at Trinity in March 1632, and he delivered the commencement oration in July 1632. When he left Cambridge again at some point after the 1632 convocation, he may have stayed in London for a while, and also in the country; apparently he soon became tutor to the son of Capt. William Stafford of Blatherwick. Randolph died in March 1635 and was buried in Blatherwick Church on 17 March. After his death, the unverifiable opinion circulated that he had killed himself with dissipation. Typical of the consensus, Anthony à Wood's remarks in *Athenae Oxonienses* (1692) sum up Randolph's life as a promising but squandered literary endeavor. Referring to the drama and verses that Randolph had produced, Wood stated: "Several other things of the like nature . . . were expected from the said young poet Tho. Randolphe, but . . . indulging himself too much with the liberal conversation of his admirers (a thing incident to poets) brought him untimely to his end. . . ."

Randolph practiced his literary crafts during the Caroline period, a fact not always reflected in his theatrical works because he depended on earlier dramatic modes for almost every component of his plays. Throughout his short career, he turned to the classics—Aristophanes, Plautus, and Terence—for standards of plot, character, and satire; and he relied on prior English drama—from moralities and interludes to the plays of Shakespeare, Jonson, and Fletcher—for a variety of comedic patterns. Jonson's work exerted the greatest influence on Randolph's somewhat academic canon. Although it sometimes proves difficult to separate Jonson's effect from that of the classics, Jonson's humors and allegorical techniques appear distinctly in Randolph's plays. Like its models, most of Randolph's comedy evinces a serious dimension: it satirizes contemporary vices and follies with varying degrees of intensity.

One of Randolph's earliest dramatic efforts, *Aristippus, or The Jovial Philosopher* seems to have been prepared in 1625 or 1626 for a Cambridge audience; it often alludes to academic and specifically Cambridge matters. This one-act play with more than half-a-dozen speaking parts exists in two basically similar versions which manifest a few sig-

nificant differences: a manuscript preserves what appears to be the original text for student actors and audience; printed copies seem to represent the same comedy revised several years after it was written. John J. Parry describes the manuscript version as more satirical and chaotic than the published one: "Here we find jumbled together in hopeless confusion, humorous parodies of the text-books the students used in their college studies, satiric portrayal of the way in which these same students spent their leisure hours, ridicule of local characters well known to the college audience, disparaging allusions to Olivares, the Spanish prime minister and his general Spinola, much more biting attacks upon his ambassador Gondomar, and references to such delicate subjects as the unsuccessful expedition against Cadiz and the king's many attempts to raise money." Not surprisingly the printed text avoids giving offense by omitting or modifying objects of satire which were too delicate or outdated to appear in public. Six editions of *Aristippus* were published between 1630 and 1635, a sign that the little satire was popular even in its more tactful form.

Aristippus introduces itself through its praeludium as nothing more nor less than an amusing show (despite its content and its derivation from Aristophanes' satirical comedy *The Clouds*): "You need not fear this show, you that are bad—/It is no Parliament. . . ." and ". . . all my skill/Shall beg but honest laughter. . . ." Containing mere traces of a plot, this show offers a sequence of discourses—soliloquy, monologue, and dialogue, both long and short, prose with verse—by a handful of characters who supposedly represent various academic points of view: for instance, Aristippus stands for Arminianism, the Wild Man for Ramism. But the discourses actually focus upon less intellectual matters, as Aristippus holds forth, Falstaff-like, on the virtues of sack, and the Wild Man "stands up against the persecution of barley-broth, and will maintain a degree above the reputation of *aqua vitae.*"

The Conceited Pedlar, published with *Aristippus*, also exists in six early editions and a manuscript. Performed at Trinity College, Cambridge, on All Saints' Day 1627, the manuscript version was somewhat revised and cut for printing: the later form omits a few topical and academic references (although many erudite allusions remain) and includes a number of minor verbal alterations. Neither a play nor a show, *The Conceited Pedlar* is a benign satirical monologue in verse and prose delivered by the Pedlar (probably Randolph), who describes himself as "an *individuum vagum,* or the *primum mobile* of tradesmen, a walking-burse or movable exchange, a Socratical citizen of·the vast universe, or a peripatetical journeyman, that, like another Atlas, carries his heavenly shop on's shoulders."

Using his wares as metaphors, the Pedlar comments on a wide range of contemporary vices and follies, from dishonesty and ignorance in general to usury and the sale of church livings in particular. The looking glass which he brings forth and raises to the audience anticipates the governing idea of Randolph's later, full-length comedy *The Muses' Looking Glass,* where the mirror is a symbol of comedy which reflects human nature in order to improve it. In *The Conceited Pedlar* it represents simply an objective point of view which reveals the truth about moral and ethical weaknesses concealed by social behavior: "An usurer cannot see his conscience in it, nor a scrivener his ears. . . . Corrupt takers of bribes may read the price of their consciences in it."

Hey for Honesty, Down with Knavery was published sixteen years after Randolph's death by "F. J.," who remains unidentified. Although some critics have disagreed with the ascription to Randolph, various kinds of evidence—Randolph's name on the title page, stylistic parallels with his other works—have convinced the majority of scholars, including the play's most recent editor, Phyllis Brooks Toback (Ph.D. dissertation, New York University, 1971), of his authorship. "F. J." made changes in the original text of *Hey for Honesty* which prove difficult to isolate, except for the obvious allusions to events that occurred after Randolph's death. Nevertheless, this layered edition of Randolph's first full-length comedy, which he composed circa 1626-1628 possibly for a Cambridge audience, clearly reveals the playwright's dramaturgical themes and style.

A free translation of Aristophanes' *Plutus*— in fact, the first English rendering of this playwright's work—*Hey for Honesty* testifies to Randolph's continuing interest in classical literature. Directed toward antique comedy by his university education and the influence of Jonson, Randolph found in *Plutus* a comical satire which could be adjusted to comment on seventeenth-century society. He modified his source, which satirized the negative aspects of wealth, so that it became a critical reflection of contemporary inequities and corruption stemming from the acquisition of wealth.

In Randolph's plot, Chremylus, "an honest decayed gentleman," learns from Apollo's oracle how to repair his fortunes: he must follow the first man he encounters, who turns out to be Plutus, "the old blind God of Wealth," in disguise. By the time Chremylus celebrates his good fortune with virtuous neighbors—and dishonest acquaintances fail to rejoice—Randolph's narrative has established its patently allegoric level: Plutus regains his sight at the Temple of Esculapius; and the Goddess Poverty, revealing that her scepter has been destroyed, proceeds to lose the war she incites. As a result, knaves become poor and the Pope himself starves. At the conclusion, the defeated party of rogues and evildoers receives the ultimate affront when the God of Wealth appears married to Honesty.

More than twice as long as *Plutus, Hey for Honesty* adds sixteen characters not in its source to create a social spectrum. The range of dramatis personae, typical of Randolph's theatrics, extends from classical types to rustic English figures and contemporary stereotypical characters, from scholars and rascally servants to farmers, old women, and stage Puritans. Randolph creates an English ambience by adding not only familiar characters, but also numerous details—allusions to every phase of life in seventeenth-century England, and to many specific events and people—which combine to give a portrait of the age; and he sets the play in London.

As he modified *Plutus,* Randolph borrowed characters and details from his own earlier work and from the comedies of Jonson (for example, *Hey for Honesty* echoes both *Epicoene* and *Bartholomew Fair* at different points). Always eclectic in his working habits, he joined a classical play from mythological tradition with allegorical figures and conflicts from the morality play and a wealth of contemporary allusions. Unfortunately, one can only speculate vaguely about the reception of Randolph's heterogeneous comedy, because a mere reference survives to a performance at Oxford circa 1652.

The Drinking Academy, or The Cheaters' Holiday, not included in the early editions of Randolph's work, surfaced in an anonymous seventeenth-century manuscript which Hyder E. Rollins published in 1924 and edited with Samuel A. Tannenbaum in 1930. The play's humble advent has raised many questions about its background, particularly its authorship and date. The consensus of experts assigns this comedy to Randolph on the basis of correspondences in dramatic situation, ideas, characterization, and verbal style with the dramatist's known plays. But so far it has been impossible to determine where *The Drinking Academy* belongs chronologically in Randolph's career. Borrowings from Jonson's *The Staple of News* and James Shirley's *Love Tricks* point to a date of 1626 or after; imitation of *The Drinking Academy* in *The Jealous Lovers* fixes 1632 as the latest possible date; and the prologue (which may postdate the text) adds to the confusion by referring to Randolph's adoption into the Tribe of Ben, an event which happened at an undetermined time.

Like the question of date, that of performance remains unsettled. Scholars conjecture from the play's shortness (901 lines), its allusions to London rather than Cambridge, and its mechanics of production—an all-male cast, eight speaking parts (one with only two lines), few supernumeraries, and simple stage sets and properties—that it may have been performed originally by schoolboys, probably at Westminster. In June 1660 a play called *The Prodigal Scholar* was entered on the Stationers' Register with an attribution to Randolph; a number of critics think this lost comedy may be identical with *The Drinking Academy*.

The Drinking Academy shares part of its subject matter with Randolph's earlier show *Aristippus* and his later play *The Jealous Lovers:* all three dramatize events at a school which teaches young gentlemen how to engage in fashionable vices. In *The Drinking Academy*, Cavaliero Whiffe, master of the academy, claims that within two weeks he can instruct even Worldly, "an old doting vser" how "to drinke, quarrel roare and dice it as neatly as any gallant about the town. . . ." As the subject matter suggests, this brief five-act play is a high-spirited satire conforming with Randolph's other early works. Daniel C. Boughner has demonstrated that its principal topic had a foundation in the actual social life of seventeenth-century London, and other writers such as Thomas Dekker, Robert Greene, Ben Jonson, Thomas Middleton, and Thomas Nashe also treated it satirically: taverns served for the instruction of young men from the nouveaux riches who wanted to appear as gallants; their teachers were authentic gallants who had fallen upon economic hard times.

The Drinking Academy focuses on the gulling of Worldly, his prodigal son, Knowlittle, and Knowlittle's tutor, Whiffe, by a few swindlers with equally revealing names: Timothy Shirk (scoundrel), Tom Nimmer (filcher), and Jack Bidstand, a highwayman. Dressed as the god Plutus, the fury Alecto, and the ghost of Knowlittle's beloved Lady Pecunia, the three rogues frighten father, son, and tutor at a rendezvous in the suburbs in order to steal World-

ly's possessions and reduce the gentlemen to absurdity: "They shall . . . walke the woods without ther clothes/ . . . /Thre dayes thre nights during wich time if they/To any house or village take ther way./Ther bodies in to peces we will teare/And vnto hel with vs ther soules wee'l beare."

In the manner of *Hey for Honesty, The Drinking Academy* borrows heavily from Jonson's plays: *The Staple of News* constitutes the major influence, although Randolph's play also shows connections with *Every Man in His Humour, Every Man out of His Humour, Epicoene, Bartholomew Fair,* and *The Mask of Augurs.* Also, *The Drinking Academy* observes the unities with the conscientiousness of Jonson's *The Alchemist.* In addition, Randolph's comedy echoes Beaumont and Fletcher's *The Scornful Lady* and Shirley's *Love Tricks.* No source has been identified for the plot of *The Drinking Academy,* but a number of Randolph's scenes appear to derive from earlier plays and courtesy books, and Aristophanes' *The Clouds* may have affected the drama's conception.

Amyntas, or The Impossible Dowry represents a departure from Randolph's preceding comedies and a significant development in the history of seventeenth-century English drama. Experts in pastoral drama consider *Amyntas* one of the most important English experiments in the genre, classifying Randolph's play with Fletcher's *The Faithful Shepherdess* and Jonson's *The Sad Shepherd.* Lacking the kind of satire and the allegory that characterize Randolph's previous work, *Amyntas* fuses the conventions of Italian pastoral drama with those of English comedy. As Walter W. Greg notes, "Randolph insisted on treating the venerable proprieties of the pastoral according to the traditions of English melodrama." Randolph composed *Amyntas* during his London years, while he was growing familiar with the professional theater. Consequently, *Amyntas* smacks less of academe than Randolph's first plays (although he may have written it originally for a Cambridge audience); and its fusion of pastoral and comedy seems an attempt to popularize the Italian form for the English stage. Typically, Randolph borrows situations and characters from a variety of sources, in particular Tasso's *Aminta* and Guarini's *Pastor Fido.* For comic elements, he turns to his own earlier work and to Jonson. In this play, however, he skillfully constructs a complex, threefold plot which turns on the wrath of Ceres and Amyntas's ingenious explanation of an oracle.

The central action of *Amyntas* involves three pairs of lovers, each character individualized, whose adventures are kept distinct: each pair

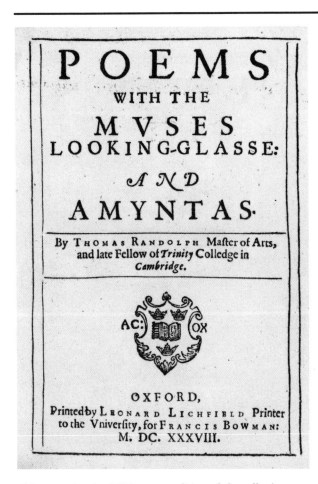

Title page for the 1638 quarto edition of the collection containing the two plays that Randolph wrote for the King's Revels company circa 1630 (Henry E. Huntington Library and Art Gallery)

Amyntas excels in dramaturgy, however, it makes almost no advances with its blank-verse dialogue, which is sometimes pointed with rhyme.)

Despite the originality of *Amyntas,* there are no records of the reception of its performances or the play's stage history. The title pages of printed editions indicate that the comedy was acted before the King and Queen at Whitehall, perhaps as one of three plays performed there by the King's Revels company in 1631; the prologue and epilogue suggest that it appeared as well at a regular theater. Apparently *Amyntas* was not revived in the seventeenth century, but an anonymous condensed prose version of the main action, called *The Fickle Shepherdess,* was performed by an all-female cast at Lincoln Inn Fields in 1703. Because *Amyntas* never appeared in print as a separate work, scholars cannot judge whether it won the approval of the reading public.

With *The Muses' Looking Glass,* Randolph again strikes out in a new direction, although he continues to use resources from his earlier plays. A self-reflective drama, *The Muses' Looking Glass* has been described by Joe Lee Davis as a comedy "primarily about the art of comedy. . . ." Like the plots of *Amyntas,* the action of *The Muses' Looking Glass* comprises a multitude of dramatic incidents and clearly distinguishes among its constituent parts. But *The Muses' Looking Glass* depends on different theatrical conventions which it shares with several analogues and probable sources. It presents a play within a play accompanied by its own master of ceremonies, Roscius, in the manner of Jonson's *Every Man out of His Humour,* Beaumont's *The Knight of the Burning Pestle,* Massinger's *The Roman Actor,* and Ford's *The Lover's Melancholy.*

In his comedy Randolph singles out two members of an audience at Blackfriars: Bird, who sells feathers, and Mistress Flowerdew, who sells pins and mirrors, both Puritan extremists opposed to the stage. Their presence allows the dramatist to engage in satire not only against Puritan theology, morals, and ethics, but also against aesthetic ignorance or literalism. The outer play thus returns to the satiric mode favored by Randolph in his dramatic works outside of *Amyntas;* and the inner play, which relies on allegory, also contributes to the satire. In about a dozen scenes, the inner play introduces twelve pairs of personified excesses and insufficiencies, deviants from the golden mean which Aristotle defined in his *Nicomachean Ethics.* According to Randolph's presentation, these deficiencies take shape as both vices and follies—for instance, Flattery, Peevishness, Presumption, De-

undergoes trials motivated by different causes and resolved in different ways. The main plot focuses on Amyntas, a shepherd, and Urania, a nymph who loves him; the minor plots concern Alexis and Laurinda, "a wavering nymph," as well as Damon (who loves Laurinda) and Amaryllis, "a distressed shepherdess," who loves Damon. In addition, a farcical subplot portrays Mopsus, "a foolish augur," and his beloved Thestylis, "an old nymph," and it unravels with the central action. The three serious plots contain comic elements, and the humorous tone of the whole play distinguishes *Amyntas* not only from Italian but from English pastoral as well. Sometimes Randolph's play parodies the very conventions in which it originated, as in its treatment of fairyland and a scene where Amyntas encounters the clowns. In the end it successfully combines dramatic modes ranging from tragicomedy and romantic comedy to farce and burlesque. (Although spair, Pride, Anger—which Roscius interprets, providing the play with a dimension of ethical and social commentary. As Davis points out, the inner play works like a dramatized book of Overburian characters. By the time it concludes with a dance of eleven Virtues, the two Puritans have been converted to accept drama and the stage.

During the process of this conversion, Randolph expresses his own views about comedy's means and ends. His attitude typifies classical and Renaissance theory on the subject: he believes that comedy should accomplish moral education in a pleasurable way. In short the genre should mirror contemporary life—especially its vices and virtues—reflecting human nature entertainingly in order to promote its improvement.

The Muses' Looking Glass, Randolph's own "comicall satyre" (Jonson's phrase), was first performed apparently in a Cambridge venue, then at London late in 1630 with the title *The Entertainment.* (Bentley argues that it opened the Salisbury Court theater after the lengthy plague closing of 14 April to 12 November and that it was introduced by Randolph's *Praeludium.*) The play assumed its present title upon publication in 1638. Between its London performance and its printing, Randolph made alterations to the text—for example, adding allusions to contemporary events—some of which may reflect the influence of William Prynne's *Histriomastix,* published in 1632. Prynne attacked four types of drama in a huge prose work that culminated Puritan hostility toward the stage, and in his revisions Randolph defends those four types in defining the qualities and purposes of dramatic art. Although scant information exists about the reception of *The Muses' Looking Glass,* evidence suggests that other seventeenth-century writers offended by Puritan extremism (such as Thomas D'Urfey) appreciated Randolph's defense. In the eighteenth century *The Muses' Looking Glass* was republished in 1706; scenes from it were performed at Covent Garden in 1748 and 1749; and it was revised as *The Mirror* by Henry Dell in the 1750s.

The Jealous Lovers is known far less for its plot, characterization, or style than for the hectic circumstances surrounding its first performance and publication. Among various entertainments, it was one of two plays written for production before King Charles and Queen Henrietta on their visit to Cambridge in March 1632. The second play, Peter Hausted's *The Rival Friends,* competed with *The Jealous Lovers* for first performance and won: it was acted by the students of Queens' College and then quickly published. In the course of establish-

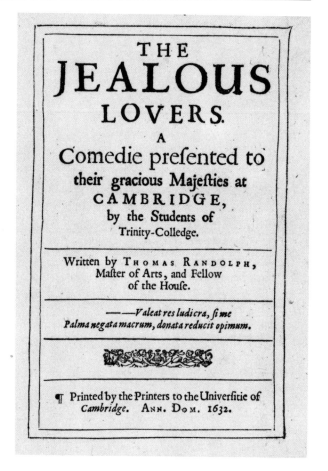

THE JEALOUS LOVERS.

A
Comedie presented to
their gracious Majesties at
CAMBRIDGE,
by the Students of
Trinity-Colledge.

Written by THOMAS RANDOLPH,
Master of Arts, and Fellow
of the House.

——*Valeat res ludicra, si me
Palma negata macrum, donata reducit opimum.*

¶ Printed by the Printers to the Universitie of
Cambridge. ANN. DOM. 1632.

Title page for the 1632 quarto edition of the Randolph play that was performed before King Charles I and Queen Henrietta Maria when they visited Cambridge in March 1632 (Henry E. Huntington Library and Art Gallery)

ing priority between the two plays, university officials became involved; a notorious academic quarrel ensued, and evidently as a result the vice-chancellor of Cambridge committed suicide. In this heated atmosphere, during one of the productions a gentleman with a lady on his arm was jostled by another gentleman, and this incident prompted another row. When the royal visit ended, the rivalry between the student factions of Trinity and Queens' continued. At convocation the following July, Randolph made his *Oratio Praevaricatoria* an attack on Hausted. When, at the end of 1632, Cambridge published *The Jealous Lovers*—revised since its performance—its title-page motto, prose dedications, dedicatory and commendatory verses, and an addition to the body of the text all referred to the animosity which must have persisted through the year.

The object of much of this attention, *The Jealous Lovers* borrows its complex intrigue pattern and many of its characters' names and types from Roman New Comedy. According to Alfred Harbage, "It is Plautine comedy pure and simple, . . ." albeit in blank verse. As usual, however, Randolph depends also on Jonson's dramaturgy. In this play he seems to use several of Jonson's characters as models: for example, Kitely in *Every Man in His Humour* for the jealous Tyndarus and Techmessa, and Asotus in *Cynthia's Revels* for his namesake in *The Jealous Lovers*. Randolph's comedy displays numerous other reflections of Jonson's work in its situations and conception of humors, and it contains several well-known echoes of *Hamlet*. But in the end, Randolph copies most extensively from himself: diction, characterization, and situation here derive mainly from *The Drinking Academy*, but *Amyntas* and *The Muses' Looking Glass* contribute as well.

On the whole, *The Jealous Lovers* differs from *Amyntas* in merging romance with Jonsonian elements. The romantic plot of the later comedy centers on two pairs of lovers—Evadne and Tyndarus, Techmessa and Pamphilus—whose courtships are obstructed by the jealous humors of Tyndarus and Techmessa. When jealousy subsides long enough to permit the lovers to wed, a statue of Hymen before them in the temple indicates disapproval by turning away. "What prodigies are these!," exclaims the priest, immediately before the threat of double incest is revealed: "This is not Tyndarus, but Demetrius' son,/Call'd Clinias, and fair Evadne's brother!/Evadne trusted in exchange to Chremylus,/For young Timarchus, whom Demetrius took/With him to Athens, when he fled from Thebes/To save the infants from the monster's jaws—/The cruel Minotaur." So the lovers change partners, "*The statue assents*," and the absurdity of the situation is enhanced by the match of Asotus, the play's prodigal-son figure, with Phryne, a courtesan. In addition to the prodigal son and his courtesan, Jonsonian characters include the pander, the gull, the cozener, and the cursed wife.

The vast sponsorship of its publication and the many verses appearing with the printed version and elsewhere suggest that *The Jealous Lovers* was very well received. In 1682 Aphra Behn revised the play for a performance at Dorset Garden; the text of this production is not extant.

Besides the dramatic works already cited, Randolph's canon includes three other items. His *Salting,* a college show discovered in a manuscript commonplace book by Fredson Bowers, was performed between late September and the first half of November 1627. A monologue of 316 lines primarily in iambic-pentameter couplets, it was part of a "salting" or initiation banquet for freshmen. After various introductory formalities, this piece continues with a series of twelve satirical sketches of named students as if they were dishes at the banquet. It concludes suddenly in the middle of a sketch. Randolph's *Praeludium* is a short dialogue of fewer than 200 lines, endorsed "T. Randall after ye last Plague" and published only once, by John J. Parry, in 1917. Bentley theorizes that this exchange between Histrio, an actor, and Gentleman, a theater patron, was Randolph's curtain raiser for the Salisbury Court theater when it reopened after the plague closing of 1630.

Randolph's poetry—much of it in print, some of it still being recovered from manuscripts as late as 1972—includes occasional poems, epithalamiums, epitaphs, elegies, and humorous verse. Within this body of work are three poems addressed to Jonson, and a group in the pastoral mode: dialogues, songs, eclogues, and an ode. Like his comedies, Randolph's poetry was influenced by classical models and Jonson, although some evidence indicates that he tried his hand at the metaphysical style. Assessing this portion of Randolph's canon, Douglas Bush concludes: "among the courtly and metaphysical poets he remained the precocious undergraduate. . . ."

In the tradition of many Renaissance literary canons, Randolph's contains some items assigned to him but not generally accepted as his. Of the four unsettled ascriptions, *The Prodigal Scholar* is a lost play known only by its 1660 Stationers' Register entry which attributes the work to Randolph. Fredson Bowers has made a circumstantial case for assigning to Randolph *The Fairy Knight, or Oberon the Second*, a play which he edited in 1942 from a unique manuscript. He argues from such evidence as sources, borrowings, and probable original date (he believes 1622-1624) that this comedy was first composed by Randolph and later transcribed and revised by another writer who remains unknown. *Cornelianum Dolium,* a witty Latin comedy mostly in prose, was ascribed to "T. R." by its printer in 1638. Although scholars have found in this play traces of Randolph's style and parallels with *The Jealous Lovers,* the attribution continues to appear extremely questionable. Similarly, the attribution of the prologues, epilogue, and praeludium accompanying *The Careless Shepherdess,* attributed to Thomas Goffe and published 1656, rests more on speculation than on substantial evidence.

The brevity of Randolph's life and canon allows few generalizations about his achievement. His dramatic career lasted less than ten years, bridging university plays and the professional theater. As a playwright, he depended on earlier models, and working from these he engaged modestly in experimentation with various dramatic genres. But his comedies remained consistently derivative; and as time went on, he borrowed not only from Aristophanes and Jonson, but also from his own previous work. A constant in his plays, satire modulates from the gentle parody of *Amyntas* to the serious moral and aesthetic comments of *The Muses' Looking Glass.* The principal target of his satire moves from university life to contemporary society. In the process, Randolph tried out a number of dramatic forms, extending from simple monologue to play within play, complex intrigue, and multilayered romance. But he seems always to have conceived his purpose as moral instruction conveyed in forms designed to give pleasure. The player Roscius articulates his author's point of view in *The Muses' Looking Glass:* "Boldly, I dare say,/There has been more by us in some one play/Laugh'd into wit and virtue, than hath been/By twenty tedious lectures drawn from sin/And foppish humours: hence the cause doth rise,/Men are not won by th' ears so well as eyes."

Bibliographies:

Samuel A. Tannenbaum and Dorothy R. Tannenbaum, *Thomas Randolph*, Elizabethan Bibliographies, no. 38 (New York: Privately printed, 1947);

Rachel Fordyce, *Caroline Drama: A Bibliographic History of Criticism* (Boston: G. K. Hall, 1978);

Terence P. Logan and Denzell S. Smith, eds., *The Later Jacobean and Caroline Dramatists: A Survey and Bibliography of Recent Studies in English Renaissance Drama* (Lincoln & London: University of Nebraska Press, 1978), pp. 251-253.

References:

Gerald Eades Bentley, *The Jacobean and Caroline Stage: Plays and Playwrights*, volume 5 (Oxford: Clarendon Press, 1956): 964-993;

Bentley, "Randolph's *Praeludium* and the Salisbury Court Theatre," in *Joseph Quincy Adams Me-* *morial Studies,* edited by James G. McManaway, Giles E. Dawson, and Edwin E. Willoughby (Washington, D.C.: Folger Shakespeare Library, 1948), pp. 775-783;

Daniel C. Boughner, "*The Drinking Academy* and Contemporary London," *Neophilologus,* 19 (October 1934): 272-283;

Fredson Bowers, "Thomas Randolph's *Salting,*" *Modern Philology,* 39 (February 1942): 275-280;

Joe Lee Davis, *The Sons of Ben: Jonsonian Comedy in Caroline England* (Detroit: Wayne State University Press, 1967);

Walter W. Greg, *Pastoral Poetry & Pastoral Drama: A Literary Inquiry, with Special Reference to the Pre-Restoration Stage in England* (London: Bullen, 1906), pp. 282-296;

Karl Kottas, *Thomas Randolph: sein Leben und seine Werke* (Vienna & Leipzig: W. Braumüller, 1909);

Kathryn Anderson McEuen, *Classical Influence upon the Tribe of Ben: A Study of Classical Elements in the Nondramatic Poetry of Ben Jonson and His Circle* (Cedar Rapids: Torch Press, 1939);

John J. Parry, "A New Version of Randolph's *Aristippus,*" *Modern Language Notes,* 32 (June 1917): 351-354;

G. C. Moore Smith, "The Canon of Randolph's Dramatic Works," *Review of English Studies,* 1 (July 1925): 309-323;

Smith, *Thomas Randolph*, Wharton Lecture on English Poetry, British Academy (London: Oxford University Press, 1927).

Papers:

The British Library has manuscripts for *Aristippus* (MS Sloane 2531, fols. 124-140b), *The Conceited Pedlar* (MS Add. 27406), and Randolph's *Praeludium* (MS Add. 37425, fols. 54-55). Another manuscript for *The Conceited Pedlar* is at the University of Edinburgh (MS Laing, iii. 493). The Henry E. Huntington Library and Art Gallery has a manuscript for *The Constant Lovers* in the manuscript commonplace book of Constance Astor (H.M. 904) and a manuscript for *The Drinking Academy* (H.M. 741). The manuscript for *The Fairy Knight,* attributed to Randolph by Fredson Bowers, is at the Folger Shakespeare Library (MS 46.1).

William Rowley

(circa 1585-February 1626)

T. H. Howard-Hill
University of South Carolina

PLAY PRODUCTIONS: *The Travels of the Three English Brothers,* by Rowley, John Day, and George Wilkins, London, Curtain theater, 1607;

A Shoemaker a Gentleman, London, Red Bull theater, circa 1608;

Fortune by Land and Sea, by Rowley and Thomas Heywood, London, Red Bull theater, circa 1609;

A New Wonder, A Woman Never Vexed, London, circa 1611-1614;

Hymen's Holiday or Cupid's Vagaries, London, circa 1612;

The Fool Without Book, London, circa 1613;

A Knave in Print or One for Another, London, circa 1613;

The Birth of Merlin, by Rowley and possibly William Shakespeare, London, Globe(?) theater, circa 1613-1615;

Wit at Several Weapons, by Rowley and Thomas Middleton, London, circa 1613-1615;

A Fair Quarrel, by Rowley and Middleton, London, Hope(?) theater, circa 1617;

The Old Law, or A New Way to Please You, by Rowley and Middleton, London, circa 1618;

All's Lost by Lust, London, circa 1619;

The World Tossed at Tennis, by Rowley and Middleton, London, Cockpit theater, 1620;

The Witch of Edmonton, by Rowley, John Ford, and Thomas Dekker, London, Cockpit theater, 1621;

The Changeling, by Rowley and Middleton, London, Cockpit theater, 1622;

A Match at Midnight, London, Red Bull theater, circa 1622;

The Maid in the Mill, by Rowley and John Fletcher, London, Globe theater, 1623;

The Four Honourable Loves, London, circa 1623;

The Nonesuch, London, circa 1623;

The Late Murder in Whitechapel or Keep the Widow Waking, London, Red Bull theater, 1624;

A Match or No Match, London, Fortune theater, 1624;

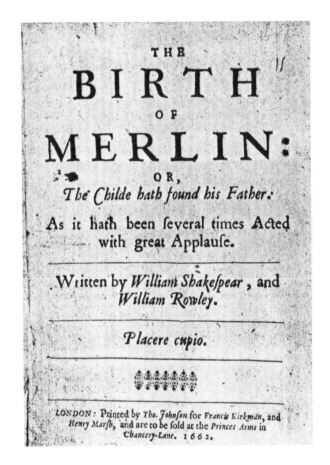

Title page for the 1662 quarto edition of the play on which Rowley may have collaborated with Shakespeare (British Library)

A Cure for a Cuckold, by Rowley and John Webster, London, circa 1624-1625.

BOOKS: *The Travailes of the Three English Brothers. Sir Thomas, Sir Anthony, M*^r^*. Robert Shirley,* by Rowley, John Day, and George Wilkins (London: Printed by G. Eld for J. Wright, 1607);

A Search for Money. Or The Lamentable Complaint for the Losse of Mounsieur l'Argent (London: Printed by G. Eld for T. Hunt, 1609);

241

A Faire Quarrell, by Rowley and Thomas Middleton (London: Printed by G. Eld for J. Trundle, sold by E. Wright, 1617);

A Courtly Masque: the Device Called the World Tost at Tennis, by Rowley and Middleton (London: Printed by G. Purslowe, sold by E. Wright, 1620);

For a Funerall Elegie on the Death of Hugh Atwell, Seruant to Prince Charles (London, 1621);

A New Wonder, A Woman Never Vext (London: Printed by G. Purslowe for F. Constable, 1632);

A Match at Mid-Night. A Pleasant Comedie (London: Printed by A. Mathewes for W. Sheares, 1633);

A Tragedy Called All's Lost by Lust (London: Printed by T. Harper, 1633);

A Merrie and Pleasant Comedy: Called A Shoo-Maker a Gentleman (London: Printed by J. Okes, sold by J. Cowper, 1638);

Wit at Several Weapons, by Rowley and Middleton; *The Maid in the Mill,* by Rowley and John Fletcher; in *Comedies and Tragedies Written by Francis Beaumont and John Fletcher, Gentlemen* (London: Printed for Humphrey Robinson & Humphrey Moseley, 1647);

The Changeling, by Rowley and Middleton (London: Printed for Humphrey Moseley, 1647);

Fortune by Land and Sea, by Rowley and Thomas Heywood (London: Printed for John Sweeting & Robert Pollard, 1655);

An Excellent Comedy, Called The Old Law, or A New Way to Please You, by Rowley and Middleton (London: Printed for Edward Archer, 1656);

The Witch of Edmonton, by Rowley, John Ford, and Thomas Dekker (London: Printed by J. Cottrel for Edward Blackmore, 1658);

A Cure for a Cuckold, by Rowley and John Webster (London: Printed by Thomas Johnson, sold by Francis Kirkman, 1661);

The Birth of Merlin, by Rowley and possibly William Shakespeare (London: Printed by T. Johnson for F. Kirkman & H. Marsh, 1662).

Editions: *William Rowley, His "All's Lost by Lust" and "A Shoemaker a Gentleman,"* edited by Charles W. Stork (Philadelphia: University of Pennsylvania, 1910);

The Changeling, by Rowley and Middleton, edited by Nigel W. Bawcutt (London: Methuen, 1958);

A Fair Quarrel, by Rowley and Middleton, edited by R. V. Holdsworth (London: Benn, 1974).

OTHER: John Taylor, *Great Britaine, all in Blacke. For the Incomparable Losse of Henry, Our Late Worthy Prince,* second edition, includes poems by Rowley (London: Printed by E. Allde for J. Wright, 1612).

Early dramatic historians placed William Rowley in the third rank of dramatic writers, and recent critics, who admire his contributions to the collaborations of his later years, have not significantly improved his standing. Four plays which Rowley wrote unaided have survived—*A Shoemaker a Gentleman, All's Lost by Lust, A Match at Midnight,* and *A New Wonder, A Woman Never Vexed*—but the greater part of his reputation was won as collaborator with some of the leading playwrights of his time. The most notable of these was Thomas Middleton, with whom Rowley wrote his two most highly regarded works, *A Fair Quarrel* and *The Changeling.* Proper appreciation of his place in dramatic history has been hampered by scanty biographical information and some difficulty in identifying his collaborations and his share in them. Nevertheless, Rowley's place in theatrical history is assured by his prominence as an actor-manager, particularly as the actor of fat-clown parts that he wrote himself or were written for him, and as a representative of that class of seventeenth-century dramatist which provided the everyday entertainments of the public stage.

The only certain facts in Rowley's biography derive from theatrical records, the early publication of plays where he was named as author, and the record of his burial at St. James's in Clerkenwell on 11 February 1626. His date of birth is conjectured from the licensing of his first collaboration, a topical play entitled *The Travels of the Three English Brothers,* with John Day and George Wilkins, on 29 June 1607. This play was performed by the Queen Anne's company of players at their theater, The Curtain. Since Rowley's comedy *A Shoemaker a Gentleman* (produced circa 1608) and his collaboration with Thomas Heywood, *Fortune by Land and Sea* (produced circa 1609), another comedy, were apparently written for the same company, it is inferred (by Gerald Eades Bentley) that he was an actor with the company. In any event by the middle of 1609 Rowley was in a position of some responsibility with the Prince Charles's Men, a fact which implies that he had had previous professional experience. He remained with the Prince Charles company until around 1623, writing, usually for the company and usually with a collaborator, the comedy *Wit at Several Weapons* (produced circa

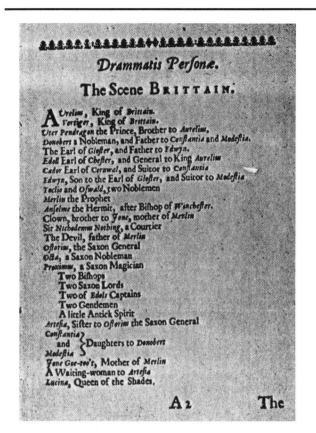

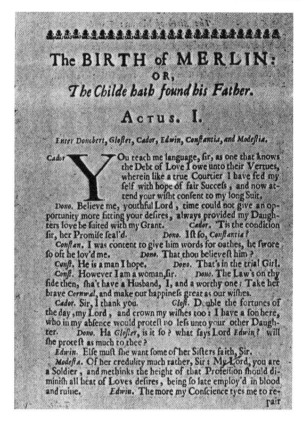

Drammatis Personæ.

The Scene BRITTAIN.

Aurelius, King of *Brittain*.
Vortiger, King of *Brittain*.
Uter Pendragon the Prince, Brother to *Aurelius*,
Donobert a Nobleman, and Father to *Constantia* and *Modestia*.
The Earl of *Gloster*, and Father to *Edwyn*.
Edoll Earl of *Chester*, and General to King *Aurelius*
Cador Earl of *Cornwal*, and Suitor to *Constantia*
Edwyn, Son to the Earl of *Gloster*, and Suitor to *Modestia*
Toclio and *Oswald*, two Noblemen
Merlin the Prophet
Anselme the Hermit, after Bishop of *Winchester*.
Clown, brother to *Jone*, mother of *Merlin*
Sir *Nichodemus Nothing*, a Courtier
The Devil, father of *Merlin*
Ostorius, the Saxon General
Octa, a Saxon Nobleman
Proximus, a Saxon Magician
   Two Bishops
   Two Saxon Lords
   Two of *Edols* Captains
   Two Gentlemen
   A little Antick Spirit
Artesia, Sister to *Ostorius* the Saxon General
Constantia}
  and }Daughters to *Donobert*
Modestia}
Jone Goe-too's, Mother of *Merlin*
A Waiting-woman to *Artesia*
Lucina, Queen of the Shades.

A2   The

The BIRTH of MERLIN:
OR,
The Childe hath found his Father.

ACTUS. I.

Enter Donobert, Gloster, Cador, Edwin, Constantia, and Modestia.

Cador. YOu teach me language, sir, as one that knows
the Debt of Love I owe unto their Vertues,
wherein like a true Courtier I have fed my
self with hope of fair Succeis, and now attend your wisht consent to my long Suit.
  Dono. Believe me, youthful Lord, time could not give an opportunity more fitting your desires, always provided my Daughters love be suited with my Grant.   *Cador.* 'Tis the condition
sir, her Promise seal'd.   *Dono.* Ist so, *Constantia?*
  Constan. I was content to give him words for oathes, he swore
so oft he lov'd me.   *Dono.* That thou believest him?
  Const. He is a man I hope.   *Dono.* That's in the trial Girl.
  Const. However I am a woman, sir.   *Dono.* The Law's on thy
side then, sha't have a Husband, I, and a worthy one: Take her
brave *Cornwal*, and make our happiness great as our wishes.
  Cador. Sir, I thank you.   *Glost.* Double the fortunes of
the day, my Lord, and crown my wishes too: I have a son here,
who in my absence would protest no less unto your other Daughter.   *Dono.* Ha *Gloster*, is it so? what says Lord *Edwin*? will
she protest as much to thee?
  Edwin. Else must she want some of her Sisters faith, Sir.
  Modesta. Of her credulity much rather, Sir: My Lord, you are
a Soldier, and methinks the height of that Profession should di-
minish all heat of Loves desires, being so late employ'd in blood
and ruine.   *Edwin.* The more my Conscience tyes me to repair

The Birth of Merlin:

pair the worlds losses in a new succession. *Modest.* Necessity it
seems ties your affections then, and at that rate I would unwilling-
ly be thrust upon you, a wife is a dish soon cloys, sir.
  Edwin. Weak and diseased appetites it may.   *Modest.* Most
of your making have dull stomacks sir.   *Dono.* If that be all Girl,
thou shalt quicken him, be kinde to him *Modesta*: Noble *Edwin*, let
it suffice what's mine in her, speaks yours;
For her consent, let your fair suit go on,
She is a woman sir, and will be won.   *Enter Toclio.*
  Edwin. You give me comfort sir.   *Dono.* Now *Toclio.*
  Toclio. The King, my honor'd Lords, requires your presence, and
calls a Council for return of answer unto the parling enemy,
whose Embassadors are on the way to Court.   *Dono.* So suddenly, *Chester* it seems has ply'd them hard at war, they sue so fast for
peace, which by my advice they ne're shall have, unless they leave
the Realm. Come noble *Gloster*, let's attend the King, it lies sir in
your Son to do me pleasure, and save the charges of a Wedding
Dinner,
If you'l make haste to end your Love affairs,
One cost may give discharge to both my cares.   *Exit Dono. Glost.*
  Edwin. I'le do my best.   *Cador.* Now *Toclio*, what stirring
news at Court?   *Toclio.* Oh my Lord, the Court's all fill'd with
rumor, the City with news, and the Country with wonder, and all
the bells i'th' Kingdom must proclaim it, we have a new Holy-
day a coming.   *Consta.* A holy-day! for whom? for thee?
  Toclio. Me, Madam! 'sfoot I'de be loath that any man should
make a holy-day for me yet: In brief 'tis thus, there's here arriv'd
at Court, sent by the Earl of *Chester* to the King, a man of rare e-
steem for holyness, a reverent Hermit, that by miracle not onely
saved our army, but without aid of man o'rethrew the pagan Host,
and with such wonder sir, as might confirm a Kingdom to his faith.
  Edwin. This is strange news indeed, where is he?
  Toclio. In conference with the King that much respects him.
  Modest. Trust me, I long to see him.   *Toclio.* Faith you will
finde no great pleasure in him, for ought that I can see Lady, they
say he is half a Prophet too, would he could tell me any news of
the lost Prince, there's twenty Talents offer'd to him that finds
him.   *Cador.* Such news was breeding in the morning.
                        Toclio.

Dramatis personae and beginning of act one from the 1662 quarto edition of The Birth of Merlin *(British Library)*

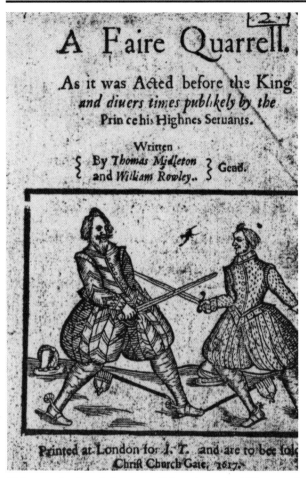

Title page for the 1617 quarto edition of one of Middleton and Rowley's most successful collaborations (Henry E. Huntington Library and Art Gallery)

1613-1615) with Middleton, *A New Wonder, A Woman Never Vexed* (produced circa 1611-1614; previously dated 1625 for no good reason but quite convincingly redated by George Cheatham), the tragicomedy *A Fair Quarrel* (produced circa 1617) and the comedy *The Old Law* (produced circa 1618) with Middleton, his tragedy *All's Lost by Lust* (produced circa 1619), the masque *The World Tossed at Tennis* (produced in 1620) with Middleton, and the tragicomedy *The Witch of Edmonton* (produced in 1621) with Thomas Dekker and John Ford. Rowley's major work, the tragedy of *The Changeling*, was written with Middleton in 1622 for the Lady Elizabeth's company, the successor of the Prince's Men, and was followed by a comedy, *A Match at Midnight*, in the same year. In 1623 he collaborated with John Fletcher on *The Maid in the Mill*, a comedy for the King's Men, his new company; around 1624 or 1625 he wrote another comedy, *A Cure for a Cuckold*, with John Webster.

To the above may be added the following lost comedies listed in Samuel Schoenbaum's 1964 revision of Alfred Harbage's *Annals of English Drama* with their conjectured dates of composition: *Hymen's Holiday, or Cupid's Vagaries* (1612), *A Knave in Print or One for Another* (1613), *The Fool Without Book* (1613), *The Four Honourable Loves* (1623), *The Nonesuch* (1623), *The Late Murder in Whitechapel, or Keep the Widow Waking* (1624; a comedy and tragedy with Dekker, Ford, and Webster), and—if not by Samuel Rowley (to whom he was not related)—*A Match or No Match* (1624). Rowley has often been assigned a share in *The Spanish Gypsy*, a tragicomedy licensed for performance on 9 July 1623, but David J. Lake finds it a Ford-Dekker collaboration, while MacDonald P. Jackson says it is "probably the work of Ford and another dramatist—Dekker, Rowley, or Brome." Because the evidence of Rowley's collaboration is very slight, it is probably best to exclude it from consideration among his works (although Michael E. Mooney's dissertation discusses it). On the other hand Dewar M. Robb finds convincing evidence of Rowley's hand in the scenes containing the clown and the story of Merlin's birth in the romance *The Birth of Merlin*, attributed to Shakespeare and Rowley by the publisher Francis Kirkman in a 1661 playlist. The composition date of the play has been placed variously between 1608 and 1621, Mark Dominik (who supports the title-page attribution) placing it in 1613-1615 (Shakespeare died in April 1616). Jackson concludes that "a poet and dramatist of stature must have participated with Rowley in *The Birth of Merlin*, but his identity remains unknown." The date of composition and the precise extent of Rowley's share in the play remain doubtful even though it is similar in its use of romance material drawn from fabulous English history to Rowley's unaided *A Shoemaker a Gentleman*.

His nondramatic works include the mildly satirical pamphlet, *A Search for Money* (1609), verses on the death of Prince Henry printed in John Taylor's *Great Britain All in Black* (1612) and in William Drummond's compilation *Mausoleum or the choicest Flowers of the Epitaphs Written on the Death of . . . Prince Henry* (1613). Publications more nearly related to his professional activities include a couplet on the death of Thomas Greene, a fellow comedian of Queen Anne's company, that he contributed to Joshua Cooke's *Green's Tu Quoque* (1614), his *Funeral Elegy on the Death of Hugh Atwell* (1621), his fellow in the Prince Charles's company, and commendatory verses for the 1623 edition of Webster's *The Duchess of Malfi*. The small extent of his writ-

Title page for a 1620 quarto edition of the masque in which Rowley may have acted the part of Simplicity, probably the figure at far right in the woodcut above (from an undated Pickering & Chatto catalogue)

ings, their occasional character, and the fact that he paid little if any attention to the publication of his plays suggests that he regarded himself primarily as an actor who occasionally wrote plays rather than as a dramatist. The kind and quality of his dramatic achievement make the conclusion easy to accept.

Because of his acting specialization and probably the effect of increasing age on his girth, Row-

ley's plays contain good roles for fat clowns. He acted Plumporridge in Middleton's *The Inner Temple Masque* (produced in 1619) and the Fat Bishop in Middleton's *A Game at Chess* (produced in 1624), a role apparently added to the play for his benefit. Thomas W. Baldwin assigns him parts in other plays. He also acted the part of Jacques, "a simple clownish gentleman," in his own *All's Lost by Lust,* possibly Simplicity's part in *The World Tossed at Ten-*

nis (according to Bentley, but Richard H. Barker disagrees), and Bustopha in *The Maid in the Mill*. Lollio in *The Changeling*, "Young Cuddy Banks, the Clown" in *The Witch of Edmonton*, Roger in *A Woman Never Vexed*, the Clown in *Fortune by Land and Sea*, and Sin in *A Match at Midnight* also exemplify Rowley's interest in clownish characters.

From studies by Robb and, more recently, Lake and Jackson in relation to Rowley's connection with the Middleton canon, Rowley's part in his collaborations is fairly well defined. Nevertheless, in collaborative works there must always occur questions about responsibility for the original conception and plot of the play, or of the extent to which one collaborator revised the work of another. These questions do not arise with Rowley's unaided works which, therefore, would seem to point clearly to his part in the collaborative works. However, there can be little doubt that Rowley was more successful in bending his talents to those of superior dramatists such as Dekker, Ford, and Middleton than he was when writing alone.

That Rowley should be famed mainly for his comedies is appropriate not only to his own contributions to that genre in his own and collaborative works alike but also to his comparative lack of prowess in the tragic kind. *All's Lost by Lust* is an early dramatic treatment of a theme which attracted much attention from later writers, as Charles A. Stork mentions, but the conquest of Spain by the Moors led by Muly Mumen serves merely as an occasion that assists Roderigo, King of Spain, to send his general Julianus out of the way in order to rape his daughter Jacinta. To revenge himself on the King, Julianus enlists the defeated Moors to aid him, but eventually he is betrayed by Muly Mumen who tricks him into killing his own daughter. This variation on the old Appius and Virginia situation is more sensational than satisfying, and the success of *All's Lost by Lust* on the contemporary stage is evidence rather of the degradation of tragedy in the middle of the century than of dramatic merit. Rowley's small achievement in this play makes his participation in *The Changeling* only a few years afterward all the more remarkable.

On the other hand, the comic elements of *A Shoemaker a Gentleman* retain a boisterous appeal which goes far to mitigate the sentimental piety of the main romantic plot. Maximinus and Dioclesian, the Emperors of Rome, are devoted to suppressing the British Christians, and Winifred, "a Virgin of Wales," Saint Hugh, and Saint Alban come to appropriate ends in the play; their story was drawn partly from Holinshed's chronicle history and

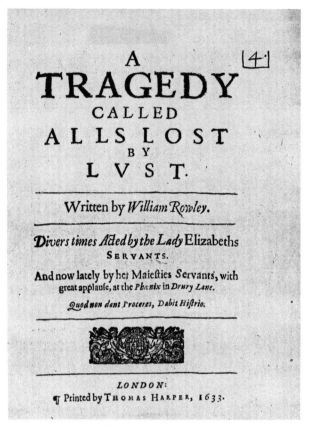

Title page for the 1633 quarto edition of the only surviving tragedy written solely by Rowley (Anderson Galleries, sale no. 1405, 4-5 March 1919)

partly from Thomas Deloney's *The Gentle Craft* (circa 1598). For the ostensibly realistic comic elements of the plot, the house of shoemakers (in which the sons of the defeated King of Britain find refuge and at last fame and restoration of their dignities), Rowley depended mainly on Deloney's first tale of patriotic shoemakers (the source also of Thomas Dekker's *The Shoemakers' Holiday* eight or nine years before). The master shoemaker, Sisley, his wife, and their men, Barnaby (especially) and Raph, are rendered with broad, often bawdy humor as figures of characteristic English common humanity: they have a vigor that does not animate the other conventional personages of the romantic comedy. The printer of the first edition of 1638 claimed that its frequent performances met with much applause, and it is easy to believe that Rowley's undemanding but satisfying romantic play appealed to the patriotic artisans to whom mainly it seems to have been directed.

The central character of *A Woman Never Vexed* is a widow who, having been blessed by fortune

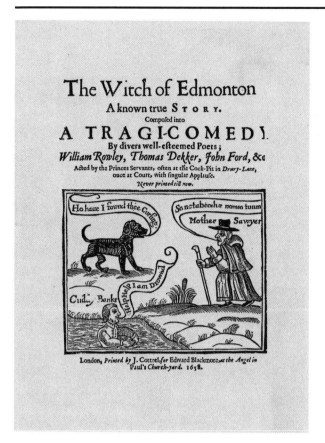

The Witch of Edmonton
A known true S T O R Y.
Compofed into
A TRAGI-COMEDY.
By divers well-efteemed Poets;
William Rowley, Thomas Dekker, John Ford, &c
Acted by the Princes Servants, often at the Cock-Pit in *Drury-Lane,*
once at Court, with fingular Applaufe.
Never printed till now.

London, *Printed by* J. Cottrel, *for* Edward Blackmore, *at the Angel in*
Paul's Church-yard. 1658.

*Title page for the 1658 quarto edition of the play in which
Rowley acted the part of "Young Cuddy Banks, the Clown"
(Fredson Bowers, ed.,* The Dramatic Works of Thomas
Dekker, *volume 3, 1958)*

and escaped the "many tribulations" promised in a biblical passage, marries Stephen Foster, a profligate, in the hope of receiving her portion of woes. However, marriage almost immediately transforms him into an exemplary husband and careful manager of his wife's estate. After resolution of quarrels and misfortunes involving his brother, Old Foster, and the affections of his nephew Robert, Stephen becomes a city benefactor and his wife remains "a woman never vexed." The form is that of romantic citizen comedy of a kind shortly to become unfashionable. Rowley's next unaided venture is less congenial, being in a sense more sophisticated and ambitious. *A Match at Midnight* is a comedy of romantic intrigue, set in the city and involving common types: the wealthy Widow, the object of the usurer Bloodhound's matrimonial intentions, soldiers false (Captain Carvegut, Lieutenant Bottom) and true (Ancient Young), young men idle (Alexander Bloodhound) and foolish (Tim Bloodhound, Randall a Welshman, Ear-lack the scrivener, and—

like Alexander—all deceived suitors). The denouement when the Widow reveals that she has been married all along, to Jarvis her servant, is, like the original situation, contrived and unsatisfying. Indeed, although the characters are presented with a fair degree of vivacity, they lack the intrinsic interest which would persuade a reader to be concerned for their fortunes in the play. Such flat characters require performance to round them out.

Rowley's contributions to his two most successful collaborations exemplify to a point the qualities of his comedies: monochromatic characters dominated by a single passion or trait, what Samuel Schoenbaum calls "whimsical and droll, broad and exaggerated" humor with frequent punning and bawdry, and, in final situations, moral sententiousness. While Middleton wrote the main plot of *A Fair Quarrel,* Rowley contributed mainly the scenes dealing with Russell's plots to frustrate the marriage of his daughter Jane to Fitzallen and the "roaring" scenes in which a foolish Cornish gentleman, Chough (with his servant Trimtram), receives instruction in fashionable city roistering. (For the division of the play see Holdsworth.) Here as in *The Changeling* Rowley wrote most of the first and last acts, which comprise the protasis and catastrophe respectively and give compelling witness to the closeness of the collaboration between the two playwrights. Bawcutt notes that *The Changeling* "has a remarkable consistency and continuity, and there is a complete absence of the discrepancies in detail between one part and the next which are often the sign of a work written by several authors." Collaboration with Middleton raised Rowley's verse to almost Middletonian intensity. Often rough and awkward Rowley rarely manages to build up long passages of blank verse. In V.ii of *The Changeling,* however, where the situation is tense, the relatively disjointed verses convey a nervous intensity completely in accord with the process of the action. As Bawcutt observes, "Rowley was responsible for the most famous lines in the play, Beatrice's speech at V.iii.149ff." She and De Flores are more psychologically complex than any of the characters in which Rowley had shared so far, and his achievement here is not much diminished by comparison with Middleton's.

Nevertheless, it remains true that were it not for his collaboration with Middleton, Rowley's name would be unknown to the modern theatergoer. The height of his achievement as a playwright was not sufficient to elevate his plays above the circumstances and dramatic fashions that gave them rise, and the vivacity of his comic characters—

who are rarely as witty as they perceive themselves—is mostly shrouded by the passage of time and the evolution of taste.

References:

Thomas W. Baldwin, *The Organization and Personnel of the Shakespearean Company* (Princeton: Princeton University Press, 1927);

Richard H. Barker, *Thomas Middleton* (New York: Columbia University Press, 1958);

Gerald Eades Bentley, *The Jacobean and Caroline Stage,* volume 2 (Oxford: Clarendon Press, 1941), pp. 555-558; volume 5 (Oxford: Clarendon Press, 1956), pp. 1014-1027;

George Cheatham, "The Date of William Rowley's *A New Wonder, A Woman Never Vext,*" *Publications of the Bibliographical Society of America,* 75 (1981): 437-442;

Mark Dominik, *William Shakespeare and "The Birth of Merlin"* (New York: Philosophical Library, 1985);

Wilbur D. Dunkel, "Did Not Rowley Merely Revise Middleton?," *Publication of the Modern Language Association,* 48 (September 1933): 799-805;

Henry D. Gray, "*A Cure for a Cuckold* by Heywood, Rowley and Webster," *Modern Language Review,* 22 (October 1927): 389-397;

MacDonald P. Jackson, *Studies in Attribution; Middleton and Shakespeare* (Salzburg: Institut für Englische Sprache und Literatur, Universität Salzburg, 1979);

David J. Lake, *The Canon of Thomas Middleton's Plays; Internal Evidence for the Major Problems of Authorship* (Cambridge: Cambridge University Press, 1975);

Terence P. Logan and Denzell S. Smith, eds., *The Popular School* (Lincoln: University of Nebraska Press, 1975), pp. 263-269;

Michael E. Mooney, " 'The Common Sight' and 'Dramatic Form'; Rowley's Embedded Jig in *A Faire Quarrel,*" *Studies in English Literature,* 20 (Spring 1980): 306-323;

Mooney, "Framing as Collaborative Technique; two Middleton-Rowley Plays," *Comparative Drama,* 13 (Summer 1979): 127-141;

Mooney, "William Rowley, Jacobean Playwright," Ph.D. dissertation, University of Southern California, 1976;

George R. Price, "The Authorship and the Manuscript of *The Old Law,*" *Huntington Library Quarterly,* 16 (February 1953): 117-139;

Dewar M. Robb, "The Canon of William Rowley's Plays," *Modern Language Review,* 45 (April 1950): 129-141;

Samuel Schoenbaum, *Middleton's Tragedies: A Critical Study* (New York: Columbia University Press, 1955), pp. 203-226.

James Shirley
(1596-October 1666)

Gordon Braden
University of Virginia

PLAY PRODUCTIONS: *Love Tricks* (*The School of Compliment*), London, Phoenix theater, 1625;

The Maid's Revenge, London, Phoenix theater, 1626;

The Brothers (probably not the surviving play of the same name; possibly the same play as *The Wedding*), London, Phoenix theater(?), 1626;

The Wedding, London, Phoenix theater, 1626-1629;

The Witty Fair One, London, Phoenix theater, 1628;

The Grateful Servant (*The Faithful Servant*), London, Phoenix theater, 1629;

The Duke (possibly the same play as *The Humorous Courtier*), London, Phoenix theater, 1631;

Love's Cruelty, London, Phoenix theater, 1631;

The Traitor, London, Phoenix theater, 1631;

The Ball, London, Phoenix theater, 1632;

Changes, or Love in a Maze, London, Salisbury Court theater, 1632;

Hyde Park, London, Phoenix theater, 1632;

The Arcadia, London, Phoenix theater, 1632(?);

The Bird in a Cage, London, Phoenix theater, 1632-1633;

A Contention for Honor and Riches (early version of *Honoria and Mammon*), privately performed (?), before 1633;

The Gamester, London, Phoenix theater, 1633;

The Young Admiral, London, Phoenix theater, 1633;

The Night Walker, by John Fletcher, revised by Shirley, London, Phoenix theater, 1633;

The Triumph of Peace, Westminster, Whitehall Palace, 3 February 1634;

The Example, London, Phoenix theater, 1634;

The Opportunity, London, Phoenix theater, 1634;

The Coronation, London, Phoenix theater, 1635;

The Tragedy of Chabot Admiral of France, by George Chapman, revised by Shirley, London, Phoenix theater, 1635;

The Lady of Pleasure, London, Phoenix theater, 1635;

The Duke's Mistress, London, Phoenix theater, 1636;

The Royal Master, Dublin, Werburgh Street theater, 1637; London, Salisbury Court theater(?), 1638;

The Humorous Courtier (perhaps the same play as *The Duke*), Dublin, Werburgh Street theater, 1637-1639;

The Constant Maid (*Love Will Find Out the Way*), Dublin, Werburgh Street theater(?), 1637-1640;

St. Patrick for Ireland, Dublin, Werburgh Street theater, 1637-1640;

The Doubtful Heir (*Rosania, or Love's Victory*), Dublin, Werburgh Street theater, 1638(?); London, Blackfriars theater, 1640;

No Wit, No Help Like a Woman's, by Thomas Middleton, possibly revised by Shirley, Dublin, Werburgh Street theater, 1638;

The Gentleman of Venice, Dublin, Werburgh Street theater, 1639(?); London, Salisbury Court theater, 1639;

The Politician, Dublin, Werburgh Street theater, 1639(?); London, Salisbury Court theater, 1639(?);

The Tragedy of St. Albans, unknown theater, before 1640;

The Imposture, London, Blackfriars theater, 1640;

The Brothers (*The Politic Father*), London, Blackfriars theater, 1641;

The Cardinal, London, Blackfriars theater, 1641;

The Sisters, London, Blackfriars theater, 1642;

The Court Secret, London, Blackfriars theater, "never acted but prepared for the scene," 1642; eventually performed London, Theatre Royal, 1664;

The Triumph of Beauty, privately performed, before 1646;

Cupid and Death, unknown location, 26 March 1653;

Honoria and Mammon, possibly performed, before 1659;

The Contention of Ajax and Ulysses for the Armor of Achilles, privately performed (at Shirley's grammar school?), before 1659.

BOOKS: *The Wedding* (London: Printed by J. Okes for J. Grove, 1629);

The Gratefull Servant. A Comedie (London: Printed by B. Alsop & T. Fawcet for J. Grove, 1630);

James Shirley (by permission of the Bodleian Library, Oxford)

The Schoole of Complement (London: Printed by E. Allde for F. Constable, 1631); republished as *Love Tricks* (London: Printed for R. T., sold by Thomas Dring, Jr., 1667);

Changes: or, Love in a Maze. A Comedie (London: Printed by G. Purslowe for W. Cooke, 1632);

A Contention for Honour and Riches (London: Printed by E. Allde for W. Cooke, 1633);

The Wittie Faire One. A Comedie (London: Printed by B. Alsop & T. Fawcet for W. Cooke, 1633);

The Bird in a Cage. A Comedie (London: Printed by B. Alsop & T. Fawcet for W. Cooke, 1633);

The Triumph of Peace. A Masque (London: Printed by J. Norton for W. Cooke, 1633);

The Traytor. A Tragedie (London: Printed by J. Norton for W. Cooke, 1635);

Hide Park. A Comedie (London: Printed by T. Cotes for A. Crooke & W. Cooke, 1637);

The Lady of Pleasure. A Comedie (London: Printed by T. Cotes for A. Crooke & W. Cooke, 1637);

The Young Admirall (London: Printed by T. Cotes for A. Crooke & W. Cooke, 1637);

The Example (London: Printed by J. Norton for A. Crooke & W. Cooke, 1637);

The Gamester (London: Printed by J. Norton for A. Crooke & W. Cooke, 1637);

The Dukes Mistris (London: Printed by J. Norton for A. Crooke, 1638);

The Royall Master (London: Printed by T. Cotes, sold by J. Crooke & R. Serger, 1638);

The Ball. A Comedie (London: Printed by T. Cotes for A. Crooke & W. Cooke, 1639);

The Tragedie of Chabot Admirall of France, by George Chapman, revised by Shirley (London: Printed by T. Cotes for A. Crooke & W. Cooke, 1639);

The Maides Revenge. A Tragedy (London: Printed by T. Cotes for W. Cooke, 1639);

The Coronation: A Comedy (London: Printed by T. Cotes for A. Crooke & W. Cooke, 1640);

The Night-Walker, or The Little Theife, by John Fletcher, revised by Shirley (London: Printed by T. Cotes for A. Crooke & W. Cooke, 1640);

Loves Crueltie. A Tragedy (London: Printed by T. Cotes for A. Crooke, 1640);

The Opportunitie: A Comedy (London: Printed by T. Cotes for A. Crooke & W. Cooke, 1640);

The Humorous Courtier. A Comedy (London: Printed by T. Cotes for W. Cooke, sold by J. Becket, 1640);

A Pastorall Called The Arcadia (London: Printed by J. Dawson for J. Williams & F. Eglesfeild, 1640);

The Constant Maid. A Comedy (London: Printed by J. Raworth for R. Whitaker, 1640); republished as *Love Will Finde Out the Way* (London: Printed by Ja: Cottrel for Samuel Speed, 1661);

St. Patrick for Ireland. The First Part (London: Printed by J. Raworth for R. Whitaker, 1640);

Poems &c. (London: Printed for Humphrey Moseley, 1646);

Via ad Latinam linguam complanata; The Way Made Plaine to the Latine Tongue, the Rules Composed in English and Latine Verse (London: Printed by R. W. for John Stephenson, 1649); republished as *Grammatica Anglo-Latina. An English and Latine Grammar* (London: Printed for Richard Lowndes, 1651);

Cupid and Death. A Masque (London: Printed by T. W. for J. Crook & J. Baker, 1653);

Six New Playes, viz. The Brothers. The Sisters. The Doubtful Heir. The Imposture. The Cardinall. The Court Secret (London: Printed for Humphrey Robinson & Humphrey Moseley, 1653);

The Gentleman of Venice: A Tragi-Comedie (London: Printed for Humphrey Moseley, 1655);

The Polititian, A Tragedy (London: Printed for Humphrey Moseley, 1655);

[*Eisagogae*]:*sive, Introductorium Anglo-Latino-Graecum* (London: Printed by J. G., sold by J. Crook, 1656);

The Rudiments of Grammar (London: Printed by J. Macock for R. Lownds, 1656); enlarged as *Manductio; or, A Leading of Children by the Hand through the Principles of Grammar* (London: Printed for Richard Lowndes, 1660);

No Wit, No Help Like a Woman's, by Thomas Middleton, possibly revised by Shirley (London: Printed for Humphrey Moseley, 1657);

Honoria and Mammon . . . Whereunto Is Added The Contention of Ajax and Ulisses, for the Armour of Achilles (London: Printed for John Crook, 1659);

An Ode upon the Happy Return of King Charles II. To His Languishing Nations, May 29, 1660 (London, 1660);

The True Impartial History and Wars of the Kingdom of Ireland, possibly by Shirley (London: Printed for Nicholas Boddington, 1692);

An Essay Towards an Universal and Rational Grammar; Together with Rules for Learning Latin, in English Verse, edited by Jenkin Thomas Philipps (London: Printed by J. Downing, 1726).

Edition: *The Dramatic Works and Poems of James Shirley*, edited by William Gifford and Alexander Dyce, 6 volumes (London: John Murray, 1833)—comprises *Love Tricks, or, The School of Compliment*; *The Maid's Revenge*; *The Brothers*; *The Witty Fair One*; *The Wedding*; *The Grateful Servant*; *The Traitor*; *Love's Cruelty*; *Love in a Maze*; *The Bird in a Cage*; *Hyde Park*; *The Ball*; *The Young Admiral*; *The Gamester*; *The Example*; *The Opportunity*; *The Coronation*; *The Lady of Pleasure*; *The Royal Master*; *The Duke's Mistress*; *The Doubtful Heir*; *St. Patrick for Ireland*; *The Constant Maid*; *The Humorous Courtier*; *The Gentleman of Venice*; *The Politician*; *The Imposture*; *The Cardinal*; *The Sisters*; *The Court Secret*; *Honoria and Mammon*; *Chabot, Admiral of France*; *The Arcadia*; *The Triumph of Peace*; *A Contention for Honor and Riches*; *The Triumph of Beauty*; *Cupid and Death*; *The Contention of Ajax and Ulysses for the Armour of Achilles*; and *Poems*.

James Shirley dominated the last generation of English Renaissance drama with an industrious fluency unapproached by any other playwright during the reign of Charles I. Others, notably John Ford, wrote plays of greater power and more enduring interest; Shirley's taste was too sure to attempt anything as memorable or extreme as *'Tis Pity She's a Whore*. His instinct for experiment and innovation was slight, and the general ethos of his plays is the official gentility of the Caroline court: cleverly risqué but fundamentally conservative in its sophisticated decorum. But by the same token, none of Shirley's thirty-odd plays fall below a high level of artful competence. The capable heir to greater predecessors, he absorbed their lessons into a skillful conventionality that showed how natural a certain kind of theatrical deftness had become for the English stage.

He was probably the "James the sonne of James Sharlie" who was baptized in London on 7 September 1596. His parents and ancestry are otherwise unknown, though he styled himself "Gent." throughout his career and is reported to have displayed a coat of arms. He attended the Merchant Taylors' School—where Edmund Spenser and Thomas Kyd had also gone—from 1608 until at least 1612. In that year, according to Anthony à Wood's *Athenae Oxonienses*, Shirley entered St. John's College, Oxford, where William Laud, then master of the college, dissuaded him from the ministry because of an unsightly mole on his cheek. The mole is otherwise attested, but his attendance at Oxford is not; some evidence suggests that Shirley may actually have been an apprentice scrivener at the time. In 1615, however, he enrolled at Catherine Hall, Cambridge; he received his B.A. in 1617 and may have proceeded to the M.A. in 1619 or 1620. By then he had married Elizabeth Gilmet, had been ordained an Anglican priest, and had accepted a living at Wheathampstead in Hertfordshire.

In 1621 he left that post to become headmaster at a grammar school in nearby St. Albans. Wood attributes this move to a conversion to Catholicism that has proved impossible to document; oblique evidence on the matter pulls both ways. The profession of schoolteacher would seem to have been congenial to Shirley; it was in such a position that he was to spend the last twenty years of his life. In 1624, however, he changed tack again, and more drastically: resigning from St. Albans, he moved himself and his family to London. No specific reason is known. His Catholicism may have continued to cause problems, but there is also reason to think that secular ambitions had been chafing in the obscurity of provincial life. In 1618

Shirley had published *Echo, or The Infortunate Lovers*; no copy of that edition survives, but the work in question was probably the poem *Narcissus* printed in Shirley's 1646 *Poems &c.* A neo-Ovidian fable about a nymph's fatal passion for an unresponsive youth, it is the sort of gracefully decorative and languorously erotic poem that ambitious young writers of an earlier generation had written to display their wit and secure attention—a poem indeed conspicuously like Shakespeare's *Venus and Adonis*, to which Shirley unmistakably alludes. The tracks of such a career pointed in one direction. In London, as Wood put it, Shirley "set up for a playmaker"; in 1625 Lady Elizabeth's Men performed *Love Tricks*, the "first fruits of a Muse, that before this/Never saluted audience."

Love Tricks, a comedy, seems to have been a success, as was a tragedy, *The Maid's Revenge*, licensed the next year. There followed seventeen years of steady productivity and increasing reputation. After the accession of Charles in 1625, Lady Elizabeth's Men became Queen Henrietta's Men; Shirley continued to do most of his writing for them until 1636, when the London theaters were closed because of the plague. He then left for Dublin, where in Werburgh Street John Ogilby had established the first English theater outside of London; Shirley was its mainstay, as prolific as ever, until 1640. In that year, after the death of Philip Massinger, Shirley returned to London to become chief dramatist for the King's Men: Shakespeare's institutional successor. A new play, *The Court Secret*, was in rehearsal when Parliament closed the theaters for good in 1642.

Shirley's theatrical career is thus almost exactly coextensive with the ascendancy of the Caroline court, with which he seems to have had particularly good relations. Charles's Master of the Revels, Sir Henry Herbert, censored *The Ball* in 1632 to remove what seemed like scandalous topicality; but, if Shirley was being taught a lesson, he learned it quickly. The next year Herbert was praising Shirley's *The Young Admiral* as a model of theatrical good taste: "being free from oaths, profaness, or obscenes, [it] may serve for a patterne to other poetts, not only for the bettring of maners and language, but for the improvement of the quality, which hath received some brushings of late." Shirley's plays were frequently presented, and liked, at court; Charles is said to have suggested the plot for *The Gamester*, and, when it was performed before him early in 1634, he pronounced it "the best play he had seen for seven years." According to Wood, Shirley was especially favored by

Portions of pages from the Register of St. Mary Woolchurch, London (top), recording the baptism of "James the sonne of James Sharlie," and the "probation and triall" register of the Merchant Taylors' School, London (bottom), ranking Shirley first in the fifth form on 11 September 1610 (Arthur Huntington Nason, James Shirley, Dramatist, *1915)*

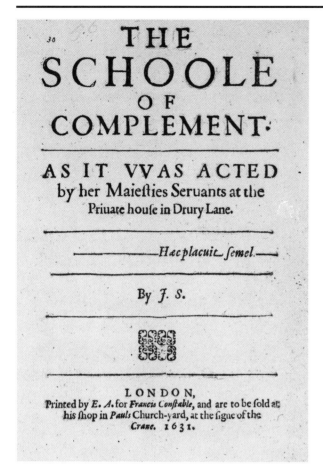

THE SCHOOLE OF COMPLEMENT·

AS IT VVAS ACTED
by her Maiefties Seruants at the
Priuate houfe in Drury Lane.

Hæc placuit_ femel.

By *J. S.*

LONDON,
Printed by *E. A.* for *Francis Conftable*, and are to be fold at
his fhop in *Pauls* Church-yard, at the figne of the
Crane. 1631.

*Title page for the 1631 quarto edition of Shirley's first play,
republished in 1667 as* Love Tricks *(Henry E. Huntington
Library and Art Gallery)*

the Catholic Queen Henrietta; he became an honorific valet of her chamber. By 1634 he was a member of Gray's Inn, which early in that year presented Shirley's masque *The Triumph of Peace* at Whitehall as a rejoinder to Puritan attacks on the court's morality (including the queen's fondness for the theater):

> To you, great king and queen, whose smile
> Doth scatter blessings through this isle,
> > To make it best
> > And wonder of the rest,
> We pay the duty of our birth;
> Proud to wait upon that earth
> > Whereon you move,
> > Which shall be nam'd
> And by your chaste embraces fam'd,
> > The paradise of love.

The production, designed by Inigo Jones, was one of the age's most sumptuous; the total cost was reported to be more than £20,000, almost half of it for costumes alone. The king and queen were so taken with it that they asked for a second performance ten days later.

Shirley was able to survive the disaster that awaited this world, but his interest in being a playwright did not. After the outbreak of the civil war, he served on the royalist side under the earl of Newcastle. Newcastle left the country after the battle of Marston Moor in 1644; Shirley made his way back to London and found a measure of security in the circle of the gentleman-scholar Thomas Stanley. He settled in the Whitefriars district and returned to school teaching, and seems to have been treated fairly leniently by the new regime. He published his poems, several of his plays, and a few other dramatic scripts; one of them was in fact a masque, *Cupid and Death*, commissioned for official performance before the Portuguese ambassador. But in a note "to the candid reader" introducing *Honoria and Mammon* (1659), Shirley overtly, and with a sound of irritable relief, announced the end of his theatrical career: *"It is now public, to satisfy the importunity of friends: I will only add, it is like to be the last, for in my resolve, nothing of this nature shall, after this, engage either my pen or invention."*

The resolve was kept. The Restoration saw the revival of a number of Shirley's plays—including the delayed performance of *The Court Secret*—and a general reestablishment of his reputation (a song from *The Contention of Ajax and Ulysses* is said to have become a personal favorite with Charles II). But Shirley wrote no new plays; he gave his pen and invention wholly over to the material of his pedagogy. In 1649 he published a Latin textbook; what poetic impulse remained went into the composition of rhymed mnemonics: "In *di, do, dum,* the Gerunds chime and close;/*Um* the first Supine, *u* the latter shews." Similar volumes appeared in 1656 and 1660. His last years were given over to attempts at a "universal and rational grammar," edited from notes after his death. A will signed in July 1666 names a second wife, Frances, and five children; Shirley and his wife both died in October of that year, in the aftermath of the great fire.

The most substantial critical study of Shirley's drama remains *The Relations of Shirley's Plays to the Elizabethan Drama* (1914), by Robert Stanley Forsythe: a laborious compendium of sources and analogues for particular characters, scenes, and plot devices. Such lists can be compiled for any of Shirley's colleagues, but for none of them—or at least for none of them of comparable stature—does the effort seem so appropriate as for Shirley. He was

Inigo Jones's costume designs for the Sons of Peace in Shirley's The Triumph of Peace *(Stephen Orgel and Roy Strong,* Inigo Jones, *1973)*

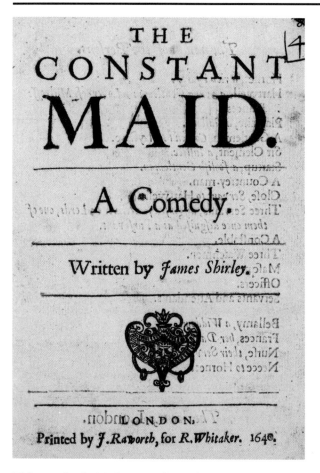

Title page for the 1640 quarto edition of one of the plays Shirley wrote in Dublin, where he went in 1636 to write for John Ogilby's Werburgh Street theater after an outbreak of the plague forced the closing of the London theaters (Henry E. Huntington Library and Art Gallery)

a dramatist generally content to work with interchangeable parts; his art is the art of their arrangement and combination. Where he is visibly original, it is usually by going the convention one or two better: as in, for instance, a double reversal of the familiar Renaissance bed trick on which the plot of *The Gamester* pivots. Characters seldom acquire any memorable individuality; they rarely soliloquize and are not allowed much in the way of introspection, but are realized almost wholly through their place in the plot. "*The poet's art,*" Shirley declared in his prologue to *The Cardinal*, "*is to lead on your thought/Through subtle paths and workings of a plot*"; his story lines are for the most part conspicuously complicated but also conspicuously lucid and well managed. They often have a mathematical quality to them, structured around matched pairs of characters: brothers, sisters, close friends, caught in

chiastic or triangular situations. (*The Maid's Revenge* uses both: two friends, each in love with the other's sister; and two sisters, each in love with the same man.) The action depends heavily on arranged surprises, when mistaken identity or information is set right. Shirley is particularly fond of scenes of unannounced testing, where someone feigns a certain kind of behavior or motive in order to check out someone else's response; in one case, *The Humorous Courtier*, the entire story turns out to be such a test. Shirley made plays for those who enjoy watching witty machinery.

With such detachment comes versatility, and Shirley alternated among the genres throughout his career; it does not sort out into clear phases. Yet his touch also now seems more suited to some kinds of plays than to others—and perhaps least suited to tragedy. A sense of manipulative distance from convention edges unavoidably toward amusement. The kind of language, for instance, that in Shakespeare and Webster could be a potent expression of tragic endurance—"I am Antony yet," "I am Duchess of Malfi still"—would have reached Shirley's ears, from Massinger's *The Duke of Milan*, as a cliché—"I would be Sforza still"—and in *The Maid's Revenge* becomes a joke: "my name's Sforza still," "still my name is Sforza," "My name is Sforza then," "My name's Sforza, sir," "and still my name is Sforza," says a minor character, all in the course of one scene. Shirley's management of tone in his later tragedies is more even, but they are now generally regarded as the least successful part of his theatrical oeuvre.

The most impressive tragedy to bear his name is *The Tragedy of Chabot Admiral of France*, published in 1639 as the joint effort of Shirley and George Chapman. Chapman had died five years before, after a decade of apparent inactivity; Shirley's role in the composition is almost certainly that of a belated reviser. (Chapman's name is also linked with Shirley's on the title page of *The Ball*, but in this case the older playwright is now thought to have had no significant part.) The action and dialogue of *Chabot* have a clarity and cleanness of line uncharacteristic of Chapman, and that finish is probably Shirley's contribution; but the play seems fundamentally Chapman's in conception, a grave study of the fatal paradoxes of patronage and service in a Renaissance court. A plot of Machiavellian intrigue is important primarily for delivering the title character into a situation in which his integrity and worth become political liabilities, in a clear variation of the theme played out in Chapman's Bussy and Byron plays.

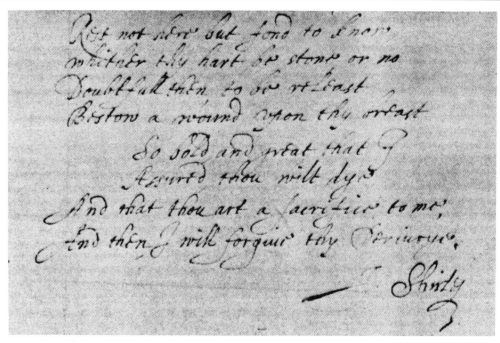

A portion of a page from a manuscript volume of Shirley's poems thought to be in his own hand and preserved at the Bodleian Library (MS Rawl. poet. 88, p. 78; by permission of the Bodleian Library)

In Shirley's own tragedies the intrigue, usually sexual as well as political, is central and its choreography often the main focus of interest. *The Traitor* (licensed in 1631) is a textbook example. The secret schemer Lorenzo plots to supplant the Duke of Florence by exploiting the Duke's designs on the virtuous Amidea; Lorenzo works her hotheaded brother Sciarrha into a coconspirator who will kill the Duke to preserve the family honor. Shirley's ingenuity is on display halfway through when Amidea's resolute chastity brings the Duke to a bedroom conversion; Sciarrha, moved, confesses all and comes close to ending the play happily, two acts early. Lorenzo's adroit avoidance of exposure is an electric moment, and his deft manipulation of a hitherto tangential subplot to neutralize Sciarrha and revive his conspiracy is impressively handled. The conclusion, however, is a derivative holocaust, "a heap of tragedies": Amidea killed by her brother, the deconverted Duke killed by Lorenzo after kissing her corpse in bed, Lorenzo and Sciarrha killing each other. The moral is similarly all-inclusive: " 'Tis a sad night, my lords; by these you see/There is no stay in proud mortality."

Love's Cruelty (also licensed in 1631), a dark fable about lust's implacable wittiness, has a focus and intensity that have gained a measure of special notice from critics. Also set in an Italian ducal court, its plot is political only insofar as the Duke of Ferrara attempts to seduce the innocent Eubella with the temptations of advancement; assigned to serve his lord's purpose, the courtier Hippolito is racily articulate: "come, you do not know what it is to be a duke's mistress, to enjoy the pleasures of the court, to have all heads bare, all knees bow to you, every door fly open as you tread; with your breath to raise this gentleman, pull down that lord, and new-mould the t'other lady; wear upon a tire the wealth of a province." On virginity he is an insidious student of Falstaff on honor: "Your maidenhead? where is it? who ever saw it? Is it a thing in nature? what marks has it? many have been lost you'll say; who ever found them? and could say and justify, this is such or such a woman's maidenhead? A mere fiction." Yet Eubella holds her ground, and in so doing saves herself; it is the ironically named Hippolito who, for all his insouciant knowingness, is in fact at risk, the unreckoning stress point of some unforgiving erotic geometry.

In what his friend Bellamente calls an act of "unexampled virtue," he has refused to meet Clariana, the woman Bellamente is about to marry: "He knows not what may thieve upon his senses,/Or what temptation may rise from him,/To undo us all." Yet like Oedipus, Hippolito runs to just that fate in attempting to avoid it. His reticence intrigues Clariana: "I must see this strange friend."

The portrait of Shirley by W. Marshall that was published in the 1646 octavo edition of Poems &c. *(Arthur Huntington Nason,* James Shirley, Dramatist, *1915)*

She meets him incognita, and they fall effortlessly into the flirtatious banter that he does so well. By the time he learns her identity, they are obsessed with each other. After Clariana's marriage, they consummate their affair; frisky in bed, she confirms that Eros is indeed most powerful when he is least lawful:

> Lawful! that would take much from the delight
> And value. . . .

'Tis no glory to take a town without some hazard; that victory is sweetest, which is got in the face of danger. . . . What makes a maidenhead the richer purchase, think you?

The rest of the action is a tragic deduction from this axiom, as the lovers' pleasure is destroyed by the danger that makes it desirable. Bellamente discovers them, almost kills them, then arranges instead a tense cover-up that proves even more explosive. Hippolito, shaken, falls in love with Eubella's virtue and even wins the Duke's consent to their marriage, but again his attempt to escape dooms him. Clariana finds her own desire reinflamed, and in an interview with Hippolito both fails to win him back and compromises herself again with her newly vengeful husband. She stabs Hippolito in despair, and he runs her through almost on reflex; dying, she makes explicit a final equation of desire and death:

> Thy sword was gentle to me; search't again,
> And thou shalt see how my embracing blood
> Will keep it warm, and kiss the kind destroyer.

The actual slaughter is minimal; but, as Ben Lucow says, Shirley here comes perhaps his closest to the harrowing nihilism of his Jacobean masters.

Shirley's reputation as a tragedian, however, traditionally rests on *The Cardinal* (licensed in 1641), which he himself called in his dedication "*the best of my flock*." Fredson Bowers singles it out as "the last great tragedy of revenge" on the English Renaissance stage. Much seems directly owed to Thomas Kyd's *The Spanish Tragedy* in both general ethos and specific plot construction, but Shirley makes things brisker with a cunning doubling of the revenge story. At the start of the play the title character, the all-powerful favorite of the King of Navarre, has arranged the engagement of his nephew Columbo to the widowed Duchess Rosaura—an arrangement which she apparently accepts but secretly resists. Their twin intrigues proceed to feed off one another, working their way through intermediary goals and victims, until both Columbo and Rosaura's real love, Alvarez, are dead and the two principals finally destroy one another.

Rosaura, the play's Hieronimo or Hamlet, is one of the powerful heroines of Renaissance drama: "This woman has a spirit, that may rise/To tame the devil's." Her gender adds to the avenger's traditional feeling of impotence and gives new dramatic force to her resourcefulness under pressure: "Do not I walk upon the teeth of serpents,/And, as I had a charm against their poison,/Play with their stings?" After the murder of Alvarez, her quest for vengeance becomes an almost ascetic purity of intent:

> I so much
> Desire to sacrifice to that hovering ghost
> Columbo's life, that I am not ambitious

To keep my own two minutes after it.

It is a purity partly compromised by a tentative promise of love to the soldier Hernando, who becomes her vengeful agent; but the promise is never put to the test and would seem to be astutely tactical. That is certainly the case with the derangement she assumes in the later stages, less showy than Hieronimo's and Hamlet's and more sly: "they say/I have lost my wits; but they are safe enough,/And I shall have them when the Cardinal dies." Her adversary is interestingly less of a piece. He looms as a villain from the start, and Rosaura is emphatic about his moral degradation: "How gross your avarice, eating up whole families!/How vast are your corruptions and abuse/Of the king's ear." Yet for about half the play he is if anything a moderating influence. He is angry about Rosaura's affront to the family honor in escaping from her engagement with Columbo; but he is not an accessory to Columbo's murder of Alvarez and does not defend it: " 'Twas violent and cruel, a black deed." When he uses his power to prevent Columbo's punishment, that seems to him simple decency on his part: "Could I do less for one so near my blood?" He is nevertheless being lured across important moral boundaries; when Rosaura executes her own justice on Columbo, the Cardinal is instantly vicious in the Senecan mode:

>   'tis too cheap
> A satisfaction for Columbo's death,
> Only to kill her by soft charm or force.
> I'll rifle first her darling chastity;
> It will be after time enough to poison her.

Yet he never gains control of his own villainy; the attempted rape is unexpected in its effect:

> I have took a strong enchantment from her lips,
> And fear I shall forgive Columbo's death,
> If she consent to my embrace.

The final action is a comedy of mortal errors. Believing himself fatally wounded, the Cardinal feigns repentance to trick Rosaura into taking a poison that he calls an antidote; as a proof of good faith he takes some first himself. When Rosaura has drunk as well, a surgeon pronounces his wounds "not desperate": dying, he sees Rosaura's blood guilt lifted and his own compounded with an unnecessary suicide. The audience is treated to the frisson of an indifferent sinner finally securing

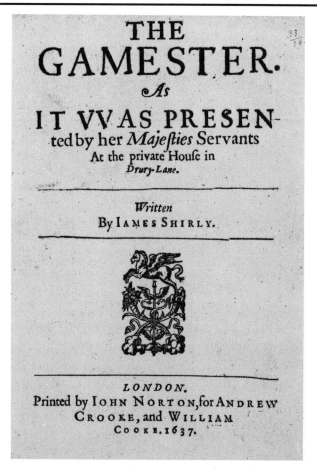

THE GAMESTER.

As

IT VVAS PRESEN-

ted by her *Majesties* Servants
At the private House in
Drury-Lane.

Written
By IAMES SHIRLY.

LONDON.
Printed by IOHN NORTON, for ANDREW
CROOKE, and WILLIAM
COOKE. 1637.

Title page for the 1637 quarto edition of the Shirley play for which King Charles I is said to have suggested the plot. When he saw The Gamester *in early 1634, Charles called it "the best play he had seen for seven years" (Henry E. Huntington Library and Art Gallery).*

his own damnation through sheer confusion at almost the last possible minute.

The effect is memorable but risks being funny; Shirley's instinct for last-act surprises is in general more appropriate for happy endings, and that is in fact the purpose they serve in most of his plays. A number of them fall into the Renaissance category of tragicomedy: potentially tragic situations adroitly resolved by unpredictable rearrangements. Beaumont and Fletcher had made such plays a staple of the English stage, and Shirley—whose first play was produced in the year of Fletcher's death and who contributed an adulatory preface to a collection from their canon in 1647—is their direct and attentive heir. The genre intimates evil's insufficiency in an ultimately benign universe. In *The Imposture* (licensed in 1640), for instance, the machinations of Flaviano begin as the kind of Machiavellian intrigue that in other plays would bring ruin to almost everyone about him:

So, so! Fortune, thou shalt have eyes again,
If thou would'st smile on mischief; I will build thee
An altar, and upon it sacrifice
Folly, and all her children.

But Flaviano's immensely complex plot finally baffles his powers of improvisation and is halted by a virtuous counterscheme and the defection of an accomplice before any permanent harm is done. He tries a defiant snarl at the end—

Whose witty brain must sentence me? Let it
Be home and handsome; I shall else despise,
And scorn your coarse inventions.

—but it is not necessary to subject him to anything harsher or wittier than banishment. Other happy endings suggest the semimagical tradition of romance. At the end of *The Coronation* (licensed as

Shirley's in 1635 but ascribed to Fletcher on its first publication in 1640), the brutal usurper Seleucus, placed on the throne through a cynical claim to be the dead king's lost son, turns out to be indeed the dead king's lost son; and the discovery itself changes him for the better: "Nature has rectified in me . . . / The wanderings of ambition." In an interesting variation of this trick, Shirley has the happy ending of *The Sisters* (licensed in 1642) hinge on the discovery that the presumably highborn but unamiable Paulina ("Of a kin to Lucifer for pride") is in fact the child of peasants, and that her estate actually belongs to the more tractably feminine Angellina ("every hair of her head worth stellifying"). Such revelations testify to the enveloping sense of a providential order, though one less religious than social.

The Gamester—the play which King Charles liked so well and which David Garrick adapted and revived in the eighteenth century—moves this genre to the border of comedy pure and simple. An almost tragic context is provided by the love story of two sets of friends. The men, Delamore and Beaumont, quarrel—"wine made them fall out, some say, about their mistresses"—and Delamore is wounded and reported dead. The father of Delamore's beloved Leonora tries to enforce his own inclination and have her marry Beaumont: that marriage is made the price of a pardon. Beaumont's determined fidelity to Leonora's friend Violante eventually draws from the father the news that Delamore is in fact recovering: "I see heaven has decreed him for thy husband," he tells his daughter, "And shalt have my consent too." Beaumont himself experiences a sense of grace beyond words: "I feel a blessing/That only can be thought; silence, my tongue,/And let our hearts discourse." The story's real force, however, is to help locate the title character, Will Hazard, as the play's moral center. His attitude toward the kind of dueling that almost ruins four lives is bracingly sensible:

> There may be causes, that have women in them:
> But I confess, no polecats, or lewd strumpets,
> Though I do use the trick o' the flesh, shall drive
> Me to the surgeon.

In the first scene he talks a group of Delamore's friends out of escalating the quarrel:

> I believe the stoutest
> That now would seem all fire and sword, will go
> With as ill will to hanging, as another,
> And will become't as scurvily.

> . . . .
> Come, be yourselves; these are not acts of gentlemen,
> Where shame, not honour, must reward your daring.

Himself an unapologetic gambler and man-about-town, Hazard stands for the principle that a masculine enjoyment of the pleasures of the city is compatible with, indeed entails a certain genteel decorum and self-control; his arguments on dueling have their parallel in "A Rapture," the well-known paean to sexual license by Shirley's courtly contemporary Thomas Carew. Yet in the play's central action Hazard proves, despite his predilection for the trick of the flesh, a guardian of marital chastity as well. As part of another erotic quadrilateral involving his rakish friend Wilding, Wilding's wife, and Wilding's ward Penelope, he engineers another apparent disaster that not only prevents Wilding's attempted adultery but also brings him to his sexual senses:

> I am asham'd; pray give me all forgiveness.
> I see my follies; heaven invites me gently
> To thy chaste bed: be thou again my dearest,
> Thy virtue shall instruct me.

Hazard himself marries Penelope—won over, he says, precisely by her resistance to some earlier importuning: " 'twas a trial of thee:/That humour made me love thee, and since that,/Thy virtue." Hazard's championship of lawful love requires some prompting from the women, but nothing so dramatic as a conversion; in him Shirley depicts an ideal of sophisticated hedonism that is also easily congruent with conventional morality.

That ideal is one self-image of the privileged class of Caroline London, and what now seem Shirley's best plays are the comedies that depict, in bright and playful colors, the life and values of that class. Though set in contemporary London, they are not city comedies in the Jacobean mode; there is a satiric subplot in *The Gamester* about an aspiring merchant and his son—"we that had/Our breeding from a trade, cits, as you call us"—but it is subordinate and circumscribed. Shirley's comic focus is on the nobility and the gentry, and his tone festive and celebratory. *The Ball*, despite the offense it apparently gave, seems in fact intended to defend the social style of its highborn personnel from the charge of immorality; Diana triumphs in the climactic masque:

> *Cupid, if you mean to stay,*
> *Throw your licentious shafts away,*

R. Gaywood's engraved copy of G. Phenik's painting of Shirley; from the 1659 edition of Honoria and Mammon *and* The Contention of Ajax and Ulysses *(Arthur Huntington Nason,* James Shirley, Dramatist, *1915)*

Then you are Love, then be embrac'd,
Love is welcome while he's chaste.

The sense of humor at work is less Jonsonian scorn than the anatomizing of amiable absurdity. In *Love in a Maze* (licensed in 1632) the poet Caperwit ("the midwife wrapt my head up in a sheet of sir Philip Sidney") comes out with a memorable encomium of the adjective:

would you have a poem without adjectives?
They are the flowers, the grace of all our language:
A well chose epithet doth give new soul
To fainting poesy; and makes every verse
A bride . . .

His patron reins him in a bit with a different theory of poetry ("Poets write masculine numbers") and a request for more in the way of "stately substan-

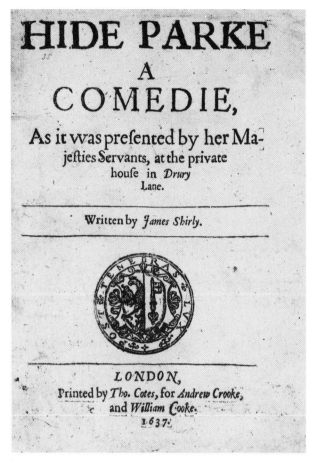

Title page for the 1637 quarto edition of the play that Shirley set in part at the popular foot and horse races in London's Hyde Park
(Henry E. Huntington Library and Art Gallery)

tives," but without getting nasty: good sense need not spoil the fun. In the surrounding play Shirley puts his instinct for schematic plotting to one of its best uses in the young Gerard's utter inability to decide which of two matched sisters to love:

> The scales are even still; that one had less
> Perfection, to make the doubtful balance
> Give different in their value! but I wrong
> Their virtues to wish either any want,
> That equally involve my soul to love them.

His solution is to ask his friend Thornay to pick one of them for himself, so that he may choose the leftover: "Thou art not thus my rival, but my friend." The results are predictable: Gerard finds that he loves the one that Thornay prefers. Complications ramify as this plot gears with others into an elaborate demonstration of the force of third persons in erotic attachments. This is the theme of *Love's Cruelty* adapted for comedy; and the eventual

sorting out of the various pairs in a way that manages to respect the initial premise attests the potential joviality of that theme. A happy ending becomes possible when love is recognized as essentially not a private but a social experience.

A related text informs the most interesting plot in *Hyde Park* (licensed in 1632): "What women are forbidden/They're mad to execute." The woman in question is the notoriously unwinnable Carol:

> None that have eyes will follow the direction
> Of a blind guide, and what do you think of Cupid?
> Women are either fools, or very wise,
> Take that from me; the foolish women are
> Not worth your love, and if a woman know
> How to be wise, she will not care for you.

The rebuffed Fairfield cannily responds by tricking her into a promise "never to desire my company/ Hereafter; for no reason to affect me." Coupled with the pretended courtship of another woman, this does the trick, but also moves Carol to revenge. Professing love, she tricks Fairfield into releasing her from her oath, and then pretends to have been pretending and unleashes some of her nastiest wit in a description of his face ("you have eyes,/Especially when you goggle thus, not much/Unlike a Jew's"). Fairfield is sent into a "scurvy melancholy" that evens the score. Meeting again, they engineer a touchy accommodation:

> CAROL. I know you love me still; do not refuse me.
>   If I go once more back, you ne'er recover me.
> FAIRFIELD. I am as ticklish.
> CAROL. Then let's clap it up wisely,
>   While we are both i' the humour; I do find
>   A grudging, and your last words stick in my
>   stomach.
>   Say, is't a match? speak quickly, or for ever
>   Hereafter hold your peace.
> FAIRFIELD. Done!
> CAROL. Why, done!

They are not unworthy kin of Shakespeare's Beatrice and Benedick and Congreve's Millamant and Mirabell. Their demonstration of the compatibility of love and independence is interwoven with gentler reconciliations: a virtuous wife's lost husband returns in time to prevent the consummation of her second marriage; a virgin's confident chastity moves a promiscuous lord to reform. All these stories pass through the newly established Hyde Park, where the third and fourth acts take place: an urban pastoral scene, complete with milkmaids, where the urban elite gather to enjoy a syllabub and one another's company and to bet on the races. Their communal wit and manners make a green world of romantic providence in the midst of London.

The best known of Shirley's comedies—"the best comedy of its generation," according to Alfred Harbage—is somewhat harsher on London high society. The title of *The Lady of Pleasure* (licensed in 1635) is contemporary slang for "whore"; the two upper-class women around whom its action revolves have names—Aretina and Celestina—drawn from the annals of Renaissance pornography and prostitution. Lady Aretina Bornwell, herself of even nobler family than her husband, seems clearly meant as a symbol for a willfully corrupt aristocracy. She has harassed her husband into moving to London (an action officially discouraged by the King) to allow her to pursue her "pleasure"; she finds him still offensively unwilling to spend his money to that end:

> though you veil your avaricious meaning
> With handsome names of modesty and thrift,
> I find you would intrench and wound the liberty
> I was born with. Were my desires unprivileged
> By example, while my judgment thought 'em fit,
> You ought not to oppose; but when the practice
> And track of every honourable lady
> Authorise me, I take it great injustice
> To have my pleasures circumscribed, and taught me.

She is not contesting her husband's enumeration of those pleasures, some merely expensive—"the superfluous plate,/Antique and novel; vanities of tires;/Fourscore-pound suppers for my lord, your kinsman"—but some worse:

> Your meetings call'd THE BALL, to which repair,
> As to the court of pleasure, all your gallants,
> And ladies, thither bound by a subpoena
> Of Venus, and small Cupid's high displeasure;
> 'Tis but the Family of Love translated
> Into more costly sin!

Bornwell goes on to mention Shirley's own play as a scandalous whitewash of such gatherings. And Aretina indeed has adultery on her mind. When she discovers that one of the city women of her acquaintance is an accomplished pimp, she proceeds to it with single-minded efficiency.

Aretina is not a lost soul, however. The last part of the play presents her reformation:

> Heaven has dissolved the clouds that hung upon
> My eyes, and if you can with mercy meet
> A penitent, I throw my own will off,
> And now in all things obey your's.

This change is prompted in part by her husband's comic counterplot, in which he has abandoned his insistence on sobriety and pretended to become a creature of pleasure himself, flirting with Celestina and gambling his estate away. But other spectacles sicken her as well, including her lover's report of their anonymous night together: " 'Twas a she devil too, a most insatiate,/Abominable devil, with a tail/Thus long." Aretina herself is tellingly inarticulate; the morning after brings her a *malheur* that Shirley subtly dramatizes mainly through her impression on others ("What! melancholy,/After so sweet a night's work?"). He also allows her change of heart to take place without any exposure of her adultery, even to her husband; her precautions to ensure secrecy remain effective, and no official humiliation is demanded of her. Female sexual transgres-

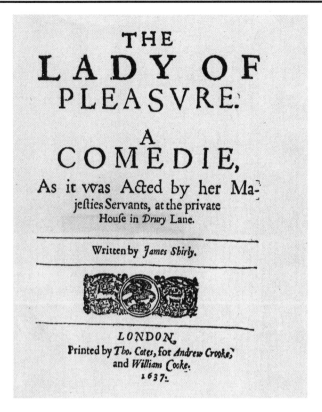

THE
LADY OF
PLEASVRE.

A
COMEDIE,

As it was Acted by her Majefties Servants, at the private
Houfe in *Drury* Lane.

Written by *James Shirly.*

LONDON,
Printed by *Tho. Cotes*, for *Andrew Crooks*,
and *William Cooke.*
1637.

Title page for the 1637 quarto edition of Shirley's best-known comedy (Henry E. Huntington Library and Art Gallery)

sion is seldom treated so gently in the Renaissance, though the dramatic purpose is to underscore the depth and inwardness of Aretina's repentance:

> I feel a cure upon my soul, and promise
> My after life to virtue. Pardon, heaven,
> My shame, yet hid from the world's eye.

Yet the other woman in the case gives this repentance yet another twist. Celestina is there to show that Aretina's crime was not necessarily a consequence of her announced program, but in a way a betrayal of it. In her own opening scene, Celestina is no less high-handedly hedonistic than Aretina as she dresses down her cautious steward:

> Must I be limited to please your honour,
> Or, for the vulgar breath, confine my pleasures?
> I will pursue 'em in what shapes I fancy,
> Here, and abroad; my entertainments shall
> Be oftener, and more rich. Who shall control me?

As a widow she is better set to pursue such whims than Aretina, who constantly feels herself bested in their competition. Yet Celestina also knows a rule

of the game that Aretina has not figured out: "jest, but love not."

> Some ladies are so expensive in their graces,
> To those that honour them, and so prodigal,
> That in a little time they have nothing but
> The naked sin left to reward their servants;
> Whereas, a thrift in our rewards will keep
> Men long in their devotion, and preserve
> Ourselves in stock, to encourage those that honour
>   us.
> ....
> It takes not from the freedom of our mirth,
> But seems to advance it, when we can possess
> Our pleasures with security of our honour;
> And, that preserv'd, I welcome all the joys
> My fancy can let in.

She holds to those principles. Her flirtation with Bornwell is recognized by both as an act, and she later successfully resists the more serious suit of a noble relative of Aretina's who woos her with, in fact, speeches based on Carew's "A Rapture." Celestina takes her cue from another branch of the libertine tradition, that of a chaste libertinage which values courtship and foreplay over "fruition" and its resultant *tristesse*. The Bornwells return to the country after their taste of London's pleasures, but Celestina stays, having grasped what it takes to enjoy those pleasures properly. Her stance has affinities with the courtly Platonism that Queen Henrietta cultivated and that the Puritans attacked as hypocritical; Celestina is in effect Shirley's attempt to close that gap, to show, even more clearly than in Will Hazard, how valuing one's pleasures can be the basis for a serious moral discipline. She keeps her virtue precisely so as not to spoil her fragile and expensive earthly delights.

Bibliography:
Ruth K. Zimmer, *James Shirley: A Reference Guide* (Boston: G. K. Hall, 1980).

References:
Fredson Bowers, *Elizabethan Revenge Tragedy 1587-1642* (Princeton: Princeton University Press, 1940);

Robert Stanley Forsythe, *The Relations of Shirley's Plays to the Elizabethan Drama* (New York: Columbia University Press, 1914);

Alfred Harbage, *Cavalier Drama* (New York: MLA, 1936);

Ben Lucow, *James Shirley* (Boston: Twayne, 1981);

Arthur Huntington Nason, *James Shirley, Dramatist* (New York: Privately printed, 1915).

Papers:
The Bodleian Library has a manuscript volume of poems (MS Rawl. poet, 88) thought to be in Shirley's hand. A manuscript for an early version of *The Court Secret,* in the hand of a scribe with later revisions in another hand, is at Worcester College, Oxford (MS 1200). The British Library has a manuscript for *Cupid and Death* (Add. MS 17799), and Shirley's will, in his own hand and dated July 1666, is at Somerset House.

Sir John Suckling

(February 1609-1642)

Charles L. Squier
University of Colorado-Boulder

PLAY PRODUCTIONS: *Aglaura*, London, at Court, 1638; tragicomic version, London, Cockpit theater, 3 April 1638;
The Goblins, London, Blackfriars theater, 1641(?);
Brennoralt, or The Discontented Colonel, London, Blackfriars theater, 1641(?).

BOOKS: *Aglaura* (London: Printed by J. Haviland, Thomas Walkley, 1638);
The Discontented Colonell (London: Printed by Edward Griffin for Francis Eaglesfield, 1642);
Fragmenta Aurea (London: Printed for Humphrey Moseley, 1646)—comprises *Poems, Letters, An Account of Religion by Reason, Aglaura, The Goblins*, and *Brennoralt;*
The Last Remains of Sir John Suckling. Being a Full Collection of All His Poems and Letters (London: Printed for Humphrey Moseley, 1659).
Editions: *The Works of Sir John Suckling, the Non-Dramatic Works*, edited by Thomas Clayton (Oxford: Oxford University Press, 1971);
The Works of Sir John Suckling, the Plays, edited by L. A. Beaurline (Oxford: Oxford University Press, 1971).

Sir John Suckling was, according to the seventeenth-century gossip and biographer John Aubrey, "The greatest gallant of his time and the greatest gamester both for Bowling and Cards, so that no Shopkeeper would trust him for 6d, as today, for instance, he might by winning, be worth 200 pounds, and the next day he might not be worth half so much, or perhaps sometimes be *minus nihilo.*" A recent biographer, Herbert Berry, points out that Suckling's greatness as a gambler is best measured by the substantial amounts of money he lost. In the course of a few years he managed to gamble away the large estate left him by his father. Suckling's dramatic ventures are not unconnected with the constantly fluctuating and usually depressed state of his exchequer. He was not a professional playwright but a gentleman amateur, a courtier who saw the drama as a means of courtly advancement. He was sufficiently talented, how-

ever, to draw the fire of forty-two lines of irritated verse from the professional playwright Richard Brome. If the times had been different and his life longer, Suckling might well have become a professional playwright himself.

As it is, Suckling's literary reputation rests primarily on his poems, on his skill as a witty and graceful lyricist. His three plays are so firmly set in the world of the seventeenth century that it is highly unlikely they will ever be produced on a modern stage, even under academic auspices. Nonetheless, the plays merit attention and respect for moments of skillful artifice, spectacle, and song and above all for the creation of a fashionable stage language for gentlemen to be assiduously emulated in the Restoration. Suckling chose to have Anthony Van Dyck paint him with a folio volume of Shakespeare, open to *Hamlet*, in his hand. If the plays seem slight today, at least Sir John could imagine himself within the great dramatic tradition. His plays, moreover, did hold the stage well into the Restoration, until, in fact, their mode was dead.

John Suckling's life was brief and ended tragically in suicide, but he was born in fortunate circumstances in 1609 in Twickenham Parish, Middlesex, where his father, also John Suckling, a prosperous landowner and courtier, had an estate at Whitton. The elder Suckling became a member of the Privy Council and held court positions as Master of Requests and Comptroller of the King's Household. Suckling's mother, Martha, who died when he was four and a half, was the sister of Lionel Cranfield, who was to become Lord Treasurer of England and Earl of Middlesex. Theophilus Cibber's report in his *Lives of the Poets* (1753) that Suckling was born "with the remarkable circumstance of his mother's going eleven months with him" seems as questionable as Gerard Langbaine's statement in *An Account of the English Dramatic Poets* (1691) that he "spoke Latin at Five Years old and writ it at Nine." What is certain is that Suckling was born to a rich and influential family.

He was probably privately tutored at home until he matriculated as a fellow commoner at Trin-

Sir John Suckling, portrait by Sir Anthony Van Dyck (copyright the Frick Collection, New York)

ity College, Cambridge, in the Easter term of 1623. He left Cambridge without a degree to continue his education at Gray's Inn, where he was admitted in February 1627. His studies—such as they may have been, surely a smattering of law with a mixture of gambling, poetry, and wenching—were interrupted by the death of his father in March 1627. The elder Suckling had wisely provided that his lands and large fortune be held in trust until his son was twenty-five, but the provision was of little

use in controlling so resolute a spendthrift as young Suckling. The following years are a record of military service abroad, gambling, courtship, both amorous and political, and the beginning of his literary and dramatic career.

In May of 1627 Suckling probably joined the ill-fated expedition to the Island of Rhé led by the Duke of Buckingham; badly planned and supplied, more than half the British troops were lost, the majority through disease. It was hardly a glamorous introduction to the life of a Cavalier. His military career, however, continued in 1629 as a volunteer in the Low Countries under Lord Wimbledon. His letters from this period give a glimpse of a young man trying to make his way in the world, dutifully reporting political news to his influential uncle while writing witty, cynical commentary to his friends. His name is found on the rolls of Leyden University, but his study of astrology there was brief. In September 1630 Suckling was knighted by King Charles, but since the knighthood was purchased it is a mark of the amplitude of his fortune rather than merit. Still, the glitter, and perhaps the prospects, of the witty courtier must have been enhanced by the new title.

In 1631 Sir John was in the service of Sir Henry Vane, ambassador extraordinary to King Gustavas Adolphus of Sweden, who was then campaigning in Germany; but his travels abroad ended when he returned to England with dispatches for the court in April 1632. John Aubrey credits Suckling with the invention of cribbage; the attribution is vexed and unresolved. His gambling, however, begins in earnest about this time. The record includes his winning nearly £2,000 from Lord Dunluce at ninepins, but even such a stunning take could not offset the losses, and in a relatively short time Sir John had gambled away his patrimony, amounting to more than £7,000. It is not surprising that in 1634 Suckling devoted considerable effort to an unsuccessful attempt to win a rich bride. The enterprise reads like a comedy of intrigue. Servants were corrupted; the heiress, Anne Willoughby, was induced to sign a statement saying she wanted to marry Suckling; Sir John challenged Sir Henry Willoughby, the outraged father, to a duel; Willoughby's marital choice for his daughter, Sir John Digby (brother of the noted pirate, alchemist, and scholar Sir Kenelm Digby), cudgeled Suckling, who retaliated by hiring a gang of thugs to assault Sir John Digby outside Blackfriars theater.

At least the location serves as a reminder that Suckling combined literary activities with his rakehell life. His earliest literary remains are juvenile poems going back to 1626. But his real beginnings as a poet and his first attempt at play writing belong to the 1630s, after his return from the Continent. "A Song to a Lute," a brilliant parody of Ben Jonson's song "Have You Seen But the Bright Lily Grow" in *The Devil Is an Ass*, comes from this period and is dramatically set in Suckling's incomplete play, *The Sad One*. *The Sad One* was a trial run, a practice play filled with the commonplaces of Caroline theater—a Sicilian setting, an intrigue-ridden

court, a revenge theme, a lecherous king, an immoral but repentant lady with a brother for bawd, attempted regicide, and an abundance of talk and high sentiments. *The Sad One* is undeniably pretty bad; perhaps that was the reason Suckling left it unfinished. The plot, however, provided some of the material for his first complete play, *Aglaura;* and Suckling, ever thrifty in art if not in life, also reworked many of the lines of *The Sad One* in *Aglaura*. In addition to the parody of Jonson's lyric Suckling parodies the man himself in *Aglaura* in the figure of the poet Multecarni busily and boastfully producing an obviously execrable masque: "If it does not take, my masters, it lies not upon me, I have provided well; and if the stomack of the times be naught, the fault's not in the meat or in the Cook." Suckling's dramatic allegiance was to Shakespeare and Fletcher; Jonson remained a lifelong aversion.

Certainly Jonson would have found nothing to admire in Suckling's first complete play, the splashy and spectacular *Aglaura*. Sir John made sure that his debut in the theatrical world would not go unnoticed. The play was produced by the King's Company at court and at Blackfriars in late January or early February 1638, apparently at Suckling's own cost. In a letter to the Earl of Strafford John Gerrard reported, "*Sutlin's* Play cost three or four hundred pounds setting out, eight or ten Suits of new Cloaths he gave the Players; an unheard of Prodigality," and John Aubrey described the costumes as "very rich; no tinsell, all the lace pure gold and silver. . . ." Not content with the lavish productions, Suckling also printed *Aglaura* in a handsome, wide-margined folio for presentation to the court audience, and the extant manuscript of the play, formerly in the Royal Library, was probably made as a presentation copy for the king.

In 1638 Suckling sold his last estate, Roos Hall, and was appointed a Gentleman of the Privy Chamber Extraordinary. That either event is connected with *Aglaura* is uncertain, but the production of *Aglaura* certainly was a deliberate attempt to capture the attention of the court. The play can be seen as a courtly flourish, a dazzling demonstration of the versatility of the ambitious young courtier—even to the point of equipping the play with two interchangeable last acts, tragic and tragicomic.

Suckling's comments on the double ending are lighthearted:

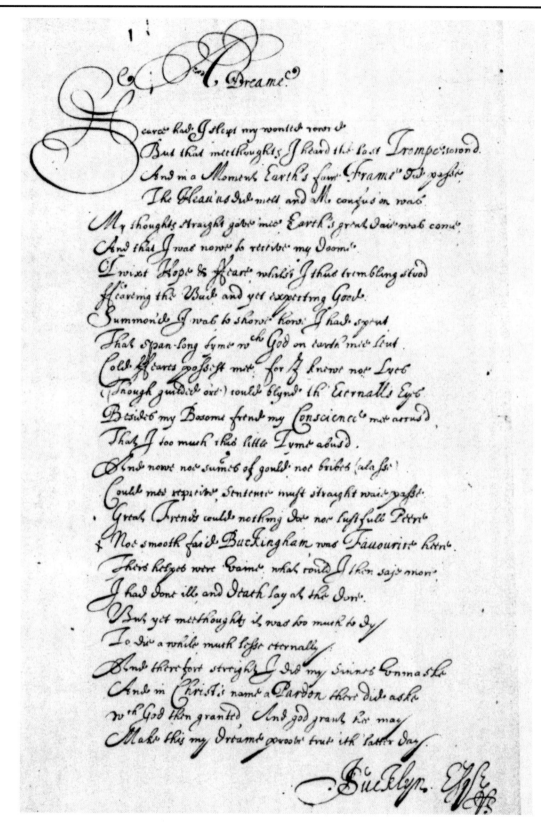

Manuscript for a poem written by Suckling probably between 1624 and 1632. He adapted lines seventeen and eighteen for use in his unfinished first play, The Sad One *(by permission of Hugh Sackville West, agent for Knole Estates; Cranfield Papers, U. 269. F. 36, No. 38, f. 2ʳ).*

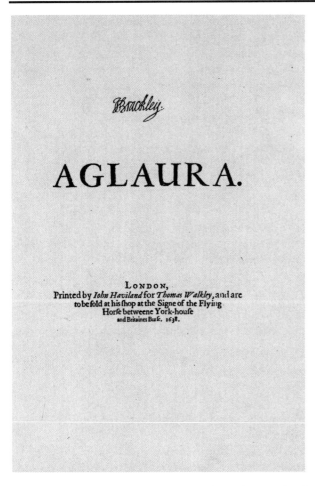

Title page for the 1638 folio edition of Suckling's first completed play (Henry E. Huntington Library and Art Gallery)

Tis strange perchance (you'll thinke) that she that di'de
At Christmas, should at Easter be a Bride:
But 'tis a privilege the Poets have,
To take the long-since dead out of the grave.

They point to the conclusion that we are not meant to take the lurid and complex materials of the plot with much seriousness. In the tragic version Thersames, the good prince, dies, as does his bride, the object of the lustful attentions of King Orsames, who also dies. In fact, virtually everyone is stabbed, poisoned, or, like *Aglaura,* dies heartbroken. In the tragicomic version forgiveness, penitence, and reform triumph.

When Samuel Pepys read *Aglaura* in 1664, he found it "but a mean play; nothing of design in it." Suckling's own view of dramatic design, however, as expressed in the epilogue to the tragicomic version, is that "Plays are like Feasts, and everie Act

should bee/Another Course, and still varietie." That description fits both Suckling's intent and achievement in *Aglaura. Aglaura* contains elements of the revenge play, Platonic and anti-Platonic libertine drama, and Fletcherian theater of court intrigue. It does not try for consistency but for variety. As well as rich and elaborate costuming, *Aglaura* also apparently made use of painted scenes, a device Suckling's friend Sir William Davenant would transfer to the public theater in the Restoration.

Suckling saw his play as spectacle and as fashionable entertainment, the fashionable quality asserted not only by the masquelike elegance of its mounting but by the language—witty, graceful, and copious. The wit, that of the similitude and of infinite variation of commonplaces, aims at making the ordinary surprising. The language of *Aglaura* is often essentially detached from the action. Conversations, figures, jokes exist for themselves. The audience listens for elegancies of wit, not for revelation of character or for language tied to the characters in image or tone. One way of looking at *Aglaura* is to see it as a kind of revue with a series of "turns" of language and scene. Two of Suckling's songs—"Why so pale and wan fond Lover" and "No, no, fair Heretique"—are included in the play and reinforce the sense of the play as a sort of revue.

Aglaura, with a plot derived directly or indirectly from Plutarch's *Life of Artaxerxes,* is set in a Persian never-never land of fantastic intrigue and overblown emotions. Through this dream world of impossible dangers, spectacle, sex, and sentiment wander characters speaking the witty language of courtly fashion and creating an oddly distorted, but recognizable, mirror image of the court of Charles I. *Aglaura* shows Suckling at home with the theatrical conventions and themes of his day. If it is the play of an amateur, he is a highly skilled amateur. *Aglaura* certainly caused comment in its day and was revived with apparent success after the Restoration. If Samuel Pepys did not like it, Gerard Langbaine was still able to write of it as late as 1691, "This play is much priz'd at this day."

Aglaura provided its audience with a colorful escape from the political realities around them. In 1639 the First Bishops' War marks the first skirmish of the oncoming civil war. Suckling, however, met the event quite as if it were a scene in *Aglaura.* He raised a cavalry troop of "100 very handsome young proper men, whom he clad in white doubletts and scarlett breeches, and scarlet Coates, hatts, and feathers, well horsed and armed." They must have been an impressive sight. Unfortunately the Cavaliers, weary with dysentery, took one look at the superior Scottish army and retreated. The campaign ended with the inconclusive Treaty of Berwick.

Suckling's growing reputation as a literary figure can be seen in the dedications to him by Thomas Nabbes of his play *Covent Garden* (1638) and by Wye Saltonstall of his *Ovid de Ponto* (1639). His poems circulated in manuscript, and such a poem as "The Wits" or "A Session of the Poets," written in the same year as *Aglaura,* indicates that Suckling's literary contacts extended beyond the court to the intellectual circle associated with Lucius Cary, Lord Falkland, at Great-Tew, a group which included such luminaries as John Hales of Eton, John Selden, and William Chillingsworth. Suckling's prose tract *An Account of Religion by Reason* (first published in *Fragmenta Aurea,* 1646) attests to the breadth of his interests.

Suckling's last two plays, *The Goblins* and *Brennoralt,* both reflect the increasingly troubled times. In April 1640 he was elected to Parliament as the member from Bramber, Sussex, but his parliamentary career lasted only five days. After the dissolution of Parliament he was commissioned a captain for the Second Bishops' War, which ended in defeat for the English at Newborn Ford near Newcastle. Suckling participated in the general retreat and is rumored to have lost some horses and his coach with money and clothes in it. *The Goblins* is escapist romantic comedy; *Brennoralt* more directly reflects the military and political situation in Britain. While Suckling was creating this stage echo of Britain's problems he was becoming increasingly involved in the conspiracy that would end in his flight from England and death in France, the Army Plot, a plan to use the army to gain control of Parliament and restore the King to a position of strength.

The date of *The Goblins* is not exactly established. It appears in a list of plays belonging to the King's Men dated 7 August 1641, and in January 1667 Pepys mentions its revival as a play "not acted these twenty-five years." The play is about the reconciliation of a postwar world, a romance dream of a happy ending to a civil war, and provides a momentary theatrical respite from the realities of Charles I's kingdom. Pepys saw only the last two acts of the play and reported that it was "a play I could not make anything of by these two last. . . ." If he had seen more of the play he might still have been in difficulty for the action of *The Goblins* is undeniably chaotic and confusing.

The scene is Francelia at the end of the civil war between the Orsabins and the Tamorens. The play is filled with all the trappings of romance— the royal brother lost and restored, courtly intrigue, complexities of love, and what amounts to the dramatic centerpiece, "*Theeves disguised in Devils habits, living underground by the Woods.*" These thieves, suggestive of the duke and his foresters in *As You Like It,* are the remnants of the defeated Tamorens, led by the younger brother of Old Tamoren. The heir of the Tamorens, Reginella, an innocent girl modeled on Shakespeare's Miranda, lives with the Robin Hood-like band and obligingly falls in love with Orsabrin, the lost brother of the Prince of the Orsabrins, as soon as he is captured by the amiable thieves. After a dizzying series of escapes and captures, alarms and confusions, the essential discoveries are made and peace is brought through the union of the warring sides with the marriage of Reginella and Orsabrin. The play is filled with escapes, disguises, duels, mistaken identities, social satire, witty chatter, talk of love, a few songs and a bit of dance, a good deal of lively stage action and language, and not much substance.

But nothing in *The Goblins* pretends to substance. The epilogue warns off critics: "who goes about/To take asunder oft destroyes (we know)/ What altogether made a pretty shew." The Shakespearean echoes from *The Tempest* and other plays are clear and unmistakable, from Reginella and Orsabrin as Suckling's version of Miranda and Ferdinand to Orsabrin's outrageous parody of Hamlet's most famous soliloquy:

> To die! yea what's that?
> For yet I never thought on't seriously;
> It may be 'tis.—hum.—It may be 'tis not too.—

But to see *The Goblins* as a serious attempt at Shakespearean romance is to demand too much of the play. The Shakespearean influence is in scenes, character types, techniques such as the mid-conversation entrance, in sum in bits and pieces, not in the broader informing Shakespearean spirit.

The Goblins really has no enlarging comic theme. Its surfaces are bright and shiny; it is purely entertainment. Individual scenes, however, are clearly the work of a craftsman of no little skill and sometimes of real genius. It is an engaging mélange of stage excitement, song, and lively dialogue. Moreover, the closer *The Goblins* comes to witty, quasi-realistic comedy, to the comedy of cynical, bright, conversational courtiers, in short to the kind of comedy most fully developed after the Resto-

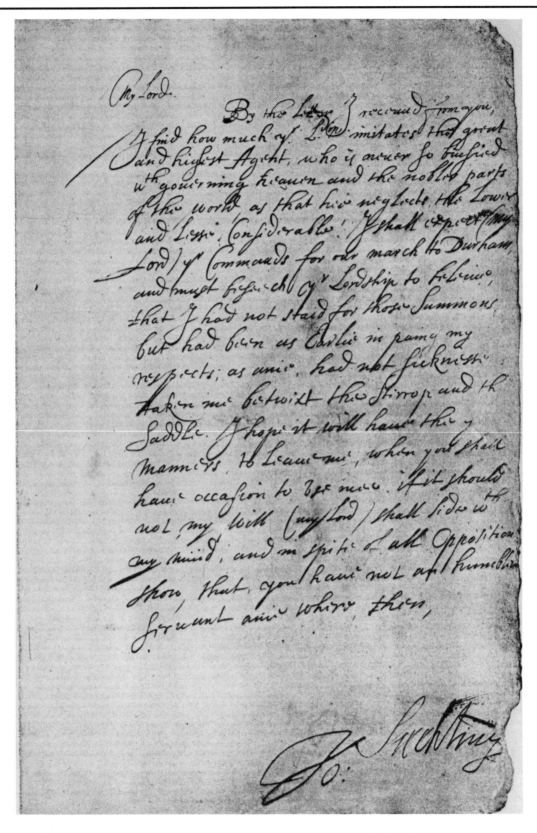

Letter from Suckling to Edward Viscount Conway, written circa April-May 1640 while Suckling was serving as a captain in the
Second Bishops' War (by permission of Viscountess Eccles)

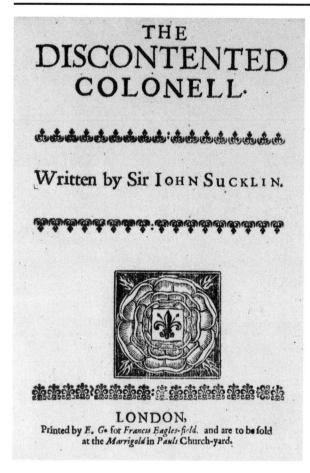

THE DISCONTENTED COLONELL.

Written by Sir IOHN SUCKLIN.

LONDON,
Printed by *E. G.* for *Francis Eagles-field.* and are to be fold
at the *Marrigold* in *Pauls* Church-yard.

Title page for the 1642 quarto edition of the play that was republished as Brennoralt *in Suckling's* Fragmenta Aurea *(Henry E. Huntington Library and Art Gallery)*

that the King should adopt a hard line against his enemies. It is first mentioned under its alternate title, *The Discontented Colonel,* in the 7 August 1641 list of plays belonging to the King's Men which were not to be published without permission. On 5 April 1642, however, Francis Eaglesfield entered *The Discontented Colonel* in the Stationers' Register and a quarto edition was published. By this time, however, Sir John was in exile and probably dead.

The date of the first performance is not known; nor is there any record of a court performance. L. A. Beaurline speculates that the paucity of allusions to *Brennoralt* before the Restoration indicates that "the play may have come too late to achieve notoriety before the closing of the theatres."

The substance of the plot is borrowed from Jean Pierre Camus's French romance *L'Iphigene,* published in Paris in 1625. The action is set in Poland, but clearly Suckling chose the story because of the obvious parallels between the rebellion of the Lithuanians against their Polish king and the rebellion of the Scottish Presbyterians against King Charles. The hero of the piece, the discontented colonel, is a conventional heroic soldier-lover, but his unexalted rank and the topicality of his attitudes suggest that he represents a recognizable contemporary figure, perhaps Col. George Goring or even Suckling himself. Whatever the identity of the discontented colonel, the play divides itself between love and war and extremes of realistic topicality and romantic tragedy.

Brennoralt, the discontented loyalist colonel, is in love with Francelia, the daughter of a leading rebel. Francelia, unfortunately for Brennoralt, is betrothed to a gallant rebel officer, Almerin. This familiar romantic situation is complicated by the presence of Almerin's friend, Iphigene. Iphigene is not just a loyalist but she is a girl disguised as a man and has been, oddly enough, so disguised all her life. It is hardly surprising that when Iphigene is taken prisoner by the rebels Francelia falls in love with him/her. All ends unhappily when in quick succession Almerin stabs Francelia in a jealous rage; Brennoralt kills Iphigene, assuming her to have murdered Francelia; and, after kissing the lips of their dead loves (for Almerin has found he loves Iphigene), the two heroes fight. The rebel Almerin is killed. The King offers Brennoralt a generous reward for his courage, but with a direct reference to Charles I's inadequacies in this regard Brennoralt rejects it and retires to private life: "A Princely gift! But Sir it comes too late."

ration, the better it is. The most outstanding aspect of *The Goblins* and of Suckling's dramatic achievement in general is in creating the "conversation of gentlemen" that John Dryden admired in Beaumont and Fletcher, the creation of a truly effective dramatic language capable of conveying the illusion of witty, genteel conversation.

If *The Goblins* shows Suckling's stagecraft to advantage, it is displayed to his advantage even more in *Brennoralt, or The Discontented Colonel.* At least the action of *Brennoralt* is far easier to follow. *Brennoralt* is not a pleasing play by modern standards, but it is reasonably well constructed, is filled with considerable action, and makes a substantial attempt at distinctive characterization. *Brennoralt* was probably written after Sir John's return from Scotland and the First Bishop's War. The play is filled with political and military allusions reflecting Suckling's irritation with the Treaty of Berwick, the petitions of the Scottish Covenanters, and his belief

The portrait of Suckling by William Marshall that was published in the 1646 octavo edition of Fragmenta Aurea *(Bernard Quaritch, Ltd., catalogue no. 436, 1930)*

The ending of the play with Brennoralt's speech focusing on the royal distribution of rewards and his withdrawal to private life directs attention away from the heroic-romantic unreality of the love stories to the unromantic realities of the court of King Charles I and the troubled politics of the day. The political allusions are the real heart of the play; the romantic complications provided the requisite dramatic stuff onto which the playwright's real concerns could be attached. Additionally the love scenes supplied the opportunity for poetic embellishment and stylized scenes. The lovers, as lovers, do not really matter. The sight of Francelia in her bed leads Brennoralt to a burst of poetry, admirable as decoration but of no significance otherwise. The pleasure is in the decoration, in the skill of the artifice. An audience cannot really care about the love plot except as decorated convention; the love plot serves to set off and heighten the political commentary and certain quasi-realistic scenes.

These scenes feature the sparkling conversation of the witty and cynical Cavaliers under Brennoralt. The officers provide a glimpse of camp life and offer a sharp contrast to the romantic fantasy of the heroic love plot. In one of the liveliest scenes of the play the officers engage in a drinking and extempore-poetry contest. The great issues are casually dismissed and give place to song: "Shee's pretty to walke with:/And witty to talke with. . . ." This scene and others like it belong to the world of realistic comedy. The carefree gaiety, the *sprezzatura* of the Cavaliers establish something of the court tone, if not of its actuality, at least of its aspirations. The conversation of the Cavaliers plays ironically against the heroic-romantic language of the serious plot. Six performances of *Brennoralt* between 1661 and 1669 and another production in the 1670s attest to its popularity in the Restoration, no doubt assisted by the excellent breeches role provided by Iphigene.

Suckling's limited dramatic career ended with his flight to France on the pinnace *Roebuck* on 6 May 1641 after the discovery of the Army Plot. He reached Paris on 14 May, but after that nothing is certain. He was probably dead by the end of 1641. John Aubrey's account of his death is most likely as true as any we shall have: "He went into France, where after sometime, being come to the bottom of his Found, reflecting on the miserable and despicable condition he should be reduced to, having nothing left to maintain him, he (having a convenience for that purpose, lyeing at an apothecarie's house in Paris) took poyson, which killed him miserably with vomiting."

Suckling's three plays survived into the Restoration and represent a fairly substantial achievement for an amateur playwright whose time was also devoted to military expeditions, court politics, gambling, wenching, and poetry. He mastered the dramatic conventions of his day and was able to create worlds of extravagant adventure, high romance, noble poses, as well as a variety of dramatic languages. In particular his realistic comic dialogue is distinctive and brilliant and his dramatic genius is most evident in comic scenes filled with song and witty conversation. His voice is the authentic voice of imagined gentlemen, urbane, artfully artless, wry, and humorous.

The first collection of Suckling's poems and plays, *Fragmenta Aurea,* appeared in 1646; with the exception of the period from 1725 to 1750 an edition or reprint of his works appeared at least every quarter century. Suckling's secure but minor place in English literature, it is true, rests on his poems. His plays are essentially of historical interest, but they do show that Suckling could write for the stage with real competence. Under different circumstances he might have become a far more substantial playwright.

References:

Gerald Eades Bentley, *The Jacobean and Caroline Stage,* volume 5 (Oxford: Oxford University Press, 1956), pp. 1197-1214;

John Frehafer, "*The Italian Night Piece* and Suckling's *Aglaura,*" *Journal of English and Germanic Philology,* 67 (April 1968): 249-265;

Charles L. Squier, *Sir John Suckling* (Boston: Twayne, 1978);

Ruth Wallerstein, "Suckling's Imitation of Shakespeare," *Review of English Studies,* 19 (July 1943): 290-295.

Papers:

Some poems and letters are found in the Cranfield papers, originally the personal papers of Lionel Cranfield, the first Earl of Middlesex, Suckling's uncle. The papers are in the collection of Lord Sackville of Knole, Sevenoaks, Kent, in the care of the Historical Manuscripts Commission. A manuscript for *Aglaura* is in the British Library.

Cyril Tourneur

(circa 1580-28 February 1626)

Paul A. Cantor
University of Virginia

PLAY PRODUCTIONS: *The Revenger's Tragedy*, attributed to Tourneur, London, Globe theater(?), 1606;

The Atheist's Tragedy, London, unknown theater, circa 1610-1611;

The Nobleman, London at Court, 23 February 1612;

The Arraignment of London (The Bellman of London?), by Tourneur and Robert Daborne, London, Whitefriars theater, after 9 December 1613.

BOOKS: *The Transformed Metamorphosis* (London: Printed by V. Sims, 1600);

Laugh and Lie Downe: Or, The Worldes Folly, attributed to Tourneur (London: Printed by W. Jaggard for J. Chorlton, 1605);

The Revengers Tragœdie, attributed to Tourneur (London: Printed by G. Eld, 1607);

A Funerall Poeme. Upon the Death of Sir Francis Vere (London: Printed by J. Windet for E. Edgar, 1609);

The Atheist's Tragedie: Or The Honest Man's Revenge (London: Printed for John Stepney & Richard Redmere, 1611);

A Griefe on the Death of Prince Henrie (London: Printed by F. Kingston for W. Welbie, 1613).

Editions: *The Works of Cyril Tourneur*, edited by Allardyce Nicoll (London: Fanfrolico Press, 1929)—comprises *The Transformed Metamorphosis, The Revenger's Tragedy, A Funeral Poem upon the Death of Sir Francis Vere, The Atheist's Tragedy, The Character of Robert Earl of Salisbury, A Griefe On the Death of Prince Henry*, and *Laugh and Lie down;*

The Plays of Cyril Tourneur, edited by George Parfitt (Cambridge: Cambridge University Press, 1978)—comprises *The Revenger's Tragedy* and *The Atheist's Tragedy*.

Among the many shadowy figures in the ranks of English Renaissance dramatists, Cyril Tourneur is one of the most elusive. Very little is known about his life, and we cannot even be sure that he actually wrote the work for which he is most celebrated, *The Revenger's Tragedy* (first performed

in 1606). Yet despite the almost complete absence of biographical facts concerning Tourneur, he seems to come alive through his works and to speak with one of the most distinct voices in Renaissance drama. Tourneur is arguably the quintessential Jacobean playwright, the one in whom the dark vision we associate with early-seventeenth-century drama achieves its purest form. He is a master of intricate plotting and counterplotting and seems to share his characters' delight in intrigue and deception. He played a key role in the development of the revenge play; no longer accepting the conventions of the genre uncritically, he raised the issue of the morality of revenge and in the process deepened his portrait of the psychology of the revenger. Above all, together his plays create a unique imaginative world, a world gone insane with evil. He portrays petty courts that have become grotesque in their corruption and focuses on a sexual perversity so pervasive as to suggest a general decay of the moral universe his characters inhabit.

We have no record of the year of Tourneur's birth, but most scholars assume that he was born around 1575 or 1580. We also know nothing of the family into which he was born or of the circumstances of his upbringing. The fact that Tourneur worked at times for the powerful Cecil family has led scholars to conjecture that he may have been related to a Capt. Richard Turnor (or Turner), who served under Sir Thomas Cecil in the Netherlands and became lieutenant governor of the Dutch town of Brill in 1596. The few facts that we have suggest that Tourneur was a typical young man on the make in Elizabethan society, hoping to rise in the world by exploiting family connections and attaching himself to a powerful courtier. He served for a while in the 1590s as secretary to Sir Francis Vere and as a result may have been involved in the raid on Cádiz in 1596 led by the Earl of Essex.

When Tourneur later surfaces, he is caught up in the tangled world of Renaissance diplomacy and statecraft. He functioned as a courier in 1613, carrying letters from London to Brussels, and also performed some service in the Netherlands, since we know that the United Provinces granted him a pension of sixty pounds a year. In 1617 he was brought before the Privy Council and briefly imprisoned, for what reason we—as usual—do not know. The fact that Sir Edward Cecil secured his release suggests that Tourneur may have run afoul of the authorities in the course of some kind of secret service or espionage, a specialty of the Cecil family. Allardyce Nicoll has speculated that Tourneur may in fact have been a double agent for the Cecils and tentatively suggests that Cyril Tourneur and a suspicious character named William Turner, who crops up in historical records, may have been one and the same man. In 1625 Tourneur was serving as secretary to Edward Cecil and as such participated in the disastrous second expedition against Cádiz. Amid the miserable conditions of this abortive raid, Tourneur evidently grew ill, and when the English forces turned back after failing to achieve any of their objectives, Tourneur was left to die in Kinsale, Ireland, on 28 February 1626. It is only at this point that we learn that Tourneur was married. His widow, Mary, sent a petition to the council of war begging to be granted her husband's back pay to avoid being left destitute.

Given what we know of Tourneur's career as a minor civil servant and courtier, his literary activities seem to have been a sideline for him. A number of his works are occasional in nature and were probably intended to advance his cause in court by ingratiating him with important patrons. He may have turned to the theater to supplement his income when his fortunes as a courtier were sagging. There is no evidence to suggest that he thought of himself primarily as a dramatist or that he was known in his day as a significant contributor to the Jacobean stage.

Tourneur's first published work is a weird poem called *The Transformed Metamorphosis* (1600). Growing out of the Elizabethan tradition of crabbed satire, as practiced by Joseph Hall and John Marston, the work is impossibly obscure and seems to cry out for some kind of allegorical reading. Unfortunately, no two interpreters have been able to agree on what the subject of the allegory is, though it does seem clearly political in nature, and the central character of the poem has been identified with figures such as Essex, Raleigh, and even Edmund Spenser. All one can say with certainty is that in Tourneur's first work his characteristic theme of corruption in the court already emerges. In 1605 a prose pamphlet called *Laugh and Lie Downe: Or, The Worldes Folly* appeared with the signature "C. T.," and this work is frequently attrib-

uted to Tourneur. It shares the bitter, cynical, and disillusioned spirit of *The Transformed Metamorphosis* and thus also seems consistent with the tone of Tourneur's plays. Tourneur wrote a handful of other works, including elegies on the deaths of Sir Francis Vere (1609) and of the young Prince Henry (1613) and a prose sketch of the character of Robert Cecil, Earl of Salisbury (1612). These works have little literary merit and are chiefly important for what they show about Tourneur's life and his connections at court. The elegy on Vere and the character of Cecil reveal a certain toughmindedness and clear-eyed understanding of the realities of practical politics and military command.

If Tourneur's literary output seems small, it may be due to the fact that several of his works have been lost. The Stationers' Register records under 1612 a play called *The Nobleman* written by Cyril Tourneur. The play seems to have been performed at court by the King's Players on 23 February 1612 and then again at Christmas. Nicoll includes in his edition of Tourneur's works a fragment of music which may have been written for this play and, if it is authentic, it is all that now remains of the play. In 1613 the minor dramatist Robert Daborne wrote to Philip Henslowe that he had "givn Cyril Tourneur an act of ye Arreignment of London to write." This play is thought to be the one whose title has come down to us as *The Bellman of London*, though nothing of the work itself survives. Daborne's reference is tantalizing in the way it conjures up an image of Tourneur eking out a living in London doing dramatic hackwork. But we have no way of knowing if this commission was an isolated event or typical of Tourneur's career in the theatrical world of London.

Tourneur's fame must of necessity rest on the two plays of his which have come down to us, *The Revenger's Tragedy* and *The Atheist's Tragedy* (published in 1611). Unfortunately his reputation will always have an insecure foundation because the attribution of *The Revenger's Tragedy* to Tourneur is at best conjectural. The play was probably written and first performed in 1606, by the "Kings Majesties Servants," according to the title page of the first edition. The play was printed anonymously in 1607 and was not attributed to Tourneur until 1656, by a dramatist named Edward Archer. Aside from the internal evidence of the play's resemblance to Tourneur's unquestioned work, *The Atheist's Tragedy*, Archer's attribution is the only ground we have for claiming Tourneur as the author (Francis Kirkman repeated Archer's attribution in play lists in 1661 and 1671). Some scholars have doubted the reliability of Archer's testimony, which comes some fifty years after the fact. But he remains the closest to a contemporary witness for documenting who wrote *The Revenger's Tragedy*, and one must wonder why he would have gone out of his way to attribute the play to an obscure figure like Tourneur if he did not have some evidence for doing so.

Archer's attribution was generally accepted until the late nineteenth century, when scholars began to put forward other candidates as the author of *The Revenger's Tragedy*, most notably Thomas Middleton. (See also the Thomas Middleton entry.) The controversy has gone on ever since, with critical opinion evenly divided as to whether Tourneur or Middleton wrote the play. Barring the discovery of some genuine hard evidence, it seems as if the issue will never be settled decisively. But if only for heuristic purposes, we may accept Tourneur as the author of *The Revenger's Tragedy*. *The Atheist's Tragedy* is clearly linked to the work in terms of mood, atmosphere, and themes, and, if Tourneur did not write both, he seems to have had *The Revenger's Tragedy* in mind when composing the later play.

The opening scene of *The Revenger's Tragedy* sets the tone of the whole work and quickly and effectively introduces the decadent world of a petty Italian dukedom. The protagonist Vindice—the revenger of the title—enters carrying the skull of his once beautiful beloved, Gloriana, who was poisoned by the Duke when she would not yield to his lustful invitations. Vowing vengeance, Vindice in the course of the play is able to exploit the internal tensions in the Duke's household, which consists of a lecherous and would-be unfaithful Duchess, a worthless son, a bastard, and three stepchildren, all of whom are easily pitted against each other to bring about the Duke's ruin and their own. In order to pursue his revenge, Vindice enters into the service of the Duke's son, Lussurioso, and eventually offers to assist the Duke's amorous adventures as well. The disguises Vindice adopts land him in some rather peculiar roles, such as serving as pimp for his own sister. At one point he is even engaged in his real identity to kill himself in one of his disguises, a situation which amuses Vindice ("I'm hired to kill myself ") but which points to the underlying suicidal impulse that seems to infect Tourneur's dramatic world.

Tourneur seems fascinated by such dramatic ironies as a man hired to kill himself and loads his plot with turns and counterturns that keep an audience off balance, never knowing what compli-

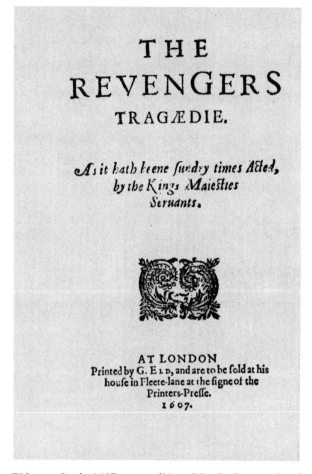

Title page for the 1607 quarto edition of the play long attributed to Tourneur but now believed by many scholars to be the work of Thomas Middleton (British Library)

cation to expect next. The unsettling of audience expectations reflects a more basic unsettling of the moral order in the work. By the time Tourneur is through, all normal moral values have been inverted, and in the imagery of the play day becomes night and night day. When the Duke justifiably sentences the Duchess's youngest son to death for attempted rape, she tries to get revenge by seducing the Duke's illegitimate son, Spurio. The Duke's stepchildren try to have their stepbrother, Lussurioso, executed but only succeed in procuring the death of their natural brother. In the culminating reversal of the work—a scene unsurpassed in Renaissance drama for horror and shock value—the Duke thinks Vindice is taking him to a midnight romantic tryst but is instead given the poisoned lips of Gloriana's skull to kiss. Before the Duke dies, Vindice forces him to watch his wife seducing his bastard son.

The action of *The Revenger's Tragedy* may appear crude and at times even barbaric, and the outlandish turns of villainy in the play could tempt twentieth-century readers into interpreting it as a forerunner of black comedy, piling horror upon horror until tragedy topples over into farce. The play seems to have served as the chief model for the absurdist Jacobean tragedy Thomas Pynchon invents in *The Crying of Lot 49* (1966), Richard Wharfinger's *The Courier's Tragedy,* about which one of Pynchon's characters comments: "It was written to entertain people. Like horror movies. It isn't literature, it doesn't mean anything. Wharfinger was no Shakespeare." One might be inclined to dismiss *The Revenger's Tragedy* similarly, but Tourneur's play seems to have a thematic core and in its own way a fierce artistic integrity.

What lifts *The Revenger's Tragedy* above the level of horror for horror's sake and makes it stand out amid the general run of Renaissance revenge plays is Tourneur's interest in the psychology of the revenger and what strikes us as a very modern concern with the problem of role playing and identity. The central question posed by the play is whether Vindice will be drawn into the very corruption he is trying to stamp out. He feels that he is merely playing the part of a pimp and an assassin, but in the course of the drama he seems to become a captive of the roles he adopts. Changing roles as often as he does, his faith in his own stable identity is shaken: "O, I'm in doubt/Whether I'm myself or no!," and he gradually turns into a mirror image of everything he hates. He prides himself on his successful scheming and takes genuine delight in accomplishing his revenge in the most fiendish ways imaginable. In the end, when he has destroyed all his enemies without anyone knowing of his role in their destruction, he voluntarily reveals what he has done and is himself sentenced to death. In a wonderful illustration of Edgar Allan Poe's idea of the Imp of the Perverse, Vindice cannot allow himself to get away with his murders unpunished and shows that the perfect crime is not perfect if nobody knows about it. Vindice has the instincts of a playwright: what good is a brilliant plot if one cannot publish it for all the world to see? Ultimately, then, *The Revenger's Tragedy* portrays how the very task of revenge corrupts the man who undertakes it and eventually destroys him.

The main reason for linking *The Revenger's Tragedy* with *The Atheist's Tragedy* is that the later play seems to continue the earlier one's questioning of the morality of revenge, raising the possibility that a good man might have to reject the task of vengeance entirely, leaving it to God. The play was published in 1611 with this title page: *The Atheist's Tragedie: Or The Honest Man's Revenge. As in divers places it hath often beene Acted.* Scholars have taken the publisher's assurance of the stage popularity of the play with a grain of salt; no independent evidence of a contemporary performance can be found. *The Atheist's Tragedy* is generally regarded as inferior to *The Revenger's Tragedy,* which has led some scholars to conjecture that it was in fact written earlier and merely published later. There is, however, no evidence for this claim. Given the fact that *The Atheist's Tragedy* shows signs of having been influenced by *King Lear* and *Macbeth,* as well as by the Bussy d'Ambois plays of George Chapman, a date of composition in 1610 or 1611 seems quite plausible for the play, and any date before 1606 seems highly unlikely.

The Atheist's Tragedy is dominated by a single character, the atheist of the title, a man named D'Amville, brother to the Baron Montferrers. D'Amville spends the whole play trying to prevent Montferrers's son, Charlemont, from coming into his legitimate inheritance and instead to win it for his own line, including his two sons, the sickly and impotent Roussard and the healthy and sexually active Sebastian. D'Amville is a kind of Marlovian overreacher, combining elements of Tamburlaine, Barabas, and Doctor Faustus in his tyrannical soul, incessant scheming, insatiable avarice, and defiance of God. But as his name suggests, he is also related to Chapman's Bussy d'Ambois, and Chapman's influence may have led Tourneur to deepen the philosophic content of his work. *The Atheist's Tragedy* is, as the title implies, a tragedy of ideas: D'Amville's naturalistic, skeptical philosophy leads him into a life of crime. He schemes to send Charlemont off to war and in his absence manages to marry off Charlemont's beloved, Castabella, to Roussard. D'Amville spreads a false report of Charlemont's death and then has Montferrers killed, thereby allowing himself to inherit the Baron's estate. In a major reversal of revenge-play tradition, Montferrers's ghost appears to his son on the battlefield and counsels him against taking vengeance: "Attend with patience the success of things/But leave revenge unto the king of kings." Despite an internal struggle, Charlemont obeys this command. Even when he returns to confront D'Amville, after a brief fight with Sebastian, he refrains from using violence. The plot is complicated by a number of erotic entanglements, chiefly involving Castabella's lecherous mother, Levidulcia, and one of those marvelous caricatures of Puritans that populate the

Jacobean stage, the self-proclaimed and hypocritical clergyman, Languebeau Snuff.

The play builds up to a climax of the macabre in IV. iii, in which half the cast shows up in a graveyard for a variety of innocent and lewd purposes. Tourneur flirts with an extraordinary range of titillating and indecent possibilities. Snuff mistakes the corpse of D'Amville's henchman for the whore he was supposed to meet and is barely saved from committing an act of homo-necrophilia ("Now purity defend me from the sin of Sodom"). D'Amville, convinced that Roussard is incapable of siring the grandson he needs to continue his line, tries to carry out an incestuous rape upon his daughter-in-law, dismissing Castabella's moral horror cavalierly: "Incest? Tush, these distances affinity observes are articles of bondage cast upon our freedoms by our own subjections." Charlemont scares off D'Amville from the attempted rape, but his triumph is short-lived, for both Charlemont and Castabella are arrested and, by the fifth act, lie at D'Amville's mercy. Tourneur begins killing off his characters in a series of conflicts, and when D'Amville discovers that both his sons are dead, he realizes that his hopes for founding an unending dynasty have died as well. His mental balance begins to unhinge, and when he goes to execute Charlemont and Castabella, we get one of the immortal stage directions in Renaissance drama: "*As he raises up the axe strikes out his own brains.*" Charlemont lives to inherit more wealth than he was born to and pronounces what appears to be the play's motto: "patience is the honest man's revenge." At the end of the play he proves to be more of a hero than the traditional active avenger. Indeed the courage with which he faces the prospect of death is what shakes up D'Amville and brings on his mental breakdown. Tourneur has found a way to make the Christian renunciation of revenge appear superior, even in strength of spirit, to the conventional aristocratic revenge ethic.

It is difficult to know exactly what to make of *The Atheist's Tragedy*. On the surface, the play seems to have a moral message, and many critics have interpreted it as the work of a deeply moral man in the kind of belated canonization that twentieth-century scholarship has conferred on many Renaissance figures. *The Atheist's Tragedy* does seem to teach that evil will eventually destroy itself and that a passive trust in divine justice will in the end triumph over all apparent obstacles. But for all the moralism of the ending, for most of the play Tourneur's villain is the focus of dramatic interest, and the good characters are pale by comparison. One

suspects that Tourneur may have felt at least a secret sympathy for his D'Amville, who is after all the playwright's surrogate, the principal plotter, the controlling intelligence of the action. And one must question whether a deeply moral man would have chosen this subject to portray or have put on stage scenes of such sheer depravity. *The Atheist's Tragedy* is exactly the kind of play Renaissance moralists were always inveighing against, and one doubts that contemporary preachers would have welcomed its publication, let alone recommended it as uplifting reading in their Sunday sermons. *The Atheist's Tragedy* provides an excellent test case for raising the larger question of whether the Jacobean theater is to be interpreted as a moral or an aesthetic phenomenon. Do the playwrights include sensational elements in order to attract an audience, who can then be properly taught a moral lesson? Or do they tack on moral lessons to their plays in order to have a publicly defensible reason for staging the kind of sensational drama they really wanted to write in the first place? In short, is the sensationalism for the sake of the moralism or the moralism for the sake of the sensationalism? These are the kind of questions that can be answered only in the context of a critic's broader understanding of the nature of drama and of the English Renaissance, and as such they are likely to provoke continuing controversy over a play such as *The Atheist's Tragedy* and Tourneur's achievement in general.

The relationship of Tourneur to Shakespeare is another issue that has elicited a great deal of critical debate. We are used to studying Shakespeare in the light of his contemporaries, showing what he was able to learn from the lesser figures who surrounded him. Less attention has been paid to the equally intriguing question of what Shakespeare's contemporaries were able to learn from him. Tourneur seems to be a classic case of a writer who was lifted to a higher level of achievement because he had the example of Shakespeare before his eyes. Individual lines and images in Tourneur, sometimes whole scenes, seem to be borrowed from Shakespeare's great tragedies. Clearly the play which made the deepest impression on Tourneur was *Hamlet*. In a way what we have in *The Revenger's Tragedy* is an indication of what a practicing playwright in Shakespeare's day thought he was seeing when he viewed *Hamlet*. We cannot say that Tourneur was consciously trying to imitate *Hamlet*, but it does seem that he was groping for the formula that had made the play such a theatrical success. If imitation is the sincerest form of flattery, Tourneur

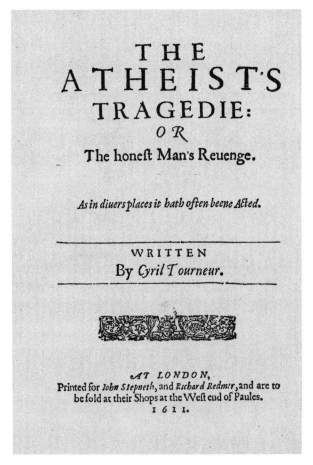

THE ATHEIST'S TRAGEDIE:

OR

The honeſt Man's Reuenge.

As in diuers places it hath often beene Acted.

WRITTEN

By *Cyril Tourneur.*

AT LONDON,
Printed for *Iohn Stepneth,* and *Richard Redmer,* and are to
be fold at their Shops at the Weſt end of Paules.
1 6 1 1.

Title page for the 1611 quarto edition of the only surviving play that is unquestionably the work of Tourneur (British Library)

evidently admired the gravedigger scene in *Hamlet* and the scene where Hamlet reproaches his mother for her moral failings (which Tourneur copies in IV. iv of *The Revenger's Tragedy,* when Vindice and his brother Hippolito get their mother to repent her sin in encouraging her daughter to yield to the lust of Lussurioso).

For Tourneur, *Hamlet* evidently consisted of one striking coup de theatre after another, and when he went to imitate it, he captured only parts and not the whole, giving us in effect *Hamlet* with everything except the Prince of Denmark. Moreover, in what may be an effort to outdo Shakespeare, Tourneur leaves any conception of good taste behind. Where Shakespeare brings a skull on stage, Tourneur drags out the whole skeleton. Where Shakespeare raises the issue of incest in the technical form of a widow marrying her dead husband's brother, Tourneur pictures a court where genuine incest is an open topic of conversation and

almost, it seems, a way of life. By comparison with *The Revenger's Tragedy, Hamlet* is a model of neoclassical decorum. But to judge Tourneur by the standard of Shakespeare is unfair. Even if Tourneur himself invites the comparison, its value lies chiefly in showing us what a contemporary of Shakespeare thought was theatrically effective in his plays.

Cyril Tourneur is admittedly not a major figure in the history of world drama. From what we can tell, his plays did not enjoy great popularity in his own time, and they have never broken into the standard dramatic repertory. *The Atheist's Tragedy* may very well never have been produced professionally; *The Revenger's Tragedy* has in recent years been revived in university theaters in both England and America and has received at least one major professional production. Trevor Nunn directed the play for the Royal Shakespeare Company at Stratford in 1966, with a cast that included Ian Richardson as Vindice. Nunn was attracted by the play's modernity and viewed it in the light of twentieth-century analogues: "It seemed to me a play that was extraordinarily about aspects of our own world . . . where the relationship between sex, violence and money was becoming increasingly popular, and expressed through all sorts of things—spy novels—James Bond." The play was considerably modified for performance, with a reordering of certain scenes, minor changes in the dialogue throughout, and the addition of seven substantial passages written specifically for this production by John Barton. Not anticipating a huge box-office success, the company planned only eight performances and saved money wherever they could (the set, for example, was borrowed from a concurrent production of *Hamlet*). The production received mixed reviews but did well enough to be brought back for nine more performances in 1967. In 1969 the company took the production to its Aldwych Theatre in London, where it was presented thirty-one times, including a gala performance which Princess Margaret attended.

Though Tourneur has never gained a large theatrical following, he has fared better with readers over the centuries. His two plays have, for example, been translated into French, and beginning in the nineteenth century he began to acquire some ardent admirers, among them Charles Lamb and A. C. Swinburne. In the twentieth century he has attracted increasing attention from critics. In reviewing Nicoll's edition, T. S. Eliot, for example, wrote a perceptive and generally laudatory appreciation of Tourneur, praising especially the quality of his versification and singling out *The Revenger's Tragedy* as a work of genius: "What gives Tourneur his place as a great poet is this one play, in which a horror of life, singular in his own or any age, finds exactly the right words and the right rhythms." Tourneur's literary output was as far as we can tell not large, and even within that small body of work his range was narrow. One cannot imagine him writing a light romantic comedy or realistically portraying a distant historical era. Yet within the realm he staked out for himself he reigns supreme as a master of stage horror. None of his contemporaries more fully achieve the abrupt shifts of tone, the prevailing mood of paradox, and the sense of moral chaos that we think of as peculiarly Jacobean, as Tourneur brilliantly mixes the sacred and the profane, the angelic and the demonic, the tragic and the grotesque, and the macabre and the obscene.

Bibliography:

Charles R. Forker, "Cyril Tourneur," in *The New Intellectuals*, edited by Terence P. Logan and Denzell S. Smith (Lincoln: University of Nebraska Press, 1977), pp. 248-280.

References:

Fredson T. Bowers, *Elizabethan Revenge Tragedy* (Princeton: Princeton University Press, 1940);

Jonathan Dollimore, *Radical Tragedy* (Chicago: University of Chicago Press, 1984);

T. S. Eliot, "Cyril Tourneur," in his *Selected Essays* (New York: Harcourt, Brace, 1950), pp. 159-169;

Una Ellis-Fermor, *The Jacobean Drama* (London: Methuen, 1958);

Peter Murray, *A Study of Cyril Tourneur* (Philadelphia: University of Pennsylvania Press, 1964);

L. G. Salingar, "Tourneur and the Tragedy of Revenge," in *The Age of Shakespeare*, edited by Boris Ford (New York: Penguin Books, 1955), pp. 334-354;

Samuel Schuman, *Cyril Tourneur* (Boston: Twayne, 1977);

Stanley Wells, "*The Revenger's Tragedy* Revived," in *The Elizabethan Theatre VI*, edited by G. R. Hibbard (Toronto: Macmillan, 1978), pp. 105-133.

John Webster

(1579 or 1580-1634?)

Antony Hammond
McMaster University

PLAY PRODUCTIONS: *Caesar's Fall or The Two Shapes,* by Webster, Anthony Munday, Michael Drayton, Thomas Middleton, and Thomas Dekker, London, Fortune theater, May 1602;

Sir Thomas Wyatt (presumably the same play as *Lady Jane*), by Webster, Henry Chettle, Dekker, Thomas Heywood, and Wentworth Smith, London, Boar's Head or Rose theater, October 1602;

Christmas Comes But Once a Year, by Webster, Heywood, Chettle, and Dekker, London, Boar's Head or Rose theater, November 1602;

Westward Ho, by Webster and Dekker, London, Paul's theater, late 1604;

Northward Ho, by Webster and Dekker, London, Paul's theater, 1605;

The White Devil, London, Red Bull theater, January-March 1612;

The Duchess of Malfi, London, Blackfriars theater, 1614;

Guise, unknown theater and date;

The Devil's Law-Case, London, Cockpit theater, circa 1619-1622;

Anything for a Quiet Life, by Middleton and perhaps Webster, London, Globe theater, 1621(?);

The Late Murder of the Son upon the Mother, or Keep the Widow Waking, by Webster, Dekker, John Ford, and William Rowley, London, Red Bull theater, September 1624;

A Cure for a Cuckold, by Webster and Rowley, London, Cockpit or Curtain theater, circa 1624-1625;

The Fair Maid of the Inn, by John Fletcher, Philip Massinger, and perhaps Webster and Ford, London, Blackfriars theater, licensed 22 January 1626;

Appius and Virginia, by Webster and perhaps Heywood, London, Phoenix theater, 1634.

BOOKS: *The Famous History of Sir T. Wyat,* by Webster, Thomas Dekker, Henry Chettle, Thomas Heywood, and Wentworth Smith (London: Printed by E. Allde for Thomas Archer, 1607);

West-ward Hoe, by Webster and Dekker (London: Printed by W. Jaggard, sold by John Hodges, 1607);

North-ward Hoe, by Webster and Dekker (London: Printed by G. Eld, 1607);

The White Divel (London: Printed by N. Okes for Thomas Archer, 1612);

A Monumental Columne, Erected to the Memory of Henry, Late Prince of Wales (London: Printed by N. Okes for William Welby, 1613);

The Tragedy of the Dutchesse of Malfy (London: Printed by Nicholas Okes for John Waterson, 1623);

The Devils Law-Case (London: Printed by A. Mathewes for John Grismand, 1623);

Monuments of Honor. Derived from Remarkable Antiquity, and Celebrated in London. At the Confirmation of John Gore (London: Printed by Nicholas Okes, 1624);

The Fair Maid of the Inn, by John Fletcher, Philip Massinger, and perhaps Webster and John Ford, in *Comedies and Tragedies Written by Francis Beaumont and John Fletcher, Gentlemen* (London: Printed for Humphrey Robinson & Humphrey Moseley, 1647);

Appius and Virginia, by Webster and Heywood (London: Printed for Richard Marriot, 1654);

A Cure for a Cuckold, by Webster and William Rowley (London: Printed by Thomas Johnson, sold by Francis Kirkman, 1661);

Anything for a Quiet Life, by Thomas Middleton, perhaps with Webster (London: Printed by Thomas Johnson for Francis Kirkman & H. Marsh, 1662).

Editions: *The Complete Works of John Webster,* 4 volumes, edited by F. L. Lucas (London: Chatto & Windus, 1927)—comprises *The White Devil, The Duchess of Malfi, The Devil's Law-Case, Cure for a Cuckold, Appius and Virginia, Shorter Poems, A Monumental Column,* Induction to *The Malcontent, Monuments of Honour, Characters,*

Anything for a Quiet Life, and *The Fair Maid of the Inn*;

The Famous History of Sir Thomas Wyat, in *The Dramatic Works of Thomas Dekker,* edited by Fredson Bowers, volume one (Cambridge: Cambridge University Press, 1953);

Westward Ho and *Northward Ho,* in *The Dramatic Works of Thomas Dekker,* edited by Bowers, volume two (Cambridge: Cambridge University Press, 1955);

The White Devil, edited by John Russell Brown (London: Methuen, 1960);

The Duchess of Malfi, edited by Brown (London: Methuen, 1964);

The Devil's Law-Case, edited by Elizabeth M. Brennan (London: Benn, 1975).

OTHER: Anthony Munday, trans., *The Third and Last Part of Palmerin of England,* includes prefatory verses by Webster (London: Printed by J. Roberts for W. Leake, 1602);

Samuel Harrison, *The Arch's of Triumph Erected in Honor of James, the First at His Entrance and Passage Through London,* includes an ode by Webster (London: Printed by J. Windet, 1604);

John Marston, *The Malcontent,* augmented edition, includes an induction by Webster (London: Printed by V. Simmes for William Aspley, 1604);

Thomas Heywood, *An Apology for Actors,* includes prefatory verses by Webster (London: Printed by N. Okes, 1612);

Sir Thomas Overbury, *New and Choise Characters, of Seuerall Authors . . . Sixt Impression,* includes thirty-two "New Characters" attributed to Webster (London: Printed by Thomas Creede for Laurence L'Isle, 1615);

Henry Cockeram, *The English Dictionarie,* includes prefatory verses by Webster (London: Printed for N. Butter, 1623).

Despite his seminal importance in Jacobean drama (most critics rank him as second only to Shakespeare as a tragedian), very little was known about John Webster's life until recently. However, the researches of Mary Edmond and the discovery in 1985 of a fragment of a manuscript play which may be in Webster's hand have materially changed the information available about him. Webster has been the subject of much critical enthusiasm this century, and his two tragedies, *The White Devil* and *The Duchess of Malfi,* are more frequently revived than any Jacobean plays other than Shakespeare's.

Yet most of this critical and theatrical attention is paid to only a small portion of Webster's output. Part of the reason for this is that beyond reasonable question *The White Devil* and *The Duchess of Malfi* are his finest surviving achievements. But these masterpieces need to be seen in context.

Edmond established that Webster was the son of a prosperous coachmaker, John Webster the elder, who was a member of the prestigious Company of Merchant Taylors (coachmaking was a relatively new trade, which did not have its own livery company). The Websters lived at the corner of Hosier Lane and Smithfield Street (then called Cow Lane), right next to what is now the Central Smithfield Meat Markets, and was in Webster's day the location of the famous St. Bartholomew's Fair, as well as a great horse fair, and center for other dealings in livestock. Webster's father married in 1577, and it is a reasonable inference that the baby who was to become the dramatist was born shortly afterward. (Webster had a brother, Edward, who was presumably younger.) Unfortunately, the parish records of St. Sepulchre, Holborn, were destroyed in the Great Fire of London, so it is not possible to obtain precise dates of birth, marriage, and death for Webster's family. Even so, a number of documentary items survive, and it is possible to draw some reasonable inferences.

It seems very probable that Webster was sent to the Merchant Taylors' School, probably in about 1587. Certainly his father had the right to send him there, and as a prosperous man, was in a position to do so. In *John Webster, Citizen and Dramatist* (1980) Muriel C. Bradbrook comments, "It would have been an act not merely of eccentricity but of ostracism for a member of the company to send his child anywhere else." The point is of importance, for the Merchant Taylors' School was an important educational institution, whose High Master from 1561 to 1586 was the influential Richard Mulcaster. (It is interesting that Thomas Jenkins, the Stratford schoolmaster who taught the young William Shakespeare, was probably a product of Mulcaster's teaching, so that Mulcaster's influence may have extended to Shakespeare as well as to Webster.) Mulcaster was succeeded by Henry Wilkinson, who continued the tradition Mulcaster had established; as boys could be admitted to the school at the age of nine, Webster probably arrived there shortly after Wilkinson's tenure began. Mulcaster's curriculum was unusual in several ways: he believed in teaching in English rather than exclusively in Latin, and he encouraged the performance of music and plays to encourage discipline and self-confidence in his students. Earlier, the boys had performed even at Court, but after the opening of the Theatre in 1576 their main outlets were in City of London pageants and other civic events, in some of which Webster must surely have participated.

A John Webster was entered at the Middle Temple in 1598. The evidence that this was the playwright is not positive, but it does seem likely. Certainly there is more than a suggestion of legal training in Webster's plays: there are centrally important trial scenes in *The White Devil, The Devil's Law-Case,* and *Appius and Virginia;* a point of law is the focus of the comic subplot of *A Cure for a Cuckold;* and a vein of legal imagery runs in the other works besides. Webster had connections with a number of Templars, such as Sir Thomas Overbury, and the dramatists John Marston and John Ford. Certainly, if Webster did attend the Temple, this would not only account for his preoccupation with legal matters, but this great legal university also would have acquainted him with its lively inmates, his fellow students. He would have met such writers as John Davies, and participated in such events as the Revels, with their satirical sports. The Inns of Court were celebrated for their connections with the literary life of the times, and there can be no question, from the quantity of borrowings detected in Webster's work, that he was very alert to the writings of his contemporaries. But one must not hypothesize beyond the facts, and there were certainly other John Websters in Elizabethan London.

Whatever his training, his practical career in the theater began with collaborative work for Philip Henslowe. If we discount *The Weakest Goeth to the Wall* (no one has made an even remotely convincing case for Webster's authorship of this play), the earliest reference to his work as a professional author comes in May 1602, when Henslowe paid an advance to a group of authors, Anthony Munday, Michael Drayton, Webster, and Thomas Middleton, for a play titled *Caesar's Fall* (or, in Henslowe's spelling, "sesers ffale"); a few days later Henslowe made "fulle paymente" to the same group (with the addition of Thomas Dekker), but now the play is called "too shapes" (the inserted title in the Diary is not in Henslowe's hand). It seems unlikely that the same consortium was working on two plays at once, so, odd as the name seems, *Caesar's Fall or The Two Shapes* is generally accepted as the title of the lost play in question.

In October of the same year Henslowe paid Henry Chettle, Dekker, Heywood, Wentworth Smith, and Webster two amounts for a play called

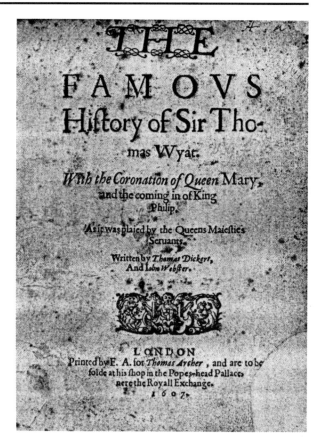

Title page for the 1607 quarto edition of the play that is probably an abridgement of the two-part play Lady Jane, *on which Webster collaborated with Thomas Dekker, Henry Chettle, Thomas Heywood, and Wentworth Smith (British Library)*

"Ladey Jane"; he also paid Dekker an advance on a second part of it later in November. The other dramatists are not mentioned, and it may be that not all of them were engaged in the second part: Webster was already working on another play. *Lady Jane* survives only as a bad quarto, printed in 1607 and titled *The Famous History of Sir T. Wyat.* According to Cyrus Hoy (1980) this text probably represents an abridgment of both parts. Such of *Lady Jane* as survives in *Sir T. Wyat* is an uninspired history play, heavily influenced by Shakespeare, in which motivation is glossed over, action is fast and confusing, and the odd mixture of comedy and sentimentality suggests that the authors had not quite got their act together. But the condition of the text makes any attempt at critical assessment, or even guesses toward the dramatists' shares in the play, virtually impossible.

In October 1602 Webster and Heywood were advanced money by Henslowe for a play called *Christmas Comes But Once a Year;* in November more payments were made, to Chettle and Dekker, and again to Chettle alone, for the same play, which was in production in November and December. The omission of Webster's name from these later entries does not imply that he had dropped out, since Henslowe's bookkeeping was always erratic. At this time his connection with Henslowe seems to have ceased. Webster's only other literary activity in 1602 was to produce a set of stilted verses prefixed to the third part of Anthony Munday's translation of *Palmerin of England,* printed in 1602.

Toward the end of 1604, Dekker and Webster collaborated in *Westward Ho,* which was produced by the Children of Paul's. This satirical and scandalous city comedy engendered a riposte: the even more scandalous *Eastward Ho,* produced by the Children of Her Majesty's Revels at the Blackfriars and written by Marston, George Chapman and Ben Jonson; Dekker and Webster returned to the fray in *Northward Ho,* presumably in 1605. Both *Westward Ho* and *Northward Ho* were printed in 1607.

Critical opinion is unanimous in thinking *Northward Ho* to be the better of the two Dekker/Webster plays, but there is good satirical comedy in both of them, and unmistakable signs of Webster's style as early as the first scene of *Westward Ho.* In a 1980 article Charles R. Forker makes a good case that these plays have been undervalued and stresses their self-conscious theatricality and the ambiguity of their support for middle-class morality. Despite their predictable, and rather confusing plots, they might well bear revival.

However, though Webster remained a life-long collaborator with Dekker, Heywood, and others, he did not follow them into an entirely professional career. His next work was done for an entirely different company, the King's Men, and consisted of an induction to Marston's revised version of his play *The Malcontent,* which the King's acted probably in 1604; it was printed in 1604. The early editions of *The Malcontent* are a considerable bibliographical and textual puzzle, the chief ques-

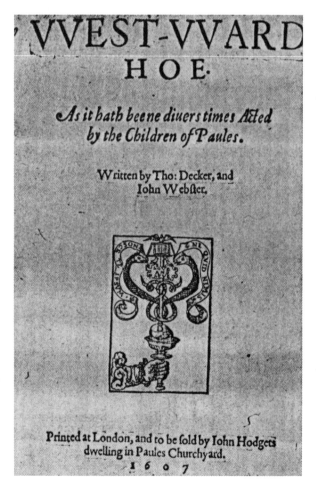

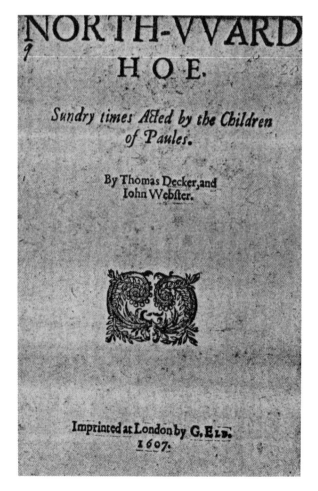

Title pages for the 1607 quarto editions of Webster and Dekker's controversial city comedies (British Library)

First and last pages of text from the 1607 quarto edition of Westward Ho *(British Library)*

tion being whether Webster contributed more than the induction to this "augmented" version of *The Malcontent*. The studies of the most recent scholar to examine the problem, Adrian Weiss, conclude very plausibly that only the induction is Webster's. The induction shows Webster's undoubted talent for satirical comedy directed at the citizen class (a vein much exploited in the plays in which he collaborated with Dekker) and his interest in matters theatrical.

Shortly after this, Webster married Sara Peniall and started a family. His eldest born, also called John, was baptized in 1606; the record survives because the baby evidently was born in the house of Webster's in-laws, whose parish, St. Dunstan's in the West, escaped the Great Fire. Sara, the eldest girl in the Peniall family, had been born in 1589; she was thus about ten years younger than Webster, and a mere seventeen years old when the baby was born. Other baptismal records are lacking, but from a neighbor's will it is clear that the Websters had a large family and were citizens in good standing with the community. But records are very sparse, and Webster's poetic and dramatic work seemed to have come to a halt; instead of pursuing his connection with the King's Men, he evidently had sufficient means to live an independent life. His next published work is *The White Devil*, which was printed in 1612.

In 1985, however, Edward Saunders and Felix Pryor made a fascinating discovery in the muniments room of Melbourne Hall: a folded leaf which had originally been used as a wrapper for a bundle of Sir John Coke's correspondence and was now in a box containing plans for the garden. Upon examination, this leaf was found to consist of four manuscript pages of a hitherto unknown Jacobean play. The manuscript is "foul papers," (that is, an author's final working draft) much corrected in the course of composition. Its unique significance is that it is the only fragment of foul papers yet discovered. The handwriting is unlike that of any known Jacobean dramatist (though of course there are no surviving autographs of many dramatists, such as Beaumont, Ford, and William Rowley, as well as Webster). The subject of the scene is a conversation between Alexander de Medici, the Duke of Florence, and his favorite, his kinsman Lorenzo, in which Lorenzo manages to deflect Alexander's suspicions of him. The style very much resembles the sort of scenes Webster wrote in *The White Devil* between Bracciano and Flamineo.

Pryor claimed that the manuscript was a fragment of a hitherto unknown play by Webster, and tentatively titled it *The Duke of Florence*. This manuscript was put up for auction on 20 June 1986, but failed to reach its reserve price. The evidence for attributing this play fragment to Webster is equivocal, but his authorship is by no means impossible, and the similarities with Webster's style make the identification attractive. Against such an attribution must be set the entire lack of external evidence, and the fact that of Webster's habitual linguistic preferences, his fondness for contractions such as "i'th'," "o'th'," and " 's" as an abbreviation for "his" do not occur in the fragment. It is true that aspects of the Moor, Zanche, in *The White Devil* might derive from the fact that Alexander's mother was Moorish: the association might well have lodged in Webster's mind. And the image of the "Jacobs staffe" which occurs in the manuscript is an uncommon one, yet one that recurs in Webster. At present the matter must be regarded as undecided, but if it should turn out that the balance of evidence confirms Webster's authorship, then it will add a new work to his canon, and a further evidence that after 1605 (an allusion in the fragment to Jonson's *Sejanus* shows that it cannot have been written earlier) Webster determined to mine the increasingly popular area of Italianate intrigue tragedy.

This, at any rate, is the subject of *The White Devil*, which was printed (very badly) by Nicholas Okes in 1612, having been acted by the Queen's Men in the Red Bull theater sometime in the period January-March of that year. Webster complains in his preface that "it was acted, in so dull a time of winter, presented in so open and black a theater, that it wanted (that which is the only grace and setting out of a tragedy) a full and understanding auditory." Clearly it had not been a success, despite its sensational subject matter, and Webster in publishing the play was hoping to restore his good name. In a postscript he praised the acting and especially the work of Richard Perkins (who almost certainly played Flamineo): the first such tribute in the history of English drama.

The play deals with the adulterous passion of the Duke of Bracciano for Vittoria, which leads to his murder of his Duchess and of Vittoria's husband. His careless arrogance earns him the enmity of his Duchess's powerful brother, Francisco, Duke of Florence, and of the Cardinal Monticelso, who in the course of the play becomes Pope. Bracciano is ensnared in a plot and poisoned; subsequently Francisco's hired killers end Vittoria's life. It is an immensely powerful play, in which the conventional structures of social restraint (religious, political, and personal moralities) no longer have the

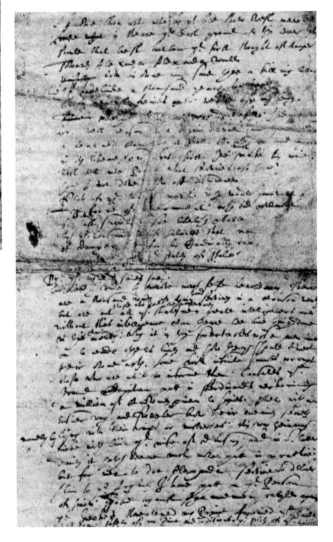

The Melbourne Manuscript (pages 1 and 4, left; 2 and 3, right), a fragment of a final working draft, discovered in 1985, of a previously unknown Jacobean play that has been assigned the title The Duke of Florence. *There are no surviving examples of Webster's handwriting with which to compare this fragment, but stylistic evidence suggests Webster's authorship (Bloomsbury Book Auctions, 20 June 1986).*

capacity to control the characters' vigorous passions. Francisco succeeds in his plan of revenge not because he is in any sense a better man than Bracciano, but because he is more astute, a better Machiavel, a smarter operator. At the center of the play is the ambivalent figure of Flamineo, Bracciano's secretary and Vittoria's brother. Whatever moral scruples he may have had have been overgrown by a lifetime of dependency; the corrupting atmosphere of the court has warped all his ethical reactions. He has no objections whatever to soliciting his sister for his master; his only complaint throughout the play is that his dedicated service to Bracciano's willful sensuality has never brought material rewards. He dies, as he has lived, in a state of lack of knowledge. Flamineo is a classic malcontent (Marston's play, with which Webster's had a close association, is an undoubted influence). He is

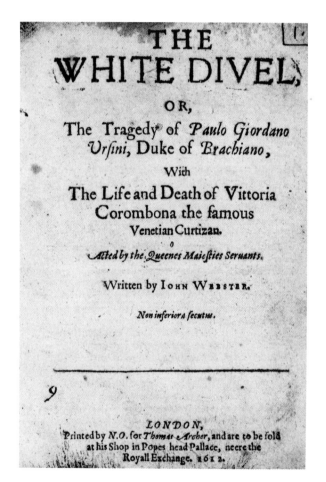

Title page for the 1612 quarto edition of one of Webster's best-known plays. Though it has been successfully revived as late as 1983, Webster complained in his preface that its first production "wanted . . . a full and understanding auditory" (Henry E. Huntington Library and Art Gallery) .

a kind of litmus paper, through whose reactions we can sense the level of tension of the rest of the court, and through whose corruption we can gauge the decay of the entire society.

Vittoria herself marks a new departure in Jacobean drama, a heroine whose morality is thoroughly corrupt, but with whom it is impossible not to sympathize. She has elected to live by the truth of her own sensations, and this decision leads her to welcome the passionate relationship with Bracciano, so different from the milksop Camillo to whom she is married. When Bracciano's injudicious actions land her in court, she seizes the opportunity to defend her life-style in the vigorous and characterful scene called "The Arraignment of Vittoria," in which she eloquently challenges the mean and narrow-minded morality expressed by her accuser, Monticelso. It is a great scene for a self-confident actress and is succeeded by two more: the great quarrel scene in the House of Convertites to which she is condemned, where her fury at Bracciano's allowing her to take the blame melts gradually under his masterful influence; and the final scene, in which she confronts death first at the hands of her malcontent brother, and then in the persons of Francisco's assassins. No one who saw Glenda Jackson's superb performance at the Old Vic in 1976 will ever forget the way she reconciled the conflicting aspects of Vittoria's character into a performance of great power and consistency. No other heroine in Jacobean drama is quite such a challenge to the actress or the audience: not even Cleopatra, who for all her moral evasions is never party to a pair of nasty murders of convenience. Yet because she is a woman, Vittoria's freedom of action is very much circumscribed by a wholly male-oriented society, a society which she must manipulate as best she can in defense of that independence of mind which characterizes her. The only quality which remains to Flamineo and to Vittoria in the long-drawn-out scene of their deaths is a sort of personal integrity, a courage in the face of unavoidable suffering.

Neither Vittoria nor Flamineo is in any sense an admirable character, but Webster creates for them, and the other denizens of his corrupt world, a language so full of vitality and poetic strength and energy—Webster is by far the most "conceited" of the Jacobean dramatists—that they cannot fail to attract attention and even sympathy from the audience. Their evil actions are largely inexplicable to themselves, which leaves them intriguing enigmas to the audience. The work of scholars such as Fredson T. Bowers, Harold Jenkins, and Richard

W. Hillman has shown that both *The White Devil* and *The Duchess of Malfi* employ many of the techniques of the revenge play, but not at all for the usual purposes of such plays. In *The White Devil* Francisco carries out the role of revenger, but is never subject to the moral dilemmas that most revengers suffer from, which makes their plays interesting. Nor is the corrosive evil of the revenge ethic the subject of the play. In many ways, Flamineo is evil, but his evil is not the explanation (in dramatic terms) of either his character or the structure of events in *The White Devil*. Nor are the plays structured according to the revenge-tragedy paradigm; as A. J. Smith has suggested—in an essay in *John Webster* (1970), edited by Brian Morris—Webster's way of re-creating reality, by a series of seemingly random juxtapositions of scenes of very different tone and style, reflects powerfully the instability of the imaginary yet persuasively real-seeming world he has created.

Many critics have held *The White Devil* to be inferior to *The Duchess of Malfi* on the grounds that there is little or no sense of hope in the earlier play and that it is impossible to identify wholly with any of the characters. These objections have led more sophisticated critics to search for structures of meaning at a deeper level in *The White Devil*, with some success; there is also the undeniable fact that it is an overwhelmingly powerful play in performance. It can be played as a very bleak representation of the selfishness and carelessness of worldly people, revealing as grim a view of society as some of Samuel Beckett's plays. It is also possible to play it more in sorrow than in anger, so that the excesses of the characters seem to arise from a society which has lost its roots in traditional morality and religion, people who have no star of guidance to steer their lives by. This, surely, is the more intelligible understanding of the play and aligns it with such other works as *Macbeth* and *Antony and Cleopatra*, plays which show individuals trying to derive from their own personal resources the moral judgments to control their lives. Macbeth turns away from the values he knows perfectly well; Antony seeks in his own will a value higher than his society's. The similarities are striking, except that both Antony and Macbeth are heroic in status, which is not true of any of the characters of *The White Devil* (saving, in her special way, Vittoria). But the dramaturgy is the same: the sense of people lost in their selves, struggling and, necessarily, failing, to make sense out of their lives in a world from which sense had been banished.

Shortly after *The White Devil* was performed, an event occurred which cast down all of England: the sudden death in November 1612, at the age of eighteen, of Prince Henry, King James's eldest son. Webster expressed his grief in an elegy entitled *A Monumental Column*, which was published in two formats: on its own, and with companion elegies by Tourneur and Heywood as *Three Elegies on the Most Lamented Death of Prince Henrie*. Nicholas Okes was the printer, and the elegies were published in 1613. Webster dedicated his poem to Sir Robert Carr, who was one of James's favorites and shortly to be created Earl of Somerset; almost immediately Carr became involved in the Overbury scandal, which also produced a connection with Webster. (Robert Bennett's suggestion that the dedication was ironical and cynical is preposterous.) Clearly Webster felt powerfully the untimely death of this hopeful prince; he compares him in the elegy to the Black Prince and uses all the usual elegiac machinery. But the poem remains obstinately earthbound: the brilliance and originality of Webster's imagery seemingly deserts him in the formal couplets of this poem. Nonetheless, as has often been remarked, some of the ideas stillborn here come to vivid life in *The Duchess of Malfi*, which Webster was probably already at work upon: the play becomes, as it were, the objective correlative for the grief occasioned by Henry's death which the elegy choked upon.

The Duchess of Malfi, by common consent Webster's greatest play, was probably written in 1613 or 1614; it was performed by the prestigious King's Men and must have been staged before 16 December 1614, because William Ostler, who played Antonio in the original production, died that day. Unique among dramatic quartos of its period, that of the *Duchess* (printed by Nicholas Okes in 1623) gives two partial casts for the play, one for the original production, the other presumably for a revival near the date of publication (John Thompson, who played Julia, apparently did not join the company until 1621). In both performances the bluff, portly John Lowin, rather surprisingly, played Bosola (his other roles included Shakespeare's Henry VIII, Falstaff, Volpone, and Sir Epicure Mammon). Burbage played Ferdinand in 1614; in the revival, the part went to Joseph Taylor. Richard Sharpe, who is listed as playing the Duchess, probably did so at the revival; the principal boy actor in 1614 was Richard Robinson, whose name was favorably brought by Jonson into *The Devil is an Ass*. It seems clear that the play was initially given at the Blackfriars theater, though the

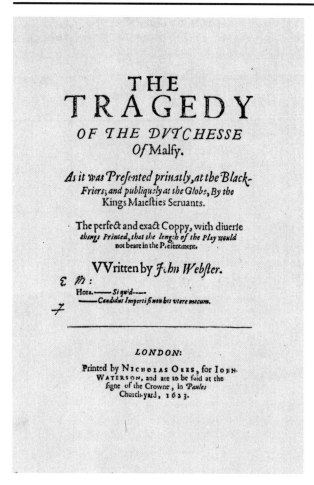

THE
TRAGEDY
OF THE DVTCHESSE
Of Malfy.

As it was Prefented privatly, at the Black-
Friers; and publiquely at the Globe, By the
Kings Maiesties Seruants.

The perfect and exact Coppy, with diuerfe
things Printed, that the length of the Play would
not beare in the Prefentment.

VVritten by John Webster.

ɛ m :
Hora.——Si quid——
——Candidus Imperti fi non his vtere mecum.

LONDON:

Printed by Nicholas Okes, for Iohn-
Waterson, and are to be fold at the
figne of the Crowne, in Paules
Church-yard, 1623.

Title page for the 1623 quarto edition of Webster's most successful play (Anderson Galleries, sale no. 2217,
10 January 1928)

title page of the quarto adds that it was publicly acted at the Globe. Many writers have commented on the advantages the Blackfriars would have had for the scenes of the Duchess's torment and murder; but the idea that the stage could have been artificially darkened for these scenes has been exploded, and the fact that they worked on the Globe's daylit stage shows that the "special effects" were emblematically, rather than "realistically" achieved.

It seems evident that in Webster's own time, as subsequently, *The Duchess of Malfi* was his greatest success. In the Duchess herself, we are given one of the greatest of tragic heroines, who tries to establish a good, Christian life in the context of the deranged hostility of her brother Ferdinand and the less unstable, but equally cruel, machinations of the Cardinal. Despite her brothers' urging against her remarriage, she secretly weds Antonio,

her master of the household, and lives with him some years before Ferdinand's spy, Bosola, uncovers the truth. (The notion, expressed by several critics, that the Duchess herself becomes somehow guilty by marrying her social inferior, is, in terms of the play's overall structure and mood, grotesque.) Harried from her home, separated from husband and children, the Duchess is imprisoned and tormented in the famous masque of the madmen; she is finally murdered, in one of the most powerful scenes in all Jacobean drama. Initially she acts with stoic resignation (her celebrated line, in response to Bosola's attacks, "I am Duchess of Malfi still," is only one of many stoical responses). But at the last she attains a mood of Christian resignation, well described by David Gunby (in an essay in *John Webster*, edited by Morris). After her death, the evil that men have done lives after them and is worked out in the final act, which brings all the other principals to their deaths.

Most writers find the structure of *The Duchess of Malfi* easier to apprehend than that of *The White Devil*. The powerful conflict between the Duchess and Ferdinand—and the role of Bosola as the intermittently reluctant agent between them—provides a clear and direct dramatic organization that Webster had not attempted in *The White Devil*, and indeed, only achieved elsewhere in *Appius and Virginia*. Ferdinand's obsession with his sister is darkly motivated—there are enough hints that it arises in suppressed incestuous feelings about her to have convinced most critics—but so is the rest of his unstable, haughty personality. It is not enough for him to separate the Duchess from her family: he organizes her torment and murder, actions which finally drive him into that particular form of insanity known as lycanthropy. He has, in theatrical terms, made himself into a beast. A development of Flamineo, Bosola adds to the earlier character's readiness to do evil for personal advancement an uncertainty very characteristic of Webster. At one moment Bosola plays the spy with evident relish and skill; the next he laments his degrading employment and begs Ferdinand to abandon his campaign against the Duchess. But only after the deed has been done, and Ferdinand has refused to reward Bosola for it, does his latent hostility become overt. Like Flamineo, Bosola never becomes entirely sympathetic, or wholly unsympathetic; and he does worse things himself than Flamineo ever did. He too is a malcontent, but despite his personal confusions, his actions are crucial to the destruction of the evil brothers, and thereby to the eradication of evil from the world of the play. And in his confusion and uncertainty, he finds himself acting in ways which are deplorable but by no means inexplicable. Like *The White Devil, The Duchess of Malfi* achieves its dramatic power through the vivid, brilliant, and flexible verse in which Webster has caught his characters' dilemmas. The play continues to excite the admiration of critics and the enthusiasm of theatrical companies. Without wishing to belittle Webster's other achievements, there is no doubt that common consent is that *The Duchess of Malfi* is Webster's supreme achievement.

At the height of his success, he was obliged to suffer the grief of his father's death: Webster senior must have died by 1615, because in that year Webster was admitted free of the Merchant Taylors by patrimony; his brother had been already admitted through apprenticeship in 1612, and it was Edward who carried on the family business after the elder Webster's death. The image of John Webster and his family that one arrives at is of successful and prosperous members of the urban middle class. Unfortunately the biographical record for the dramatist fades out in his middle years. However, in 1615 Webster contributed thirty-two new "Characters" to the sixth edition of Sir Thomas Overbury's popular Theophrastic collection, *New and Choice Characters, of Several Authors*. Whether Webster knew him before the *Characters* were published is unknown, but as Overbury had been a member of the Middle Temple, it is not inherently unlikely. Overbury's death rather cast into shade his life and literary achievements: he was poisoned by agents of Frances Howard, Countess of Somerset, who brought suit of nullity against her first husband, the Earl of Essex, in order to marry Robert Carr, the Earl of Somerset, King James's favorite. Overbury was Carr's friend, and allegedly he wrote the poem, "The Wife," printed in *New and Choice Characters*, to dissuade Carr from marrying Frances. The King had Overbury imprisoned in the Tower for refusing to accept a diplomatic appointment, and there he died, in September 1613, probably with Somerset's connivance. The tale became a public scandal of monumental proportions, and led to the fall from favor of the entire Howard family.

Overbury may be credited with the fashion in England for "characters"—generalized thumbnail sketches of classes of people, often satirically pointed. They survived as an essential aspect of biographical treatments and fictional handling of biography for more than 200 years: one can still find the descendants of the "character" in Dickens's novels. Webster liked them, and had already writ-

ten some into *The White Devil*: Flamineo gives a "character" of the cuckold in his description of Camillo in I.ii; Monticelso has his famous "character of a whore" in "The Arraignment of Vittoria" (III.ii): "This character 'scapes me" ripostes Vittoria, dryly. There are also Antonio's "characters" of Ferdinand and the Cardinal to Delio in *The Duchess of Malfi*, and many more. The thirty-two "New Characters" in the sixth edition generally believed to be by Webster (on the basis of close parallels with *The White Devil* and *The Duchess of Malfi*) include the celebrated "An excellent Actor," apparently written as a rejoinder to the abusive character of "A Common Player," in J. Stephens's *Satirical Essays, Characters, and Others*, also published in 1615. This precipitated a reply from Stephens, who criticizes Webster's "hackney similitudes" (without actually naming him); and another satirist, Henry Fitzgeffrey, attacks Webster in his book *Satyres and Satyricall Epigrams* (1617), which contains a poem (in execrable verse) called "Notes from Blackfryers":

> But h'st! with him Crabbed (*Websterio*)
> The *Play-wright, Cart-wright*: whether? either! (*ho*—
> No further. Looke as yee'd bee look't into:
> Sit as ye woo'd be *Read: Lord!* who woo'd know him?
> Was ever man so mangl'd with a *Poem*?
> See how he drawes his mouth awry of late,
> How he scrubs: wrings his wrests: scratches his Pate.
> A *Midwife*! helpe! By his *Braines coitus*
> Some *Centaure* strange: some huge *Bucephalus*,
> Or *Pallas* (sure) ingendred in his *Braine*—
> Strike *Vulcan* with thy hammer once againe.

> This is the *Crittick* that (of all the rest)
> I'de not have view mee, yet I feare him least,
> Heer's not one word *cursively* I have *Writ*,
> But hee'l *Industriously* examine it.
> And it some 12. monthes hence (or there *about*)
> Set in a shamefull sheete, my errors *out*.
> But what care I it *will* be so obscure,
> That none shall understand him (I am sure).

Behind the petty malice of this libel can be distinguished that both Stephens and Fitzgeffrey knew enough to associate Webster with the coaching trade, that Fitzgeffrey knew of his association with Dekker in the *Ho* plays, knew of his liking for Italianate plots (hence "Websterio"), and was aware of his reputation for slow composition. Before one takes this poem too seriously (no author in those heady days escaped detraction), it is worth recalling the respectful and generous poems that Middleton,

Rowley, and Ford contributed to *The Duchess of Malfi*.

The major enigma of this period is the lost play, *Guise*. Webster refers to it in his dedication of *The Devil's Law-Case*, where he lists it with *The White Devil, The Duchess of Malfi*, "and others" which his dedicatee, Sir Thomas Finch, has seen. Whether this means "seen in print" or "seen on the stage," no one can tell; and what the "others" are—did he mean the collaborative plays, or was he hinting at other lost plays (perhaps *The Duke of Florence?*)—can only be guessed at. It seems fair to assume that a play about the notorious Duke of Guise would be a tragedy of intrigue; that the *Guise* was written before *The Devil's Law-Case* is only a plausible inference.

The Devil's Law-Case was written for the Cockpit (later known as the Phoenix), built by John Best in 1609, and converted by Inigo Jones to its final form in 1616, when Christopher Beeston leased it for Queen Anne's Men, the same company as had formerly produced *The White Devil*. It is a reasonable inference that Richard Perkins, the actor Webster had praised in *The White Devil*, was entrusted with the leading role of Romelio in *The Devil's Law-Case*, though no cast list survives. The play was printed in 1623, the same year as *The Duchess of Malfi*, but by a different printer (Augustine Mathewes). The date of composition is uncertain: the title page described it as "A new Tragecomoedy," but such assertions are not to be trusted. There are some lines which seem to be derived from Jonson's *The Devil is an Ass*, which was acted in 1616, but the topical allusions discovered in the play are difficult to depend on: such as they are, they suggest 1619, which in itself is a plausible enough date; it must have been played before 1622, when Queen Anne's Men disbanded.

Most critics agree in finding it the most difficult of Webster's works to assess. It uses many of the materials and styles of *The White Devil* and *The Duchess of Malfi*, but for an entirely different dramatic end. The key event in the play is the law case itself, where Leonora attempts to disinherit her son Romelio by alleging his bastardy. Unfortunately for her scheme, the judge trying the case turns out to be the man she is claiming to be Romelio's father. But this is only one of a huge number of plots in the play, many of them originated by Romelio himself, whose scheming is untinged by moral considerations, and who goes so far in his designs as to disguise himself as a Jewish doctor and attempt to stab to death the wounded Contarino. By an ironic reversal, the blood-letting actually saves Contari-

no's life, and none of the other immoral plots in the play actually come to fruition. Both David Gunby (in a 1968 article) and Elizabeth Brennan (in her 1975 edition of the play) have argued that there is a providential moral in this plotting, without carrying conviction to all critics. The chief obstacle to finding *The Devil's Law-Case* intelligible is the incoherence of the plot (though Ralph Berry amazingly calls it the "most skillful" of the plays). Wildly different from the Fletcherian model of tragicomedy, *The Devil's Law-Case* is full of actions which are both absurd and shocking. Romelio seems to owe something to Marlowe's Barabas, and certainly to Jonson's Volpone, and the general tone of corruption and folly is hard to reconcile with the overly hasty, careless ending. No account of the play has made a wholly plausible case for its unity, least of all Lee Bliss's extraordinary view that the conclusion was *deliberately* made unsatisfactory. The one test that remains is that of performance, which might show possibilities that have eluded the critics. But, alas, apart from a production in York, England, in 1980, *The Devil's Law-Case* has not been revived since its initial production.

The years 1623-1624 mark the high point of Webster's public celebrity. Both *The Duchess of Malfi* and *The Devil's Law-Case* were printed in that year, as were his verses prefixed to Henry Cockeram's *The English Dictionarie*. In 1624 he was responsible for the most public activity of his life, the Lord Mayor's Pageant of 1624, which represents the uniting of his poetical career with his position as a Merchant Taylor and important citizen of London. (The reason Webster was given the job is that John Gore, the incoming mayor, was also a Merchant Taylor: the guild therefore produced the pageant.) There were two water tableaux, then in Paul's churchyard a Temple of Honor was erected with Troynovant (that is, London) surrounded by presentations of other famous cities and celebrated poets, doing her honor. Following this was a triumphal chariot containing eight famous English Kings who had been free of the Company, preceded by the representation of Sir John de Hawkwood, an eminent Merchant Taylor soldier in the time of Edward III. A troupe of famous notables who also had been free of the Company followed, all costumed; there were also representations of famous maritime events. These were succeeded by two more pageants, the first the Monument of Charity, fashioned like a garden, which represented the foundation of St. John's College, Oxford, by Sir Thomas White, a former Mayor and Merchant Taylor; a speech by Learning was included as part

The Deuils Law-cafe.

OR,

When Women goe to Law, the
Deuill is full of Bufineffe.

A new Tragecomædy.

The true and perfeEt Copie from the Originall.

As it was approouedly well Acted
by her Maiefties Seruants.

Written by IOHN WEBSTER.

Non quam diu,, fed quam bene.

LONDON,
Printed by *A. M.* for *Iohn Grifmand,* and are
to be fold at his Shop in Pauls Alley at the
Signe of the Gunne. 1623.

Title page for the 1623 quarto edition of one of the plays that lends credence to the theory that the dramatist was the John Webster who entered the Middle Temple to study law in 1598 (Anderson Galleries, sale no. 1405, 4-5 March 1919)

of this pageant. The last pageant was the Monument of Gratitude, focused on the figure of the late Prince Henry, presented on a rock of jewels. This last pageant is the original note to what was otherwise a grand but entirely conventional set of pageants. The praise of Henry represented a kind of indirect criticism of the government of James I. According to Bradbrook in *John Webster, Citizen and Dramatist,* "Henry represented a decency in the monarchy which Webster's commentary spells out, and which had vanished in the final squalid stages of James's ignoble reign." (In "The Politics of Pageantry," 1981, Bradbrook discusses the City pageants and their political and theatrical connections in general.)

In September of the same year (1624) was licensed a play called *The Late Murder of the Son upon the Mother* (also known as *Keep the Widow Wak-*

ing), by Webster and Ford, in which Dekker and Rowley probably also had a share. The text is lost, but seems to have been a topical piece about a foolish widow intimidated into marriage, a scandal that was a nine-days wonder at the time. The dating of the other plays with which Webster is more or less securely associated is virtually impossible. *Appius and Virginia,* which was acted by Christopher Beeston's company at the Phoenix in 1634, was printed with Webster's name on the title page, in 1654. However, most scholars believe the play to have been written in collaboration with Heywood (for the most recent bibliographical and linguistic discussion of it, see MacDonald P. Jackson's article in *Studies in Bibliography,* 1985). Most writers also think on the basis of prosodic tests that the play dates from the end of Webster's career. Such tests, however, are only marginally reliable in view of the entirely different character of *Appius and Virginia* from Webster's other plays. Michael Steppat suggests it should be dated 1615, as Robert Anton of Cambridge included a reference to "Virgineaes rape" in a diatribe (published in 1616) against the "lustfull Theatres" of the time. The context hardly suits Webster's chaste tragedy; it is conceivable that Anton had another (lost) play in mind. *Appius and Virginia* is a Roman tragedy about a corrupt judge, Appius, who seeks to possess the heroic general Virginius's daughter, by claiming her to be the child of a dead slave of one of his corrupt associates. The centerpiece of the play is another trial scene (IV.i), in which Virginius fails to defeat Appius's schemes, and kills Virginia rather than allow her to fall into Appius's hands. The army rises in support of its general, and Appius and his associates fall. The play was much liked by nineteenth-century critics, who felt relief at the absence from it of the sort of irregularity and horror that characterize *The White Devil* and *The Duchess of Malfi;* in the twentieth century its status has slipped. Bradbrook accounts for its formal style and classical simplicity by supposing it to have been written for a children's company.

The other plays, *A Cure for a Cuckold, Anything for a Quiet Life,* and *The Thracian Wonder,* form a bibliographical group: they were part of a series of plays printed by Thomas Johnson for the bookseller Francis Kirkman in 1661-1662. Kirkman obviously had obtained a number of theatrical manuscripts and was anxious to get them into print as quickly and as inexpensively as possible. The quartos are monuments to meanness in printing, with almost all the verse printed as prose and the layout as squeezed as possible, in order to contain the plays within as few sheets as could be managed. In the circumstances, much of the evidence that would have helped to date the plays and to assign shares in them to the various authors, has disappeared. Most scholars agree in refusing Webster any share in *The Thracian Wonder,* a very foolish play indeed cobbled up out of Robert Greene's *Menaphon* and Shakespeare's *The Winter's Tale.* But Webster is by general consent allowed a share in *A Cure for a Cuckold* (Webster's name appears with Rowley's on the title page) and (less universally) *Anything for a Quiet Life* (which Kirkman published as by Middleton).

A Cure for a Cuckold is a peculiar play: it has a preposterous main plot, involving a totally unnecessary duel between two friends at the instigation of Lessingham's beloved, Clare, "whose acts are so obscure as to be indecipherable," according to Bradbrook. Although a most tedious traversal of some of the love-and-honor territory that the Fletcherian tragicomedy had made popular, this main plot is in some respects not unlike the plotting of *The Devil's Law-Case.* But the virtue of *A Cure for a Cuckold* lies entirely in the subplot, which almost certainly featured its fat coauthor, William Rowley, as the mariner Compass, who returns home after having been given up as drowned to find that his wife has had a child by a gentleman, Franckford. Both Franckford and Compass wish to keep the child, and the issue is decided in a comic trial in a tavern, where Compass's arguments in favor of maternal rights persuade everyone: a surprising conclusion in an age so dominated by partilinear thinking. Compass divorces his wife and instantly remarries her thus obviating the cuckoldry he has sustained. If the whole play lived up to the subplot, *A Cure for a Cuckold* would be well worth revival, but the obscurity and tediousness of the main plot are insurmountable obstacles. There is no plausible indication of date, nor any that the play was ever revived. Rowley, as a leader of Prince Charles's Men, presumably presented it with his company, either at the Phoenix or at the Curtain.

Even less can be said about *Anything for a Quiet Life.* As Middleton died in 1627 it must be earlier than that; Lucas draws attention to a reference to the Standard in Cheapside as new; this monument was restored in 1621, and as none of the other allusions in the play are of much help in dating it, it seems plausible to locate it sometime in the early 1620s. Sykes was the chief champion for Webster's presence in the play, and though his methodology has come under attack subsequently, his attribution was accepted by Lucas, and by Richard Barker and

David Lake in their books on Middleton. Many recent authors have tended to bypass it, and the most that can be said is that at present the majority opinion concurs in assigning Webster some share in it. Cyrus Hoy has given good reasons for thinking that Webster had a share in *The Fair Maid of the Inn,* which he assigns to a team of Massinger, Webster, Ford and Fletcher. It was printed in the Beaumont and Fletcher folio of 1647. He thinks it was the last play on which Fletcher worked; it was licensed in 1626. Another play claimed in part for Webster from the Beaumont and Fletcher folio is *The Honest Man's Fortune,* which also survives in a scribal manuscript written by the prompter of the King's Men, Edward Knight. It appears that the play was originally written in 1613 and subsequently revived in 1625. Although some of the play recalls Flamineo's satirical vein, Cyrus Hoy dismisses Webster's participation, showing that on linguistic grounds Nathan Field probably wrote most of the play, with Massinger working in act three and Fletcher in act five.

It seems as well at this point to reject two other ascriptions to Webster. There is a very bad pseudo-history play called *The Valiant Scot,* printed in 1637 and described on the title page as being "By J. W. Gent."; the publisher was John Waterson, and the identity of his initials with the author's is suggestive. In a 1965 article R. G. Howarth made a vague, impressionistic case for Webster as author, which was refuted by George F. Byers in his 1980 edition of the play. There is also a letter-writing manual called *A Speedie Post,* by I. W., printed in 1625, which was also claimed for Webster by Howarth in another 1965 article on the grounds that the phrase "worms in libraries" occurs in it and in *The Duchess of Malfi.* This does not by any means exhaust the number of works which have been attributed to Webster (see, for instance, Carol A. Chillington's 1981 article in *ELH*). So far, computer-aided studies of authorship have not produced any evidence of an unequivocal or self-evidently reliable nature which would enable them to be applied to the Webster canon. There can be no question that computer applications will continue in the future, and little doubt that at some stage a program will be devised which can add data to the kind of linguistic tests perfected by Hoy, which so far are the most reliable indicators in authorship determination. But even these are subject to uncertainty. One of Webster's most characteristic uses in *The White Devil* and *The Duchess of Malfi* is a very strong preference for "hath" rather than "has." Yet in *The Devil's Law-Case* we find "has" almost universally. Is this a change in linguistic habit? Or is the fact that *The Devil's Law-Case* was printed by Augustine Mathewes, while the two other plays come from Nicholas Okes's shop relevant?

The date of Webster's death is unknown: Heywood mentions him in the past tense in *The Hierarchie of the Blessed Angels* (licensed 7 November 1634) along with other dramatists then dead, but how long before that he died cannot be determined. (Howarth, in 1954, tried to discount the Heywood reference because a John Webster was buried in Clerkenwell in March 1638, but as this John Webster was not described as a householder, it was almost certainly not the poet.)

Webster's critical reputation, like those of most of his Jacobean contemporaries, has fluctuated enormously (Don D. Moore has made a good survey of this subject). His work never vanished entirely from critical or theatrical awareness: he was one of the relatively few Jacobean dramatists whose plays continued to be given in the Restoration. John Downes, the prompter, described *The Duchess of Malfi* in his *Roscius Anglicanus* (1708), as "one of the Best of Stock Tragedies," noting that it had "fill'd the House 8 days Successively"—a very good run indeed; he also lists *The White Devil* as an old play that was acted now and then. In the period during which adaptations were popular, three of Webster's plays were so treated. Joseph Harris adapted *A Cure for a Cuckold* as *The City Bride* in 1696; more surprisingly, Nahum Tate altered *The White Devil* as *Injur'd Love* in 1707, and Lewis Theobald in 1735 produced a version of *The Duchess of Malfi* which he called *The Fatal Secret*.

Revival of critical interest in Webster really begins with Charles Lamb's *Specimens of the English Dramatic Poets* (1808), which printed excerpts from the plays, with a commentary which stressed Webster as a master of the emotions of fear and horror and of intenseness of feeling generally. This view was reiterated through the nineteenth century, culminating in an enthusiastic article by Swinburne (1886, republished in his *The Age of Shakespeare*, 1908), which ranked Webster next to Shakespeare, chiefly on the grounds of his poetic genius. There was an opposition party, which grumbled about the violence and extravagance of the plays, and complained that Webster could not construct: this school of thought reached its apex in the writings of William Archer, between 1893 and 1924. Archer complained that the Webster enthusiasts only concentrated upon selected passages of poetic splendor, ignoring the structural weaknesses and unrealistic tone of the plays. Archer's complaints

were responded to by T. S. Eliot, among others, who pointed out that Archer's criteria were those of the late-nineteenth-century well made play, and thus totally inappropriate to Renaissance poetic drama.

In the meantime scholars had been working on Webster, beginning with the first collected edition (by the Reverend Alexander Dyce, in 1830). Much nineteenth-century scholarship was devoted to the attempt to establish the canon, and if possible to assign shares in the collaborative plays. The major figures in this work are H. Dugdale Sykes and E. H. C. Oliphant (who is still worth reading, though superseded by the more analytical studies of Cyrus Hoy). Both Sykes and Oliphant attempted to use various kinds of internal evidence to establish authorship; and although the detail of their work and many aspects of its methodology have been questioned, on the whole their opinions are still widely accepted. Their conclusions were at any rate enshrined in what is still the standard edition of Webster, Lucas's *Complete Works* of 1927, which includes many of the doubtful texts.

Since the 1920s an extraordinary amount has been published on Webster: the first 70 pages of Schuman's bibliography take us up to the watershed year of 1927; another 184 pages are needed to bring the record up to 1981, and more than 100 of these pages record the preceding mere twenty years. By far the great majority of studies stay with *The White Devil* and *The Duchess of Malfi*, since—as Hoy remarked in 1976—many critics feel uneasy in attempting structural analysis or close reading of the other texts, whose authorship rests upon a thin thread of inference. Many writers find the central issue of Webster's work to be whether or not he was expressing any kind of coherent moral or spiritual concepts in the plays. Eliot, though more sympathetic to Webster's dramaturgy than Archer, believed that his was "a very great literary and dramatic genius directed towards chaos," and his lines from "Whispers of Immortality" (1920) have been used as catch phrases by critics and directors alike:

Webster was much possessed by death
And saw the skull beneath the skin;
And breastless creatures under ground
Leaned backward with a lipless grin.

Daffodil bulbs instead of balls
Stared from the sockets of the eyes!
He knew that thought clings round dead limbs ·
Tightening its lusts and luxuries.

The critics who feel that Webster's outlook was fundamentally negative outnumber those who believe his plays to express positive values (Ian Jack's attack on him is one of the most vigorous); and those who find him truly positive (such as Gunby) are in turn outnumbered by those, such as Travis Bogard, who will allow only that in the existentially chaotic universe Webster's plays reveal, an individual can still assert personal integrity. This view makes Webster into a kind of stoic-Senecal dramatist, a view appropriate enough to the ideology of the later-twentieth century, but not, one hopes, the last word. A number of influential studies, such as Hereward Price's, have sought to find structural patterns in Webster in his imagery, while others have focused on particular texts or upon staging questions. Among the more influential studies have been Clifford Leech's book (1951) and Inga-Stina Ekeblad's celebrated essay on Webster's "Impure Art" (1958), which shows how the images of dance in the Duchess's death scene are emblems; instead of stressing the unity of creation they reveal the disordered state of the Duchess's collapsing world.

One of the most important developments has been the systematic study of Webster's sources and methods of composition. Dent and Boklund both deal with this subject and reveal that Webster was more of a borrower than perhaps any of his contemporaries, that he wrote, as it were, with commonplace book open before him. Some critics, unreasonably, have felt that this diminishes his imaginative originality; they might have pondered on Eliot's *The Waste Land* (1922), and Eliot's (or Joyce's) compositional methods: "These fragments I have shored against my ruins." That Webster was a great borrower is interesting information, but marginal to the indisputable fact that he was a great tragedian.

Interest in Webster continues to increase. The publication in 1979 of the concordance to Webster by Cornballis and Harding provided an essential tool (though they did not include *Anything for a Quiet Life* and *The Fair Maid of the Inn*). A new full-length critical study by Charles Forker was published in 1986, and the Cambridge University Press will publish a new, complete, critical edition in old-spelling in the near future. Performances of at least *The White Devil* and *The Duchess of Malfi* continue to be fairly common (the former at the Bristol Old Vic in 1983; the latter in a disappointing production by the National Theatre of Britain in 1985); David Carnegie's list of productions is surprisingly long. It is reasonable to conclude that Webster's

remoteness, the very difficulty of seizing the "author's intention" that has led so many critics to disagree so violently, will ensure continuing controversy, while the undeniable power and passion of his best work will continue to attract readers and audiences. It is to be hoped that the subsidized theaters will take the risk of producing one or more of the other works, to give them the only true test of drama, a professional staging.

Bibliographies:
William E. Mahaney, *John Webster: A Classified Bibliography* (Salzburg: Institut für Anglistik und Amerikanistik, 1973);
Inga-Stina Ewbank, "Webster, Tourneur, and Ford," in *English Drama (Excluding Shakespeare): Select Bibliographical Guides,* edited by Stanley Wells (London: Oxford University Press, 1975);
David Carnegie, "A Preliminary Checklist of Professional Productions of the Plays of John Webster," *Research Opportunities in Renaissance Drama,* 26 (1983): 55-63;
Samuel Schuman, *John Webster: A Reference Guide* (Boston: G. K. Hall, 1985).

References:
William Archer, *The Old Drama and the New* (London: Heinemann, 1923);
Richard H. Barker, *Thomas Middleton* (New York: Columbia University Press, 1958);
Robert B. Bennett, "John Webster's Strange Dedication: An Inquiry into Literary Patronage and Jacobean Court Intrigue," *English Literary Renaissance,* 7 (Autumn 1977): 352-367;
Ralph T. Berry, *The Art of John Webster* (Oxford: Clarendon Press, 1972);
Lee Bliss, "Destructive Will and Social Chaos in *The Devil's Law-Case,*" *Modern Language Review,* 72 (July 1977): 513-525;
Bliss, *The World's Perspective: John Webster and the Jacobean Drama* (New Brunswick: Rutgers University Press, 1983);
Travis Bogard, *The Tragic Satire of John Webster* (Berkeley: University of California Press, 1955);
Gunnar Boklund, *"The Duchess of Malfi" Sources, Themes, Characters* (Cambridge: Harvard University Press, 1962);
Boklund, *The Sources of "The White Devil"* (Uppsala: Lundequistska Bokhandeln/Cambridge: Harvard University Press, 1957);

Fredson T. Bowers, *Elizabethan Revenge Tragedy 1587-1642* (Princeton: Princeton University Press, 1940);

Muriel C. Bradbrook, *John Webster, Citizen and Dramatist* (London: Weidenfeld & Nicolson, 1980);

Bradbrook, "The Politics of Pageantry: Social Implications in Jacobean London," in *Poetry and Drama 1570-1700: Essays in Honour of Harold F. Brooks*, edited by Antony Coleman and Antony Hammond (London: Methuen, 1981), pp. 60-75;

Nicholas Brooke, *Horrid Laughter in Jacobean Tragedy* (London: Open Books, 1979);

Rupert Brooke, *John Webster and the Elizabethan Drama* (New York: John Lane, 1916);

John Russell Brown, "The Printing of John Webster's Plays," *Studies in Bibliography*, 6 (1954): 117-140; 8 (1956): 113-127; 15 (1962): 57-69;

George F. Byers, ed., *"The Valiant Scot" by J. W.: A Critical Edition* (New York: Garland, 1980);

Carol A. Chillington, "Playwrights at Work: Henslowe's, not Shakespeare's, *Book of Sir Thomas More*," *ELH*, 11 (1981): 439-479;

Richard Cornballis and J. M. Harding, *A Concordance to the Works of John Webster*, 4 volumes (Salzburg: Institut für Anglistik und Amerikanistik, 1979);

Robert W. Dent, *John Webster's Borrowing* (Berkeley: University of California Press, 1960);

Jonathan Dollimore, *Radical Tragedy: Religion, Ideology and Power in the Drama of Shakespeare and his Contemporaries* (London: Harvester Press, 1984);

Mary Edmond, "In Search of John Webster," *Times Literary Supplement*, 24 December 1976, pp. 1621-1622;

Inga-Stina Ekeblad, "The 'Impure Art' of John Webster," *Review of English Studies*, new series 9, no. 35 (1958): 253-267;

Ekeblad, "Storm Imagery in *Appius and Virginia*," *Notes and Queries*, new series 3 (January 1956): 5-7;

Ekeblad, "Webster's Constructional Rhythm," *ELH*, 24 (September 1957): 165-176;

T. S. Eliot, "Four Elizabethan Dramatists: A Preface to an Unwritten Book," in his *Selected Essays* (London: Faber & Faber, 1932);

Una Ellis-Fermor, *The Jacobean Drama: An Interpretation* (London: Methuen, 1936);

Charles R. Forker, *Skull Beneath the Skin: The Achievement of John Webster* (Carbondale & Edwardsville: Southern Illinois University Press, 1986);

Forker, "*Westward Ho* and *Northward Ho*: A Revaluation," *Publications of the Arkansas Philological Association*, 6 (1980): 1-42;

H. Bruce Franklin, "The Trial Scene of Webster's *The White Devil* Examined in Terms of Renaissance Rhetoric," *Studies in English Literature*, 1 (Spring 1961): 35-51;

J. Gerritsen, ed., *The Honest Man's Fortune: A Critical Edition of MS Dyce 9 (1625)* (Groningen, Djakarta: J. B. Wolters, 1952);

David Gunby, "*The Devil's Law-Case*: An Interpretation," *Modern Language Review*, 63 (July 1968): 545-558;

Antony Hammond, "*The White Devil* in Nicholas Okes's Shop," *Studies in Bibliography*, 39 (1986): 135-176;

Hammond and Doreen DelVecchio, "The Melbourne Manuscript and John Webster," *Studies in Bibliography*, 40 (forthcoming 1987);

Richard W. Hillman, "Meaning and Morality in Some Renaissance Revenge Plays," *University of Toronto Quarterly*, 49 (Fall 1979): 1-17;

R. G. Howarth, " John Webster's Burial," *Notes and Queries*, new series 1 (March 1954): 114-115;

Howarth, "*The Valiant Scot* as a Play by John Webster," *Bulletin of the English Association, South African Branch*, 9/10 (1965): 3-8;

Howarth, "Worms in Libraries," *Notes and Queries*, new series 12 (June 1965): 236-237;

Cyrus Hoy, "Critical and Aesthetic Problems of Collaboration in Renaissance Drama," *Research Opportunities in Renaissance Drama*, 19 (1976): 3-6;

Hoy, *Introductions, Notes, and Commentaries to Texts in "The Dramatic Works of Thomas Dekker" Edited by Fredson Bowers*, 4 volumes (Cambridge: Cambridge University Press, 1980);

Hoy, "The Shares of Fletcher and his Collaborators in the Beaumont and Fletcher Canon," parts 4 and 5, *Studies in Bibliography*, 12 (1959): 91-116; 13 (1960): 77-108;

Ian Jack, "The Case of John Webster," *Scrutiny*, 16 (March 1949): 38-43;

MacDonald P. Jackson, " John Webster and Thomas Heywood in *Appius and Virginia*: A Bibliographical Approach to the Problem of Authorship," *Studies in Bibliography*, 38 (1985): 217-235;

Harold Jenkins, "The Tragedy of Revenge in Shakespeare and Webster," *Shakespeare Survey*, 14 (1961): 45-55;

David J. Lake, *The Canon of Middleton's Plays* (Cambridge: Cambridge University Press, 1975);

Clifford Leech, *John Webster: A Critical Study* (London: Hogarth Press, 1951);

Leech, *Webster: "The Duchess of Malfi"* (London: Arnold, 1963);

Don D. Moore, *John Webster and his Critics 1617-1964* (Baton Rouge: Louisiana State University Press, 1966);

Brian Morris, ed., *John Webster*, Mermaid Critical Commentaries (London: Benn, 1970);

Peter B. Murray, *A Study of John Webster* (The Hague: Mouton, 1969);

E. C. H. Oliphant, *The Plays of Beaumont and Fletcher: An Attempt to Determine their Respective Shares and the Shares of Others* (New Haven: Yale University Press, 1927);

Robert Ornstein, *The Moral Vision of Jacobean Tragedy* (Madison: University of Wisconsin Press, 1965);

Jacqueline Pearson, *Tragedy and Tragicomedy in the Plays of John Webster* (Manchester: Manchester University Press, 1980);

Hereward T. Price, "The Function of Imagery in Webster," *PMLA,* 70 (September 1955): 717-739;

Samuel Schuman, *"The Theatre of Fine Devices": The Visual Drama of John Webster* (Salzburg: Institut für Anglistik und Amerikanistik, 1982);

Michael P. Steppat, "John Webster's *Appius and Virginia*," *American Notes and Queries,* 20 (March/April 1982): 101;

E. E. Stoll, *John Webster: The Periods of his Work* (Boston: Mudge, 1905);

H. Dugdale Sykes, "A Webster-Middleton Play: *Anything for a Quiet Life*," *Notes and Queries,* 141 (5 March 1921): 181-182, 202-204; (19 March 1921): 225-226; (9 April 1921): 300.

Arthur Wilson
(1595-1652)

Linda V. Itzoe
Pennsylvania State University

PLAY PRODUCTIONS: *The Inconstant Lady (or Better Late Than Never)*, London, Hampton Court, 30 September 1630;
The Swisser, London, Blackfriars theater, 1631;
The Corporal, London, Blackfriars theater, 1633(?).

BOOKS: *The History of Great Britain, Being the Life and Reign of King James the First, Relating to What Passed from His First Access to the Crown, Till His Death* (London: Printed for R. Lownds, 1653);
The Inconstant Lady, A Play, edited by Philip Bliss (Oxford: Printed by Samuel Collingwood, 1814);
Wilson's The Swisser, edited by Albert Feuillerat (Paris: Libraire Fischbacher, 1904).
Editions: *Arthur Wilson's The Inconstant Lady: A Critical Edition*, edited by Linda V. Itzoe (New York & London: Garland, 1980);
Arthur Wilson's The Swisser: A Critical Edition, edited by Itzoe (New York & London: Garland, 1984).

OTHER: "Observations of God's Providence in the Tract of My Life," in *Desiderata Curiosa*, 2 volumes, edited by Francis Peck (London: Privately printed, 1732, 1735), II: 460-483.

Although Arthur Wilson has been known chiefly as a historian since the publication of his *The History of Great Britain, Being the Life and Reign of King James the First* in 1653, he is also recognized as a Caroline playwright whose three plays—*The Inconstant Lady (or Better Late Than Never)*, *The Swisser*, and *The Corporal*—were performed by the King's Men in the 1630s but were not subsequently published. In the late 1700s Philip Bliss discovered a manuscript for *The Inconstant Lady* in the Rawlinson collection at the Bodleian Library, Oxford, and in 1814 published an edition of the play. With the further discoveries of the manuscript for *The Swisser* (now in the British Library), edited by Albert Feuillerat and published in 1904, and of the Lambarde manuscript of *The Inconstant Lady* (now in the

Folger Shakespeare Library) in 1924, Wilson's reputation as a playwright has been clearly established.

Playwright, historian, and poet—Arthur Wilson was born in Yarmouth, England, the son of John and Suzan Wilson, and baptized on 14 December 1595. Most of what is known about his life derives from his autobiography ("Observations of God's Providence in the Tract of My Life" in *Desiderata Curiosa*), which he began in 1642 in an attempt, he explained, to identify the presence of divine providence in his life.

At age fourteen he traveled to France, where he remained for two years. Upon his return he studied calligraphy for six months under John Davies and shortly thereafter became a clerk in the Exchequer Office, only to be dismissed after two years, when some religious verses he had written for his own amusement gave offense. Through a relative acquainted with the steward of Robert Devereux, the Third Earl of Essex, Wilson, now jobless and unsettled, visited the Essex estate at Chartley, where his rescue of a maiden who had fallen into the moat brought him not just notice but an invitation to enter into service as Essex's secretary. Thus, in 1614, Wilson gained entry to the social, cultural, and political world in which he would write the plays and other works for which he is remembered.

For the next fifteen years Wilson served Essex, accompanying him to court and on military campaigns in the Palatinate, Holland, and Spain (1620-1625), observing the events and personages that he would record in his *The History of Great Britain, Being the Life and Reign of King James the First*, which he began at Essex's suggestion. This history, which focuses on the official aspects of James's reign, includes descriptions of rivalries among the noblemen, a first-person account of England's involvement in the wars of the Palatinate, and accounts showing the growing dissatisfaction among those unsympathetic to the Crown, as well as copies of communications between the King and members of Parliament. The work is criticized for being clearly biased against the Stuart monarchy.

Not published until a year after Wilson's death, it is said to have been altered by those who saw it into print. Because Wilson's manuscript of the work has been lost, the extent of these emendations is not known, though differences in style between this work and those known to be in Wilson's handwriting suggest that the changes were considerable.

It was also during these years that Wilson wrote at least one and quite possibly all three of his known plays. In his only reference in his autobiography to his plays, he comments that as a member of the Essex retinue, he spent winters at the various estates of Essex's family, most especially at the home of Essex's grandmother, the Countess of Leicester, where he saw performances of plays of which he was he writes, "a contriver both of words and matter."

It was during this segment of his life that he wrote the tragicomedy *The Inconstant Lady,* which a playbill indicates was performed at Hampton Court by the King's Men on 30 September 1630. In the play Wilson presents a basically optimistic view of life, creating a world composed of good and ill, with the good triumphing in the end.

The story focuses on Emilia, the beautiful but ambitious "inconstant lady," who, interested in wealth and prestige, calls off her marriage to Aramant when she learns that his father, unhappy with the impending marriage, has disinherited him. She turns her affections to Millecert, Aramant's younger brother, to whom the entire estate has been given, and so enthralls him that they marry immediately. Their happiness is short-lived, however, for Emilia becomes envious of her sister, the virtuous Cloris, whom the long-widowed duke wishes to take as his wife, and Millecert, already melancholy because he has the inheritance and the wife which were to have been Aramant's, now must endure his wife's scheming attempts to make herself the next duchess. Meanwhile, Cloris has fallen in love with the spurned Aramant and he with her, though they believe their love to be hopeless because of the duke's determination to make Cloris his wife.

Millecert seems to disappear, but, in fact, he disguises himself as Gratus, a faithful courtier who quickly earns the confidence of the duke and his corrupt adviser Busiro as well as of the unsuspecting Emilia, Cloris, and Aramant. Thus he is able to work as an agent of good in their lives. He thwarts Emilia's plot to poison Cloris and bring the duke to her own bed; further, he brings the wicked Busiro to confess that years earlier, influenced by witches, he had abandoned and then reported the

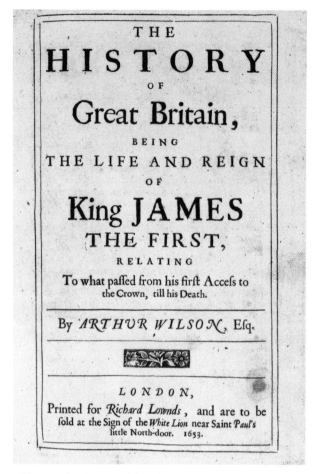

THE
HISTORY
OF
Great Britain,
BEING
THE LIFE AND REIGN
OF
King JAMES
THE FIRST,
RELATING
To what paſſed from his firſt Acceſs to
the Crown, till his Death.

By *ARTHUR WILSON,* Eſq.

LONDON,
Printed for *Richard Lownds,* and are to be
ſold at the Sign of the *White Lion* near Saint *Paul's*
little North-door. 1653.

Title page for the 1653 folio edition of the only work by Wilson published in the seventeenth century (Henry E. Huntington Library and Art Gallery)

death of the duke's only child, a daughter, Bellaura. Moreover, after learning that Cloris is an adopted foundling, not Emilia's real sister, Gratus determines that she is the supposedly dead Bellaura, and a scarf and a birthmark verify her identity. Overjoyed that his daughter lives, the duke readily consents to her marriage to Aramant, promising an ample dowry, and Emilia, chastened by the exposure of her scheme and touched by the ready forgiveness of her husband and Cloris, promises to reform, albeit "better late than never."

The play is in many ways a comedy typical of the Caroline period. For example, it is ostensibly set it France, though the exact location of the action is unimportant, and the characters are seventeenth-century men and women. It uses as its central theme the joining of lovers in marriage, with the marriage of Emilia and Millecert early in the play and the betrothal of Cloris to Aramant at the conclusion, and in a comic subplot the marriage of a

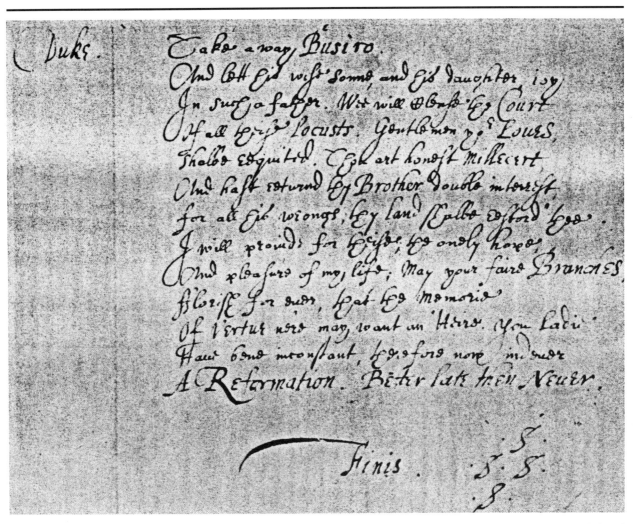

A portion of the last page of the manuscript for The Inconstant Lady *preserved at the Bodleian Library. This manuscript is believed to be in Wilson's hand (MS Rawl. poet.9, fol. 45ᵃ; by permission of the Bodleian Library)*.

bawdy-house madam to Busiro's foppish son, whose extravagant speeches ironically end up expressing a promise of marriage.

Other motifs popular in the Caroline drama occur in the play: Wilson combines the threat-of-incest and the recovery-of-the-lost-child motifs in the attraction of the duke to the virtuous Cloris. Likewise, Wilson makes use of a disguise motif, first with Millecert, who as Gratus possesses a special ability to induce Busiro's confession of villainy and Emilia's repentance and promise of reform, and second with Emilia, disguised as Cloris, who hopes to bring the duke to her bed. Further, in a more general sense this motif permeates the play, disguising good and bad alike, so that time and again things are not what they seem on the surface: Emilia is not in love with Aramant; Busiro is not the good and wise counselor the duke believes him to

be; Cloris is not Emilia's sister; Bellaura is not dead.

The play also contains the chance and artifice typical of Caroline drama. For example, the duke's daughter conveniently has a birthmark—"a strange blue mark upon her arm"—that can help verify her identity. Further, the scarf that aids in her identification "just happens" to be at hand, for Emilia used it only moments before to disguise herself as Cloris; moreover, Emilia remembers that it was with Cloris when she was found, and the duke recognizes it as having belonged to Bellaura's mother.

The King's Men considered this Caroline play worthy of performance at Hampton Court and again at Blackfriars in 1635. In 1641 they included it on a list of plays protected from being printed except with their consent, and in 1653 it was entered in the Stationers' Register, though not subsequently printed. It was not until the Bliss edition in 1814 that the play became accessible to the literary public.

In the same year as the performance of *The Inconstant Lady* at court, Wilson had a falling out with Essex's bride, and so at age thirty-five, set with a pension from Essex and determined, as he wrote in his autobiography, to be "free from the troubles of the world," he left Essex's service to attend Trinity College, Oxford, where he remained for the next two years. While there, he may have completed his other two plays (if he had not already finished them before leaving Essex's service) and worked on his history of James I. A classmate, Edward Bathurst, in a note penned in later years in a Trinity College copy of Wilson's history, wrote of Wilson, "He made some Comedies, which were acted at Black-Friars in London, by the King's players, and in the Act time at Oxon, with good applause, himself being present. Part of this book he composed in Trinity College."

A second play by Wilson, a comedy titled *The Swisser*, was presented by the King's Men at Blackfriars in 1631. Like *The Inconstant Lady* it depicts a world comprised of good and ill ("The same soil brings forth ill and well," Wilson wrote in the epilogue), but unlike the earlier play, its mood and tone are somber. It is set in Lombardy, Italy, against the backdrop of the Lombards' battle with their neighbors, the Raveneans. Early in the play the Lombard army, under the able leadership of Arioldus, routs the Raveneans, taking some prisoners, among them a beautiful maiden, Eurinia. Her goodness so impresses Arioldus that he gives her sanctuary in his own home. The king, hearing of her beauty, visits Arioldus and, when Eurinia refuses his advances, takes her by force to his palace, where he traps her alone and ravishes her. Arioldus is so incensed by this that he threatens to challenge the king to a duel. However, he is dissuaded by "the Swisser," Andrucho, whom he knows is really the banished Lord Aribert now disguised as a Swiss guard, who, behaving as a sort of gadfly, now counsels his king through barbs and jests.

Andrucho argues that even an act as odious as the king's does not give just cause to raise a hand against a sovereign—" 'tis sacred blood," he argues, "precious as tears of dying saints"; he urges, "Preserve't and leave our justice to the gods." To persuade Arioldus further, Andrucho confides that Eurinia is none other than his own daughter Eugenia in disguise, whose earlier refusal of the king's hand in marriage had caused the banishment of the family. Arioldus endeavors to convince the king to rectify his actions by marrying Eurinia, but the king scoffs at the idea of his marrying a peasant. However, when he learns that she is in fact his Eugenia, he readily makes an offer of marriage, which she now accepts, and he rescinds the banishment order.

The play has two subplots. One focuses on Timentes, a cowardly general, literally scared of his shadow. A ruse to make him think some disgruntled soldiers are seeking to do violence to him frightens him into such a deep faint that the perpetrators of the joke, Andrucho and two friends, think he is dead. Thus, in a comic turnabout, the trio, fearful of being hanged for murder, end up almost as frightened as Timentes.

In the second subplot two young lovers—Alcidonus and Selina, children of rival lords—have secretly married. After Antharis, the wicked father of Alcidonus, seeks to break up the pair by "confessing" that Alcidonus was born of Selina's mother, the pair, thinking their love incestuous, plan to poison themselves. However, Selina's father, the noble Lord Clephis, ever vigilant, learns of the lie and the couple's plan in time to substitute a harmless sleeping potion for the poison. Antharis discovers the pair in their deathlike sleep and, thinking his treachery has caused the death of his son, wanders off hopelessly distracted. In the end the lovers have their marriage publicly acknowledged, and the king orders all of Antharis's goods and property turned over to the happy pair.

Also in the end, Arioldus and the king's sister Panopia announce their plans to marry, so the play concludes with the banished Lord Aribert welcomed back to Lombardy and the three couples joined in marriage.

In addition to the theme of lovers joined in marriage, *The Swisser*, like *The Inconstant Lady*, contains other themes popular in Caroline dramas—the substitution of a sleeping potion for poison, the threat of incest, and the recovery of a lost child. However, here the threat of incest is not real. The child, Eurinia, is lost in the sense that she has been violated but is "recovered" through marriage to the king. Also, as in *The Inconstant Lady*, disguise is central to the play. In the opening scene Andrucho strikes the keynote in his comment "We . . . are not what we seem; all are disguised." Throughout the play the masking of good and bad alike takes place, as, for example, in Andrucho's advice to the king presented as barb and jest, in Alcidonus and Selina's secret marriage, and in Eurinia's acquiescence finally to marrying the king. Similarly, in this play Wilson makes literal use of the disguise motif to enable a character to work as an agent of good,

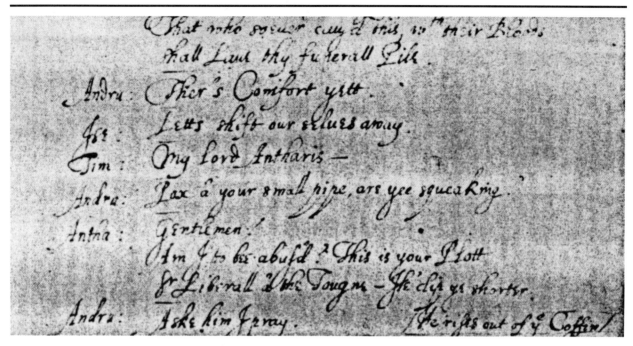

A portion of a page from the manuscript for The Swisser *preserved at the British Library. This manuscript is believed to be in Wilson's hand (MS Addit. 36759, fol 33ª; by permission of the British Library).*

for, like the disguised Millecert in *The Inconstant Lady,* Lord Aribert, in the guise of Andrucho, is able to calm Arioldus's fury and affect the fate of his wronged daughter.

According to the dramatis personae list in Wilson's manuscript of *The Swisser,* when the play was acted by the King's Men at Blackfriars in 1631, the role of Andrucho was performed by the company's key player, John Lowin. Two references to Andrucho's size suggest that Wilson may well have had Lowin, a large man, in mind for the part: at one point the king addresses Andrucho as "my tall Swisser," and in the comic subplot, when Andrucho and his cohorts fear they have frightened Timentes to death, Andrucho responds to the comment "Then thy great beard and bulk/Will grace the gallows well" with "I shall take it heavily." Other actors of the major roles were Joseph Taylor (Arioldus), Richard Sharpe (the king), and Alexander Gough (Eurinia).

Extant records list only this one performance of *The Swisser*; however, the King's Men kept the play in their repertoire, as evidenced by its being listed in 1641 as one of the plays protected from being printed except by consent of the company. In 1646 it was entered in the Stationers' Register but was not printed. There is no record of the play receiving any further attention until a manuscript in Wilson's hand, sold at Hodgson's in 1903 and added to the collection in the British Museum, was edited by Albert Feuillerat in 1904.

Wilson's third known play, *The Corporal,* was also in the repertoire of the King's Men. Unfortunately only fragments of the work survive—two fragments in Wilson's hand and what is apparently a transcription, in an unknown eighteenth-century hand, of the first act and part of the second. One of the surviving pages notes that the play, which was acted at Blackfriars, is set in Lorraine and has a cast of twelve, with the corporal, the titular character, listed third. An entry in Sir Henry Herbert's office book indicates that it was peformed in 1633. This play was also on the 1641 list of plays of the King's Men protected from unauthorized printing. In 1646 it was entered in the Stationers' Register but was not printed; subsequent entries were made in 1673 and 1683. The fact that a partial transcription was made in the eighteenth century suggests that there was some interest in the play at that time. Unfortunately, as most of Wilson's manuscript of it is apparently lost, the play in its complete form is no longer available.

Although very little of Wilson's poetry survives, his reputation as a poet as well as a playwright while at Oxford is attested to by his classmate Bathurst, who describes him as "a commendable poet"; further, Wilson had the honor of seeing his elegy on John Donne, "Upon Mr. J. Donne and

His Poems," included in the 1633 edition of Donne's *Poems*.

In his autobiography Wilson confesses that by 1632 he had grown weary of his life of retirement and thus accepted an offer to serve as steward to Robert Rich, Second Earl of Warwick, a cousin of Wilson's previous master, the Third Earl of Essex. He took up residence at Leighs Priory, Warwick's estate outside of Felsted in Essex, and, two years later, in 1634, married Susan Spitty. His life in the Warwick household lacked much of the glamor he had known in his younger years in Essex's service; Warwick was a leader of the Parliamentary cause and a champion of the Puritan religion, and his family, the most powerful in Essex, held much sway in the community. In his autobiography Wilson comments on how profoundly this environment affected him: "Since I came into this noble family, whether it were age and experience creeping upon me, . . . or by a clearer light received from a powerful ministry, or by the example of others whose lives were fit patterns to follow, or by a divine spirit . . . , I know not . . . , but I found in myself a greater affection to good duties."

It is not surprising then that in 1644 Wilson heeded advice in a sermon to examine his life in order to apprehend the "hand of Divine Goodness" present there. The result was his autobiographical "Observations of God's Providence in the Tract of My Life," his most significant work in the years he served Warwick. In this account, first published by Francis Peck in volume two of *Desiderata Curiosa* in 1735 and included by Philip Bliss in his 1814 edition of *The Inconstant Lady*, Wilson presents incidents in which he perceived that a higher power was watching over him. In addition to being the source of almost all of what is known about Wilson's life, the work, introspective but not confessional, provides an unaffected collection of vignettes capturing Wilson's own character and sensibilities, and, more importantly, it provides candid glimpses of life in his age. For instance, he tells of Charles I's difficulty with Parliament in the very first year of his reign when, despite the plague raging in London and in Oxford, Charles summoned Parliament to meet at Oxford and then dissolved the body after they refused to submit to his will. Likewise he captures the mood of his countrymen during England's civil war, when the whole town of Sudbury seemed to set upon him as he attempted to pass through in the company of a suspected royalist. One of his most vivid accounts is the storming of the Warwick estate by royalist sympathizers in

Essex to obtain the arms which they used in the battle at Colchester in 1648.

Even though the civil war caused a political division among the Essex citizenry, Wilson apparently did not let these differences disrupt his literary friendships. When *Theophilia, or Love's Sacrifice*, by his royalist neighbor Edward Benlowes, was printed in 1652 it contained Wilson's commendatory poem "For the Much Honoured Author."

Besides the autobiography and this verse to Benlowes, Wilson's other known writings during his years with Warwick are some meditations (in essay, poetic, and letter form) included in the same volume in which he wrote his autobiography and an elegy on the death of Ann Rich.

Wilson died in the fall of 1652 and was buried in the chancel of the church in Felsted, Essex. At the time of his death, all of his writings—except a few poems—were still unpublished. He had been a secretary to Essex and a steward to Warwick—a commoner in the company of two of the most influential families of the age; he had spent his life observing his world and had recorded his impressions of it. As a result, his writings—in both their form and their content—provide a glimpse of the first half of the seventeenth century by a man, sensitive and artistic, responding to his age rather than helping to shape it. This view that he provides of his age makes him a minor but nonetheless important literary figure of the early seventeenth century.

References:

Robert C. Bald, "Arthur Wilson's *The Inconstant Lady*," *Library: A Quarterly Review of Bibliography*, fourth series 18 (1937-1938): 287-313;

Gerald E. Bentley, *Jacobean and Caroline Stage: Dramatic Companies and Players*, volume 5 (Oxford: Clarendon Press, 1956), pp. 1266-1274;

Christopher Gordon-Craig, "Arthur Wilson's *The Inconstant Lady*," Ph.D. dissertation, University of New Brunswick, 1969;

Review of *The Inconstant Lady, a play*, edited by Philip Bliss, *Gentleman's Magazine*, 84 (September 1814): 254-257.

Papers:

The Bodleian Library, Oxford, holds a manuscript for *The Inconstant Lady*, a manuscript fragment of *The Corporal*, and an altered version of *The Inconstant Lady* in an unknown eighteenth-century hand (all in the Rawlinson collection), plus some poetry and a fragment of *The Corporal*, both in unknown eighteenth-century hands (Douce collection). The British Library houses the complete manuscript for *The Swisser* and a letter; Cambridge University Library has a manuscript book containing "Observations of God's Providence in the Tract of My Life," some copies of letters, and meditational essays and poems. The Folger Shakespeare Library holds a manuscript for *The Inconstant Lady* (Lambarde collection); the Victoria and Albert Museum has a fragment of a manuscript for *The Corporal* (Forster collection).

A Yorkshire Tragedy

Gordon Braden
University of Virginia

PRODUCTION: London, Globe theater, 1605(?).

FIRST PUBLICATION: *A Yorkshire Tragedy* (London: Printed by R. B. for Thomas Pavier, 1608).

Edition: *A Yorkshire Tragedy*, edited by A. C. Cawley and Barry Gaines, The Revels Plays (Manchester: Manchester University Press, 1986).

This spare, fierce play, not quite like anything else in Renaissance drama, is based, with journalistic urgency, on a contemporary episode of family violence. In April 1605 Walter Calverley, of fairly distinguished Yorkshire gentry, murdered two of his children, attempted to kill the third, and seriously wounded his wife in a rage apparently occasioned by mounting debts. The story was publicized in June of that year in an anonymous pamphlet, *Two Unnatural Murders*. The dramatic version published three years later as *A Yorkshire Tragedy* contains no definite reference to Calverley's execution in August 1605, and so probably was composed before then; it deletes the proper names of the principals but generally follows the account of the pamphlet quite closely, at times to the point of virtual transcription, and with remarkably economical results: in the Revels edition the text runs to 703 lines.

A handful of scholarly questions surround the play. Its brevity makes credible the announcement in the first quarto edition that it is "One of the four plays in one," but none of the others in the set have been identified. An unusually talkative first scene dilates on a subplot—Calverley's jilting of an earlier lover—only briefly dealt with in the pamphlet and barely alluded to in the rest of the play, and also seems, unaccountably, to locate the rest of the play in London. The scene may well have been added later, and by another hand. The best-known question raised by the first quarto, however, is occasioned by the title-page attribution of the whole work to "W. Shakspeare": an attribution substantiated not only by the second quarto edition (1619) but also by the Stationers' Register and by the play's eventual inclusion in the third and fourth folio collections of Shakespeare's works. Weighing against this claim are the shady reputation of the publisher of the quartos, Thomas Pavier, the play's absence from the first folio of Shakespeare's works, as well as the incongruity of its comparatively simple style with Shakespeare's, especially the Shakespeare of 1605-1608. The disparity of style has been decisive for most scholars, though plausible arguments have been made for Shakespeare's commissioned authorship of the first scene as part of an attempt to conceal the topical references. Authorship has been attributed to a number of other Jacobean tragedians as well. Particular attention has focused in the past on George Wilkins, whose *Miseries of Enforced Marriage* (1607) dramatizes the earlier part of Calverley's story, though with changed names and a new ending; again, serious dissimilarity of styles, coupled in this case with manifest inequality of dramatic competence, argues otherwise. Recent close studies of the play's language have made a case for Thomas Middleton's hand in the text, and his is the strongest claim now standing. (See also the Thomas Middleton entry.)

Whoever did write *A Yorkshire Tragedy* produced an indelible work. At its center is a powerful portrait of the lead character's psychopathic despair, "A fearful melancholy, ungodly sorrow":

Title page for the 1608 quarto edition of one of the best-known plays in the Shakespeare apocrypha (Bodleian Library)

Not as a man repentant but half mad
His fortunes cannot answer his expense,
He sits and sullenly locks up his arms;
Forgetting heaven, looks downward, which makes him

Appear so dreadful that he frights my heart;
Walks heavily, as if his soul were earth,
Not penitent for those his sins are past,
But vexed his money cannot make them last.

Events are driven swiftly by the anger that lashes out of this brooding:

WIFE. Dear husband—
HUSBAND. O, most punishment of all, I have a wife.
WIFE. I do entreat you as you love your soul
   Tell me the cause of this your discontent.
HUSBAND. A vengeance strip thee naked, thou art cause,
   Effect, quality, property; thou, thou, thou!

The virtuous and devoted wife hears that she is a "harlot,/Whom, though for fashion sake I married,/I never could abide," that her children are "bastards, bastards, bastards; begot in tricks, begot in tricks." The historical Calverley claimed that his wife, Philippa, taunted him with such news; the playwright, following the pamphleteer, simplifies the conflict to powerful effect, distilling a domestic rage that becomes horribly convincing precisely in its stark injustice.

The clarity of responsibility gives the work something of the feel of a morality play, an impression strengthened by the abstraction of the main characters into "Husband" and "Wife" and the general simplicity of presentation. The story to some extent fits the pattern of an especially popular parable on the English stage, that of the prodigal son—"fond and peevish,/An unclean rioter"—raised to a new pitch of moral extremity, where the motive force is effectively demonic: "as if some vexèd spirit/Had got his form upon him." The Husband himself makes that diagnosis explicit in the last scene—"now glides the devil from me"—as part of the remorse that fulfills further expectations of the morality tradition:

      Let him not rise
To make men act unnatural tragedies,
To spread into a father and, in fury,
Make him his children's executioners;
Murder his wife, his servants, and who not?
For that man's dark where heaven is quite forgot.

His speech wins from the Wife a benediction that tempers his coming fate—"O my repentant husband!/. . . Thou shouldst not, be assured, for these faults die/If the law could forgive as soon as I"— and he departs offering himself as a cautionary exemplum: "Let every father look into my deeds,/ And then their heirs may prosper while mine bleeds."

Yet the pattern to hand is also darker than the morality tradition would predict, to the point even of being what A. C. Cawley and Barry Gaines call "a grim parody of the morality play." By previous standards the Husband's repentance is inefficacious; it does not appear to bring "the trust in God's mercy that is needed to make repentance complete," and he seems about to die with the conviction that he is damned: "Farewell ye bloody ashes of my boys;/My punishments are their eternal joys." It is, moreover, an earlier effort at repentance that leads the Husband into criminality beyond mere dissipation. Faced with the news of the

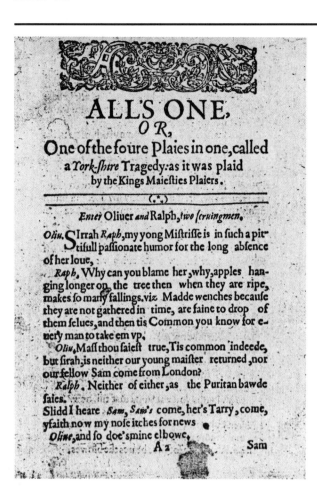

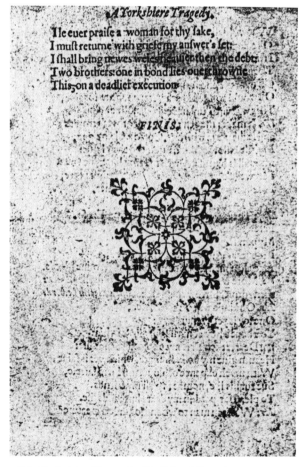

First and last text pages from the 1608 quarto edition of A Yorkshire Tragedy *(Bodleian Library)*

imprisonment of the brother who had guaranteed some of his debts, he takes harsh stock of his prodigality: " 'Tis done; I ha' done't, i'faith; terrible, horrible misery! . . . In my seed five are made miserable besides myself. My riot is now my brother's jailor, my wife's sighing, my three boys' penury, and my own confusion!" With a specificity of motivation undocumented in his source, the playwright makes this remorse the electrifying justification for the killing of the children:

> My eldest beggar, thou shalt not live to ask
> an usurer bread, to cry at a great man's gate,
> or follow "good your honor" by a coach; no,
> nor your brother. 'Tis charity to brain
> you. . . . Bleed, bleed rather than beg, beg.
> Be not thy name's disgrace; Spurn thou thy
> fortunes first if they be base.

What sparks the murders is not the Husband's hatred of his family but a protective obsession with its integrity.

His perverse logic is made credible by the play's social geography, within which aristocratic pride faces an economic corrosion whose resonance is greater than that of individual improvidence: "Thy lands and credit/Lie now both sick of a consumption." The Husband himself tells the Wife that the "true cause of [his] discontent" is "Money, money, money"; hoping to repair their finances, she takes what seems the natural step: "My uncle, glad of your kindness to me and mild usage (for so I made it to him), has in pity of your declining fortunes provided a place for you at court of worth and credit." But she succeeds only in enraging the Husband further: "Thou politic whore, subtler than nine devils." The nuance of "politic" is specifically "political": "Shall I that dedicated myself to pleasure be now confined in service, to crouch and stand like an old man i'th'hams, my hat off, I that never could abide to uncover my head i'th'church?" The Wife's imagined whoredom grades into that of the Renaissance court, dominating a once free nobility, as the Husband's irreligion merges with an angry refusal to accept the new power arrangements of the age. Those arrangements, whatever their rewards, compromise a ferociously guarded independence: "He calls it slavery to be preferred,/A place of credit a base servitude." His murderousness is ultimately a reassertion of power over his destiny, destroying what no one else will now be able to rule:

> Fates,
> My children's blood shall spin into your faces;
> You shall see how confidently we scorn beggary!

Strongly pagan values inhere in such a stance, and the dramatic model that looms perhaps more powerfully in the background than the Christian morality play is Senecan tragedy, with its titanic figures of despairing and defiant rage. The Husband is in many ways of their company—"Nothing will please him until all be nothing"—and at his capture indeed boasts like an Atreus or a Medea: "My glory 'tis to have my action known." His story, of a man who murders his own children, exemplifies one of the Senecan themes that the Renaissance would find especially riveting, and may make us specifically think of *Hercules Furens*; the pamphlet illustrator who gave Calverley a club rather than the dagger that was actually used seems to have had such a memory. Of the unknown playwright's achievement, we may say that, without a single classical allusion or more than a hint of the trademark rant, he was able to make us feel the classical tragedy of nihilistic pride in all its cosmic force within the little room of contemporary private life.

Contributors

Gordon Braden..*University of Virginia*
James C. Bulman..*Allegheny College*
Paul A. Cantor..*University of Virginia*
Irby B. Cauthen, Jr..*University of Virginia*
Larry S. Champion..*North Carolina State University*
Philip Edwards..*University of Liverpool*
George L. Geckle..*University of South Carolina*
Allan P. Green..*Spring Lake, New Jersey*
Virginia J. Haas..*University of Wisconsin-Milwaukee*
Anthony Hammond..*McMaster University*
T. H. Howard-Hill..*University of South Carolina*
Cyrus Hoy..*University of Rochester*
Linda V. Itzoe..*Pennsylvania State University*
Donald S. Lawless..*Rome, New York*
Jill L. Levenson..*Trinity College, University of Toronto*
David Lindley..*University of Leeds*
John S. Nania..*Richmond, Virginia*
Susan Gushee O'Malley...*Kingsborough Community College, City University of New York*
Norman Sanders..*University of Tennessee*
Charles L. Squier..*University of Colorado-Boulder*
Karen Wood..*University of California, Berkeley*

Cumulative Index

Dictionary of Literary Biography, Volumes 1-58
Dictionary of Literary Biography Yearbook, 1980-1986
Dictionary of Literary Biography Documentary Series, Volumes 1-4

Cumulative Index

DLB before number: *Dictionary of Literary Biography,* Volumes 1-58
Y before number: *Dictionary of Literary Biography Yearbook,* 1980-1986
DS before number: *Dictionary of Literary Biography Documentary Series,* Volumes 1-4

C

H

I

J

L

M

N

O

P

Q

S

Y